soups

soups

MURDOCH BOOKS

contents

soup kitchen

Someone once said 'Soup is cuisine's kindest course'. Soup soothes us when we're ill, feeds us when we're short on time (or money!), curtain-raises at our dinner parties and provides the best use possible for almost any seasonal produce.

Soup spans seasons, continents and the whole gamut of ingredients and cooking skills. Soups can be hot or chilled and can even take us travelling to exotic places; to Vietnam, Tunisia, Thailand or Spain. It is suited to any occasion and comes in a mind-boggling number of colours, consistencies and textures. It can be as familiar a friend as a creamy pumpkin purée, a thick clam chowder or cheesy French onion soup — menu stalwarts that are never out of vogue.

A soup can have the suave sophistication of classic crab bisque, or be as down-home rustic as pasta and bean or pea and ham. These may be fashioned from humble everyday staples but they're the soups we arguably most love to cook and eat.

Soup loves an accompaniment or two (rolls, dumplings, toast or croutons) but is equally happy served solo. In fact, the only thing that soup really isn't capable of doing is making itself. Lucky for you, the eager soup cooks of the world, here are all your favourite soup recipes in one indispensable volume.

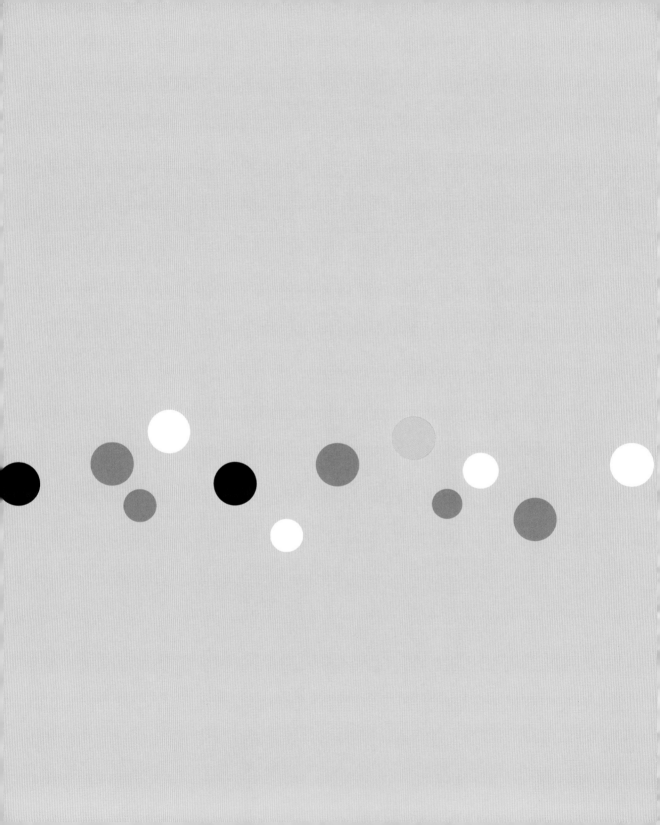

classic

French onion soup

50 g (1¾ oz) butter
750 g (1 lb 10 oz) onions, finely sliced
2 garlic cloves, finely chopped
45 g (1½ oz/⅓ cup) plain (all-purpose) flour
2 litres (70 fl oz/8 cups) beef or chicken stock
250 ml (9 fl oz/1 cup) dry white wine
1 bay leaf
2 thyme sprigs
12 slices stale baguette
100 g (3½ oz) gruyère cheese, finely grated

Melt the butter in a heavy-based saucepan and add the onion. Cook over low heat, stirring occasionally, for 25 minutes, or until the onion is deep golden brown and beginning to caramelise.

Add the garlic and flour and stir continuously for 2 minutes. Gradually blend in the stock and the wine, stirring continuously, and bring to the boil. Add the bay leaf and thyme and season. Cover the pan and simmer for 25 minutes. Remove the bay leaf and thyme. Preheat the grill (broiler).

Toast the baguette slices, then divide among six soup bowls. Ladle the soup over the top and sprinkle with the grated cheese. Grill (broil) until the cheese melts and turns light golden brown. Serve immediately.

SERVES 6

Lentil and silverbeet soup

Chicken stock

1 kg (2 lb 8 oz) chicken
    trimmings (neck, ribs, wings),
    fat removed
1 small onion, roughly chopped
1 bay leaf
3–4 flat-leaf (Italian) parsley
    sprigs
1–2 oregano or thyme sprigs

280 g (10 oz) brown lentils
850 g (1 lb 14 oz) silverbeet
    (Swiss chard)
3 tablespoons olive oil
1 large onion, finely chopped
4 garlic cloves, crushed
25 g (1 oz) coriander (cilantro)
    leaves, finely chopped
4 tablespoons lemon juice
lemon wedges, to serve

To make the stock, put all the ingredients in a large saucepan. Add 3 litres (104 fl oz/ 12 cups) of water and bring to the boil. Skim any scum from the surface. Reduce the heat and simmer for 2 hours. Strain the stock, discarding the trimmings, onion and herbs. Chill overnight. You will need about 1 litre (35 fl oz/4 cups).

Skim any fat from the stock. Put the lentils in a large saucepan, add the stock and 1 litre (35 fl oz/4 cups) of water. Bring to the boil, then reduce the heat and simmer, covered, for 1 hour.

Meanwhile, remove the stems from the silverbeet and shred the leaves. Heat the oil in a saucepan over medium heat and cook the onion for 2–3 minutes, or until transparent. Add the garlic and cook for 1 minute. Add the silverbeet and toss for 2–3 minutes, or until wilted. Stir the mixture into the lentils. Add the coriander and lemon juice, season, and simmer, covered for 15–20 minutes. Serve with lemon wedges.

SERVES 6

Pumpkin soup

500 ml (17 fl oz/2 cups) vegetable stock
750 g (1 lb 10 oz) butternut pumpkin (squash),
    cut into 1.5 cm (⅝ inch) cubes
2 onions, chopped
2 garlic cloves, halved
3 tablespoons pouring (whipping) cream
¼ teaspoon ground nutmeg

Put the stock and 500 ml (17 fl oz/2 cups) of water in a large heavy-based saucepan and bring to the boil. Add the pumpkin, onion and garlic and return to the boil. Reduce the heat slightly and cook for 15 minutes, or until the pumpkin is soft.

Drain the vegetables in a colander, reserving the liquid. Cool the pumpkin mixture slightly, then purée in a blender until smooth (you may need to add some of the reserved liquid). Return the pumpkin purée to the pan and stir in enough of the reserved liquid to reach the desired consistency.

Serve with cream swirled on top and season to taste with nutmeg, salt and pepper.

SERVES 4

Spring vegetable
soup with basil pesto

1.25 litres (44 fl oz/5 cups) vegetable or chicken stock
1 tablespoon extra virgin olive oil
8 spring onions (scallions), finely sliced
2 celery stalks, finely sliced
12 baby (dutch) carrots, sliced
310 g (11 oz) asparagus, woody ends removed,
   cut into 3 cm (1¼ inch) lengths
150 g (5½ oz) baby corn, cut into 3 cm (1¼ inch) lengths
60 g (2¼ oz/¼ cup) fresh or bottled pesto
extra virgin olive oil, to thin pesto (see Note)
shaved parmesan cheese, to garnish

Bring the stock to the boil in a large saucepan. Meanwhile, heat the olive oil in a large heavy-based saucepan and add the spring onion and celery. Cover and cook over medium heat for 5 minutes, or until softened.

Add the stock to the spring onion mixture and mix well. Add the carrot, asparagus and corn to the pan. Return the mixture to the boil, then reduce the heat and simmer for 10 minutes.

Top with a dollop of pesto, season to taste, and garnish with shaved parmesan.

SERVES 4

NOTE: Homemade pesto or fresh pesto from a deli will give a better flavour than bottled pesto. If you prefer a thinner pesto, mix it with a little olive oil to give it a runnier consistency.

Crab bisque

50 g (1¾ oz) butter
½ carrot, finely chopped
½ onion, finely chopped
1 celery stalk, finely chopped
1 bay leaf
2 thyme sprigs
1 kg (2 lb 4 oz) live crabs,
    cleaned and claws detached

2 tablespoons tomato paste
    (concentrated purée)
2 tablespoons brandy
150 ml (5 fl oz) dry white wine
1 litre (35 fl oz/4 cups) fish stock
60 g (2¼ oz) rice
3 tablespoons thick
    (double/heavy) cream
¼ teaspoon cayenne pepper

Heat the butter in a large saucepan. Add the vegetables, bay leaf and thyme and cook over medium heat for 3 minutes, without allowing the vegetables to colour. Add the crab claws, legs and bodies and cook for 5 minutes, or until the crab shells turn red. Add the tomato paste, brandy and white wine and simmer for 2 minutes, or until reduced by half.

Add the stock and 500 ml (17 fl oz/2 cups) of water and bring to the boil. Reduce the heat and simmer for 5 minutes. Remove the shells, leaving the crab meat in the stock, and reserve the claws to use as a garnish. Finely crush the shells in a mortar and pestle (or in a food processor with a little of the stock).

Return the crushed shells to the soup with the rice. Bring to the boil, reduce the heat, cover and simmer for about 20 minutes, or until the rice is soft.

Immediately strain the bisque into a clean saucepan through a fine sieve lined with damp muslin (cheesecloth), pressing down firmly on the solids to extract all the liquid. Add the cream and season with salt and cayenne pepper, then gently reheat. Garnish with the crab claws.

SERVES 4

Spinach soup

30 g (1 oz) butter
1 onion, finely chopped
500 g (1 lb 2 oz) floury potatoes, grated
1 litre (35 fl oz/4 cups) vegetable or chicken stock
500 g (1 lb 2 oz) frozen chopped English spinach
¼ teaspoon ground nutmeg
sour cream, to serve

Melt the butter in a large saucepan over medium heat. Add the chopped onion and cook, stirring occasionally, until soft but not browned.

Add the potato and stock to the pan and mix well, scraping the onion from the bottom of the pan. Add the unthawed spinach and cook, covered, until the spinach has thawed and broken up, stirring occasionally. Uncover and simmer, stirring often, for 10–15 minutes, or until the potato is very soft. Allow to cool slightly, then transfer to a blender or food processor and blend in batches until smooth.

Return the soup to the pan and gently reheat. Add the nutmeg and season. Serve with sour cream swirled on top.

SERVES 4

Chicken and vegetable soup

1.5 kg (3 lb 5 oz) chicken
1 onion
2 large leeks, halved lengthwise
  and well washed
3 large celery stalks
5 black peppercorns
1 bay leaf
2 large carrots, peeled and
  diced

1 large swede (rutabaga),
  peeled and diced
2 large tomatoes, peeled,
  seeded and finely chopped
165 g (5¾ oz/¾ cup) barley
1 tablespoon tomato paste
  (concentrated purée)
2 tablespoons finely chopped
  flat-leaf (Italian) parsley

Put the chicken, onion, 1 leek, 1 celery stalk, halved, the peppercorns and bay leaf in a large saucepan and add enough water to cover. Bring to the boil, then reduce the heat and simmer for 1½ hours, skimming any impurities that rise to the surface.

Strain the stock through a fine sieve and return to the cleaned saucepan. Discard the onion, leek, celery, peppercorns and bay leaf, and set the chicken aside to cool slightly. Discard the fat and bones, then shred the flesh. Cover with plastic wrap and refrigerate.

Allow the stock to cool, then refrigerate overnight. Skim the fat from the surface. Put the stock in a large saucepan and bring to the boil. Dice the remaining leek and celery and add to the soup with the carrot, swede, tomato, barley and tomato paste. Simmer for 45–50 minutes, or until the vegetables are cooked and the barley is tender. Stir in the parsley and shredded chicken. Simmer until warmed through and season. Serve immediately.

SERVES 4–6

Leek and potato soup

50 g (1¾ oz) butter
1 onion, finely chopped
3 leeks, white part only, sliced
1 celery stalk, finely chopped
1 garlic clove, finely chopped
200 g (7 oz) potatoes, chopped
750 ml (26 fl oz/3 cups) chicken stock
220 ml (7½ fl oz) pouring (whipping) cream
2 tablespoons chopped chives, to garnish

Melt the butter in a large saucepan and add the onion, leek, celery and garlic. Cover the pan and cook, stirring occasionally, over low heat for 15 minutes, or until the vegetables are softened but not browned. Add the potato and stock and bring to the boil.

Reduce the heat and leave to simmer, covered, for 20 minutes. Allow the soup to cool slightly, then purée in a blender or food processor. Return to the saucepan.

Bring the soup back to the boil and stir in the cream. Season and serve hot or well chilled, garnished with chives.

SERVES 6

Minestrone

80 g (2¾ oz/½ cup) macaroni
1 tablespoon olive oil
1 leek, sliced
2 garlic cloves, crushed
1 carrot, sliced
1 waxy potato, chopped
1 zucchini (courgette), sliced
2 celery stalks, sliced
100 g (3½ oz) green beans,
   cut into short lengths
425 g (15 oz) tinned chopped
   tomatoes

2 litres (70 fl oz/8 cups)
   vegetable or beef stock
2 tablespoons tomato paste
   (concentrated purée)
425 g (15 oz) tinned cannellini
   beans, rinsed and drained
2 tablespoons chopped flat-leaf
   (Italian) parsley
shaved parmesan cheese,
   to serve

Bring a saucepan of water to the boil. Add the macaroni and cook for about 10–12 minutes, or until *al dente*. Drain and return to the pan to keep warm.

Meanwhile, heat the oil in a large heavy-based saucepan. Add the leek and garlic and cook over medium heat for 3–4 minutes.

Add the carrot, potato, zucchini, celery, green beans, tomato, stock and tomato paste. Bring to the boil, then reduce the heat and simmer for 10 minutes, or until the vegetables are tender.

Stir in the cooked pasta and the cannellini beans and heat through. Garnish with the parsley and shaved parmesan.

SERVES 4

NOTE: Just about any vegetable can be added to minestrone, so this is a great recipe for using up odds and ends.

Caramelised onion and parsnip soup

30 g (1 oz) butter
3 large onions, halved and thinly sliced
2 tablespoons soft brown sugar
250 ml (9 fl oz/1 cup) dry white wine
3 large parsnips, peeled and chopped
1.25 litres (44 fl oz/5 cups) vegetable stock
3 tablespoons pouring (whipping) cream
thyme leaves, to garnish

Melt the butter in a large saucepan. Add the onion and sugar, and cook over low heat for 10 minutes. Add the wine and parsnip, and simmer, covered, for 20 minutes, or until the onion and parsnip are golden and tender.

Pour in the stock, bring to the boil, then reduce the heat and simmer, covered, for 10 minutes. Cool slightly, then place in a blender or food processor and blend in batches until smooth. Season and drizzle with a little cream. Sprinkle the thyme leaves over the top.

SERVES 4

Mushroom soup

40 g (1½ oz) butter
1 onion, finely chopped
12 large (about 1.4 kg/3 lb 2 oz) field mushrooms,
    finely chopped
2 garlic cloves, crushed
2 tablespoons dry sherry
1 litre (35 fl oz/4 cups) chicken or vegetable stock
2 tablespoons flat-leaf (Italian) parsley, finely chopped
pouring (whipping) cream, to serve

Melt the butter in a large saucepan and fry the onion until the onion is translucent but not browned.

Add the mushroom and garlic and continue frying. The mushrooms might give off a lot of liquid, so fry for 15–20 minutes, or until it is all absorbed back into the mixture.

Add the sherry to the pan, increase the heat and let the mixture bubble — this burns off the alcohol but leaves the flavour. Cool slightly, then transfer to a blender. Process until a smooth paste forms, then add the stock and blend until smooth. Add a couple of tablespoons of cream and blend together. Pour back into the saucepan and heat gently. Garnish with the parsley.

SERVES 4

Gazpacho

1 kg (2 lb 4 oz) vine-ripened tomatoes, chopped
1 Lebanese (short) cucumber, chopped
1 small red capsicum (pepper), seeded and chopped
1 red onion, chopped
3 garlic cloves
80 g (2¾ oz) sourdough bread, crusts removed
2 tablespoons sherry vinegar
Tabasco sauce

Dressing
2 teaspoons each of finely diced tomato, red capsicum (pepper),
    red onion, Lebanese (short) cucumber
2 teaspoons finely chopped flat-leaf (Italian) parsley
1 tablespoon extra virgin olive oil
1 teaspoon lemon juice

Combine the tomatoes, cucumber, capsicum, onion, garlic, sourdough and 250 ml
(9 fl oz/1 cup) of cold water in a blender and blend until smooth. Pass through a
strainer into a bowl, and add the sherry vinegar. Season to taste with salt and
Tabasco, then cover and refrigerate for at least 2 hours, or overnight, to allow the
flavours to develop.

To make the dressing, combine all the ingredients in a small bowl. Season.

Stir the gazpacho well. Spoon the dressing over the top before serving.

SERVES 4

Bouillabaisse

Rouille
1 small red capsicum (pepper)
1 slice white bread
1 red chilli
2 garlic cloves
1 egg yolk
4 tablespoons olive oil

Soup
2 tablespoons oil
1 fennel bulb, thinly sliced

1 onion, chopped
750 g (1 lb 10 oz) ripe tomatoes
1.25 litres (44 fl oz/5 cups) fish
    stock
pinch of saffron threads
bouquet garni
5 cm (2 inch) piece orange zest
1.5 kg (3 lb 5 oz) monkfish
    fillets, cut into pieces
18 black mussels, cleaned

To make the rouille, cut the capsicum in half, remove the seeds and membrane and place, skin-side up, under the grill (broiler) until the skin blackens. Cool, then peel away the skin. Chop the capsicum flesh. Soak the bread in 3 tablespoons of water, then squeeze dry. Put the capsicum, bread, chilli, garlic and egg yolk in a food processor and process. Add the oil, mixing until smooth. Cover and refrigerate.

Heat the oil in a large saucepan. Cook the fennel and onion for 5 minutes.

Score a cross in the base of each tomato. Cover with boiling water for 30 seconds, then plunge into cold water. Drain and peel the skin. Chop the tomatoes.

Add the tomato to the saucepan and cook for 3 minutes. Stir in the stock, saffron, bouquet garni and orange zest, bring to the boil and boil for 10 minutes. Remove the bouquet garni and orange zest and purée in a blender. Return to the saucepan, season and bring back to the boil. Reduce the heat to a simmer and add the fish and mussels. Cook for 5 minutes, or until the fish is tender and the mussels have opened. Discard any mussels that haven't opened. Serve the soup with rouille.

SERVES 6

Pea and ham soup

500 g (1 lb 2 oz) yellow or green split peas
1½ tablespoons olive oil
2 onions, chopped
1 carrot, diced
3 celery stalks, finely chopped
1 kg (2 lb 4 oz) ham bones or smoked hock, chopped
1 bay leaf
2 thyme sprigs
lemon juice, to taste (optional)

Put the split peas in a large bowl, cover with cold water and soak for 6 hours. Drain well.

Heat the oil in a large saucepan, add the onion, carrot, and celery, and cook over low heat for 6–7 minutes, or until vegetables are soft.

Add the split peas, ham bones, bay leaf, thyme and 2.5 litres (88 fl oz/10 cups) of cold water and bring to the boil. Reduce the heat and simmer, stirring occasionally for 2 hours, or until the split peas are tender. Discard the bay leaf and thyme sprigs.

Remove the ham bones from the soup and cool slightly. Remove the meat from the bone, discard the bones and chop the meat. Return the ham to the soup and reheat. Season to taste and add lemon juice, if desired.

SERVES 4

Asparagus soup

750 g (1 lb 10 oz) asparagus spears
1 litre (35 fl oz/4 cups) vegetable or chicken stock
30 g (1 oz) butter
1 tablespoon plain (all-purpose) flour
½ teaspoon finely grated lemon zest, plus extra, to garnish

Trim and discard any woody ends from the asparagus spears and cut into 2 cm
(¾ inch) lengths. Put in a large saucepan and add 500 ml (17 fl oz/2 cups) of the
stock. Cover and bring to the boil, then cook for 10 minutes, or until the asparagus
is tender. Allow to cool slightly.

Transfer the asparagus and the stock to a blender or food processor, and purée in
batches until smooth.

Melt the butter in the saucepan over low heat, add the flour, then cook, stirring, for
1 minute, or until pale and foaming. Remove from the heat and gradually add the
remaining stock, stirring until smooth after each addition. When all the stock has
been added, return the saucepan to the heat, bring to the boil, then simmer for
2 minutes.

Add the asparagus purée to the pan and stir until combined. When heated through,
stir in the lemon zest and season. Garnish with the extra lemon zest.

SERVES 4

Borscht

6 large (1.5 kg/3 lb 5 oz) beetroot, peeled
1½ tablespoons caster (superfine) sugar
125 ml (4 fl oz/½ cup) lemon juice
3 eggs
sour cream, to serve (optional)

Grate the beetroot, and put in a saucepan with the caster sugar and 2.25 litres (79 fl oz/9 cups) of water. Stir over low heat until the sugar has dissolved. Simmer, partially covered, for about 30 minutes, skimming the surface occasionally.

Add the lemon juice and simmer, uncovered, for 10 minutes. Remove the pan from the heat.

Whisk the eggs in a bowl. Gradually pour the eggs into the beetroot mixture, whisking constantly and taking care not to curdle the eggs. Season to taste. Allow the soup to cool, then cover and refrigerate until cold. Served with a dollop of sour cream, if desired.

SERVES 6

Vegetable soup

105 g (3½ oz/½ cup) dried red kidney beans or borlotti beans
1 tablespoon olive oil
1 leek, halved lengthways and chopped
1 small onion, diced
2 carrots, chopped
2 celery stalks, chopped
1 large zucchini (courgette), chopped
1 tablespoon tomato paste (concentrated purée)
1 litre (35 fl oz/4 cups) vegetable stock
400 g (14 oz) butternut pumpkin (squash), cut into
    2 cm (¾ inch) cubes
2 potatoes, cut into 2 cm (¾ inch) cubes
3 tablespoons chopped flat-leaf (Italian) parsley

Put the beans in a large bowl, cover with cold water and soak overnight. Rinse, then transfer to a saucepan, cover with cold water and cook for 45 minutes, or until just tender. Drain.

Heat the olive oil in a saucepan. Add the leek and onion and cook over medium heat for 2–3 minutes, without browning, or until they start to soften. Add the carrot, celery and zucchini and cook for 3–4 minutes. Add the tomato paste and stir for 1 minute. Pour in the vegetable stock and 1.25 litres (44 fl oz/5 cups) of water and bring to the boil. Reduce the heat to low and simmer for 20 minutes.

Add the pumpkin, potato, parsley and beans and simmer for a further 20 minutes, or until the vegetables are tender and the beans are cooked. Season well.

SERVES 6

Cabbage soup

100 g (3½ oz/½ cup) dried haricot beans
125 g (4½ oz) bacon, cubed
40 g (1½ oz) butter
1 carrot, sliced
1 onion, chopped
1 leek, white part only, roughly chopped
1 turnip, peeled and chopped
bouquet garni
1.25 litres (44 fl oz/5 cups) chicken stock
400 g (14 oz) white cabbage, finely shredded

Soak the beans overnight in cold water. Drain, put in a saucepan and cover with cold water. Bring to the boil and simmer for 5 minutes, then drain. Put the bacon in the same saucepan, cover with water and simmer for 5 minutes. Drain and pat dry with paper towels.

Melt the butter in a large heavy-based saucepan. Add the bacon and cook for 5 minutes, without browning. Add the beans, carrot, onion, leek and turnip and cook for 5 minutes. Add the bouquet garni and chicken stock and bring to the boil. Cover and simmer for 30 minutes. Add the cabbage, uncover and simmer for 30 minutes, or until the beans are tender. Remove the bouquet garni before serving and season to taste.

SERVES 4

hot

Sweet potato and chilli soup

1 tablespoon oil
1 onion, chopped
2 garlic cloves, finely chopped
1–2 small red chillies, finely chopped
¼ teaspoon paprika
750 g (1 lb 10 oz) orange sweet potato,
   chopped into small pieces
1 litre (35 fl oz/4 cups) vegetable or beef stock
chopped dried chilli, to garnish

Heat the oil in a large heavy-based saucepan. Add the onion and cook for about
1–2 minutes, or until soft. Add the garlic, chilli and paprika and cook for a further
2 minutes, or until aromatic. Add the sweet potato to the pan and toss to coat with
the spices.

Pour in the stock and bring to the boil. Reduce the heat and simmer for 15 minutes,
or until the vegetables are tender. Cool slightly, then transfer to a blender or food
processor and blend in batches until smooth, adding extra water if needed to reach
the desired consistency.

Season to taste and sprinkle with dried chilli before serving.

SERVES 4

Laksa

200 g (7 oz) dried rice vermicelli
2 tablespoons peanut oil
2–3 tablespoons laksa paste
1 litre (35 fl oz/4 cups) vegetable stock
750 ml (26 fl oz/3 cups) coconut milk
250 g (9 oz) snow peas (mangetout), halved diagonally
5 spring onions (scallions), cut into 3 cm (1¼ inch) lengths
2 tablespoons lime juice
125 g (4½ oz) bean sprouts, trimmed
200 g (7 oz) fried tofu puffs, halved
3 tablespoons roughly chopped Vietnamese mint
20 g (¾ oz) coriander (cilantro) leaves

Put the vermicelli in a large bowl, cover with boiling water and soak for 5 minutes.

Heat the oil in a large saucepan, add the laksa paste and cook, stirring, over medium heat for 1 minute, or until fragrant. Add the stock, coconut milk, snow peas and spring onion and simmer for 5 minutes. Pour in the lime juice and season to taste.

Drain the vermicelli and add the bean sprouts and fried tofu puffs. Ladle the hot soup over the vermicelli. Serve immediately, sprinkled with the mint and coriander.

SERVES 4

Curried chicken noodle soup

175 g (6 oz) dried thin egg noodles
2 tablespoons peanut oil
2 boneless, skinless chicken breasts (250 g/9 oz each)
1 onion, sliced
1 small fresh red chilli, seeded and finely chopped
1 tablespoon finely chopped fresh ginger

2 tablespoons Indian curry powder
750 ml (26 fl oz/3 cups) chicken stock
800 ml (28 fl oz) coconut milk
300 g (10½ oz) baby bok choy (pak choy), cut into long strips
20 g (¾ oz) basil, torn

Cook the noodles in a large saucepan of boiling water for 3–4 minutes, or until soft. Drain well and set aside.

Heat the oil in a large saucepan and add the chicken. Cook on each side for 5 minutes, or until cooked through. Remove the chicken and keep warm.

Put the onion in the pan and cook over low heat for 8 minutes, or until softened but not browned. Add the chilli, ginger and curry powder and cook for a further 2 minutes. Add the chicken stock and bring to the boil. Reduce the heat and simmer for 20 minutes. Thinly slice the chicken on the diagonal.

Add the coconut milk to the saucepan and simmer for 10 minutes. Add the bok choy and cook for 3 minutes, then stir in the basil.

To serve, divide the noodles among four deep serving bowls. Top with slices of chicken and ladle in the soup. Serve immediately.

SERVES 4

Caribbean fish soup

2 tomatoes
2 tablespoons oil
4 French shallots, finely chopped
2 celery stalks, chopped
1 large red capsicum (pepper),
    chopped
1 Scotch bonnet chilli, deseeded
    and finely chopped (see Note)
½ teaspoon ground allspice
½ teaspoon freshly grated
    nutmeg

875 ml (30 fl oz) fish stock
275 g (9¾ oz) orange sweet
    potato, peeled and cut
    into cubes
3 tablespoons lime juice
500 g (1 lb 2 oz) skinless sea
    bream fillets, cut into chunks

Fish substitution
sea bass, cod

Score a cross in the base of each tomato. Soak in boiling water for 30 seconds, then plunge into cold water. Drain and peel the skin away from the cross. Chop the tomatoes, discarding the cores, and reserving any juices.

Heat the oil in a large saucepan, then add the shallots, celery, capsicum, chilli, allspice and nutmeg. Cook for 4–5 minutes, or until the vegetables have softened, stirring occasionally. Add the chopped tomatoes (including their juices) and stock and bring to the boil. Reduce the heat to medium and add the cubes of sweet potato. Season to taste and cook for about 15 minutes, or until the sweet potato is tender.

Add the lime juice and chunks of fish to the saucepan and poach gently for 4–5 minutes, or until the fish is cooked through. Season to taste.

SERVES 6

NOTE: Scotch bonnet chillies looks like a mini capsicum (pepper) and can be green, red or orange. They are extremely hot but have a good, slightly acidic flavour.

Chicken and galangal soup

5 cm x 2 cm (2 in x ¾ inch) piece fresh galangal, peeled and
  cut into thin slices
500 ml (17 fl oz/2 cups) coconut milk
250 ml (9 fl oz/1 cup) chicken stock
4 makrut (kaffir lime) leaves, torn
1 tablespoon finely chopped coriander (cilantro) roots
500 g (1 lb 2 oz) chicken breast fillets, cut into thin strips
1–2 teaspoons finely chopped fresh red chillies
2 tablespoons fish sauce
1½ tablespoons lime juice
3 teaspoons palm sugar or soft brown sugar
1 small handful coriander (cilantro) leaves, chopped

Place the galangal in a saucepan with the coconut milk, stock, makrut leaves and coriander roots. Bring to the boil, reduce the heat to low and simmer for 10 minutes, stirring occasionally.

Add the chicken and chilli to the pan and simmer for 8 minutes.

Stir in the fish sauce, lime juice and palm sugar and cook for 1 minute. Stir in the coriander leaves. Serve immediately garnished with extra coriander, if desired.

SERVES 4

Beef pho

200 g (7 oz) rice noodle sticks
1.5 litres (52 fl oz/6 cups) beef
   stock
1 star anise
4 cm (1½ inch) piece fresh
   ginger, sliced
2 pigs trotters
½ onion, studded with 2 cloves
2 lemon grass stems, pounded
2 garlic cloves, pounded
¼ teaspoon white pepper
1 tablespoon fish sauce
400 g (14 oz) beef fillet,
   partially frozen, and
   thinly sliced

90 g (3¼ oz/1 cup) bean sprouts,
   trimmed
2 spring onions (scallions), thinly
   sliced on the diagonal
25 g (1 oz) coriander (cilantro)
   leaves, chopped
25 g (1 oz) Vietnamese mint,
   chopped
1 fresh red chilli, thinly sliced
fresh red chillies, extra, to serve
Vietnamese mint, extra, to serve
coriander (cilantro) leaves,
   extra, to serve
2 limes, cut into quarters
fish sauce, extra, to serve

Soak the noodles in boiling water for 15–20 minutes. Drain.

Bring the stock, star anise, ginger, trotters, onion, lemongrass, garlic and white pepper to the boil in a large saucepan. Reduce the heat and simmer for 30 minutes. Strain, return to the same pan and stir in the fish sauce.

Divide the noodles among bowls, then top with beef strips, sprouts, spring onion, coriander, mint and chilli. Ladle on the broth.

Pute the extra chilli, mint, coriander, lime quarters and fish sauce in small bowls on a platter and serve with the soup.

SERVES 4

Mexican soup with salsa

3 tablespoons olive oil
1 large onion, chopped
1 large celery stalk, chopped
3 garlic cloves, crushed
2 thin red chillies, chopped
200 ml (7 fl oz) fish stock
800 g (1 lb 12 oz) tinned
   chopped tomatoes
2 bay leaves
1 teaspoon dried oregano
1 teaspoon caster (superfine)
   sugar
2 corn cobs, kernels removed
500 g (1 lb 2 oz) halibut fillets

2 tablespoons chopped
   coriander (cilantro) leaves
juice of 2 limes
12 prawns (shrimp), tails intact
8 scallops, cleaned
12 clams, cleaned
125 g (4½ oz/½ cup) thick
   (double/heavy) cream

Salsa
½ small avocado
1 tablespoon coriander
   (cilantro) leaves
grated zest and juice of 1 lime
½ red onion, finely chopped

Heat the oil in a saucepan. Add the onion and celery and cook over medium heat for 10 minutes. Add the garlic and chilli and cook for 1 minute, stirring. Add the fish stock and tomatoes. Stir in the bay leaves, oregano and sugar and bring to the boil. Reduce the heat to low and simmer for 10 minutes. Remove the bay leaves, then tip the slightly cooled tomato mixture into a food processor and whiz until smooth. Return the tomato sauce to the pan and season. Add the corn kernels and bring back to the boil. Reduce the heat and simmer for 3 minutes. Cut the fish into chunks. Stir the coriander and the lime juice into the sauce, add the fish, then simmer for 1 minute. Add the prawns, scallops and clams. Cover with a lid and cook for a further 2–3 minutes, or until the seafood is cooked through.

To make the salsa, chop the avocado into cubes and mix with the coriander, the lime zest and juice, and red onion. Stir the cream into the soup and top with salsa.

SERVES 4

Thai spicy sour soup

750 ml (26 fl oz/3 cups) vegetable stock
2 tablespoons tom yum paste (see Note)
2 cm x 2 cm (¾ inch x ¾ inch) piece galangal,
    peeled and cut into thin slices
1 lemongrass stem, lightly crushed and cut into 4 lengths
3 makrut (kaffir lime) leaves
1 small red chilli, finely sliced on the diagonal (optional)
200 g (7 oz) button mushrooms, halved
200 g (7 oz) silken firm tofu, cut into 1.5 cm (⅝ inch) cubes
200 g (7 oz) baby bok choy (pak choi), roughly shredded
2 tablespoons lime juice
1 small handful coriander (cilantro) leaves

Place the stock, Tom Yum paste, galangal, lemongrass, makrut leaves, chilli and 750 ml (26 fl oz/3 cups) of water in a saucepan. Cover and bring to the boil, then reduce the heat and simmer for 5 minutes.

Add the mushrooms and tofu and simmer for 5 minutes, or until the mushrooms are tender. Add the bok choy and simmer for a further minute, or until wilted. Remove the pan from the heat and stir in the lime juice and coriander leaves before serving.

SERVES 4–6

NOTE: For vegetarian cooking, make sure you buy a brand of tom yum paste that does not contain shrimp paste or fish sauce.

Chicken and pumpkin laksa

Paste
2 bird's eye chillies, chopped
2 lemongrass stems, white part
  only, chopped
4 red Asian shallots, peeled
1 tablespoon chopped ginger
1 teaspoon ground turmeric
3 candlenuts (optional)

110 g (3¾ oz) dried rice noodle
  sticks
1 tablespoon peanut oil

250 g (9 oz) butternut pumpkin
  (squash), cut into chunks
800 ml (28 fl oz) coconut milk
600 g (1 lb 5 oz) chicken breast
  fillets, cut into cubes
2 tablespoons lime juice
1 tablespoon fish sauce
90 g (3¼ oz) bean sprouts
15 g (½ oz) torn basil
10 g (¼ oz) torn mint
50 g (1¾ oz/½ cup) unsalted
  peanuts, toasted and chopped
1 lime, cut into quarters

Put all the paste ingredients in a food processor with 1 tablespoon of water and blend until smooth.

Soak the noodles in boiling water for 15–20 minutes. Drain.

Meanwhile, heat the oil in a wok and swirl to coat. Add the paste and stir over low heat for 5 minutes, or until aromatic. Add the pumpkin and coconut milk and simmer for 10 minutes. Add the chicken and simmer for 20 minutes. Stir in the lime juice and fish sauce.

Divide the noodles among four deep serving bowls, then ladle the soup over them. Top with the bean sprouts, basil, mint, peanuts and lime.

SERVES 4

Curried lentil, carrot and cashew soup

1.5 litres (52 fl oz/6 cups) vegetable or chicken stock
750 g (1 lb 10 oz) carrots, grated
185 g (6½ oz/¾ cup) red lentils, rinsed and drained
1 tablespoon olive oil
1 large onion, chopped
80 g (2¾ oz/½ cup) unsalted cashew nuts
1 tablespoon Madras curry paste
25 g (1 oz/½ cup) chopped coriander (cilantro) leaves and stems
125 g (4½ oz/½ cup) Greek-style yoghurt
coriander (cilantro) leaves, to garnish

Bring the stock to the boil in a large saucepan. Add the carrots and lentils, bring the mixture back to the boil. Simmer over low heat for about 8 minutes, or until the carrot and lentils are soft.

Meanwhile, heat the oil in a large frying pan. Add the onion and cashews and cook over medium heat for 2–3 minutes, or until the onion is soft and browned. Add the curry paste and coriander and cook for a further 1 minute, or until fragrant. Stir the paste into the carrot and lentil mixture. Allow to cool slightly.

Transfer to a food processor or blender and process in batches until smooth. Return the mixture to the pan and reheat over medium heat until hot. Season to taste and serve with a dollop of yoghurt and a sprinkling of coriander.

SERVES 6

NOTE: Garnish the soup with a pinch of chilli flakes to give it an extra kick.

Vietnamese beef soup

400 g (14 oz) rump steak, trimmed
½ onion
1½ tablespoons fish sauce
1 star anise
1 cinnamon stick
pinch ground white pepper
1.5 litres (52 fl oz/6 cups) beef stock
300 g (10½ oz) fresh thin rice noodles
3 spring onions (scallions), thinly sliced
15 g (½ oz) Vietnamese mint leaves
90 g (3¼ oz) bean sprouts, trimmed
1 small white onion, cut in half and thinly sliced
1 small red chilli, thinly sliced on the diagonal
lemon wedges, to serve

Wrap the rump steak in plastic wrap and freeze for 40 minutes.

Meanwhile, put the onion, fish sauce, star anise, cinnamon stick, pepper, stock and 500 ml (17 fl oz/2 cups) of water in a large saucepan. Bring to the boil, then reduce the heat, cover and simmer for 20 minutes. Discard the onion, star anise and cinnamon stick.

Cover the noodles with boiling water and gently separate the strands. Drain and refresh under cold water.

Remove the meat from the freezer and thinly slice it across the grain.

Divide the noodles and spring onion among four deep bowls. Top with the beef, mint, bean sprouts, onion and chilli. Ladle the hot broth over the top and serve with the lemon wedges.

SERVES 4

NOTE: In Vietnam, noodle soups are called pho — beef noodle soup, pho bo, is one of the most popular.

Pumpkin and red lentil soup

1 tablespoon olive oil
1 long red chilli, seeded and chopped
1 onion, finely chopped
500 g (1 lb 2 oz) butternut pumpkin (squash), chopped
350 g (12 oz) orange sweet potato, chopped
1.5 litres (52 fl oz/6 cups) vegetable stock
125 g (4½ oz/½ cup) red lentils
1 tablespoon tahini
red chilli, extra, to garnish

Heat the oil in a large saucepan over medium heat. Add the chilli and onion and cook for 2–3 minutes, or until the onion is soft. Reduce the heat to low, add the pumpkin and sweet potato and cook, covered, for 8 minutes, stirring occasionally.

Increase the heat to high, add the stock and bring to the boil. Reduce the heat to low, and simmer, covered, for 10 minutes. Add the red lentils and cook, covered, for 7 minutes, or until tender.

Process the soup in batches in a blender or food processor. Add the tahini and blend until smooth. Return to the saucepan and gently heat until warmed through. Garnish with chilli.

SERVES 4

Rice noodle soup with duck

1 whole Chinese roast duck
4 coriander (cilantro) roots and
  stems, well rinsed
5 slices fresh galangal
4 spring onions (scallions), sliced
  on the diagonal into 3 cm
  (1¼ inch) lengths
400 g (14 oz) Chinese broccoli,
  cut into 5 cm (2 inch) lengths
2 garlic cloves, crushed
3 tablespoons fish sauce

1 tablespoon hoisin sauce
2 teaspoons grated palm sugar
  or soft brown sugar
½ teaspoon ground white
  pepper
500 g (1 lb 2 oz) fresh rice
  noodles
crispy fried garlic flakes,
  to garnish (optional)
coriander (cilantro) leaves,
  to garnish (optional)

To make the stock, cut off the duck's head and discard. Remove the skin and fat, leaving the neck intact. Remove the flesh from the bones and set aside. Cut any fat from the carcass along with the parson's nose, then discard. Break the carcass into pieces, then put in a stockpot with 2 litres (70 fl oz/8 cups) of water.

Bruise the coriander roots and stems with the back of a knife. Add to the pot with the galangal and bring to the boil. Skim off any foam from the surface. Boil over medium heat for 15 minutes. Strain the stock through a fine sieve, discard the carcass, and return the stock to a clean saucepan.

Slice the duck flesh into strips. Add to the stock with the spring onion, Chinese broccoli, garlic, fish sauce, hoisin sauce, palm sugar and white pepper. Gently bring to the boil.

Cook the noodles in boiling water for 2–3 minutes, or until tender. Drain well. Divide the noodles and soup evenly among the serving bowls. If desired, garnish with the garlic flakes and coriander leaves.

SERVES 4–6

Hot and sour
prawn soup

350 g (12 oz) raw medium
  prawns (shrimp)
1 tablespoon oil
3 lemongrass stems, white part
  only
3 thin slices fresh galangal
3–5 small fresh red chillies
5 makrut (kaffir lime) leaves,
  finely shredded
2 tablespoons fish sauce

2 spring onions (scallions), sliced
70 g (2½ oz/½ cup) tinned
  straw mushrooms, drained,
  or quartered button
  mushrooms
3 tablespoons lime juice
1–2 tablespoons chilli paste, or
  to taste
coriander (cilantro) leaves,
  to garnish (optional)

Peel and devein the prawns, leaving the tails intact and reserving the heads and shells.

Heat the oil in a large stockpot or wok and add the prawn heads and shells. Cook for 5 minutes, or until the shells turn bright orange. Bruise 1 stem of the lemongrass with the back of a knife. Add to the pan with the galangal and 2 litres (70 fl oz/8 cups) of water. Bring to the boil, then reduce the heat and simmer for 20 minutes. Strain the stock and return to the pan. Discard the shells and herbs.

Finely slice the chillies and remaining lemongrass. Add to the liquid with the makrut leaves, fish sauce, spring onion and mushrooms. Cook gently for 2 minutes.

Add the prawns and cook for 3 minutes, or until the prawns are tender. Add the lime juice and chilli paste (adjust to taste with extra lime juice or fish sauce). If desired, garnish with coriander leaves.

SERVES 4–6

Green curry
vegetable soup

2 teaspoons peanut oil
1 tablespoon green curry paste
3 makrut (kaffir lime) leaves
1.25 litres (44 fl oz/5 cups) vegetable or chicken stock
670 ml (23 fl oz/2⅔ cups) coconut milk
600 g (1 lb 5 oz) butternut pumpkin (squash),
   cut into 1.5 cm (⅝ inch) cubes
250 g (9 oz) small yellow (pattypan) squash, sliced
115 g (4 oz) fresh baby corn spears, halved lengthways
2 tablespoons mushroom soy sauce
2 tablespoons lime juice
1 teaspoon sugar
1½ tablespoons Vietnamese mint, finely chopped

Heat the oil in a large saucepan and add the curry paste and makrut leaves. Cook, stirring, over medium heat for 1 minute, or until fragrant.

Bring the stock to the boil in a separate saucepan.

Gradually add the stock and coconut milk to the curry mixture and bring to the boil. Add the pumpkin, squash and corn, and simmer over low heat for 12 minutes, or until the pumpkin is tender.

Add the soy sauce and lime juice, and season to taste with sugar, salt and black pepper. Garnish with the mint before serving.

SERVES 6

Beef and chilli bean soup

1 tablespoon oil
1 red onion, finely chopped
2 garlic cloves, crushed
2½ teaspoons chilli flakes
2½ teaspoons ground cumin
2½ tablespoons finely chopped coriander (cilantro) root and stem
1½ teaspoons ground coriander
500 g (1 lb 2 oz) lean minced (ground) beef
1 tablespoon tomato paste (concentrated purée)
4 tomatoes, peeled, seeded and diced
420 g (15 oz) tinned red kidney beans, drained and rinsed
2 litres (70 fl oz/8 cups) beef stock
3 tablespoons chopped coriander (cilantro) leaves
80 g (2¾ oz/⅓ cup) sour cream, to serve

Heat the oil in a large saucepan over medium heat. Cook the onion for about
2–3 minutes, or until softened. Add the garlic, chilli flakes, cumin, fresh and ground
coriander, and cook for 1 minute. Add the beef and cook for 3–4 minutes, or until
cooked through — break up any lumps with a spoon.

Add the tomato paste, tomato, beans and stock and bring to the boil. Reduce the
heat and simmer for 15–20 minutes, or until reduced slightly. Remove any scum
on the surface. Stir in the chopped coriander. Serve with sour cream.

SERVES 4

Gumbo

Roux
4 tablespoons oil
75 g (2½ oz/⅔ cup) plain
  (all-purpose) flour
1 onion, finely chopped

4 crabs, cleaned
450 g (1 lb) chorizo sausage, cut
  into bite-sized pieces
6 spring onions (scallions), sliced

1 green capsicum (pepper),
  roughly chopped
3 tablespoons chopped flat-leaf
  (Italian) parsley
¼ teaspoon chilli powder
500 g (1 lb 2 oz) prawns (shrimp),
  peeled and deveined
24 oysters, shucked
½ teaspoon filé powder (see
  Note)
1½ tablespoons long-grain rice

To make the roux, pour the oil into a heavy-based saucepan over low heat. Add the flour, stirring after each addition, to make a thin roux. Continue to stir over low heat for 35 minutes, or until dark brown. Add the onion and cook for 4 minutes, or until tender. Pour in 1.5 litres (52 fl oz/6 cups) of boiling water, stirring to dissolve the roux, and bring to a simmer.

Cut the crabs into pieces. Add the crab, sausage, spring onion, capsicum, parsley and chilli powder to the roux. Cook for 30 minutes, then add the prawns and the oysters and their juices and cook for a further 5 minutes, or until the prawns are pink. Season well, then stir in the filé powder.

Meanwhile, cook the rice in salted boiling water for about 10 minutes, or until just cooked through. Put a couple of tablespoons of rice in the bottom of each bowl and ladle over the gumbo. Serve immediately.

SERVES 6

NOTE: Filé powder is a flavouring often used in Creole cooking. It is made by drying, then grinding sassafras leaves.

Tom yum goong

1 tablespoon oil
500 g (1 lb 2 oz) prawns
   (shrimp), peeled and
   deveined, reserving the heads
   and shells
2 tablespoons Thai red curry
   paste or tom yum paste
2 tablespoons tamarind purée
   (see Note)
2 teaspoons ground turmeric

1 teaspoon chopped red chillies
4 makrut (kaffir lime) leaves,
   shredded
2 tablespoons fish sauce
2 tablespoons lime juice
2 teaspoons grated palm sugar
   or soft brown sugar
2 tablespoons coriander
   (cilantro) leaves

Heat the oil in a large saucepan or wok and cook the prawn heads and shells for 10 minutes over medium heat, stirring frequently, until the heads are deep orange in colour.

Add 250 ml (9 fl oz/1 cup) of water and the curry paste to the saucepan. Bring to the boil and cook for 5 minutes, or until reduced slightly. Add another 2 litres (70 fl oz/ 8 cups) of water and simmer for 20 minutes. Strain, discarding the shells and heads, and pour the stock back into the pan.

Add the tamarind, turmeric, chillies and makrut leaves to the saucepan. Bring to the boil and cook for 2 minutes. Add the prawns and cook for 5 minutes, or until pink. Stir in the fish sauce, lime juice and sugar. Serve sprinkled with coriander leaves.

SERVES 4–6

NOTE: If you are unable to find tamarind purée, you can make your own by soaking a 225 g (8 oz) packet of tamarind pulp in 500 ml (17 fl oz/2 cups) of boiling water for 1–2 hours, crushing occasionally. Push through a sieve and discard the fibres. Alternatively, use lemon juice.

Chilli, corn and red capsicum soup

1 coriander (cilantro) sprig
4 sweet corn cobs
30 g (1 oz) butter
2 red capsicums (peppers), diced
1 small onion, finely chopped
1 small red chilli, finely chopped
1 tablespoon plain (all-purpose) flour
500 ml (17 fl oz/2 cups) vegetable stock
125 ml (4 fl oz/½ cup) pouring (whipping) cream

Trim the leaves off the coriander and finely chop the root and stems. Cut the kernels off the corn cobs.

Heat the butter in a saucepan over medium heat. Add the corn kernels, capsicum, onion and chilli and stir to coat in the butter. Cook, covered, over low heat, stirring occasionally, for 10 minutes, or until soft. Increase the heat to medium, add the coriander root and stem and cook, stirring, for 30 seconds, or until fragrant. Sprinkle with the flour and stir for 1 minute. Remove from the heat and gradually stir in the stock. Add 500 ml (17 fl oz/2 cups) of water and return to the heat. Bring to the boil, reduce the heat to low and simmer, covered, for 30 minutes, or until the vegetables are tender. Cool slightly.

Pour 500 ml (17 fl oz/2 cups) of the soup into a blender and purée until smooth. Return the purée to the soup in the pan, pour in the cream and gently heat until warmed through. Season. Sprinkle with the coriander leaves.

SERVES 4

creamy

Zucchini pesto soup

1 tablespoon olive oil
1 large onion, finely chopped
2 garlic cloves, crushed
750 ml (26 fl oz/3 cups)
   vegetable or chicken stock
750 g (1 lb 10 oz) zucchini
   (courgettes), thinly sliced
3 tablespoons pouring
   (whipping) cream
toasted ciabatta, to serve

Pesto
50 g (1¾ oz) basil
25 g (1 oz/¼ cup) finely grated
   parmesan cheese
2 tablespoons pine nuts, toasted
2 tablespoons extra virgin
   olive oil

Heat the oil in a large heavy-based saucepan. Add the onion and garlic and cook over medium heat for 5 minutes, or until the onion is soft.

Bring the stock to the boil in a separate saucepan. Add the zucchini and hot stock to the onion mixture. Bring to the boil, then reduce the heat. Cover and simmer for 10 minutes, or until the zucchini is very soft.

To make the pesto, process the basil, parmesan and pine nuts in a food processor for 20 seconds, or until finely chopped. Gradually add the olive oil and process until smooth. Spoon into a small bowl.

Transfer the zucchini mixture to a blender or food processor and blend in batches until smooth. Return the mixture to the pan, stir in the cream and 2 tablespoons of the pesto, and reheat over medium heat until hot. Season and serve with toasted ciabatta, if desired.

SERVES 4

Orange
sweet potato soup

40 g (1½ oz) butter
2 onions, chopped
2 garlic cloves, crushed
1 kg (2 lb 4 oz) orange sweet potato, peeled and chopped
1 large celery stalk, chopped
1 large green apple, peeled, cored and chopped
1½ teaspoons ground cumin
2 litres (70 fl oz/8 cups) chicken stock
125 g (4½ oz/½ cup) natural yoghurt
lavash bread, to serve (optional)

Melt the butter in a large saucepan over low heat. Add the onion and cook, stirring occasionally, for 10 minutes, or until soft. Add the garlic, sweet potato, celery, apple and 1 teaspoon of the cumin and cook for 5–7 minutes, or until well coated. Add the chicken stock and the remaining cumin and bring to the boil over high heat. Reduce the heat and simmer for 25–30 minutes, or until the sweet potato is very soft.

Cool the soup slightly and blend in batches until smooth. Return to the pan and gently stir over medium heat until warmed through. Season and serve with a dollop of yoghurt and toasted lavash, if desired.

SERVES 4–6

Prawn, potato and corn chowder

600 g (lb 5 oz) raw medium
  prawns (shrimp)
3 corn cobs, husks removed
1 tablespoon olive oil
2 leeks, white part only,
  finely chopped
2 garlic cloves, crushed
650 g (1 lb 7 oz) potatoes, cut
  into 1.5 cm (⅝ inch) cubes

750 ml (26 fl oz/3 cups) fish or
  chicken stock
375 ml (13 fl oz/1½ cups) milk
250 ml (9 fl oz/1 cup) pouring
  (whipping) cream
pinch cayenne pepper
3 tablespoons finely chopped
  flat-leaf (Italian) parsley

Peel and devein the prawns, then chop into 1.5 cm (⅝ inch) pieces. Cut the kernels from the corn cobs.

Heat the oil in a large saucepan and add the leek. Cook over medium–low heat for about 5 minutes, or until soft and lightly golden. Add the garlic and cook for 30 seconds, then add the corn, potato, stock and milk.

Bring to the boil, then reduce the heat. Simmer, partially covered, for 20 minutes, or until the potato is soft but still holds its shape. Remove the lid and simmer for a further 10 minutes to allow the soup to thicken. Reduce the heat to low. Put 500 ml (17 fl oz/2 cups) of the soup in a blender and blend until very smooth.

Return the blended soup to the saucepan and add the prawns. Increase the heat to medium and simmer for 2 minutes, or until the prawns are pink and cooked through. Stir in the cream, cayenne pepper and 2 tablespoons of the parsley. Season to taste, then serve garnished with the remaining parsley.

SERVES 4–6

Fresh mushroom,
shallot and sour cream soup

40 g (1½ oz) butter
100 g (3½ oz) French shallots, roughly chopped
3 garlic cloves, crushed
30 g (1 oz) flat-leaf (Italian) parsley
315 ml (10¾ fl oz/1¼ cups) vegetable or chicken stock
315 ml (10¾ fl oz/1¼ cups) milk
600 g (1 lb 5 oz) button mushrooms, chopped,
    plus extra to garnish (optional)
¼ teaspoon ground nutmeg
¼ teaspoon cayenne pepper, plus extra to garnish
150 g (5½ oz) light sour cream

Melt the butter in a large heavy-based saucepan and add the shallots, garlic and parsley. Cook over medium heat for 2–3 minutes.

Put the stock and milk in a separate saucepan and bring to the boil.

Add the mushrooms to the shallot mixture. Season, then stir in the nutmeg and cayenne pepper. Cook, stirring, for 1 minute. Add the stock and milk, bring to the boil, then reduce the heat and simmer for 5 minutes. Transfer the soup to a blender or food processor and blend until smooth. Return to the pan.

Stir in the sour cream and reheat gently. Season to taste and serve sprinkled with cayenne pepper. Garnish with the extra mushrooms, lightly fried in butter, if desired.

SERVES 4

Watercress soup

30 g (1 oz) butter
1 onion, finely chopped
250 g (9 oz) potatoes, diced
625 ml (21½ fl oz/2½ cups) chicken stock
1 kg (2 lb 4 oz) watercress, trimmed and chopped
125 ml (4 fl oz/½ cup) pouring (whipping) cream
125 ml (4 fl oz/½ cup) milk
freshly grated nutmeg
2 tablespoons chopped chives

Melt the butter in a large saucepan and add the onion. Cover the pan and cook over low heat until the onion is softened. Add the potato and chicken stock and simmer for 12 minutes, or until the potato is tender. Add the watercress and cook for 1 minute.

Remove from the heat and leave the soup to cool a little. Pour into a blender or food processor and blend until smooth. Return to the saucepan.

Bring the soup gently back to the boil and stir in the cream and milk. Season with nutmeg, salt and pepper and reheat without boiling. Serve garnished with chives.

SERVES 4

Creamy chicken and corn soup

20 g (¾ oz) butter
1 tablespoon olive oil
500 g (1 lb 2 oz) chicken thigh
    fillets, trimmed and
    thinly sliced
2 garlic cloves, chopped
1 leek, chopped
1 large celery stalk, chopped
1 bay leaf
½ teaspoon thyme

1 litre (35 fl oz/4 cups) chicken
    stock
3 tablespoons sherry
550 g (1 lb 4 oz) corn kernels
    (fresh, canned or frozen)
1 large floury potato, cut into
    1 cm (½ inch) cubes
185 ml (6 fl oz/¾ cup) pouring
    (whipping) cream
chives, to garnish

Melt the butter and oil in a large saucepan over high heat. Cook the chicken in batches for 3 minutes, or until lightly golden and just cooked through. Place in a bowl, cover and refrigerate until needed.

Reduce the heat to medium and stir in the garlic, leek, celery, bay leaf and thyme. Cook for 2 minutes, or until the leek softens. Add the stock, sherry and 500 ml (17 fl oz/2 cups) of water and stir to combine. Add the corn and potato and bring to the boil. Reduce the heat and simmer for 1 hour, skimming any scum off the surface. Cool slightly.

Remove the bay leaf and purée the soup in a blender or food processor. Return to the pan and add the cream and chicken. Stir over medium heat for 2–3 minutes, or until heated through. Season. Serve with extra cream and garnish with chives.

SERVES 4–6

Corn and lemon grass soup with yabbies

4 corn cobs
1 tablespoon oil
1 leek, white part only, chopped
1 celery stick, chopped
3 lemon grass stems, white part
  only, bruised
5 garlic cloves, crushed
1 teaspoon ground cumin
1 teaspoon ground coriander
¾ teaspoon ground white pepper
3 makrut (kaffir lime) leaves

750 ml (26 fl oz/3 cups) chicken
  stock
800 ml (28 fl oz) coconut milk
125 ml (4 fl oz/½ cup) pouring
  (whipping) cream
2 teaspoons butter
½ teaspoon sambal oelek
1.2 kg (2 lb 10 oz) cooked
  yabbies or crayfish, shredded
1 tablespoon finely chopped
  coriander (cilantro) leaves

Trim the kernels from the corn. Heat the oil in a saucepan over medium heat. Add the leek, celery and lemongrass. Stir for 10 minutes, or until the leek is soft. Add half the garlic, and the cumin, coriander and ½ teaspoon of the pepper. Cook, stirring, for 1–2 minutes, or until fragrant. Add the corn, makrut leaves, stock and coconut milk, stir well and simmer for 1½ hours. Remove from the heat and cool. Remove the lemongrass and makrut leaves and blend the mixture in batches in a food processor.

Push the mixture through a sieve. Repeat. Return to a saucepan, add the cream and warm gently.

Melt the butter in a frying pan over medium heat, add the remaining garlic, sambal oelek, remaining pepper and a pinch of salt and stir for 1 minute. Add the yabby meat, stir for a further minute, then remove from the heat and stir in the coriander.

SERVES 4

Cauliflower and almond soup with hot cheese rolls

75 g (2½ oz/½ cup) blanched
   almonds
1 tablespoon olive oil
1 leek, white part only, chopped
2 garlic cloves, crushed
1 kg (2 lb 4 oz) cauliflower, cut
   into small florets
2 desiree potatoes, cut into
   1.5 cm (5⁄8 inch) pieces

1.75 litres (60 fl oz/7 cups)
   chicken stock

Cheese rolls
4 round bread rolls
40 g (1½ oz) softened butter
125 g (4½ oz) cheddar cheese,
   grated
50 g (1¾ oz) parmesan cheese,
   grated

Preheat the oven to 180°C (350°F/Gas 4). Put the almonds on a baking tray and toast for 5 minutes, or until golden.

Heat the oil in a large saucepan over medium heat and cook the leek for 2–3 minutes, or until softened. Add the garlic and cook for 30 seconds, then add the cauliflower, potato and stock. Bring to the boil, then reduce the heat and simmer for 15 minutes, or until the vegetables are very tender. Cool for 5 minutes.

Blend the soup with the almonds in batches in a blender until smooth. Season to taste. Return to the pan and stir over medium heat until heated through. Serve with the cheese rolls, if desired.

To make the cheese rolls, split the rolls and butter both sides. Combine the grated cheeses and divide evenly among the rolls. Sandwich together and wrap in foil. Bake in the oven for 15–20 minutes, or until the cheese has melted.

SERVES 4

Potato and sweet corn chowder

6 sweet corn cobs
2 tablespoons vegetable oil
1 onion, finely diced
3 garlic cloves, crushed
1 celery stalk, diced
1 carrot, peeled and diced
2 large potatoes, peeled and diced
1 litre (35 fl oz/4 cups) vegetable or chicken stock
2 tablespoons finely chopped flat-leaf (Italian) parsley

Bring a large saucepan of salted water to the boil. Cook the sweet corn for 5 minutes. Reserve 250 ml (9 fl oz/1 cup) of the cooking water. Cut the corn kernels from the cob, place half in a blender with the reserved cooking water, and blend until smooth.

Heat the oil in a large saucepan. Add the onion, garlic, celery and a large pinch of salt and cook for 5 minutes. Add the carrot and potatoes, cook for a further 5 minutes, then add the stock, corn kernels and blended corn mixture. Reduce the heat and simmer for 20 minutes, or until the vegetables are tender. Season well and stir in the chopped parsley before serving.

SERVES 6

Cream of fennel and leek soup

30 g (1 oz) butter
2 large fennel bulbs, thinly
   sliced
2 leeks, thinly sliced
1 litre (35 fl oz/4 cups) hot
   vegetable or chicken stock
2 rosemary sprigs
1/8 teaspoon ground nutmeg
80 g (2¾ oz/⅓ cup) sour cream

25 g (1 oz/¼ cup) finely grated
   parmesan cheese
1 tablespoon oil
1 leek, extra, cut in half
   lengthways, and cut into
   4 cm (1½ inch) lengths
grated parmesan cheese, extra,
   to garnish
sour cream, extra, to garnish

Heat the butter in a large heavy-based saucepan and add the sliced fennel and leek. Cook, covered, over medium heat for 2–3 minutes, stirring occasionally.

Put the hot stock, rosemary sprigs and nutmeg in a saucepan and bring to the boil. Simmer over low heat for about 15 minutes, then remove the rosemary sprigs and add the fennel and leek mixture to the pan.

Transfer the soup to a blender or food processor and blend in batches until smooth. Return to the pan and stir in the sour cream and parmesan. Reheat over medium heat until hot. Season to taste and keep warm.

Heat the oil in a frying pan and cook the extra leek for 2–3 minutes, or until soft but not browned.

Top with the fried leek and garnish with the extra parmesan and sour cream. Serve immediately.

SERVES 6

Chicken, mushroom and Madeira soup

10 g (¼ oz) dried porcini
  mushrooms
25 g (1 oz) butter
1 leek, white part only,
  thinly sliced
250 g (9 oz) pancetta, chopped
200 g (7 oz) Swiss brown
  mushrooms, roughly chopped
300 g (10½ oz) large field
  mushrooms, chopped
2 tablespoons plain
  (all-purpose) flour

125 ml (4 fl oz/½ cup) Madeira
1.25 litres (44 fl oz/5 cups)
  chicken stock
1 tablespoon olive oil
2 chicken breast fillets (about
  200 g/7 oz each)
80 g (2¾ oz/⅓ cup) light sour
  cream
2 teaspoons chopped marjoram,
  plus whole leaves, to garnish

Soak the porcini in 250 ml (9 fl oz/1 cup) of boiling water for 20 minutes.

Melt the butter in a large saucepan over medium heat and add the leek and pancetta.
Cook for 5 minutes, or until the leek is softened. Add all the mushrooms and the
porcini soaking liquid and cook for 10 minutes. Stir in the flour and cook for 1 minute.
Add the Madeira and cook, stirring, for 10 minutes. Stir in the stock, bring to the
boil, then reduce the heat and simmer for 45 minutes. Cool slightly.

Heat the oil in a frying pan and cook the chicken for 4–5 minutes each side, or until
cooked through. Remove from the pan and thinly slice.

Blend the soup until smooth. Return to the saucepan, add the sour cream and
chopped marjoram and stir over medium heat for about 1–2 minutes to warm
through. Season. Top with the chicken and garnish with marjoram.

SERVES 4

Creamy clam soup

1.75 kg (4 lb) clams, cleaned
50 g (1¾ oz) butter
1 onion, chopped
1 celery stalk, chopped
1 large carrot, chopped
1 large leek, sliced into rings
250 g (9 oz) swede (rutabaga), diced
800 ml–1 litre (28–35 fl oz) fish stock

1 bay leaf
75 g (2½ oz/⅓ cup) medium- or short-grain rice
200 ml (7 fl oz) pouring (whipping) cream
3 tablespoons finely chopped flat-leaf (Italian) parsley

Fish substitution
pipis

Put the clams and 250 ml (9 fl oz/1 cup) of water in a large saucepan. Bring to the boil, then reduce the heat to medium and cover with a tight-fitting lid. Cook for 3–4 minutes, or until the shells open. Strain into a bowl. Add enough stock to make up to 1 litre (35 fl oz/4 cups). Discard any clams that haven't opened. Remove all but eight of the clams from their shells.

Melt the butter in a saucepan. Add the vegetables and cook, covered, over medium heat for 10 minutes, stirring occasionally. Add the stock and bay leaf, bring to the boil, then reduce the heat and simmer for 10 minutes. Add the rice, bring back to the boil, cover and cook over medium heat for 15 minutes, or until the rice and vegetables are tender. Remove from the heat and stir in the clam meat. Remove the bay leaf and allow to cool for 10 minutes.

Purée the soup in a blender until smooth, then return to a saucepan. Stir in the cream and season. Gently reheat the soup. Add the parsley and two clams in the shell to each bowl.

SERVES 4

Sweet potato and pear soup

25 g (1 oz) butter
1 small white onion, finely chopped
750 g (1 lb 10 oz) orange sweet potato,
    peeled and cut into 2 cm (¾ inch) cubes
2 firm pears (500 g/1 lb 2 oz), peeled,
    cored and cut into 2 cm (¾ inch) cubes
750 ml (26 fl oz/3 cups) vegetable or chicken stock
250 ml (9 fl oz/1 cup) pouring (whipping) cream
mint leaves, to garnish

Melt the butter in a saucepan over medium heat. Add the onion and cook for 2–3 minutes, or until softened. Add the sweet potato and pear, and cook, stirring, for 1–2 minutes. Add the stock, bring to the boil and cook for 20 minutes, or until the sweet potato and pear are soft.

Cool slightly, then place the mixture in a blender or food processor and blend in batches until smooth. Return to the pan, stir in the cream and gently reheat without boiling. Season and garnish with the mint.

SERVES 4

New England
clam chowder

1.5 kg (3 lb 5 oz) clams, cleaned
2 teaspoons oil
3 bacon slices, chopped
1 onion, chopped
1 garlic clove, crushed
750 g (1 lb 10 oz) potatoes, diced
330 ml (11¼ fl oz/1⅓ cups) fish stock

500 ml (17 fl oz/2 cups) milk
125 ml (4 fl oz/½ cup) pouring (whipping) cream
3 tablespoons chopped flat-leaf (Italian) parsley

Put the clams in a large heavy-based saucepan with 250 ml (9 fl oz/1 cup) of water. Cover and simmer for about 4 minutes, or until they open. Discard any that do not open. Strain the liquid through a muslin (cheesecloth)-lined sieve and reserve. Pull most of the clams out of their shells, leaving a few intact as a garnish.

Heat the oil in a saucepan. Add the bacon, onion and garlic and cook, stirring, over medium heat until the onion is soft and the bacon golden. Add the potato and stir well.

Add enough water to the reserved clam liquid to make 330 ml (11¼ fl oz/1⅓ cups) of liquid in total. Pour this and the stock into the saucepan and bring to the boil. Pour in the milk and bring back to the boil. Reduce the heat, cover and simmer for 20 minutes, or until the potato is tender. Uncover and simmer for 10 minutes, or until slightly thickened. Add the cream, clam meat and parsley and season. Heat through gently, but do not allow to boil. Serve with the clams in shells as a garnish.

SERVES 4

Jerusalem artichoke
and roast garlic soup

1 garlic head
40 g (1½ oz) butter
1 tablespoon olive oil
1 onion, chopped
1 leek, white part only, chopped
1 celery stalk, chopped
700 g (1 lb 9 oz) Jerusalem artichokes, peeled and chopped
1 small potato, chopped
1.5 litres (52 fl oz/6 cups) vegetable or chicken stock
olive oil, to serve
finely chopped chives, to garnish

Preheat the oven to 200°C (400°F/Gas 6). Slice the base from the head of garlic, wrap it in foil and roast for 30 minutes, or until soft. When cool enough to handle, remove from the foil and slip the cloves from the skin. Set aside.

Heat the butter and oil in a large heavy-based saucepan over medium heat. Add the onion, leek and celery and a large pinch of salt and cook for 10 minutes, or until soft. Add the Jerusalem artichokes, potato and garlic and cook for a further 10 minutes. Pour in the stock and bring the mixture to the boil. Reduce the heat and simmer for 30 minutes, or until the vegetables are soft. Allow to cool slightly.

Purée the mixture in a blender until smooth, and season well. Serve with a drizzle of olive oil and garnish with chives.

SERVES 4

Lobster soup with zucchini and avocado

50 g (1¾ oz) butter
1 garlic clove, crushed
2 French shallots, finely chopped
1 onion, chopped
1 zucchini (courgette), diced
2½ tablespoons dry white wine
400 ml (14 fl oz) fish stock
250 g (9 oz) raw lobster meat,
    chopped
250 ml (9 fl oz/1 cup) thick
    (double/heavy) cream

1 avocado, diced
1 tablespoon chopped coriander
    (cilantro) leaves
1 tablespoon chopped flat-leaf
    (Italian) parsley
lemon juice, to serve

Fish substitution
crayfish, prawns (shrimp)

Melt the butter in a large saucepan over medium heat. Add the garlic, chopped shallots, onion and zucchini and cook for 8–10 minutes, or until the vegetables are just soft.

Add the wine and bring to the boil, then simmer for 3 minutes. Pour in the stock and bring to the boil again. Reduce the heat to low, add the lobster and simmer for 3–4 minutes, or until the lobster meat is opaque and tinged pink. Gently stir in the cream and season well.

Ladle the soup into four bowls and stir some of the avocado, coriander and parsley into each one. Squeeze a little lemon juice over the soup before serving.

SERVES 4

spicy

Vegetable and lentil soup with spiced yoghurt

2 tablespoons olive oil
1 leek, white part only, chopped
2 garlic cloves, crushed
2 teaspoons curry powder
1 teaspoon ground cumin
1 teaspoon garam masala
1 litre (35 fl oz/4 cups) vegetable stock
1 bay leaf
185 g (6½ oz/1 cup) brown lentils
450 g (1 lb) butternut pumpkin (squash), peeled and cut into 1 cm (½ inch) cubes
2 zucchini (courgettes), cut in half lengthways and sliced

400 g (14 oz) tinned chopped tomatoes
200 g (7 oz) broccoli, cut into small florets
1 small carrot, diced
80 g (2¾ oz/½ cup) peas
1 tablespoon chopped mint

Spiced yoghurt

250 g (9 oz/1 cup) plain yoghurt
1 tablespoon chopped coriander (cilantro) leaves
1 garlic clove, crushed
3 dashes Tabasco sauce

Heat the oil in a saucepan over medium heat. Add the leek and garlic and cook for 4 minutes. Add the curry powder, cumin and garam masala and cook for 1 minute. Add the stock, bay leaf, lentils and pumpkin. Bring to the boil, then reduce the heat and simmer for 10–15 minutes, or until the lentils are tender. Season. Add the zucchini, tomatoes, broccoli, carrot and 500 ml (17 fl oz/2 cups) of water and simmer for 10 minutes, or until the vegetables are tender. Add the peas and simmer for 2–3 minutes.

To make the spiced yoghurt, put the yoghurt, coriander, garlic and Tabasco in a bowl and stir until combined. Serve with the soup and garnish with the mint.

SERVES 6

Spicy pumpkin and coconut soup

1 small red chilli, seeded and chopped
1 lemon grass stem, white part only, sliced
1 teaspoon ground coriander
1 tablespoon chopped fresh ginger
500 ml (17 fl oz/2 cups) vegetable stock
2 tablespoons oil
1 onion, finely chopped
800 g (1 lb 12 oz) pumpkin (squash) flesh, cubed (see Note)
375 ml (13 oz/1½ cups) coconut milk
3 tablespoons chopped coriander (cilantro) leaves
2 teaspoons shaved palm sugar or soft brown sugar
extra coriander (cilantro) leaves, to garnish

Put the chilli, lemongrass, ground coriander, ginger and 2 tablespoons of vegetable stock in a food processor and process until smooth.

Heat the oil in a large saucepan over medium heat. Add the onion and cook for 5 minutes. Add the spice paste and cook, stirring, for 1 minute.

Add the pumpkin and remaining vegetable stock. Bring to the boil, then reduce the heat and simmer, covered, for 15–20 minutes, or until the pumpkin is tender. Cool slightly, then process in a food processor or blender until smooth. Return to the pan, stir in the coconut milk, coriander and palm sugar and simmer until hot. Garnish with the extra coriander leaves.

SERVES 4

NOTE: You will need to buy 1.5 kg (3 lb 5 oz) pumpkin with the skin on to yield 800 g (1 lb 12 oz) flesh.

Tunisian fish soup

3 tablespoons olive oil
1 onion, chopped
1 celery stalk, chopped
4 garlic cloves, crushed
2 tablespoons tomato paste
   (concentrated purée)
1½ teaspoons ground turmeric
1½ teaspoons ground cumin
2 teaspoons harissa
1 litre (35 fl oz/4 cups) fish stock
2 bay leaves
200 g (7 oz/1 cup) orzo or other
   small pasta

500 g (1 lb 2 oz) mixed skinless
   snapper and sea bass fillets,
   cut into bite-sized chunks
2 tablespoons chopped mint,
   plus some extra leaves,
   to garnish
2 tablespoons lemon juice
pitta bread, to serve (optional)

Fish substitution
cod, haddock, ocean perch,
   coral trout

Heat the oil in a large saucepan over medium heat. Add the onion and celery and cook for 8–10 minutes, or until softened. Add the garlic and cook for a further minute. Stir in the tomato paste, turmeric, cumin and harissa and cook, stirring constantly, for an extra 30 seconds.

Pour the fish stock into the saucepan and add the bay leaves. Bring the liquid to the boil, then reduce the heat to low and simmer gently for 15 minutes.

Add the orzo to the liquid and cook for 2–3 minutes, or until *al dente*. Add the fish to the liquid and poach gently for 3–4 minutes, or until the fish is opaque. Stir in the mint and lemon juice and season to taste. Serve with warm pitta bread, if desired. Garnish with mint leaves.

SERVES 6

Japanese prawn,
scallop and noodle soup

4 dried shiitake mushrooms
100 g (3½ oz) dried soba or
    somen noodles
10 g (¼ oz) sachet bonito-
    flavoured soup stock
75 g (2½ oz) carrot, cut into
    thin batons
150 g (5½ oz) firm tofu, cut into
    cubes
16 prawns (shrimp), peeled and
    deveined, tails intact

8 scallops, cleaned
2 spring onions (scallions), finely
    chopped
1 tablespoon mirin
shichimi togarashi, to serve
    (see Note)

Fish substitution
chunks of firm white fish,
    fish balls

Soak the mushrooms in 300 ml (10½ fl oz) of boiling water for 30 minutes. Cook the noodles in a saucepan of boiling water for 2 minutes, then drain and rinse with cold water. Return the noodles to the pan and cover.

In a saucepan, mix the stock with 1 litre (35 fl oz/4 cups) of water. Drain the mushrooms and add the soaking liquid to the pan. Chop the mushroom caps. Add the mushrooms and carrot to the pan and bring to the boil. Reduce the heat to a simmer and cook for 5 minutes. Add the tofu, prawns, scallops, spring onion and mirin. Simmer for 4 minutes, or until the prawns are pink.

Meanwhile, pour hot water over the noodles. Drain. Divide the noodles among four large bowls and pour the soup over, dividing the seafood equally. Serve sprinkled with shichimi togarashi.

SERVES 4

NOTE: Shichimi togarashi is a Japanese condiment.

Split pea and vegetable soup

1 tablespoon peanut or vegetable oil
1 onion, chopped
2 garlic cloves, chopped
1½ teaspoons chopped fresh ginger
1½ tablespoons Madras curry paste
100 g (3½ oz) yellow split peas, rinsed and drained
1 large zucchini (courgette), peeled and chopped
1 large carrot, roughly chopped
170 g (6 oz) button mushrooms, roughly chopped
1 celery stalk, roughly chopped
1 litre (35 fl oz/4 cups) vegetable stock
125 ml (4 fl oz/½ cup) pouring (whipping) cream

Heat the oil in a saucepan, add the onion and cook over low heat for 5 minutes, or until soft. Add the garlic, ginger and curry paste and cook over medium heat for 2 minutes. Stir in the split peas until well coated with paste, then add the zucchini, carrot, mushroom and celery and cook for 2 minutes.

Add the stock, bring to the boil, then reduce the heat and simmer, partly covered, for 1 hour. Remove from the heat and allow to cool slightly.

Transfer the soup to a blender or food processor and process in batches until smooth. Return to the pan, stir in the cream and gently heat until warmed through. Serve with naan bread, if desired.

SERVES 4

Moroccan lamb, chickpea and coriander soup

165 g (5¾ oz/¾ cup) dried chickpeas
1 tablespoon olive oil
850 g (1 lb 14 oz) boned lamb leg, cut into 1 cm
   (½ inch) cubes
1 onion, chopped
2 garlic cloves, crushed
½ teaspoon ground cinnamon
½ teaspoon ground turmeric
½ teaspoon ground ginger
4 tablespoons chopped coriander (cilantro) leaves
800 g (1 lb 12 oz) tinned chopped tomatoes
1 litre (35 fl oz/4 cups) chicken stock
160 g (5¾ oz/⅔ cup) dried red lentils, rinsed
coriander (cilantro) leaves, to garnish

Soak the chickpeas in cold water overnight. Drain and rinse well.

Heat the oil in a large saucepan over high heat and brown the lamb in batches for 2–3 minutes. Reduce the heat to medium, return the lamb to the pan with the onion and garlic and cook for 5 minutes. Add the spices, season and cook for 2 minutes. Add the coriander, tomato, stock and 500 ml (17 fl oz/2 cups) of water and bring to the boil over high heat.

Add the lentils and chickpeas and simmer, covered, over low heat for 1½ hours. Uncover and cook for 30 minutes, or until the lamb is tender and the soup is thick. Season. Garnish with coriander.

SERVES 4–6

Saffron and Jerusalem artichoke soup

1 pinch saffron threads
250 g (9 oz) Jerusalem artichokes
2 tablespoons lemon juice
1 tablespoon olive oil
1 large onion, finely chopped
1 litre (35 fl oz/4 cups) vegetable or chicken stock
3 teaspoons ground cumin
500 g (1 lb 2 oz) desiree potatoes, grated
2 teaspoons lemon juice, extra

Put the saffron threads in a bowl with 2 tablespoons of boiling water and set aside.

Peel and thinly slice the artichokes, dropping the slices into a bowl of water mixed with lemon juice to prevent discolouration.

Heat the oil in a large heavy-based saucepan over medium heat. Add the onion and cook for 2–3 minutes, or until the onion is softened. Bring the stock to the boil in a large saucepan. Add the cumin to the onion mixture and cook for a further 30 seconds, or until fragrant. Add the drained artichokes, potato, saffron mixture, stock and extra lemon juice. Bring to the boil, then reduce the heat and simmer for 15–18 minutes, or until the artichokes are very soft.

Transfer to a blender and process in batches until smooth. Return the soup to the pan and season to taste. Reheat over medium heat and serve immediately.

SERVES 4

Cold spicy roast capsicum soup

4 red capsicums (peppers)
2 teaspoons oil
2 garlic cloves, crushed
4 spring onions (scallions), sliced
1 teaspoon finely chopped seeded chillies
425 g (15 oz) tinned crushed tomatoes
125 ml (4 fl oz/½ cup) chilled vegetable stock
1 teaspoon balsamic vinegar
2 tablespoons chopped basil

Cut the capsicums into quarters and remove the seeds and membrane. Put the capsicums skin side up under a hot grill (broiler) and grill until the skins blacken and blister. Cool in a plastic bag, then peel away the skin and roughly chop the flesh.

Heat the oil in a small saucepan. Add the garlic, spring onion and chilli and cook over low heat for 1–2 minutes, or until softened.

Transfer to a food processor or blender, and add the capsicum, crushed tomatoes and stock. Blend until smooth, then stir in the vinegar and basil. Season to taste. Refrigerate, then serve cold.

SERVES 4

Carrot and ginger soup

750 ml (26 fl oz/3 cups) vegetable stock
1 tablespoon oil
1 onion, chopped
1 tablespoon grated fresh ginger
1 kg (2 lb 4 oz) carrots, chopped
2 tablespoons chopped coriander (cilantro) leaves

Put the stock in a saucepan and bring to the boil.

Heat the oil in a large heavy-based saucepan over medium heat. Add the onion and ginger and cook for 2 minutes, or until the onion has softened.

Add the stock and carrots. Bring to the boil, then reduce the heat and simmer for 10–15 minutes, or until the carrot is cooked and tender.

Pour into a blender or food processor and process in batches until smooth. Return to the pan and add a little more stock or water if needed.

Stir in the coriander and season to taste. Heat gently before serving.

SERVES 4

Pork congee

300 g (10½ oz/1½ cups) long-
    grain rice, thoroughly rinsed
½ star anise
2 spring onions (scallions), white
    part only
4 x 4 cm (1½ x 1½ inch) piece
    ginger, cut into slices
3.5 litres (122 fl oz/14 cups)
    chicken stock
1 tablespoon peanut oil

2 garlic cloves, crushed
1 teaspoon grated ginger, extra
400 g (14 oz) minced (ground)
    pork
ground white pepper
3 tablespoons light soy sauce
sesame oil, to drizzle
6 fried dough sticks (optional,
    see Note)

Put the rice in a large saucepan with the star anise, spring onions, sliced ginger and chicken stock. Bring to the boil, then reduce the heat to low and simmer for 1½ hours, stirring occasionally.

Heat the oil in a frying pan over high heat. Cook the garlic and grated ginger for 30 seconds. Add the pork and cook for 5 minutes, or until browned, breaking up any lumps with a spoon.

Remove the star anise, spring onions and ginger from the soup and discard. Add the pork mixture and simmer for 10 minutes. Season with white pepper and stir in the soy sauce. Serve with a drizzle of sesame oil and fried dough sticks, if desired.

SERVES 4–6

NOTE: Fried dough sticks are available at Chinese bakeries and speciality shops and are best eaten soon after purchasing. If not, reheat in a 200°C (400°F/Gas 6) oven for 5 minutes, then serve.

Soba noodle and vegetable soup

250 g (9 oz) soba noodles
2 dried shiitake mushrooms
2 litres (70 fl oz/8 cups) vegetable stock
120 g (4 oz) snowpeas (mangetout), cut into strips
2 small carrots, cut into thin 5 cm (2 inch) strips
2 garlic cloves, finely chopped
6 spring onions (scallions), cut into 5 cm (2 inch) lengths
    and thinly sliced lengthways
3 cm (1¼ inch) piece ginger, cut into julienne strips
4 tablespoons soy sauce
3 tablespoons mirin or sake
90 g (3¼ oz) bean sprouts, trimmed
coriander (cilantro) leaves, to garnish

Cook the noodles according to the packet instructions. Drain.

Soak the mushrooms in 125 ml (4 fl oz/½ cup) of boiling water until soft. Drain, reserving the liquid. Remove the stalk and slice the mushrooms.

Combine the stock, mushrooms, reserved liquid, snowpeas, carrot, garlic, spring onion and ginger in a large saucepan. Bring slowly to the boil, then reduce the heat to low and simmer for 5 minutes, or until the vegetables are tender. Add the soy sauce, mirin and bean sprouts. Cook for a further 3 minutes.

Divide the noodles among four large serving bowls. Ladle the hot liquid and vegetables over the top and garnish with coriander.

SERVES 4

Spicy tomato soup
with chorizo

500 g (1 lb 2 oz) chorizo sausage
2 tablespoons olive oil
3 onions, halved and sliced
3 garlic cloves, thinly sliced
½ teaspoon ground cumin
1 teaspoon paprika
1–2 small red chillies, seeded and finely chopped
1.5 litres (52 fl oz/6 cups) chicken stock
800 g (1 lb 12 oz) tinned chopped tomatoes
4 tablespoons chopped flat-leaf (Italian) parsley

Fill a large deep frying pan with about 3 cm (1¼ inches) of cold water. Add the chorizo sausage, then bring to the boil over high heat. Reduce the heat and simmer, turning occasionally, for 15 minutes, or until the water evaporates, then continue to cook in any fat left in the pan for 3–4 minutes, or until the chorizo is lightly browned. Allow to cool slightly and break into bite-sized pieces.

Heat the oil in a large saucepan over medium heat. Cook the onion and garlic for 5–6 minutes, or until soft. Stir in the cumin and paprika, chilli, chicken stock, tomato and half the parsley. Bring to the boil and add the chorizo. Reduce the heat and simmer for 20 minutes. Stir in the remaining parsley and serve immediately.

SERVES 4–6

Duck, mushrooms and rice noodle broth

3 dried shiitake mushrooms
1 Chinese roast duck (1.5 kg/
   3 lb 5 oz)
500 ml (17 fl oz/2 cups) chicken
   stock
2 tablespoons light soy sauce
1 tablespoon Chinese rice wine
2 teaspoons sugar
400 g (14 oz) fresh flat rice
   noodles

2 tablespoons oil
3 spring onions (scallions), thinly
   sliced
1 teaspoon finely chopped
   ginger
400 g (14 oz) bok choy (pak
   choi), trimmed and leaves
   separated
¼ teaspoon sesame oil

Place the shiitake mushrooms in a bowl, cover with 250 ml (9 fl oz/1 cup) of boiling water and soak for 20 minutes. Drain, reserving the liquid and squeezing the excess liquid from the mushrooms. Discard the woody stems and slice the caps.

Remove the skin and flesh from the roast duck. Discard the fat and carcass. Finely slice the duck meat and the skin.

Place the chicken stock, soy sauce, rice wine, sugar and the reserved mushroom liquid in a saucepan over medium heat. Bring to a simmer and cook for 5 minutes.

Meanwhile, place the rice noodles in a heatproof bowl, cover with boiling water and soak. Gently separate the noodles and drain. Divide among soup bowls.

Heat the oil in a wok over high heat. Add the spring onion, ginger and shiitake mushrooms and cook for several seconds. Transfer to the broth with the bok choy and duck meat and simmer for 1 minute, or until the duck has warmed through. Ladle the soup over the noodles and drizzle sesame oil on each serving.

SERVES 4–6

Spicy Portuguese
chicken soup

2.5 litres (87 fl oz/10 cups) chicken stock
1 onion, cut into thin wedges
1 celery stalk, finely chopped
1 teaspoon grated lemon zest
3 tomatoes, peeled, seeded and chopped
1 mint sprig
1 tablespoon olive oil
2 chicken breast fillets
200 g (7 oz/1 cup) long-grain rice
2 tablespoons lemon juice
2 tablespoons shredded mint

Combine the chicken stock, onion, celery, lemon zest, tomatoes, mint and olive oil in a large saucepan. Slowly bring to the boil, then reduce the heat, add the chicken and simmer gently for 20–25 minutes, or until the chicken is cooked through.

Remove the chicken from the saucepan and discard the mint sprig. Allow the chicken to cool, then thinly slice.

Meanwhile, add the rice to the pan and simmer for 25–30 minutes, or until the rice is tender. Return the sliced chicken to the pan, add the lemon juice and stir for 1–2 minutes, or until the chicken is warmed through. Season and stir through the mint.

SERVES 6

Spicy parsnip soup

1.25 litres (44 fl oz/5 cups) vegetable or chicken stock
30 g (1 oz) butter
1 white onion, cut into quarters and finely sliced
1 leek, finely sliced
500 g (1 lb 2 oz) parsnips, peeled and finely sliced
1 tablespoon Madras curry powder
1 teaspoon ground cumin
315 ml (11 oz/1¼ cups) pouring (whipping) cream (see Note)
10 g (¼ oz) coriander (cilantro) leaves

Bring the stock to the boil in a saucepan and keep at a low simmer.

Melt the butter in a large saucepan over medium heat. Add the onion, leek and parsnip and cook, covered, for 5 minutes. Add the curry powder and cumin and cook for 1 minute. Stir in the stock and cook, covered, over medium heat for about 10 minutes, or until tender.

Transfer the soup to a blender or food processor and blend in batches until smooth. Return to the pan. Stir in the cream and warm through over low heat. Season to taste and scatter with coriander leaves.

SERVES 6

NOTE: This soup is also delicious without the cream, if you prefer not to add it.

Spicy seafood and roasted corn soup

2 corn cobs (700 g/1 lb 9 oz)
1 tablespoon olive oil
1 red onion, finely chopped
1 small red chilli, finely chopped
½ teaspoon ground allspice
4 vine-ripened tomatoes, peeled
   and finely diced
1.5 litres (52 fl oz/6 cups) fish
   stock or light chicken stock
300 g (10½ oz) boneless firm
   white fish fillets, diced
200 g (7 oz) fresh crab meat

200 g (7 oz) peeled raw prawns
   (shrimp), roughly chopped
1 tablespoon lime juice

Quesadillas
4 flour tortillas (19 cm/7½ inch)
85 g (3 oz/⅔ cup) grated
   cheddar cheese
1 large handful coriander
   (cilantro) leaves
2 tablespoons olive oil

Preheat the oven to 200°C (400°F/Gas 6). Peel back the husks on the corn cobs and remove the silks. Fold the husks back over the corn, put in a baking dish and bake for 1 hour, or until the corn is tender.

Heat the oil in a saucepan over medium heat. Add the onion and cook until soft. Add the chilli and allspice and cook for 1 minute, then add the tomato and stock and bring to the boil. Reduce the heat and simmer, covered, for 45 minutes. Slice the kernels from the corn cobs, add to the soup and simmer for 15 minutes. Add the fish, crab and prawn meat and simmer for 5 minutes. Add the lime juice.

Meanwhile, to make the quesadillas, top one tortilla with half the cheese and half the coriander. Season, then top with another tortilla. Heat 1 tablespoon of the oil in a frying pan and cook the quesadilla for 30 seconds on each side. Repeat. Cut into wedges and serve with the soup.

SERVES 4

Five-spice duck and somen noodle soup

4 duck breasts, skin on
1 teaspoon Chinese five-spice
1 teaspoon peanut oil
200 g (7 oz) dried somen noodles

Star anise broth
1 litre (35 fl oz/4 cups) chicken stock
3 whole star anise
5 spring onions (scallions), chopped
1 large handful coriander (cilantro) leaves, chopped

Preheat the oven to 200°C (400°F/Gas 6). Trim the duck breast of excess fat, then lightly sprinkle both sides with the five-spice powder.

Heat the oil in a large frying pan over medium heat. Add the duck, skin side down, and cook for 2–3 minutes, or until brown and crisp. Turn and cook the other side for 3 minutes. Transfer to a baking tray and cook, skin side up, for a further 8–10 minutes, or until cooked to your liking.

Meanwhile, put the chicken stock and star anise in a small saucepan. Bring to the boil, then reduce the heat and simmer for 5 minutes. Add the spring onion and coriander and simmer for 5 minutes.

Cook the noodles in a saucepan of boiling water for 2 minutes, or until soft. Drain and divide among four bowls. Ladle the broth the noodles and top each bowl with one sliced duck breast.

SERVES 4

Chickpea, potato and spinach soup

1 litre (35 fl oz/4 cups) vegetable stock
1½ tablespoons olive oil
1 onion, finely chopped
1 large potato, cut into 1.5 cm (⅝ inch) cubes
1½ teaspoons paprika
2 garlic cloves, crushed
400 g (14 oz) tinned chickpeas, drained
1 large tomato, cut into small cubes
50 g (1¾ oz) English spinach, coarsely shredded
25 g (1 oz/¼ cup) grated parmesan cheese

Put the stock in a saucepan, then cover and slowly bring to the boil.

Heat the olive oil in a large heavy-based saucepan. Cook the onion for 2 minutes, or until soft. Add the potato to the onion, and stir in the paprika, garlic and chickpeas. Add the onion mixture to the stock and bring to the boil. Stir in the tomato, and season.

Simmer for 10 minutes, or until the potato is tender. Add the spinach and cook until wilted. Top with parmesan and season to taste.

SERVES 4

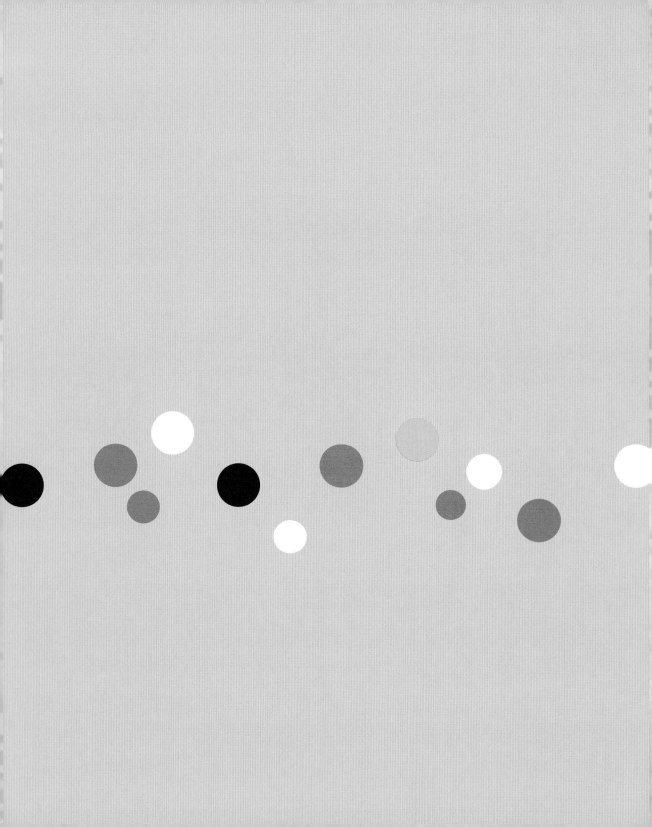

hearty

Capsicum, spinach and chickpea soup

1 tablespoon olive oil
8 spring onions (scallions), finely sliced
1 red capsicum (pepper)
1 garlic clove, crushed
1 teaspoon cumin seeds
375 ml (13 fl oz/1½ cups) Italian tomato passata (puréed tomatoes)
750 ml (26 fl oz/3 cups) vegetable or beef stock
300 g (10½ oz) tinned chickpeas, rinsed and drained
2 teaspoons red wine vinegar
1–2 teaspoons sugar
100 g (3½ oz) baby English spinach leaves

Heat the oil in a large heavy-based saucepan over medium heat and stir in the spring onion. Reduce the heat and cook, covered, for 2–3 minutes, or until softened.

Remove the seeds and membrane from the capsicum and finely dice. Add the capsicum, garlic and cumin seeds to the pan and cook for 1 minute.

Add the passata and stock and bring the mixture to the boil. Reduce the heat and simmer for 10 minutes. Add the chickpeas, vinegar and sugar to the soup and simmer for a further 5 minutes. Stir in the baby spinach and season to taste. Cook until the spinach begins to wilt. Serve immediately.

SERVES 4

Chicken and
spinach risoni soup

1 tablespoon olive oil
1 leek, quartered lengthways and thinly sliced
2 garlic cloves, crushed
1 teaspoon ground cumin
1.5 litres (52 fl oz/6 cups) chicken stock
2 boneless, skinless chicken breast fillets
205 g (7¼ oz/1 cup) risoni
150 g (5½ oz) baby English spinach leaves, roughly chopped
1 tablespoon chopped dill
2 teaspoons lemon juice

Heat the oil in a large saucepan over low heat. Add the leek and cook for about 8–10 minutes, or until soft. Add the garlic and cumin and cook for 1 minute. Pour the stock into the pan, increase the heat to high and bring to the boil. Reduce the heat to low, add the chicken fillets and simmer, covered, for 8 minutes. Remove the chicken from the broth, allow to cool slightly, then shred.

Stir the risoni into the broth and simmer for 12 minutes, or until *al dente*.

Return the chicken to the broth along with the spinach and dill. Simmer for 2 minutes, or until the spinach has wilted. Stir in the lemon juice and season to taste.

SERVES 4

Pasta and bean soup

200 g (7 oz/1 cup) dried borlotti
  beans
3 tablespoons olive oil
90 g (3¼ oz) pancetta or bacon,
  finely diced
1 onion, finely chopped
2 garlic cloves, crushed
1 celery stalk, thinly sliced
1 carrot, diced
1 bay leaf
1 rosemary sprig
1 flat-leaf (Italian) parsley sprig

400 g (14 oz) tinned chopped
  tomatoes, drained
1.625 litres (55 fl oz/6½ cups)
  vegetable stock
2 tablespoons finely chopped
  flat-leaf (Italian) parsley
150 g (5½ oz) ditalini or other
  small dried pasta
extra virgin olive oil, to drizzle
freshly grated parmesan cheese,
  to serve

Put the borlotti beans in a large bowl, cover with cold water and leave to soak
overnight. Drain and rinse.

Heat the oil in a large saucepan over medium heat. Add the pancetta, onion, garlic,
celery and carrot and cook for 5 minutes, or until golden. Season with black pepper.
Add the bay leaf, rosemary, parsley, tomato, stock and beans and bring to the boil.
Reduce the heat and simmer for 1½ hours, or until the beans are tender. Add more
boiling water if necessary to maintain the liquid level.

Discard the bay leaf, rosemary and parsley sprigs. Scoop out 250 ml (9 fl oz/1 cup)
of the bean mixture and purée in a food processor or blender. Return to the pan,
season and add the parsley and pasta. Simmer for 6 minutes, or until the pasta is
al dente. Remove from the heat and set aside for 10 minutes. Serve drizzled with
extra virgin olive oil and sprinkled with parmesan.

SERVES 4

Broth with ravioli

1.5 litres (52 fl oz/6 cups) vegetable or chicken stock
500 g (1 lb 2 oz) spinach and ricotta ravioli
175 g (6 oz) snowpeas (mangetout), sliced on the diagonal
4 tablespoons chopped flat-leaf (Italian) parsley
4 tablespoons chopped basil
grated parmesan cheese, to garnish

Place the stock in a large heavy-based saucepan and bring to the boil. Add the ravioli and cook for 8–10 minutes, or until the pasta is *al dente*.

Season to taste and stir in the snowpeas, parsley and basil. Sprinkle with grated parmesan just before serving.

SERVES 2

Manhattan-style
seafood chowder

60 g (2¼ oz) butter
3 bacon slices, chopped
2 onions, chopped
2 garlic cloves, finely chopped
2 celery stalks, sliced
3 potatoes, diced
3 teaspoons chopped thyme
1.25 litres (44 fl oz/5 cups) fish
   stock
1 kg (2 lb 4 oz) baby clams
1 tablespoon tomato paste
   (concentrated purée)

400 g (14 oz) tinned chopped
   tomatoes
375 g (13 oz) skinless ling fillets,
   cut into bite-sized pieces
12 large prawns (shrimp),
   peeled and deveined, tails
   intact
2 tablespoons chopped flat-leaf
   (Italian) parsley

Fish substitution
cod, flake, hake

Melt the butter in a saucepan over low heat. Add the bacon, onion, garlic and celery and cook, stirring occasionally, for 5 minutes, or until soft. Add the potato, thyme and 1 litre (35 fl oz/4 cups) of the stock to the saucepan and bring to the boil. Reduce the heat and simmer, covered, for 15 minutes. Pour the remaining stock into a saucepan and bring to the boil. Add the clams, cover and cook for 3–5 minutes, or until they open. Discard any that do not open. Drain the clam liquid through a muslin-lined sieve and add to the soup mixture. Pull most of the clams out of their shells, leaving a few intact to garnish.

Stir the tomato paste and chopped tomatoes into the soup and bring back to the boil. Add the fish, clams and prawns and simmer over low heat for 3 minutes, or until the seafood is cooked. Season and stir in the parsley. Serve garnished with the clams in their shells.

SERVES 4

Mushroom and tortellini soup

1 tablespoon olive oil
175 g (6 oz) small flat mushrooms, sliced
6 spring onions (scallions), sliced
1 small garlic clove, crushed
1.25 litres (44 fl oz/5 cups) vegetable or chicken stock
1 tablespoon port
2 teaspoons worcestershire sauce
200 g (7 oz) fresh large ricotta tortellini
shaved parmesan cheese, to garnish

Heat the oil in a large heavy-based saucepan over high heat. Add the mushrooms and cook for 2 minutes, browning the mushrooms before turning. Add the spring onion and garlic and cook for a further 1 minute.

Meanwhile, bring the stock to the boil in a separate saucepan. Add the stock, port and worcestershire sauce to the mushroom mixture and bring to the boil. Add the tortellini and simmer for 8 minutes, or until the tortellini is *al dente*.

Season to taste and serve topped with shaved parmesan.

SERVES 4

Seafood soup with rouille

Rouille
1 cooked floury potato, peeled
   and diced
1 red capsicum (pepper), grilled
   and peeled
2 garlic cloves, chopped
1 egg yolk
125 ml (4 fl oz/½ cup) olive oil

1 litre (35 fl oz/4 cups) fish stock
½ teaspoon saffron threads
4 thyme sprigs

5 cm (2 inch) piece orange peel
1 small baguette
olive oil, for brushing
300 g (10½ oz) salmon fillet,
   cut into 4 pieces
300 g (10½ oz) ling fillet, cut
   into 4 pieces
1 squid tube, cleaned and
   cut into rings
8 raw king prawns, shelled and
   deveined

To make the rouille, place the potato, capsicum, garlic and egg yolk in a food processor and process until smooth. With the motor running, gradually add the olive oil until the mixture has the consistency of mayonnaise.

Preheat the oven to 180°C (350°F/Gas 4). Put the stock in a large saucepan and bring to the boil. Add the saffron, thyme and orange peel. Remove from the heat and leave to stand for 10 minutes to allow the flavours to infuse.

Meanwhile, cut the baguette into 1 cm (½ inch) slices. Brush with oil and put on a baking tray. Bake for 10 minutes, or until crisp and golden.

Strain the stock and return to the boil, then add the salmon, ling, squid rings and prawns. Remove the stock from the heat and leave for 2 minutes, or until the seafood is cooked. Serve with the rouille and croutons.

SERVES 4

Zuppa di faggioli

800 g (1 lb 12 oz) tinned
  cannellini beans
1 tablespoon extra virgin olive oil
1 leek, finely chopped
2 garlic cloves, crushed
1 teaspoon thyme leaves
2 celery stalks, diced
1 carrot, diced
1 kg (2 lb 4 oz) silverbeet (Swiss
  chard), trimmed and roughly
  chopped

1 ripe tomato, diced
1 litre (35 fl oz/4 cups) vegetable
  stock
2 small crusty rolls, each cut into
  4 slices
2 teaspoons balsamic vinegar
35 g (1¼ oz/⅓ cup) finely
  grated parmesan cheese

Put half of the cannellini beans and half of the liquid in a blender or food processor and blend until smooth. Drain the remaining beans and set aside.

Heat the oil in a large heavy-based saucepan over medium heat. Add the leek, garlic and thyme and cook for 2–3 minutes, or until soft and aromatic. Add the celery, carrot, silverbeet and tomato and cook for a further 2–3 minutes, or until the silverbeet has wilted. Heat the stock in a separate saucepan.

Stir the puréed cannellini beans and stock into the vegetable mixture. Bring to the boil, then reduce the heat and simmer for 5–10 minutes, or until the vegetables are tender. Add the drained beans and stir until heated through. Season to taste.

Arrange 2 slices of bread in the base of each soup bowl. Stir the balsamic vinegar into the soup and ladle over the bread. Serve topped with grated parmesan.

SERVES 4

Chunky fish soup with bacon and dumplings

2 tablespoons olive oil
1 onion, chopped
1 small red capsicum (pepper), chopped
1 small zucchini (courgette), diced
150 g (5½ oz) smoked bacon, chopped
1 garlic clove, crushed
2 tablespoons paprika
400 g (14 oz) tinned chopped tomatoes
400 g (14 oz) tinned chickpeas

450 g (1 lb) skinless pike fillet, cut into large pieces
2 tablespoons chopped flat-leaf (Italian) parsley

Dumplings
75 g (2½ oz) self-raising flour
1 egg, lightly beaten
1½ tablespoons milk
2 teaspoons finely chopped marjoram

Fish substitution
bream, char, trout

Heat the oil in a saucepan over low heat. Add the onion and cook for 8 minutes, or until softened. Add the capsicum, zucchini, bacon and garlic and cook over medium heat for 5 minutes, stirring occasionally.

Meanwhile, to make the dumplings, combine the flour, egg, milk and marjoram in a bowl and mix with a wooden spoon.

Add the paprika, tomato, chickpeas and 800 ml (28 fl oz) water to the vegetables. Bring the liquid to the boil, then reduce the heat to low and simmer for 10 minutes, or until thickened slightly. Using two tablespoons to help you form the dumplings, add six rounds of the dumpling mixture to the soup. Poach for about 2 minutes, then slide the pieces of fish into the liquid. Poach for a further 2–3 minutes, or until the fish is cooked. Season to taste and sprinkle with parsley

SERVES 6

Minestrone alla Milanese

225 g (8 oz) dried borlotti beans
55 g (2 oz) butter
1 onion, finely chopped
1 garlic clove, finely chopped
3 tablespoons flat-leaf (Italian)
    parsley, finely chopped
2 sage leaves
100 g (3½ oz) pancetta, cubed
2 celery stalks, halved, then sliced
2 carrots, sliced
3 potatoes, peeled but left whole
1 teaspoon tomato paste
    (concentrated purée)

400 g (14 oz) tinned chopped
    tomatoes
8 basil leaves
3 litres (101 fl oz/12 cups)
    chicken or vegetable stock
2 zucchini (courgettes), sliced
225 g (8 oz) shelled peas
125 g (4½ oz) runner beans, cut
    into 4 cm (1½ inch) lengths
¼ cabbage, shredded
220 g (7¾ oz/1 cup) risotto rice
grated parmesan cheese,
    to serve

Put the dried beans in a large bowl, cover with cold water and soak overnight. Drain and rinse under cold water.

Melt the butter in a saucepan and add the onion, garlic, parsley, sage and pancetta. Cook over low heat, stirring until the onion is soft.

Add the celery, carrot and potatoes, and cook for 5 minutes. Stir in the tomato paste, tomatoes, basil and borlotti beans. Season with pepper. Add the stock and bring slowly to the boil. Cover and leave to simmer for 2 hours, stirring once or twice.

If the potatoes have not broken up, roughly break them with a fork. Season to taste and add the zucchini, peas, runner beans, cabbage and rice. Simmer until the rice is cooked. Serve with the parmesan cheese.

SERVES 6

Goulash soup with dumplings

3 tablespoons olive oil
1 kg (2 lb 4 oz) chuck steak, cut into 1 cm (½ inch) cubes
2 large onions, chopped
3 garlic cloves, crushed
1 green capsicum (pepper), chopped
1½ teaspoons caraway seeds, ground
3 tablespoons sweet paprika
¼ teaspoon ground nutmeg
pinch cayenne pepper
½ teaspoon sea salt
400 g (14 oz) tinned chopped tomatoes
2 litres (70 fl oz/8 cups) chicken stock
350 g (12 oz) potatoes, diced
1 green capsicum (pepper), julienned
2 tablespoons sour cream

Dumplings
1 egg
3 tablespoons finely grated parmesan cheese
75 g (2½ oz/⅔ cup) self-raising flour
pinch cayenne pepper

Heat half the oil in a saucepan over medium heat. Cook the beef in batches for 1–2 minutes. Remove and set aside. Heat the remaining oil in the pan over low heat. Add the onion, garlic and chopped capsicum and cook for 5–6 minutes, or until softened. Stir in the spices and salt. Return the beef to the pan. Stir in the tomato and stock and bring to the boil. Reduce the heat to low and simmer, covered, for 1¼ hours. Add the potato and cook for 30 minutes. Stir in the julienned capsicum and sour cream.

To make the dumplings, combine the ingredients and a pinch of salt to form a dough. Turn onto a floured surface and knead for 5 minutes. Roll ½ teaspoonfuls of the dough into balls, drop into the soup and cook for 6 minutes.

SERVES 4–6

Spaghetti and meatball soup

150 g (5½ oz) spaghetti, broken
   into 8 cm (3 inch) lengths
1.5 litres (52 fl oz/6 cups) beef
   stock
3 teaspoons tomato paste
   (concentrated purée)
400 g (14 oz) tinned chopped
   tomatoes
3 tablespoons basil leaves, torn
shaved parmesan cheese,
   to garnish

Meatballs
1 tablespoon oil
1 onion, finely chopped
2 garlic cloves, crushed
500 g (1 lb 2 oz) lean minced
   (ground) beef
3 tablespoons finely chopped
   flat-leaf (Italian) parsley
3 tablespoons fresh breadcrumbs
2 tablespoons finely grated
   parmesan cheese
1 egg, lightly beaten

Cook the spaghetti in a large saucepan of boiling water according to packet instructions until *al dente*. Drain. Put the stock and 500 ml (17 fl oz/2 cups) of water in a large saucepan and slowly bring to a simmer.

Meanwhile, to make the meatballs, heat the oil in a frying pan over medium heat. Cook the onion for 2 minutes, or until soft. Add the garlic. Cook for 30 seconds. Allow to cool. Combine the beef, parsley, breadcrumbs, parmesan, egg, the onion mixture and season. Roll heaped teaspoons of mixture into balls, making 40 balls.

Stir the tomato paste and tomato into the beef stock and simmer for 2–3 minutes. Drop in the meatballs, return to a simmer and cook for 10 minutes, or until cooked through. Stir in the spaghetti and basil to warm through. Season and top with shaved parmesan.

SERVES 4

Winter lamb shank soup

1 tablespoon olive oil
1.25 kg (2 lb 12 oz) lamb shanks
2 onions, chopped
4 garlic cloves, chopped
250 ml (9 fl oz/1 cup) red wine
2 bay leaves
1 tablespoon chopped rosemary
2.5 litres (87 fl oz/10 cups) beef stock
425 g (15 oz) tinned crushed tomatoes

165 g (5¾ oz/¾ cup) pearl barley, rinsed and drained
1 large carrot, diced
1 potato, diced
1 turnip, diced
1 parsnip, diced
2 tablespoons redcurrant jelly (optional)

Heat the oil in a saucepan over high heat. Cook the lamb shanks for 2–3 minutes, or until brown. Remove from the pan.

Add the onion to the pan and cook over low heat for 8 minutes, or until soft. Add the garlic and cook for 30 seconds, then add the wine and simmer for 5 minutes.

Add the shanks, bay leaves, half the rosemary and 1.5 litres (52 fl oz/6 cups) of the stock to the pan. Season. Bring to the boil over high heat. Reduce the heat and simmer, covered, for 2 hours, or until the meat falls off the bone. Remove the shanks and cool slightly.

Remove the meat off the bone and roughly chop. Add to the broth with the tomato, barley, the remaining rosemary and stock and simmer for 30 minutes. Add the vegetables and cook for 1 hour, or until the barley is tender. Remove the bay leaves, then stir in the redcurrant jelly.

SERVES 4

Silverbeet and risoni soup with gruyère croutons

30 g (1 oz) butter
1 large onion, finely chopped
1 garlic clove, crushed
2 litres (70 fl oz/8 cups) vegetable or chicken stock
200 g (1 cup) risoni
½ baguette, cut into 6 slices
15 g (½ oz) butter, extra, melted
1 teaspoon dijon mustard
50 g (1¾ oz) gruyère cheese, coarsely grated
500 g (1 lb 2 oz) silverbeet (Swiss chard), shredded
30 g (1 oz) basil, torn

Heat the butter in a large heavy-based saucepan over medium heat. Add the onion and garlic and cook for 2–3 minutes, or until the onion is softened.

Meanwhile, put the stock in a large saucepan and bring to the boil.

Add the stock to the onion mixture and bring to the boil. Add the risoni, reduce the heat and simmer for 8 minutes, stirring occasionally.

Meanwhile, put the baguette slices in a single layer on a baking tray and cook under a preheated grill (broiler) until golden brown on one side. Turn the slices over and brush with the combined melted butter and mustard. Top with the gruyère and grill until the cheese has melted.

Add the silverbeet and basil to the risoni mixture and simmer for about 1 minute, or until the risoni is *al dente*. Season and serve with the gruyère croutons.

SERVES 6

Tomato and pasta soup

1.25 litres (44 fl oz/5 cups) vegetable or chicken stock
90 g (3¼ oz/1 cup) spiral pasta
2 carrots, sliced
1 zucchini (courgette), sliced
4 ripe tomatoes, roughly chopped
2 tablespoons shredded basil

Place the stock in a heavy-based saucepan and bring to the boil. Reduce the heat, add the pasta, carrot and zucchini and cook for about 5–10 minutes, or until the pasta is *al dente*.

Add the tomato and heat through gently for a few minutes. Season to taste.

Serve the soup sprinkled with the basil over the top.

SERVES 4

NOTE: To give this soup a slightly different flavour, serve with a dollop of fresh pesto.

Hearty seafood soup

2 tablespoons dried shrimp

3 tablespoons olive oil

1 large onion, finely chopped

3 garlic cloves, crushed

1 small red chilli, deseeded and finely chopped

1 teaspoon finely grated fresh ginger

3 tablespoons crunchy peanut butter

800 g (1 lb 12 oz) tinned chopped tomatoes

50 g (1¾ oz) creamed coconut, chopped

400 ml (14 fl oz) coconut milk

generous pinch of ground cloves

4 tablespoons chopped coriander (cilantro) leaves

700 g (1 lb 9 oz) swordfish, cut into large chunks

100 g (3½ oz) small prawns (shrimp), peeled and deveined

2 tablespoons chopped cashew nuts

Fish substitution

marlin, tuna, monkfish

Soak the dried shrimp in boiling water for 10 minutes, then drain.

Heat the oil in a saucepan over medium heat. Cook the onion for 5 minutes. Add the garlic, chilli and ginger and cook for 2 minutes. Stir in the dried shrimp, peanut butter, tomato, creamed coconut, coconut milk, ground cloves and half of the coriander. Bring the mixture to the boil and simmer gently for 10 minutes. Remove from the heat, allow to cool slightly, then tip the sauce into a food processor or blender and blend until thick and smooth.

Return the sauce to the pan over medium heat. Add the swordfish and cook for 2 minutes, then add the prawns and continue to simmer until all the seafood is cooked — the prawns will be pink and the fish opaque. Serve with the cashews and remaining coriander sprinkled over the top.

SERVES 4

Tomato bread soup

750 g (1 lb 10 oz) vine-ripened tomatoes
1 loaf day-old crusty Italian bread
1 tablespoon olive oil
3 garlic cloves, crushed
1 tablespoon tomato paste (concentrated purée)
1.25 litres (44 fl oz/5 cups) hot vegetable stock
4 tablespoons torn basil leaves
2–3 tablespoons extra virgin olive oil
extra virgin olive oil, extra, to serve

Score a cross in the base of each tomato. Put in a bowl of boiling water for 1 minute, then plunge into cold water and peel the skin away from the cross. Cut the tomatoes in half and scoop out the seeds with a teaspoon. Chop the tomato flesh.

Remove most of the crust from the bread and discard. Cut the bread into 3 cm (1¼ inch) pieces.

Heat the oil in a large saucepan over medium heat. Add the garlic, tomato and tomato paste, then reduce the heat and simmer, stirring occasionally, for about 10–15 minutes, or until reduced and thickened. Add the stock and bring to the boil, stirring for 2–3 minutes. Reduce the heat to medium, add the bread pieces and cook, stirring, for 5 minutes, or until the bread softens and absorbs most of the liquid. Add more stock or water if necessary.

Stir in the torn basil leaves and extra virgin olive oil, and leave for 5 minutes to allow the flavours to develop. Drizzle with a little extra virgin olive oil to serve.

SERVES 4

Beef ball and white bean soup

600 g (1 lb 5 oz) minced
   (ground) beef
2 garlic cloves, crushed
1 tablespoon flat-leaf (Italian)
   parsley, finely chopped
large pinch ground cinnamon
large pinch freshly grated
   nutmeg
2 eggs, lightly beaten

1.5 litres (52 fl oz/6 cups) beef
   stock
2 carrots, thinly sliced
800 g (1 lb 12 oz) tinned white
   beans, drained
½ savoy cabbage, finely
   shredded
grated parmesan cheese,
   to serve

Put the beef in a bowl with the garlic, parsley, cinnamon, nutmeg and half of the egg. Mix to combine and season well. If the mixture is dry, add the rest of the egg — it needs to be sticky enough so that forming small balls is easy.

Roll the beef mixture into small balls — they should be small enough to scoop up on a spoon and eat in one mouthful.

Put the beef stock and the carrot in a saucepan and bring to the boil. Add the meatballs, one at a time, and reduce the heat. Simmer for 3 minutes. Add the beans and cabbage and cook for a further 4–5 minutes. Season to taste. Serve with grated parmesan.

SERVES 4

index

First published in 2008 by Murdoch Books Pty Limited

Murdoch Books Australia
Pier 8/9, 23 Hickson Road
Millers Point NSW 2000
Phone: +61 (0) 2 8220 2000
Fax: +61 (0) 2 8220 2558
www.murdochbooks.com.au

Murdoch Books UK Limited
Erico House, 6th Floor
93–99 Upper Richmond Road,
Putney, London SW15 2TG
Phone: +44 (0) 20 8785 5995
Fax: +44 (0) 20 8785 5985
www.murdochbooks.co.uk

Chief Executive: Juliet Rogers
Publishing Director: Kay Scarlett

Design Manager: Vivien Valk
Project manager and editor: Gordana Trifunovic
Design concept: Alex Frampton
Designer: Susanne Geppert
Production: Nikla Martin
Introduction text: Leanne Kitchen
Recipes developed by the Murdoch Books Test Kitchen

PRINTED IN CHINA.
Reprinted 2008, 2009.

ISBN 978 1 74196 101 0

A catalogue record for this book is available from the British Library.

IMPORTANT: Those who might be at risk from the effects of salmonella poisoning (the elderly, pregnant women, young children and those suffering from immune deficiency diseases) should consult their doctor with any concerns about eating raw eggs.

CONVERSION GUIDE: You may find cooking times vary depending on the oven you are using. For fan-forced ovens, as a general rule, set the oven temperature to 20°C (35°F) lower than indicated in the recipe.

eBay® Business

ALL-IN-ONE

4th Edition

by Marsha Collier

eBay® Business All-in-One For Dummies®, 4th Edition

Published by: **John Wiley & Sons, Inc.,** 111 River Street, Hoboken, NJ 07030-5774, www.wiley.com

Copyright © 2018 by John Wiley & Sons, Inc., Hoboken, New Jersey

Published simultaneously in Canada

No part of this publication may be reproduced, stored in a retrieval system or transmitted in any form or by any means, electronic, mechanical, photocopying, recording, scanning or otherwise, except as permitted under Sections 107 or 108 of the 1976 United States Copyright Act, without the prior written permission of the Publisher. Requests to the Publisher for permission should be addressed to the Permissions Department, John Wiley & Sons, Inc., 111 River Street, Hoboken, NJ 07030, (201) 748-6011, fax (201) 748-6008, or online at http://www.wiley.com/go/permissions.

Trademarks: Wiley, For Dummies, the Dummies Man logo, Dummies.com, Making Everything Easier, and related trade dress are trademarks or registered trademarks of John Wiley & Sons, Inc. and may not be used without written permission. eBay is a registered trademark of eBay, Inc. All other trademarks are the property of their respective owners. John Wiley & Sons, Inc. is not associated with any product or vendor mentioned in this book.

For general information on our other products and services, please contact our Customer Care Department within the U.S. at 877-762-2974, outside the U.S. at 317-572-3993, or fax 317-572-4002. For technical support, please visit https://hub.wiley.com/community/support/dummies.

Wiley publishes in a variety of print and electronic formats and by print-on-demand. Some material included with standard print versions of this book may not be included in ebooks or in print-on-demand. If this book refers to media such as a CD or DVD that is not included in the version you purchased, you may download this material at http://booksupport.wiley.com. For more information about Wiley products, visit www.wiley.com.

Library of Congress Control Number: 2017962213

ISBN: 978-1-119-42771-1

ISBN: 978-1-119-42774-2 (ePDF)

ISBN: 978-1-119-42770-4 (ePub)

Manufactured in the United States of America

10 9 8 7 6 5 4 3 2 1

Contents at a Glance

Table of Contents

Introduction

'''ve been selling on eBay for over two decades, since before it was eBay. My fascination with ecommerce made me realize that online sellers may not have business backgrounds, and a business book would help them set up their new business professionally. The Internet changes from year to year (as does the ecommerce market), and I am obsessive about keeping my advice for small businesses updated.

My books about eBay don't just give you the information you can find in help pages; they give you the ins and outs of selling and connecting online, based on my daily experience and research. I also stay on top of the current trends in online and social marketing, test them out, and pass the results back to you. This book gives you more information than even many longtime sellers know.

I am lucky enough to have watched eBay evolve since 1996, a charter member of the PowerSeller program, and now a Top Rated Plus Seller. Running a business online has given me the opportunity to spend more time with my loved ones and have better control of my life. I can make my own schedule and enjoy what I'm doing because my business makes money. Owning a small business is empowering — and profitable.

But those of us who run a small business (even part time) always seem to be doing *something*. Buying, selling, and communicating — even when going on a vacation, our businesses keep humming. There's no 9-to-5 schedule, no regular weekends or holidays. Our stores on eBay can always be open.

Alas, all that success and freedom takes some work. That's why you have this book.

About This Book

This book will give you the basics, the hows and whys of setting up a business selling on eBay and on your own website. I've authored several best-selling books about running a business and marketing online. This book gives you the information you need to get started in one nifty (albeit heavy) volume. You can get the info found in several books about eBay all in one place. Here are some good-to-know features of this All-in-One:

>> There's no need to read straight through all the chapters and minibooks in order. Use the Table of Contents to find information you want to learn. When you have a question, use the Index to find your answer, as you might do with a Google search.

>> Within this book, you may note that some printed web addresses break across two lines of text. If you're reading this book in print and want to visit one of these web pages, simply type in the web address exactly as it's noted in the text, pretending as though the line break doesn't exist. If you're reading this as an ebook, you've got it easy — just click the web address to be taken directly to the web page.

>> When instructions in the book tell you exactly what to type on your keyboard, you'll see those letters, numbers, and symbols in **boldface** type. Of course, if the instruction itself is boldface, **you'll see what to type in** non-bold **type**.

>> I occasionally give you key combinations to use as keyboard shortcuts. For example, when you see something like *Ctrl+S,* that means to hold down the *Ctrl* key and press *S.*

Foolish Assumptions

While writing this book, I've made a few assumptions about you. Because you bought this book, naturally I assume you're an intelligent person with refined tastes. Kidding aside, that may well be true — but the main assumption I've really made about you is that you want to find out more about eBay and selling online.

I assume also that you

>> Have a computer and/or mobile device and an Internet connection

>> Are comfortable browsing the Internet

>> Are familiar with email

>> Are looking for a way to make some extra money

>> Have checked out eBay and bought more than a few items

You've probably also sold a few items and made a couple of dollars. Maybe you think eBay just might be a good place to earn a regular stream of extra income. It also helps if you've read my current edition of *eBay For Dummies* where you get familiar with the basics of eBay.

Note that eBay changes regularly, adding features and new layouts. This book keeps you focused on what's important rather than being written about the latest shiny promotions. The location of links changes regularly too. I've noted the important places you need to go to and what to look out for.

If you can accept that nothing comes without a bit of effort, you might just be on the track of a new career — or a very profitable side gig.

Icons Used in This Book

I've written quite a few books in the *For Dummies* series, and all the books have cute little icons to draw your attention to special comments. Following are the ones I use, along with what they mean.

AUTHOR SAYS

This icon indicates a story about a real event. The story may come from one of my dealings or from a fellow eBay user. I hope you find the stories interesting and learn from another user's mistake (or dumb luck).

REMEMBER

When you see this icon, it's a friendly reminder to keep in mind the short fact that follows. No doubt it will come up again, and you'll be ahead of the game if you remember it.

TIP

Here are a few words from me to you, to help you do things the easy way. I've made the mistakes, but you don't have to make them too.

WARNING

This little bomb of a fact will keep you out of trouble. Often these facts are not generally known. Be sure to read them to avoid common pitfalls.

Also, you will see sidebars (with light gray behind the text); these are important things that I like to emphasize — so don't forget to read them.

Beyond the Book

Here, in one volume, are nine individual minibooks related to becoming an expert on eBay and online sales. Each book is broken down into individual chapters to give you more in-depth information on the subject at hand.

You will notice title pages at the beginning of each minibook (we call them *parts pages*) where you see what's included in the associated minibook, and where you can go online to find more.

And don't forget the book's related Cheat Sheet, which is another source of quick reference information. Find it online at `www.dummies.com/business/online-business/ebay`.

Where to Go from Here

It's time to open the book and dive in. For ongoing eBay-related adventures in cyberspace (the latest frontier), here are some handy destinations:

>> You can find current editions of my *For Dummies* books at `www.dummies.com`.

>> For updates on the topics I cover in this book, be sure to visit my website, `http://www.coolebaytools.com`. You'll find articles about things going on at eBay, online business, and social media.

>> For time-sensitive and technology oriented posts, I have a blog at `http://mcollier.blogspot.com`.

If you'd like to ask me questions personally, you can find me active on the following social media sites:

>> **Twitter:** @MarshaCollier

`https://twitter.com/MarshaCollier`

>> **Facebook:** `Marsha Collier`

`https://www.facebook.com/MarshaCollierFanPage`

>> **Google+:** `Marsha Collier` Circle me?

`https://plus.google.com/101540468776840533944`

>> **YouTube:** DealingDiva (don't judge — I opened that account a long time ago). I post videos to answer many questions I receive.

`http://www.youtube.com/user/dealingdiva`

You can contact me directly from the Contact page on my website. I read all emails and try to answer as many as I can. But please remember that I'm just me. No giant staff, no big offices. I write books, research new products to help online citizens, consult with eBay sellers just like you, run an eBay business, and try to have a life.

Thank you for buying this book. Please email me and let me know about your eBay successes.

1

eBay Basics

Contents at a Glance

Chapter **1**

Connecting with Up-to-Date Technology

I f the whole idea of *technology* gives you the creeps, don't back out now. I feel your pain. Every bit of new tech knowledge that's entered my brain has penetrated only after a great deal of mental whining. I suffered the pain so that you wouldn't have to.

Better yet, you don't need to know much technology (in the true sense of the word) to run a successful online business. Most online sellers have about as much knowledge as you will after you read this chapter.

Starting with the Right Device

You don't have to know a lot of fancy computer mumbo-jumbo to do well on eBay, but you must *have* a computing device. (Okay, if you have your heart set on using eBay from a mobile device, I give you tips for using them throughout the book.) If you're in the market for a computer, you can buy a new, used, or refurbished system, depending on your computing needs. Consider laptops or tablets for portability as well.

The absolute necessities

Although the following list is geared mainly toward the purchase of new PCs (which you can get for a few hundred bucks), you should read this info even if you're thinking of buying a used computer:

>> **Look for a computer with a good-size hard drive.** Remember how the classic movie *The Time Machine* sent a traveler thousands of years into the future? Imagine if each of those years was a computer file. The more time you spend using your computer, the more stuff you want to save on your hard drive. The more stuffed your drive, the bigger the timespan it represents — and the less you'd want to lose it. I recommend buying the biggest hard drive your budget affords you — because no matter how large your hard drive is, you'll find a way to fill it up. And while you're at it . . .

>> **Consider an external backup drive of at least 1.5TB.** Backing up your data on a regular basis can help save you from the many disasters that sometimes befall a computer that's active on the Internet. You can find new 1.5TB drives for sale on eBay for under $50.

>> **Make sure you have a top-quality modem.** Your modem connects your computer to the Internet, normally using a broadband cable or (mostly in days of yore) a telephone line. Even if you have a high-speed connection (see later in this chapter), you need a modem that transfers lots of data quickly (we're talking many thousands of megabits per second, or *Mbps*). The fastest cable modem currently in use is DOCSIS 3.0 (backward-compatible with older standards). DOCSIS 3.0 has more channels than previous versions, and can bond multiple channels for higher speeds. If you rent your modem from your Internet provider, request an upgrade to the latest standards.

>> **Get a big screen.** An LCD or LED monitor that has at least a 23-inch screen with high resolution can make a huge difference after several hours of rabid listing, bidding, or proofreading your item descriptions. (If your monitor is smaller, you may have a hard time actually seeing the listings and images.)

>> **Make sure the computer's central processing unit (CPU) is fast.** A CPU (also known as a "chip") is your computer's brain. It should be the fastest you can afford. You can always opt for the top of the line, but even a slower 2 GHz (gigahertz) processor could suffice. One of my computers is an antique slowpoke, but it's still fast enough that it won't choke when I ask it to do some minor multitasking. If you want lightning-fast speed (imagine a Daytona 500 race car with jet assist), you have to move up to an octa-core processor.

>> **You must have a keyboard.** No keyboard, no typing. In the case of a tablet, if you're comfortable with an on screen keyboard, go for it, the basic keyboard is fine. They do make ingenious ergonomic models, but if the standard keyboard feels comfortable to you, stick with it.

Different keyboards have different feels. I like a keyboard with "clicky" keys, because their action lets my fingers know that the letters I type actually appear. Test out several keyboards prior to purchase and see which one suits your typing style.

>> **You need a pointing device, usually a mouse.** Some laptops come with touchpads or trackballs designed to do the same thing — give you a quick way to move the pointer around the screen so you can select options by clicking or tapping.

Buying a used computer

If you don't have much money to spend, you might want to investigate the used market. Thousands of perfectly good used machines are floating around looking for a caring home. You can pick up a model that's a few years old for a couple of hundred dollars, and it will serve your budding eBay needs just fine. The same holds true for used Macs. Make sure a monitor is included in the purchase price (or buy a new one). The good news: eBay's sellers sell their old computers when upgrading. You can get some great deals.

Buying a refurbished computer or device

If you don't feel comfortable buying a used machine, you may want to consider a factory-refurbished model. These are new machines that were returned to the manufacturer for one reason or another. The factory fixes them so they're just like new and then sweetens the deal with a warranty. Some companies even offer optional, extended, on-site repairs. What you're getting is a new computer at a deep discount because the machine can't be resold legally as new.

TIP

For the most part, refurbished computers are defined as returns, units with blemishes (scratches, dents, and so on), or evaluation units. The factories rebuild them to the original working condition, using new parts (or sometimes used parts that meet or exceed performance specs for new parts). They come with 60- to 90-day warranties that cover repairs and returns. Warranty information is available on the manufacturers' websites. Be sure to read it before you purchase a refurbished computer.

Major computer manufacturers such as Dell, Lenovo, Hewlett-Packard, and Apple provide refurbished computers. Check whether their websites have stores on eBay, or go direct to their sites. For example, you can visit, www.apple.com/shop/browse/home/specialdeals/mac, www.hp.com/go/refurbished, http://outlet.lenovo.com/outlet_us/, and www.dell.com/outlet, and check for closeouts and refurbished goods. I do it and have never been burned!

TIP

Because the inventory of refurbished computers changes daily (as do the prices), there's no way of telling exactly how much money you can save by buying refurbished instead of new. I suggest that you find a new computer you like (and can afford) in a store or a catalog, and then compare it with refurbished systems. If you're thinking about buying from the web or a catalog, don't forget to include the cost of shipping in the total price. Even with shipping costs, however, a refurbished computer may save you between 30 and 60 percent, depending on the deal you find.

Upgrading your devices with the help of eBay

TIP

I've seen eBay listings for workable, older PCs and laptops (a few years old), fully outfitted, for $200. For that matter, you can get great deals on used tablets and smartphones to use for your listings.

You can also find on eBay all the bits and pieces you need to upgrade your computing system. The items you may find most useful include

>> Digital cameras and scanners

>> Flash drives and memory cards

>> Wireless routers

>> Monitors

>> Printers

TIP

Home wireless networks are becoming *de rigueur;* many people have them set up even if they don't have a business at home (Book 9 Chapter 5 shows you how to set up your own network). I have a wireless printer/scanner combination that allows me to send scans through my network from my scanner to any device located elsewhere in my home.

You may have to keep checking in and monitoring the different listings on eBay or manufacturers' sites; they change daily. On eBay, put in your best bid, and check back later to see whether you've won! (If you want to find out about the fine art of auction sniping — bidding at the last minute — skip to Chapter 6 in this minibook. I won't be insulted if you leave me in Chapter 1 for a while now. Honest.)

Connecting to eBay without a Computer or While at Home

Selling on eBay isn't as easy without a computer; it can be done, but eventually you'll want to buy one. That said, I do a large proportion of my eBay work on mobile devices, and it's very convenient.

I'll be referring to the use of the eBay mobile app throughout the book because it is easy to use. I generally start posting drafts of my listings from a smartphone (using an older phone with a good camera) and finish the listings on my laptop.

I find it easier to be sure my listing is competitive when I can check other active (and sold) items on the site at the same time. Also, I often tend leave out some details when I'm posting from a phone or tablet.

If you're going to run a professional business, complete with a postage service and bookkeeping, you'll need to use the features of a computer at some point in your online selling career.

If you get a long lunch at work or have to kill time waiting for clients to call back, you may want to get started on eBay from your work computer. But give it a lot of thought before you do. Pink slips can come to those who run online business on company time.

FREE WI-FI AT STARBUCKS AND MORE!

If you love Starbucks already, you're going to love it even more now that you can buy a cuppa joe and get free Wi-Fi all day. Researching items and shopping on eBay is easy when you don't want to be home alone. Other business locations like Barnes & Noble, McDonalds, Peet's Coffee, and Panera Bread Company also graciously provide free Wi-Fi for customers.

Type the words *free wifi near me* in a Google search text box to find a free Wi-Fi hotspot close to you.

Choosing an ISP

Okay, so you have a computer, and you're ready to surf eBay. Hold on a minute — before you start surfing, you need *access* to the Internet. (Details, details. . . .) The way to access the Internet is through an ISP, or *Internet service provider*, such as Spectrum, Comcast, or AT&T. If you don't already belong to one of these, don't worry; joining is easy.

TIP

If you have a need for speed, and your time is worth a bit more than an increase in ISP cost, you need to look into getting a broadband connection. The quality of the different types of broadband (DSL and cable) can vary greatly from area to area, even from street to street.

Before you decide what kind of broadband connection you want, go to the following site, shown in Figure 1-1:

        www.dslreports.com

Although the site is named DSLReports, they cover all types of ISPs in North America. Just type your Zip code in the appropriate text box next to the Review Finder on the home page, and click the Go button. You'll see a page similar to Figure 1-1. From the resulting list, read the reports from other users in your area. You can also click the Reviews in Detail link to see which broadband service provider is doing the best job. You can read reviews, post questions, and get all the information you need to decide what kind of high-speed connection will work best for your setup.

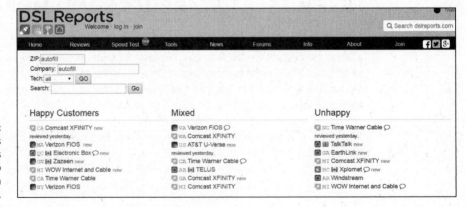

FIGURE 1-1:
The DSLReports website has handy tools to help you select an ISP in your area.

Broadband (high-speed) connections can be a boon to your eBay business. Here's the skinny on the different types:

» **DSL:** Short for *Digital Subscriber Line*. For as little as $12.95 a month, you can move quickly over regular copper phone lines and always be connected to the Internet. A DSL line can move data as fast as three megabits per second (3 Mbps) — that's three thousand kilobits per second. At that speed, a DSL connection can greatly enhance your eBay and Internet experiences.

» **Cable:** An Internet cable connection is the most reliable, fastest, and most expensive method for Internet access (whether or not you have digital cable TV). Using the DOCSIS 3.0 modems mentioned before, you can theoretically get speeds over 150 Mbps. Your Internet connection runs through a cable and is regulated by the provider. With the advent of digital cable, this reliable and speedy Internet connection is an excellent alternative. (See my speed report from my wireless network in Figure 1-2.)

FIGURE 1-2:
Wireless speed results from an 801.11ac router on the 2.4 GHz band.

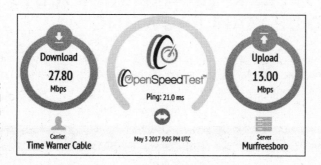

Browsing for a Browser

When you get a computer, you get an Internet browser for free. A *browser* is the software program that lets your computer talk to the Internet. It's like having your own private cyberchauffeur. Type the address (also known as the *URL*, for *Uniform Resource Locator*) of the website you want to visit, and boom, you're there. For example, to get to eBay's home page, type `www.ebay.com` and press Enter. (It's sort of a low-tech version of "Beam me up, Scotty!" — and almost as fast.)

Windows 10 comes with a speedy new browser called Edge (which replaces the venerable Internet Explorer). Other most-used browsers are Safari for iOS and Google Chrome (available both for iOS and the PC), with the previous champ, Firefox, still hanging in. All four programs are powerful and user-friendly.

TIP

You get Microsoft Edge and updates as part of the Windows 10 operating system. If you'd like to try Chrome or Firefox, you can download them for free. To find out more information (or to make sure you're using the most up-to-date version of the software)

» Go to www.google.com/chrome for Google's Chrome browser.

» Go to www.mozilla.com/firefox for Firefox.

If you're a web-browsing veteran, have you ever wondered what happened to all those buttons and drop-down lists at the top of your browser? They're going the way of VHS. According to recent statistics from StatCounter, 53.72 percent of Internet users are using Chrome to surf the web, 14.63 percent use Apple's Safari, and 6.32 percent Firefox. In the accompanying sidebar, I explain in depth how you can use keyboard shortcuts to browse the web more efficiently. Read on while we browse together.

USE EXPERT KEYBOARD SHORTCUTS TO SPEED UP YOUR BROWSING

I'm all about using keystrokes instead of clicking! I also love the controls available on my mouse. The table below gives you a list of all the shortcuts I could find. I hope these tips help cut down your desk time.

Press This	To Make This Happen
F1	Open a help window
Ctrl+F	Open the Search box so you can perform a search on the current page for a word
F5	Refresh the current page
F11	Display full screen, reducing the number of icons and amount of stuff displayed
Esc	Stop loading the current page
Fn+Home	Go back to the top of the web page
Fn+End	Jump to the bottom of the current page
Ctrl and mouse wheel	Enlarge or reduce the text on the screen
Ctrl+D	Add the current page to your favorites list (don't forget to organize this list once in a while)

Backspace	Go to the previous page you've viewed
Ctrl+O	Open a window to open files from your computer
Ctrl+U	Open a new tab to view page source (to study HTML)
Ctrl+P	Print the page
Ctrl+S	Save the current web page to a file on your computer
Ctrl++ or Ctrl+-	Enlarge or reduce the text on the screen
Ctrl+1 through Ctrl+8	Switch to the tab at the specified position number
Ctrl+9	Switch to the last tab that is open in your browser
Ctrl+Shift+T	Reopen the last closed tab
Ctrl+D	Bookmark the current page
Ctrl+Shift+N	New Incognito window; websites you browse in this tab will not be recorded in your Internet history
Ctrl+T	Open a new tab; when you want to visit another web page and want to leave the current one open

» Going places lightning-fast with the navigation bar

» Browsing categories

» Using the home page quick search

Chapter **2**

Navigating through eBay

A s I've said before, the writer Thomas Wolfe was wrong: You *can* go home again — and again. At least with eBay you can! Day after day, millions of people land at eBay's home page without wearing out the welcome mat. The eBay home page is the front door to the most popular ecommerce site on the Internet.

Everything you need to know about navigating eBay begins right here. In this chapter, I give you the grand tour of the areas you can reach right from the home page with the help of links.

Homing In on the Home Page

If you're visiting eBay for the first time (or are returning after deleting the cookies in your browser), you'll arrive at a vibrant marketplace showing you some of the best deals on the site that day. The new eBay home page is shown in Figure 2-1. It includes several key areas:

» A navigation bar at the top of the page with eBay links that can zip you straight to any of the many eBay areas

» An important link to your eBay shopping cart

>> A bar with links to product categories

>> A bottom-of-page set of universal links to important eBay areas

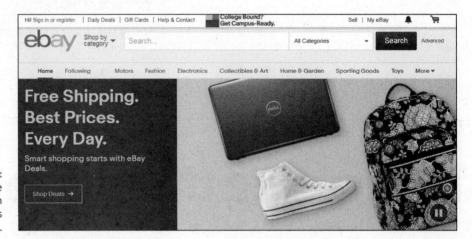

FIGURE 2-1:
New users are presented with great deals upon arrival.

After you've logged on to eBay and performed a few searches, eBay uses AI (artificial intelligence) to customize the home page you see with items that relate to others that you've previously searched for.

TIP

At the top of almost every eBay page is a search box that helps you find items by keywords.

REMEMBER

Do not adjust your computer monitor. You're not going crazy. You may notice that a link was on the eBay home page one minute but gone the next minute.

eBay Daily Deals and Seasonal Specials

If you look carefully on the home page, you can see several other areas that give you express service to several key parts of the site.

Click the link on the home page (it's the same as www.ebay.com/deals) to visit the highly discounted items of the day. Here at eBay, deals are the draw, so a Top Rated Seller can deeply discount an item, offer free shipping, and get eBay to feature his or her listing on the home page. eBay rotates several items each day; during that timeframe, these items are replaced with other items only when the inventory of a featured item has been fully depleted.

You can find everything from homemade crafts to online stores built by major brands to sell their items on eBay. Featured items are not for mere mortal sellers.

They've been lifted to that exalted status because sellers met eBay's stringent requirements for Top Rated Sellers and have assured eBay that they have enough stock to fulfill a huge swath of orders.

Based on your previous searches, you'll see many related items that might just tempt you to buy.

Bottoming out

At the very bottom of the home page, nested into category titles, is an unassuming group of hierarchical links to some seriously handy pages. Here's a guide to a few of the links you'll find:

>> **Tools:** A link to delve into the depths of eBay technology. There are links to eBay software downloads and tools. (See Book 2 for more on these super tools.) If you have a hankering to create some eBay-compatible software, there's a link to the developers' network. You can also visit the Security Center from here. This link takes you to a page where concerns about fraud and safety are addressed. Before buying or selling, it's a good idea to check out the Security Center details in Chapter 3 of this minibook.

   Clicking the eBay Sitemap link provides you with a bird's-eye view of the eBay world. Every top-level (or main) link available on eBay is listed on the Sitemap page. If you're ever confused about finding a specific area, try the sitemap first. If a top-level link isn't listed here, it's not on eBay — yet. When you get lost on eBay (it happens), the Sitemap page will generally get you going in the right direction.

>> **About eBay:** This is always a fun place to visit. You can get company info, investor information, company history, and more. If you think you might want to work *for* eBay instead of *through* eBay, there's a link to jobs available all over the globe.

   You will also find the Policies link, the place to go to brush up on the site's policies and guidelines.

   eBay invites their sellers to get active in the politics of online selling and buying through their Government Relations group. Join in, share your views, and send letters to congresspeople — make a difference!

>> **Contact:** The link to contact eBay often seems elusive just when you really need it. You will find a Contact Us link at the bottom of the Help and Contact links heading.

>> **Affiliates:** If you have your own website and want to make a few bucks, click this link under the Sell header. If you sign up for the program and put a link to eBay on your web page, eBay pays you for new users who sign up directly from your website (plus other bonuses). Click the link for the current details.

>> **Community:** When you want to know about new features on eBay or about any late-breaking news, look here. You will also see links to preview eBay's latest innovations.

REMEMBER

On other eBay pages, the bottom navigation bar looks different. You can access these special, categorized links only on the eBay home page.

The links at the bottom of the page can be critical. They will take you to some very important places on the site. How they're arranged can vary from page to page; Figure 2-2 shows you the two different versions of the bottom-of-the-home-page links.

FIGURE 2-2:
Depending on your screen resolution, you'll see these links.

Since your mileage may vary, let me tell you about the links I feel are the most important.

>> **Sitemap:** I always find that when I get lost on a website, the sitemap can help me find what I'm looking for. By clicking the tabs on the top of the page, you'll find many useful links. You can find the eBay sitemap here:

http://pages.ebay.com/sitemap.html

>> **Announcements:** When eBay makes a policy change or has a new feature, they will post it here. You can also see the quarterly seller policy updates as they are announced. Here's the link:

http://community.ebay.com/t5/Announcements/bg-p/Announcements

>> **Security Center:** On this page you'll find links to much of the official informa-
tion you'll need when you run into rough seas. Again, click the tabs at the top
of the page to home in on your area of interest.

`http://pages.ebay.com/securitycenter/`

>> **StubHub:** At `www.stubhub.com`, you'll find a service that acts as an online
marketplace for buyers and sellers of tickets for sports, concerts, theater, and
other live entertainment events. StubHub takes a commission of the total
amount of the sale.

>> **eBay sites:** Links you to eBay's international ecommerce sites. From a pop-up
menu, you may enter eBay Austria, Australia, Belgium, Canada, China, France,
Germany, Hong Kong, India, Ireland, Italy, Japan, Korea, Malaysia, Netherlands,
Philippines, Poland, Singapore, Spain, Sweden, Switzerland, Taiwan, Thailand,
Turkey, United Kingdom, and (whew) Vietnam. The international sites are in
the country's native language. It might be a good place to practice your
third-year French — or maybe not! Remember that after you leave eBay USA,
you're subject to the contractual and privacy laws of the country you're
visiting.

Navigating eBay the Easy Way

The navigation bar is at the top of the eBay home page and lists six eBay links that
take you directly to different eBay areas. Using the navigation bar is kind of like
doing one-stop clicking. You can find this bar at the top of every page on eBay.
Hovering over some of the links reveals a subnavigation list with links to other,
related (and important) places.

Links to main areas

Here, without further ado, are the links on the navigation bar — and where they
take you:

>> **My eBay:** Clicking the top level, the My eBay link, may bring you to different
places. If you are new to the site, it will bring you to your personal My eBay
transactions page. This is where you keep track of all your buying and selling
activities and account information.

If you've been selling on the site and are using Seller Hub, clicking this link will
take you to those pages. (Find the pertinent details on this area in Book 2,
Chapter 5.)

By mousing over (and not clicking) the My eBay link, you produce a drop-down menu that offers additional links:

- **Summary:** Clicking here takes you to your eBay Overview page or Seller Hub, based on how you've been using the site.

- **Recently Viewed:** A handy graphical list of each item you've recently viewed on the site.

- **Bids/Offers:** Clicking here takes you to a page that tracks any bids you've placed on items up for auction. It also shows any fixed-price listing in which you've placed an offer. (For more about how to make an offer on a fixed-price item, see Chapter 6 in this minibook.)

- **Watch List:** Every eBay item has a link you can click to Watch that item. Doing so gives you the opportunity to bookmark an item for possible future purchase, or to keep an eye on bidding in an auction. Any item you've marked to Watch will be listed on this page.

- **Purchase History:** If you buy on eBay, the site keeps an online record of every purchase you make. Clicking, and going to the Purchase History page, allows you to view all your purchases as far back as three years ago.

- **Selling:** Here you'll find an interactive list of all the items you currently have up for sale on eBay.

- **Saved Searches:** If (like me) you have many different things you search for, eBay gives you a tool for saving certain searches you make. (Book 2, Chapter 5 gives you more info on this.) On the Saved Searches page, you can view, edit, or add product searches.

- **Messages:** Click this link and you'll be brought to the eBay message area. When someone wants to contact you regarding an eBay item, that person's email will appear here. You'll also find messages from eBay — which it also sends to your registered eBay email address.

  This is eBay's private messaging system where you can reply without exposing your personal email address.

REMEMBER

>> **Sell:** Takes you to a page where you can find drafts of listings made from your mobile device and saved for later — or create a new listing. I explain how to navigate this form in Book 3, Chapter 3.

WARNING

Keep in mind that many informational links provided to you by eBay are just that: from eBay. They may be influenced by sponsorship deals or alliances with providers . . . get the drift? Don't consider the information you get on eBay to be, um, commercially unbiased. This book is unbiased — I have no sponsors or advertisers to please.

>> **Help and Contact:** Clicking here will take you to an area where you may find answers to your questions about eBay.

» **Gift Cards:** Send an eBay gift card for any special occasion. Digital gift cards will be sent to any mail or email address you provide. The gift certificate is good for any item on the site. This page also lists other brand's gift cards for sale.

» **Cart:** When you're in a shopping frenzy on eBay, you'll see your cart fill up. Click here to check out and pay for your items all at once.

Links to register, sign in, or shop

On the eBay navigation bar (next to the Sign In link) is a link to eBay's Daily Deals. It's clear they don't want you to miss the deals, so click the link to see the discounts! To the left, on the same line is the Sign In/Sign Out link. It toggles between Sign In and Sign Out depending on your current status. Your browser (and eBay) remember you and whether you're signed in or out; this link will also read *Hi*, followed by your User ID. You can also reach your Account Settings in the drop-down menu.

You'll also find a big honking search bar which enables you to perform a quick search site-wide or directly within a category selectable from a drop-down menu. (Find more on searching in the section "Exploring Home Page Search Options" later in this chapter.)

Just above the topmost graphic promotion are tabs (shown in Figure 2-3) that represent the main top-level categories on eBay.

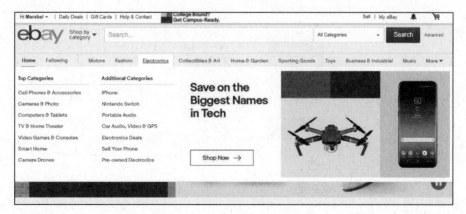

FIGURE 2-3:
Click a category from the drop-down menu.

In similar fashion, a drop-down menu, to the right of the eBay logo, beckons you to Shop by Category. Clicking any of the links in these two areas will bring you to the hub page for the category. This page lists the main subcategories of that category. Click your desired department, and you arrive at the subcategory page with top brands or deals at the top, and you can scroll down to see sort tabs at the top of the listings.

>> **All Listings:** Clicking here will show you everything for sale within the category you've selected.

>> **Auction:** Here you see only the items that are up for auction.

>> **Buy It Now:** This box isolates a view of all items listed as fixed-price or with the Buy It Now feature where the item is up for immediate sale. To the left of the items, you'll find a way to just see the different formats of listing.

>> **Active Listings:** This is the default setting for the page. This option delivers on its promise — you see all items, including auctions and those items that can be purchased immediately using Buy It Now.

>> **Sold Listings:** Here you find items in the category that have ended and have been sold.

>> **Completed Listings:** Any item that has been up for sale and has closed (sold or not) appears here.

Also, to the right of the listings tabs is a drop-down menu of options (see Figure 2-4) that allows you to sort your category results. You can sort from a search in these ways:

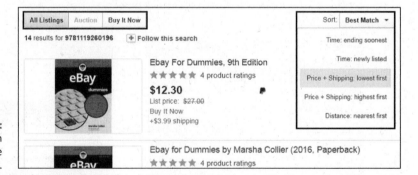

FIGURE 2-4:
Sort your search
with these
options.

>> **Best Match** is the default search option; it sorts the listings you see by their relevance. A listing's relevance is based, in part, on past successful buyer behavior for similar items. The added reasoning behind this sort order is to identify sellers who provide great buying experiences and sellers who don't, all gauged by the use of Detailed Seller Ratings and feedback ratings.

>> **Time: ending soonest** allows you to view the category listings in time order, with the soonest to end on top. (This is the way I always sort when I'm browsing.)

>> **Time: newly listed** shows the items that have recently been listed in the category.

>> **Price + Shipping: lowest first** sorting can be deceiving. Many sellers list their items at an extremely low starting price to attract bidders. You may have to wade through 20 pages of 99-cent items before you reach the dollar ones — a huge waste of time.

>> **Price + Shipping: highest first** sorting is a good choice if you're looking for high-ticket items in a category.

>> **Distance: nearest first** is the best search if you want to buy a large item (sofa? refrigerator? car?) and would rather save on shipping or want to drop by to inspect the item.

You can also search through the category. Type some keywords in the Search box to find, for example, a particular book. Because more than 20 million items are up for auction at any given time, finding just one (say, a book on antique Vermont milk cans) is no easy task.

Maneuvering the Categories

So how does eBay keep track of the millions of items up for sale at any given moment? The brilliant minds at eBay decided to group items into nice, neat little storage systems called *categories.* The home page lists most of the main categories, but eBay also lists tens of thousands of subcategories, ranging from Antiques to Weird Stuff. And don't ask how many sub-subcategories (categories within categories) eBay has — I can't count that high.

Well, okay, I *could* list all the categories and subcategories currently available on eBay — if you wouldn't mind squinting at a dozen pages of really small, eye-burning text. But a category browse is an adventure that's unique for each individual, and I wouldn't think of depriving you of it. Suffice to say that if you like to hunt around for that perfect something, you're in browsing heaven now.

WARNING

If you're a bargain hunter by habit, you may find some pretty weird stuff while browsing the categories and subcategories of items at eBay — some of it super-cheap and some of it just cheap. There's even a Weird Stuff category (under Everything Else)! Remember that (as with any marketplace) you're responsible for finding out as much as possible about an item before you buy — and definitely before you bid. So if you're the type who sometimes can't resist a good deal, ask yourself what you plan to *do* with the pile of stuff you can get for 15 cents — and ask yourself *now*, before it arrives on your doorstep. (Book 1, Chapter 6 offers more information on savvy bidding techniques.)

Exploring Home Page Search Options

There's an old Chinese expression that says, "Every journey begins with the first eBay search." Okay, so I updated the quote. They're very wise words nonetheless. You can start a search from the home page in one of two ways:

>> **Use the Search box.** It's right there at the top of the home page (and most eBay pages), and it's a fast way of finding item listings.

>> **Use the Advanced link (which is next to the Search box).** This link will take you to the sophisticated Advanced Search area (explained in Book 2, Chapter 1), where you can do all kinds of specialized searches.

To launch a title search from the home page, follow these steps:

1. **In the Search box, type no more than a few keywords that describe the item you're looking for.**

Refer to Figure 2-1 to see the Search box.

2. **Click the Search button.**

The results of your search appear in a matter of seconds.

You can type just about anything in the Search box and get some information. Say you're looking for *Star Trek* memorabilia. If so, you're not alone. The original television show premiered on September 8, 1966, and even though it was canceled in 1969 because of low ratings, *Star Trek* has become one of the most successful science-fiction franchises in history. You can use the Search box on the eBay home page to find all sorts of *Star Trek* stuff. I just ran a search and found around 478,327 items in numerous categories on eBay with *Star Trek* in their titles.

WARNING

When you search for popular items at eBay (a classic example is *Star Trek* memorabilia), you may get inundated with thousands of auctions that match your search criteria. Even if you're traveling at warp speed, you could spend hours checking each item individually. ("Scotty, we need more power *now!*") If you're pressed for time like the rest of us, eBay has not-so-mysterious ways for you to narrow down your search to make finding a specific item much more manageable. Turn to Chapter 4 for insider techniques that can help you slim down those searches and beef up those results.

IN THIS CHAPTER

» **Registering with eBay**

» **Choosing a password**

» **Selecting a User ID**

» **Signing in**

» **Following eBay's rules**

Chapter **3**

Signing Up and Getting Started

The prospect of getting started on eBay is exciting — and daunting. Perhaps you've visited the eBay website once or twice with the idea that you might buy something. Maybe you've heard your friends talk about the things they've bought. Did you look up something simple, such as a golf club? Did eBay come up with several thousand listings? Or maybe you figured you'd get smart and narrow the search down to a 3 iron, but you still got more than a thousand listings?

Did you consider buying something and then just left the site, for fear you'd get ripped off? eBay works much better for me than any quasi-convenient TV shopping. On eBay, you have the opportunity to give an item a leisurely once-over, read the description and terms, and click a link to ask the seller a question *before* you bid or buy — and there's eBay's Money Back Guarantee! That's the great thing about eBay: There's always another seller — and always another item.

Registering on eBay

You can browse eBay all you want without registering, but before you transact any sort of business on eBay, you must register. I recommend registering right now — while you're reading this book.

You don't have to be a rocket scientist to become a member on eBay. The only hard-and-fast rule is that you have to be 18 or older. Don't worry; the Age Police won't come to your house to card you — they have other ways to discreetly ensure that you're at least 18 years old. (*Hint:* Credit cards do more than satisfy account charges.)

If you're having a momentary brain cramp and you've forgotten your age, just think back to your childhood. If your first memory is watching *Saved by the Bell* on TV, you're in. Head to the eBay home page and register. The entire process takes only a few minutes.

AUTHOR SAYS

During the early days of online trading, I was selling *Star Trek* memorabilia on Auction Web (the original eBay site) and doing quite well. I ran into William Shatner (Captain Kirk of *Star Trek* fame) at a marketing meeting in mid-1997. Anxious to let him know how well I was doing with my merchandise online, I tried to explain Auction Web (soon to become the awesome eBay). Shatner scoffed, "No one will ever make any money on the Internet." (Really, I have witnesses — remember, this is the future Mr. Priceline.com.) Ah, well. The future is full of surprises.

Before you can sign up, you have to be connected to the web, so now's the time to fire up your computer. After you open your Internet browser, you're ready to sign up. In the address box of your browser, type www.ebay.com and press Enter.

Your next stop is the eBay home page. Right there, where you can't miss it, is the Hi! Sign In or Register set of links. Click the word *register* and let the sign-up process begin.

When you're at the Registration form, you go through a three-step process. Here's an overview:

1. **Enter the basic required info.**

2. **Read and accept the User Agreement.**

3. **Confirm your email address.**

The following sections fill you in on all the details.

You register on eBay through an encrypted (supersecret) connection called SSL (Secure Sockets Layer). You can tell because the normal http at the beginning of the web address is now https.

The SSL certificate verification (in a lower corner of the Get Started on eBay page) means that eBay is a secure place that is safe from unauthorized people seeing or receiving your information. Your information is treated with the highest security, and you can fill out these forms with the utmost level of confidence. I could tell you how SSL works, but instead I'll just give you the bottom line: It *does* work, so trust me and use it. The more precautions eBay (and you) takes, the harder it is for some hyper-caffeinated kid to get into your data.

Filling in required information

After you click the Register link, you go to the first registration page. At the top of the page, you will see that you are creating a personal account. If you'd prefer to start a business account, click the appropriate link. Why not start with a personal account — just to get your feet wet. eBay asks you to fill in some required information (see Figure 3-1).

TIP

You can change your personal eBay account from a personal into a business account when and if you decide it's time. A quick link to that page is

```
https://scgi.ebay.com/ws/eBayISAPI.dll?ChangeRegistrationAccountType
```

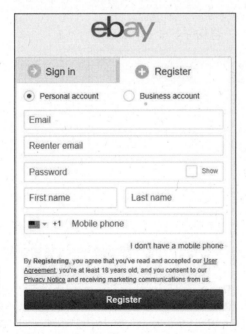

FIGURE 3-1: Required information for your eBay registration.

To get started, follow these steps:

1. **eBay needs to know stuff about you. Enter the following information:**

   - Your full name

   - Your mobile phone number

   - Your email address (*yourname@my ISP . com*)

WARNING

   If you register with an *anonymous email service* such as Yahoo!, Gmail, or Hotmail, you may go to a page that requires additional information for authentication. You must provide valid credit card information for identification purposes. Your information is protected by eBay's privacy policy, and your credit card won't be charged.

   After you input your personal information, you're ready to create your eBay persona.

2. **Type in your new eBay User ID.**

   Your User ID is the name that will be shown to other users when you bid, buy, or sell. But don't strain your brain too much right now over your choice of User ID. You can change your User ID once every 30 days. (See "Selecting Your User ID," later in this chapter, for some tips on making your selection.) If your chosen ID is already taken, eBay has a handy tool to help you select another one, as shown in Figure 3-2.

---

eBay user ID ?

▶ marsha_c

   Sorry, that user ID is not available. Please try again.

   Suggestions:

   marshac.2012

   marshac_2012

   marshac-2012

   2012marshac

   2012_marshac

- I have read and accepted the User Agreement and Privacy Policy.
- I may receive communications from eBay and can change my notification
- I am at least 18 years old.

FIGURE 3-2: eBay's instant User ID suggestion form.

---

3. **Choose a password, enter it in the Password box, and then type it a second time in the Confirm Password box to confirm it.**

   The best passwords for eBay or any website are more than six characters long and include a combination of letters (upper- and lowercase) and numbers. Never use your User ID, name, pet's name, address, birthdate, or anything that may be easily known by others. C'mon, get a little cagey. For more information on choosing your password, see "Picking a Pickproof Password," later in this chapter.

4. **Read the not-so-fine print and click the Register button.**

At this point, eBay tells you that they will send an email to your email address for confirmation (see Figure 3-3). If that's OK, click the Yes, Continue button. If you'd prefer the email be sent to a different email address, click the No, Please Send to Another Email Address link. eBay will prompt you to type the alternate email address in the original Email Address text box. So give them the correct one the first time.

The upcoming section will tip you in on what to expect in the "fine print."

FIGURE 3-3:
Clicking Submit will help confirm your email address.

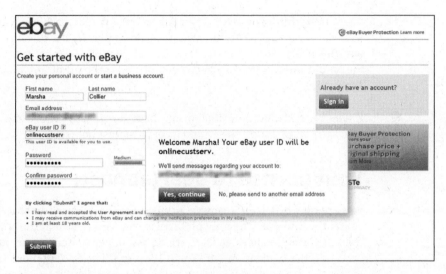

Do you solemnly swear?

After you fill in your required information and scroll down, you should click the links to see the eBay User Agreement and Privacy Policy. At this page, you take an oath to keep eBay safe for democracy and commerce. You promise to play well with others, to not cheat, and to follow the golden rule. No, you're not auditioning for a superhero club, but don't ever forget that eBay takes this stuff seriously. You can be kicked off eBay or worse. (Can you say, "federal investigation"?)

Be sure to read the User Agreement thoroughly when you register. So that you don't have to put down this riveting book to read the legalese right this minute, I provide the nuts and bolts here:

>> You understand that every transaction is a legally binding contract. (Click the User Agreement link at the bottom of any eBay page for the current eBay rules and regulations.)

» You agree that you can pay for the items you buy and the eBay fees that you incur.

» You understand that you're responsible for paying any taxes.

» You're aware that if you sell prohibited items, eBay can forward your personal information to law enforcement for further investigation.

» eBay makes clear that it is just a *venue,* which means it's a place where people with similar interests can meet, greet, and do business.

When everything goes well, the eBay website is like a school gym that opens for Saturday swap meets. At the gym, if you don't play by the rules, you can get tossed out. But if you don't play by the rules at eBay, the venue gets un-gymlike in a hurry. But fair's fair; eBay keeps you posted by email of any updates in the User Agreement.

If you're a stickler for fine print, head to `pages.ebay.com/help/policies/overview.html` for all the *Ps* and *Qs* of the latest policies.

Your license to deal (almost)

You are now officially a *newbie,* or eBay rookie, licensed to shop to your heart's content on the site. The only problem is that you're still at the window-shopping level. If you're ready to go from window shopper to item seller, just click the Sell button in the navigation bar. You'll have to fill out a few more forms, shown in Figure 3-4, and before you know it, you can start running your own sales on eBay.

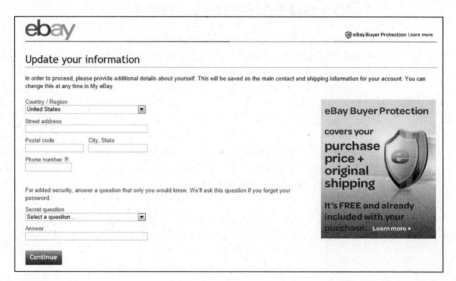

FIGURE 3-4: Fill out more details to register to sell on the site.

DON'T TELL ANYONE, BUT YOUR INFO IS SAFE ON eBay

eBay keeps most personal information secret. The basics (your name, phone number, city, and state) go out only to answer the specific request of another registered eBay user (if you are involved in a transaction with that person), law enforcement, or members of the eBay Verified Rights Owner program (eBay's copyright-watchdog program). Other users may need your basic access info for several reasons — a seller may want to verify your location, get your phone number to call you regarding your auction, or double-check who you are. If somebody does request your info, you get an email from eBay giving you the name, phone number, city, and state of the person making the request. Just one more reason you need to keep the information on your My eBay page up to date. If you don't, you risk being suspended from the site.

eBay will ask for your business address and phone number, and ask you to create your secret question and input the answer. Once you've filled that out, click Continue. You're brought to the Sell Your Item page.

TIP

eBay uses the secret question you select here as a security test should you need help to remember your password. There are six choices. I suggest you do not select the "What is your mother's maiden name?" question because banks and financial institutions often use this question for identification. Guard your mother's maiden name and don't give it out to anyone blithely. Select one of the other questions and fill in the answer. For more info on secret questions and their power, visit Book 9, Chapter 4.

Picking a Pickproof Password

Choosing a good password is not as easy (but is twice as important) as it may seem. Whoever has your password can (in effect) "be you" at eBay — running auctions, bidding on auctions, and leaving possibly litigious feedback for others. Basically, such an impostor can ruin your eBay career — and possibly cause you serious financial grief.

WARNING

Many passwords can be cracked by the right person in a matter of seconds. Your goal is to set a password that takes too much of the hackers' time. With the number of available users on eBay or PayPal, odds are they'll go to the next potential victim's password rather than spend too many minutes (or even hours) trying to crack yours.

As with any online password, you should follow these commonsense rules to protect your privacy:

» **Don't** choose anything too obvious, such as your birthday, your first name, or (*never* use this) your Social Security number. (**Hint:** If it's too easy to remember, it's probably too easy to crack.)

» **Do** make things tough on the bad guys — combine numbers, letters (use uppercase and lowercase), and symbols — or create a punctuated phrase (maybe a quote from your favorite movie?).

» **Don't** give out your password to anyone — it's like giving away the keys to the front door of your house.

» **Do** change your password *immediately* if you ever suspect someone has it. You can change your password by going to the Account Information area of your My eBay page or to the following address:

> signin.ebay.com/ws/eBayISAPI.dll?ChangePasswordAndCreateHint

» **Do** change your password every few months just to be on the safe side.

TIP

For more information on passwords and other security stuff, check out Book 9.

Selecting Your User ID

Making up a User ID is always a pleasant chore. If you've never liked your real name or never had a nickname, here's your chance to correct that situation. Choose an ID that tells a little about you. Of course, if your interests change, you may regret too narrow a User ID.

You can call yourself just about anything, but remember that this ID is how other eBay users will know you. Here are some guidelines:

» **Don't** use a name that would embarrass your mother.

» **Don't** use a name with a negative connotation, such as *scam-guy*. If people don't trust you, they won't buy from you.

» **Don't** use a name that's too weird, you know, something like *baby-vampire-penguin*. People may chuckle, but they may also question your sanity.

» **Remember** that eBay doesn't allow spaces in User IDs, so make sure that the ID makes sense when putting two or more words together. A friend of mine intended to register as "gang of one." She forgot the hyphens, so her ID reads *gangofone*.

TIP

If you're dying to have several short words as your User ID, you can use underscores or hyphens to separate them, as in *super-shop-a-holic*. And if you sign in to eBay for the whole day, you won't have to worry about repeatedly typing a complicated ID.

REMEMBER

You can change your User ID once every 30 days if you want to, but I don't recommend it because people come to know you by your User ID. If you change your ID, your past does play tagalong and attaches itself to the new ID. But if you change your User ID too many times, people may think you're trying to hide something.

eBay also has some User ID rules to live by:

>> No offensive names (such as &*#@guy).

>> No names with *eBay* in them. (It makes you look like you work for eBay, and eBay takes a dim view of that.)

>> No names with & (even if you *do* have both looks&brains).

>> No names with @ (such as @Aboy).

>> No symbols, such as the greater than or less than symbol (> <), and no consecutive underscores (__).

>> No IDs that begin with an *e* followed by numbers, an underscore, a hyphen, a period, or *dot* (as in dot.com).

>> No names of one letter (such as Q from *Star Trek*).

When you choose your User ID, make sure that it *isn't* a good clue for guessing your password. For example, if you use *Natasha* as your User ID, don't choose *Boris* as your password. Even Bullwinkle could figure that one out.

Signing In to Deal

You don't have to wear one of those tacky "Hello, my name is" stickers on your shirt, but you and several million other folks will be roaming around eBay's online treasure trove. eBay needs to know who's who when we're browsing. So, keeping that in mind, sign in when you first go on to the eBay website, please! By clicking Sign In on the eBay home page, you're ready to shop or sell.

TIP

If you're the only one who uses your computer, be sure to select the check box that says "Stay signed in." This way, you're signed in to eBay every time you go to the site. The sign-in process places a *cookie* (a techno-related piece-of-code thingy) on your computer that remains a part of your browser until you sign out.

If you don't select the check box, you will be signed in only while you're on the site. If you do select it, your password will be saved in the browser until you sign out, even if you disconnect from the Internet, close your browser, or turn off your computer.

Here's how to get to the eBay Sign In page and sign in:

1. **Click the Sign In link near the eBay logo on the eBay home page.**

2. **Enter your User ID and password.**

3. **Click the Sign In button.**

You're now signed in to eBay and can travel the site with ease. You may go to your My eBay page's eBay Preferences to tell eBay where you want to land after you sign in.

eBay's Trust & Safety Is Watching

The Security Center is where eBay's Trust & Safety gurus focus on protecting the website from members who aren't playing by the rules. Through this department, eBay issues warnings and policy changes — and in some cases, it gives eBay bad guys the old heave-ho.

You can find eBay's Security Center by clicking the Security Center link at the bottom of most eBay pages. The Security Center page is more than just a link to policies and information. It also connects you to a customer support database. eBay staffers look at complaints on a case-by-case basis, in the order they receive them. Most complaints they receive are about these problems:

>> Shill bidders (see the section on "Selling abuses" in this chapter)

>> Feedback issues and abuses (see the section on "Feedback abuses" in this chapter)

TIP

Keep in mind that eBay is a community of people, most of whom have never met each other. No matter what you buy or sell on eBay, don't expect eBay transactions to be any safer than buying or selling from a complete stranger. If you go in with this attitude and stay personable-but-vigilant, you won't be disappointed.

Staying Notified about the Rules

For an up-close online look at eBay's rules and regulations, click the Policies link (which is at the bottom of most eBay pages) and then read the User Agreement. (The agreement is revised regularly, so check it often.)

To visit the User Agreement page, go to

`http://pages.ebay.com/help/policies/user-agreement.html`

If you plan on being an active eBay member, it's probably worth your while to regularly check eBay's announcements at

`http://community.ebay.com/t5/Announcements/bg-p/Announcements`

You can also find a link in the footer of eBay pages.

Abuses You Might Report

Before you even consider blowing the whistle by reporting someone who (gasp!) gave you negative feedback to Trust & Safety, make sure that what you're encountering is *actually* a misuse of eBay. Some behavior isn't nice (no argument there), but it *also* isn't a violation of eBay rules — in which case, eBay can't do much about it. The following sections list the primary reasons you may start investigations.

Selling abuses

If you're on eBay long enough, you're bound to find an abuse of the service. It may happen on an auction you're bidding on, or it may be one of the sellers who compete with your listings. Stay safe and be on the lookout for the following:

>> **Shill bidding:** A seller uses multiple User IDs to bid, or has accomplices place bids to boost the price of his or her auction items. eBay looks for telltale signs, including a single bidder putting in a really high bid, a bidder with really low feedback but a really high number of bids on items, a bidder with low feedback who has been an eBay member for a while but who's never won an auction, or excessive bids between two users.

>> **Auction interception:** An unscrupulous user, pretending to be the actual seller, contacts the winner to set up terms of payment and shipping in an effort to make off with the buyer's payment. This violation can be easily avoided by paying with PayPal directly through the eBay site.

>> **Fee avoidance:** A user reports a lower-than-actual final price or illegally submits a Final Value Fee credit. (I explain Final Value Fees in Book 3, Chapter 1.)

>> **Bid manipulation:** A user, with the help of accomplices, enters dozens of phony bids to make the auction appear to have a lot of bidding action. Let the experts at eBay decide on this one; but you may wonder if loads of bids come in rapid succession but the price moves very little.

TIP

To report issues with individual eBay listings, look for the *Report Item* link on the far right of the *Description* and *Shipping and Payments* tabs on the item page.

Bidding abuses

If you want to know more about bidding in general, see Chapter 6. Here's a list of bidding abuses that eBay wants to know about:

>> **Bid shielding:** Two users work in tandem. User A, with the help of accomplices, intentionally bids an unreasonably high amount and then retracts the bid in the closing moments of the auction — leaving a lower bid (which the offender or an accomplice places) as the winning bid.

>> **Bid siphoning:** Users send email to bidders of a current auction to offer the same merchandise for a lower price elsewhere.

>> **Auction interference:** Users warn other bidders through email to stay clear of a seller *during a current auction*, presumably to decrease the number of bids and keep the prices low.

>> **Bid manipulation (or invalid bid retraction):** A user bids a ridiculously high amount, raising the next highest bidder to the maximum bid. The manipulator then retracts the bid and rebids *slightly* over the previous high bidder's maximum.

>> **Unpaid item (nonpaying bidder):** No matter how eBay chooses to couch it by fancy verbiage, I call these bidders deadbeats. The bottom line is that these people win auctions but never pay.

>> **Unwelcome bidder:** A user bids on a specific seller's auction despite the seller's warning that he or she won't accept that user's bid (as in the case of not selling internationally and receiving international bids). This practice is impolite and obnoxious. If you want to ban specific bidders from your auctions, you can exclude them in your My eBay area links.

Feedback abuses

All you have at eBay is your reputation, and that reputation is made up of your feedback history. eBay takes any violation of its feedback system seriously. Because eBay's feedback is transaction-related, unscrupulous eBay members find that manipulating the system is much harder. Here's a checklist of feedback abuses that you should report to Trust & Safety:

>> **Feedback extortion:** A member threatens to post negative feedback if another eBay member doesn't follow through on some unwarranted demand.

>> **Personal exposure:** A member leaves feedback for a user that exposes personal information that doesn't relate to transactions on eBay.

WARNING

>> **–4.3 feedback:** Any user reaching a net feedback score of –4.3 is subject to suspension.

Identity abuses

Who you are on eBay is as important as what you sell (or buy). eBay monitors the identities of its members closely — and asks that you report any great pretenders in this area to the Security Center. Here's a checklist of identity abuses:

>> **Identity misrepresentation:** A user claims to be an eBay staff member or another eBay user, or registers under the name of another user.

>> **False or missing contact information:** A user deliberately registers with false contact information or an invalid email address.

>> **Underage:** A user falsely claims to be 18 or older. (You must be at least 18 to enter into a legally binding contract.)

>> **Dead or invalid email address:** When emails bounce repeatedly from a user's registered email address, chances are good that the address is dead. Usually return email indicates that the address is unknown.

>> **Contact information:** One user publishes another user's contact information on the eBay site.

Operational abuses

If you see someone trying to interfere with eBay's operation, eBay staffers want you to tell them about it. Here are two roguish operational abuses:

>> **Hacking:** A user purposely interferes with eBay's computer operations (for example, by breaking into unauthorized files).

>> **Spamming:** The user sends unsolicited commercial email to eBay users.

Miscellaneous abuses

The following are additional problems that you should alert eBay about:

>> A user is threatening physical harm to another eBay member.

>> A person uses racist, obscene, or harassing language in a public area of eBay.

For a complete list of offenses and how eBay runs each investigation, go to the following address:

pages.ebay.com/help/buy/report-trading.html

Don't Get Caught in a Trading Violation

Playing by eBay's rules keeps you off the Security Center radar. If you start violating eBay policies, the company's going to keep a close eye on you. Depending on the infraction, eBay may be all over you like jelly on peanut butter. Or you may safely lurk in the fringes until your feedback rating is lower than the temperature in Nome in November.

Here's the docket of eBay no-no's that can get members flogged and keelhauled — or at least suspended:

>> Feedback rating of –4.3

>> Three instances of deadbeat bidding

>> Repeated warning for the same infraction

>> Feedback extortion

- » Bid shielding

- » Unwelcome bidding after a warning from the seller

- » Shill bidding

- » Auction interception

- » Fee avoidance

- » Fraudulent selling

- » Identity misrepresentation

- » Bidding when younger than age 18

- » Hacking

- » Physical threats

TIP

If you get a suspension but think you're innocent, respond directly to the person who suspended you to plead your case. Reversals do occur. But *don't* broadcast your suspicions on chat boards. If you're wrong, you may regret it. Even if you're right, it's oh-so-gauche.

WARNING

Be careful about accusing members of cheating. Unless you're involved in a transaction, you don't know all the facts. CSI moments are great on television, but they're fictional for a reason. In real life, drawing yourself into a possible confrontation is senseless. Start the complaint process, keep it businesslike, and let eBay's staff figure out what's going on.

Signing Up and
Getting Started

Chapter **4**

Understanding eBay Transactions

Sometimes, when you know exactly what you want to buy, you find not one but many auctions and fixed-price listings with that same item for sale. In this situation, knowing the different eBay sales formats is important. In this chapter, I go over the various types of sales and show you the ways to use each type to your advantage.

Checking Out the Listing Page

All item pages on eBay — whether auctions, fixed-price items, or Buy It Now items — look about the same. Figure 4-1 shows your options on a conventional auction-item page. If you were viewing the entire auction page, you could scroll down and see a complete description of the item, along with shipping information.

eBay auction listings have some subtle differences. (With a venue as big as eBay, you gotta have some flexibility.) You may see the words *PayPal Credit* (which indicates you can use PayPal's payment plan) or an option to add a *Protection plan from Square Trade*. Most listings also have preset item specifics that appear above the description written by the seller. If you're looking at an item in a fixed-price sale, you'll see the words *Buy It Now* with no option to bid, as shown in Figure 4-2.

FIGURE 4-1:
Either place a bid, or buy the item outright.

FIGURE 4-2:
Buy on the spot or put the item in your shopping cart to combine with other sellers' items.

Examining listing info

Here's a list of stuff you see as you scroll down a typical item page:

>> **Item category:** Located just above the item title, you can click the category listing and do some comparison shopping. (Book 2, Chapter 1 offers some more searching strategies.)

>> **Item title and number:** The title and number identify the item. Keep track of this info for inquiries later. You will find the item number cleverly hidden at the top-right of the Description tab, just above Item Specifics.

TIP

If you're interested in a particular type of item, take note of the keywords used in the title (you're likely to see them again in future titles). Doing so helps you narrow down your searches.

>> **Add to Watch list:** Click this box, and the item is magically added to the Watch list on your My eBay Lists page so you can keep an eye on the progress of an auction — without actually bidding. If you haven't signed in, you have to do so before you can save a listing to your My eBay.

>> **Email, Facebook, Twitter, and Pinterest icons:** Next to another option to *Add to Watch list,* you see four social-sharing icons. Clicking any one of these opens a share window that allows you to post a link to the listing for all your social media friends to see. If the listing is an auction, however, this kind of sharing may not be in your immediate best interest. After all, the less competition you have, the lower your win price will be.

>> **Time left:** Although the clock never stops ticking on eBay, you must continue to refresh your browser on an auction to see the time remaining on the *official* clock. When the item gets down to the last hour, you'll see the time updated automatically in minutes and seconds. You'll also see the date and time that the listing will close.

Timing is the key in an eBay bidding strategy (covered in Chapter 6), so don't forget that eBay uses Pacific Standard Time (PST) or Pacific Daylight Time (PDT) as the standard, depending on the season.

REMEMBER

>> **Quantity:** This field appears only when multiple items are available. If it's a multiple-item, fixed-price sale, you have no opportunity to bid — you use Buy It Now to purchase whatever quantity of the item you want. You'll be prompted for a quantity when you buy.

>> **Seller information:** This area, on the right side of the page, gives you information about the seller. *Know thy seller* ranks right after *caveat emptor* as a phrase that pays at eBay. As I tell you nearly a million times in this book, *read the feedback rating!* (Okay, maybe not a million — it would drive the editors bonkers.) Like any community, eBay has its share of good folks and bad folks. Your chance for a flawless transaction is to read the seller's feedback. You'll see several things in the Seller Information box (as shown in Figure 4-3).

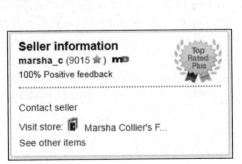

FIGURE 4-3:
Lots of data on the seller is accessible here.

● **Seller icons:** Various icons that show the status of the seller. A varicolored star reflects the feedback level of the seller. If the seller is a Top Rated, you see the Top Rated icon. The *me* icon links to a seller's Profile page where you'll find out more about the person or business behind the sale (not every seller sets one up). Click the blue-and-red *me* icon — or the seller's User ID — to get there.

- **Feedback rating:** This number is also to the right of the seller's name in parentheses. Click the number next to the seller's ID to view his or her Feedback profile and entire feedback history. There, you can click any positive or negative feedbacks you find to see what really transpired. Read as much of the feedback as you want; the idea is to ensure that you feel comfortable doing business with this person.

Keep in mind that no matter what the seller's rating is, your purchase is covered under eBay's Money Back Guarantee to be exactly as described.

- **Positive feedback percentage:** The eBay computers calculate this figure. It's derived from all the positive and negative feedback that a user receives.

» **Starting bid or Current bid:** In an auction listing, this is the dollar amount that the bidding has reached. The amount changes throughout the auction as people place bids. If no bids have been placed on the item, it will read *Starting bid*.

Sometimes, next to the current dollar amount, you see *Reserve not met* or *Reserve met.* This means the seller has set a *reserve price* for the item — a secret price that must be reached before the seller will sell the item. Most auctions do not have reserve prices.

» **Buy It Now price:** If you want an item immediately and the price listed in this area is okay with you, click Buy It Now. You will be taken to a page where you can complete your purchase. Buy It Now is an option in auctions and does not appear in all listings.

» **Number of bids:** Clicking this number takes you to a page that shows you the bids that have been placed in an auction. The starting bid is listed on this page as well, in light gray, below the list of bids. When the listing is live, you can click the number of bids to find out when bids were placed. (Only the seller can view the true User IDs of the bidders.)

When you're bidding, eBay hides your bidder ID by using anonymous names. Your actual User ID is shown to the seller of this item only. Bidders are assigned anonymous names, such as a***k.

You can click the number of bids to see how the bidding action is going, but you won't be able to see the high bidder's proxy bid (more about proxy bids later in this chapter).

Sometimes an item has no bids because everyone is waiting until the last minute. Then you see a flurry of activity as bidders try to outbid each other (called *sniping,* which Chapter 6 in this minibook explains). It's all part of the fun of eBay.

>> **Shipping:** If the seller is willing to ship the item anywhere in the U.S. for free (or for a flat rate), you'll see that here. This area may also link to eBay's shipping calculator if the seller customizes the shipping expense according to weight and distance.

>> **Item location:** This field tells you, at the very least, the country where the seller is located. You may also see more specific info, such as the seller's city and geographic area. (What you see depends on how detailed the seller chooses to be.)

>> **Ships to:** If the seller ships to only the United States, it will state so here. If the seller ships to any other countries, this is where they will be listed.

Moving on to the tabs

If you scroll on down the listing page, you see tabs that give you even more detailed information about the item that's for sale or auction, as follows. When you click the Description tab, you find the item description, which will state "revised" if the seller has made any revisions to the description during the run of the listing. Read all this information carefully before buying or bidding:

>> **Item Specifics:** At the top of the Description tab, you will see a box containing specific descriptors about the item for sale. The seller generally adds the information you see here, but often, information is pulled from eBay's product catalog (based on a product's SKU, UPC, or ISBN).

>> **Detailed item info:** Depending on the type of item, this box may just contain a few lines — or, in the case of media or electronics, a bucketload of data (as shown in Figure 4-4). This type of information is also supplied from eBay's catalog.

Detailed item info

Synopsis
Everything you need to know to start and run a successful eBay business. Everything you need to know to start and run a successful eBay business eBay now has 100 million active users and just keeps growing. And those have turned to For Dummies books and bestselling eBay author Marsha Collier, to help guide them through buying and selling on eBay for over a decade. This nine-books-in-one guide has now been updated to cover all the newest eBay seller tools, new techniques to drive sales, new ways to enhance an eBay business using social media, and more. Marsha Collier covers the basics, essential tools, professional selling tips, where to find merchandise, how to showcase and promote your stuff, storage and shipping, advice for Power Sellers, and legal/tax issues. A complete update of the bestselling eBay business guide Covers getting the necessary eBay selling tools, how to do product research and set up payment systems, and tips on setting prices, creating good listings, and organizing sales Helps you find things to sell at prices that will make a profit, create listings that get attention, take great merchandise photos, and promote your items on social media sites Offers advice on providing customer service, safely storing and shipping your merchandise, and handling necessary bookkeeping and tax chores Includes how to analyze data and establish the needed resources to become a Power Seller eBay Business All-in-One For Dummies, 3rd Edition is the soup-to-nuts guide for running a successful eBay business.

Product Identifiers
ISBN-10	1118401662
ISBN-13	9781118401668

Key Details
Author	Marsha Collier
Number Of Pages	840 pages
Format	Paperback
Publication Date	2013-08-05
Language	English
Publisher	Wiley & Sons, Incorporated, John
Publication Year	20130000

Additional Details
Edition Number	3
Copyright Date	2012

Dimensions
Weight	38.3 Oz
Height	1.8 In.
Width	7.4 In.
Length	9.2 In.

Target Audience
Group	Trade

Classification Method
LC Classification Number	HF5476
Dewey Decimal	381.177
Dewey Edition	23

FIGURE 4-4: Catalog details on the item for sale in a standardized format.

By clicking the Shipping and Payments tab, you'll find some other important data on the typical listing page, as shown in Figures 4-5.

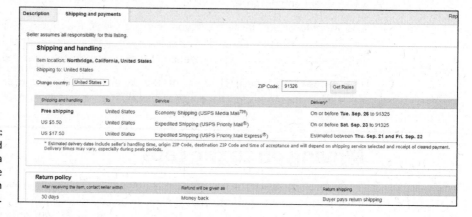

>> Who pays

>> Whether the seller is charging flat-rate shipping or is offering more than one shipping option through a shipping calculator

>> The estimated delivery date

>> Which states have to pay sales tax (if any) and the sales tax rate

>> Whether the seller is willing to ship to your area

TIP

Sometimes sellers won't ship internationally; if that's the case, they'll let you know here. Be sure to also check the item description for other shipping information and terms.

The seller's return policy will be listed here too, so if you want the option to return an item (if it doesn't fit?) you'd better check here first.

The Payment details area tells you the payment methods that the seller accepts: PayPal or their own merchant credit card service. Often, you are directed to read the item description for more details.

TIP

Be sure to use the Watch This Item feature when shopping around. Organization is the name of the game on eBay, especially if you plan to bid on multiple auctions or compare pricing in fixed-price listings. I figure you're in the bidding game to win, so start keeping track of items now.

Getting even more info (if you want to)

Links in the Seller Information area and on the item's Description tab give you access to details about the seller as well as enable you to contact the seller. For example, you can find the date the seller joined eBay and the country in which he or she registered by clicking the Feedback number link to the right of the seller's User ID.

Clicking the Ask a Question link (scroll down to find it at the bottom of the Description tab) hooks you up with eBay's email system so you can ask the seller a question regarding the item.

To ask a seller a question, follow these steps:

1. **Scroll all the way to the bottom of the Description tab and click the Ask a Question link.**

   You're presented with the Find Answers form.

2. **Select a topic from the drop-down list that most closely matches your query.**

   The seller may have posted common answers to questions. If you haven't found your answer, click other, and a Continue button will appear.

3. **Click the Continue button to get a message form.**

4. **Fill in the topic and the message area; then click Send Message.**

TIP

Expect to hear back from the seller within a day. If it takes the seller more than a day to respond (unless it's over the weekend — eBay sellers are entitled to a little rest), and you get no explanation for the delay, consider buying from someone else.

Also in the Seller Information area is a *See Other Items* link. This link takes you to a page that lists all the seller's current auctions and fixed-price sales. If the seller has an eBay Store, a link to it appears in the Seller Information area as well. I tell you about eBay Stores in the later section "Shopping eBay Stores."

Bidding on Auctions

To give you a sense of the auction process, here's a real-world example of my addictions put to the eBay test. I searched and found an item that I wanted, "Homemade Snickerdoodle cookies." (Yes, you can find real food in the Home and Garden⇨Food and Beverages⇨Cookies & Biscotti category!) After reading the seller's feedback (and skipping lunch), I wanted the item even more! As a matter of fact, no one seems able to say enough good things about the quality of their food. Yum! (If I buy cookies for research for this book, it makes my baked goods a tax write-off, no?)

For a dozen cookies, the starting bid is $6.95, and the auction ends in over four days. So I need to observe several things about the auction. How many more are up for sale on the eBay site? A simple search shows that only one is up for auction. What did they sell for in the past? I run a Sold Listings search and see that they've sold in both auctions and fixed-price listings for up to $20. (Shipping is free.)

You have to make some decisions and observations as a buyer, even if all you're after is snacks. I have observed that these cookie auctions have an active bidding pattern, so at this early stage I bid the minimum amount just to get the item to show up as one of the items in the My eBay page⇨Buy⇨Bids/Offers area.

REMEMBER

Bidding can be like a game of poker. If you want to win a one-of-a-kind item, don't show your hand to other bidders. Simply mark the auction to watch. Note, however, that this strategy isn't necessary for an item that will be sure to be listed again (like those Snickerdoodle cookies).

When it comes to auctions, the highest bid wins. *Remember this, please.* People are constantly boo-hooing because they've been outbid at the last minute (or *sniped*, as I explain in Chapter 6). You can't be outbid if you're the high bidder!

Automatic bidding

Bidding on eBay goes up by a *prescribed bid increment,* which is the minimum amount by which your bid can be raised. But what if you're not able to sit in on an auction 24 hours a day, 7 days a week, upping your bid every time someone bids against you? (You mean you have a life?)

You do receive email messages from eBay (or notifications on your smartphone app) to let you know that you've been outbid, but you may be busy doing other things and you might not get the notice in time to place a new successful bid.

If you're interested in an item but you don't have the time to follow it closely from the beginning of the auction to its conclusion, you can place a *proxy bid* using eBay's automatic bidding system to place your bid for the highest amount you're willing to pay for an item — without spending your valuable time constantly following the auction. eBay will increase your bid automatically on your behalf (using the prescribed bid increment) up to your maximum bid — to maintain your position as the high bidder or to meet the item's reserve price.

TIP

Instead of waiting it out with eBay's automatic bidding, you can also go to the seller's eBay Store to see whether a duplicate item is for sale at a fixed price. Or, if the seller has set a Buy It Now price and (again) you're too impatient to wait until the end of the auction to win, click Buy It Now and go from there.

Before you place your proxy bid, you should give serious thought to how much you want to pay for the item. When you place an automatic bid (a proxy bid) on eBay, eBay's bidding engine places only enough of your bid to outbid the previous bidder. If there are no previous bidders and the seller has not entered a reserve price, your bid appears as the minimum auction bid until someone bids against you. Your bid increases incrementally in response to other bids against yours. Table 4-1 lists eBay's bidding increments.

TABLE 4-1

eBay's Bidding Increments

Current High Bid ($)	Next Bid Increased By ($)
0.01–0.99	0.05
1.00–4.99	0.25
5.00–24.99	0.50
25.00–99.99	1.00
100.00–249.99	2.50
250.00–499.99	5.00
500.00–999.99	10.00
1,000.00–2,499.99	25.00
2,500.00–4,999.99	50.00
5,000.00 and up	100.00

No one will know how much your proxy bid is — unless someone outbids you and becomes the high bidder. To place a proxy bid in an auction, follow these steps:

1. **Type your maximum bid in the appropriate box, or click the Place Bid button.**

   A confirmation page appears, and you have one last chance to back out.

2. **If everything is in order, click Confirm Bid, as shown in Figure 4-6.**

   After you've placed your bid, the next page lets you know whether you're the high bidder.

FIGURE 4-6:
Enter your
maximum bid.

3. **The confirmation page tells you if you are the high bidder (as shown in Figure 4-7). If you're not the high bidder, just click the Increase max bid button and place another bid.**

FIGURE 4-7:
I'm a winner.

REMEMBER

You'll often come across auctions that have the words *Reserve not met* next to the bid amount. By placing a reserve price on the auction, the seller ensures that the item will not sell until the bidding reaches that mysterious reserve figure.

Private auctions

Private auctions are handled in the same way as plain-vanilla auctions, except only the buyer and seller know who the winner is. As a matter of fact, all bidders' names are hidden from anyone other than the seller.

After you've been on eBay for a while, you might see the same group of names bidding on the same auctions as you. I like bidding in private auctions because they're handy for snaring items secretly.

Buying an Item Outright

Although eBay's success was built on auctions, eBay also allows sellers to handle outright sales. You can make a direct purchase

>> By using the Buy It Now feature in an eBay auction

>> In a fixed-price sale

>> In one of eBay's Stores

Buy It Now

You may have already looked at auctions and seen a Buy It Now price located below the minimum or starting bid amount. That little indicator means that if you want the item badly enough, and the Buy It Now price is within your budget, you can end the auction right then and there by buying the item for the stated amount.

WARNING

Before using the Buy It Now option (because you think you've hit upon a bargain), be sure to check the seller's shipping charges. Many sellers set a low Buy It Now price but place a high shipping amount on the item to make up their missing prof-its. A Buy It Now transaction is *final*; you can't withdraw your commitment to buy. It's best to know what you're getting into beforehand.

If you decide that you want to buy, click the Buy It Now button. An eBay confirma-tion page appears. If you still want to make the purchase, you can click Confirm to tell eBay that you're willing to pay the purchase price. Then all you have to do is go through the checkout process and pay the seller.

TIP

You can still place a bid on an auction that has a Buy It Now option. When you do, the option to immediately buy disappears and the item goes into auction mode. If the item has a reserve, the Buy It Now option doesn't disappear until the bidding surpasses the reserve amount.

Fixed-price sales

eBay also offers items for sale without the option to bid. These *fixed-price* listings may be for a single item or for multiple items. When multiple items are offered, you can buy as many as you like. Just backspace over the default 1 in the Quantity box, and type in the number of items you want to buy (see Figure 4-8).

Add to cart

It's almost like having a shopping cart at the market — eBay has its own online version. When you click the Add to Cart button, the item is added to your shopping cart. When you put an item in your shopping cart, just as in real life, you haven't bought it yet. Only when you check out is the purchase transaction completed.

WARNING

If the seller has only one of the item you put in your cart for sale, it behooves you to check out swiftly. The item is not yours until you confirm the purchase.

Shopping eBay Stores

eBay Stores are the secret weapon for knowledgeable eBay shoppers. First, of course, you can consistently find great deals. But you can also help small businesses make it against the behemoths. Sellers open eBay Stores to make searching merchandise easier for buyers; these stores also help save sellers money because sellers don't need to set up private ecommerce websites. Translation? Sellers can list items in their eBay Stores for even lower fees, passing their savings on to you, the savvy bargain hunter.

TIP

Before you buy any item from a listing on eBay, check to see whether the seller has the small, blue *stores* icon next to his or her User ID. If so, be sure to click the icon *before* you bid on the item. Most sellers run auctions for items to draw people into their eBay Stores, where you may be able to find even more interesting merchandise you can buy, and then have the seller put it in the same crate along with your auction item, which saves on shipping.

You can get to the eBay Stores hub by typing the following web address:

```
http://stores.ebay.com
```

At the center of the eBay Stores hub page, as shown in Figure 4-9, you see a small group of store logos. These logos change every few minutes as eBay rotates its *anchor stores* through the area. Store owners pay a considerable amount to have their stores listed as anchor stores.

FIGURE 4-9: The eBay Stores consumer home page is the place to go to browse and buy.

Strolling through an eBay Store

When you finally arrive at the eBay Store of your choice, you see a page that looks similar to the one in Figure 4-10. An eBay Store displays every active auction or Buy It Now item the seller has placed on the eBay site.

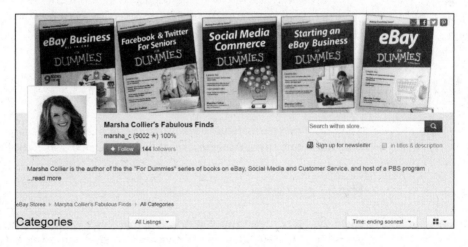

FIGURE 4-10: The home page for my eBay Store.

Most eBay Stores home pages display the following:

>> **Store Search:** To the right of the store name banner is a search box that allows you to search all the items this seller has for sale.

>> **Store Categories:** eBay Store owners may assign their own custom categories to the items they sell to better organize things within the store. You may click individual categories to see items in that classification from that seller.

>> **Display:** You can decide how you'd like to view the items in the seller's store, in Gallery style or List views.

At the top and bottom of the store home page, you'll see a variety of things:

>> **The store name:** This is the name the store owner has chosen for the store. Each eBay Store has its own address that ends in the eBay Store's name, like this: `www.stores.ebay.com/`*`insertstorename`*. For example, my store's URL is

```
http://stores.ebay.com/Marsha-Colliers-Fabulous-Finds
```

>> **Seller's User ID and feedback rating:** Some stores choose to put this on the home page; others replace it with graphics. Next to the seller's User ID is the ubiquitous feedback rating.

>> **Save the Seller:** If you click this link, the store is added to the Saved Sellers list in your My eBay.

>> **Store logo and description:** At the top of the page is the store's graphic logo, and below that is the seller's description of the store. (This is the area that is searched when you search Stores by store name *and* description.)

Supercategories and Specialties

Aside from partnering with PayPal (the world's largest online payment service), eBay runs some special categories that make up a good deal of the business on eBay.

Real estate

Since the founding of our country, land has been valued as a great commodity; passed from generation to generation. As Gerald O'Hara so eloquently put it, "It's the only thing that lasts." (Remember that scene from *Gone with the Wind?*) People buy land for investment, vacations, or retirement. It's no longer common for a family to spend their entire life in one home. Real estate, although a major purchase, is becoming more and more an everyday transaction.

The smart people at eBay are sly trend-spotters, so they opened an official category for real estate transactions in the fall of 2000. You can access eBay's Real Estate category through the category link (on the left side of the home page) or by going directly to

> http://realestate.shop.ebay.com/

Because substantial legal restrictions are involved in real estate transactions, sellers can choose to list their properties either as auctions or in the form of classified advertisements, depending on the laws in their areas.

REMEMBER

When you participate in a listing that is in an ad format, you do not place bids. At the bottom of the item's description page is a form for you to fill out that's sent to the seller. After the seller receives this information, he or she can contact you, and the two of you may negotiate privately. When you browse the Residential Homes category, such listings will have the words *Classified Ad* next to the title. Many residential home sales are handled in this manner. Land and timeshares are typically sold in the auction format.

REMEMBER

Because of a wide variety of laws governing the intricacies and legalities in real estate transactions, the auction format may be nonbinding. Before getting involved in any real estate transactions on eBay, I suggest you read the official rules, which you can find on the following page:

> http://pages.ebay.com/help/policies/real-estate.html

Cruising eBay Motors

Buying a car — that's one purchase I don't enjoy making. Please don't misunderstand. I love cars and have had a personal attachment to every car I've owned. It's just that each time I'm approached by a car salesperson, I get intimidated. The minute the salesperson says "I've got to check with my sales manager to see if I can do that," I know I'm a goner. And when I've finally decided on the car model I want, I still have to face *the deal,* when the finance manager tries to sell me warranties, alarms, and extras that I never wanted or needed. I feel the need to run out of the dealership — and I usually do.

If this feeling is familiar to you, I would like to introduce you to the sweetest deal of the 21st century, eBay Motors (see Figure 4-11). eBay Motors is the largest auto mall in the universe and is consistently ranked the number-one automotive site on the web by Nielsen/NetRatings.

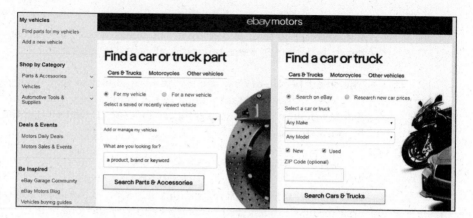

For some of us, eBay Motors is a magnificent fantasy site. I have a friend who browses the Volkswagen bus category; his eyes glaze over with hope and awe as he reads each listing. I'm sure he's reliving his hippie days of the late '60s. Another friend reads the Ferrari and Lamborghini listings; he pooh-poohs all the aftermarket changes to the classics. My best friend checks out the vintage Thunderbirds and pictures herself as Suzanne Somers flirting with the guys in *American Graffiti*. Then of course there's my fantasy car — the buttercup-yellow Rolls-Royce Corniche convertible driven by Teensy in *Ya-Ya Sisterhood*. (I've yet to find one on eBay in that color — but then again, some things are best kept a fantasy.)

FINDING MORE THAN CARS

The truly amazing part about eBay Motors is that it has more than just the usual cars and vans. In fact, the rule seems to be that if it has an engine, you'll find it here. Here's a description of the Other Vehicles categories:

- **ATVs:** Within the ATV subcategory of Powersports, you'll find a wide selection of new and used 4x4s and 2x4s, three-wheelers and four-wheelers. I even found a few six-wheel amphibious vehicles! Bidding in this category is active, and the items move quickly.

- **Aircraft:** Anything that flies can be found here, from hot-air balloons to military trainer jets. Browsing this category is amazing. Who could imagine that with a click of your mouse (and enough money) you could own your own Bell helicopter or Gulfstream jet? If you've ever dreamt of taking up flying, this might be the category to get your hobby started!

- **Boats:** This category was so full that I got seasick just browsing! It has its own sub-categories of Fishing Boats, Personal Watercraft (Sea-Doo, Yamaha, Kawasaki, and so on), Powerboats, Sailboats, and Other (kayaks, canoes, pontoons, tenders, and dinghies). I know boats, and I saw some great deals in this category. There were some beautiful Bass boats and Boston Whalers at incredible prices. It was also nice to see a wide selection of prices for sailboats. With some time spent shopping in this category, you can find just about anything you want within your price range.

- **Buses:** No kidding. You want to start your own bus line? Here's the place to find the buses — and it seems that plenty of people are interested in them! There's active bidding on old school buses in this category. (And I thought the American family was getting smaller!)

- **Commercial trucks:** Since commercial trucks are something I know jack about, I went to some experts who browsed the site and examined the deals. Here's their review for those in the know. The items are good quality and of the type they'd like to find at commercial truck auctions. They tell me the prices are bargains and that they'll be visiting the site regularly from now on — sounds like a good recommendation to me!

- **Scooters and minibikes:** Aside from what you'd expect to find here, this is the home for beautiful vintage and new Vespa motor scooters.

- **Snowmobiles:** I've never lived in a snowy part of the country, so I can only imagine how much fun these bad boys are. You'll see everything from top-of-the-line new ones to gently used examples in private sales.

- **Other:** How about a 1947 Coca-Cola vending truck — complete with fountain, cotton-candy machine, and propane-powered hot-dog cooker! Sounds like a carnival on wheels! Okay, it doesn't run, but hey — it was only $3000! There's also a Shelby Cobra kit, with no motor or tranny, but you need a hobby, don't you? I also found a Think Neighbor electric vehicle, a sandrail dune buggy four-seater, go-karts, and car haulers. There's nothing you can't find on eBay!

Many of the cars on eBay Motors are private-party sales, bank cars (repossessions), and cars that have been cherry-picked by wholesalers and dealer overstocks. In addition, professional car dealers sell rare, hard-to-find cars to a marketplace that draws millions of visitors per month. You can't get that many people through the door at a local dealership! Dealers put up the rare colors and limited-edition vehicles because this *is* an auction site — the rarer an item, the more likely bidders are to get excited. The more excited bidders are, the more they lose their heads — and the higher the price goes.

With an average of seven to eight bids per sale, eBay Motors is a competitive environment for the most desirable cars. Dealers can sell cars for less on eBay because it costs them less to sell. (They don't have to pay the finance manager to twist your arm to buy the extras.)

You can enter the eBay Motors site in two ways. Click the Motors link on the left of the home page, or go to

```
www.ebay.com/motors
```

For more on eBay Motors auction bidding strategies, check out Chapter 6 in this minibook.

Supercategories

When it comes to unique shopping, there are some supercategories worth taking a look at. On the eBay home page, take a look at the major category list of links on the top. By poking around the major category-listing links, you'll find links to unique eBay areas.

eBay has outlined these specialized categories to reflect interests that cover more than one category. Some interesting (and popular) supercategories to check out are

>> Business & Industrial

>> Collectibles

>> eBay for Charity

These supercategories come in handy when you're looking for cross-category merchandise.

Business & Industrial

If you're looking for anything to outfit a business, the Business & Industrial category is the place to go. Shown in Figure 4-12, it covers everything from tractor parts to welding equipment to computers. You can browse the subcategory of your choice and see what's available.

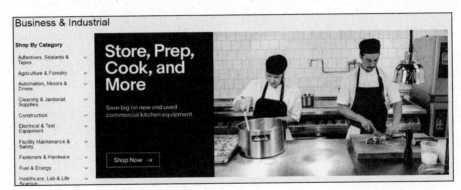

FIGURE 4-12:
The Business &
Industrial
category covers
a varied group
of items.

However, if you need a particular brand name or item, you may find it easier through eBay's search. For professional tips on eBay's search, check out Chapter 6.

eBay for Charity: Giving back to nonprofits

Many charitable organizations are selling their wares on eBay to raise money for their fine work. You can get some rare and unusual items here, such as the annual NBC *Today Show* Green Room autograph book. This one-of-a-kind book has signatures and notes from the famous guests of the *Today Show*. One of these Green Room books sold for $87,500! The super-hottest auction is the annual lunch with Warren Buffet (the CEO of Berkshire Hathaway); in 2017 (and in 2012) it raised $3,456,789 — bidding almost tripled in the last seconds!

When you list an item on eBay, you can choose a nonprofit from a certified list and designate a percentage of the proceeds (from 10 to 100 percent) to donate. The item appears in the search results with a Charity Auction icon. When you go to the item page, you'll see the name of the nonprofit, some information about it, and the percentage of the final bid that the seller is donating. You can search eBay for your favorite nonprofits by name.

Chapter **5**

Checking Out a Seller and Leaving Feedback

When you're shopping on eBay, you're faced with hundreds of items, perhaps even hundreds of listings for the same item. How do you decide where to place your order or your bid? In this chapter, I show you the tools on eBay that guide you to a safe and positive transaction.

Understanding and Giving Feedback

Unlike Amazon, one of eBay's strong suits is a sense of community formed through its use of feedback. Many experts say the reason eBay originally succeeded where dozens of other dot-com auction sites failed is that eBay paid close attention to the needs of its users.

In the early days, the concept was clear. Pierre Omidyar and his employees figured that if users complained openly (for all other members to see), feedback would be more genuine — not so much *flaming* as *constructive.* "Do unto others as you'd have them do" prevailed as a philosophy; above all else, Pierre encouraged buyers and sellers to give each other the benefit of the doubt and to conduct themselves professionally.

It soon became clear to eBay's three employees that they did not have time to adjudicate member disputes. Thus the feedback system was born. But the *pièce de résistance* of feedback policy, the part that makes eBay work, is the fact that Pierre and his staff encouraged users to give *positive* feedback as often as they give negative or neutral feedback.

The benefits of the feedback policy are immediately clear. Before even placing a bid with a seller, a buyer (you) can check the experience other eBay buyers have had doing business with this seller. You can see whether items in a seller's previous auctions shipped quickly, whether items were packed carefully, whether communication was clear and frequent, and so on. You now have more information about an eBay seller than you have when you walk into a new store in your neighborhood!

The types of feedback

REMEMBER

Every eBay member has a feedback rating. Buyers rate sellers (more on that below), and sellers rate buyers — no one is immune. Although sellers can no longer leave negative or neutral feedback for a buyer, a seller still might comment on how quickly you paid for an item, how well you communicated, or how you reacted to a problem.

Leaving feedback for the seller comes in three exciting flavors:

>> **Positive feedback:** Someone once said, "All you have is your reputation." Reputation is what makes eBay function. If the transaction works well, you get positive feedback — and whenever it's warranted, you should give it right back.

>> **Negative feedback:** If there's a glitch (for instance, it takes six months to get your *Charlie's Angels* lunchbox, or the seller substitutes a rusty Thermos for the one you bid on, or you never get the item), you have the right to leave the seller negative feedback (and get your money back from eBay).

>> **Neutral feedback:** You can leave neutral feedback if you feel so-so about a specific transaction. It's the middle-of-the-road comment that's useful when, for example, you bought an item that has a little more wear and tear on it than the seller indicated, but you still like it and want to keep it.

TIP

Keep in mind that neutral feedback will affect the seller's feedback percentage (and reputation). The feedback percentage (next to the feedback number) is calculated based on the total number of feedback ratings received in the last 12 months. This does *not* include repeat feedback from the same buyer in the same week.

Leaving feedback for a buyer isn't quite as colorful. A seller can leave only positive feedback for a transaction — or none at all. If I've dealt with a particularly difficult buyer, there is a good chance that I won't leave any feedback at all.

REMEMBER

You're not required to leave feedback, but because it's the benchmark by which all eBay users are judged, you should *always* leave feedback comments whether you're buying or selling. Every time you complete a transaction — the minute the package arrives safely and you've checked the contents, whether you're a seller or a buyer — you should go to eBay and post your feedback.

The magic feedback number

You know how they say you are what you eat? At eBay, you are only as good as your feedback says you are. Your feedback is made up of comments — good, bad, or neutral — that people leave about you (and you leave about others). In effect, people are commenting on your overall professionalism. (Even if you're an eBay hobbyist with no thought of using eBay professionally, a little businesslike courtesy can ease your transactions with everyone.) These comments are the basis for your eBay reputation.

When you get your first feedback, the number that appears next to your User ID is your feedback rating, which follows you everywhere you go on eBay, even if you change your User ID or email address. It sticks to you like glue.

Click the number next to any User ID and get a complete look at the user's feedback profile. When you do, here are some points to recognize about the user's magic feedback number:

>> **This number is a *net figure*** of the positive and negative comments that were left for that eBay user. For example, if you get 50 positive comments and 49 negative comments, your feedback rating is 1.

For every positive comment you receive, you get a plus 1. For every negative comment, you get a minus 1. Negative comments deduct from your total of positive comments, thereby lowering the number beside your User ID.

REMEMBER

Anyone with a –4.3 rating may have their eBay membership suspended. And don't make automatic assumptions just because someone has a high feedback rating. Even if someone has a total of 1,000 feedback messages, 250 of them *could* be negative.

>> **This number shows more than how good a customer or seller you are.** As it grows, the feedback number also tells how experienced you are at doing business on the site.

>> **This number ignores neutral comments.** A neutral comment is neither negative nor positive; it doesn't change the number that appears after your User ID. Neutral comments are used most often when buyers may not be completely happy with transactions, but not so unhappy that they choose to destroy someone's reputation over the situation.

eBay riddle: When is more than 1 still 1? Gotcha, huh? The answer is, when you get more than one feedback message from the same person in the same week. Confused? This example should help: You can sell one person 100 different items, but even if the buyer gives you a glowing review 100 times, your feedback rating doesn't increase by 100. In this case, the other 99 feedback comments appear in your feedback profile, but your rating increases by only 1

Giving Detailed Seller Ratings Properly

In addition to a feedback comment and rating (positive, negative, or neutral), buyers can leave detailed seller ratings, too. After the buyer types a comment, he or she is prompted to rate the seller with one to five stars on four different factors of the transaction. Figure 5-1 shows the specific rating factors, and Table 5-1 outlines what the stars mean.

FIGURE 5-1:
eBay Detailed
Seller Rating
system.

Click on the stars to rate more details of the transaction. These ratings will not be seen by the seller.	
How accurate was the item description?	★★★★★ ·
How satisfied were you with the seller's communication?	★★★★★ ·
How quickly did the seller ship the item?	★★★★★ ·
How reasonable were the shipping and handling charges?	★★★★★ ·

In some cases, Detailed Seller Ratings (DSRs) are grayed out when you attempt to leave feedback. This situation occurs under three circumstances:

>> **Communication:** If you haven't sent any messages to the seller via eBay's message system, and the seller specifies one-day handling time and uploads tracking information by the end of the next business day, there will be no option to rate the seller.

>> **Shipping quickly:** When the seller posts tracking numbers to eBay for your shipment within the time frame promised in the listing and the package arrives within four days, eBay automatically gives the seller a five-star rating.

>> **Shipping charges:** If the seller provided free shipping, he or she automatically receives a five-star rating.

TABLE 5-1 **What the DSR Stars Mean**

Rating Question	# of Stars = Meaning	In the Real World
How accurate was the item description?	1 = Very inaccurate 2 = Inaccurate 3 = Neither inaccurate or accurate 4 = Accurate 5 = Very accurate	In Marsha's world, the item was either described right or wrong — to me, there is no in-between. So when I rate a seller, the item is either as advertised, or it isn't.
How satisfied were you with the seller's communication?	1 = Very unsatisfied 2 = Unsatisfied 3 = Neither unsatisfied or satisfied 4 = Satisfied 5 = Very satisfied	As I buyer, I lean toward being very satisfied that I got enough communication from the seller if I get a question answered, and satisfied if I at least get a tracking number notification. But if I haven't heard from a seller until the item reaches my door, I'm definitely rating in the two-star range.
How quickly did the seller ship the item?	1 = Very slowly 2 = Slowly 3 = Neither slowly or quickly 4 = Quickly 5 = Very quickly	As a buyer, you need to check the postmark on the package you receive. If the seller ships the next day or the next day after that, it's fair to click 5 (Very quickly), no matter how long the postal service took to get it to you.
How reasonable were the shipping and handling charges?	1 = Very unreasonable 2 = Unreasonable 3 = Neither unreasonable or reasonable 4 = Reasonable 5 = Very reasonable	When I purchase an item, I know what the shipping cost will be. The only surprise here is when you get an item in a small envelope and you've paid $9.00 for shipping — or if you paid for Priority Mail and it comes in another class of service. This is, to me, pretty black-and-white. It's either going to be reasonable or not.

Here are some other items to keep in mind when you're deciding on the Detailed Seller Ratings for sellers:

>> **Shipping takes time:** In most cases, as a buyer, it is your choice whether an item is to be shipped via Ground or Priority Mail. You've got to realize that Ground shipping can take up to 10 days. eBay will give you a delivery estimate based on the mode of the seller's shipping. That should be close.

>> **Shipping costs money:** Sellers have to add a little charge to cover the costs of tape, boxes, and packing materials. As a buyer, you've got to keep that in mind. If you are unfamiliar with postage rates, you should also know that a package costs a lot more to ship across the country than to ship to the next

state. So do a little homework and evaluate shipping costs before you buy. If the shipping is too high, go to another seller.

» **Ratings affect the seller's costs:** If your seller is a Top Rated Seller, you should also know that your star ratings affect the fees he or she pays to eBay. Being a good seller (with high DSRs) can save a percentage on their Final Values Fees, so your rating is a very serious matter. Visit Book 8, Chapter 3 for the lowdown on how these ratings affect the Top Rated Seller's pocketbook.

Becoming a Star

Yes, eBay *loves* the stars. When you first join eBay, it seems like everyone on eBay has a star next to the User ID except for you. It's so unfair isn't it? Well, not really. The stars of many colors are awarded based on the amount of feedback left for you. When you receive a feedback rating of 10, you get a bright new gold star (just like in school).

You may notice stars of other colors — even shooting stars; Table 5-2 gives you the lowdown on what each star color represents.

TABLE 5-2

Star Colors Reflect Feedback Rating

Star	Feedback Rating
Gold star	10 to 49
Blue star	50 to 99
Turquoise star	100 to 499
Purple star	500 to 999
Red star	1,000 to 4,999
Green star	5,000 to 9,999
Gold shooting star	10,000 to 24,999
Turquoise shooting star	25,000 to 49,999
Purple shooting star	50,000 to 99,999
Red shooting star	100,000 and higher

After you have a star and you reach a higher level, I assure you that you will get a silly tingly feeling of accomplishment. Very silly, yes, but it's all part of being an active member of the eBay community.

Leaving Feedback with Finesse

Writing feedback well takes some practice. It isn't a matter of saying things; it's a matter of saying *only the appropriate things.* Think carefully about what you want to say — because after you submit feedback, it stays with the person for the duration of his or her eBay career. I think you should always leave feedback, especially at the end of a transaction, although doing so isn't mandatory. Think of leaving feedback as voting in an election: If you don't leave feedback, you can't complain about the service.

eBay recommends that you make feedback "factual and emotionless." You won't go wrong if you comment on the details (either good or bad) of the transaction. If you have any questions about what eBay says about feedback, click the Feedback Forum link at the bottom of any member's Feedback Profile page.

In the Feedback Forum, you can perform the following feedback-related tasks:

>> **Leave Feedback:** Here you see all pending feedback for all transactions within the past 60 days — the ones for which you haven't left feedback. Fill them in, one at a time. Then, with one click, you can leave as many as 25 feedback comments at once.

>> **View a Feedback Profile:** Clicking here allows you to type any eBay member's ID to see that person's feedback profile (the same as if you clicked the number next to the member's name).

>> **Reply to feedback received:** If you've received feedback that you'd like to respond to, click this link. This comes in handy when a buyer leaves what you feel is an unwarranted negative; you can briefly state your case.

>> **Follow up to feedback left:** Here you may also leave follow-up feedback after the initial feedback should situations change.

>> **Request feedback revision:** This is possible, but before you do it, review this chapter — in particular, the "eBay will consider removing feedback if . . ." sidebar and the next section's links to current feedback policy.

>> **Make feedback public or private:** This is where you can decide to show your feedback profile to the public or keep it to yourself.

FETCHING FEEDBACK FACTS

If you're selling, here's how to get a good reputation:

- Answer any questions you receive through eBay Messages as quickly as possible.

- After you've received payment, send out the item quickly.

- Make sure that your item is exactly the way you described it.

- Package the item well and ship it with care.

- React quickly and appropriately to problems — for example, if the item's lost or damaged in the mail or the buyer is slow in paying.

If you're buying, try these good-rep tips:

- Read the entire item description before you buy.

- Send your payment fast.

- Work with the seller to resolve any problems in a courteous manner.

Of course, you should also know how some folks destroy their own businesses by alienating customers, sellers, and the eBay community — so here are some sure-fire ways to get *negative* feedback:

- Tell a major fib in the item description. (To defend truth, justice, and legitimate creative writing, see Book 3.)

- Take the money but take your time shipping the item. (That's the sure path to a bad rep.)

- Package the item poorly so that it ends up smashed, squashed, or vaporized during shipping. (To avoid this pathetic fate, see Book 7.)

If you're buying, here's how to make your status a serious mess:

- Bid on an item, win an auction, and never respond to the seller. (Rude.)

- String the seller out with constant claims of "I will go to PayPal when I get my paycheck." (Flaky.)

- Ask the seller for a refund because you changed your mind. (Flibbertigibbet.)

» **Report buyer problems:** If you feel you are having a problem with a transaction, click the link in the Feedback Forum and go to the Report a Buyer form in the Resolution Center. To report a buyer, follow these steps:

1. Select the recent transaction in question by clicking the option button next to the buyer's ID.

2. Click Continue and select the appropriate situation from the Next, Tell Us What Happened section.

3. Click the Submit button to send your complaint to eBay.

On this page, you also have more links that explain the ins and outs of the eBay feedback system. Here are the details on a few:

» **All About Feedback:** This link takes you to an exclusive help area for feedback questions.

`http://pages.ebay.com/help/feedback/allaboutfeedback.html`

» **Feedback Policies:** Learn about Feedback policies and the various forms of Feedback Abuse — and how eBay deals with them.

`http://pages.ebay.com/help/policies/feedback-ov.html`

» **Feedback FAQs:** Here you find answers to frequently asked questions about how to handle feedback — and how buyers can rephrase their knee-jerk negative or neutral feedback entries to something more accurate after sober reflection (and a request from the seller). You have 10 days to change or remove your feedback before the request expires.

`http://pages.ebay.com/services/forum/changes.html`

WARNING

In the real world (at least in the modern American version of it), anybody can sue anybody else for slander or libel; this fact holds true on the Internet, too. Be careful not to make any comments that could be libelous or slanderous. eBay is not responsible for your actions, so if you're sued because of posting slanderous feedback (or anything else you've written), you're on your own. The best way to keep yourself safe is to stick to the facts and don't get personal.

TIP

If you're angry, take a huge breather *before* you type your complaints and click the Leave Comment button. If you're convinced that negative feedback is necessary, try a cooling-off period before you send comments. Wait an hour — or a day — and then see whether you feel the same. Nasty feedback based on emotion can make you look vindictive, even if what you're saying is true.

TIP

MINCING WORDS: THE AT-A-GLANCE GUIDE TO KEEPING FEEDBACK SHORT

It is best to keep things simple. If you want to compliment, complain, or take the middle road, you have to do it in 80 characters or less. That means your comment needs to be short and sweet. If you have a lot to say but you're stumped about how to say it, here are a few examples for any occasion. String them together or mix and match!

Positive feedback:

- Very professional
- Quick email response
- Fast service
- A+++
- Good communication
- Exactly as described
- Highly recommended
- Smooth transaction
- Would deal with again
- An asset to eBay
- I'll be back!

Negative feedback:

- Never responded
- Never paid for item
- Beware track record
- Item not as described

Neutral feedback:

- Slow to ship but item as described
- Item not as described but seller made good
- Poor communication but item came OK

Ways to Leave Feedback

Several ways are available to leave feedback comments:

» In the Purchase History area of your My eBay, click the Leave Feedback link next to the transaction.

» In the Feedback Forum, `http://pages.ebay.com/services/forum/feedback.html`, click the Leave Feedback link to see a list of all your completed transactions from the last 30 days for which you haven't left feedback.

» On your My eBay Summary, scroll down and on the bottom you will see the Orders heading. You will see a Leave Feedback box next to purchases with which you can leave feedback.

To leave feedback for a seller, follow these steps:

1. **Enter the required information.**

   Note that your item number is usually filled in, but if you're placing feedback from the user's feedback page, you need to have the number at hand.

2. **Choose whether you want your feedback to be positive, negative, or neutral.**

3. **Type your feedback comment.**

4. **Fill in your star ratings by clicking the stars next to the questions (as I discuss in the earlier section, "Giving Detailed Seller Ratings Properly").**

   If you decide that the seller's description was inaccurate, you will have to explain why by clicking next to the explanations that appear (shown in Figure 5-2).

FIGURE 5-2: Be sure to select the proper reason you are giving a seller low ratings.

5. **Click the Leave Feedback button.**

You Have the Last Word — Replying to Feedback

After reading feedback you've received from others, you may feel compelled to respond. If the feedback is negative, you may want to defend yourself. If it's positive, you may want to say thank you.

EBAY WILL CONSIDER REMOVING FEEDBACK IF . . .

Only under certain, special circumstances will eBay remove feedback:

- eBay is served with a court order stating that the feedback in question is slanderous, libelous, defamatory, or otherwise illegal. eBay will also accept a settlement agreement from a resolved lawsuit submitted by both attorneys and signed by both parties.

- The feedback in question has no relation to eBay — such as comments about transactions outside eBay or personal comments about users.

- The feedback contains a link to another page, picture, or a script that can be used to make a purchase outside of eBay.

- The feedback comprises inappropriate comments.

- The feedback contains any personal identifying information about a user.

- The feedback is intended for another user, when eBay has been informed of the situation and the same feedback has been left for the appropriate user.

eBay allows buyers to withdraw or edit feedback after the transaction is righted. The seller must send a time-sensitive request to the buyer. To check on up-to-the-minute feedback removal policies, go to

```
https://pages.ebay.com/help/policies/defect-removal.
html#guidelines
```

and

```
http://pages.ebay.com/help/policies/rfe-spam-ov.html
```

WARNING

Do not confuse *replying* to feedback with *leaving* feedback. Replying does not change the other user's feedback rating; it merely adds your response below the feedback comment in your own feedback profile.

To reply to feedback, follow these steps:

1. On your My eBay Overview page, click Account, then Feedback.

You're transported to the Feedback page where you can leave feedback or request a feedback revision.

2. **Click the link at the top to go to the Feedback Forum.**

3. **Click the Reply to Feedback Received link.**

4. **When you find the feedback you want to respond to, click the Reply link.**

5. **Type your response.**

Checking Out a Seller's Reputation

You've finally found an item you'd like to buy. Don't place that bid just yet! Taking a look at the seller's feedback will supply you with a good deal of information about the reputation of your potential trading partner.

Although the eBay Money Back Guarantee covers your transaction in almost any way, it will not cover you if the seller takes a long time to ship. By looking at the seller's feedback, you can tell whether you'll get the birthday gift you bought for your sister in time for the celebration.

REMEMBER

Always look for the words Top Rated Seller or the Top Rated Plus seal (shown in Figure 5-3) when you are buying an expensive or time-sensitive item. eBay bestows this appellation on only the best sellers.

FIGURE 5-3:
The Top Rated Plus seal shows the sellers with the best customer service.

When you consider buying a more expensive item, be sure to click the seller's feedback number when you visit the item page. Clicking the number will show you the *member profile*: the Feedback Summary and the DSR ratings, as shown in Figure 5-4. After you click the feedback number, you should examine some important details if you want to be a savvy, security-minded shopper.

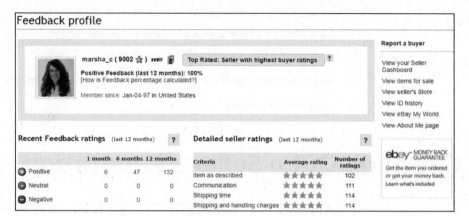

Feedback profile

marsha_c (9002 ☆) me 🔲   Top Rated: Seller with highest buyer ratings   ?

Positive Feedback (last 12 months): 100%
[How is Feedback percentage calculated?]

Member since: Jan-04-97 in United States

Report a buyer

View your Seller
Dashboard

View items for sale

View seller's Store

View ID history

View eBay My World

View About Me page

Recent Feedback ratings (last 12 months)   ?

	1 month	6 months	12 months
Positive	6	47	132
Neutral	0	0	0
Negative	0	0	0

Detailed seller ratings (last 12 months)   ?

Criteria	Average rating	Number of ratings
Item as described	★★★★★	102
Communication	★★★★★	111
Shipping time	★★★★★	114
Shipping and handling charges	★★★★★	114

ebay° MONEY BACK GUARANTEE

Get the item you ordered or get your money back.

Learn what's included

FIGURE 5-4:
A sample
member profile.

On the left side of the page you see Recent Feedback Ratings; on the right, the Detailed Seller Ratings. You also see the counts of feedback comments divided by time periods: 1 month, 6 months, and 12 months. Note the following significant entries:

» **Positive Feedback comments:** You may notice that the *actual* number of positive comments is higher than the positive figure. This is because every eBay community member can comment only once a week on another member and have it count in the feedback rating. (The net rating was previously based on comments from *unique* users.) All feedback entries count as long as they're left in different weeks.

» **Neutral comments:** Neutral comments are usually left when a party wasn't thrilled with the transaction but nothing happened that was bad enough to leave a dreaded, reputation-ruining negative comment.

» **Negative comments:** The number of negative comments may also vary, just as the positives do, for the same reason.

REMEMBER

This feedback page is where all those little stars you place when you leave feedback show up. You'll be able to see how many ratings have been left for each category and where the Average Rating lies.

Reading Feedback Reviews

Scrolling down the feedback history page, you'll be able to read the actual reviews left by other eBay members. In Figure 5-5, you'll see a sample of my feedback. You see each member's User ID, along with his or her feedback rating and comment.

9,904 Feedback received (viewing 1-25)		Revised Feedback: 1 ?
		Period: All ▼
Feedback	**From**	**When**
Good buyer, prompt payment, valued customer, highly recommended. -- (#332377478347)	Seller: bhfo (2382172 ⭐) --	During past month View Item
Nice gift for my son who is working with NASA on this project Rare NASA Journey to Mars Vinyl SLS Space Launch System Orion Bumper Sticker (#351755900992)	Buyer: arabella246 (321 ⭐) US $7.99 Best Offer Price was Accepted ②	During past month View Item
What could you expect from an expert?? Yes, excellent service and communication eBay Business All-in-One For Dummies Signed 2U Marsha Collier 3rd Ed - GirlBoss (#361960835482)	Buyer: coki-2014 (39 ⭐) US $21.59	During past month View Item
EXCELLENT QUAKE HOLD Museum Putty 2.64oz FREE SHIP Earthquake Supplies Survival Kit Wax (#351450213868)	Buyer: paupedra (649 ⭐) US $5.99	During past month View Item

FIGURE 5-5:
Feedback
comment page.

By default, you see the All Feedback Received tab. You may use the other tabs at the top of the page to sort the comments as follows:

>> **Feedback as a Seller:** These are comments from people who bought something from this seller.

>> **Feedback as a Buyer:** When you buy and play by the rules, you get some positive feedback.

>> **All Feedback:** A conglomeration of all feedback left for the particular member, regardless of whether that person was a buyer or a seller in a transaction.

>> **Feedback Left for Others:** Checking the type of feedback someone leaves about others can give you an insight into his or her personality. When considering making a big purchase, I always check this area; it helps me know the type of person I'm dealing with. When you read feedback that makes nasty slams at the other person, or if the person uses rude words or phrases when leaving feedback, it's a clue that you may be dealing with a loose cannon.

Many independent eBay sellers are experienced buyers as well as sellers — they have an excellent grasp of how eBay feels from a customer's point of view, and know how to handle any of your concerns.

TIP

Here are some tips for assessing feedback, depending on the situation:

>> When buying from a seller who sells the same item repeatedly, use the clickable links to past transactions to see whether *other* buyers of the same item were pleased with their purchases.

>> When you come across neutral or negative feedback in the numbers, click to read those specific feedbacks.

REMEMBER

The feedback system relies on the expectation that members give each other the benefit of the doubt. When you come across negative (or neutral) feedback about a seller, look for the seller's response and see whether the problem was resolved before you make your final judgment. You may even see a follow-up feedback comment from the buyer saying that everything has been settled.

Getting Protection on eBay

One thing's for sure in this world: Nothing is for sure. That's why insurance companies exist. Several forms of protection are available for eBay users:

>> eBay Money Back Guarantee

>> eBay Motors Vehicle Purchase Protection

>> Verified Rights Owner program

For more information on how to acquire various protections for your buyers, see Book 2, Chapter 4.

eBay Motors Vehicle Purchase Protection

A major benefit of buying a car on eBay is that you are covered against certain losses associated with some types of fraud. To qualify (this is the easy part), you simply need to purchase the car on eBay. (See? I told you it was simple.)

The Protection Plan gives you some pretty specific protections against conditions such as these that may result in losses:

>> You pay for a vehicle and never receive it.

>> You send a refundable deposit for a vehicle and never receive it.

>> Vehicle Purchase Protection does not cover any damage on vehicles 10 years old or older or without a clear title.

>> You pay for a vehicle and receive it but suffer losses because

• The vehicle was determined by a law enforcement agency to have been stolen at the time the listing ended.

• The vehicle has an undisclosed or unknown lien against its title.

- The vehicle make, model, or year is different from what was described in the seller's listing at the time you placed your bid or offer.

- A title is required for the vehicle by your state and the seller's state but you did not receive a title from the seller and it is not possible to obtain a title from the appropriate DMV.

- The vehicle has a title with an undisclosed salvage, rebuilt/rebuildable, unrebuildable, reconstructed, scrapped/destroyed, junk, lemon, manufacturer-buyback, or water-damage brand at the time the listing ended. (This protection is not available for vehicles listed in the Dune Buggies, Race Cars, or Trailers categories.)

- The vehicle is less than 20 years old and has more than a 5,000-mile odometer discrepancy from the mileage as stated in the seller's listing. (This protection is only available for vehicles listed in the Cars & Trucks and RVs & Campers categories.)

- The vehicle had undisclosed engine, body, transmission, and/or frame damage at the time of purchase that will cost more than $1,000 to repair. The cost of repair to any one of those components must exceed $1,000. For vehicles in the Boats (engine and hull only), Buses, Commercial Trucks, and RVs & Campers categories, the cost of the undisclosed engine, body, transmission, or frame damage must exceed $1,500. Vehicles in the Race Cars category are not eligible for this protection (gee, I wonder why).

Learn more about this protection and any current updates at

pages.ebay.com/ebaymotors/buy/purchase-protection/index.html

Verified Rights Owner program

eBay is a *venue* — a place where sellers sell their wares to smart shoppers like you. No one at eBay owns the items, and no one at eBay can guarantee that any item is as described in auction listings. That means you could, theoretically, buy a "genuine" Kate Spade purse on eBay for $24, and immediately realize when it arrives that the purse is counterfeit. That's *not* eBay's fault. (Shame on you for thinking you could get that kind of deal on a new Kate Spade purse — but if you can, for real, email me and let me know where.)

Just because eBay doesn't take the blame for its fraudulent sellers' handiwork doesn't mean that eBay doesn't care if you get duped. Their VeRO (Verified Rights Owner) program connects eBay with companies or persons who care to protect their intellectual property rights (such as a copyright, trademark, or patent) against possible infringements in eBay listings. VeRO members send proof to eBay that they own the specified intellectual property. In return, they can report infringements to eBay — and eBay's listing police will end the counterfeit listings. This is not an automatic service, however, and the property owners are responsible for finding their own infringements on the site.

Many VeRO members have their own profile pages. To see a list of links to these pages, go to

```
http://pages.ebay.com/seller-center/listing/create-effective-
listings/vero-program.html
```

Chapter **6**

Bidding to Win

Quite a few years ago, on the day after Christmas, I was on *The Today Show* with Matt Lauer talking about post-holiday bargains on eBay. This wasn't the first time I'd been on the show with him; but this time Matt seemed very interested in getting a deal on a child's lamp that I happened to be selling. He and his wife had just had a baby, and everyone likes a bargain.

If everyone likes a bargain, then I'm not like everyone — because I *love* bargains! When I was teaching classes at eBay's own eBay University (yes, there really was one), my favorite class to teach was Buying and Browsing, because I love the thrill of the chase and the acquisition of a good deal without all the haggling.

Often, the first thing that people ask me is how they can stop getting outbid at the last minute of an auction. I always say the same thing — become an expert *sniper* and bid higher than the other guy!

Okay, but how? In this chapter, I give you my tips and a few I picked up from other savvy shoppers along the way.

REMEMBER

eBay treats every bid — other than bids on some real estate sales or incorrectly placed bids — as binding. If you win an auction or buy an item and do not go through with your commitment by purchasing, the seller will file a case against you. If you establish a history as a nonpaying bidder with eBay (that is, you repeatedly back out of purchasing what you bid on), you have a strong chance of getting suspended from the community.

How much an item sells for depends on how many people see the item and how badly others want it. You may think of the *retail price* or *book value* as a standard for pricing, but neither may be accurate when it comes to shopping on eBay. In fact, I say everything has three prices:

>> The price a retailer *charges* for an item at the store

>> The price *everyone* says something is worth

>> The price an item *actually* sells for on eBay

Understanding the Bidding Action

Okay, you've found the perfect item to track (say, a really classy Hello Kitty wristwatch), and it's in your price range. You're more than interested — you're ready to bid. If this were a live auction, some stodgy-looking guy in a gray suit would see you nod your head and start the bidding at, say, $2. Then some woman with a severe hairdo would yank on her ear, and the price of the watch would jump to $3.

eBay reality is more like this: You're sitting at home in your fuzzy slippers, sipping coffee while perusing eBay on your tablet or in front of the computer. All the other bidders are cruising cyberspace in their pajamas, too, but you can't see 'em. (Be real thankful for little favors.)

When you're ready to jump into the bidding fray, find the bidding form (my name for the center square for bidding shown in Figure 6-1) with the Place Bid button. If the item includes a Buy It Now option, you see that below the Place Bid button.

FIGURE 6-1:
You can find the Place Bid button in the center of the auction page header.

Placing your auction bid

To fill out the bidding form and place a bid, first make sure that you're registered. (For help in registering, see Chapter 3.) After you make your first bid on an item, you can instantly get to auctions you're bidding on from your My eBay page. Follow these steps to place a bid:

1. **Sign in to your eBay account, and find an item that you'd like to buy.**

2. **Click the Place Bid button and in the resulting box, enter your maximum bid on your selected item's page.**

   Your bid must be higher than the current minimum bid and you are not required to place one of the bids suggested by eBay (as shown in Figure 6-2).

TIP

   You don't need to put in the dollar sign, but you do need to use a decimal point — unless you really *want* to pay $1,049.00 instead of $10.49. If you make a mistake with an incorrect decimal point, you can retract your bid (see "Retracting Your Bid in an Emergency," at the end of this chapter).

3. **Click Bid.**

   The Review and Confirm Your Bid page appears on your screen, filling it with all the costs involved in purchasing the item. This is your last chance to change your mind: Do you really want the item, and can you really buy it? The bottom line is this: If you bid on it and you win, you buy it.

4. **If you are sure you want to bid on the item and agree to the terms, click Confirm Bid.**

   After you agree, the Bid Confirmation screen appears.

FIGURE 6-2:
The serious part — where you place your bid.

5. **After you place your bid, you will either be the high bidder . . . or not.**

   You'll know where you stand because a window pops up confirming your bid or letting you know your bid wasn't high enough, as shown in Figure 6-3.

US $6.72 + $7.99 for shipping

1d 2h 11m | 3 Bids

! You've been outbid by someone else.
You can still win! Try bidding again.

Place your bid ⊘

| Bid US $8 | Bid US $9 | Bid US $12 |

OR

US $ _____   **Bid**

By placing a bid, you're committing to buy this item if you win.

FIGURE 6-3:
My bid was not
high enough to
beat another
user's proxy bid.

REMEMBER

eBay considers a bid on an item to be a binding contract. You can save yourself a lot of heartache if you promise *never to bid on an item you don't intend to buy*. Don't make spurious bids on the silly assumption that because you're new to eBay, you can't win; if you do that, you'll probably win simply because you've left yourself open to Murphy's Law. Therefore, before you click Place Bid, be sure that you're in this auction for the amount you're bidding — and make yourself another promise *to figure out the maximum you're willing to spend* — and stick to it.

If you want to practice bidding, go to eBay's Test Bid page at

http://pages.ebay.com/education/tutorial/course1/bidding/

Bidding to the max with automatic (proxy) bidding

When you make a maximum bid on an item, you actually make several small bids — again and again — until the bidding reaches where you told it to stop. For example, if the current bid is up to $19.99 and you put in a maximum of $45.02, your bid automatically increases incrementally so you're ahead of the competition — at least until someone else's maximum bid exceeds yours. Basically, you bid by *proxy*, which means the automatic-bid feature stands in for you so your bid rises incrementally in response to other bidders' bids.

No one else knows whether you're bidding automatically, and no one knows how high your maximum bid is. And the best part is that you can be out enjoying your life while the proxy bidding happens automatically.

The *bid increment* is the amount of money by which a bid is raised, and eBay's system can work in mysterious ways. Buyers and sellers have no control over the bid increments that eBay sets. The current maximum bid can jump up a nickel or a quarter or even a twenty-dollar bill, but there is a method to the madness (even though you may not think so). To determine how much to increase the bid increment, eBay uses a *bid-increment formula* that's based on the current high bid. Here are examples:

» A 5-quart bottle of cold cream has a current high bid of $14.95. The bid increment is $0.50 — meaning that if you bid by proxy, your automatic bid will be $15.45.

» A 5-ounce can of top-notch caviar has a high bid of $200. The bid increment is $2.50. If you choose to bid by proxy, your bid will be $202.50.

Table 6-1 shows you what happens when you put the proxy system and a bid-increment formula together in the same cyber-room.

TABLE 6-1   **eBay Auction Proxy Bidding Magic**

Current	Bid Increment ($)	Minimum Bid ($)	eBay Auctioneer	Bidders
2.50	0.25	2.75	"Do I hear $2.75?"	Joe Bidder tells his proxy that his maximum bid is $8.00. He's the current high bidder at $2.75.
2.75	0.25	3.00	"Do I hear $3.00?"	You tell your proxy that your maximum bid is $25.00 and take a nice, relaxing bath while your proxy calls out your $3.00 bid, making you the current high bidder.
3.00	0.25	3.25	"I hear $3.00 from proxy. Do I hear $3.25?"	Joe Bidder's proxy bids $3.25, and while Joe Bidder is out walking his dog, he becomes the high bidder.
A heated bidding war ensues between Joe Bidder's proxy and your proxy while the two of you go on with your lives. The bid increment inches from $0.25 to $0.50 as the current high bid increases.				
7.50	0.50	8.00	"Do I hear $8.00?"	Joe Bidder's proxy calls out $8.00, his final offer.
8.00	0.50	8.50	"The bid is at $8.00. Do I hear $8.50?"	Your proxy calls out $8.50 on your behalf, and having outbid your opponent, you win the auction.

The Secret's in the Timing

Brick-and-mortar auctions, such as those held by Sotheby's or Christie's, end when the bidding ends. No auctioneer is going to cut off the feverish bidding for that one-of-a-kind Van Gogh, right? As long as someone is bidding, all systems are go. The last bidder standing wins. Auctions on eBay, however, close at a pre-scribed time. Because of this fundamental difference in the way eBay runs its auctions, you need to do some special work to make sure that you time your bid as strategically as possible.

GOING, GOING, GONE

Although many people list their auctions to end at all hours of the day and night, the amount of bidders in cyberspace is higher during certain hours. Between the hours of 23:00 (that's 11:00 p.m. Pacific Standard Time) and 03:00 (that's 3:00 a.m. Pacific Standard Time), things run a bit slowly on eBay. If you're online at that time, you may be able to take advantage of some very serious bargains in auctions. So swallow a shot of espresso and have fun if you're a night owl.

Going, going, gone is the name of the game my daughter and I used to play when we wanted to go sport-shopping on eBay. Visit your favorite eBay category and have fun.

You can choose to view the auctions that are going to end in the next few hours by using the Sort By options from the drop-down menu. Here you can cruise the auctions that are closing while the world is asleep, and bid to your heart's content to get some great bargains.

TIP

You can find out what time an auction ends by simply looking at the auction page. Note that eBay runs on Pacific Time and uses a 24-hour clock (00:00 to 24:00 versus the more familiar 1:00 to 12:00).

To get the serious deals, you may want to synchronize your computer's clock with eBay's. To find out what eBay's official time is, go to

```
http://ofr.ebay.com/ws/eBayISAPI.dll?EbayTime
```

Then compare eBay's time with your computer's clock. On most Windows-based computers, the time is in the lower-right corner of the screen on the taskbar. Now you'll know how to offset your timing if necessary.

Using the lounging-around strategy

Sometimes the best strategy at the beginning of an auction is to do nothing at all. That's right; relax, take off your shoes, and loaf. You may want to make a *token bid* (the very lowest you are allowed) or mark the page to Watch on your My eBay page. I generally take this attitude through the first six days of a week-long auction I want to bid on, and it works pretty well. I do, however, check in to keep tabs on important items I'm watching on My eBay, and revise my strategy as time passes.

TIP

If an auction has received no bids 12 hours before the auction ends, the seller has the right to change the minimum bid. Also, if there is a Buy It Now option on an auction, someone can swoop in and purchase the item for the stated price. If you place the minimum as a token bid when you first see the auction, you may foil a Buy It Now from another bidder. (Buy It Now is disabled after a bid is placed in some categories. In others, it disappears once the reserve is met — if there is one.)

REMEMBER

If you see an item that you absolutely must have, mark it to watch (or make a token bid) and revise your maximum bid as the auction goes on. I can't stress enough how important this is.

As you check back each day, take a look at the other bids and the high bidder. Is someone starting a bidding war? Look at the time when the competition is bidding and note any patterns, such as lunchtime bidding. If you know what time your major competition is bidding, you can bid after he or she does.

Using the beat-the-clock strategy

You should rev up your bidding strategy during the final 24 hours of an auction and decide, once and for all, whether you really *have* to have the item you've been eyeing. Maybe you put in a maximum bid of $45.02 earlier in the week. Now's the time to decide whether you're willing to go as high as $50.02. Maybe $56.03?

No one wants to spend the day in front of the computer (ask almost anyone who does), but if you have a smartphone, you might want to use the eBay mobile app while running errands. Just place a sticky note where you're likely to see it, reminding you of the exact time the auction ends. If you're not going to be near a computer when the auction closes, you can also use an automatic bidding software program to bid for you; see "Succeeding by Sniping," later in this chapter, for details.

In the last few minutes

With half an hour left before the auction becomes ancient history, head for the computer and dig in for the last battle of the bidding war. I recommend that you sign on to eBay about 10 to 15 minutes before the auction ends. The last thing you want is to get caught in Internet gridlock and not get access to the eBay website. Go to the items you're watching and click the auction title.

With 10 minutes to go, if there's a lot of action on your auction, click reload or refresh every 30 seconds to get the most current info on how many people are bidding.

REMEMBER

Bidding in odd increments is just one of the many strategies to get you ahead of the rest of the bidding pack without paying more than you should. Many of the strategies in this chapter are for bidders who are tracking an item over the course of a week or more, so be sure you have time to track the item and plan your next move. Also, get a few auctions under your belt before you throw yourself into the middle of a bidding war.

PUT IN YOUR TWO CENTS

Your two cents does matter — at least on eBay. Here's why: Many eBay members round off their bids to the nearest dollar figure or choose familiar coin increments such as 25, 50, or 75 cents. But the most successful eBay bidders have found that adding 2 or 3 cents to a routine bid can mean the difference between winning and losing. So I recommend that you make your proxy bids in odd amounts, like $15.02 or $45.57, as an inexpensive way to edge out your competition. For the first time ever, your two cents may actually pay off!

My Favorite Bidding Strategies

There used to be a time when I would tell beginning eBay members my favorite methods of bidding and winning, and if there was an eBay employee in earshot, you could see him or her wince. Things are considerably different these days. For example, eBay used to officially oppose the use of third-party payment options — until they purchased PayPal. And when sniping swept the online auction community and became *de riguer*, the eBay Powers That Be didn't endorse the practice. Finally, after some agonizing, the eBay insiders admitted that sniping *does* work in winning auctions.

As a matter of fact, eBay's instructors are now pitching many of the strategies that I've been talking about for years — because they work! While editing this book, my editor even reminisced about just how much the eBay "party line" has changed since I wrote my first book on eBay in 1999.

Hunting for errors

Some of my best buys on eBay were the result of searching for misspellings. Many sellers are in a hurry when they set up their auction listings, and to err is human (and to win, divine). I am more than willing to forgive sellers for their mistakes because the payoff for bargain hunters is, well, a bargain.

Think of alternative spellings when you search for an item. A favorite of mine is *Von Furstenburg* for *Von Furstenberg*. Usually, I search for the correct spelling and find a bunch of items where the bidding can get steep. But when I search for the misspelled version, I may find identical items that have no bids, because I'm the only one who has found the listing. Figure 6-4 shows that eBay is often aware of misspellings when it comes to name brands.

FIGURE 6-4:
Once I clicked the link to the misspelling, there were 1,002 results (versus 32,710, spelled correctly).

You can search for both the correct and incorrect spellings by using a search such as (*furstenberg,furstenburg*). Book 2 gives you lots more search tricks.

I was also successful during one holiday season when computer-animated cats were popular (and going for extremely high prices on eBay, because they were sold out everywhere across the country). The brand name was FurReal. I searched for spellings like *fur real* and *furreal* and found many bargains.

eBay smartened up and now sometimes shows alternative spellings — but not always (what is the right way to spell L'Occitane?).

A couple of our favorite misspellings are *neckless* (instead of *necklace*) — currently 2,305 items up for sale — and *vidio* (instead of *video*), for which 180 are currently on the site. I accidentally ran a misspelled search for a popular electronics game and noticed that there were 29 items spelled *Nitendo*. Note that eBay did suggest the proper spelling of *Nintendo*, with 43,902 items.

There are a couple of websites that can help you find misspelled bargains on eBay; check out `www.fatfingers.com` and `www.typohound.com` for some stellar examples.

Researching your item

Sometimes we (that includes me *and* you) find what we think is an incredible deal on eBay. It may well be, especially if we know that the retail price is, say, $80 and we're seeing a Buy It Now or an auction closing at $40. If a low, low price works for you, just go ahead and buy the item if you want it right away. To find the best price for any item on eBay, do your homework to find out what similar items on eBay (or Amazon) tend to sell for.

When you conduct your eBay research, the best strategy is to look at the prices achieved in previous sales. Do a search for Sold auctions. Then check an auction's bid history by clicking the number of bids placed on the auction item page (the link appears next to the Winning Bid price). You'll be presented with a screen like the one in Figure 6-5. This will at least give you an idea of how many people are duking it out for the item, if not their actual IDs. You should also click the Show Automatic Bids link on the right, so you can see how many bids were placed by proxy.

Pay attention to the times when bidders are placing their bids, and you may find that the people bidding in the auction are creatures of habit — making their bids about once a day and at a particular time of day. They may be logging on before work, during lunch, or after work. Whatever their schedules, you have great info at your disposal in the event that a bidding war breaks out: Just bid after your competition traditionally logs out, and you increase your odds of winning the auction.

Bidder (i)	Bid Amount	Bid Time
g***n (311 ⭐)	$43.00	11 Jul 2017 at 6:24:57PM PDT
i***h (5)	$42.00	11 Jul 2017 at 5:58:53PM PDT
e***i (1559 ⭐)	$41.55	11 Jul 2017 at 5:24:02PM PDT
6***6 (299 ⭐)	$40.00	10 Jul 2017 at 6:34:41PM PDT
e***i (1559 ⭐)	$39.55	11 Jul 2017 at 5:23:56PM PDT
e***i (1559 ⭐)	$37.55	11 Jul 2017 at 5:23:46PM PDT
i***n (660 ⭐)	$35.00	6 Jul 2017 at 1:19:29PM PDT
6***6 (299 ⭐)	$35.00	10 Jul 2017 at 6:34:28PM PDT

FIGURE 6-5:
I don't know who they are, but their bids sure seem persistent.

Early in an auction, there may not be much of a bidding history for an item, but that doesn't mean you can't still check out the dates and times a bidder places bids. You can also tell whether a bidder practices *sniping* (discussed later in this chapter) if his or her bid is in the last few seconds of the auction. You may have a fight on your hands if the bidder uses sniping.

Quick Bidding Tips

When you get a tip, double-check to see who it's coming from. Visit eBay's community boards and chats, and listen to what the others have to say. Before taking anything to heart and changing the way you do things, check the tip-givers' experiences. Are they really experienced on eBay? Or are they selling seminars or passing on the latest misinformation? I love buying from eBay sellers who are also buyers, because they respect and understand what it's like to be a buyer on eBay!

Here are a few short tips that I know really work:

>> **Shop eBay.ca, eh!** That's right. If you're in the U.S.A., why not bid on auctions on the eBay Canada website? In fact, if you're an international bidder and are willing to pay shipping from the United States, you'll have no problem handling Canadian shipping charges.

>> **Place your bids in odd figures.** Many eBay bidders place their bids in the round numbers that match eBay's proxy system. You can win by a few cents if you place your bids in odd numbers like $10.97 or $103.01.

>> **Don't get carried away in a bidding war.** Unless the item is rare, odds are that a similar item will show up on eBay again someday soon. Don't let your ego get in the way of smart bidding. Let your opposition pay too much!

>> **Don't freak out if you find yourself in a bidding war.** Don't keel over if, at the split-second you're convinced that you're the high bidder with your $45.02, someone beats you out at $45.50.

>> **Watch for item relistings.** If you see an item that you want but it has too high an opening bid (or too high a reserve), there's a good chance that no one else will bid on the item, either. Put that auction into your Watch area of My eBay. Then, after the auction ends, double-check the seller's auctions every so often to see whether the item has been relisted with a lower starting bid and a lower (or no) reserve.

>> **Combine shipping when possible.** When you purchase an item, check the seller's other auctions and see whether you're interested in making a second purchase. If you see something else that appeals to you, message the seller to see whether he or she will combine the items in shipping. That way, you can make two purchases for a smaller single shipping bill.

>> **Never bid early, but if you do, bid high.** The only time this "bidding early" business works is if no one else is interested in the auction. Usually, though, the tactic will gear up another eBay user to outbid you because suddenly the item is valuable to at least one person. If you *must* bid before the auction's close, bid high. As a matter of fact, bid a couple of dollars more than you might want to pay. (I mean literally a couple, not a couple hundred.)

>> **Try for a Best Offer (previously Second Chance).** If you get outbid and miss the chance to increase your bid on an auction item, you'd be smart to email the seller and ask whether he or she has any more of the item. You may get lucky, and the seller can send you a Best Offer for your high bid.

A seller may send a Best Offer to up to four underbidders in the auction under three circumstances: when the winner doesn't pay, when the reserve price wasn't met, or when the seller has more than one of the items that were sold. Any purchase you make in this manner will be covered under eBay Buyer Protection, and you will have the opportunity to leave feedback.

Succeeding by Sniping

Sniping is the fine art of outbidding your competition in the very last seconds of the auction — without leaving them enough time to place a defensive bid. Sniping is my number-one favorite way to win an auction on eBay. When I first touted this method in 1999, it was a fairly new idea. Now everyone knows about sniping, and it's pretty much an accepted bidding method.

REMEMBER

Bidders (that is, losing bidders) whine and moan when they lose to a sniper, but they should remember one thing: The high bidder always wins, whether you're sniping or using the automatic bid system. If you're going to snipe, assume that the current bidder has a *very* high-dollar proxy bid in the works.

Some eBay members consider the practice of sniping unseemly and uncivilized — like when dozens of parents used to mob the department-store clerks to get to the handful of Cabbage Patch dolls that were just delivered. (Come to think of it, whatever happened to *those* collectibles?) Of course, sometimes a little uncivilized behavior can be a hoot.

TIP

Sniping is an addictive, fun part of life on eBay. I recommend that you try it. You're likely to benefit from the results and enjoy your eBay experience even more — especially if you're an adrenaline junkie.

Sniping techniques for the beginner

Here's a list of things to keep in mind when you get ready to place your snipe bid:

» **Know how high you're willing to go.** If you know you're facing a lot of competition, figure out your highest bid to the penny. You should have already researched the item and figured out its value. Raise your bid only to the level where you're sure you're getting a good return on your investment; don't go overboard. Certainly, if the item has some emotional value and you just have to have it, bid as high as you want. But remember, you'll have to pay the piper later. You win it, you own it!

» **Know how fast (or slow) your Internet connection is.** Before you start sniping, figure out how long it takes to get your bid confirmed on eBay. Test it a few times until you know how many seconds you have to spare when placing a bid.

» **Don't lose heart if you lose the auction.** Remember, this is a game.

WARNING

Although sellers love sniping because it drives up prices and bidders love it because it's fun, a sniper can ruin a week's careful work on an auction strategy. The most skillful snipers sneak in a bid so close to the end of the auction that you have no chance to counter-bid. Losing too often, especially to the same sniper, can be a drag. See the section on BidRobot further on to solve this problem (it works for me).

TIP

If your Internet connection is slow and you want to do some sniping, make your final bid two minutes before the auction ends and adjust the amount of the bid as high as you feel comfortable so you can beat out the competition. If you *can* make the highest bid with just 10 seconds left, you most likely will win. With so many bids coming in the final seconds, your bid might be the last one eBay records.

This stuff is supposed to be fun, so don't lose perspective. If you can't afford an item, don't get caught up in a bidding war. Otherwise, the only person who wins is the seller. If you're losing sleep, barking at your cat, or biting your nails over an item, it's time to rethink what you're doing. If it's taking up too much of your life or an item costs too much, be willing to walk away — or log off — and live to bid another day.

To snipe a bid manually (without a sniping service), first make sure you're signed in. Then follow these steps to snipe at the end of the auction:

1. **In the last few minutes of the auction, locate the item you want to win and press Ctrl+N to open a second window on your Internet browser.**

Keep one window open for bidding, as shown in Figure 6-6.

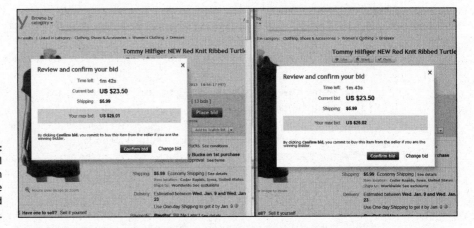

FIGURE 6-6: My manual sniping system in action (before I automated my snipes).

2. **Continuously click the Reload or Refresh button that appears in the last few minutes of an auction, just above the Place Bid button.**

By reloading the item continually, you'll be aware when you're in the last 60 seconds of bidding. You also can see instantly whether anyone else is doing any last-minute bidding.

3. **In the bid box of the second browser, type your maximum bid and then click the Place Bid button.**

You then face a page that, when you press the button, finalizes and confirms your bid on the item. Do not click the Confirm Bid button yet.

94   BOOK 1 **eBay Basics**

4. **As the auction nears its end, confirm your final bid by clicking the Confirm Bid button.**

   You know when the auction is almost over because you're reloading your first browser continually. The longer you can hold off bidding before the auction ends, the better.

If you really want an item bad enough, you may want to set up a backup for your snipe. Try my three-screen system, in which you can place a backup high bid in case you catch another sniper swooping in on your item immediately after your first snipe.

Obviously, if you win with the first snipe, the second window is unnecessary. But if you lose the first one, that second window feels like a real lifesaver! If you're outbid after two snipes, don't cry. The winner paid way more than you were willing to pay. It's not *much* consolation, but rarely is an item so rare that you only see it come on the auction block once in a lifetime.

Auto-sniping your auctions

My daughter says that I can make almost anything high-maintenance, and she may very well be right. When it comes to eBay bidding and winning, a bunch of software programs and websites can help automate your shopping and feedback process. I like that they will bid for me whether I'm near a computer or sleeping peacefully.

Here is one bidding service that I have used successfully: BidRobot. Shown in Figure 6-7, BidRobot deftly places sniping bids for you from its servers. It's won many an auction for me while I've been on the road or busy writing. The service is one of the least expensive out there, charging a low flat rate. Get a three-week free trial (all you can snipe for three weeks!) at

   www.bidrobot.com/cool

BidRobot also has a BidGroup feature to use if you're bound and determined to get the lowest price for an item. This is accomplished by planning a bidding schedule at a set price. The bidding continues until you win your item (or not). Here's how it works.

1. **Search for your item.** Search for your specific item on eBay. You may find a large number of eBay auctions that offer your item.

2. **Select the auctions you'd like to bid on**. Review the listings (checking the seller's feedback, description, and eBay Buyer Protection availability) and select six different listings.

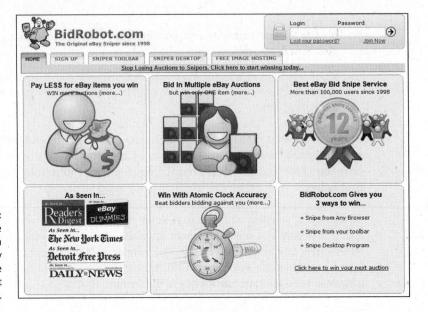

FIGURE 6-7:
Easily place snipes in advance by using the BidRobot website.

3. **Create your first snipe.** Type your first snipe bid in the pale-yellow Bid section (at the very top of the BidRobot bid screen) and select the option to indicate that you want to create a group of bids with the other five auctions.

4. **Group the other auctions.** To bid on other sellers' auctions, scroll down until you find the Pending Bid Group that contains your first item bid. Then use the form in that BidGroup area to add more snipe bids for other auctions in that specific BidGroup. You may add bids for as many additional auctions as you like to this group.

5. **Winning.** If you win any one of the auctions in your BidGroup, the remaining bids in that specific group will not be placed. This is automatic.

KNOWING WHAT YOU'RE BUYING

Before you place a bid, be sure that you know the item's *street price,* which is the price that people actually pay — not the MSRP (manufacturer's suggested retail price). You can use the Internet to check prices for many items. In fact, several consumer websites are dedicated to serving savvy consumers by offering this information. You can find prices at www.pricewatch.com or www.shopping.com. Almost everything is also sold on Amazon these days. Why not give its pricing a try at www.amazon.com. You may be comfortable paying slightly more than the street price because the sellers on eBay are small businesses, with many run by people like your neighbor. I'm a big believer in supporting small business. Plus: You have eBay's Buyer Protection behind your purchase.

Retracting Your Bid in an Emergency

We're all human, and we all make mistakes. Luckily for everyone, eBay members are allowed to retract bids under certain circumstances. You may retract your bid if you meet one of the following criteria:

>> **You accidentally typed the wrong bid amount:** Say you typed $900 but you meant $9.00. Oops. In a case like this, you can retract the bid, but you'd better rebid the proper amount (that original $9.00) immediately, or you may be in violation of eBay's policies.

>> **The seller has added information to the item description that changes the value of the item considerably:** The bull that was let loose in the seller's shop has changed the mint condition of the Ming vase you just bid on? No problem.

>> **You can't reach the seller through eBay's messages or through the telephone number you got from eBay's find members area:** Seller has gone AWOL, and you have a question about an item you've bid on? You can use eBay's message system by clicking the Ask a Question link near the bottom of the listing page. Or to get the seller's telephone number, click the Advanced link (at the top-right corner of most eBay pages) and then click the Find a Member link (on the left side of the page). Next, input your transaction number and the seller's User ID. After checking to make sure that you've begun a transaction with this person, the good people at eBay will send the seller's telephone number in an email message to your registered email address. Your phone number will also be emailed to the seller.

REMEMBER

Every time you retract a bid, it appears in the feedback area of your eBay feedback page.

Here are a couple of additional restrictions to retracting bids:

>> **You can retract a bid if it was placed during the last 12 hours of an auction.** If you bid more than once in the last 12 hours of the same auction, you can retract a bid within one hour of placing it. In this case, only that bid will be retracted; any other bid placed before the last 12 hours of the listing remains valid.

>> **When you retract a bid and the listing has more than 12 hours to go, you wipe out any of your previous bids in the auction.** To reinstate yourself as a bidder, you must bid again.

If you want to retract your bid within the last 12 hours of the auction and you placed the bid before the last 12 hours, you must send a message to the seller asking him or her to cancel your bid. It is up to the seller whether to cancel your bid. A bid retraction isn't a guarantee that you will get out of purchasing the item. Sometimes sellers simply don't have the opportunity or time to cancel a bid. That means you have to buy the item.

You'll probably never need this link, but to retract your bid (or find more information), be sure you're signed in and go to

> `http://offer.ebay.com/ws/eBayISAPI.dll?RetractBidShow`

WARNING

eBay vigorously investigates members who abuse bid retractions. Too many bid retractions and you may find yourself suspended from the system.

IN THIS CHAPTER

» **Buying an item and paying immediately**

» **Using plastic**

» **Paying through PayPal**

» **Contacting the seller**

» **Leaving feedback**

Chapter **7**

Completing the Transaction

The thrill of the chase is over, and you've won (or bought) your eBay item. Congratulations — now what do you do? You have to follow up on your victory and keep a sharp eye on what you're doing. The post-sale process is smooth as silk if you follow the proper procedure.

In this chapter, you get a handle on what's in store for you after you win an auction or buy an item. I clue you in on what the seller is supposed to do to make the transaction go smoothly and show you how to grab hold of your responsibilities as a buyer. You find out about proper post-sale etiquette, including the best ways to get organized, communicate with the seller professionally, and send your payment without hazards. I also brief you on how to handle an imperfect transaction.

Monitoring the Auction Action

TIP

Throughout the bidding process, the dollar amounts of items you're winning appear in green on your My eBay⇨Buy⇨Bids/Offers shown in Figure 7-1. If you've been outbid, the notification appears in red.

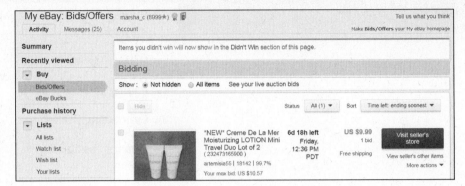

FIGURE 7-1:
Check here to see
the progress of
your bid.

After the auction ends, there's no marching band, no visit from a camera crew, no armful of roses, and no oversized check to duck behind. In fact, you're more likely to find out that you've won the auction from eBay or the Buy⇨Purchase History section of your My eBay page. That's because eBay gets its end-of-auction and transaction confirmation emails out pronto. After you win, you can go back to the item and see a checkout link on the item page or click Pay Now on the email you get from eBay. For a look at all the transaction information in the end-of-auction email, see Figure 7-2.

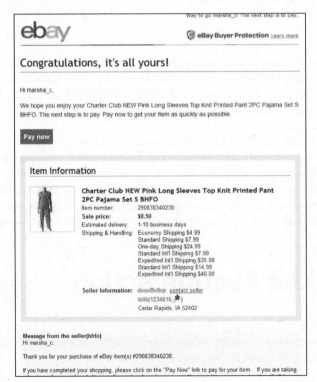

FIGURE 7-2:
Everything you
need to know
about your
transaction is
included in eBay's
Congratulations
email.

TIP

If you have a smartphone, I recommend that you get eBay's Mobile app (more about the app in Book 2, Chapter 2). With this handy tool you can bid or buy an item wherever you are. When you have bid on an auction with a proxy bid and you win, your phone will ring and let you know that you have won. Isn't the world of mobile apps fabulous?

Checking Out

When you buy something in a store, you have to check out as a part of paying. eBay isn't much different. eBay's checkout is a convenient way to pay for your completed auction or purchase with a credit card or eCheck through PayPal. You may also use checkout to pay for your item using another payment service that the seller accepts.

Checkout is integrated directly onto the item page so that you can buy and pay for an item in less than a minute.

When you click the Buy Now button, you're taken to the checkout page, where you can make an immediate payment through PayPal. To check out and pay, first take care of some important details on the Confirm Order page:

>> **Ship To address.** This will be your registered eBay address. If you want the item to be shipped elsewhere, click the Change Shipping Address link.

>> **Add Message to Seller.** If you want to send the seller a message regarding your purchase, click here; a text box appears, and that's where you type in your message.

>> **Item title.** Be sure what you're paying for is what you purchased!

>> **eBay Bucks.** If you have an eBay Bucks code to redeem, enter it here and that amount will be deducted from your purchase.

>> **Shipping options.** If the seller offers several shipping options, be sure you select the one that will get the item to you when you need it. eBay lists estimated delivery dates under each option; these are based on the seller's shipping policies.

>> **PayPal payment method.** You can choose any of the payment methods you have registered with PayPal. Before you click the Confirm and Pay button, be sure to select the appropriate credit card or bank account from the drop-down list that appears when you click the Change link.

When I talk to people about why they don't buy on eBay, the most frequent answer is that they're afraid of giving out their credit card information. The second most common reason is that they don't want to send money to strangers. In addition to all the eBay safeguards that I mention in previous chapters, the next section gives you further info on how to stay safe when sending your payment to the sellers. You may be surprised to know that there are distinct levels of safety in how you can send a payment to a seller.

Using Your Credit Card Safely

The safest way to shop on eBay is to use a credit card, whether through PayPal or direct through the seller's merchant account. eBay Buyer Protection covers your entire purchase. In the rare instance that your purchase is not covered, most credit card companies will stand behind you if you encounter problems using your card online.

Knowing your credit card company's policy

Before you start bidding, find out how your credit card company handles fraud claims. The major credit-card companies — American Express, MasterCard, and Visa — have different policies regarding how they stand behind your online purchases:

>> **American Express:** American Express offers a "Fraud Protection Guarantee" for online shoppers. The company claims that there's "no fine print and no deductible" if you need to rely on American Express to help you fight a fraudulent transaction.

www.americanexpress.com/us/content/fraud-protection-center.html

>> **MasterCard:** The MasterCard Zero Liability program is offered if MasterCard is satisfied that your account is in good standing, you haven't broadcast personal account information online frivolously, and you haven't reported more than two "unauthorized events" in the past 12 months.

REMEMBER

It appears that MasterCard's policy is conditional and that they (not you) are the final judge when it comes to determining fraud, so be careful.

www.mastercard.us/zero-liability.html

>> **Visa:** Visa likes the phrase *zero liability,* as well. Your liability for unauthorized transactions is $0. A new program, called Verified by Visa, lets you set up your own private password that you use with your Visa card any time you use it online at participating merchants.

```
http://usa.visa.com/personal/security/visa_security_program/
zero_liability.html
```

WARNING

Never — really, I mean *never ever* — send your credit card information to anyone through email. Email is the most insecure way to send information. As your email makes its way from your computer to the recipient's desktop, it makes a whole lot of micro-stops along the way. These stops may take just nanoseconds, but your information is open for reading or storing by outside parties (at least those who have the right expertise) at any stop along the journey.

Adding a layer of protection with an online checkout service

Many eBay sellers use an independent online checkout service that allows them to process shipping information, combine purchases, give an exact shipping total, and receive credit card payments. If the seller uses such a service, you probably see a clickable link in the email that's sent to you to complete the transaction. The link leads you to an online checkout page.

When you come to the point in the checkout process where you must input your credit card information (see Figure 7-3), look for the following:

>> **Check the URL for an *s*:** The URL (website address) may change from a prefix of http:// to https:// (the s stands for secure).

>> **Look for a Security Certificate or *SSL*:** You may also see the initials SSL in the website's address or somewhere on the page. SSL stands for Secure Socket Layer.

TIP

The preceding items indicate that the website uses *security encryption* methods. Translation? No one but you and the merchant can read or view your payment information.

FIGURE 7-3:
A secure credit card checkout.

Paying with PayPal

PayPal is my preferred method of payment on eBay. I've been happily using PayPal since the company was introduced to eBay, and I've always had positive results. Well, okay, not always. No service can make a slow or lazy seller into the picture of efficiency. The advantage of PayPal, though, is that you don't have to get your hands dirty.

The folks at eBay know a good thing when they see it, so they acquired PayPal late in 2002. Now PayPal payments are integrated into eBay's checkout process.

Registering at PayPal

When you register to use PayPal, you have to give your name, address, phone number, and email address. You also have to make up a password.

REMEMBER

Make your password more than six characters, and use numbers *and* letters — revisit Chapter 3 in this minibook for more information on registration security.

You have to select a security question. The safest is your first pet's name (many people on Facebook probably know your current pet's name), your city of birth, or the last four digits of your Social Security number. You have to click to put a check mark next to the paragraph that says you have read and agree to PayPal's User Agreement and Privacy policy. (There are links so you can read them.) When you're convinced that you understand what PayPal's all about and what it expects of you, click Sign Up.

PayPal sends you an email confirming your registration. The email arrives, almost instantaneously, at the email address you used at registration, and the message contains a link. When you receive the email, click the link to visit the PayPal site. Enter the password that was used to create your account. Bingo — you're in.

Giving PayPal credit card or checking account information

Of course, you also have to add a credit card number to your PayPal account if you want to pay for anything with a credit card (or plan to sell on eBay). If you don't have a credit card — or would like to occasionally pay for things directly from your bank account — you have to register your checking account.

YOUR CREDIT CARD COMPANY AND PayPal

To be a good consumer, you need to take responsibility for your transactions. Be sure you understand your credit card terms and conditions when it comes to third-party payment services. Each credit card company has its own agreement with PayPal — and each company has a different view of how to handle PayPal transactions. For example, Visa and MasterCard treat PayPal as the *merchant of record* in your transactions, meaning that PayPal ends up as the responsible party if you don't receive the merchandise or if you dispute the transaction. If you register a complaint about a charge made on your Visa or MasterCard, the credit card company just yanks the money from PayPal, and it's up to PayPal to settle things with the seller.

At the time of this writing, Discover and American Express treat PayPal transactions somewhat like a cash advance — a money transfer of sorts. I just checked a couple of my past Discover and American Express bills, and the PayPal charges look like any other charges. The only difference is how these credit card companies handle their level of liability in third-party payment services. This is why any complaints about a transaction should go to eBay (or PayPal) first as you are generally covered by Buyer Protection.

I can see you beginning to squirm; you're not comfortable giving that type of information to anyone, much less putting it out on the Internet. Relax. PayPal uses military-strength encryption technology to keep your account information safe, so don't be afraid to give up your data.

To register your credit card, you'll have to input the name on the card (the last name is already filled in with the name you registered on the account), the expiration date, and the *card verification number* — the three-digit number on the back of the card, imprinted next to the last few digits of the card number in the area where you sign. (American Express verification numbers are on the front of the card.) PayPal also asks you to supply a billing address.

TIP

On an American Express card, the card verification number is the four-digit number on the right side of the face of the card.

When you enter all the information PayPal needs, click the Add button. PayPal submits your information to your credit card company for confirmation. This process may take a minute or so, but eventually your credit card company says you are who you say you are, and the card is added to your PayPal account. You can register four active credit cards.

Registering your checking account is just as easy. You supply the information from the bottom of one of your checks, as shown in Figure 7-4.

FIGURE 7-4: Provide your bank routing number and your account number.

Getting PayPal-verified

For your account to get verified, PayPal must be able to confirm that your bank account is really yours. If you bank online, you can usually confirm your account in a few minutes. When PayPal has the information it needs, it makes two small deposits into that account. (When I say *small*, I mean small!) After a while, call your bank or check your account online and find out the amount of these two deposits. When you have the amounts, sign on to the PayPal website with your password, and type the amounts in the appropriate place. Voilà! Your account is registered — and, not coincidentally, you're verified! PayPal has confirmed that you hold an active account with your bank. All banks are required to screen their account holders, and verification authenticates your identity to anyone who does business with you.

Here are some benefits of being PayPal verified:

>> It lifts any PayPal-imposed withdrawal limits.

>> You gain a higher level of account security.

>> You present a confident image as a buyer or seller. Verified status shows other PayPal members that you have passed PayPal's security checks.

When you first sign up, there are limits on the amount of money you can withdraw from PayPal; you may only be able to withdraw $500.00 per month.

Luckily, you can remedy this feature by confirming your bank account and linking your credit cards. After you complete the steps shown here, you're in the clear.

Here's how you can view and lift your withdrawal limit:

1. **Go to PayPal.com and sign in to your account.**

2. **Click the Profile link (next to Log Off).**

3. **On the resulting page, complete the To-Do list.**

   You are now ready to roll with the "big guys."

Ways to pay through PayPal

The easiest and most efficient way to pay for eBay purchases is by credit card. If you are not a PayPal-verified buyer, you still have your credit card's fraud-protection guarantee behind you.

eBay sees to it that PayPal is incredibly easy to use because PayPal is the official payment service at eBay. After the auction is over, a link that the buyer can use to pay appears. If you prefer, wait until you hear from the seller.

You may also send money directly from your bank account (either savings or checking) through instant transfer or eCheck.

>> **Instant transfer:** An instant transfer is *immediately* debited from your bank account and deposited into the seller's account — so you'd best be sure you have the funds in your account to back up the purchase *now* (not tomorrow, not next week). PayPal requires you to back up an instant transfer with a credit card, just in case you've miscalculated your account balance.

>> **eCheck:** You may also write an eCheck, which is just like writing a check, only you don't write it with a pen. Like regular, plain-vanilla paper checks, eChecks take three to four days to clear, and do not post to the seller's account as paid until then.

REMEMBER

The seller will not ship your item until PayPal tells the seller that the eCheck has cleared your bank — so if you're in a hurry, don't use this option.

>> **Credit card:** You can use your American Express, Discover, Visa, or MasterCard to make your payment through PayPal. The cost of the item is charged to your card, and your statement reflects a PayPal payment with the seller's ID.

TIP

If you have a balance in your PayPal account, you must use that money to make your payment; so withdraw your PayPal balance first if you want to pay with a credit card. Payment will then default to using your bank account, so be sure to select a credit card (if that's the way you want to pay) when you're finalizing an eBay transaction.

Sending Payment Promptly and Securely

How many times have you heard the saying "The check is in the mail"? Yeah, I've heard it about a thousand times, too. If you're on the selling end of a transaction, hearing this line from the buyer but not getting the money is frustrating. If you're on the buying end, it's bad.

Being the good buyer that you are, you'll get your payment out pronto. If you've purchased an item and intend to pay by using PayPal, do it immediately — why wait? (The sooner you pay, the sooner you get your item.)

On October 20th, 2008, eBay changed its policies so that paper checks or money orders will no longer be allowed as payment on eBay.

TIP

Most sellers expect to get paid immediately after the close of the auction or sale. If, for some reason, you cannot send a PayPal payment right away, be sure to use eBay Messages to let the seller know when you will be paying.

REMEMBER

If you have to delay payment for any reason (you have to go out of town, you broke your leg), let the seller know as soon as possible. Most sellers understand if you send them a kind and honest email. Let the seller know what's up; give him or her a date by which the money can be expected, and then meet that deadline. If the wait is unreasonably long, the seller may cancel the transaction.

Contacting the Seller

Generally there's no need to contact the seller in a normal transaction. You pay via PayPal and your item should arrive within the timespan estimated by eBay on the item page when you made your purchase.

REMEMBER

If you've won an item, it's *de rigueur* for you to use the Pay Now link on the item page as soon as possible after you've won.

GETTING THE SELLER'S PHONE NUMBER

If you don't receive your item (or something else is amiss) and you've already tried sending an email through eBay Messages, you need to get more contact information. Remember back when you registered and eBay asked for a phone number? eBay keeps this information for times like this.

Know that the eBay Messaging system is monitored by eBay, and the information that it tracks becomes part of the transaction record. If anything weird is going on, it's better to use eBay's system instead of sending an email independently.

To get an eBay member's phone number on a transaction that you're participating in, go back to the Advanced Search: Members: Find Contact Information link. Fill out the Contact Info form by entering the seller's User ID and the number of the item that you're buying, and then click the Search button. If all the information is correct, you automatically see a request-confirmation page; then eBay generates an email message to both you and the other user.

eBay's email message includes the seller's User ID, name, company, city, state, and country of residence, as well as the seller's phone number and date of initial registration. eBay sends this same information about you to the user you want to get in touch with. Most sellers jump to attention when they receive this email from eBay and promptly get the ball rolling to complete the transaction.

If you need to contact the seller before sending payment, you have several ways to find contact information:

>> **Click the Ask a Question link** on the very bottom of the listing page, which takes you to common questions and answers written out by the seller. If your answer isn't there, you will see a text box where you can send a message through eBay Messages.

>> **Click the Advanced Search link** (at the top-right corner of all eBay pages), and then click the Find Contact Information link (on the left side of the page).

WARNING

eBay doesn't tolerate abuses of its contact system. Make sure that you use this resource to communicate with another user *only* about a specific transaction in which you are participating. To use contact information to complete a deal outside eBay is an infringement of the rules. If you abuse the contact system, eBay can investigate you and you may lose your site privileges.

Leaving Responsible Feedback

Almost any eBay seller will tell you that one of his or her pet peeves about the eBay feedback system is that new community members tend to leave neutral or (even worse) *negative* feedback the moment a shipment arrives and something is wrong. In this section, I tell you what you need to know to avoid getting a bad reputation for being too hard on sellers.

Chapter 5 gives you the long version of leaving feedback on eBay; please read it for detailed information on the new seller ratings. These DSRs (Detailed Seller Ratings) allow buyers to get more specific with their transaction feedback.

REMEMBER

The DSR part of the feedback system asks you to rate sellers by filling in one to five stars. Why be judgmental? If the transaction went through as promised, why not give the seller five stars? A five-star rating doesn't cost you anything as the buyer, and if the seller is a Top Rated Seller, it can affect a discount they receive on their eBay fees.

Late delivery

A late delivery is not always the seller's fault. Before dinging a seller's reputation for slow delivery, check the postmark on the package's label. You'll often find that the seller followed through with his or her shipping promise, but the package was held up in transit. The shipping services may deserve a one-star rating, but if the seller shipped right away, why not give that person five stars for a good-faith effort?

Missing or damaged shipment

When a package leaves the seller's hands, it is *literally* (and completely) out of his or her hands. If UPS, Federal Express Ground, or Federal Express Air ships your package, the tracking number can track the item. Here are a few things to remember:

>> Be sure you know when the seller plans to ship the merchandise, so there's less question about when it will probably arrive. At the top of each listing (under the shipping costs), you will see an estimated delivery time based on the seller's shipping policies. A Top Rated Plus Seller sends items out within 24 hours.

>> Open your packages immediately upon receipt. A seller can't make a claim on an item that you report damaged in shipping a month after it arrives, so leaving negative feedback for the seller at that point is unfair. Most shippers insist that any and all damage be reported within five days of receipt. Also, if damage has occurred, keep all packing materials for inspection by the carrier.

>> A seller can't do much about a missing package. Sellers can't even make a claim on a postal shipment until 30 days have passed since mailing. If, however, the tracking information says the package was delivered to your door (and it went missing from there), you have no recourse.

REMEMBER

>> If the item never arrives, only the sender can file a claim with the shipping company and must produce all shipping receipts. Notify the seller immediately by eBay Messages or telephone upon receiving a damaged shipment. Leaving negative feedback before contacting the seller is just plain unjust.

Item doesn't meet your expectations

If the item arrives and isn't as described in the item description, message the seller through eBay Messages. Communication is a good thing — and most sellers want to preserve their reputations. Give the seller the opportunity to work things out with you. Keep in mind these facts:

>> If a new item in a manufacturer's sealed box arrives damaged, the damage could have happened at the manufacturer and the seller wouldn't even know about it.

>> A seller may not be as experienced in a particular collectible as you are. If you didn't ask all the necessary questions before bidding, you may have received what the seller *assumed* was a collectible. It's up to the buyer to ask questions before placing a bid.

>> If you receive the wrong item, the seller might have simply mixed up labels. Don't jump to leave negative feedback. Just notify the seller, who will no doubt work out the mistake with you.

Most important, sellers should be given the chance to prove they care and make good. Most items are always covered by eBay Buyer Protection.

Choosing your words carefully

Good sellers should be rewarded, and potential buyers should be informed. That's why no eBay transaction is complete until the buyer fills out the feedback form. Before leaving any feedback, remember that sometimes no one's at fault when transactions get fouled up. Here are some handy hints on what kind of feedback to leave for a seller:

>> **Give the seller the benefit of the doubt.** Selling on eBay is a source of income, and most sellers are honest, hardworking people. If the transaction could have been a nightmare, but the seller tried to make it right and meet you halfway, that's an easy call — leave positive feedback.

>> **Whenever possible, reward someone who seems honest or tried to correct a bad situation.** For example, if the seller worked at a snail's pace but you eventually got your item and you're thrilled with it, you may want to leave positive feedback with a caveat. Something like "Item as described, good seller, but very slow to deliver" sends the right feedback message.

>> **If the seller worked at a snail's pace but packaged the item adequately and the item was kinda-sorta what you expected, you may want to leave neutral feedback.** That is, the experience wasn't bad enough for negative feedback but didn't deserve praise. Here's an example: "Really slow to deliver, didn't say item condition was good not excellent, but did deliver." Wishy-washy is okay as a response to so-so performance; at least the next buyer will know to ask specific questions.

>> **If the seller doesn't ship your item or the item doesn't match the description and the seller won't make things right, then you need to leave negative feedback.** But never write negative feedback in the heat of the moment — and *never* make it personal. Life's interesting enough without taking on extra hassles.

You are responsible for your words, which will remain on the eBay site forever (with your User ID next to them for all to see). Be sure to leave a simple, factual, and *unemotional* statement. Important things to mention in your feedback are

>> How satisfied you are with your purchase

>> The quality of the packaging

>> The promptness of shipping

>> The seller's professionalism

>> The level of communication

REMEMBER

If you must leave a negative feedback comment, know that there is karma in this life. If you couldn't resolve things without a problem, chances are the seller wasn't happy with the trading experience, either. Try to work things out first!

Completing the Transaction

Chapter **8**

Participating in the Community

eBay is more than just an Internet location for buying and selling great stuff. Most of all, eBay is about people. For years now, the byword for business has been "social media" — and eBay at one time had a large and bustling community of its own. As in real-life communities, you may participate as much as works for you.

As you've probably heard, one of the main ways to participate in the eBay community is through feedback (which I explain in detail in Chapters 5 and 7). In this chapter, I show you some other ways to become part of the eBay community. Social media has opened up many new groups — and new ways to share ideas with other sellers who may not want to hang around eBay all day. On the eBay site, you can socialize, get information from other members, leave messages, or just read what everybody's talking about on eBay's message boards, category boards, and corporate announcement board. The tools in this chapter help you solidify your place in the community that is eBay.

Your Social Profile on eBay

Want to know more about the people on eBay? You can learn by clicking their User IDs to visit their Profile pages. eBay users with active Profile pages have a Me icon (with a blue lowercase *m* and a red lowercase *e*) next to their User IDs.

If you're on eBay, you *need* a Profile page; consider it akin to your Facebook page. Checking out the Profile for each person you conduct business with gives you an opportunity to get to know those folks. Because eBay is a cyberspace market, you have no other way to let prospective bidders know that you're a real person. (Don't you shop at some stores because you like the owners or people who work there?)

The Profile page enables you to personalize yourself as a bidder to sellers and as a business to prospective bidders. (See Figure 8-1 for an example.)

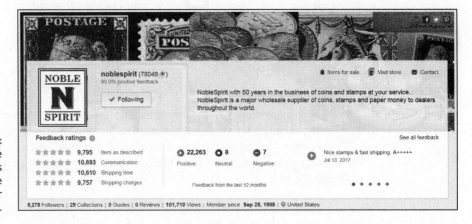

FIGURE 8-1: An example of a business Profile page from member NobleSpirit.

A Profile page benefits you also when you buy. Sellers like to know about bidders to build confidence in their trading partners. You can see an example of a personal My eBay page in Figure 8-2.

If you don't have a Profile page, put this book down for a minute and set one up. It doesn't have to be a work of art; just get something up there to tell the rest of the community who you are. You can always go back later and add to it.

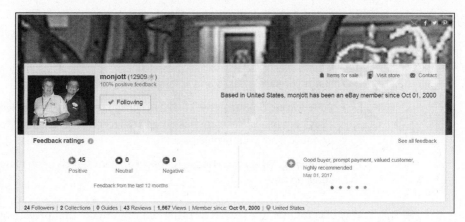

FIGURE 8-2:
Monjott tells us about their business.

AUTHOR SAYS

The Profile page can also be a deal-maker or a deal-breaker. Once I was looking around eBay for some extra-long cables, and I found several sellers selling just what I wanted. One of the lower-priced sellers had a low feedback rating because he was new on eBay. But he had a Profile (previously called an About Me page), so I clicked. I found out that the seller was a computer technician by trade, and that he and his son made these computer cables together as a family business at home in the evenings. The money they made went to pay for their father-son trips to see their favorite baseball team play. What a great family enterprise! Better yet, he guaranteed the cables. As you might have guessed, I bought the cables, and we both got positive feedback.

Reaching the World through Your Profile Page

If staying social is the key to the new web, your eBay profile is the hub of your eBay user interaction. Your Profile page is there for customers and the eBay community. People like to know about other people, and your eBay pages let folks know who they're doing business with.

To create your page, hover over the "Hi (username)" in the upper-left corner of the eBay navigation bar and click your username. (Whenever you want to check your Profile, you can also click your username anywhere it appears on eBay.)

This page will be pre-populated with items you're selling and your reviews (if you've reviewed an item on eBay), but your bio and profile picture will need to be filled in.

Participating in the Community

Your profile page contains basic information about you as a seller, your recent feedback, your eBay Store (if you have one), as well as:

>> **Items for sale:** Images and links to your current listings.

>> **Collections:** Links to items you have chosen to add to your collections from eBay item pages. You can make many collections and set them to be private or public from your profile page.

>> **Following:** When you choose to follow an item search or an eBay seller, they show up here.

TIP

If you're following a search or seller, you can make that private by clicking Public under the image on the Profile page.

Take an opportunity to edit the page. Here's the lowdown on what you can do to personalize your page after clicking the Edit Profile button under your User ID. When you click that button, small pen icons appear, showing you where you can edit the page:

>> **Upload a Profile photo:** Click the pen icon in the corner of the square next to your User ID. The page will prompt you to upload your Profile image. Choose a photo that portrays you and your personality. There are no requirements for size, so I suggest using a close-to-square headshot. If you do not select a headshot, your face might be too small for folks to see.

>> **Upload a cover photo:** Just as on Facebook, you may upload a photo for the top of your page. Keep in mind that text covers a good deal of the cover photo, so don't select a picture in which the most important spot is at the bottom. When you're selecting (or cropping) an image for use as a cover photo, keep in mind eBay's recommended size (1200 pixels x 270 pixels) for best viewing. Also eBay prefers image files to be smaller than 5MB.

>> **Add content:** Here you have 250 characters to talk about yourself, your eBay life, or the items you enjoy selling or buying.

It's easy to share a link to your Profile or to find other buyers and sellers by typing an eBay ID into an eBay URL, like this: www.ebay.com/usr/<User ID>. My Profile page, for example, is www.ebay.com/usr/marsha_c and is pictured in Figure 8-3. I can't wait to see your creativity on *your* eBay profile page!

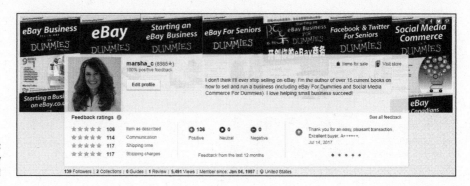

FIGURE 8-3:
Welcome to my
eBay Profile page!

Your profile page reflects your many varied interests. From here, eBay gives you other ways to express yourself (links to all these pages are also on the main Community page):

>> **Collections:** Have a hobby? Maybe enjoy an old TV series or a movie? (No cracks about my collection of the rare Star Trek collectibles: www.ebay.com/cln/marsha_c/The-Most-Rare-Star-Trek-Collectibles/59087095010). You can curate your own online image collection to share. Anytime you see a Star icon (shown in Figure 8-4) you can click to add to a collections page. I think you'll enjoy putting one together.

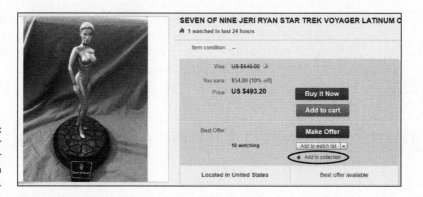

FIGURE 8-4:
Look for the Star
icon to add your
favorites to a
collection.

>> **Reviews:** Wondering what other eBay members think of a particular product, book, or movie? Better yet, contribute one of your own. Reviews you post show up when people search for an item that eBay users have posted reviews for. At the top of a listing, under the title, you will see Product ratings and Stars, as in Figure 8-5. To write a review for one of these products, simply scroll down the page to the area shown in Figure 8-6 and click the *Write a review* box.

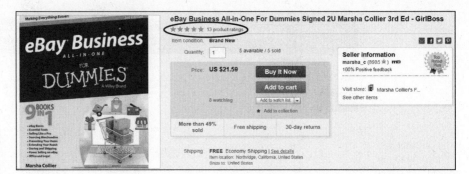

FIGURE 8-5:
eBay members
review books and
other products.

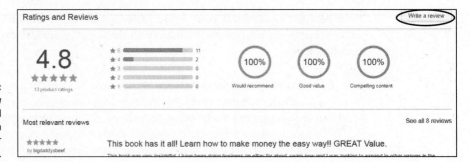

FIGURE 8-6:
Click *Write a
review* to add
your opinion
along with your
eBay User ID.

>> **Guides:** Do you have a special talent? Maybe you're an expert on antique linens and want to share that knowledge? If you aren't putting it on your own blog (which I recommend as the smartest strategy), there's still a place on eBay for you. Go to the Guides area and post your guide to help other eBay members. Just go to www.ebay.com/gds.

Playing Nice with Other eBay Members

The navigation bar has a handy Community link that connects you to the people and happenings on eBay. eBay has more than 169 million active users — a bigger population than some countries — but it can still have that small-town feel through groups and discussion boards. Start on the main page by clicking Community on bottom of eBay pages (or go directly to http://community.ebay.com/). Now you can access dozens of category-specific groups and discussion boards.

But there's a whole lot more to the eBay community, as you find out in this section. Take a little time to explore it for yourself.

News and chat, this and that

The Community Overview page is not quite like *The New York Times* ("All the News That's Fit to Print"), but it is the place to go to find all the news. Figure 8-7 shows you what the Community home page looks like.

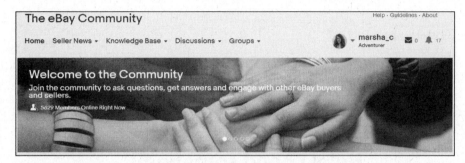

FIGURE 8-7: The main Community page features links to social places on eBay.

Hear ye, hear ye! eBay's announcements

If you were living in the 1700s, you'd see a strangely dressed guy in a funny hat ringing a bell and yelling, "Hear ye, hear ye!" every time you opened eBay's announcements. (Then again, if you were living in the 1700s, you'd have no electricity, no computer, no fast food, or anything else you probably consider fun — like eBay!) In any case, eBay's Announcements are the most important place to find out what's going on (directly from headquarters) on the website. And no one even needs to ring a bell.

The Announcements page is where eBay lists new features and policy changes. You find out about upcoming changes in categories, new promotions, and eBay goings-on. Reach this page by clicking the Announcements link at the bottom on most eBay pages or by going to the following page:

    http://announcements.ebay.com/

Figure 8-8 shows you eBay's Announcements, complete with information that could affect your listings.

AUTHOR SAYS

When you look at some of eBay's older URL addresses, you may notice a subfolder named */aw/*. The *aw* harkens back to the day when eBay wasn't eBay — but was AuctionWeb instead (way back when I joined up).

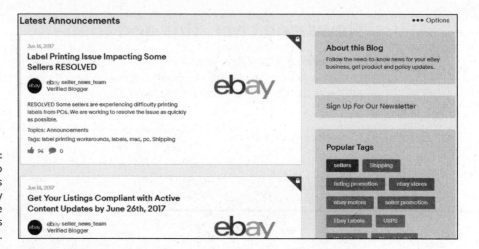

FIGURE 8-8:
Keep up to date on what's new at eBay by visiting the Announcements board.

Help! I need somebody

If you ever have specific eBay questions, I suggest you click the Help & Contact link at the top of all eBay pages and get the policy information right from eBay. If you want to get involved in a discussion, go to the community and ask a question.

To get an answer on a discussion board, you can search the community for your topic, or start a thread by clicking *Start a discussion* further down the Community home page (shown in Figure 8-9). Title your thread with your question, and you'll no doubt get an answer to your query posted swiftly.

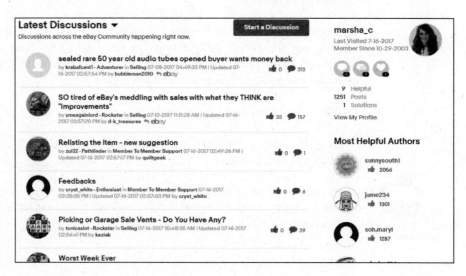

FIGURE 8-9:
Start a discussion with eBay members here.

Keep in mind that the Community area is social and is full of opinions. You can take the advice here — or not. Use your good judgment. People may have their own agendas. Note, also, that one has to know about this area to participate. Many may come here just to chat; they may not really be active in your area of expertise.

TIP

After you've finished reading (or just checking out the index) in this book, you'll have answers to the questions most commonly asked on the site. Use this book as your fun way to participate.

WARNING

The one cardinal rule for eBay chat boards and message boards is: *No doing business on the board.* No advertising items for sale! Not now. Not ever. eBay bans any repeat offenders who break this rule from participating on these boards.

Going Deeper into the Community

To find discussions you might like to join as a participant, click the downward-facing arrows at the top of the eBay Community page. Figure 8-10 shows you some current options in the Discussions area.

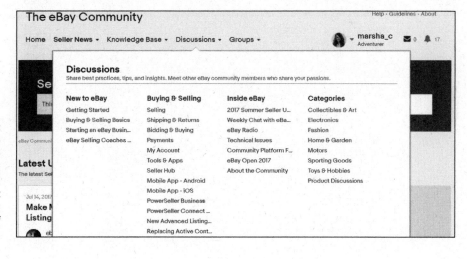

FIGURE 8-10:
There are also many active eBay groups on LinkedIn and Facebook that have an even wider selection of deep discussions.

Participating in the Community

Essential Tools

2

Contents at a Glance

Chapter **1**

Researching on eBay

Think of walking into a store and seeing thousands of aisles of shelves containing millions of items. Browsing the categories of items up for sale on eBay can be just as pleasantly boggling, without the prospect of sore feet. One of the best parts of shopping on eBay is that you can find just about everything, from that esoteric lithium battery to new designer dresses (with matching shoes) to pneumatic jackhammers. New or used, it's all here — lurking in the millions of daily listings.

Start surfing around the site, and you instantly understand the size and scope of what you can find for sale. You may feel overwhelmed at first, but the folks at eBay have come up with a multitude of ways to help you find exactly what you're looking for. But finding the nuggets (deals) can be like searching for the proverbial needle in the haystack. The search tips in this chapter will put you ahead of your competition for finding deals, and instruct the pricing and timing of your own listings.

Looking for Items with eBay's Search

Anyone can find items to purchase on eBay. Finding bargains or researching selling prices accurately, on the other hand, requires a bit more finesse. The key is to understand how to search the site for hidden treasures. Just as knowing how to browse the categories is important, knowing how to work the search engine expertly will steer you in the right direction to find your item for the lowest price.

eBay has instituted machine learning (AI) to provide those who search with what they feel are the best results. Prior to 2012, eBay's search worked in a slightly different way. The search engine was based on traditional Boolean search operators that let you refine searches in depth. Some of these operators (such as searching for two instances at once) still work. If you want to search explicitly for some particular thing, use the symbols in Table 1-1, given later in this chapter.

Going where the Search button takes you

The single most important button on any eBay page is the Search button. When you type some keywords in the search text box and click this button, you'll be presented with a list of items that closely match your keywords on eBay.

Should you want a more advanced type of search, click the Advanced link next to the Search button. You're sent to the Advanced Search: Find Items page, which will have your search options in a box on the left side of the page, as shown in Figure 1-1. Three sections of advanced searches — Items, Stores, and Members — are available; each enables you to search for items in a different way.

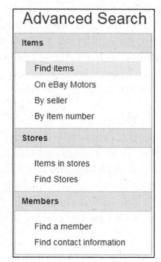

FIGURE 1-1: The various searches available in the Advanced Search area.

TIP

To enhance your search, ask eBay search to check both item titles and item descriptions. Select the check box next to Search Title and Description to open up your search. You'll get more hits if you select the Search Title and Description check box, but you may also get too many items that are out of your search range.

Under the Items section, you can choose the following types of searches:

>> **Find Items:** Search by keywords or item number. Type the keywords that describe an item (for example, *Superman lunchbox* or *antique pocket watch*) and click Search, and you can see how many matching items are available on eBay.

>> **On eBay Motors:** Looking for something related to wheels or an engine? Click here to see the form specifically designed for eBay Motors searches.

>> **By Seller:** Every person on eBay has a personal User ID (it's the name you use to conduct transactions). Use the Items by Seller search if you liked the merchandise from a seller's auction and want to see what else the seller has for sale. Type the seller's User ID, and you get a list of every item that person is selling.

>> **By Item Number:** Every item that's up for sale on eBay is assigned an item number, which is displayed on the top right of the description on its page. To find an item by number, just type the number and click Search.

The second search section is Stores. When you click the link to search in Stores, you can search by two options:

>> **Items in Stores:** eBay Stores have an additional search engine. Listings of items in eBay Stores appear on a regular search for items.

>> **Find Stores:** If you know an eBay Store name or description, you can type a store name — or portion of a store name — and find the store you're looking for.

The final search section is Members:

>> **Find a Member:** Here you can type the User ID of any eBay member to view his or her feedback profile, About Me page, or User ID history.

>> **Find Contact Information:** When you are in a transaction with someone, you can type the person's User ID and the number of the transaction to receive an email containing the phone number of your trading partner. This works only if you have a current bid or have bought an item.

Performing a basic search in Advanced

It's your choice — you can make your search as complex (or confusing) as you want by using the gazillions of options on the Advanced Search page. You can also choose to keep it somewhat basic. I know, it sounds a tad bizarre, but the basic Find Items search can be more accurate than typing keywords into the eBay general Search box. You have more options and artificial intelligence won't get in the way. Click the drop-down menu next to the text box and select an option.

On this search form, you'll see innumerable boxes. You can fill out some or all of them. The more information you type into this form, the more precise your search can be.

To illustrate this, try a basic search as you might do from the regular text Search box. It's a lot easier to find your items in that simple method. Stumped on what words to use in your search? Consider the item you're trying to find. Look at it and determine which words best describe it. Suppose that your favorite china pattern has been discontinued and you want to search eBay for some missing pieces. To find the pieces quickly, follow this process:

1. Determine the manufacturer's name.

Since I'm looking for a plate, I turn over the plate I have and look on the back for the manufacturer's name — it's Dansk!

If you don't have all the information you need, check out the manufacturer's website or a website that specializes in the item you're looking for.

2. Determine the name for the series, collection, pattern, or design.

Sometimes an item has more than one name. For example, I'm searching for Bistro (the name of the collection) and Maribo (the pattern name).

3. Narrow your search even further, if possible or necessary.

For example, I need to replace a salad plate.

4. Enter the words for your search.

I typed *Dansk Bistro Maribo salad* into the keyword box. If someone has listed an item with all those words in the title, I'll be lucky and pull up some winners. However, it's more likely that the words in your initial search have been buried in the description.

5. After you get your search results, you can narrow your search by searching in a category.

Use the category list at the left of the results to limit your search to a particular main (or *top-level*) category, for example, instead of searching all eBay categories. This might be a good idea if you know for sure where the item is listed.

I often leave the category selection alone so that my search encompasses all categories. Sometimes sellers (when listing many items at once) make mistakes and list in the wrong category. That's when you can find a real deal.

But items often cross over categories. When they do, eBay lists (on the left side of the page) the actual categories where the search items were found. From my search results (pictured in Figure 1-2), I can see that my salad plates are listed in the sub-category of Pottery & Glass. In this instance, I'm lucky that they're listed in only one area, so it's clear that I've found exactly what I'm searching for.

FIGURE 1-2:
Search results for my salad plates.

REMEMBER

eBay displays — below the core Buy-It-Nows and Auction listings — the items that both match my search.

6. **Tell eBay how you want the results arranged by using the Sort drop-down list shown in Figure 1-3.**

For example, if you want to check out auctions in order of how soon they're closing, choose Time: Ending Soonest. (This is my favorite option — you might miss the deal of the century while you're sifting through hundreds of listings in another order.) From the Sort drop-down list, choose one of the following options:

● *Best Match:* This is eBay's default when you search for an item. Searches are based on the eBay search engine's algorithms, and this search is (loosely) tied to item availability, seller reputation, and adherence to eBay policies. The precise definition of Best Match isn't public, but eBay described it this way:

Along with the listing keywords and other information, one of the most important elements in this calculation is the historical buyer behavior on the site for similar searches.

I generally prefer my searches as *Time: Ending Soonest,* but *Best Match* in my searches finds items in eBay's featured order.

I can tell you that sellers, according to their information on the Seller Dashboard, rise and fall in search results according to buyer satisfaction and detailed seller ratings (DSRs). Also, offering *free shipping* (as long as you're in good standing as a seller) will bring your items higher up in Best Match searches.

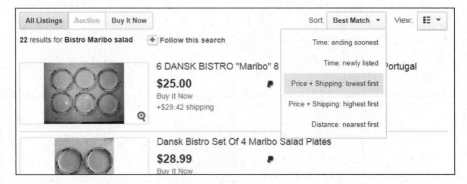

FIGURE 1-3:
Select how you want to search for your item.

REMEMBER

Here's another reason, that, as a buyer, you might not want to penalize a seller just because "I don't give *anyone* five stars." Those Star ratings mean a whole lot to sellers; please be generous when you've had a good transaction. (Rant over.)

- *Time: ending soonest:* Listings closing first appear at the top of the results.

- *Time: newly listed:* The most recently posted items are listed first.

- *Price + Shipping: lowest first:* Search results are presented based on the combined cost of shipping to your Zip code and the price of the item. They're listed in order from lowest-priced to highest-priced.

- *Price + Shipping: highest first:* This search, too, is based on the combined cost of shipping and the current cost (or high bid) on the item. Items are listed from highest- to lowest-priced.

- *Price: highest first:* This sort of ignores the shipping costs and goes right to the heart of the search; the price of the item. This is useful when you're searching for, say, a 1967 Corvette and you want to buy a car, not a Hot Wheels toy.

TIP

Keep in mind, of course, that whatever the listed price, high shipping costs can have a significant impact on how much you actually pay for an item. Always check.

- *Distance: nearest first:* If you're looking for a bunny-style, wrought-iron boot scraper or something as huge as a stove, you might want to buy from a seller who is close by to save shipping costs (you may even be able to go pick up the item).

7. **Use the View drop-down list to select how you want to view the results.**

You've got three choices:

- *List:* This view is the standard eBay format of the item picture on the left and the listing information to the right.

- *Gallery:* This view shows you the search results in boxes. By mousing (hovering the pointer) over a box, you make a magnifying glass appear so you can see the pictures larger (as shown in Figure 1-4). Personally, I prefer to click right through to the listing.

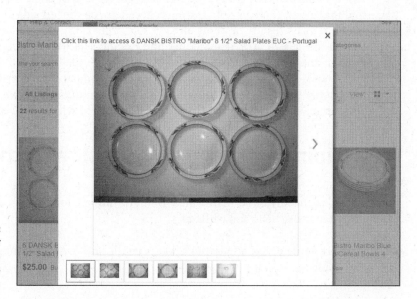

FIGURE 1-4:
In the Gallery view, each listing's image is much larger.

- *Customize:* Choosing the Customize view option opens a small window like the one in Figure 1-5, where you can preset your preferences for future searches.

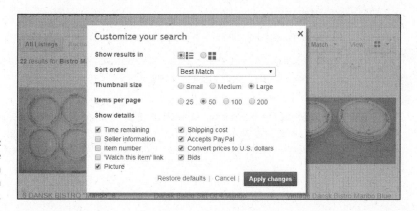

FIGURE 1-5:
Customize your search preferences in this box.

8. **Select how many items you want to see on a page.**

   eBay searches default to 50 items per page. You may want to see more or less depending on the speed of your connection. In List view, the options are 25, 50, 100, and 200.

9. **After you've filled in all your search preferences, click the Search button.**

   A list of items matching your search appears, in the order and format you selected in the Sort and View areas.

TIP

If you want to search completed items to get an idea of what the salad plate has sold for before, click the Sold Listings check box (on the left side of the page). This search returns results of items already sold. This is my favorite search option on eBay; I use it as a strategic bidding and pricing tool. How? If you're bidding on an item and want to know whether the prices are likely to go too high for your pocketbook, you can use this search option to compare the current price of the item to the selling price of similar items from auctions that have already ended. You can see Sold Listings items that have completed within the last 15 days.

Refining even the most basic search

You can refine an advanced search even further by using more of the options offered in the Advanced Search area. Don't be intimidated; you need to understand just a few more bells and whistles.

Here are some of the additional options you'll find in the Advanced Search: Find Items area:

» **Words:** You can choose to search

   - *All words, any order*

   - *Any words, any order*

   - *Exact words, exact order*

   - *Exact words, any order*

TIP

To save yourself time, scan Table 1-1. It features shortcuts you can use in the basic Search box to get the same results as the preceding options — and more.

» **Exclude words from your search:** If you're looking for some silver flatware, for instance, and you want it to be solid, not plated, you could type *plated*. That search would exclude any item listings that contain the word *plated*.

» **Price:** Here's where you can narrow your search to a specific price range. I don't recommend using this option because you never know what you might miss.

» **Buying formats:** Since eBay has three main buying formats, you can search them individually:

- *Auctions:* If you love the thrill of bidding, you can limit your search to auctions only. (But why? There may be a better deal in Buy It Now.)

- *Buy It Now:* This option comes in handy when you simply must purchase something immediately. This would work well for the pair of tickets you've found to *The Producers* or when you're about to run out of your favorite moisturizer and don't have time to make it to the store within the next week to pick some up.

- *Classified Ads:* In some categories, such as Real Estate, sellers put up classified ads that prompt you to contact the seller to find out more or complete the transaction.

» **Location:** You can elect to see your results from all items on eBay or you can search by country.

- *On eBay.com:* Search eBay, no matter which country. Other options are US Only, Worldwide, or North America.

- *Available To:* Select a country from the drop-down list, and the search engine looks for items from sellers willing to ship to that country.

- *Located In:* Use the drop-down box to find items from the country you specified.

» **Only Show Items from Specific Sellers:** If you want to locate an item being sold by up to ten sellers, you can type their User IDs here, separating each User ID from the others by a comma or a space. If you want to find items excluding certain sellers, click the drop-down list and list the offending sellers in the text box.

Also, under Show Results, you can select more options to display only particular items.

Should you not want to go through this tedious, step-by-step check-mark thing every time you want to make a thorough search, you might want to memorize the shortcuts in Table 1-1. You can type these shortcuts in any simple Search box on any eBay page to get a specialized search.

TABLE 1-1

Shortcut Symbols for Conducting Speedy Searches

Symbol	Effect on Search	Example
No symbol, multiple words	Returns auctions with all included words in the title.	*olympus mount* might return an item for an Olympus camera or an item from Greece. **Remember:** You can filter by category after you run a search.
"Term in quotes"	Searches items with the exact phrase within the quotes.	*"stuart little"* is more likely than *stuart little* to return items about the mouse because the search returns the words in the exact order you request.
Words enclosed in parentheses, separated by a comma and with no space	Finds items related to either item before or after the comma.	*(kennedy,nixon)* returns items with either president's name in the title.
Minus sign	Excludes results with the word after the minus sign.	*signed –numbered* finds limited edition items that are signed but not numbered.
Minus symbol and parentheses	Finds items with words before the parentheses but excludes those within the parentheses.	*Packard –(hewlett,bell)* finds those rare Packard auto collectibles.
Parentheses	Searches the main word plus both versions of the word in parentheses.	*political (pin,pins)* searches for *political pin* or *political pins*. Be sure not to put a space in this search.

Searching for Items by Seller

The next search option in the Items search area helps you find items by seller. After spending time on eBay, you'll find that you have favorite sellers. You can always access a seller's other items for sale by clicking the View Seller's Other Items link on a listing page.

TIP

If you intend to follow the items for sale from certain sellers, it's a good idea to save them in your My eBay page lists. (For more on that, see Chapter 5 of this minibook.)

Here's a way to see whether one of your competing sellers has an item like yours up for sale:

1. **Click the By Seller link under Items in the Advanced Search box.**

2. **On the resulting page, type the eBay User ID of the seller you want to find.**

3. **Select options to filter the listings that the search will return:**

- *Show Completed Listings Only:* Select this check box if you want to see listings that this specific seller has completed in the past. You can choose to see all current and previous auctions, as well as auctions that have ended in the last day, last week, or past 15 days.

- *Show Close and Exact User ID Matches:* Sometimes you may not remember the exact User ID of someone. For example, I am marsha_c. You might not remember the underscore between the *a* and the *c.* When you click this option, you see all IDs that are similar to mine (although without the underscore, my ID doesn't show up at all).

4. **Choose the order in which you want to see search results from the Sort By drop-down list.**

   If you want to see the auctions that are closing right away, choose Time: Ending Soonest.

5. **Choose how many items you want to see on a page from the Results per Page drop-down list.**

6. **Click the Search button.**

Refining a Search with Other Options

On the search results page are a few more options that allow you to further refine your search. Here are some you might like to use:

- ▶ **Sold Listings and Completed Listings:** At the left of the results, you'll find the perfect way to refine your search when you're doing research on how much an item will sell for — or how much you should expect to pay.

- ▶ **Free Shipping:** In the left column, you can select a box to isolate your search to only those sellers who offer free shipping.

- ▶ **Price:** Narrow your search to a specific price range.

- ▶ **Item Location:** When you're signed in, your Zip code is filled in by default, but you can type in any Zip code. You also select the mileage from a drop-down list.

TIP

In the quest for even more minutiae, a link at the bottom of this box allows you to customize the search queries even further. You can definitely take a good thing too far, and this is getting pretty close.

Finding eBay Members

With millions of eBay users on the loose, you may think it's hard to track folks down. Nope. eBay's powerful Advanced Search page kicks into high gear to help you find other eBay members in seconds.

In the Advanced Search, Members area, you can

>> **Find a member:** If you know a friend's email address, you can input it on this page to find out whether he or she is registered on eBay (after you type in a supplied verification code).

>> **Find contact information:** If you're involved in a transaction with someone, you can click this link to have the person's phone number emailed to you. Because this information is confidential, you must be involved in a transaction with the person. You'll be asked to type the other member's User ID and the transaction number you're dealing with before this information is sent out.

To protect privacy and prevent possible harassment, you'll have to be in a transaction with your friend before you get any information.

Understanding eBay's Category Hierarchy

Understanding eBay's categories was a lot easier when there were just a few. I remember thinking that the quantity of categories was daunting when the site boosted the number up to the unthinkable 4,000.

Now that the total number of categories is around 20,000 — including child (or sub-) categories — the time has come to either abandon all hope of understanding them or to take things in hand and appreciate the elegance and organization of a system that's just beyond the realm of comprehension. You may never totally understand the category structure, but that's okay — what's important is knowing which categories the sellers use most frequently.

TIP

eBay is constantly revisiting the way people search for items on the site. Understanding the tips in this chapter will give you a distinct advantage when you're shopping.

How the structure works

Go ahead, ask me what I'm interested in. Let's see; I like art, golf, photography, fashion — I won't bore you with the rest, but it sounds like a fairly benign list, doesn't it? I'm sure your list of interests is straightforward too. Right?

Well, not quite. Say you like golf as much as I do. You might just click Sporting Goods then find Golf and click.

Surprise! The Sporting Goods category is made up of hundreds of child categories of everything from golf balls to Pittsburgh Penguins jerseys. eBay's Golf landing page goes a long way to help you find what you're looking for.

This hasn't been done to confuse you, but as of this moment, there are 1,532,446 active listings in Golf. eBay's refinements allow you to visit areas where your sports interest might take you. To accommodate the countless items for sale that sports aficionados, collectors, and participants list, eBay had to create a lot of small areas.

Drilling down to your item

Depending on what you're looking for, things can get downright confusing. For example, suppose I want to find items relating to my dog, a somewhat obscure breed called Schipperke. You might think I have it made. I mean, how could a category for such an esoteric breed of dog be anything but very simple? A search for Schipperke will net me over 8,000 listings!

Schipperkes have their own category in the main category of Collectibles ⇨ Animals ⇨ Dogs ⇨ Schipperke on eBay (not real dogs, just the collectible type). eBay has categories in Collectibles for almost every breed of dogs. Know anybody who collects dog-related items? See what I mean about mystifying? Currently, 309 Schipperke items are listed in the category.

I hope you realize where I'm going with all this. Even though I chose an arcane item, searching only through the specific category designated for it would have affected my search significantly. I would have missed some of the more interesting items.

Chapter **2**

Researching Collectible Prices

As one who wants to sell products, you need to know how to price what you're selling. If you don't know what your item is worth, then your sale might not net the highest profit. If you don't know the facts or what to say, your well-written title and detailed description (combined with sharp, clear pictures) may still not be enough to get the highest price for your item. If you don't know how to make your item easy to find, it may not be noticed by even the hardiest of collectors.

Knowing your item is a crucial part of successful selling on eBay. New item pricing can be all over the board, and knowing how much an item will sell for — before you purchase it for resale — will help you make educated decisions. Collectible items may be appraised or listed online for a high value, but what *you* care about is the price at which the item will actually sell. Read on in this chapter for advice on pricing your item.

Imagine someone uncovering a hoard of the same type of item you're selling and, not knowing the value of it, dumping it on eBay with low Buy It Now prices. This scenario would drive down the value of the item within a couple of weeks. Great for buyers — but not so great for sellers.

REMEMBER

The best advice you can follow as you explore any free-market system is *caveat emptor* — let the buyer beware. Although you can't guarantee that every one of your transactions will be perfect, if you research items thoroughly before you bid, you won't lose too much of your hard-earned money — or too much sleep.

Pricing New Products for eBay via Mobile

So let's say you're out at a store that's slashing prices to liquidate stock. Lots of merchandise seems very resalable to you, but which will net the most profit?

My personal arsenal of tools for determining the sales potential of merchandise lies in my smartphone. All products have a scannable, numeric-based, Universal Product Code (UPC or barcode). Every product has a unique barcode, all of which follow an identical format (as shown in Figure 2-1).

FIGURE 2-1:
A sample layout for the UPC found on all products for sale.

This barcode carries information about a product and pricing for retailers and is scanned when you purchase a product. The barcode covers two steps in managing a retail business: monitoring the purchase and tracking inventory.

That all said, scanning a product prior to buying it and putting it up for sale will help you make smarter business decisions. Of course, your go-to app would be the eBay app, which is available for iPhone, iPad, and Android devices. You can use mobile apps on your smartphone, tablet, or *phablet* (a popular term for larger smartphones that double as small tablets). Figure 2-2 shows the eBay app on my Android tablet.

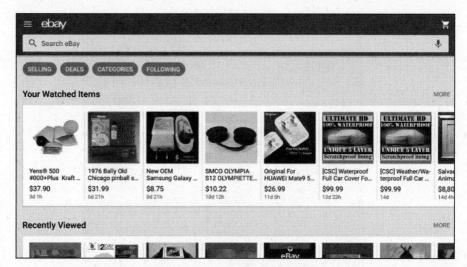

FIGURE 2-2:
The app appears
pretty much the
same on most
tablets and
smartphones.

When you tap within the Search text box, your previous searches appear. There's a Search box, prompting you to type in your search query or (in the upper right) to dictate your search (on Android), search by picture or to scan a barcode, as shown in Figure 2-3.

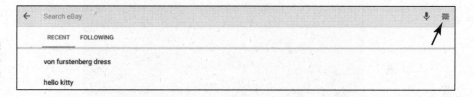

FIGURE 2-3:
Click here to
activate the
barcode scanner.

To scan a barcode, click the icon to fire up the scanning module. Scanning uses your camera to read the barcode, so line up your camera and center the barcode within the scanning boundaries shown in Figure 2-4.

TIP

Android phones also give you the option to tap the microphone icon on the app and *say* the product name. Miraculously, the name will appear in the Search box and give you results for your search.

The results of your search will show items matching your search that are currently being sold on eBay. By clicking the Refine option, you can narrow your search to Sold items and get an idea of whether the item is actually selling on eBay — and for how much.

On the off chance that the item is not being sold on eBay, you can use Google shopping to compare prices for your item, whether on the web or close to your home.

FIGURE 2-4:
Scanning a
barcode with the
eBay app.

I'm also a fan of searching for the item on the Amazon app, Walmart, and Price-grabber.com. You can never have too much information about your item.

Finding Pricing Trends on eBay

If you're just starting out on eBay, chances are you like to shop and you also col-lect items that interest you. You'll find out early in your eBay adventures that a lot of people online know as much about collecting as they do about bidding — and some are serious contenders.

UNDERSTANDING GRADING TERMS

One of the keys to establishing value is knowing an item's condition, typically referred to as an item's *grade*. The following table lists the most common grading categories that collectors use. The information in this table is used with permission from (and appreciation to) Lee Bernstein.

Category (Also Known As)	What It Means	Example
Mint (M, Fine, Mint-In-Box [MIB], 10)	A never-used collectible in perfect condition with complete packaging (including instructions, original attachments, tags, and so on) identical to how it appeared on the shelf in the original box.	Grandma got a soup tureen as a wedding present, never opened it, and stuck it in her closet for the next 50 years.
Near Mint (NM, Near Fine, Like-New, 9)	The collectible is perfect but no longer has the original packaging or the original packaging is less than perfect. Possibly used but must appear to be new.	Grandma used the soup tureen on her 25th anniversary, washed it gently, and then put it back in the closet.
Excellent (EX, 8)	Used, but barely. Excellent is just a small step under Near Mint, and many sellers mistakenly interchange the two, but Excellent can have very minor signs of wear. The wear must be a normal, desirable part of aging or so minor that it's barely noticeable and visible only upon close inspection. Damage of any sort is not "very minor." Wear or minor, normal factory flaws should be noted. (Factory flaws are small blemishes common at the time of manufacture — a tiny air bubble under paint, for example.)	Grandma liked to ring in the New Year with a cup of soup for everyone.
Very Good (VG, 7)	Looks very good but has defects, such as a minor chip or light color fading.	If you weren't looking for it, you might miss that Grandma's tureen survived the '64 earthquake, as well as Uncle Bob's infamous ladle episode.

(continued)

Researching Collectible Prices

(continued)

Category (Also Known As)	What It Means	Example
Good (G, 6)	Used with defects. More than a small amount of color loss, chips, cracks, tears, dents, abrasions, missing parts, and so on.	Grandma had the ladies in the neighborhood over for soup and bingo every month.
Poor (P or G-, 5)	Barely collectible, if at all. Severe damage or heavy use. Beyond repair.	Grandma ran a soup kitchen.

Grading is subjective. Mint to one person may be Very Good to another. Always ask a seller to define the meaning of the terms used. Also, be aware that many amateur sellers may not really know the different definitions of grading and may arbitrarily add Mint or Excellent to their item descriptions. This is where telling the story is better with many pictures accompanying the description.

How can you compete? Well, in addition to having a well-planned bidding strategy (covered in Book 1, Chapter 6), knowing your stuff gives you a winning edge. I've gathered the opinions of two collecting experts to get the info you need about online collecting basics. I also show you how one of those experts puts the information into practice, and I give you a crash course on how items for sale are (or should be) graded.

TIP

The values of collectibles go up and down. *Star Wars* items are a perfect example. Values skyrocket during the release of the latest movie, but then settle to a considerably lower level. Any published book of value listings is valid only for the *moment* the book is written. If you stay on top of your market in a few specialties, you'll be aware of these market fluctuations. If you're looking for the highest price for *Star Wars* items, for example, instead of looking to liquidate excess inventory, I'd hold those items until they hit the pop culture charts again.

Determining the "going price" of a particular item on eBay is as simple as performing a Completed Items search. I acquired a few vintage (mint) ashtrays from Disneyland, so join me as I check out the value.

1. **Type in the keywords in the Search text box at the top of every page and click the Search button.**

The resulting page shows you how many items that match your keywords are being sold on eBay at that moment. If you get too many results, add an extra keyword that further defines your item and repeat the search. I found 164 active listings (as shown in Figure 2-5).

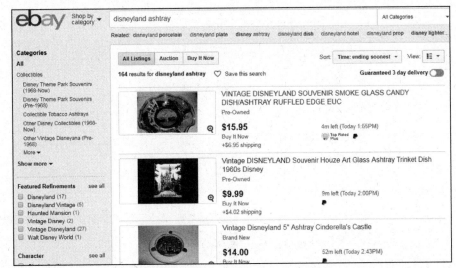

FIGURE 2-5:
One hundred sixty four listings matching "Disneyland Ashtray" up for sale.

2. **Scroll down the page and look at the images of items for sale, making note of which ones actually match your item.**

   From here, you get an idea of the prices that sellers are asking.

3. **In the column on the left, under Show Only, choose an option. They are**

   - *Sold Listings:* Shows you only the items that actually sold. To get an idea of the highest price I can get for the item, I used the sort option at the top of the page, shown in Figure 2-6, by selecting Price: Highest First from the Sort drop-down menu. What an eye-opener! These results showed me exactly which variations of my item were the most valuable — and which keywords work the best to attract customer's eyes.

   - *Completed Listings:* Clicking this option shows you how many listings have run their course and are over. If the item sold, the final price is indicated in green text. If the item hasn't sold, you see the final price in red. By studying this data, you can get an idea of a good starting price to set for your item to encourage sales and higher bids.

4. **For the deepest research, click the individual items that garnered the highest prices and see how the seller described the item.**

   Smart sellers tell the stories behind collectibles and add appropriate keywords to their titles!

TIP

In my search, I see listings for the same item that sold from $7.99 up to $103! Why? First it depends on the style and year of issue. Next, the sellers who received the lowest final sale prices put their items up for sale when several others were selling the same item. eBay is a supply-and-demand venue. Even if an item is rare, the final sale price will go down if there are too many up for sale.

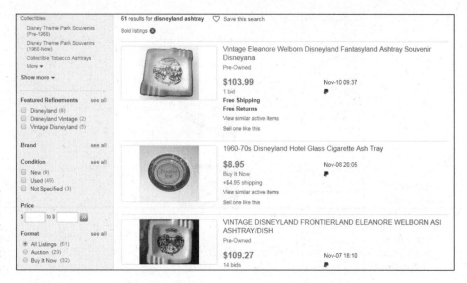

FIGURE 2-6:
Sort search
results for
Sold listings
with highest
prices first.

Following Collectible-Buying Guidelines

Buying collectibles on eBay can be a unique market unto itself. But certain rules still apply. Here are a few things to keep in mind when buying collectibles on eBay:

>> **Get all the facts before placing a bid or clicking Buy.** Study the description carefully and make your decisions accordingly. Find out whether all original parts are included and whether the item has any flaws. If the description says that the Fred Flintstone figurine has a cracked back, message the seller for a picture.

>> **Don't get caught up in the emotional thrill of bidding.** First-time buyers (known as *Under-10s* or newbies because they have fewer than ten transactions under their belts) tend to bid wildly, driven by emotions. If you're new to eBay, you can get burned if you just bid for the thrill of victory without first thinking about what you're doing.

WARNING

I can't stress how important it is to determine an item's value *before* you bid. But because value is such a flighty thing (depending on supply and demand, market trends, and all sorts of reasons), I recommend that you get a general idea of the item's *current* value and use this ballpark figure to set a maximum amount of money you're willing to bid for that item. Then *stick* to your maximum and don't even think about bidding past it. If the bidding gets too hot, there's always another auction. To find out more about bidding strategies, Book 1, Chapter 6 is just the ticket.

>> **Know what the item should cost.** Buyers used to depend on *price guides* — books on collectibles and their values — to help them bid. But price guides are becoming a thing of the past. Sure, you can find a guide that says a *Lion King* Broadway poster in excellent condition has a book price of $75, but if you do a search on eBay, you'll see that they're actually selling for under $20. (Hint: When *was* that guide published, anyway?)

TIP

When your search on eBay turns up what you're looking for, average the sold prices that you find. Doing so gives you a much better idea of what you need to spend than any price guide can.

>> **Timing is everything, and being first costs.** In the movie-poster business, if you can wait three to six months after a movie is released, you get the poster for 40 to 50 percent less. The same goes for many new releases of collectibles. Sometimes you're wiser to wait and save money.

>> **Be careful of presale items.** You may run across vendors selling items that they don't have in stock at the moment but will ship to you later. For example, before the second *Harry Potter* film came out, some vendors ran auctions on movie posters they didn't have in their possession. If you had bid and won, and for some reason the vendor had a problem getting the poster, you'd have been out of luck. Do yourself a favor and don't bid on anything that can't be delivered as soon as you make payment.

>> **Being too late can also cost.** Many collectibles become more difficult to find as time goes by. Generally, as scarcity increases, so does desirability and value. Common sense tells you that if two original and identical collectibles are offered side by side, with one in like-new condition and the other in used condition, the like-new item will have the higher value.

>> **Check out the seller.** Check the seller's feedback rating (the number in parentheses next to the person's User ID) before you buy. If the seller has many comments with very few negative ones, chances are good that this is a reputable seller. Better yet? If you find a Top Rated Seller badge next to the seller's name, you can pretty much count on a positive experience.

WARNING

If you miss winning an auction and are offered a side deal, beware! Side deals off the eBay site are strictly prohibited. If you conduct a side deal and are reported to eBay, you can be suspended. Not only that, but buyers who are ripped off by sellers in away-from-eBay transactions shouldn't look to eBay to bail them out. They're on their own. Second-chance offers, on the other hand, are eBay-legal — and safer.

Quizzing the seller

You should ask the seller certain questions when making a collectible purchase. Assume that the object of your desire is an open-box GI Joe action figure from

1964 to 1969 (by the way, these items are selling for top dollar as I write this book!). In this section, I list some questions you should ask. The information here can give you an idea of what to ask when determining your maximum bid on other collectibles as well (or whether an item is even *worth* bidding on). As you imagine, the more you know before you place a bid, the happier you're likely to be when you win.

This checklist can save you considerable hassle:

>> **Find out the item's overall condition.** For GI Joe, look at the painted hair and eyebrows. Expect some wear, but overall, a collectible worth bidding on should look good.

>> **Be sure the item's working parts are indeed working.** Most GI Joe action figures from this period have cracks on the legs and arms, but the joints should move and any cracks should not be so deep that the legs and arms fall apart easily.

>> **Ask whether the item has its original parts.** Because you can't really examine actual items in detail before buying, email the seller with specific questions relating to original or replacement parts. Many GI Joe action figures are rebuilt from parts that are not from 1964 to 1969. Sometimes the figures even have two left or right hands or feet! If you make it clear to the seller before you buy that you want a toy with only original parts, you'll be able to make a good case for a refund if the item arrives as rebuilt as the Six Million Dollar Man.

>> **Ask whether the item has original accessories.** A GI Joe from 1964 to 1969 should have his original dog tags, boots, and uniform. If any of these items are missing, you will have to pay around $25 to replace each missing item. If you're looking to bid on any other collectible, know what accessories came as standard equipment with the item.

>> **Know an item's value before you bid.** A 1964 to 1969 vintage GI Joe in decent shape, with all its parts, sells for around $500 without its original box. In a recent auction, a "1967 GI Joe Green Airborne MP Set RARE Excellent" — without box — sold for $850. If you are bidding on a GI Joe action figure and are in this price range, you're okay. If you get the item for less than $400, congratulations — you've nabbed a serious bargain.

>> **If you have any questions, ask them *before* you bid.** Check collectors' guides, research similar auctions on eBay, and Google the web for unbiased third-party advice.

Hey, experts have been buying, selling, and trading collectible items for years. But just because you're new to eBay doesn't mean you have to be a newbie for decades before you can start bartering with the collecting gods. I wouldn't leave you in the cold like that — and neither would eBay. You can get information on items you're interested in, as well as good collecting tips, right on the eBay website. Visit the category-specific discussion boards in the Community area. You can also search the rest of the web or go the old-fashioned route and check the library.

TIP

Consider visiting `Terapeak.com`, where you can find up to three years of eBay items and sales in a searchable database. They offer a 7-day free trial (with no credit card required) so you can give it a try.

Learning by reading

I used to recommend that buyers and sellers research items by going out to the local newsstand and buying a special-interest magazine based on the type of merchandise they sell. With the advent of digital publishing, finding current printed magazines is like hunting up a tool from the past. On the other hand, you may be able to find vintage copies of magazines for sale on the web, eBay, or Amazon. These magazines contain a wealth of knowledge — but remember that those articles were written at an earlier stage of the items' rarity and salability; be sure to check current market conditions. You can also find websites that specialize in selling back issues of magazines like `www.biblio.com`.

Following are a few publications (some have current websites) that can offer strategic information on collectibles:

>> **Action Figure Digest**: Find out details about the vintage action-figures biz in this monthly magazine that ceased publication around 2007.

>> **Antique Trader**: This magazine has been the bible of the antiques collecting industry for more than 40 years. Visit its online home at `www.antiquetrader.com` for more articles and subscription information.

>> **Autograph Magazine**: This online magazine gives the lowdown on the autograph business, as well as samples of many autographs for identification. Its site, `www.autographmagazine.com`, features many current articles.

>> **Barbie Bazaar**: Once this was the official Mattel magazine, packed with everything Barbie! You'll not find a website, but back issues of these magazines have valuable information on Barbie collecting.

>> **Dolls Magazine**: Still alive and with an active website, *Dolls Magazine* is filled with good info. Check the site at `www.dollsmagazine.com`.

>> **Coin World**: This respected magazine has many online services available for a free registration on their website, at `www.coinworld.com` (featured in Figure 2-7).

FIGURE 2-7:
The Coin World
website.

- » **Goldmine:** At www.goldminemag.com, this place is the hub for CD and vinyl collectors. The website has many current articles and information on rare issues.

- » **Numismatic News:** Another standard, *Numismatic News* is still publishing a print edition after more than 50 years. The website at www.numismaticnews.net has valuable current information for coin collectors and offers downloads with current coin values and identification information.

- » **Sports Collectors Digest:** Takes sports collectibles to the highest level. Visit the website at www.sportscollectorsdigest.com, read the stories, and sign up for a free email newsletter.

- » **Linn's Stamp News:** Still alive and kicking on the web at www.linns.com is the venerable *Linn's Stamp News*. First published in 1931, the magazine carries on a tradition for stamp collectors on its website.

- » **Teddy Bear & Friends:** If you're looking for information on collecting teddy bears, www.teddybearandfriends.com is the place.

It seems that every leading magazine is now digital and has its own website. In the next section, I mention some useful sites for pricing references.

Online Sources of Information

Because you're all so Internet-savvy (what's better than getting the information you want at a millisecond's notice?), I assume you plan to visit the magazine websites that I mention in the preceding section. In this section, I give you a few more fun online sources where you can pick up some more insight about your items.

Other websites

Many websites devoted to different collectible areas list prices at recently completed auctions. These auctions are the best evaluation of an item's value because they're usually directed toward specialists in the collectible category. Most of the participants in these auctions *really* know their stuff.

You may have to poke around the following websites to find the prices realized at auction, but once you do, you'll have the Holy Grail of estimated values. Look for links that point to auction archives. Many of these sites will consign an item from you as well, and sell it to their audiences:

» **Artprice:** This art auction site, at www.artprice.com, charges for its searches by artist but has an immense database.

» **Autographs and More — now part of Heritage Auctions:** Heritage has a huge free collection of collectible resources at https://www.ha.com/.

» **Collectors.com:** This is a major destination for coins, cards, stamps, and more at www.collectors.com.

» **Promotional Glass Collector's Association:** For collectible advertising glasses, check out this at www.pgcaglassclub.com (you've got to see this stuff!). And there's an online database of items at www.glass411.info.

» **Professional Coin Grading Service:** Find a U.S. coin-collecting price guide at www.pcgs.com/prices.

» **Lyn Knight Auctions:** Find currency auctions at www.lynknight.com.

TIP

If you're researching prices to buy a car on eBay, look in your local newspaper to get a good idea of prices in your community. You should also check out sites on the Internet. I've had many of my friends (and editors) visit the various sites, and we've settled on www.nadaguides.com because it seems to give the most accurate and unbiased information.

Online search engines

If you don't find the information you need on eBay, don't go ballistic — just go elsewhere. Even a site as vast as eBay doesn't have a monopoly on information. The Internet is filled with websites and Internet auction sites that can give you price comparisons.

Your tablet, phone, or computer can connect to powerful outside servers (really big computers on the Internet) that have their own fast-searching systems called *search engines.* Remember, if something is out there and you need it, you can find it in just a matter of seconds. Here are the addresses of some of the web's most highly regarded search engines or multi-search-engine sites:

» **Google** (www.google.com)

» **Bing** (www.bing.com)

» **Yahoo!** (www.yahoo.com)

WARNING

The Internet abounds with news that with Verizon merging with Yahoo! and AOL, the result will become Oath. http://www.businessinsider.com/aol-and-yahoo-will-become-oath-after-merger-closes-2017-4. Yet at the time of this book's publication, it doesn't look like the Yahoo! brand will be going away soon (https://www.cnbc.com/2017/04/04/aol-yahoo-merger-name-oath-is-about-linking-brands-and-values-aol-ceo-says.html).

The basic process of getting information from an Internet search engine is pretty simple:

1. **Type the address of the search-engine site in the Address box of your web browser.**

You're taken to the website's home page.

2. **Find the text box next to the button labeled Search or something similar.**

3. **In the text box, type a few words indicating what interests you.**

TIP

Be specific when typing search text. The more precise your entry, the better your chances of finding what you want. Look for tips, an advanced search option, or help pages on your search engine of choice for more information about how to narrow your search.

4. **Click the Search (or similar) button or press Enter on your keyboard.**

The search engine presents you with a list of Internet pages that have the requested information. The list includes brief descriptions and links to the first group of pages. You'll find links to additional listings at the bottom if your search finds more listings than can fit on one page (and if you ask for something popular, like *Twilight,* don't be surprised if you get millions of hits).

There will also be a link to click that will show you images that match your search — if you're not quite sure in identifying your item. Find the picture that matches the item to find out more.

WARNING

Always approach information on the web with caution. Not everyone is the expert he or she would like to be. Your best bet is to get lots of different opinions and then boil 'em down to what makes sense to you. And remember — *caveat emptor.* (Is there an echo in here?)

Authentication services

Some companies provide the service of *authenticating* (verifying that it's the real deal) or authenticating and *grading* (determining a value based on the item's condition and legitimacy). To have these services performed on your items, you'll have to send them to the service and pay a fee.

Following are a few excellent sites for grading coins:

>> **Professional Coin Grading Service (PCGS):** This service, at www.pcgs.com, is considered to be the top of the line in coin grading. This company's standards are strict, but coins graded by PCGS usually sell for higher prices.

To catch up on the latest pricing on American coins, go to PCGS. This site has an elaborate online price guide for all coin grades.

>> **American Numismatic Association Certification Service (ANACS):** This service was sold to Amos Press in 1990, and you can find out more at www.anacs.com.

>> **Numismatic Guaranty Corporation of America (NGCA):** The site, www.ngccoin.com, offers information as well as a mail-in grading and certification service for your coins.

>> **PCI Coin Grading Service (PCI):** PCI, the longstanding coin-grading service at http://pcicoins.com, is under new management (see Figure 2-8).

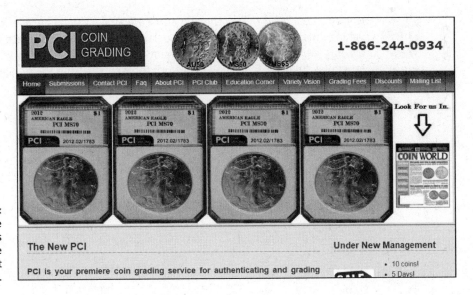

FIGURE 2-8:
The PCI website has many links and an up-to-date price guide at no charge.

Stamp collectors (or those who have just inherited a collection from Uncle Steve) can get their stamps authenticated by the American Philatelic Society. Visit this site for more information: `http://stamps.org/Stamp-Authentication`.

For comic books, Comics Guaranty, LLC (CGC) at `www.cgccomics.com/grading` will seal (enclose in plastic to preserve the quality) and grade at a discount for eBay users.

Sports cards and sports memorabilia have a bunch of authentication services. If you acquired your autograph or item of memorabilia directly from the player or team, you can ensure its authenticity. Having the item authenticated may or may not get you a higher price at eBay. Try these sites:

>> **Professional Sports Authenticator (PSA):** Go to `www.psacard.com` for more info.

>> **Online Authentics:** This service, at `www.onlineauthentics.com`, reviews autographs by scans online or by physical review.

The best way to find a good authenticator in your field is to search the items on eBay and see who is the most prominent authenticator listed in the descriptions. For example, in the coins area, coins from certain grading services get higher bids than those from other services. You can also go to an Internet search engine (such as Google or Yahoo!) and type the keywords *coin grading* (for coins). You'll come up with a host of choices; use your good sense to see which one suits your needs.

REMEMBER

Not all items need to be officially authenticated. Official authentication does add value to the item, but if you're an expert, you can comfortably rate an item on your own in your auctions. People will know from your description whether you're a specialist. Your feedback will also work for you by letting the prospective bidder or buyer know that your merchandise from past sales has been top-drawer.

Chapter **3**

Five-Star Customer Service via Personalized Communications

Business is business, yes, but you and I know that's not all there is to it. When you're in business, you must remember that your customers are number one; they deserve your very best "five-star service." Businesses become successful by inspiring a "wow" when it comes to servicing customers, shipping quickly, and selling quality merchandise. The image that you project through your messages and listings identifies you to prospective shoppers as a professional — or not. Your messages should be polite and businesslike. Your listings shouldn't make prospective buyers feel like you're hustling them, sneaking in hidden fees, or being pushy with austere rules when they're trying to make a purchase.

You don't have to have the most beautiful listings to succeed. Instead, you need products that sell — and willingness to take the time to build good customer relations. This is what gives a small-time entrepreneur a distinct advantage over a mega-company that branches its sales onto eBay. In this chapter, I cover some ways — from writing effective descriptions to sending cordial communications — to let your customers know that they're number one in your book.

Communicating Takes a Little Effort

Perhaps English class wasn't your favorite, but good grammar and proper spelling and punctuation in your communications portray you as a pro. As a writer, I constantly patrol the grammar and punctuation websites to brush up on my writing skills. (Okay, I also have brilliant editors covering up my transgressions. . . .)

Throughout the rest of this section, I provide some examples of effective email messages. Study these and also check out a few online business letter examples. And don't forget good manners. You don't want to be too formal, but you do want to be personable and polite.

When information is missing in a listing description, I find that about 20 percent of the time when I send an inquiry, I don't get a response — guaranteeing that I won't be buying that product from that source. Many folks refuse to buy from someone who doesn't care enough to respond to a question. When I do get responses, some are terse, brusquely written notes. Sellers who take the time to write short, considerate, fast replies get my business. Manners inspire confidence.

Anticipating Initial Buyer Inquiries

A relevant item description is the key to initial customer satisfaction. If you answer all the likely questions as part of a well-written description, there will be less need for the customer to deluge you with questions about your item. (In Book 3, Chapter 3, you find a full breakout of the information that your item description should include.)

Why would you want to make your item description try to pre-answer initial inquiries from buyers? Aside from immediately reassuring the buyer that you know your business, here are a couple more reasons:

>> **You may lose a sale if you don't.** Other sellers may have the same item with a more complete description, and it's just as easy for customers to buy from a seller they know is selling just what they want.

>> **Your Detailed Seller Ratings may be affected if the description is inaccurate or missing.** eBay feels that most transactions need not include communication past the buyer reading your description. For that reason, your feedback will receive an automatic five-star rating if you satisfy these three criteria:

- *You specify one-day handling time and upload tracking information within one business day.*

- *There are no buyer- or seller-initiated communications in eBay Messages.*

- *There are no requests for contact information between you and the buyer.*

Despite eBay's policy, it's not to say that communication with a prospective buyer is undesirable. The opposite is true. If you do get an inquiry, be sure to answer as quickly as humanly possible, and give the customers all the information they need. Once you do, they will most likely leave you five stars for communication.

Use eBay's options to manage communications for your buyers. This way, if your customers scroll to the bottom of your description and click *Ask a Question*, they're taken to your Auto Answers.

Follow these steps to set up your Auto Answers:

1. **Go to your My eBay page by clicking the link in the upper-right corner of most eBay pages.**

2. **Mouse over the Account tab, and click the *Manage Communications with Buyers* option, as shown in Figure 3-1.**

You arrive at an area where you can customize your questions and email messages. (I discuss email best practices in the later sections of this chapter.)

FIGURE 3-1: Accessing your buyer communications options.

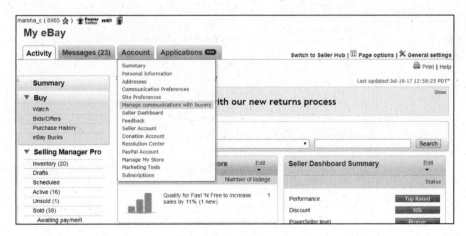

3. **Scroll down the page to the** *What your buyers can do* **section and click Edit.**

4. **On the resulting page, select the check boxes to indicate which communications you want to provide for your buyers, or go directly to**

   `http://contact.ebay.com/ws/eBayISAPI.dll?ManageSellerFAQ`

   As shown in Figure 3-2, your options are

   - *Include a message at checkout when they pay.* This option is most important because buyers may have special instructions for delivery or may just want to reach out and say Hi. (Both are part of making your customer happy.)

   - *Send you messages on eBay while they're shopping.* If you don't indicate (in the *See answers to your FAQs* box) that you want to have Auto Answers for your listing, you must select the check box here.

   - *Have your phone number.* If you'd like prospective buyers to be able to give you a call, put your number here. This might be beneficial if you're selling expensive and unique items.

   - *See answers to your FAQs.* When a buyer clicks Ask a Question, your Q&A appears on the listing page.

FIGURE 3-2:
Click the check box to indicate your preferences for communication.

5. **Scroll down the page and click a topic shown to see what eBay supplies as an Auto Answer.**

   These Auto Answers are automatically generated from the details you input (or have on file with eBay) when you list your item.

6. **(Optional) Create your own questions and answers if you have other specifications you want the customer to know about.**

To do so, here's the drill:

a. *From the list, select the topic to which your answer applies.*

b. *Click the Add a Question link.*

c. *In the Add Your Own Q&A dialog box that appears, type your question and answer, as I show in Figure 3-3.*

7. **Type in as many custom Q&As as you wish, changing topics in the Topic list as needed. When you're finished, click the Submit button at the bottom.**

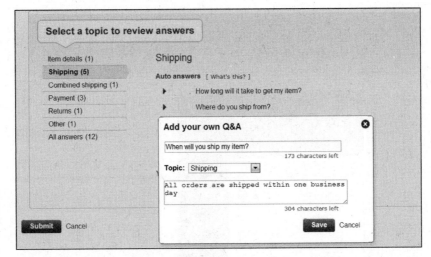

FIGURE 3-3: Create your own questions to appear in your Auto Answers.

Communicating through eBay Messages

When a prospective buyer has a question or wants to send you an offer on an item, and you permit such communications, you will know about it in two ways: through email or your eBay mobile app. You'll get a notification from eBay, alerting you that a question has been asked; it looks something like the message in Figure 3-4. A best offer email will arrive in your email inbox and notifications on mobile.

Responding to an eBay query

When you receive an email message from a buyer, you *can* click the Respond button in the email and go directly to the online question to post your response, or (for safety's sake it's best not to click links in email) go directly to your My eBay page and click the Messages tab.

FIGURE 3-4:
Email notification
of a best offer on
one of my listings.

You can also respond from the eBay mobile app: Just open the app, tap the hamburger icon, and a side menu will appear. Then select Messages or Notifications as shown in Figure 3-5.

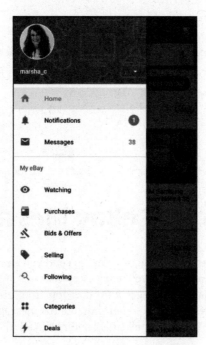

FIGURE 3-5:
Accessing eBay
messages from
the mobile app.

When you visit your eBay message box, you can find, read, and respond to your customer's message.

You can also go directly to the item page, where you'll see a notice that you have a question to answer. Click the link and you're taken to the message page where you can respond to the question. (This is the same page that the email links to.)

Making your response friendly, helpful, and productive

When answering a question, a brief and straightforward response is good. For example, I wrote the following note in response to a question regarding the condition of the Christmas tree in one of my auctions:

Hello,

Yes, the aluminum Christmas tree in my listing is in excellent condition. The 58 branches are full and lush and will look great for the holidays. Please write again if you have any more questions or concerns.

Don't forget to check my other listings for a color wheel and a revolving tree turner. They would look great with this tree, and I can combine them for shipping.

Thank you for writing,

Marsha

Isn't that pleasant? The note addresses the question in a respectful and personable manner. Writing a note like this doesn't take long. You should be doing it.

TIP

Putting your eBay Store URL in your signature is a great way to get new customers to view your other merchandise.

Personalizing Your Buyer's Communication

Your eBay business can easily run on autopilot because eBay will automatically send email messages to buyers at various points in the transaction:

>> The moment a buyer purchases an item

>> Once a buyer completes checkout and has paid

>> When the buyer hasn't paid after a few days

>> When an order is updated with tracking and shipping information

>> To remind the buyer to leave Feedback (about a month after the transaction)

WARNING

Have you ever received a bulk-generated, boilerplate email? The other party hasn't bothered to fill in half the blanks, and you're almost insulted just by having to read it? Receiving a note like this after you've requested that the seller combine purchases (and the letter pays no attention to your request) is especially annoying. Emails can cross, but a personal approach goes a long way with customers.

Sending an email when you must

When you feel you need to communicate with a customer, remember that you do have the customer's email address from your PayPal transaction. Since eBay looks down on too much on-site communication between buyer and seller, you might just want to try a direct email instead of going through eBay if your message is innocuous.

I email my buyers only under certain circumstances:

>> When I upgrade shipping

>> When I see from tracking that an item is hung up in shipping

>> When the buyer has written a question in the PayPal buyer comment box

Under no circumstances do I email a buyer for any other reason. When there's a problem with a transaction, the messages that are sent through eBay are critical, as they are used by eBay to judge the outcome of a dispute. Such emails need to be part of the transaction record.

Include a thank-you note in the package

Every time I ship an item, I enclose a slip of paper thanking the buyer for their purchase. These notes aren't big or fancy. I print them on a color printer, four to a page, stack them, and cut them up for package inclusion.

When I receive a package with a note of thanks inside, I remember the seller. It's a smart way to get the attention of your buyer. If you have a website, you can print the URL on the note along with a social media contact, so your buyers can get to know you better. Personalization is the name of the game these days.

Chapter **4**

Letting PayPal Help You Manage the Money

I n the early days of online auctions, eBay transactions were an iffy proposition. You would send a check to your trading partner, wait for the check to clear, and then wait for the item to arrive, all of which seemed interminable. There was little feedback in the beginning, so it was difficult to separate the good sellers from the bad. The most widely accepted form of payment was the money order, but that wasn't as reliable as a check since you had no way to know when the money order cleared. Yet, in our small (but growing) community, we weren't afraid to send money orders to strangers. Heck, some sellers even shipped merchandise *before* they received payment! Things were a lot simpler, if riskier, in the old days.

Now that eBay is a huge, global marketplace, having a secure and reliable method for accepting (and making) payments for your eBay transactions is crucial. PayPal fits the bill, and it has a great track record. See the nearby sidebar, "From x.com to PayPal . . . what a story!" for a brief look at PayPal's origin and the foundation of its position as a trusted method of exchanging money.

If you've read any of my other books, you know that I've been a huge fan of PayPal from the beginning. PayPal is one of the safest and least-expensive ways for an online seller to accept payments. For a small retailer, PayPal fees can be much more cost-effective than those associated with a credit card merchant account. In this chapter, I tell you about the types of PayPal accounts, how you use PayPal to accept payments, and also, how PayPal can help you pay for your own purchases or personal money transfers. You also find out how PayPal supports your efforts to keep accurate records of all your transactions, which is a big help at tax time!

Understanding How PayPal Works

Joining PayPal is just the beginning, and the benefits far outweigh any fees charged to sellers. There's no charge to the buyer to pay for an online purchase — or to send money to anyone.

FROM X.COM TO PayPal . . . WHAT A STORY!

To solve the problem of *no-good-way-to-pay-for-online-auctions,* a bright man, Elon Musk (yes, the same person who founded Tesla Motors and SpaceX), came up with the concept of emailing money; you could even beam cash to someone's Palm Pilot! There was no charge for using this service, which was even more amazing! Signing up for the program gave you a $10 credit for becoming a member. You also received a $10 bonus for each friend you convinced to join. (The maximum amount that any user could get in bonuses was $1,000, but that's no small change!)

With numbers like that, the early eBay (née AuctionWeb) crowd signed up quickly, and x.com became the most widely used service on the Internet, the first mover and shaker in online person-to-person payments.

eBay countered, acquiring Billpoint in the spring of 1999 with hopes of launching its own payment service in a partnership with Wells Fargo. In a disaster of bad timing, the service was not available to eBay members until the second quarter of 2000. Meanwhile, x.com — now reborn as PayPal — was growing by leaps and bounds and quietly taking over the market.

PayPal went public in February of 2002 to an encouraging Wall Street. The feud between PayPal and Billpoint heated up. The number of customers who signed up with Billpoint couldn't keep pace with the number joining PayPal. PayPal posted a profit, while Billpoint was losing millions per year. In October 2002, eBay bit the bullet and acquired PayPal in a deal valued at $1.5 billion. Billpoint was then simply phased out of the site.

In 2015, after some stockholder wrangling, PayPal was spun off from eBay to become its own, publicly traded, company.

Payment methods supported by PayPal

You have several ways to fund the money you send to another party through PayPal:

>> **Instant Transfer:** Sending money this way means the money is immediately credited to the recipient's account. That person can then transfer the money to his or her personal bank account without delay. If you want to send an Instant Transfer, you must have a credit or debit card registered with PayPal as a backup for your funds.

>> **eCheck:** Sending an eCheck isn't as "instant" as an Instant Transfer. It's just like writing a check from your checking account; it can take from three to six business days for an eCheck to clear. You don't need a backup source of funds when you use eCheck.

>> **PayPal balance:** If someone sent you money through PayPal or you've sold something on eBay, you have a balance in your PayPal account. This balance can be first applied to any purchases you've made. Then the balance can be paid by credit card or from your bank account. It's simplest to keep your books balanced if you withdraw any PayPal balance to your business checking account *before* you make a purchase.

>> **Credit card:** Putting your PayPal purchases on a credit card is a good idea. Not only are you protected by PayPal, but your credit card company also backs you up in case of fraud.

TIP

You can register multiple credit cards on your PayPal account and select a different one for different types of purchases. That way, you can place personal purchases on one account and business purchases on another. It makes end-of-year bookkeeping a lot easier!

Sending money

PayPal breaks types of payments into categories based on what you're paying for. You can pay for *almost* anything in the world on the PayPal system (as long as the recipient has an email address). A few things that you *can't* pay for with PayPal include most items related to gambling, adult content or services, and buying or selling prescription drugs from noncertified sellers. If you're planning to send payments for something that may be a tad questionable, I recommend a visit to the PayPal help area to be sure your item is currently in the clear. You can find the User Agreement, Acceptable Use Policy, and Privacy Policy here:

```
www.paypal.com/us/webapps/mpp/ua/legalhub-full
```

After you sign into your PayPal account and click the Tools⇨Send Money tab, you can send money from PayPal in the following ways:

>> **Paying for eBay items:** When you buy an eBay item on eBay, you need to pay through the eBay Checkout system.

>> **Goods (other):** By clicking this radio button, you can send money to anyone in the world for goods purchased anywhere other than eBay.

>> **Services:** You can send payment for a service performed (see Figure 4-1) for you or your business, such as web design, bookkeeping, psychic readings — your imagination can get carried away here.

>> **Personal:** Use this when you need to send money to your kid in college or pay back your roommate for saving you from great embarrassment when you left your wallet at home on a double date. You can pay the transfer fee.

FIGURE 4-1:
Enter the recipient's email address, mobile number, or name to send money for goods through PayPal.

Sorting Out PayPal's Different Accounts

PayPal has three types of accounts to accommodate everyone from the casual seller to the professional business: Personal, Business, and Premier accounts.

PayPal Personal account

When you begin your business relationship with PayPal, you may want to sign up for a Personal account. With this basic account from PayPal, you can send and receive money (non–credit-card payments) for free. PayPal Personal accounts are for only one person and not for a business. (You can't have a joint Personal account, either.)

Business accounts

The PayPal accounts for the professional seller, Business accounts allow you to accept credit card payments and get a debit card. A Business account can be held in a business name and allows multiple login names. At these account levels, you have access to a customer service phone number.

A fee is levied on all money you receive through PayPal at this level. PayPal has a standard rate of 2.9% + 30¢ U.S.

Note: If you receive payment from a buyer in another country, you are charged a 4.4 percent transaction fee, plus a fixed fee based on the currency received.

The fees (for any type of account) when accepting payments via the PayPal Here card swipe or Bluetooth Chip Card reader and smartphone app (shown in Figure 4-2) are as follows:

>> 2.7 percent when you swipe a credit card in the reader

>> 3.5 percent + 15¢ per transaction when you key in a card number into the app

FIGURE 4-2: PayPal Here allows you to swipe credit cards and the Bluetooth reader accepts chips or contactless payments like Apple Pay.

PayPal's Protection Plans

Safety: Isn't that what paying for things online is all about? Safety for the buyer *and* safety for the seller are primary concerns in the minds of those doing business online. PayPal has created protection policies for both parties.

PayPal Purchase Protection

As a buyer who pays for eBay items through PayPal, you are protected under these circumstances:

>> **You didn't receive the item you paid for with PayPal.** PayPal refers to this as an *item not received dispute.* When you pay for an item through PayPal, the seller must produce a tracking number that you can use to chart the transit of your package. If the item is valued over a certain amount, you may be required to sign a delivery confirmation when it gets to your door.

>> **You received an item you paid for with PayPal but it is "significantly not as described."** This can mean many things, such as you received a completely different item, the condition was misrepresented, parts were missing, the item was damaged in transport, or you received a counterfeit version of the item.

REMEMBER

This kind of protection doesn't cover you when you're merely disappointed with an item when you open the box. It also won't cover downloadable software or digital items — even if you buy them on eBay.

>> **You were charged for something you didn't purchase, and you report it within 60 days**. With PayPal, you're covered by the $0 Liability for Eligible Unauthorized Transactions program.

TIP

When your purchase is made on eBay, it's covered by eBay Buyer Protection. PayPal is used by many online merchants for payment processing.

PayPal Seller Protection

Don't think that sellers get left out of the protection scenario. You do have some protection against unwarranted claims made on your online and eBay sales; it's called (logically enough) *Seller Protection.*

To see whether your transaction is covered under seller protection, follow these steps:

1. **Sign in to your PayPal account and click on the transaction.**

2. **Look for the words, *Seller Protection;* underneath those words, it will say *Eligible*.**

3. **Under Eligible there may be some requirements:**

   - Ship to the address on this page.
   - Save your tracking or shipping info.

- Follow the requirements for seller protection. The current Seller Protection requirements will be found in the User Agreement at

www.paypal.com/us/webapps/mpp/ua/useragreement-full

You'll see whether the shipping address is confirmed by a notation below the address. (PayPal confirms the address by making sure that the credit card billing address matches the shipping address.) If it is confirmed, you must ship to that address to be protected.

While your transaction is protected, should any fraud be involved (a stolen credit card or identity hoax), you will not lose the money. In such a case, PayPal invalidates the transaction.

TIP

If you receive a PayPal payment and the buyer requests you ship to an address other than the address on the transaction details page, drop the buyer a note and ask about the address. At this point, depending on the reply you receive, decide for yourself whether you're willing to take the risk. Remember that you will not be covered under seller protection if you ship to an unconfirmed address.

Surprise! There are a few other rules and restrictions. For sellers to be protected, here are some of the musts:

>> **Ship to a confirmed address.** You must ship to the buyer's address exactly as displayed on the transaction details page.

>> **Ship within seven days.** The item must leave your place of business within seven days of your receiving payment. In the case of a pre-sale or customized item, you must post the delivery time in your listing.

>> **Accept single payment from a single account.** You must have accepted one payment from one PayPal account to pay for the purchase. (No multiple-account payments for an item.)

>> **Ship tangible goods.** Seller protection is not available for services, digital goods, and other electronically delivered items.

>> **Provide proof of shipping.** You need to provide a tracking number so the shipment can be tracked online. The transaction details page must show that you shipped to the buyer's address. For items valued at $750 and over, you must be able to produce a signed signature-delivery confirmation.

TIP

If you use an automated shipping solution such as Endicia (at www.endicia.com), you also just copy and paste the delivery confirmation numbers onto the PayPal page. PayPal will send an email to the buyer with the information for the buyer's records. If the item is an eBay purchase, it's best to input the Tracking number onto the eBay transaction as well.

Letting PayPal Help You
Manage the Money

WARNING

If PayPal is required by the buyer's issuing credit card company to respond immediately to resolve a chargeback situation, you must provide all information within three days.

At this writing, seller protection is available for many International sites. Check with the PayPal site by going to this page

`www.paypal.com/us/webapps/mpp/country-worldwide`

and clicking the individual country to check for any changes in this policy.

Downloading Your Transaction History from PayPal

I've been running a home-based business since the mid-1980s. Because I came from a corporate background working in the newspaper business, I've always known that keeping my books clean is of utmost importance. Even so, record-keeping has always been the bane of my existence. When I began my home-based business, the first thing I did was to hire a lawyer and a CPA to teach me what I had to do.

Recordkeeping means keeping track of everything: Every penny, sou, farthing, or ruble that you spend or take in. In the United States (and in most other countries), we have a pesky thing called taxes. We all have to turn in tax returns of several types when we run a business — and they'd better be correct. There may come a day when you receive a letter from a State or Federal tax agency asking to take a look at your books. This is simply a nice way of saying the dreaded word, *audit.*

TIP

The best defense against an audit is to have backup records. The more records you have proving your business income and expenses, the less painful your audit will be. One excellent piece of data to have at your fingertips is your PayPal transaction history.

Besides meeting tax-reporting requirements, keeping accurate records keeps you on top of your business dealings. (See Book 9 for more about how good record-keeping helps your business succeed.) PayPal helps you with this all-important recordkeeping by providing reports on your buying and selling activity with these features:

» **24/7 availability:** PayPal allows you to customize and download your transaction reports at any time. You might want to consider downloading your reports on a monthly or quarterly basis — as well as generating one big report at the end of the year.

Or you may want to download the reports to coincide with your state sales-tax payments (for backup documentation) or to keep a record of your monthly totals.

» **Various formats:** You can download reports in several formats. A flexible option is a comma-delimited file that you can open and edit in a spreadsheet program, such as Excel or Google Sheets. There's also a downloadable QuickBooks IIF file that can be imported into that bookkeeping program.

Chapter **5**

Using eBay's Management Tools

e Bay offers you a variety of tools. Because the site is constantly changing, few of us know where all the Easter eggs are or even how to use them. It's always an eye-opener when I poke around the site and find a useful shortcut.

TIP

Although I use eBay's management tools, there are many solid third-party services and tools are available. Book 8 lets you in on some of the most popular.

Signing In to Get Going

Before you start doing business on eBay, it's best to sign in. What would be more painful than to find an item you want, at the price you'd love to pay, with only two minutes to go — and not be signed in? (See the sidebar "The lowdown on sign-ins" for more information.) You must be signed in to bid, sell, or buy, so just do it!

1. **Click the Sign In link at the top of any eBay page.**

   (If you're already signed in, the link will read Sign Out.) You're sent to the Sign In page.

2. **Type your User ID and password, as shown in Figure 5-1.**

   Type your registered eBay User ID (not your email address). Your User ID and email address aren't interchangeable on the site.

TIP

   If you ever forget your eBay password, you can click the Forgot your User ID or Password links or go directly to the following:

   ```
   https://scgi.ebay.com/ws/eBayISAPI.dll?FYPShow
   ```

   If you remember the answer to the question you were asked during the eBay registration process, you can create a new password immediately.

3. **Click the Sign In button.**

   You're now signed in and ready to do almost anything on eBay!

THE LOWDOWN ON SIGN-INS

Your computer holds your sign-in information until you sign out.

When you check the *Stay signed in* check box, you will remain signed in. You'll also be set up to pay if you've saved your payment info. You can always turn off this feature in My eBay.

If you have more than one User ID or share a computer with other people, be sure to sign out when you're finished. For your protection, you still may have to type your password for actions involving financial or personal information such as these:

- Changing your user information such as email address, User ID, payment methods, or credit card information

- Going from a buyer account to a seller account

- Selling an item in a different browser session

- If you clear your browser cookies

- Posting in the Community Discussion Boards, Chat, Answer Center, or Groups

Occasionally, eBay may ask you to enter a verification code when you sign in. This is simply an additional security feature that prevents people from using the site inappropriately through automated registrations.

FIGURE 5-1:
Click Sign In and
you are ready
to deal!

Taking Charge on Your My eBay Hub

The number-one tool available at no cost to every eBay user is the My eBay page. This area of the site is designed to organize your buying and selling activities. After you've registered on the site, you have a My eBay page automatically, so let's delve into exactly what it can do for you.

I call My eBay a page, but it's really an *area* — a group of several pages held together with links. The My eBay area gives you control of everything you are doing (or would like to do) on eBay.

To get to My eBay, hover over the My eBay link at the top right of the page and a drop-down menu will appear as shown in Figure 5-2.

FIGURE 5-2:
Navigation
links to the My
eBay hub.

REMEMBER

You will always have access to My eBay when you're on the site. When eBay feels that your sales are growing, they may unceremoniously move you the Seller Hub. (Discussed in Book 8, Chapter 1).

As I said, eBay is constantly making changes. Your My eBay may be divided into two pages or it may appear all on one page. The main Summary page covers all your shopping needs and the My eBay: All Selling page gives you information on your selling activities. As of this moment, I'm seeing three variations on different accounts.

Figure 5-3 shows you My eBay views. You'll note they all have common links. Most are described in Table 5-1.

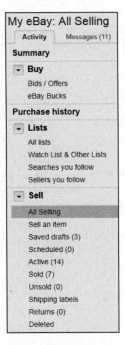

FIGURE 5-3:
Variations in the navigation links on the My eBay pages.

You can visit each activity by clicking links in the column on the left side of the Summary page. The top-level links of each My eBay area presents you with a summary of the activity in that area. The links below the top link take you to specific data, without making you scroll through a long page.

TABLE 5-1   **In a Snapshot: Selected Views of the My eBay:
All Selling Area**

Click Here	To See This on Your My eBay Page
Summary	A page summarizing your My eBay area, with notifications of actions that need follow-up on the balance of the My eBay pages.
Buy	Every item for sale that you're watching, bidding on, or have made offers on, as well as any auctions you've lost.
Lists	A collection of links to the items on your wish list, Watch list, and any custom list you chose to make: favorite categories, searches, sellers, and stores.
Saved Searches	When you perform a search on eBay, you are prompted to save the search. When you save, that search will appear in this area.
Saved Sellers	When you come across a seller who sells the types of items that interest you, click to save, and that seller will appear here. (**Hint:** My User ID is marsha_c.)
Purchase History	When you make a purchase on eBay, the transaction information lands here. When your seller ships the item, the tracking number will be posted so you can check on the status of the shipment.
Sell: All Selling	All the information about any items you're selling on eBay.
Tab: Messages	A separate tab to a direct and secure place to view the latest information about eBay. You no longer have to worry about phishing spam that pretends to be from eBay. When eBay has something to tell you, it appears here.
Tab: Applications	Clicking here will take you to eBay's App store and show you the ones that you are subscribed to.
Tab: Account	This contains links to several important areas: your eBay account information, such as seller's fees and invoices; the most recent feedback comments about you, links that send you to all the feedback you've left and received, an area where you can respond to feedback; and finally, preferences you can specify so that eBay performs just as you want it to.

Below the My eBay: All Selling links are convenient shortcuts to services and answers you may need while doing business on eBay (see the left of Figure 5-4). You can choose to specify which links appear here by clicking the *Edit Shortcuts* link. Clicking this link presents you with a box of options. You may then select topic links for display on your page, as shown on the right in Figure 5-4.

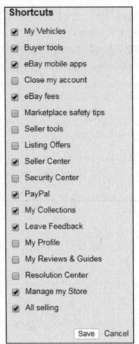

FIGURE 5-4:
Your Shortcuts
links (left) and all
those available
(right).

Looking at the My eBay Summary Page

Until you set your preferences (as to which page you want to automatically open your My eBay area to — see the "Site Preferences link" section further on), you land on the Summary page. Mine is shown in Figure 5-5, my Selling shows up on a different page.

FIGURE 5-5:
My eBay Activity
Summary — the
heart of your
eBay activities.

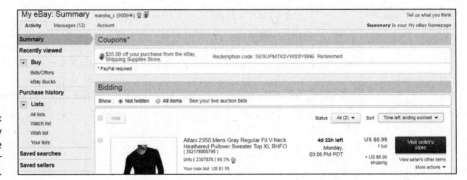

The Summary page gives you a snapshot of your current eBay business. It provides data about your buying and selling business, and supplies links to the items.

When you are a buyer, this area tells you about

>> Items you're watching

>> Items you're bidding on

>> Items you've been outbid on (for which you may need to up your bid)

>> Feedback that you need to leave for items you've purchased

If you have a Watch list (more on that further on), it will appear front and center on this page, as well as in the Lists category.

When you sell on eBay, the eBay: All Selling area will provide info on

>> Questions about items pending from prospective customers

>> Items you have sold

>> Any items that are in the Returns process

>> Items you're selling

>> How many items you haven't sold

Should you subscribe to any of eBay's paid services such as eBay Stores, there will also be a link to your subscription area. In addition, a link is provided to any important notices from eBay regarding changes in its policies or services.

Tracking Your Buying Activity on My eBay

The Buy page is the hub for keeping track of your bids, your wins, items you're watching, and any items you didn't win. This area of My eBay helps you control everything you're currently shopping for on the site. I check this page several times a day to see the progress of items I'm interested in.

Bids/Offers

When you place a bid, eBay registers it in the Bids/Offers area, as shown in Figure 5-6, and displays a clickable link to the item.

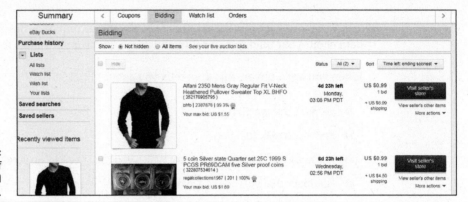

FIGURE 5-6:
Keeping track of your bidding and buying activity.

When shopping, if you don't check on your mobile device, make the bidding page a daily stop on eBay, so you can see the status of your bids:

>> Bid amounts in green indicate that you're the high bidder in the auction.

>> Bid amounts in red indicate that your bid is losing. If you want to increase your bid, simply click the auction title to go to the auction.

>> As auctions on which you've bid end, they are transferred to the Purchase History or the Didn't Win section, depending (respectively) on your success or failure in the bidding process.

TIP

You can make notations on your bidding or item-watching. Just click the Add Note button which appears as you mouse over the item on your list and then add the information.

eBay Bucks

Loyalty programs keep you coming back for more, and eBay Bucks (shown in Figure 5-7) gives you rewards for the money you spend on eBay. Every calendar quarter, eBay totals up the amount you've spent on the site in qualifying categories and issues (currently) an eBay Bucks certificate worth one percent of your total. This certificate can be used toward the purchase of any item on the site for the following quarter after it's issued.

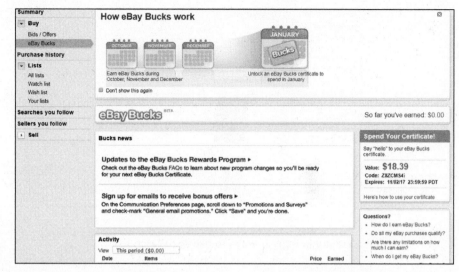

FIGURE 5-7:
Keep track of
your eBay Bucks
earnings on this
page.

Organizing My eBay Lists, Searches, and Purchases

If you sell and have an interest in a few categories, eBay lists can make your search for new items easier. The list of Saved Sellers can bring you back to product specialists you like; Saved Searches help you track trends and find some bargains to resell on eBay.

Lists: Watch list

I'll bet you've seen an item that made you think . . .

> *I don't want to bid (or buy) this just now, but I'd like to buy it if it's a bargain!*

And you've probably seen the *Add to watch list* link on each listing page. Click it to add that item to your Watch list, which is available from your My eBay page.

Clicking the Watch list link from My eBay brings you to the Watch list (see Figure 5-8), one of the most powerful features of the My eBay Lists area. If you're watching items, you'll see a notation on the page, indicating how many auctions you're currently watching. This page lists each watched item with a countdown (time left) timer, so you know exactly when the auction will close. When a listing on your watch list gets close to ending, you can swoop down and make the kill — if the price is right.

FIGURE 5-8:
Sit back and observe with the My eBay Watch list.

Here are two great ways to use the Watch list:

>> **As a buyer:** Are you interested in an item? You can observe the bidding action — the number of bids and how fast the price is rising (or not) — without showing your hand to the competition.

TIP

The watch-list function helps me keep my bargain-hunting quiet. Everybody knows when you're bidding on an item; nobody knows when you're watching the deals like a hawk. When you're looking for bargains to buy and resell, you may not want to tip off the competition by letting them know you're bidding.

>> **As a seller:** Also a handy marketing tool, the Watch list allows you to store listings from competitive sellers. That way, you can monitor the status of items similar to ones you plan to sell later — and see whether the items are selling high or low, which helps you to decide whether it's a good time to sell.

Saved Searches link

A tool that comes in handy for sellers as well as buyers is the Saved Searches area of My eBay where you can accumulate a bucket load of your favorite searches. When you want to see whether any of your searched-for items are available for sale, simply click the View Items link. If there are no items matching your search, you see the words *Your search returned 0 items* below the search words in the list.

Are you always looking for certain things on eBay? For example, maybe you plan to search frequently for a Callaway Seven Heaven Wood — whatever. Add it to your list of saved searches and you won't have to type *Callaway Seven Heaven Wood* more than once. By organizing your saved searches, you can search for your favorite items with a click of your mouse on the title links.

You can view saved searches, change them, delete them, or indicate that you'd like to receive email notification when a new matching item is listed. To add an item search to the list, run a search from the search box on any eBay page and click the Save button with a star icon that appears next to your search text. The next time you reload your My eBay Saved Searches page, your new favorite search will be listed.

When you click the Save button, a window pops up, asking you to name the search and giving you the option to receive emails when new items match your search. Click the check box next to this option, and you won't have to go to your Saved Searches area; you'll be notified by email instead (refer to Figure 5-9). eBay sends its robot to check listings each night, so you'll get a notification of new listings the next morning.

FIGURE 5-9:
Save in your
Saved searches
and/or opt out
to receive
daily emails
notifying you.

TIP

Be sure to use all the search tricks and shortcuts I show you in the table in Chapter 1 of this minibook. These are single-line searches that you normally would perform from the search boxes on the eBay pages.

Keeping track of favorite searches is a valuable tool when you're looking for particular items to resell and want to find them at bargain prices. Also, when you have a unique collectible for sale, you can monitor the current selling prices.

Saved Sellers link

When you've been on eBay for awhile, you will find that certain sellers carry a specific type of merchandise that interests you. By saving their User IDs in the Saved Sellers area, you'll be able to revisit their current items for sale without having to run a seller search. Remember that the purpose of the My eBay page is to have all your controls in one area.

From a seller's point of view, Saved Sellers is where you can keep a list of people who sell items similar to what you sell. You can check up on them and see what they're selling, when they're selling it, and for how much. It's a helpful timing tool that can prevent you from listing a similar item at the same time as their auctions.

Saved Sellers is handy also when your competition is selling an item that you plan to sell, but at a deeply discounted price. When that happens, don't offer yours until they sell out of the item, at which time the price will most likely go back up — supply and demand, remember? I have a few quality wholesalers and liquidators under Saved Sellers, too, and search for lots that I can resell at a profit.

To add a seller to your Saved Sellers list, just go to one of their items for sale. If you are actively searching items, and find a seller with goods you like, just click the Save this Seller link in the Seller Information box on the item page.

Purchase History link

Clicking the Purchase History link in the My eBay navigation area displays all the items you've won as far back as the last 60 days, as shown in Figure 5-10.

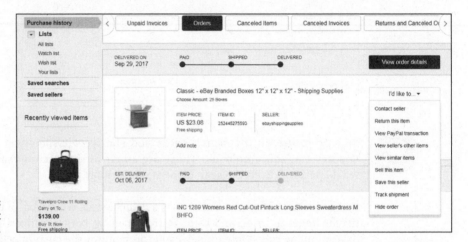

FIGURE 5-10:
What I just
bought on eBay.

The Purchase History page is the go-to place to check on any items that you're waiting to receive. It's also a convenient way to keep track of your expenditures, especially if you are buying for resale.

Helpful features on the Purchase History vary whether the item has been delivered or is still in transit.

>> **Drop-down menu:** Click the More Actions drop-down menu to the far right of any item you've purchased, and you'll be able to perform actions related to your transaction. Here are some important ones:

- *Contact Seller:* This link sends you to the seller's smart answers page. If you don't see the answer to your question, you can send a message to the seller through eBay messaging.

- *I didn't receive it:* If the item is hasn't arrived by the estimated delivery date, click here to make an inquiry.

- *Return This Item:* If the seller has a return policy, you can use this link to initiate a return and resulting refund.

- *Sell This Item:* If you purchased the item to resell, or just figured out you really don't want it, click here and you go to a Sell an Item page.

Clicking on the View order details link takes you to a page where you can check the status of your item. It includes

» **Listing title:** A link to the listing. I always use this when an item arrives so I can be sure that the item I received is exactly as advertised.

» **Item sale date and price paid:** Helps you remember when you purchased the item.

» **Leave Feedback.** Here's where you can leave the all-important feedback for the seller.

» **Estimated delivery date:** Based on the seller's mode of transit, eBay estimates how long the item should take to get to your door. If it hasn't arrived within a day or so (barring snowstorms and natural disasters), it doesn't hurt to contact the seller to check on the shipping status.

» **Show shipping details:** When the seller has shipped, you can click this link to see the progress (or delivery confirmation) of your item, as I did in Figure 5-11.

FIGURE 5-11:
This item shipped
First Class Mail
from New Jersey
and got to my
door in one day!

USING MY eBay TO MANAGE YOUR SALES

For the new seller, the tools on the Selling pages are great. They're simple and get right to the point. To run an eBay business, small sellers can use the All Selling page with the Sell an Item form for individual listings, and these tools should be sufficient.

On the Selling page, you can view details like these for your active listings:

- **Links to listings:** Each listing title is a clickable link you can use to go instantly to an item's page.

- **Current price:** This is the starting price of your item (if you have no bids) or the current price based on bids received.

- **Reserve price:** This handy feature reminds you of the reserve price that you've set on an item. There's nowhere else to check this.

- **Quantity available:** Here's where you can see how many of the item are still available for purchase on the site. When an eBay store item is listed, this feature shows you how many are left, as well as the original quantity you listed.

- **# of bids:** When you see that the price is rising on an item, check out this column to see how many bids have been placed to date.

- **Views/Watchers:** This is the number of views your item page received, and the number of people who have selected the item for their Watch list.

- **Time left:** In this column, you can see how much time is left (to the minute) in your listing.

- **Actions:** This is the handiest column of all. Here you have a link that lets you list a similar item. This is particularly handy if you want to use a template again for another item. It also allows you to revise a listing, add to the description, end a listing, or edit promotions if you have a store.

Visit Book 3, Chapter 4 for an in-depth look at how the My eBay: All Selling area can help you manage your eBay business.

My eBay: Account Tab

On the My eBay: All Selling page, you'll find the Account tab (which links to the My Account page) lets you know how much you owe eBay and how much they'll charge your credit card that month. This is a quick and easy way to check your most recent invoice, payments and credits, and your account; all these links are located in one area. You can also access your PayPal account to see, for example, when deposits were sent to your checking account.

The Account tab is also a place where you can find a drop-down menu that links to the many areas that affect your selling procedures and account data (you can see mine in Figure 5-12). This section tells you about some of the important links you'll find on this menu.

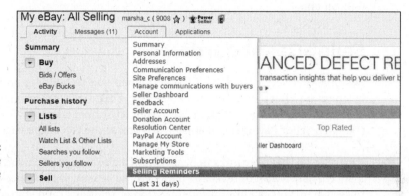

FIGURE 5-12:
Links available
from the
Account tab.

Personal Information link

Click the Personal Information link to get to the Personal Information page, which holds all the links to your personal information on eBay. This is where you can change your email address, User ID (without losing your feedback), password, and credit card information — and also edit or create your About Me page. You can also change or access any registration or credit card information that you have on file at eBay. There's even a link you can use to change your home address on record.

Keeping all your contact information up to date on eBay is important. If the eBay folks should ever find that any of the contact information is wrong, they may suspend your membership.

Another link, Communication Preferences, takes you to where you can specify how you want to receive information from eBay and handle your member-to-member communications.

TIP

By using the eBay mobile app, you can get instantaneous notifications on your smartphone. My personal favorite is the cash register sound I hear when someone pays for one of my items on PayPal.

Site Preferences link

A handy feature of the Site Preferences area is the opportunity to customize the settings you see here by clicking the Show link and then the Edit link for that preference. For example, under General Preferences, you can save extra clicks by changing preferences to keep yourself "Signed in on this computer."

You may as well click through every option every once in a while. That way, you'll be sure you have things set up just the way you want them for conducting business on eBay.

Seller Dashboard

Customer service is what it's all about when you're building and maintaining a business on eBay, so this space should be a regular stop for you. It'll keep you apprised of how you're doing with your customer service. Your average DSR (Detailed Seller Ratings) will appear in a box at the top of the page.

TIP

Each title on this page links to deeper information on your personal seller performance. There's a lot of revealing data here, so be sure to click these links regularly to see where you can improve your customer relations (and status with eBay).

REMEMBER

If you're a Top Rated Seller, the Seller Dashboard is a very important place — because this is where you can keep track of your Final Value fee discount (which is based on your ratings). Click the arrows to expand the information and then click links to generate reports on how your feedback has fared.

Feedback link

In Book 1, I talk all about the importance of feedback to the eBay community. In the Feedback area of the Account page, you can keep track of all your feedback duties. Feedback is a most important function of your eBay transactions; don't forget to leave some for your trading partners!

When you click the Feedback link, you can see your listings from the last 30 days. You see a star to the far right of a transaction if you've left feedback. (The star will be grayed out if you haven't.) If your trading partner has left feedback for you, you see a sign in a comment-cloud icon — a plus sign means positive feedback and a minus sign means negative.

TIP

At the very bottom of the page, eBay shows you recent feedback that has been left for you. But it's much easier to click the feedback number next to your User ID to see your most recent feedback.

There's also a link on the top that takes you to the Feedback Forum, where you can perform many feedback-related functions, including these crucial two:

>> **Reply and Follow Up:** Responding to feedback left for you is especially important, especially if the feedback is less than stellar. Every story has two sides. Make sure yours is prompt and professional.

>> **Request Feedback Revision:** If you've solved a problem and turned an unhappy customer into a happy one, you can request that the person re-examine the feedback left earlier.

Should you want to check feedback for a specific eBay member, there's a Find a Member search box where you can type in his or her User ID and go to the Find a Member page.

Subscriptions link

Click the Subscriptions link, and you'll be able to see just which additional selling tools you're paying for. From here, you can upgrade, downgrade, or unsubscribe.

3

Selling Like a Pro

Contents at a Glance

Chapter **1**

Be Sure Your Listings Make Cents

S elling on eBay is a good idea for anyone. You clean out your garage, sell things you might have thrown away anyway, and make a profit. What a wonder–ful marketplace! You can make money in your spare time and enhance your lifestyle with just a few clicks on your keyboard and mouse.

When you decide to sell on eBay in earnest, however, you can run into business problems like tight profit margins. Few eBay sellers have a background in retail–ing or marketing, and eBay is all about retailing and marketing. In this chapter, I give you tips on pricing strategies. The first item on the agenda is to understand all the fees involved with running an ecommerce business on eBay.

Keeping an Eye on Where the Pennies Go

It doesn't seem so much to list an item, plus pay a small Final Value Fee. Of course, a few cents (maybe dollars) go to PayPal. One by one, these minute amounts tend to breeze by even the most experienced seller. You don't really see your eBay fees, because they're not directly deducted from your sales. eBay bills you at the end of the month. It's easy to lose track of your costs unless you are keeping *very* good books (more about tracking costs in Book 9, Chapter 3).

TIP

All those nickels, dimes, and quarters add up. The hundreds (thousands?) of people who are selling items on the site for $1 can't be making much of a profit — not even enough for a pack of gum! To avoid this low-profit trap, you must be keenly aware of every penny you spend on listing fees, Final Value Fees, listing options, and PayPal fees. Keep in mind that if you have slim profit margins on an item but are constantly selling it, you may be making up for the low margin in sheer volume.

Becoming complacent ignoring your eBay costs as you list items for sale can be easy to do. As a person in business for yourself, you must take into account outgoing expenses as well as incoming revenues. The cost of your initial listing (does your time to write and photograph not have a cost?) is just the beginning of your advertising budget for that item. You have to factor in the cost of all the listing options and features you use as well. After all that, you also pay a Final Value Fee to eBay after the item sells. (For the fees that are relevant to your eBay Store, check out Book 8, Chapter 4.)

REMEMBER

In this section, I review the costs for listing an item to sell on eBay. But if you use a credit card payment service, those folks also charge a fee. Later in this chapter, I examine the costs of some popular credit card payment services.

AUTHOR
SAYS

BE SURE YOU'RE MAKING A PROFIT

I recently purchased a selection of women's apparel to sell. My cost per item was $9.99. To remain competitive, I offered free shipping, which probably will cost me another $4 (including the cost of the mailer). Other eBay sellers smartly zeroed in on the same items of apparel — and I don't mind the competition, as long as my items sell. But some of the other sellers didn't continue to be so smart — and may be cheating themselves out of money. They priced their listings at $14.99 and offered free shipping. At this point, I have to say: Do the math. Is it worth the time to source an item and then sell it for just a few pennies' profit? Unless it's a high-volume loss-leader, not in my book. When you price your items, price them within the going market. Selling an item cheaply will not give you the kind of ROI (return on investment) that will make you happy in the long run. Truth.

Insertion (listing) fees

If you don't have an eBay Store, you are entitled to 50 free listings per calendar month (beginning at 12:00:00 a.m. Pacific Time on the first day of each month and ending at 11:59:59 p.m. Pacific Time on the last day of the month). That means the listings are free of *insertion fees*. After that, the fee is a straightforward: $.30 per listing, whether it's a fixed-price listing or an auction in most categories. Adding extra listing features adds more to the listing fee. For example, when you place a reserve on an auction, you're charged an *insertion listing upgrade fee* based on the *amount* of the reserve price.

Free listings are not available in the Real Estate, Motors: Boats, Cars & Trucks, Motorcycles, Other Vehicles & Trailers, Powersports, and some Business & Industrial categories.

What listings count toward your free limit? See the following:

>> New listings (whether auction or fixed price)

>> Relisted items when eligible (that is, when you relist an item that didn't sell the first time)

>> Listings ended early, or those that eBay ends early due to an eBay policy violation

>> Duplicate identical auction listings (even if eBay removes one or more of those listings for policy violation)

REMEMBER

If your item doesn't sell, you do have the option of relisting your unsuccessful item. Your relisted item will count as an additional listing for the month. Writing a better title, starting with a lower opening bid, or adding a snappier description and better pictures may help in selling the item.

Reserve-price auction fees

In a *reserve-price auction*, you're able to set an undisclosed minimum price for which your item will sell, thereby giving yourself a safety net. Using a reserve-price auction protects the investment you have in an item. If, at the end of the auction, no bidder has met your undisclosed reserve price, you aren't obligated to sell the item and the high bidder isn't required to purchase the item. For example, if you have a rare coin to sell, you can start the bidding at a low price to attract bidders to click your auction and read your description. If you start your bidding at too high a price, you might dissuade prospective bidders from even looking at your auction, and you won't tempt them even to bid. They may feel that the final selling price will be too high for their budgets. You want to get the auction fever going with lots of bidders!

SECOND CHANCE TO SELL!

If your auction goes above the target sales price and you have more of the item in stock, you can offer items in stock to your underbidders. The figure shows you where you can click from your My eBay Sold Items area to make a Second Chance Offer. Click to offer the item to underbidders for their most recent high bids. You will also find a link to make a Second Chance Offer on the Closed Item page.

You will be charged only Final Value Fees — not a second relisting (insertion) fee — if the person purchases the item. The Second Chance Offer will also not count toward your free listings per month.

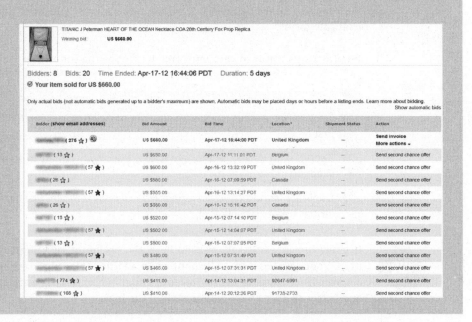

Everyone on eBay is looking for a deal or a truly rare item. If you can combine the mystical force of both of these needs in one auction, you have something special. The reserve-price auction enables you to attempt — and perhaps achieve — this feat.

Although the reserve-price auction is a safety net for the seller, it's often an uncomfortable guessing game for the prospective bidder. To alleviate buyer anxiety, many sellers put reserve prices in the item description, allowing bidders to decide whether the item will fit into their bidding budgets.

REMEMBER

Should you have a change of heart, you can lower or even remove your reserve price after you receive a bid on the item.

Placing a reserve price on one of your auctions means that the item will not sell until the bidding reaches the reserve price. When your reserve-price item does sell, you've sold your item at a profit (let's hear it for optimism!). The *reserve fee* is based on the reserve price you set, as outlined in Table 1-1, so be sure to set the reserve high enough to cover the fee and *still* give you a profit.

TABLE 1-1

eBay Reserve Auction Fees*

Starting Price ($)	Fee
0.01–74.99	$3.00
75.00 and up	4% of reserve price (maximum of $100.00)

Reserve fee for eBay Motors is $40.00 for items selling up to $75,000.

REMEMBER

If your item doesn't sell the first time with a low starting price and a reserve, you can always relist it at a slightly higher starting price without a reserve.

eBay's Optional Listing Features

eBay listings have many options and upgrades. Figure 1-1 shows how even a random search on eBay listings can yield examples of some very popular listing options.

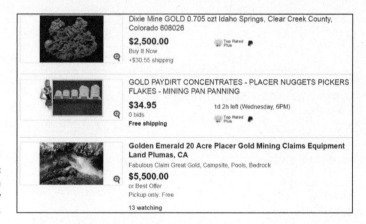

FIGURE 1-1:
A search showing eBay option upgrades.

When the process of listing your item brings you to eBay's optional listing features, you see the headline, "Get more bids with these optional features! Make your item stand out from the crowd!" Sounds pretty good, doesn't it? But getting carried away with these options is easy — and can lead to spending all your expected profits before you earn them.

When I was teaching eBay University's Advanced Selling class, I quoted statistical success rates for the different features, but in the real life of *your* business, success varies from item to item and category to category.

If you take the boldface option and then your listing appears in a category full of boldface titles, the bold just doesn't have the potential to boost your return on investment. In fact, your listing might stand out more *without* the bold option.

I recap the cost of the various eBay listing options in Table 1-2. Weigh the pros and cons in terms of how these options affect your eBay business. Will spending a little extra money enhance your item enough to justify the extra cost? Will you be able to make the money back in profits? You must have a good understanding of what the options are — and when and how you can use them to fullest advantage.

TABLE 1-2   ## eBay Listing Upgrade Fees

Option	Buy It Now or Starting Price UNDER $150 1-, 3-, 5-, 7-, and 10-day	Buy It Now or Starting Price UNDER $150 30-day and Good 'Til Cancelled (GTC)	Buy It Now or Starting Price OVER $150 1-, 3-, 5-, 7-, and 10-day	Buy It Now or Starting Price OVER $150 30-day and Good 'Til Cancelled (GTC)
Subtitle	$0.50	$1.50	$1.00	$3.00
Boldface title	$2.00	$4.00	$3.00	$6.00
Listing Designer	$0.10	$0.30	$0.20	$0.60
Gallery Plus	$0.35	$1.00	$0.70	$2.00
International site visibility	Auctions (Starting price – all durations) $0.01–$9.99: $0.10; $10.–$49.99: $0.20; $50. and up: $0.40	Buy It Now (all durations) $0.50		
List in two categories	Double insertion and listing upgrade fees			
Value Pack (Gallery Plus, Listing Designer, and subtitle)	$0.65	$2.00	$1.30	$4.00

REMEMBER

When doing business on eBay, you may have to pay a store fee, an insertion fee, and a Final Value Fee. If you accept credit card payments, you must pay an additional fee to the payment service. Estimate your expenses from these basics before you consider spending money for advertising.

Subtitle

You may use a maximum of 80 characters for your item's title. Title search is the de-facto search standard on eBay. From the statistics I've seen during years on the site, more than 98 percent of searches were made for title only, versus title and description. So how can you make your item stand out when it shows up with hundreds of other items that look the same? Use the subtitle option!

Notice the subtitle under one of the listings in Figure 1-2. This is your opportunity to add just enough tantalizing text to your listing — text that is readable by prospective buyers as they quickly scan search results or browse category offerings. Subtitles work very well if you are one of several sellers selling the same item at a similar price — it sets your listing apart from the others. A caveat: This additional text will be picked up in a search only if the person chooses to search both titles *and* descriptions, but will be visible on any page where your item shows up. The fee for this option is $.50 to $3.00.

FIGURE 1-2: Set your items apart from the competition by using subtitles.

When your item has something special about it or could use some extra description, the subtitle option allows you more space to give the browsing shopper vital information.

Listing Designer

eBay comes up with options to fill the needs (or wants, in this case) of users. Some sellers enjoy putting colorful graphics around their descriptions. Listing Designer will include pretty graphics and help you design your description, placing pictures in different locations on the page. But if you have a good description (creatively done with HTML color and emphasis), plus a good picture (inserted creatively with the HTML code I give you in Book 5), your item will draw bids just the same as if you spent up to $.60 extra (per listing) for the Listing Designer option.

TIP

Using a graphics template to brand your listings on eBay — giving them a uniform look — is a great idea. If you want to use a template, decide on one and make it your signature look.

Boldface

The Boldface option is a favorite and probably the most-used option in the eBay stable. A listing title in **boldface type** stands out in a crowd, unless . . . you got it, unless it's in a category loaded with boldface titles. If the $2 to $6 that eBay charges for this benefit is in your budget, odds are it might get you a good deal more views (depending on your item) than if you didn't use it.

Applying boldface to your item title pulls it off the page right into the reader's eye. Unfortunately, bold type tacks additional money onto your listing cost — so you'd better be in a position to make a good profit from the item. Also make sure your research shows that the item can sell for your target price.

Buy It Now

The Buy It Now feature for auctions, shown in Figure 1-3, has a few significant benefits. If you have a target price for the item you're listing, make that your Buy It Now price. You can also use this option during frenzied holiday shopping times or with hot items. Be sure to stay within the rules and post a Buy It Now price of at least 30 percent above your opening bid and perhaps you'll get a bite, er, sale.

The Buy It Now feature disappears when someone bids on the item or, if you've placed a reserve on the auction, when a bidder meets your reserve price.

FIGURE 1-3:
See the Buy It
Now button just
below the Place
Bid button?

Adding the Final Value Fees

eBay's version of the Hollywood back-end deal is the Final Value Fee. Big stars get a bonus when their movies do well at the box office; eBay gets a cut when your item sells. When the revenue is posted, eBay charges the Final Value Fee to your account in a matter of seconds. Then, if you don't have an eBay Store, you generally pay a flat 10 percent of your final selling price including any shipping you charge the buyer.

If you have an eBay Store, the fee varies by category. You can find the Final Value Fee structure for eBay Stores in Book 8, Chapter 4.

TIP

A classified ad in the Real Estate category is *not* charged a Final Value Fee, and eBay doesn't charge a percentage Final Value Fee on an auction in the Real Estate category (as it does in other categories). You pay a flat FVF of $35 for Timeshares, Manufactured Homes, and Land and no FVF for Commercial or Residential. See this page for any late updates

http://pages.ebay.com/help/sell/realestatefees.html

But in the Automotive category, you pay a flat Successful Listing Fee of up to $125 for vehicles if your auction ends with a winning bidder (and the reserve has been met). For current fees for eBay Motors, visit

http://pages.ebay.com/help/sell/motorfees.html

Know Your Options in Auctions

An auction is an auction is an auction, right? Wrong! eBay has four types of auctions for your selling pleasure. Most of the time you'll run traditional auctions, but other auctions have their special uses, too. After you've been selling on eBay for a while, you may find that one of the other types of auctions better suits your needs. In this section, I review these auctions so you fully understand what they are and when to use them.

Traditional auctions

Traditional auctions are what made eBay famous. You can run a traditional auction for 1, 3, 5, 7, or 10 days, and when the auction closes, the highest bidder wins. I'm sure you've bid on several and won at least a few. I bet you've also made money running some of your own.

You begin the auction with an opening bid, and bidders will bid up your opening price into a healthy profit for you (I hope).

Best Offer

If you've got a fixed-price listing, you can opt to insert a button under your sales price that encourages buyers to make you an offer on your item. This is probably one of the oldest sales methods around. (In some countries, it's an insult to buy something at the posted price; haggling is part of their retail culture.)

So, if you love the thrill of haggling (I don't, really), you can insert the Make Offer button into your listings at no extra charge. See Figure 1-4 for an example. When someone makes an offer on one of your items, eBay sends you an email asking that you reply to indicate whether the proposed price is acceptable to you.

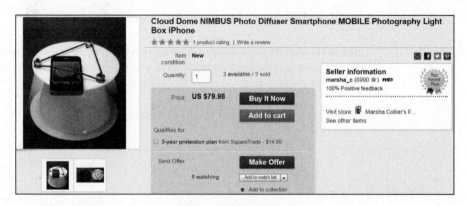

FIGURE 1-4:
Maybe I'll make a deal on this.

Restricted-access auctions

eBay won't allow certain items to be sold in nonrestricted categories, so you must list them in the Adult Only category of eBay. eBay makes it easy for the user to find or avoid these types of items by making this area accessible only after the user agrees to the terms and conditions. Items in the Adult Only category are not openly accessible through the regular eBay title search, nor are they listed in Newly Listed Items. Anyone who participates in auctions for items in the Adult Only category on eBay, whether as a bidder or a seller, must have a credit card on file on eBay for verification.

WARNING

Do not attempt to slip an adults-only auction into a nonrestricted category. eBay doesn't have a sense of humor when it comes to this violation of policy, and may relocate or end your auction. eBay might even suspend you from its site.

Private listings

The eBay Advanced Search page features an area where you can conduct a bidder search. You can find a list of the items that you've bid on in the past 30 days. Anyone not signing in on your eBay account sees a list of only the items you've won — but that's no real help. One December, my daughter told me that she didn't want a particular item — something that I had just bid on — for Christmas. My creative daughter had been regularly perusing my bidding action on eBay to see what I was buying for the holidays! A private listing would have kept my shopping secret.

Private sales also work well for the buyers who avail themselves of the services of the psychics, card readers, and fortunetellers on eBay and don't want their friends to think they are . . . well, you know. Sometimes it's just best to keep things quiet. No one needs to know just how much you choose to pay for something. As a seller, you have the option (at no extra charge) of listing your item as private.

TIP

The private auction is a useful tool for sellers who are selling bulk lots to other sellers. It maintains the privacy of the bidders, and customers can't do a bidder search to find out what sellers are paying for the loot they plan to resell on eBay.

The private auction can save you the potential embarrassment associated with buying a girdle or the tie that flips over to reveal a racy half-nude on the back.

Although the private auction is a useful tool, it may intimidate a novice user. If your customer base comes from experienced eBay users and you're selling an item that may benefit from being auctioned in secret, you might want to try this option.

NOT QUITE ADULT ENOUGH . . .

I was surprised to see a private auction listed on one of my favorite eBay seller's list. She usually doesn't sell items like "Fringe Black BRA 36B SEXY SEXY SEXY," so I looked through this seller's past auctions. I saw that she didn't get any bids when she listed the bra in the restricted (adults-only) area of eBay in the category Everything Else: Mature Audiences: Clothing, Accessory. When she put the bra up for private auction in the category Clothing & Accessories: Women's Clothing: Lingerie: Bras: General, she got five bidders and sold the item. I guess it wasn't sexy enough for the "adult" crowd!

PayPal Gets Its Cut

When you've sold your item, do you think that's the end of the fees? Nope! If your customer pays using PayPal, you're faced with additional fees. However, having a PayPal Premier or Business account is important for building your commerce for these reasons:

>> eBay buyers look for the PayPal option because it offers them a high level of protection against fraud.

>> Most customers prefer to pay with a credit card, either to delay the expense or to have complete records of their purchases.

>> From a seller's point of view, using PayPal can be cheaper than having a direct-merchant credit card account.

>> PayPal helps with your paperwork by offering downloadable logs of your sales that include all PayPal fees. eBay fees are not included; you're on your own for the recordkeeping on those.

REMEMBER

A PayPal Business account requires the account to be registered in a business name. A Premier account allows you to do business under your own name.

Check out Book 2, Chapter 4, which covers the PayPal services and fees in depth.

FOREWARNED IS SMART

After you know all the eBay fees involved in selling your item, you can play around with the pricing and figure out how much your Buy It Now (or target selling) price should be. Remember to include the following costs when pricing your items:

- How much you paid for the item you want to resell

- The "Freight In" amount (the cost of shipping the item to you)

- The cost of shipping the item to your buyer

Setting Sensible Shipping Costs

Buyers who visit the eBay site are bargain shoppers. They want to get their items at the lowest possible prices. They're also more cognizant about the "hidden" expense buried in the item's shipping and handling fees. When you set these fees, you must take into account every expense involved in your packing and shipping. You can't make your shipping area a losing proposition.

However, many eBay sellers have increased their shipping prices to outrageous amounts. But when the shipping fee equals a third of the item's cost, a prospective bidder may think twice about placing a bid. Of course, if the item is big or the buyer wants it fast, he or she may feel better about paying higher shipping costs.

TIP

eBay penalizes sellers who charge high shipping fees and rewards sellers who offer Free Shipping by giving the free shippers better visibility in the Best Match search results. Try listing your item by including the shipping amount in your selling price and offer Free Shipping. Then offer buyers a second shipping option for Priority Mail (faster shipping) at a charge. Your item will still get the benefit of eBay's Free Shipping search preference.

Business is business, and when you're on eBay to make a profit, every penny counts. In this section, I tell you how to evaluate all the costs involved with packing and shipping the items you sell. I also show you how to use the tools at your disposal — such as eBay's shipping calculator — to make the best decisions about how much to charge your buyers for shipping costs.

For information on organizing your shipping area, be sure to read Book 7.

REMEMBER

When calculating shipping costs, don't assume that all you have to worry about is just the cost of your postage. You also have per–item costs for boxes, padded mailers, shipping tape, labels, and pickup or service fees from your carriers. Now and again, you may even pay the college kid across the street five bucks to schlep your boxes for you. Expenses show up in the strangest places.

In addition to adding up the packing and shipping supplies, you need to amortize the monthly fees from any online postage shipping services. Should you occasionally pay for a pickup from the carrier, you need to add that expense to the shipping charges, too. The following list runs down some of the expenses involved:

>> **Padded bubble or vinyl mailers:** Select an average-size padded mailer that works for several types of items you sell. Selecting a few average sizes for all your products works well because it's cheaper to buy in quantity. Even if a few of your items could fit in the next-size-down mailers, buying the bigger size by the case gives you a considerable discount. Why keep five sizes of mailers in stock in quantities of 100 if you don't have to? If you don't use all the bigger ones, you can always sell them. And besides, envelopes don't go bad.

TIP

Don't be misled by packaging suppliers' claims of low-cost mailers. They *usually* don't include the shipping costs in these price estimates.

When you price your cost-per-piece, be sure to include (as part of your cost) what you have to pay to get the item shipped to you. For example, if you purchase your mailers — say #4s (9½ x 14½) — by the hundred, they may cost you $.39 each. If you buy a case of 500, they may cost only $.29 each. By buying in quantity, you save $.10 per mailing envelope! The more business you do, the more significant the savings.

>> **Packing peanuts:** I must admit that storing all those packing peanuts is a real drag. But here's where buying in bulk equates to huge cost savings. I just checked one of my favorite vendors, www.bubblefast.com, and found a *free-shipping* offer. From BubbleFAST, you can purchase antistatic packing peanuts in lots of various sizes:

3.25 cubic feet for $11.50 = $3.54 per cubic foot

7 cubic feet for $22.00 = $3.14 per cubic foot

14 cubic feet for $42.00 = $3.00 per cubic foot

It's no surprise that the 14-cubic-foot deal turns out to be the most economical. eBay sellers such as BubbleFAST sell packing peanuts for almost *half* what they cost when purchased from a brick-and-mortar retailer. (That's because a store you can walk into has to use up square footage to store these babies, which means a higher cost.)

TIP

Here, in a nutshell (sorry, I couldn't resist), is my solution to peanut storage: Fill a drawstring-type trash bag with packing peanuts, and then tie the drawstring. Screw some cup hooks into the rafters of your garage and hang the bags from the rafters. You can store a bunch of peanuts there! *Be sure to recycle!*

» **Packing tape:** You need a stock of clear packing tape. The common size for a roll is 2 inches wide by 110 feet long. Shipping tape comes in two thicknesses, 1.6 mil and 2 mil; the heavier tape makes a better seal in larger packages and costs pennies more. I searched eBay and found these deals on 2-mil tape, and the following prices *include* shipping:

    6 rolls = $14.98 = $ 2.50 per roll

    12 rolls = $21.45 = $ 1.79 per roll

    18 rolls = $26.45 = $1.47 per roll

Again, compare prices before buying.

» **Boxes:** I won't take you through the various costs of boxes because *hundreds* of sizes are available. Shop eBay (but often the shipping prices are too high), and also check out www.uline.com for boxes at reasonable prices. For the example, let's just say a typical box will cost $.55 each.

» **G&A (general and administrative) costs:** For the uninitiated (translation: you never had to do budgets at a large corporation), G&A represents the costs incurred in running a company. But the principle is familiar: Time is money. For example, the time it takes you to research the costs of mailers, tapes, and boxes on eBay is costing you money. The time it takes you to drive to the post office costs you money. You won't actually put a figure on this just now, but it's something you need to think about — especially if you spend half an hour at the post office every other day. In effect, that's time wasted. You could be finding new sources of merchandise instead.

» **Online postage service:** If you're paying around $10 a month for the convenience of buying at a discount and printing online postage, that's an expense too. If you ship 100 packages a month, that amortizes to $.10 per package.

REMEMBER

If you're questioning whether you need an online postage service, here's my two cents: Being able to hand your packages to the postal carrier beats standing in line at the post office, and having records of all your shipments on your own computer is worth the monthly fee.

Table 1-3 shows you the cost for mailing a tiny padded envelope cushioned with packing peanuts. Before you even put postage on the package, you could possibly be spending $.52 — not including your time or postage.

TABLE 1-3

Sample Shipping Costs

Item	Estimated Cost per Shipment ($)
Padded mailer	0.29
Peanuts	0.07
Tape	0.02
Mailing label	0.04
Postage service	0.10
Total	0.52

If you're shipping many packages a month, read Book 9, which tells you how to use QuickBooks to easily and simply track your shipping costs.

Chapter **2**

Understanding the Finer Points of Selling

E commerce has made a turnaround. Auctions are in a rut. And as the brick-and-mortar businesses opened online web stores, shoppers looked for more traditional transactions. Customers wanted to just "buy" products.

In the last three months of 2016, only 13 percent of gross merchandise sales come from auctions. This is not to say that auctions are not popular; many high-dollar profits are made from auctioning unique, rare, and high-demand items. Understanding how eBay sales work is important to anyone who wants to sell on the site.

You can buy the "inside secrets" of eBay from lots of places; ebooks and webinars abound these days. Some of these authors and instructors try to convince you that only *they* have the surreptitious bits of knowledge — gleaned from years (months?) of experience on the site — that reveal what's really going on.

Sure, you hear mysterious rumors of the way to sure-fire profits (cue up *The X-Files* theme in the background). Start an auction at a certain day and time, run a fixed-price listing a certain amount of days, and you'll automatically make more money? Puh-leez! The only one who rakes in profits with that information is the guy who's selling it to you! In addition to reflecting market deviations, eBay changes its search metrics continually — so there is no hard-and-fast answer for securing high profits.

TIP

Before deciding to hire an eBay mentor or pay for a program, ask for the mentor's or instructor's eBay User ID. By taking a look at the type(s) of items the person sells (are they varied?), the frequency of sales, feedback, and where that seller's items show up in a Best Match search, you'll get a good idea of how successful the seller really is.

I've interviewed many eBay high-volume sellers (*PowerSellers*) including the most elite, those who have attained Top Seller status. Almost all agree that eBay theories are bunk; you've got to watch the site and follow its change announcements. However, the sellers do have some practical preferences for when and how they conduct their eBay business. This chapter gets to the gist of these preferences — and the corresponding best practices.

Auction Selling Strategies

The basic plan for running an auction is the same for everyone, except for decisions regarding the timing of the auction and the starting price. If you speak to 20 eBay sellers, you'll probably get 20 different answers about effective starting bids and when to end your auction. The big answer is "it depends" — it depends on your category, your seller status, how you describe your item, and even your photos. Until you develop your own philosophy based on a success ratio, I'd like to give you the tools to make a sound decision. What works for one seller may not work as well (or at all) for another.

You can also successfully promote your eBay sales online and offline, and you can legally offer your item to the next highest bidder if an auction winner doesn't come through with payment — or even if you have more than one of the item in stock. I discuss a few of these practices in this section.

REMEMBER

The ideas in this chapter come from my own experience and discussions with current eBay PowerSellers. These ideas are merely suggestions of methods and starting points that work for others. You definitely need to test them out to find out which practices work — for you and for the types of items you sell.

Starting the auction bidding

The most generally accepted theory about starting bids is that setting the bidding too high scares away new bids. But again, the variable is based on how much the item is worth or even how much it costs.

TIP

Some sellers begin the bidding at the price they paid for the item, including known eBay and PayPal fees, thereby protecting their investment. This is a good tactic, especially if you bought the item at a price far below the current going rate on eBay.

To determine the current going value for your item, I recommend searching for the item through the sold listings, which I explain in Book 2, Chapter 1. If you know that the item is selling on eBay for a certain price and that there is a demand for it, starting the bidding at a reasonably low level can be a great way to increase bidding and attract prospective bidders to view your auction.

REMEMBER

Years of advertising experience can't be wrong. If your item is in demand and people are actively buying, start the bidding low. Retail stores have done this for years with ads that feature prices starting at $9.99 or $14.98.

When sellers know that they have an item that will sell, they often begin their bidding as low as 99 cents. Because of the eBay *proxy bidding system* (which maintains your highest bid as a secret, increasing it incrementally when you're bid against), it takes *more* bids (due to the smaller bidding increments) to bring the item up to the final selling price.

The downside is that new bidders who aren't familiar with the system may bid only the minimum required increment each time they bid. This can be frustrating, and they may quit bidding because it might take them several bids to top the current bid placed by someone who is familiar with the proxy bid system. eBay offers up a tip when the bidder places a bid that doesn't meet the current bid in the system, as shown in Figure 2-1.

FIGURE 2-1:
After bidding, eBay suggested placing a bid of $55.01 or more.

Very few of us remember the proxy increments by heart, so as a refresher, I give you the goods in Table 2-1.

Auction Proxy Bidding Increments

Current High Bid ($)	Bid Increment ($)
0.01–0.99	0.05
1.00–4.99	0.25
5.00–24.99	0.50
25.00–99.99	1.00
100.00–249.99	2.50
250.00–499.99	5.00
500.00–999.99	10.00
1,000.00–2,499.99	25.00
2,500.00–4,999.99	50.00
5,000.00 and up	100.00

Auction length

Another debatable philosophy is auction timing. People are always asking me how long to run auctions and what's the best day to end an auction. You have to evaluate your item and decide which of the following is the best plan:

>> **One-day auction:** Did you just get in a load of an item that sells as fast as you post it on the site? A Buy It Now feature on any auction can bring great results, but that will work only if the item is super-hot!

If people are aggressively bidding up an item — and they really gotta have it — you may do best by starting the bidding low and listing the item with a one-day format.

The best way to use a one-day listing is if your item is time-sensitive, for example, event tickets, airline tickets, vacation packages, or tee times. A one-day listing gives you the immediacy — and the time to ship a physical ticket — if necessary.

Short-term auctions (1-to-3-day) incur an additional "Special Duration" $1 fee.

REMEMBER

When you list in a one-day format, your listing goes right to the top of the *Time: Ending Soonest* sort. Many savvy shoppers view their searches by Listings Ending First (rather than the eBay default of Best Match). With a one-day format, you can pretty much choose the time of day your item will be at the top.

This format can also be successful if you have an item that's the current hot ticket in pop culture. I used this format when I sold some *Friends* TV-show memorabilia a while back. The 24-hour auction opened at midday before the final episode of the show — and ended the next day — at a healthy profit!

REMEMBER

Buy It Now pricing must be at least 30 percent over your listing's starting price.

>> **Three-day auction:** If the item's price will shoot up right after you post it, a three-day auction works just fine. And it's great for those last-minute holiday shoppers looking for hard-to-find items.

A three-day auction is good, for the same reasons that a one-day auction is good — only it's better for the faint of heart and nervous Nellies (like me) because it gives your item more time on the site — more of a chance to sell.

TIP

With the Buy It Now feature, you can pretty much accomplish the same thing as you would with a short-term auction. When you list your item for sale, set a price at which you're willing to sell the item immediately; this is your Buy It Now price.

>> **Five-day auction:** A five-day auction gives you two days more than a three-day auction and two days less than a seven-day auction. That's about the size of it. If you just want an extended weekend auction or your item is a hot one, use it. Five-day auctions are useful during holiday rushes, when gift-buying is the main reason for bidding.

>> **Seven-day auction:** Tried-and-true advertising theory says that the longer you advertise your item, the more people will see it. On eBay, this means that you have more opportunities for people to bid on it. The seven-day auction is a staple for the bulk of eBay vendors. Seven days is long enough to cover weekend browsers and short enough to keep the auction interesting.

>> **Ten-day auction:** Many veteran eBay sellers swear by the ten-day auction. The extra three days of exposure (it can encompass two weekends) can easily net you extra profits.

TIP

A ten-day auction is good for special collectibles or an expensive item that isn't normally on the site. Putting up a ten-day auction (start Friday night so you get exposure over two weekends) is a near-perfect way to attract bidders.

REMEMBER

Your auction closes exactly one, three, five, seven, or ten days — *to the minute* — after you start the auction. Try not to begin your auctions when you're up late at night and can't sleep: You don't want your auction to end at two in the morning when no one else is awake to bid on it.

The specific day you close your auction can also be important. eBay is full of weekend browsers, so including a weekend of browsing in your auction time is a definite plus. Often auctions that end late Sunday evening through Monday close with high bids.

You'll need to do some research to determine the best times to run your auctions and for how long. The best person to figure out the closing information for your auctions is you. Use the tools and, over time, you'll work out a pattern that works best for you.

Figuring out What Day to End an Auction

Back when eBay counted its listings by the hundreds (and then low thousands), it clearly made a difference what day of the week you chose to end an auction. That is, when the number of buyers and sellers on eBay was relatively small, matching your auction time with the bidders' online habits was important. Now that eBay spawns millions of listings a day — with countless buyers and lookie-loos visiting the site — you find the eBay shoppers looking for bargains at virtually all hours of the day and night. So for a traditional auction, you can choose almost any ending time and know that you'll still have some healthy bidding action.

TIP

The wildcards in the mix are the Buy It Now and fixed-price transactions, which are popular — and successful. Although they don't always follow a daily pattern of sales, they can still follow the preferred auction-ending days you find in this section.

To figure out when to end an auction, you need to know when to start it. Figures 2-2, 2-3, and 2-4 are the top preferred timelines for running a sale on eBay.

Sunday	Monday	Tuesday	Wednesday	Thursday	Friday	Saturday
1	2	3	4	5 8:00 PM PST	6	7
8 8:00 PM PST	9	10	11	12	13	14
15	16	17	18	19	20	21

FIGURE 2-2: A timeline for a three-day auction.

You may notice that all these preferred datelines end on a Sunday. Sunday is the top-ranked ending day for auctions by eBay sellers.

Sunday	Monday	Tuesday	Wednesday	Thursday	Friday	Saturday
				1	2	3
4 8:00 PM PST	5	6	7	8	9	10
11 8:00 PM PST	12	13	14	15	16	17
18	19	20	21	22	23	24

FIGURE 2-3: This is seven days of auction action.

Sunday	Monday	Tuesday	Wednesday	Thursday	Friday	Saturday
	1	2	3	4 8:00 PM PST	5	6
7	8	9	10	11	12	13
14 8:00 PM PST	15	16	17	18	19	20
21	22	23	24	25	26	27

FIGURE 2-4: A full ten days of bidding frenzy (if you're lucky).

I can't list everyone's opinions on the subject — that would probably confuse you anyway — so here are the item-ending days ranked in order from most to least popular:

1. Sunday
2. Monday
3. Thursday
4. Tuesday
5. Wednesday
6. Saturday
7. Friday

TIP

Test out auction-ending days to coordinate these dates with the specific type of items you sell. Some buyers (say, men who buy golf goods during lunch hour and women who buy collectibles while their husbands are out golfing on weekends) can throw these days a curve.

Knowing What Time to Start Your Auction

The only way to figure out when to end your auction is by planning when to start it. An auction beginning at 12:00 will end at that same time on the ending day.

eBay time is military time in the Pacific time zone. Table 2-2 converts the eBay clock to real time for your time zone. Make a photocopy of this table and keep it by your computer. (Even after all these years, it still takes too much time to decipher eBay time without a printed chart.)

If you ever need to check your time zone or want to know exactly what time it is in eBay-land, point your browser to

`http://ofr.ebay.com/ws/eBayISAPI.dll?EbayTime` and you'll see the map pictured in Figure 2-5.

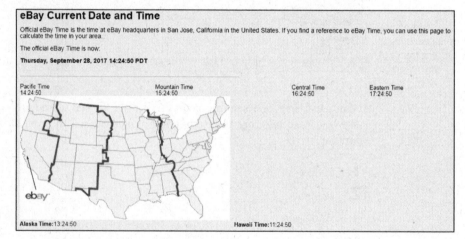

FIGURE 2-5: eBay official time.

Here's the consensus of some experts in order of ending-time preference (in eBay time; check the table for a translation):

1. 18:00 to 22:00

2. 21:00 to 0:00

3. 15:00 to 18:00

4. 13:00 to 16:00

TABLE 2-2

eBay Time versus Continental U.S. Time

eBay Time	Pacific	Mountain	Central	Eastern
0:00	12:00 a.m.	1:00 a.m.	2:00 a.m.	3:00 a.m.
1:00	1:00 a.m.	2:00 a.m.	3:00 a.m.	4:00 a.m.
2:00	2:00 a.m.	3:00 a.m.	4:00 a.m.	5:00 a.m.
3:00	3:00 a.m.	4:00 a.m.	5:00 a.m.	6:00 a.m.
4:00	4:00 a.m.	5:00 a.m.	6:00 a.m.	7:00 a.m.
5:00	5:00 a.m.	6:00 a.m.	7:00 a.m.	8:00 a.m.
6:00	6:00 a.m.	7:00 a.m.	8:00 a.m.	9:00 a.m.
7:00	7:00 a.m.	8:00 a.m.	9:00 a.m.	10:00 a.m.
8:00	8:00 a.m.	9:00 a.m.	10:00 a.m.	11:00 a.m.
9:00	9:00 a.m.	10:00 a.m.	11:00 a.m.	12:00 p.m.
10:00	10:00 a.m.	11:00 a.m.	12:00 p.m.	1:00 p.m.
11:00	11:00 a.m.	12:00 p.m.	1:00 p.m.	2:00 p.m.
12:00	12:00 p.m.	1:00 p.m.	2:00 p.m.	3:00 p.m.
13:00	1:00 p.m.	2:00 p.m.	3:00 p.m.	4:00 p.m.
14:00	2:00 p.m.	3:00 p.m.	4:00 p.m.	5:00 p.m.
15:00	3:00 p.m.	4:00 p.m.	5:00 p.m.	6:00 p.m.
16:00	4:00 p.m.	5:00 p.m.	6:00 p.m.	7:00 p.m.
17:00	5:00 p.m.	6:00 p.m.	7:00 p.m.	8:00 p.m.
18:00	6:00 p.m.	7:00 p.m.	8:00 p.m.	9:00 p.m.
19:00	7:00 p.m.	8:00 p.m.	9:00 p.m.	10:00 p.m.
20:00	8:00 p.m.	9:00 p.m.	10:00 p.m.	11:00 p.m.
21:00	9:00 p.m.	10:00 p.m.	11:00 p.m.	12:00 a.m.
22:00	10:00 p.m.	11:00 p.m.	12:00 a.m.	1:00 a.m.
23:00	11:00 p.m.	12:00 a.m.	1:00 a.m.	2:00 a.m.

Here are the worst eBay times to end an auction:

1. 2:00 to 6:00

2. 0:00 to 3:00

This information should give you some good ideas for your own auction sales.

Selling Items through Fixed-Price Sales

Because ecommerce has morphed and consumer preferences have changed, you need to consider a more balanced approach to your sales. Only after trial and error will you know how your specific products sell best — and what combination of listings will help you hit that sweet spot. In the recent era of ecommerce, folks like to come to a site to buy items outright at a given price as well as participate in auctions.

eBay Stores are a great way to offer fixed-price items, but even without a store, you can list fixed-price items on the regular eBay site. (Find out more about the costs of running an eBay Store in Book 8.)

Fixed-price listings have a slightly different pricing structure on the site. You are given a certain amount of insertion-fee-free listings on the site each month.

>> **No eBay Store:** Sellers without an eBay Store get up to 50 free auction or fixed-price listings.

>> **Basic Store sellers:** Up to 250 free listings a month.

>> **Premium Store sellers:** Up to 1,000 free listings a month.

>> **Anchor Store sellers:** Up to 10,000 free listings a month.

After you've used your initial free listings, any fixed-price listing — regardless of starting price or number of items for sale — costs up to 30 cents. This is for a 1-, 3-, 5-, 7-, 10-, or 30-day listing, or a Good Till Cancelled listing. Great news, eh?

Sounds great, huh? Well, there's a catch. (You knew there'd be a catch, didn't you?) You've got Final Value Fees to consider. Chapter 1 (in this minibook) charts them all; Book 8, Chapter 4 provides further insights.

Making Money in Other eBay Zones

There's more to eBay than just the auction site. Don't lose a selling opportunity by not checking into the other viable areas described in this section.

Automotive? Go eBay Motors

Anything and everything automotive can go in the eBay Motors category (see Figure 2-6), and it will sell like giant tires at a monster truck rally. Following are just a few of the car-related items that fit in this category.

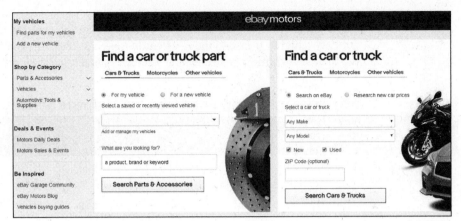

FIGURE 2-6:
The eBay Motors home page.

Car parts

Got used car parts? eBay has an enormous market in used car parts. One seller I know goes to police impound sales and buys wrecks — just to get some valuable parts that he can resell on eBay.

New car parts are in demand, too. If your local auto-parts store is blasting out door handles for a 1967 Corvette (a vehicle for which it's hard to find parts), it wouldn't hurt to pick up a few to resell on Motors. Sooner or later, someone's bound to search eBay looking for them. If you're lucky enough to catch the trend, you'll make a healthy profit.

Cars

Yes, you can sell cars on eBay. In fact, used-car sales have skyrocketed online thanks to all the people who find eBay to be a trusted place to buy and sell used vehicles. The most expensive vehicle ever sold on eBay was a 1959 Ferrari 250 GT California; it sold for $3,260,100. Sold via the mobile app was a Mercedes SLR McLaren for $240,001. (I told you those odd amount bids can make a difference.)

Selling vehicles on eBay is a natural business for you if you have access to good used cars, work as a mechanic, or have a contact at a dealership that lets you sell cars on eBay for a commission or on a consignment basis. (For the ins and outs of consignment selling, check out Book 4, Chapter 3.)

To complete your sale, eBay Motors features Vehicle Purchase Protection that covers up to $50,000, vehicle history reports, vehicle inspection and escrow services, and one-click access to vehicle shipping quotes from uShip. Access eBay Motors and its services from the eBay home page or by going directly to www.ebay.com/motors.

Different fees apply when you sell a vehicle on eBay Motors nationally. To encourage sellers to list and sell vehicles on the site, eBay has set up a tiered system of fees.

The first six vehicles you list in a 12-month period are charged no insertion fees, but have a higher transaction fee when the sale is successful. The fees are based on the final selling price. Take a look at Tables 2-3 and 2-4 for significant differences.

TABLE 2-3   ## National Insertion Fees for Low-Volume Sellers

Category	Insertion Fee	Sale of up to $2,000	Sale over $2,000
Cars & Trucks, RVs & Campers, and Commercial Trucks	Free	$60	$125
Motorcycles, Powersports, Trailers, and Boats	Free	$60	$125
Powersports under 50cc	Free	$10	$10
All other vehicles	Free	$60	$125

TABLE 2-4   ## National Insertion Fees for High-Volume Sellers

Category	Insertion Fee	Sale of up to $5,000	Sale over $5,000
Cars & Trucks, RVs & Campers, and Commercial Trucks	$50	Free	Free
Motorcycles, Powersports, Trailers, and Boats	$20	$30	$60
Powersports under 50cc	$10	$10	$10
All other vehicles	$20	$30	$60

Although many people who have found the vehicle of their dreams on eBay are more than happy to take a one-way flight to the vehicle location and drive it home, shipping a vehicle is a reasonably priced alternative. On your listing, eBay can supply a link to give you a quick estimate of shipping fees to the buyer's Zip code. Figure 2-7 shows the estimates I got to ship a car from Indianapolis, Indiana to Northridge, California.

Here are just a few things to keep in mind if you plan to sell cars on eBay:

>> To sell a vehicle on eBay Motors, you must enter the Vehicle Identification Number (VIN) on the Sell an Item page. This way, prospective buyers can access a vehicle history report to get an idea of the condition of the car.

>> An item that you've listed on eBay Motors will appear in any search, whether a potential buyer conducts a regular eBay search or a search in eBay Motors.

REMEMBER

FIGURE 2-7:
Quick shipping
estimates in
eBay Motors.

TIP

>> If your reserve isn't met in an eBay Motors auction, you may still offer the vehicle to the high bidder through the Best Offer option. You may also reduce your reserve during the auction if you feel you've set your target price too high.

Real estate: Not always an auction

eBay Real Estate at www.ebay.com/realestate isn't always an auction. Because of the wide variety of laws governing the sale of real estate, eBay auctions of real property are *not* legally binding offers to buy and sell. However, putting your real estate on eBay (see Figure 2-8) is an excellent way to advertise and attract potential buyers. When the auction ends, neither party is obligated (as they are in other eBay auctions) to complete the real estate transaction. The buyer and seller must get together to consummate the deal.

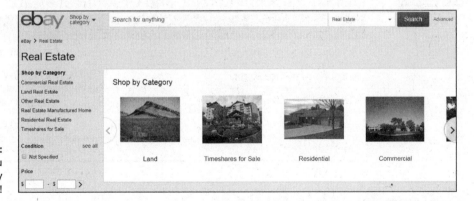

FIGURE 2-8:
Search and you
can even buy
gold mines!

Nonetheless, eBay real estate sales are popular and the sales are growing by leaps and bounds. You don't have to be a professional real estate agent to use this category, although it may help when it comes to closing the deal. If you know land and your local real estate laws, eBay gives you the perfect venue for subdividing those 160 acres in Wyoming that Uncle Regis left you in his will.

Understanding the Finer Points of Selling

For less than the cost of a newspaper ad, you can sell your home, condo, land, or even timeshare on eBay Real Estate in the auction format. You can also choose to list your property in an ad format, accepting not bids but *inquiries* from prospective buyers from around the world. On the Sell an Item form, you must specify special information about your piece of real estate.

In Tables 2-5 and 2-6, I provide a listing of fees that you can expect to encounter on eBay Real Estate. *Note:* When your listing sells in the Land, Manufactured Home, and Timeshares for Sale categories, you're charged a Notice Fee of $35.00.

TABLE 2-5

Timeshare, Land, and Manufactured Homes

Type of Fee	Fee Amount
Auction/Fixed Price listing for 1-, 3-, 5-, 7-, or 10-day listing	$35.00
Auction/Fixed Price 30-day	$50.00
Classified Ad 30 days	$150.00
Classified Ad 90 days	$300.00
Final value (Notice) fee	$35.00
Reserve fee (refunded when property sells)	$0.01 to $74.99: $3.00; $75.00 and up: 4% of reserve price (up to $100.00)

TABLE 2-6

Residential, Commercial, and Other Real Estate

Type of Fee	Fee Amount ($)
Auction/Fixed Price listing for 1-, 3-, 5-, 7-, or 10-day auction.	$100.00
Auction/Fixed Price 30-day	$150.00
Classified Ad 30 days	$150.00
Classified Ad 90 days	$300.00
Final Value (Notice) Fee	0

Selling by the Rules

There are a lot of *shoulds* in this world. You *should* do this and you *should* do that. I don't know who is in charge of the *shoulds*, but certain things just make life work better. If you follow the advice on these pages, your eBay business will thrive with a minimum of anguish. If you've ever had a listing pulled by eBay, you know that anguish firsthand and don't want to have it again.

In the real world, we have to take responsibility for our own actions. If we buy a flat-screen TV set (in the box) for $25 from some guy selling them out of the back of a truck, who do we have to blame when we take it home and the box is full of cardboard? You get what you pay for, and you have no consumer protection from a seller of possibly "hot" (or nonexistent) TVs. Responsible consumerism is every buyer's job. Lawsuit upon lawsuit gets filed — and some are won — when buyers feel they've been ripped off, but my best advice is that if you stay clean in your online business, you'll keep clean.

eBay is a community, and the community thrives on the five basic values listed here:

>> We believe people are basically good.

>> We believe everyone has something to contribute.

>> We believe that an honest, open environment can bring out the best in people.

>> We recognize and respect everyone as a unique individual.

>> We encourage you to treat others the way that you want to be treated.

eBay is committed to these values, and it says so right on its website. eBay believes that community members should "honor these values — whether buying, selling, or chatting." So *should* we all.

Is what you want to sell legal?

Although eBay is based in California and therefore must abide by California law, sellers do business all over the United States. Therefore, items sold at eBay must be governed by the laws of every other state as well. As a seller, you're ultimately responsible for both the legality of the items you sell *and* the way that you transact business on eBay. Yes, you can sell thousands of different items on eBay. But do you know what you *aren't* allowed to sell?

REMEMBER

The eBay User Agreement outlines the rules and regulations regarding what you can and can't sell, as well as all aspects of doing business on eBay. If you haven't read it in a while, do so. You can find it at the following address:

`http://pages.ebay.com/help/policies/user-agreement.html`

eBay's policies can change from time to time. As an active seller, you should make sure that you're notified of any changes. You'll be notified when eBay makes changes to the User Agreement, through your eBay Message Center.

By now, you should have a firm grasp of the rules and regulations for listing items. But in addition to knowing the rules for listing items, you must consider the items themselves. In this section, I detail the three categories of items to be wary of: prohibited, questionable, and potentially infringing. Some are banned, period. Others fall in a gray area. You're responsible for what you sell, so you'd better know what's legal and what's not.

If you're found in violation of eBay's listing restrictions, you may be penalized in a variety of ways, including

>> Listing cancellation

>> Limits on account privileges

>> Account suspension

>> Forfeit of eBay fees on cancelled listings

>> Loss of PowerSeller status

Prohibited and restricted items

A prohibited item is banned from sale at eBay. You can't sell a prohibited item under any circumstances. Take a look at the upcoming list. A little common sense tells you there's good reason for not selling these items, including liability issues for the seller. (For example, what if you sold alcohol to a minor? That's against the law!)

Restricted items involve more shades of gray. They may involve the sale of dangerous or sensitive items that may not be prohibited by law. eBay sets these limitations as a result of input by members of the eBay Community and others. eBay has a strong Offensive Material Policy which covers items of merchandise that "promote or glorify hatred, violence, racial or religious intolerance, or items that promote organizations with such views." As you can imagine, this is a slippery slope for some sellers.

The following is just a partial list; the current complete list can be found at `http://pages.ebay.com/help/policies/items-ov.html`

    Adult Material

    Alcohol*

Animals and wildlife products

Art

Artifacts, grave-related items, and Native American arts and crafts

Counterfeit currency or stamps

Counterfeit items

Credit cards

Drugs and drug paraphernalia

Embargoed goods from prohibited countries

Firearms, ammunition, replicas, and militaria

Government IDs and licenses

Human remains and body parts

Lockpicking devices

Lottery tickets

Mailing lists and personal information

Medical devices

Multilevel marketing

Postage meters

Prescription drugs

Recalled items

Satellite and cable TV descramblers

Stocks and other securities**

Stolen property

Surveillance equipment

Tobacco

Travel***

USDA-prohibited plants and seeds

*No alcoholic beverages can be sold on the eBay U.S. website, except for pre-approved sales of wine.

**Old or collectible stock certificates may be sold, provided that they're canceled or are from a company that no longer exists.

***All sellers wanting to rent out their own lodging must first register with eBay Travel verification.

Check the following address for updates:

http://pages.ebay.com/help/sell/questions/prohibited-items.html

Questionable items

Determining whether you can sell a *questionable item* is tricky. Under certain circumstances, you may be able to list the item for sale at eBay. To fully understand when and if you can list a questionable item, visit the links that I highlight in Table 2-7.

Potentially infringing items

Potentially infringing items follow a slippery slope. If you list a *potentially infringing item,* you may infringe on existing copyrights, trademarks, registrations, or the like. Get the idea? These items are prohibited for your own protection.

Items falling under the "potentially infringing" category are generally copyrighted or trademarked items, such as software, promotional items, and games. Even using a brand name in your auction as part of a description (known as *keyword spamming*) may get you into trouble.

WARNING

Repeating various un-trademarked keywords can get you in trouble as well. eBay permits the use of as many as five synonyms when listing an item for sale. A permissible example of this might be: purse, handbag, pocketbook, satchel, and bag. Adding many un-trademarked keywords would cause the auction to come up in more searches.

TABLE 2-7

Partial List of Questionable Items and Where to Find the Rules Regulating Them

Can I Sell This?	Go Here to Find Out*
Alcohol	/alcohol.html
Art	selling-art.html
Artifacts	/artifacts.html
Autographed Items	/autographs.html
Batteries	/hazardous-materials.html
Contracts and tickets	/contracts.html
Electronics equipment	/electronics.html
Event tickets	/event-tickets.html
Food	/food.html
Freon and other refrigerants	/hazardous-materials.html
Hazardous materials	/hazardous-materials.html
Human parts and remains	/remains.html
International trading — sellers	/international-trading.html
Mature audiences	/mature-audiences.html
Offensive material	/offensive.html
Pesticides	/pesticides.html
Police-related items	/police.html
Presale listings	/pre-sale.html
Recalled Items	/recalled.html
Stamps	/selling-stamps.html
Stocks and other securities	/stocks.html
Slot machines	/slot-machines.html
Used clothing	/used-clothing.html
Used medical devices	/medical-devices.html
Weapons and knives	/firearms-weapons-knives.html

*All URLs begin with http://pages.ebay.com/help/policies.

Understanding the
Finer Points of Selling

THE CHANEL-STYLE PURSE

In the early days on the site, I listed a quilted leather women's purse that had a gold chain strap, which I described as a Chanel-style purse. Within two hours, I received an informational alert from the eBay listing police. I described the item to the best of my ability, but found that it became a potentially infringing item. My use of the brand name *Chanel* caused my auction to come under the violation of keyword spamming.

In its informational alert, eBay described my violation:

> "Keyword spamming is the practice of adding words, including brand names, which do not directly describe the item you are selling. The addition of these words may not have been intentional, but including them in this manner diverts members to your listing inappropriately."

Ooops! You can see how my ingenuous listing was actually a violation of policy. Think twice before you add brand names to your auction description. Thankfully, the eBay police judge each violation on a case-by-case basis. Because my record is clear, I merely got a reprimand. Had my violation been more deliberate, I might have been suspended.

Knowing eBay's Listing Policies

eBay itself does not sell merchandise. eBay is merely a venue that provides the location where *others* can put on a giant ecommerce party (in other words, *sell stuff*). To provide a safe and profitable venue for its sellers, eBay must govern auctions that take place on its site. eBay makes the rules; you and I follow the rules. I like to think of eBay as the place that lets you hold your senior prom in its gym. When I was in school, my classmates and I had to follow the rules or see our prom cancelled. If we don't agree to follow eBay's rules, a safe and trusted eBay community can't exist.

WHEN ALCOHOL WAS A COLLECTIBLE

Many people collect rare and antique bottles of liquor or wine. I even sold a bottle of Korbel champagne (whose bottle artwork was designed by Frank Sinatra) on eBay in 1998. Korbel bottles have featured artwork by designer Nicole Miller and comedienne Whoopi Goldberg, as well as designs by Tony Bennett, Frank Sinatra, and Jane Seymour.

People also collect Jim Beam bottles, Dug decanters, and miniatures that are even more valuable when they're full. You *can* sell these on eBay as long as you show in the photograph that they are empty.

eBay has some hard-and-fast rules about listing your items. One rule is that you must list your item in the appropriate category (that only makes sense). In this section, I highlight a few other rules that you should keep in mind when listing. What I discuss isn't a definitive list of eBay listing policies and rules. Take time to familiarize yourself with the User Agreement (which details all eBay policies and rules) at the following address:

```
http://pages.ebay.com/help/policies/user-agreement.html
```

I recommend that you check the eBay User Agreement regularly for any policy changes.

Duplicate listings

Remember the old supply-and-demand theory from your economics class? When people list the same items repeatedly, they drive down the item's going price while ruining all the other sellers' opportunities to sell the item during that time frame.

eBay allows you to list as many identical auctions as you want, but only one without bids will show on eBay at a time. And you may not have more than one listing of a fixed-price item. Sellers who want to "game" the system in this way, by listing a huge number of the same item, need to think twice.

REMEMBER

eBay policy states that the display of multiple identical items from the same seller will be *limited to only one at a time without bids* in search results. So what's the point? If you're going to list an item that many times, at the very least be sure to list it in different categories. That's a rule, but it also makes sense. Nothing drives down the price of an item faster than closing identical auctions, one after another, in the same category. eBay also requires that you list your item in a category that's relevant to it.

State it up front: Drop-shipping and product-sourcing listings

In many situations, being the first seller to put a popular item up for sale can get you some high bids. And if you can guarantee in your auction description that the item will be available to ship within 30 days of the purchase or the auction closing, you can sell items from a product sourcer or drop-shipper. However, if you're not completely sure that you'll have the item in time, I don't recommend that you even attempt such a listing.

PRE-SELLING: RARELY WORTH THE HASSLE

A seller I once knew presold Beanie Babies on eBay. She had a regular source that supplied her when the new toys came out, so she fell into a complacent attitude about listing presales. Then her supplier didn't get the shipment. Motivated by the need to protect her feedback rating (and by the fear that she'd be accused of fraud), she ran all over town desperately trying to get the Beanies she needed to fill her orders. The Beanies were so rare that she ended up spending several hundred dollars more than what she had originally sold the toys for, just to keep her customers happy.

TIP

Before you set up such listings (for presale or drop-shipping), check out the Federal Trade Commission 30-day rule covering these matters, which you can find at the following address:

```
www.ftc.gov/tips-advice/business-center/guidance/
selling-internet-prompt-delivery-rules
```

Ix-nay on bonuses, giveaways, raffles, or prizes

Because eBay sells to every state in the United States, it must follow explicit laws governing giveaways and prizes. Each state has its own set of rules and regulations, so eBay doesn't allow individual sellers to come up with their own promotions.

If your auction violates this rule, eBay might end your listing.

Search and browse manipulation by keyword spamming

Keyword spamming happens when you add words, usually brand names, to your auction description that don't describe what you're selling (for example, describing that little black dress as Givenchy-style when Givenchy has nothing to do with it). Keyword spamming manipulates the eBay search engine by including an unrelated item in the listing for a copyrighted or trademarked item, and then diverting bidders to an auction of other merchandise. Sellers use keyword spamming to pull viewers to their auctions after viewers have searched for the brand name. To attract attention to their listings, some sellers use *not* or *like* along with the brand name, such as *like Givenchy*.

Here are the problems with keyword spamming:

>> It's a listing violation and causes your auction to fall under potentially infringing items for sale on eBay. The wording you choose when you run this kind of auction manipulates the eBay search engine and prospective bidders.

>> It's frustrating to the potential buyers trying to use the search engine to find a particular item, and it's unfair to other eBay sellers who've properly listed their items.

Keyword spamming can take many forms. Some merely mislead the prospective bidder; others are infringements on legal rights. A few of the most common are

>> Superfluous brand names in the title or item description

>> Using something like "not brand X" in the title or item description

>> Improper trademark usage

>> Lists of keywords

>> Hidden text

TIP

This violation is often white text on a white background or hidden text in HTML code. The white text resides in the auction HTML, so it shows up in the search but is not visible to the naked eye. Sneaky, eh? And prohibited.

>> Drop-down lists

To get the latest on eBay's keyword spamming policy, go to

```
http://pages.ebay.com/help/policies/search-manipulation.html
```

Limited linking from your listings

Few issues set sellers to arguing more than eBay's rules on linking. In your auction item description, you *can* use the following links:

>> One link to an additional page that gives further information about the item you're selling, such as product videos, freight shipping services, and other legally required information.

>> A link that sends a member to eBay messages so that the buyer can send you an email.

TIP

THE eBay VERIFIED RIGHTS OWNER PROGRAM

eBay can't possibly check every auction for authenticity. But to help protect trade-marked items, it formed the Verified Rights Owner (VeRO) program.

Trademark and copyright owners expend large amounts of energy to develop and maintain control over the quality of their products. If you buy a "designer" purse from a guy on the street for $20, it's probably counterfeit, so don't go selling it on eBay.

eBay works with VeRO program participants to educate the community about such items. They work also with verified owners of trademarks and copyrights to remove auctions that infringe on their products. If eBay doesn't close a suspicious or blatantly infringing auction, then both you and eBay are liable for the violation.

To participate in the VeRO program, the owners of copyrights and trademarks must supply eBay with proof of ownership. To view the VeRO program information, go to

```
http://pages.ebay.com/seller-center/listing/create-effective-
listings/vero-program.html
```

To report a violation of something you have legal rights to, download this form on eBay:

```
http://pics.ebay.com/aw/pics/pdf/us/help/community/NOCI1.pdf
```

Note: eBay cooperates with law enforcement and may give your name and street address to a VeRO program member.

>> Links to your other listings on eBay.

>> One link to your Profile page, besides the link next to your User ID that eBay provides.

Here's where you can get the official (ever changing) word from eBay:

```
http://pages.ebay.com/help/policies/listing-links.html
```

Chapter **3**

Listing Items for Sale

A re you ready to make some money? Yes? (Call it an inspired guess.) Are you on the threshold of adding your items to the hundreds of thousands that go up for auction (or fixed-price sale) on eBay every day? Some items are so hot that the sellers quadruple their investments. Other items, unfortunately, are so stone-cold that they may not even register a single bid.

In this chapter, I explain all the facets of listing an item to get your merchandise posted on the site for sale. You get some advice that can increase your odds of making money, and you find out the best way to position your item so buyers can see it, bid on it, or buy it outright. I also show you how to modify, relist, and end your listing. These steps are required whether you are listing from a mobile device or from a computer.

Getting Ready to List Your Item

After you decide what you want to sell, find out as much as you can about it and conduct a little market research. Then you should have a good idea of the item's popularity and value.

Before you list, make sure that you have the following bases covered:

TIP

>> **The specific category under which you want the item listed:** Ask your friends or family where they'd look for such an item — and remember the categories that were most successful when you conducted your market research with the eBay search function. Use the product UPC (or ISBN) number when you search to give you insight as to the best category to use when you list your item.

To find out which category will pay off best for your item, run a search and then select the Sold Listings option. See how many fixed-price listings and auctions of that item are running for your item (and whether people are bidding or buying them). Then click the Sold Listings on the left of your search results. Sort the results by Price and Shipping: Highest First, and then look over the most successful transactions to see which categories they're listed in. For more information on eBay's search, visit Book 2, Chapter 1.

>> **What you want to say in your item title and description:** Jot down your ideas. Take a good look at your item and make a list of keywords that describe your item. *Keywords* are single descriptive words that can include

- Brand names

- Size of the item (citing measurements if appropriate)

- Age or date of manufacture

- Condition

- Rarity

- Color

- Size

- Material (fabric)

- . . . and more

>> **An idea of what picture (or pictures) of your item you want to post at the top and/or put inside your description:** Pictures sell items, but you don't have to use them if you're selling currently available media items (eBay will supply them for you). If you want to know more about using pictures in your auctions, see Book 5.

>> **The price at which you think you can sell the item:** Be as realistic as you can. (That's where the market research comes in.)

The Sell an Item form is where your listing is born. Filling out your paperwork requires a few minutes of clicking, typing, and answering all kinds of questions. The good news is that when you're finished, your sale is up for all to see.

REMEMBER

Before you begin, you have to be registered with eBay as a seller. If you still need to do so, go to Book 1, Chapter 3 and see how to fill out the preliminary cyber-paperwork. If you've registered but haven't provided eBay with your financial information (credit card or checking account), you'll be asked for this information before you proceed to sell. Fill in the data on the secure form. Then you're ready to set up your listing.

Deciding on a Sales Format

Selling an item can be like the dizzying menu in a Chinese restaurant: You have three ways to sell an item on eBay. Three ways may not seem to be very dizzying, unless you're trying to decide just which format is the best for you.

Here's what you need to know about each type:

>> **Online auction:** This is the tried-and-true traditional sale format on eBay. You can combine this auction with the Buy It Now feature, for those who want the item immediately. Often, if you're selling a collectible item, letting it go to auction may net you a much higher profit — remember to do your research before listing.

>> **Fixed-price listing:** A fixed-price sale is easy for the buyer to complete; it's just like shopping at the corner store. The only problem is that many potential buyers may lean toward an auction because of the perception that they *may* get a better deal.

>> **Classified Ad:** If you don't want to put real estate, services, travel, businesses, virtual currency, and more up for auction and you'd like to correspond with the prospective buyers, this is the option for you.

Say, for example, that you want to list a traditional eBay auction. Or perhaps you want to sell your item for a fixed price. In any case, to find eBay's Sell an Item page from the eBay home page, just click Sell in the upper-right navigation bar and select Create listing.

Getting Your Sales Specifics in Order

Yes, the Sell an Item form looks daunting, but filling out its many sections doesn't take as long as you may think. Some of the questions you're asked aren't things you even have to think about; just click an answer and off you go. Other questions

Listing Items for Sale

ask you to type information. Don't sweat a thing; all the answers you need are right here.

When listing your item, here's the info you're asked to fill out (each of these items is discussed in detail later in this chapter):

>> **User ID and password:** If you're not signed in, you need to do so before you list an item for sale.

>> **Category:** The category where you've decided to list your item (required).

>> **Title:** The name of your item (required).

>> **Description:** What you want to tell eBay buyers about your item (required). After you've written a brilliant title for your listing, prospective buyers click and scroll down to your description. Do they have to dodge through pointless verbiage, losing interest along the way? Or do you get right down to business and state the facts about your item?

>> **Adding Pictures:** Decide which images of your item you want to upload to show off your listing. Book 5 has more information on using images in sales.

>> **Quantity:** The number of items you're offering in an auction is always one, but you can run a fixed-price listing with multiple items.

>> **Starting Price:** This would be the Minimum bid for an auction or the sale price for a fixed-price listing.

>> **Duration:** The number of days you want the listing to run (required).

>> **Reserve price:** The hidden target price you set for an auction. This is the price that bidders must meet before you'll sell this item (optional). eBay charges you a fee for this feature.

>> **Private listing:** You can keep the identity of all bidders secret with this option (optional). This option is used only in rare circumstances (such as when you're selling psychic readings and your customers might not want their proclivities made public).

>> **Buy It Now:** You can sell your auction item directly to the first buyer who meets this price (optional).

>> **List item in two categories:** If you want to double your exposure, you can list your item in two categories. Note that double exposure equals double your listing fees (optional). For some items, eBay does not permit a two-category listing.

>> **Boldface title:** A selling option to make your item listing stand out. eBay charges $2 to $4 for this feature (optional).

>> **Ship-to locations:** Here's where you can indicate where you're willing to ship an item. If you don't want to ship out of the United States, check the *Ship to the United States only* option. You can select individual countries as well (optional).

You may want to consider whether you want to be in the international shipping business. If you don't ship internationally, you're blocking possible big spenders. Give it a try when you're ready and see how it works for you.

>> **How you will ship:** Select the options that apply as to how you plan to ship the item.

>> **Shipping charges:** Your listing will get preference in search if you offer free shipping. Consider building that expense into your price.

>> **Immediate payment:** Fill out this area if you want to require the buyer to pay immediately through PayPal (optional).

Since I'm talking here about listing an item for sale, I briefly go over some high points on strategies — but be sure you also check out Chapter 1 to get some serious insight on listing strategies.

Selecting a Category: The How and Why

Many eBay sellers will tell you that selecting the exact category isn't crucial to achieving the highest price for your item — and they're right. The bulk of buyers (who know what they're looking for) just input search keywords into eBay's search box and look for their items. Potential buyers also may select a category and — just as if they were window-shopping in the mall — peruse the items and see whether one strikes their fancy.

For best positioning in search results, be sure to select the appropriate category for your item. If you pick an unrelated category, you run the risk of your listing being removed from the site as a listing violation.

On the first page of the Create a Listing form, you will select the main category for your item. After you select your main category, you land on the official working portion of the Sell an Item page.

With tens of thousands of categories, finding the right place for your item can be daunting. You need to apply some marketing techniques when deciding where to place your auctions. You can list an item in two categories, but you have to pay double for that. Does your budget allow for it?

Consider these ideas and techniques for finding the right category for your item:

TIP

>> **Find out who's currently selling your item (and where):** Check the active listings; are lots of people selling your item? If you see that you're one of 40 or 50 people selling the item, you need to get exacting about where to list yours. Evaluate the item and its potential buyers. In what categories would someone shopping for your item search?

>> **Use appropriate subcategories to catch in-the-know buyers:** Most bidders scan for specific items in subcategories. For example, if you're selling a Bakelite fruit pin, don't just list it under Jewelry; keep narrowing your choices. In this case, you can put it in a costume jewelry category that's especially for Bakelite. I guarantee that the real Bakelite jewelry collectors out there know where to look to find the jewelry they love.

As you start the listing process, eBay gives you a tool to find where the bulk of sellers are selling your item. Simply type three or four keywords (or a UPC or ISBN number in case of media) in the first step's search box and click Search to answer the question: "Tell us what you're selling." If eBay has your item in its catalog, the item's category will be automatically suggested. Figure 3-1 shows you how easy it is to find where your item is being sold.

FIGURE 3-1:
eBay will suggest
the proper
category for
your item.

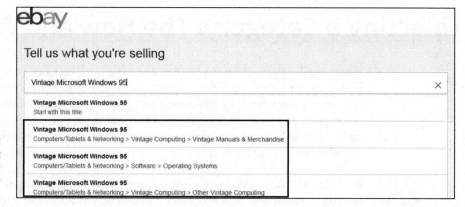

Alternatively, you can select your item's category from this Browse Categories tab for a deeper look. eBay offers you a wealth of choices in a handy point-and-click way. If you're unfamiliar with the types of items you can actually find in those categories, you may want to check out a category before you choose it to describe your item. Figure 3-2 shows you how to use the Browse Categories tool to narrow down subcategory selection.

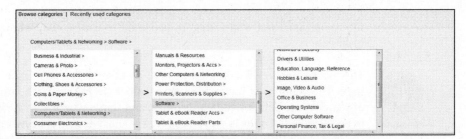

FIGURE 3-2:
Narrowing to subcategories.

To select a category, here's the drill:

1. **Click one of the main categories in the pane on the left.**

On the next pane to the right, you see a list of subcategories.

2. **Select the most appropriate subcategory in the pane to the right.**

eBay makes it easy to narrow the category of your item: Just keep clicking until you hit the end of the line.

3. **Move to the next pane and continue selecting subcategories until you've narrowed your listing category as much as possible.**

You know you've come to the last subcategory when eBay sends you to the listing form.

REMEMBER

If you've chosen to list an item, bid on an item, or even just browse in the Everything Else: Adult Only category, you need to follow separate, specific guidelines because that category contains graphic nudity or sexual content that may offend some community members. You must

>> Be at least 18 years of age (but you already know that all eBay customers must be 18 or older)

>> Have a valid credit card

>> Complete a waiver stating that you're voluntarily choosing to access adults-only materials

Listing Items for Sale

If you have erotic items that are not quite that racy, you might like to sell them in a private auction; see the "I Want to Be Alone: The Private Auction" section, later in this chapter.

Creating the Perfect Item Title

After you figure out what category you want to list in, eBay wants to get down to business.

REMEMBER

The most valuable onscreen real estate on eBay is the 80-character title of your item. The majority of buyers do title searches (in my research, around 98 percent of searches are performed by *title* only), and that's where your item must come up to be seen! So the onus is on you to give the most essential keywords right away to grab the eye of the reader who's just browsing. Be clear and informative enough to get noticed by eBay's search engine.

Here are some ideas to help you write your item title:

>> Use the most common name for the item.

>> If the item is rare or hard to find, mention that.

>> Mention the item's condition and whether it's new.

>> Mention the item's special qualities, such as its style, model, or edition.

>> Avoid jargon or unusual characters, such as $, hyphens, and L@@K (or WOW), because they just clutter up the title — buyers rarely search for them.

Ordinarily, I don't throw out French phrases just for the fun of it. But when making a profit is an issue, I definitely have to agree with the French that choosing or not choosing *le mot juste* can mean the difference between having potential buyers passing by your item and having an all-out bidding war on your hands. Read on for tips about picking *the best words* to let your auction item shine.

Look for a phrase that pays

Here's a crash course in eBay lingo that can help bring you up to speed on attracting buyers to your auction. The following words are used frequently in eBay auctions and can do wonders to jump-start your title:

>> Mint

>> One of a kind (OOAK)

- » Vintage

- » Collectible

- » Rare

- » Unique

- » Primitive

- » Well-loved

There's a science to figuring out the value of a collectible (called *grading*). Do your homework before you assign a grade to your item. If you need more information on what these grades actually mean, Book 2, Chapter 2 provides a translation.

Getting eyes on your listing

Keywords! Keywords! Keywords! I can't stress enough that keywords are essential in your title. *Keywords* are single words that people would naturally use to search for an item. For example, if you're selling a shirt, common keywords for your title might include words that tell

- » Color

- » Size

- » Fabric

- » Manufacturer's name

- » Whether it's a men's, women's, or children's garment

- » Whether it's new or used, such as NWT (New With Tags)

eBay acronyms and initialisms at a glance

The initialisms and the phrases described previously in the section "Look for a phrase that pays" aren't the only marketing standards you have at your eBay disposal. As eBay has grown, so has the lingo that members use as shortcuts to describe their merchandise. Table 3-1 gives you a handy list of common abbreviations and phrases used to describe items. (*Hint:* "Mint" means "may as well be brand new," not "cool chocolate treat attached.")

TABLE 3-1

A Quick List of eBay Abbreviations

eBay	What It Abbreviates	What It Means
MIB	Mint in Box	The item is in the original box, in great shape, and just the way you'd expect to find it in a store.
MIMB	Mint in Mint Box	The box has never been opened and looks like it just left the factory.
MOC	Mint on Card	The item is mounted on its original display card, attached with the original fastenings, in store-new condition.
NRFB	Never Removed from Box	The item has never been opened.
COA	Certificate of Authenticity	Documentation that vouches for the genuineness of an item, such as an autograph or painting.
NOS	New Old Stock	Merchandise is new and unopened, but may have been stocked (or on the shelf) for a while.
OEM	Original Equipment Manufacture	You're selling the item and all the equipment that originally came with it, but you don't have the original box, owner's manual, or instructions.
OOAK	One of a Kind	You are selling the only one in existence!
NR	No Reserve Price	A reserve price is the price you can set when you begin your auction. If bids don't meet the reserve, you don't have to sell. Many buyers don't like reserve prices because they don't think that they can get a bargain. (For tips on how to allay these fears and get bids in reserve price auctions, see the "Creating Your Item Description" section.) If you're *not* listing a reserve for your item, be sure to let bidders know.
NWT	New with Tags	An item, possibly apparel, is in new condition with the tags from the manufacturer still affixed.
NWOT	New, but Without Store Tags	Generally a new article of apparel that is missing the store tags, but is unused.
HTF, OOP	Hard to Find, Out of Print	Out of print, only a few ever made, or people grabbed up all there were. (HTF *doesn't* mean you spent a week looking for it in the attic.)

Normally, you can rely on eBay abbreviations to get your point across, but make sure that you mean it and that you're using it accurately. Don't label something MIB (Mint in Box) when it looks like it's been Mashed in Box. You'll find more eBay (and social media) abbreviations on my website at

www.coolebaytools.com/tools/online-acronyms-and-ebay-abbreviations

Or you can click the Tools tab at www.coolebaytools.com, and then click the FAQ on Online Acronyms and eBay Abbreviations.

Don't let your title ruin your listing

Imagine going to a supermarket and asking where you can find the *stringy stuff that you boil* instead of asking where the spaghetti is. You might end up with mung bean sprouts — delicious to some, but hardly what you had in mind. That's why you should check and recheck your spelling. Savvy buyers use the eBay search engine to find merchandise; if the name of your item is spelled wrong, the search engine may not find it. Poor spelling and incomprehensible grammar in descriptions also reflect badly on you. If you're in competition with another seller, the buyer is likelier to trust the seller *hoo nose gud speling.*

AUTHOR SAYS

In my travels, I meet so many interesting people with lots of great stories about their forays on eBay. One of my favorites is the story told to me by a lovely lady in Salt Lake City. She brought to my class her biggest eBay bargain. She won a Shaquille O'Neill–signed basketball on eBay for 1 cent! Yep, one red cent (plus shipping). I'll bet that seller had a rude surprise when his listing closed! Oh, you want to know why such a valuable collectible sold for so little? The seller couldn't spell Shaquille and listed the all-important name in the item's title as *Schackeel.*

WARNING

If you've finished writing your item title and you have spaces left over, *please* fight the urge to dress the title up with lots of exclamation points and asterisks. No matter how gung-ho you are about your item, the eBay search engine may overlook your item if the title is encrusted with meaningless **** and !!!! symbols. If bidders do see your title, they may become annoyed by the virtual shrillness and ignore it anyway!!!!!!!! (See what I mean?)

WARNING

Another distracting habit is overdoing capital letters. To buyers, seeing everything in caps is LIKE SEEING A HYSTERICAL SALESPERSON SCREAMING AT THEM TO BUY NOW! All that is considered *shouting,* which is rude and tough on the eyes. Use capitalization SPARINGLY, and ONLY to finesse a particular point or keyword.

Giving the title punch with a subtitle

A useful feature on eBay is the availability of subtitles. eBay allows you to buy an additional 55 characters as a subtitle, which will appear under your item title in a list-formatted search. The fee for this extra promotion is $0.50 (up to $3 depending on price and duration), and in a few circumstances, it is definitely worth your while. Any text that you input will really make your item stand out in the crowd — but (you knew there would be a *but,* didn't you?) these additional 55 characters won't come up in a title search. So if you have all those words in your description, the words will be found either way with a title-and-description search.

Creating Your Item Description

After you hook potential bidders with your title, reel 'em in with a fabulous description. Don't think Hemingway here; think infomercial (the classier the better). Figure 3-3 shows a concise description of the item for sale. You can write a magnificent description, as well — all you have to do is click the box and start typing.

> ### Karen Neuburger Size M Night Shirt - Brand New w tags
>
> I just love this nightshirt with the Cappuccino, latte, coffee espresso print! Dream the softest, coziest dreams in Karen Neuburger sleepwear. Always in the softest knits. Always relaxed in silhouette. And so comfortable, you'll never want to take them off.
>
> *Chosen as one of Oprah's favorite things:*
> *"These are my favorite pajamas! Made with the finest brushed cotton, they come in a variety of colors."*—Oprah
>
> - Soft and cozy interlock knit fabric
> - Pullover nightshirt falls above the knee
> - Three button Henley placket
> - Machine wash cold, tumble dry low
> - 60% cotton 40% polyester
>
> Sizing: S (6-8) M (10-12) L (14-16) XL (18-20)

Composing the description

Here's a list of suggestions for writing an item description:

>> **Write a factual description.** Do you carefully describe the item, stating every fact you know about it? Do you avoid the use of jargon? Does the description answer almost any question a potential buyer might ask? If not, do some revising.

>> **Accentuate the positive.** Be enthusiastic when you list all the reasons everyone should buy the item. Unlike the title, the description can take up as much space as you want. Even if you use a photo, be precise in your description — tell the reader, for example, the item's size, color, and fabric. Refer to "Creating the Perfect Item Title," earlier in this chapter, for ideas on what to emphasize.

>> **Include the negative.** Don't hide the truth of your item's condition. Trying to conceal flaws costs you in the long run: You'll not only get tagged with bad feedback, but the buyer can get his or her money back from PayPal if it arrives "not as described." If your vintage item has a scratch, a nick, a dent, a crack, a ding, a tear, a rip, missing pieces, replacement parts, faded color, dirty smudges, or a bad smell (especially if cleaning might damage the item), mention it in the description. If your item has been overhauled, rebuilt, repainted, or hot-rodded, say so. You don't want the buyer to send back

your merchandise because you weren't truthful about imperfections or modifications. This type of omission can lead to losing the item and having the money taken out of your PayPal account.

>> **Include short, friendly banter.** You want to make the customer feel comfortable shopping with you. Don't be afraid to let your personality show!

>> **Limit the number of auction rules (or terms of sale).** Some sellers include a list of rules that's longer than the item's description. Nothing turns off a prospective buyer like paragraph after paragraph of rules and regulations. If you really *must* put in a litany of rules, use the following bit of HTML to make the size of the text smaller: ‹font size=–1›.

>> **Choose a reasonable typeface size.** Many users are now looking at eBay on mobile devices. If you design your listings for a large computer display, your typefaces may be way too large for the average user. Forcing a user to scroll leads to frustrated customers. I recommend something in the range of 10 to 14 points, depending on the typeface you choose.

>> **Be concise and to the point — don't ramble!** As my sixth-grade English teacher used to say, "Make it like a woman's skirt: long enough to cover the subject, yet short enough to keep it interesting." Too many sellers these days drone on and on, causing bidders to have to scroll down the page several times. You can quickly lose your audience this way. They'll look for a listing with a less complicated look.

Jazzing it up with HTML

When you type in your description, you have the option of jazzing things up with a bit of HTML coding, or you can use eBay's HTML text editor, described in Book 5, Chapter 3. If you know how to use a word processor, you'll have no trouble dressing up your text with this tool. Table 3-2 shows you a few HTML codes that you can insert into your text to help you pretty things up.

TIP

You can go back and forth from the HTML text editor to regular input and add additional codes here and there by selecting the View/Edit HTML check box (when you're in the HTML text editor). You can prepare your listings ahead of time in an HTML composer in the Mozilla SeaMonkey suite (see Book 5, Chapter 3 for more details) and save them to your computer as plain TXT files (I do). That way, pre-designed listings are always retrievable for use (just copy and paste) no matter what program or form you're using to list them.

TABLE 3-2   ## A Short List of HTML Codes

HTML Code	How to Use It	What It Does
`<b></b>`	`<b>cool collectible</b>`	**cool collectible** (bold type)
`<i></i>`	`<i>cool collectible</i>`	*cool collectible* (italic type)
`<b><i></b></i>`	`<b><i>cool collectible</i></b>`	***cool collectible*** (bold and italic type)
`<font color=red></font>`	`<font color=red>cool collectible</font>`	Selected text appears in red
`<font size=+1></font>`	`<font size=+3>cool</font> collectible`	COOl collectible (font size normal+1 through 4, increases size *x* times)
` `	`cool collectible`	cool collectible (inserts line break)
`<p>`	`cool<p>collectible`	Cool collectible (inserts paragraph space)
`<hr>`	`cool collectible <hr>cheap`	cool collectible _____ cheap (inserts horizontal rule)
`<h1></h1>`	`<h1>cool collectible</h1>`	**cool collectible** (converts text to headline size)

Listing Multiples of an Item for Sale with Variations

Whether you have 20 of one item, or the same item in different variations (size or color), eBay has a handy way to list multiple items in one listing. For a fixed-price sale for multiple items that are all the same, just indicate the number you have in the appropriate box on the Create a listing page.

When you have different sizes or colors for your fixed-price listing, you'll want to list with variations. A listing with variations will look similar to regular listings, but there the buyer can choose size, type, color, and so on from drop-down lists.

The option to include variations in a listing will not show up on the Create a listing page, but after you select one of the categories where variations are permitted, an option will appear to Create Variations. Click those words and you'll be taken to a page with appropriate options for the item you are selling.

Currently, you can create listings with variations in the following categories:

>> Baby

>> Clothing, Shoes & Accessories

>> Crafts

>> Health & Beauty

>> Home & Garden (most sub-categories)

>> Jewelry & Watches

>> Pet Supplies

>> Sporting Goods

eBay provides you with a list of common variation details when you click the Add Variation Detail link. If you have custom variations, click Add More Details. You can select up to five variation details — such as Color, Size, Width, Material, and Style — with up to 60 values for each detail.

TIP

A multi-variation listing may appear higher in search results. Putting up multiple listings for the same item is fruitless; eBay won't show more than one identical listing from a single seller at one time in search results and may remove identical listings from the site.

Setting Bids, Prices, and Reserves

What do a baseball autographed by JFK, a used walkie-talkie, and a Jaguar sports car have in common? They all started with a $.99 minimum bid. eBay requires you to set a *minimum bid,* the lowest bid allowed in an auction. You may be surprised to see stuff worth tens of thousands of dollars offered for auctions starting just under a buck. These sellers haven't lost their minds. Neither are they worried someone could end up tooling down the highway in their $100,000 sports car for the price of a burger. They protect their final sale price with a reserve. (Keep reading; I explain in the later section "Using your secret safety net — reserve price.")

WARNING

Before you set a minimum bid, do your homework and make some savvy marketing decisions. If your auction isn't going as you hoped, you *could* end up selling Grandma Ethel's Ming vase for a dollar. See "Making Midcourse Corrections," later in this chapter, to see how you can make changes in your listing if you've made some egregious error.

Estimate costs with a fee calculator

For years I have looked to the Internet to find accurate ecommerce fee calculators. These tools calculate eBay and PayPal fees and allow you to input your expenses to get an idea of how to profitably price a specific item.

The most comprehensive calculator I've found is at `salecalc.com`, but it hasn't been updated as of this writing. I did find an updated eBay and PayPal fee calculator at `finalfeecalc.com`. They also have a calculator app in the Android Play Store.

Setting a minimum bid — how low can you go?

Setting an incredibly low minimum is a subtle strategy that gives you more bang for your buck. You can use a low minimum bid to attract more bidders who will, in turn, drive up the price to the item's real value — especially if, after doing your research, you know that the item is particularly hot.

REMEMBER

The more bids you get, the more people will want to bid on your item because they perceive it as hot.

If you're worried about the outcome of the final bid, you can protect your item by using a *reserve price* (the price the bidding needs to reach before the item can be sold). This ensures that you won't have to sell your item for a bargain-basement price because your reserve price protects your investment. The best advice is to set a reserve price that is the lowest amount you'll take for your item, and then set a minimum bid that is ridiculously low. However, use a reserve only when absolutely necessary; some bidders just pass up reserve auctions.

Going with a Buy It Now price

eBay's Buy It Now (*BIN* in eBay-speak) is available for single-item listings. This feature allows buyers to purchase an item *now*. Have you ever wanted an item really badly and you didn't want to wait until the end of an auction? If the seller offers Buy It Now, you can purchase that item immediately.

When listing an item this way, just specify the amount the item can sell for in the Buy It Now price area — the amount can be whatever you want. If you choose to sell a hot item during the holiday rush, for example, you can make the BIN price as high as you think it can go. If you just want the item to move, make your BIN price the average price you see the item go for on eBay.

After your item receives a bid, the BIN option disappears and the item goes through the normal auction process. If you have a reserve price (as well as a BIN price) on your item, the BIN feature doesn't disappear until a bidder meets your reserve price through the normal bidding process. To list an auction with Buy It Now, the price needs to be at least 30 percent higher than the starting price.

Using your secret safety net — reserve price

Here's a little secret: The reason sellers list big-ticket items such as Ferraris, grand pianos, and high-end computer equipment with a starting bid of $.99 is because they're protected from losing money with a reserve price. The *reserve price* is the lowest price that must be met before the item can be sold. It is not required by eBay but can protect you. For this feature, eBay charges an additional fee that varies depending on how high your reserve is.

For example, say you list a first-edition book — John Steinbeck's *The Grapes of Wrath*. You set the starting price at $.99 and the reserve price at $80. That means people can start bidding at $.99, and if at the end of the auction the book hasn't reached the $80 reserve, you don't have to sell the book.

As with everything in life, using a reserve price for your auctions has an upside and a downside. Many choosy bidders and bargain hunters blast past reserve-price auctions because they see a reserve price as a sign that proclaims "No bargains here!" Many bidders figure they can get a better deal on the same item with an auction that proudly declares *NR* (for *no reserve*) in its description. As an enticement to those bidders, you see lots of NR listings in auction titles.

TIP

If you need to set a reserve on your item, help the bidder out. Many bidders shy away from an auction that has a reserve, but if they're really interested, they will read the item description. To dispel their fears that the item is way too expensive or out of their price range, add a line in your description that states the amount of your reserve price. "I have put a reserve of $75 on this item to protect my investment; the highest bid over $75 will win the item." A phrase such as this takes away the vagueness of the reserve auction and allows you to place a reserve with a low opening bid. (You want to reel 'em in, remember?)

TIP

On lower-priced items, I suggest that you set a higher minimum bid and set no reserve.

If bids don't reach a set reserve price, some sellers offer an underbidder a Second Chance (also known as Best Offer) or relist the item for another whack at the buying public.

Listing Items for Sale

Timing Your Auction: Is It Everything?

Visit Chapter 2 of this minibook to learn about timing your eBay listings. Just know that if what you're listing is in demand, it will sell at the going rate without worries.

I Want to Be Alone: The Private Auction

In a *private* auction, bidders' User IDs are kept under wraps. Sellers typically use this option to protect the identities of bidders during auctions for high-priced big-ticket items (say, that restored World War II fighter). Wealthy eBay members may not want the world to know that they have the resources to buy expensive items. Private auctions are also held for items from the Adult Only category. (Gee, there's a shocker.)

AUTHOR SAYS

The famous sign pictured in almost every piece of Disney promotion (for the first 40 or so years of Disneyland's existence) was put up for sale on eBay in 2000. The sign was purchased by actor John Stamos for a high bid of $30,700. Unfortunately for John, the Disney auctions did not use the Private Auction feature. After news of the winner's name hit the tabloids, the entire world knew John's eBay User ID! He had to change his ID in a hurry to end the throngs of lovey-dovey email messages headed to his computer!

Adding Visuals to Highlight Your Item

With so many listings posted daily on eBay, you need some way to get your listing noticed. Adding visual interest to catch a potential buyer's eye is one way. As you fill out the listing page, take advantage of the visual elements that eBay offers.

eBay requires that you have at least one image to illustrate what you are selling. You can add up to 12 pictures on your listing for free, as shown in Figure 3-4. You can find the images (after the listing is over) in My eBay⇨Completed Listings for 60 days.

If you want to host your pictures on a website or other server, you can use the *import from the web* uploader. Your pictures will then be optimized automatically for use on eBay. You may also add web-hosted images to your description. See Book 5, Chapter 4 for the necessary coding and instructions.

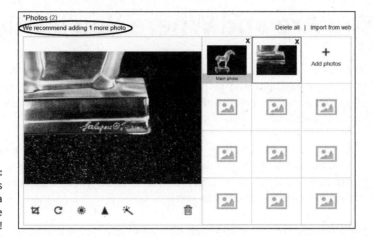

FIGURE 3-4:
Upload images
to eBay with a
couple of mouse
clicks!

TIP

For the best quality, eBay recommends that you upload images that are 1600 pixels in height or width (although the minimum suggested size is 800 pixels).

Listing the Payment Methods You'll Accept

Yeah, sure, eBay is loads of fun, but the bottom line to selling is the phrase "Show me the money!" You make the call on what you're willing to take as money from your auction's high bidder. eBay offers the following payment options — just select the ones that you like:

>> **Personal check, cashier's check, bank transfers, or money orders:** These are only permissible as payment for capital equipment, Real Estate, Adult Only, and some Motors categories, or when a customer picks up an item in person. For more information on the variables, check http://pages.ebay.com/help/policies/accepted-payments-policy.html#categories. As a seller, you want to get paid with as little risk as possible. The only drawback? You have to wait for the buyer to send the money.

>> **Credit cards:** If you accept credit cards, using PayPal is the cheapest and most convenient way to go. If you have a merchant account through a retail store, be sure to select the check boxes next to the credit cards you accept. eBay also allows sellers to accept credit card payments from Allpay.net, CertaPay, hyperwallet.com, Fiserv, Nochex.com, XOOM, or the merchant credit card account you've set up for your business.

>> **Online escrow:** An option for selling vehicles in eBay motors, an escrow service, escrow.com, acts as a referee, a neutral third party. This service charges you a percentage of the sale price.

Listing Items for Sale

Where You Are and Where You'll Ship To

When listing an item for sale on eBay, you come to the area where you need to input your payment and shipping information. You have the option of offering free shipping, a flat rate, or offer calculated shipping. The charges appear in a box at the top and the bottom of your item description.

But how you handle shipping — and its associated cost for your buyers — depends on what you're shipping (how big it is), where you're shipping it, and the carrier you decide to use. So take a bit of time to consider your location and your shipping options before you fill out this section.

TIP

Offering free shipping helps sell items and gets you a better place in Best Match search. Customers always prefer to buy items online that offer free shipping.

eBay has some rules about shipping

eBay has rules about how much you can charge for shipping in certain categories. Some greedy sellers would charge egregious amounts for shipping their items, so eBay cracked down and made maximum shipping limits. Table 3-3 gives you the current shipping charge limits as of October 9, 2017.

TABLE 3-3 ## Shipping Charge Limits by Category

Category: Books		
Subcategory	Type of Merchandise	Maximum Shipping Charge
Accessories	Address Books	$20.00
	Blank Diaries & Journals	$20.00
	Book Covers	$20.00
	Book Plates	$20.00
	Bookmarks	$25.00
	Other	$20.00
Antiquarian & Collectible	Antiquarian & Collectible	$25.00
Audiobooks	Audiobooks	$20.00
Catalogs	Catalogs	$30.00
Children's Books	Children's Books	$20.00
Cookbooks	Cookbooks	$20.00
Fiction Books	Fiction Books	$20.00

Magazine Back Issues	Magazine Back Issues	$25.00
Nonfiction Books	Nonfiction Books	$20.00
Other	Other	$20.00
Textbooks, Education	Textbooks, Education	$20.00
Wholesale & Bulk Lots	Audiobooks	$35.00
	Books > up to 5	$20.00
	Books > 6-10 Items	$25.00
	Books > 11-50 Items	$30.00
	Books > 51-100 Items	$35.00
	Books > 101- 500	$40.00
	Books > More than 500 Items	$45.00
	Magazines	$35.00
	Other	$35.00

Category: DVDs & Movies		
Subcategory	Type of Merchandise	Maximum Shipping Charge
DVD, HD DVD, & Blu-ray	DVD & Blu-ray	$20.00
Film	Film	$40.00
Laserdisc	Laserdisc	$25.00
Other Formats	Other Formats	$20.00
UMD	UMD	$20.00
VHS	VHS	$30.00
Wholesale Lots	Other	$45.00

Category: Music		
Subcategory	Type of Merchandise	Maximum Shipping Charge
Storage & Media Accessories	Storage & Media Accessories	$25.00
Cassettes	Cassettes	$25.00
CDs	CDs	$25.00
Other Formats	Other Formats	$25.00
Records	Records	$40.00
Wholesale Lots	Cassettes	$40.00
	Other Formats	$40.00

(continued)

TABLE 3-3 *(continued)*

Category: Video Games		
Subcategory	Type of Merchandise	Maximum Shipping Charge
Video Games	Video Games	$20.00
Video Game Console	Video Game Console	$50.00
Accessories	Accessory Bundles	$40.00
	Other	$20.00
Games & Consoles	Other	$20.00
Consoles	Other	$50.00
Wholesale Lots	Accessories	$40.00
	Console Systems	$50.00
	Games	$40.00
	Other	$40.00

Setting shipping and handling terms

Before you list your item, think about the details related to shipping your merchandise. Here are some of your choices for where you'll ship:

>> **Ship to the United States only:** This option is selected by default; it means you ship only domestically.

>> **Will ship worldwide:** The world is your oyster. But make sure that you can afford it.

>> **Will ship to United States and the following countries:** If you're comfortable shipping to certain countries but not to others, make your selections here. Your choices appear on the item page.

TIP

When you indicate that you will ship internationally, your listing can show up on the international eBay sites (for a small fee), which is a fantastic way to attract new buyers! eBay has lots of international users, so you may want to consider selling your items around the world. If you do, be sure to clearly state in the description all extra shipping costs and customs charges.

You also get to set the method and fees related to shipping. eBay buyers love seeing a flat shipping fee. If you can convince yourself to find a reasonable midway point, a fixed shipping price may just beat your competition.

Also in the form's shipping details, you can set a handling time, which is more attractive when you say you will ship the same day (or within a business day) of receiving the customer's money. eBay puts the phrase "Get it fast" on these listings when you also offer overnight shipping. Offering speedy handling also gets you leverage in Best Match searches.

TIP

Combining free shipping with 1-day handling earns your listing the designation *Fast 'n Free*, as shown in Figure 3-5. This delivery-truck icon attracts a lot of eyes when customers are searching. Plus, eBay gives a boost to items having this designation in Best Match search results.

FIGURE 3-5:
Get your item
shipped Fast 'n
Free!

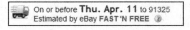

Using eBay's shipping calculator

When your item weighs two pounds or more, you may want to use eBay's versatile shipping calculator to determine your flat shipping-and-handling cost or to quote a calculated shipping cost. Using the shipping calculator has these advantages:

>> **It accounts for variable rates:** Because UPS and the U.S. Postal Service now charge variable rates for packages of the same weight, based on distance, using the calculator simplifies things for your customers (and for you). ***Note:*** Be sure you've weighed the item.

>> **It includes your handling amount:** The calculator allows you to input a handling amount and adds it to the overall shipping total — but does not break out these amounts separately for the customer.

Figure 3-6 shows how simple the calculator is. You may select up to three levels of shipping per item.

TIP

You can check out the associated costs by clicking the Show Rates button, which shows you all shipping costs, so you can decide to ship with either the U.S. Postal Service or UPS. I always test my packages from a California Zip code (because that's where I live) to a New York Zip code. Doing this gives me an estimate for Zone 8, which is the most expensive option (coast-to-coast by distance) when shipping in the U.S.

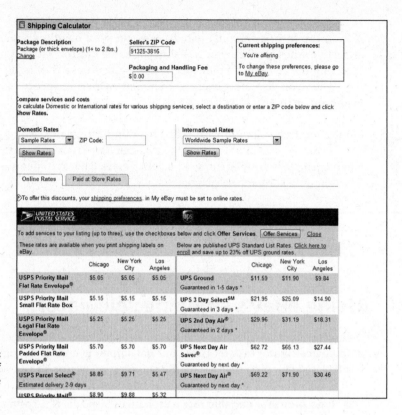

FIGURE 3-6:
The results of checking out the shipping costs.

WARNING

eBay's shipping calculator does not include Domestic First class (can be used for up to a 1-pound package) or First Class International (can be used for up to a 4-pound package). It also does not offer the options for domestic Regional Flat Rate Priority boxes (see Book 7 for more details).

You can check out the fees for different shipping services also (after signing in) by using the full eBay shipping calculator located at

```
http://payments.ebay.com/ws/eBayISAPI.dll?emitsellershipping
calculator
```

The proper shipping price appears on the item page based on the shopper's registered Zip code, so they will know immediately how much shipping will be to their location. Follow these steps in the Create a Listing process to have eBay calculate the charges for you:

1. **In the Shipping area, choose Calculated: Cost Varies by Buyer Location from the drop-down menu.**

2. **Select your package's type and weight from the drop-down lists, and fill in package dimensions as needed.**

3. **Select a carrier from the drop-down lists.**

4. **In the additional options, click to add a Handling Cost to cover your shipping expenses.**

   When adding your packaging and handling charges, don't worry that the buyers will see these individual fees. eBay combines this amount with the shipping cost and shows the total as one shipping price.

After you've input all your information, you can forget about shipping charges, because eBay takes over. Check out Book 7 for more information on shipping options — and on how to mechanize the process.

Checking Your Work and Starting the Sale

After you've filled in all the blanks on the Sell an Item page and you feel ready to join the world of ecommerce, follow these steps:

1. **Click the Review button at the bottom of the Sell an Item page.**

   You go to the Verification page, the place where you can catch mistakes before your item is listed. The Verification page shows you a condensed version of all your information and tallies how much eBay is charging you in fees and options to run this auction. You can also click to see a preview of how your auction description and pictures will look on the site.

   You also may find the Verification page helpful as a last-minute chance to get your bearings. If you've chosen a general category, eBay asks you whether you're certain there isn't a more appropriate category. You can go back to any of the pages that need correcting by clicking the appropriate tab at the top of the Verification page. Make category changes or any other changes and additions, and then head for the Verification page again.

2. **Check for mistakes.**

   Nitpick for common, careless errors; you won't be sorry. I've seen eBay members make goofs such as the wrong category listing, spelling and grammatical errors, and missing information about shipping, handling, and payment methods.

3. **When you're sure everything is accurate and you're happy with your item listing, click the Submit My Listing button.**

   A Listing Confirmation page pops up. At that precise moment, your sale begins, even though it *may* be as much as an hour before it appears in eBay's search and listings updates. If you want to see your listing right away and check for bids, your Confirmation page provides a link for that purpose. Click the link, and you're there.

WARNING

All listing pages come with this friendly warning: *Seller assumes all responsibility for listing this item.* Some eBay veterans just gloss over this warning after they've been wheeling and dealing for a while, but it's an important rule to remember. Whether you're buying or selling, you're always responsible for your actions.

Making Midcourse Corrections

If you made a mistake filling out the item listing page but didn't notice it until after the item is up and running, don't worry. Pencils have erasers, and eBay allows revisions. You can make changes at two stages of the game: before the first bid is placed and after the bidding war is underway. This section explains what you can (and can't) correct — and when you have to accept the little imperfections of the Create a listing page.

Making changes before bidding begins

Here's what you can change about your auction before bids have been placed, as long as your auction does not end within 12 hours:

- >> The title, subtitle, or description
- >> The item category
- >> The item's Minimum Bid price
- >> The item's Buy It Now price (you can add or change it)
- >> The reserve price (you can add, change, or remove it)
- >> The URL of the picture you're including with your auction
- >> A private-auction designation (you can add or remove it)

When you revise a listing, eBay puts a little notation on your page that reads: Description (revised).

To revise a listing (or auction before bids have been received), follow these steps:

1. Go to the item page and click the Revise Your Item link.

This link appears only if you've signed in to eBay. If the item hasn't received any bids, a message appears on your screen to indicate that you may update the item.

You're taken to the Revise Your Item page, which outlines the rules for revising your item's listing. At the bottom, the item number is filled in.

2. **Click Revise Item.**

   You arrive at the Revise Your Item page which looks uncannily like the Create a listing form.

3. **Scroll down to the area you'd like to change.**

4. **Make changes to the item information.**

5. **When you've finished making changes, click the Continue button at the bottom of the page.**

   A summary of how your newly revised listing appears in search is on your screen. If you've incurred any additional fees, the amount is listed at the bottom of the page. If you want to make more changes, click the Back button of your browser or the Edit Listing link.

6. **When you're happy with your revisions, click Submit Revisions.**

Making changes in the last 12 hours

If your auction is up and running and already receiving bids, you can still make some slight modifications to it. Newly added information is clearly separated from the original text and pictures. In addition, eBay puts a timestamp on the additional info in case questions from early bidders crop up later.

After your item receives bids, eBay allows you to add to your item's description. If you feel you were at a loss for words in writing your item's description — or if a lot of potential bidders are asking the same questions — go ahead and make all the additions you want. But keep in mind that whatever you put there the first time around stays in the description as well.

Follow the same procedure for making changes before bidding begins. When you arrive at the Revise Your Item page, you can *only* add to your description, add features, or add further payment information.

REMEMBER

Always check your My eBay messages to see whether bidders have questions about your item. If a bidder wants to know about flaws, be truthful and courteous when returning emails. As you get more familiar with eBay (and with writing descriptions), the number of email questions will decrease. If you enjoy good customer service in your day-to-day shopping, here's your chance to give some back.

Chapter 4

Running Your Business on eBay

I n my 20 years of selling on (and writing about) eBay, there have always been rearrangements to the management tools. As I write this book, more changes are being made. The My eBay page may not even exist in the coming year, but the tools mentioned in this chapter will always be available. Read here so you'll know what's important to look out for.

In Book 8, Chapter 1, I give you more information on the new Seller Hub. Know that the tools mentioned in this chapter will also be in Seller Hub, but in a different format.

If you're a beginning or small seller, the My eBay page helps you manage sales by providing an overview of what's going on in your eBay business.

This chapter explains how you can get the most out of the My eBay: All Selling page, and how it can benefit your business.

Managing Your My eBay: All Selling Area

eBay provides some smooth management tools on your My eBay: All Selling summary page. You can track items you currently have up for sale and items you've sold. The All Selling page is a quick way to get a snapshot of the dollar value of your auctions and fixed-price listings.

The My eBay: All Selling home page, which is shown in Figure 4-1, is a long page if you have many items for sale. The left-hand navigation links on the Activity tab let you quickly hop to the area you want to examine. This page has several areas:

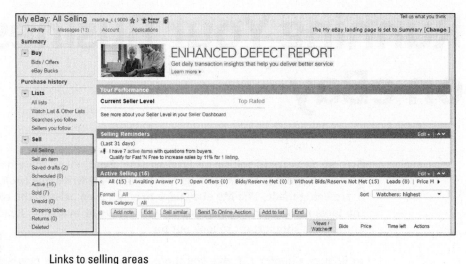

FIGURE 4-1:
All Selling Hub at
My eBay.

Links to selling areas

>> **Sell an item:** Click here to list a new item for sale or auction.

>> **Saved drafts:** Here's where you'll find listings you started and saved for later. I often start listings on my phone and finish them on my PC.

>> **Scheduled:** If you've scheduled listings to begin at a later time, you can link to them here.

>> **Active:** The listings shown in the middle of the page give you a clear idea of what's going on with your eBay sales.

>> **Sold:** Click this link and find the list of items you've (thankfully) sold.

>> **Unsold:** Follow this link to the netherworld of unsold items. It's time to relist or put these items in your store. (Find out how in the section "Relisting Items without Extra Work," later in this chapter.)

>> **Shipping Labels:** Clicking this link takes you to a searchable archive of the shipping labels you've printed. You can also check tracking information in this area.

>> **Returns:** If a customer initiates a return through eBay, the progress of the return appears in this area.

>> **Deleted:** After you process a return, the transaction goes into the Deleted folder where you can view it for up to 60 days.

TIP

If you manually scroll waaaay down the page, you'll see far too much information. To avoid all that scrolling, click the links on the left side of the page to go to each individual area on its own page.

eBay's HANDY ICONS

On the My eBay page (and other pages on eBay), eBay uses a handy group of icons to signify tasks to be accomplished or to indicate certain actions. Take a look at the figure to see the icons and what they stand for.

Icon Legend

✎	Auction Format
🔒	Fixed Price Format
$	Best Offer Format
▤	Classified ad Format
⟳	Second chance offer
✔	Checkout complete
$	Item Paid
🛒	Item Shipped
★	Left Feedback
✉	Feedback Received
$⁺	Payment was refunded
$	Item Partially Paid
◕	Request Total
🗂	Relisted

Organizing with My eBay: Active Selling

Click on the Active link on the left and you'll arrive at the Active Selling page. Here you can keep an eye on any questions you receive from buyers, open offers, bids/reserves met, your fixed-price sales, and the progress of your auctions.

The general layout

At the bottom of the left-hand column of links, you'll see your Totals, which give you an idea of your sales during the past 31 days. eBay also shows the total items currently up for sale. The total dollar amount of the items that have been bid on appears with these totals.

Depending on how you customize the view (which I describe in the next section), you can see how many bids your auctions have, whether your reserves have been met, and how much time remains before the auction closes. By clicking a listing title, you can visit the listing to make sure your pictures are appearing or to edit your description.

TIP

Don't be frustrated if you don't have a ton of bids. Many, many people watch auctions and don't bid until the last minute, so you may not see a lot of bidding activity on your page when you drop in to look.

Filtering your view

You can perform several actions via the links and drop-down menus at the top of the Active Selling page. Here's the rundown:

>> **View:** Beneath the Active Selling title bar, a group of links enable you to filter important listings. You can select for viewing

   All to see all your active listings.

   Awaiting Answer to view eBay Messages that are unanswered in your mailbox.

   Open Offers to find out when eBay members have made offers on fixed-price listings (those for which you say that you would entertain offers).

   Bids/Reserve Met to look at auctions where you've had some bidding activity.

   Without Bids/Reserve Not Met to see those auctions without bids or with bids that are too low.

>> **Sort:** Next to Sort, click the down-facing arrow to order your listings by

> **Time left:** Ending soonest or newly listed

> **Price:** Lowest first or highest first

> **Watchers:** Lowest or highest first

> **Views:** Lowest or highest first

> **Format:** Auctions first

> **High bidder ID**

> **Available Quantity:** Highest or lowest number

Taking action when necessary

Make sure you pay attention to the More actions drop-down menu that appears at the end of each listing line (see Figure 4-2). This menu has powerful options that allow you to do the following:

>> **Sell Similar:** List an item similar to the one on your page (more on making Sell Similar work for you in later sections of this chapter).

>> **Revise:** Change a listing that has no bids.

>> **End Item:** When the dog plays tug-of-war with your item, you can end the listing. (Find more about ending a listing in the "Ending your listing early" section near the end of the chapter.)

>> **Mark as answered:** If there's an Unanswered Question alert on the item, and you've responded via the mobile app or on eBay Messages, you can "Mark as answered" to make the alert disappear.

>> **Add Note:** If you want to add a notation (which only you can see and only on this page), select the check box to the left of the item title and then click the Add Note button at the top of the listings. Just type your comment on the page that appears and click Save.

>> **Add to List:** If you want to make a list that contains some of your items, you can and add them here.

TIP

Auction prices that appear in green have received one or more bids (and met any reserves you've set). Auctions in red haven't received any bids or the reserve price hasn't been met.

FIGURE 4-2:
Action options for
active listings.

Using the Tools on the My eBay: Sold Page

Clicking the Sold link (on the Activity tab at the left side of the page under the Sell header) takes you to a list of all the items you've sold.

The Sold page keeps a concise view of your sales in one place, as shown in Figure 4-3. You can use this page in lieu of fancy management software; it actually offers you some very accessible actions. If you're selling hundreds of items, your list will probably be too long to monitor individual items — but for items that did sell, you can view their total current price on the left.

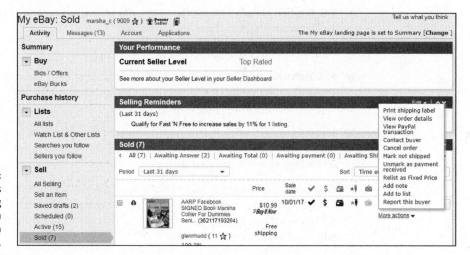

FIGURE 4-3:
The Sold items
page (showing
drop-down
menu) in
My eBay.

The Sold items page has the following features and information, which I'm sure you'll find helpful in completing your transactions:

» **Check box:** Select the check box next to an item listing to perform a task on one or more of them. Options you see at the top of the list of items include Add to List, Add Note, Add Tracking Number, and Print Shipping Labels.

» **Buyer's User ID, name, and feedback rating:** The eBay User ID of the winner of the sale.

- » **Total Items:** If the transaction was for multiple items, the number of items is displayed here.

- » **Item title:** A direct link to the auction. You can click this link to check on your auction and see the other bidders, should you want to make a Best Offer (also known as Second Chance).

- » **Tracking number:** You can add or edit a shipment tracking number here — as well as click the number to view the shipment's progress and when it was delivered.

- » **Sale price:** The final selling price for your item.

- » **Shipping price:** If the buyer paid extra for shipping, the amount will appear under the sale price, or you will see the word *Free*.

- » **Sale date:** Keep an eye on the end date so you can be sure you get your payment as agreed.

- » **Actions:** Under this heading, you find a hidden drop-down list (More Actions) that works with the transaction, offering options for various actions you can take. Here are a few of the more important ones:

  - *Contact Buyer:* When you choose this option, a window appears where you can send a buyer a note regarding his or her order.

  - *View PayPal Transaction:* This option takes you to the transaction's page on PayPal. (You'll have to sign in to your PayPal account.)

  - *Print Shipping Label:* You can print a shipping label from here. See Book 7, Chapter 2 for other professional-shipping label options.

  - *Leave Feedback:* Leave feedback with a single click once you've heard that the item arrived safely and your customer is happy.

  - *Second Chance Offer:* This option appears only in the case of an auction where there were underbidders (losers). Click here to make a Second Chance offer to one of your underbidders if you have multiple items for sale.

  - *Sell Similar:* When you want to list a similar item (or relist a sold one) you can do it quickly here.

  - *Report This Buyer:* If you have a problem with your transaction because a buyer violates any rules, click here to let eBay know.

  - *Relist:* Use this option to relist your item on the site.

» **Icons:** My eBay has several icons that appear dimmed until you perform an action from the Actions drop-down menu. You may also click the icons at the top of the list to sort your listings by auctions completed, although most sellers prefer to keep the listings in the default chronological order (with newest sale date on top). Here's what the icons mean:

- **Dollar sign:** The buyer has paid using PayPal, or you've noted that the buyer has paid with a different form of payment available on the drop-down list within the sale record.

- **Shipping box:** You've indicated that the item has shipped.

- **Star with pen:** You've left feedback for the buyer.

- **Star on an envelope:** The buyer has left you feedback.

Connecting with Your Customers and Checking the Money

Thank goodness — somebody submitted a winning bid on one of your items in an auction. It's a good feeling. When I get those end-of-transaction emails from eBay, I whisper a silent *yeah!* In the case of an auction, I hold my breath to see whether the buyer will go directly to PayPal and make the payment. Usually that's what happens. More and more buyers are savvy and understand about paying immediately after winning an item: It's good form.

New buyers and those who buy or win multiple items from you (my favorite kind of buyer!) may wait to hear from you regarding payment and shipping. Many newbies feel more comfortable hearing from you and knowing whom they're doing business with. Also, in the case of multiple purchases, you may have to recalculate the postage. The sooner you contact the buyer, the sooner you'll get your payment.

Notifying winners

eBay sends out an end-of-transaction email to both the buyer and the seller. The email is informative to the seller and a welcome email for the buyer.

The email to the buyer has a Pay Now button, but includes more concrete information about the transaction:

» Item title and number.

» The final bid or sale price.

>> Quantity (if the purchase was for more than one).

>> Seller and buyer's User ID.

>> A link for viewing the item. This link is good for up to 90 days. Note that this is the only place you get this link, and unless you subscribe to eBay's Selling Manager, you'd better keep hold of it. Sold items remain on your My eBay page for 60 days, but the items disappear from the eBay search engine within two weeks.

>> A link so that the buyer can contact the seller.

>> A buyer's link to complete checkout and pay.

>> If the seller has set up custom emails to go along with these notices, that message will appear at the bottom of the confirmation.

That's a lot of information, and I'll bet the average user just glances over it and either deletes it (bad idea) or files it in a special folder in his or her email program.

REMEMBER

If you think eBay's notification is good enough, it's time to rethink your customer service policy. An email to the buyer at this point is important. Customer contact is the key to a good transaction. If the buyer sprints directly to PayPal and sends you some money to pay for a purchase, a special email from you would be nice. Thank the buyer for the payment and mention when the item will ship, as detailed in the next section, "Sending invoices."

Sending invoices

Sometimes buyers don't pay immediately, so when the sale is final, the items go into the Sold area. Here's where you can keep track of the sale. You can check whether the buyer has paid with PayPal as well as the transaction status. If the buyer has completed checkout, you can get his or her information by clicking the Next Steps/Status link. If the buyer hasn't completed checkout, you can click the Send Invoice button to send the buyer an invoice. Very handy.

If you haven't heard from the buyer after three days (the prescribed eBay deadline for contact), you may need to resend your invoice or send a message.

After the transaction is complete (which means the item has arrived and the buyer is happy with his or her purchase), you can click the handy Leave Feedback link to leave feedback about the buyer.

Tracking payments in My eBay: Sold

You've created a winning ad, run a successful auction or sale, notified the winner, and sent off an invoice. Now it's time for the big payoff: getting the money in hand for your item. eBay and PayPal work in concert to offer several tools to notify you when a payment is made.

Once again, the Sold items area of My eBay comes to the rescue. As if by magic, every time one of your buyers makes a payment through the PayPal service, your My eBay page indicates that the item has been paid by changing the dollar-sign icon from dimmed to solid. Take a look back at Figure 4-3, and note that items have been paid using PayPal.

Stimulating Sales from the My eBay: Unsold Page

The Unsold page indicates the items that didn't sell. To get to that area, scroll way down the page or click the Unsold link under the Sell header (on the Activity tab at the left side of the page).

TIP

You may customize this page in the same way that I illustrated for the Active Selling page in the earlier section "Filtering your view."

You can take several actions on this page to get your items back up for sale. You can bulk-relist by placing check marks in the boxes to the left of the listings and then clicking the Relist button at the top.

REMEMBER

But wait! Before you automatically relist, find out whether there's a reason your item didn't sell. Run a search on the item to see whether someone else is selling the same thing at a bargain-basement price. If so, perhaps you could lower your price, or better yet, rethink your title and description. You can also opt to wait a few weeks to see if the competition runs out of stock.

Some of the actions you can easily perform on this page:

>> **Relist:** Use this option so that you can get a free relist credit for the first run of an auction if your item sells the second time. You may relist in bulk or one item at a time, hopefully giving your listing a thorough once over (and tweaking the title or description) to better improve the listing's appearance in search results.

>> **Sell Similar:** Try this if the item hasn't sold after a second auction relisting (or if the item is a similar fixed-price item). This option starts the cycle in eBay's computer fresh as new.

>> **Relist as Fixed Price:** If an auction didn't succeed, perhaps the item would be best as a Fixed Price listing (consider adding the Best Offer option as well). I tell you more about changing up your listings in the next section.

>> **Add to List:** Use this option for items that you would like to add to a list. You can start a new list or use eBay's suggestions for Watch List, Wish List, Research, or Gift Ideas.

Relisting Items without Extra Work

One of the most efficient ways to run an eBay business is to stock the same item in quantity. After getting some eBay experience under your belt, you're bound to find several items that you're comfortable selling. And if you follow my suggestions in Book 4, you'll buy multiples (dozens? cases? pallets?) of the items at a seriously discounted price. When you have all these items lying around the garage, your goal is to get them into buyers' hands at a profit.

In Book 8, I talk about opening an eBay Store. But in addition to your own store, you should be running auctions or GTC (Good 'Til Cancelled) fixed-price listings. Why? They are the key to drawing buyers into your store to purchase (or notice) your other items.

TIP

I know several sellers who bought items in such bulk that they're stocked with the item to sell once a week for the next few years! That's a good thing only if the product is a staple item that will always have a market on eBay.

Relisting after a sale

Yeah! Your space-age can opener with a built-in DVD player sold at auction! Since you have three dozen more to sell, the quicker you can get that item back up on the site, the sooner you'll connect with the next customer.

When bidders lose an auction on eBay, one of the first things they do is search for somebody offering the same item. The sooner you get an item relisted (or similarly listed in a fixed-price sale), the sooner a disappointed underbidder will find your item. Of course, relisting the item also makes it available to other interested bidders who may not have seen the item before.

If at first you don't succeed

Boo! Your Dansk Maribo dinner plate didn't sell. Don't take it personally. It's not that someone out there doesn't love you. It doesn't mean your merchandise is trash. It's just that this particular week, no one was looking for Maribo plates (go figure).

Often eBay shoppers shop with no discernable pattern. No one may want your item at a certain price one week, and then you may sell five or six the next week. It happens to me all the time.

When relisting, you often need to make adjustments. Perhaps the keywords in your title aren't drawing people to your listing. To help you figure out whether the problem is you or the market, search for other, similar items to see whether anyone is buying. If there's just no bidding activity (you're selling bikinis in January?), perhaps that item needs to be retired from eBay for a while.

Consider some other variables. Are other items selling on the site with a lower starting price? If you can comfortably lower your price, do so. If not, wait until other sellers run out of the item. Then put yours up for auction — you may just get more bidding action if you're one of the few sellers offering the same item.

I have quite a few items that I purchased by the case — right along with a bunch of other eBay sellers. They desperately dumped theirs on the site, without paying any attention to the competition. I waited and got my target price for the item the following season.

REMEMBER

eBay is a supply and demand marketplace. If the supply exceeds the demand, prices go down. If you have an item that sells as fast as you can list it, prices go up.

eBay Bidding Management Tools

Most eBay users don't know the extent of eBay's seller-specific services. And sometimes sellers are so involved with selling that they don't take the time to find out about new helper tools. So I've gone deep into the eBay pond to dig up a few excellent tools to help you with your online business. Even if you've used some of these before, it might be time to revisit them because eBay has implemented quite a few changes during the past year.

Canceling bids

Did you know that you don't have to accept bids from just anyone? Part of the business is watching your bidders. With bidding-management tools, you can save yourself a good deal of grief.

You could have any number of reasons for wanting to cancel someone's bid. Here are a few more legitimate reasons for canceling a bid:

>> The bidder contacts you to back out of the bid; choosing to be a nice guy, you let him or her out of the deal.

>> You're unable to verify the bidder's identity through email or the phone.

>> You need to end the listing early.

If you have trouble finding a direct link, you can get to the cancellation form shown in Figure 4-4 directly by typing the following into your browser's search window:

```
http://offer.ebay.com/ws/eBayISAPI.dll?CancelBidShow
```

FIGURE 4-4: Cancel bids on your auctions here.

Setting eBay buyer requirements

If you don't want certain buyers bidding on your auctions, you can remove their capability to do so. Setting up a list of bidders that you don't want to do business with is legal on eBay. If someone that you've blocked tries to bid on your auction, the bid won't go through. A message will be displayed notifying the bidder that he or she can't bid on the listing and should contact the seller for more information.

Many eBay sellers bemoan the fact that international buyers bid on their items, when the items clearly state that they do not ship internationally. Also, they get upset when a bidder with minus-level feedback wins an item.

Quit whining and do something about it! On your My eBay⇨Account⇨Site Preferences page, you can set defaults that will affect your bidders. On this page, scroll to Site Preferences: Buyer Requirements.

Click the Show, then Edit link to change your preferences. On the Select Requirements page click the check boxes for those buyers you don't want to be permitted to bid on your items. Some of the requirements you can set will block buyers who

>> Don't have a PayPal account

>> Have unpaid items recorded on their account

>> Are registered in countries to which you don't ship

>> Have reportedly violated eBay policies

>> Have a negative feedback score

>> Have bought a specified number of your items in the last 10 days, and would exceed that limit

If any of your bidders meet the requirements for blocking and attempt to bid, they will see a notice saying they are unable to bid. Figure 4-5 shows the results of my edits,

Buyer requirements

Block buyers who:	Don't have a PayPal account	Edit
	Have received 2 Unpaid Item strike(s) within 1 Month(s)	
	Have a primary shipping address in a location I don't ship to	
	Have 4 Policy Violation report(s) within 1 Month(s)	
	Have a feedback score of -1 or lower	
	Are currently winning or have bought 2 of my items in the last 10 days and have a feedback score of 5 or lower	

Buyer Requirements Activity Log
List of buyers you blocked in the past 60 days using Buyer Requirements. Learn more

FIGURE 4-5:
My seller account sets these requirements for bidders.

You can block as many as 5,000 users from buying your items. However, I recommend that you use this option only when absolutely necessary. Situations — and people — change, and it's best to try to clear up problems with particular bidders.

AUTHOR SAYS

In the case of some international buyers, I found that they send me a message to ask me to ship to them. I check their feedback, and if it's clear to me that they know the ropes, I can put their User IDs on my Buyer Requirements Exception list and they're free to win my item.

You can block buyers from the Buyer/Bidders Management page. You may find a link at the bottom of your Selling Manager Pro page or go directly to

http://pages.ebay.com/services/buyandsell/biddermanagement.html

or

```
http://cgi1.ebay.com/ws/eBayISAPI.dll?bidderblocklogin
```

You can reinstate a bidder at any time by going to the Blocked Bidder/Buyer List and deleting the bidder's User ID from the list.

Ending your listing early

You may decide to end a listing early for any number of reasons. If any bids are on your auction before ending it, you are duty-bound to sell to the highest bidder. So before ending an auction early, it's polite to email everyone in your bidder list, explaining why you're canceling bids and closing the auction. If an egregious error in the item's description is forcing you to take this action, let your bidders know whether you're planning to relist the item with the correct information.

After you've emailed all the bidders, you must then cancel their bids by using the bid-cancelation form; for the link to this form, see the earlier section "Canceling bids."

TIP

When ending a listing that has bids, the seller has the option of canceling all bids or leaving the bids, thus making the high bidder the winner of the closed listing.

To end a listing, use the drop-down list next to the listing on the Active Selling page. Click the More Actions drop-down menu next to the item and choose End Item to end your listing. You can also go directly to

```
http://offer.ebay.com/ws/eBayISAPI.dll?EndingMyAuction
```

Following are some legitimate reasons for ending your sale:

>> **An error occurred in the minimum bid or reserve amount.** Perhaps your spouse really loves that lamp and said you'd better get some good money for it, but you started the auction at $1.00 with no reserve. In this case, it is better to go to the listing and make revisions.

>> **The listing has a major error in it.** Maybe you misspelled a critical keyword in the title.

>> **The item was somehow lost or broken.** Your dog ate it?

WARNING

I don't recommend canceling an auction unless you absolutely have to because it's just bad business. People rely on your auctions being up for the stated amount of time. They may be planning to bid at the last minute, or they may just want to watch the action for a while. Also, if you have bids on the item, you may be in violation of one of eBay's policies. It pays to mind the details.

4

Sourcing Merchandise

Contents at a Glance

Chapter **1**

Understanding eRetail Marketing

'll bet it's no surprise to you that most eBay sellers lack a solid retail background or education. Most of us come from different walks of life, and just about all that most of us know about retailing is shopping — that's probably how we first found eBay. Now that game is about to change. The more we choose to sell, the more our businesses grow, and the more we need to know about the business of retail.

eBay sellers use many types of business models. Some sellers are continually on the prowl for new products, and stock their merchandise as soon as they find a deal. Others follow the trends and try to get stock of the latest and greatest gadget that they hope will take the country (and eBay) by storm. And sellers who run their businesses by selling for others are constantly beating the pavement for new customers to serve. Then there's the new eBay entrepreneur. Just like brick-and-mortar retailers, today's online sellers have to keep up on the trends so they can stock up on the most popular items for the coming seasons.

Be sure you understand how you want to run your own business. Ask yourself the following questions and give some thought to your answers:

1. **Who is your customer?** Know their demographics and where you can find them. (Book 6 gives you solid insights on how to use social media to your best advantage.)

2. **Do you want to theme your sales with specific items?** For that matter, are there some products you just wouldn't carry — no matter how profitable they might be?

3. **What is your price-point policy?** Do you have a specific profit margin in mind?

4. **How important is customer service to your business?** How far will you go to please buyers?

After you've faced these issues and given your business an identity, you're ready for the next steps. In this chapter, I help you see how to organize and run your business like a pro.

Marketing to Your Customers

When you're in business, you can't just consider yourself a retailer; you have to be a marketer too. The Internet enables sellers in the United States to market across the globe. I'm sure you know how large the area is, but what about the *people* you sell to? You've heard of advertising being targeted to the lucrative 18-to-49 age demographic, but what about all the other age groups? Who are *they*? If you learn about your customers, you'll know how to sell to them. It's all about targeting.

Decide who buys what you want to sell — or, better yet, decide with whom you want to deal. If you don't want to deal with emails from teenage gamers, for example, perhaps you shouldn't be selling items that Gen Y (defined in a moment) is going to want.

Marketers often provide blanket definitions about the population based on their stages in life, what they're expected to buy, and in which activities they participate. Generational cohorts are formed less by biological dates than by life experiences and influences. We all know that outside influences make a big difference in how we look at things; they also affect how and why we buy things.

TIP

My personal marketing theory is based on *psychographics* versus demographics. Psychographics means that you forget about the calendar age, and concern yourself more with the activities and interests of a group. For example, I know many highly technical Boomers who are the perfect market for gadgets, but a demographic profile wouldn't agree.

Since such generational marketing is all the rage, names have been applied to each cohort. The birthdates vary widely (depending on the source), but the approximate accepted dates are as follows:

>> Gen Z   1996 and later

>> Gen Y (Millennials)   1982-1995

>> Gen X   1965-1981

>> Baby Boomers   1946-1964

>> Greatest Generation   1924-1945

>> Silents   1901-1924

Table 1-1 gives you the current U.S. population grouped by age, showing how much of the total each group represents. With the knowledge from this table, you can better decide just how many people are potential shoppers for your products in the future.

TABLE 1-1

U.S. Population by Age Range

Age Range	Population	Percent of Population
18–24	30.8 million	9.5%
25–34	44.7 million	13.8%
35–44	40.5 million	12.5%
45–54	42.8 million	13.2%
55–64	41.5 million	12.8%
65–74	28.6 million	8.9%
75+	20.6 million	6.4%

Knowing the Current Market

Just as successful stockbrokers know about individual companies, they also need to know about the marketplace as a whole. Sure, I know about the newly reissued Furbies out there, and so does nearly everyone else. To get a leg up on your competition, you need to know the big picture as well. Here are some questions you should ask yourself as you contemplate making buckets of money by selling items on eBay:

>> **What items attract the buzz?** If you see everyone around you rushing to the store to buy a particular item, chances are good that the item will become more valuable as stocks of it diminish. The simple rule of supply and demand says that whoever has something everyone else wants stands to gain major profits.

>> **Do I see a growing interest in a specific item that might make it a big seller?** If you're starting to hear talk about a particular item, or even an era ('70s nostalgia? '60s aluminum Christmas trees? Who knew?), listen carefully and think of what you own — or can get your hands on — that can help you catch a piece of the trend's action.

>> **Should I hold on to this item and wait for its value to increase, or should I sell now?** Knowing when to sell an item that you think people may want is a tricky business. Sometimes you catch the trend too early — and find out later that you left money on the table by selling too early. You might have commanded a better price if you'd waited.

   Other times you may catch a fad that's already passé. It's best to test the market with a small quantity of your hoard, dribbling items individually into the market (and watching the sold prices) until you've made back the money you spent to acquire them. When you have your cash back, the rest will be gravy.

>> **Is a company discontinuing an item I should stockpile now and sell later?** Pay attention to discontinued items, especially toys and collectibles. If you find an item that a manufacturer has a limited supply of, you could make a tidy profit. If the manufacturer ends up reissuing the item, don't forget that the original run is still the most coveted and valuable.

>> **Was there a recall (due to non-safety issues), an error, or a legal proceeding associated with my item?** If so, how will it affect the value of the item? For example, a toy recalled for reasons other than safety may no longer be appropriate, but it could be rare and collectible if sealed and intact.

TIP

Some people like to go with their gut feeling about when and what to buy for resale at eBay. By all means, if instinct has worked for you in the past, factor instinct in here, too. If your research looks optimistic but your gut says, "I'm not sure," listen to it; don't assume you're just hearing that lunchtime taco talking. Test the waters by purchasing a couple of the prospective items for resale. If that sale doesn't work out, you won't have a lot of money invested, and you can credit your gut with saving you some bucks.

MONETIZING YOUR EXPERTISE

If you're talented in any way, you can sell your services on eBay. Home artisans, chefs, and even stay-at-home psychics are transacting business daily on the site. What a great way to make money on eBay — make your own product!

Many custom items do well on eBay. People go to trendy places (when they have the time) such as Soho, the Grove, or the Village to find unique custom jewelry. They also go to eBay.

There's a big demand today for personalized invitations, cards, and calligraphic work, as well as laser- and computer-designed items, but no one seems to have the time to make them. A simple search of the word *handmade* or *personalized* will give you some ideas. Savvy sellers with talent can fill this market niche.

Catching Trends in the Media

Catching trends is all about listening and looking. You can find all kinds of inside information from magazines, television, and of course, the Internet. Believe it or not, you can even find out what people are interested in these days by asking a kid to provide you with a wish list. Keep your eyes and ears open.

In the news

The media (online or on paper) is bombarded with press releases and inside information from companies the world over. Look for stories about celebrities and upcoming movies and see whether any old fads are experiencing a resurgence. (You can sell such items as *retro chic*.)

Read the accounts from trade conventions, such as the New York Toy Fair or the Consumer Electronics show. New products are introduced and given the thumbs-up or thumbs-down by journalists. Use that information to help determine the direction for your area of expertise.

On television

No matter what you think of television, it has an enormous effect on which trends come and go — and which ones stick. Why else would advertisers sink billions of dollars into TV commercials? For example, at the zenith of its popularity, *The Oprah Winfrey Show* could turn a book into an overnight bestseller with one appearance by its author. Tune in to morning news and afternoon talk shows. The producers of these shows are on top of pop culture and move fast to be the first to bring you the next big thing. Take what they feature and think of a marketing angle. If you don't, you can be sure somebody else will.

Catch up with youth culture . . .

. . . or at least keep good tabs on it. If you remember cranking up the Beatles, the Partridge Family, or KISS (say what?) until your parents screamed, "Shut off that awful noise," you may be at that awkward time of life when you hardly see the appeal of what young folks are doing or listening to. But if you want tips for hot items, ignore the noise and listen to the kids around you. Children, especially preteens and teens, may be the best trend-spotters on the planet.

Check out other media

Websites and blogs geared to the 18-to-34 age group (and sometimes to younger teens) can help you stay on top of what's hot. See what the big companies are pitching to this target audience (and whether they're succeeding). If a celebrity is suddenly visible in every other headline, be on the lookout for merchandise relating to that person. (Are we talking hysteria-plus-cash-flow here, or just hysteria?)

Join social networks

So, you say you haven't been to Facebook, haven't started to use Twitter, and don't have a blog or boards on Pinterest? Wow, you're living in the days of low-res TV! This online social scene is the place to be. The *social web* (as it's called) is branded with the top of the top; the most happening things and products. Join the fun on some social networks, and you'll soon have a clue to what the kids are doing now. Book 6 gives you insight on the where, how, and when to jump in.

Finding eBay's Soon-to-Be-Hot Sellers

Everyone wants to know what the hot ticket is on the eBay site. They want to know what's selling best so that they can run out, buy it, and *make big money* on eBay. Whoa, there, big fella.

As you may know, I'm not a believer in the notion that eBay is a get-rich-quick program. Nobody has, or can give you, secret information that magically transforms you from a garage seller to a warehouse tycoon overnight. You get there by studying the market and finding out what works and what doesn't. There are no shortcuts. That said, you can find up-to-the-minute information by typing the link below to view eBay's Trending searches. Each of the "Top 10" items listed will show you a bar graph to indicate if the item is on the way up — or on the way down (see Figure 1-1).

www.ebay.com/trending

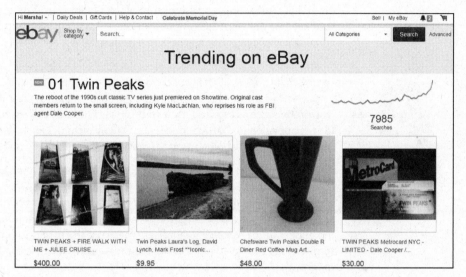

FIGURE 1-1:
Learning "what's hot" on eBay.

Now wouldn't I be the smart one if I were to list items that coincided with the top-selling items on the site? You bet! It's a great place to start. Just remember to review those top items from time to time. And stay tuned for tips on how to keep your business healthy in the midst of the dynamic eBay environment.

Taking Aim with a Six-Month Merchandise Plan

The eBay seller buys merchandise to sell on eBay and perhaps also on other marketplaces. These online sellers are always looking for new sources and wholesalers. But many of the folks who sell on eBay specialize in particular types of item, such as dolls, sports cards, lighting fixtures, or apparel. Their eBay business is organized; they sell their merchandise and then buy more to replenish their stock. Is this the best way to handle things? It definitely works for most, but those who study retailing know that there's a far more organized way.

One of the first things you learn when studying retail buying is the use of a six-month merchandise plan. It's the ultimate tool in the arsenal of a successful retail buyer. Although it was originally designed for brick-and-mortar retailers, I've adapted it here for online sellers.

Here's what establishing a six-month merchandising plan gives you:

REMEMBER

>> **A clear, concise look at your business activity:** After you fill out the plan, you'll be able to combine it with the reports generated by your bookkeeping program to get a clear, concise picture of your online business. (I explain bookkeeping best practices in Book 9.) This is a business and not a guessing game, and handling your business in a professional manner will save you a great deal of time and money.

I admit that running by the seat of your pants is fun and exciting (and perfect *if* eBay selling is your side gig), but it's not a solid long-term business practice. One of the reasons I started my own business is that an unorganized business format appealed to me. (Ah, innocence.) To my dismay, I soon learned that organization and planning really *did* make a difference in my bottom line.

>> **A basis for growth plans:** Anyone who has participated in management in a corporation knows about the annual plan. Every year in many organizations, management gets together (apparently with Ouija and dart boards) to project sales, expenses, and profits for the coming year. From this annual exercise, the budget for the coming year arises. These are the magic numbers that form the basis for everyone's annual raises — along with the company's plans for growth.

>> **A set of attainable and repeatable goals:** So, assuming that eBay sellers are online retailers, retail evaluation could help eBay sellers make sound business decisions. Making a merchandise plan is a good step in that direction. A merchandise plan covers six months at a time and sets sales goals. It also helps you estimate how much money must be spent on merchandise (and when) so that a particular season's success can be replicated and magnified.

Pulling Together Your Inventory Data

When you reach a point where your online sales are your main business, it's time to get serious. You need a few numbers to get your merchandising plan on paper. If you aren't using bookkeeping software yet, you still need to put together a report that reflects the dollar value of your existing inventory. (Book 9, Chapters 2 and 3 give you more insights into that process.) If you are using bookkeeping software, you can get these numbers easily from the program's Inventory Valuation report:

>> **BOM:** The value, in dollars, of your beginning-of-month inventory

>> **EOM:** The value, in dollars, of your end-of-month inventory

    The EOM figure for a specific month is the same as the BOM figure for the following month. For example, the end-of-month figure for April is the same as the beginning-of-month figure for May.

>> **Gross sales:** Total revenue from sales (not including shipping and handling)

>> **Markdowns:** Total revenue of merchandise you have sold on eBay below your target price

To put together your six-month plan, you need to have sales history for a six-month period. To get a good historical picture of your sales, however, it's preferable to have at least an entire year's worth of figures.

REMEMBER

Your six-month plan can be based on your total online sales or only one segment of your business. For example, if you sell musical instruments along with many other sundry items, but you want to evaluate your musical-instrument sales, you can use just those figures for a six-month plan for your music department.

What you're going to establish is your *inventory turnover* — that is, the measure of how much inventory sells out in a specified period of time. The faster you turn over merchandise, the sooner you can bring in new merchandise and increase your bottom line. You can also evaluate whether you need to lower your starting price to move out stale inventory to get cash to buy new inventory.

TIP

When you prepare your six-month plan, set out the months not by the regular calendar but by a *retail calendar,* which divides the year into the seasons of fall/winter (August 1 through January 31) and spring/summer (February 1 through July 31). This way, if you want to refer to top national performance figures in trade publications or on the Internet, you can base your figures on the same standardized retail seasons.

Using Formulas to Calculate Business Data

Okay, I can admit that bigger minds than mine came up with standard formulas for calculating business success. These formulas are used by retailers around the world. If you're not pulling the figures from a bookkeeping program, you can do the calculations yourself, as follows:

>> EOM stock = BOM stock + Purchases – Sales

>> BOM stock = EOM stock from the previous month

>> Sales + EOM – BOM = monthly planned purchases

You can make your calculations in dollar amounts or in the number of units of the item. To figure out how much of an item to buy, you must know how much you have left in stock.

Prepare a chart for your own business, similar to the one shown in Table 1-2. Study your results and find out which months are your strongest. Let the table tell you when you might have to boost your merchandise selection in lagging months. It will help you bring your planning from Ouija board to reality.

TABLE 1-2   **Sample Six-Month eBay Merchandise Plan**

Fall/Winter	Aug	Sept	Oct	Nov	Dec	Jan	Total
Total sales	$2,875.00	$3,320.00	$3,775.00	$4,150.00	$3,950.00	$4,350.00	$22,420.00
+ Retail EOM	$1,750.00	$3,870.00	$4,250.00	$3,985.00	$4,795.00	$4,240.00	$22,890.00
+ Reductions	$575.00	$275.00	$250.00	$175.00	$425.00	$275.00	$1,975.00
– Retail BOM	$3,150.00	$1,750.00	$3,870.00	$4,250.00	$3,985.00	$4,795.00	$21,800.00
= Retail purchases	$2,050.00	$5,715.00	$4,405.00	$4,060.00	$5,185.00	$4,070.00	$25,485.00
Cost purchases	$3,310.00	$3,540.00	$4,725.00	$5,150.00	$2,775.00	$3,450.00	$22,950.00
% of season's sales	12.82%	14.81%	16.84%	18.51%	17.62%	19.40%	
% of season's reductions	29.11%	13.92%	12.66%	8.86%	21.52%	13.92%	
Average stock	$3,815.00						
Average sales	$3,735.00						
Basic stock	$1,000.00						

Chapter **2**

Sourcing Merchandise Like a Pro

'm often asked, "Where do I find merchandise to sell?" This, of course, is followed by "What can I sell to make the highest profit?" Good questions. But what successful seller has an answer they want to give to the competition? Did Macy's tell Gimbel's?

When eBay PowerSellers have a good, solid source of merchandise, they're not likely to share the name of that source with anyone — nor would any offline retailer. (Think about it a minute.) When I was teaching a class for advanced sellers at eBay Live (an eBay user convention back in the day), I was asked *the* question in an auditorium-size room filled with PowerSellers. I answered a question with a question: Were there any PowerSellers in the audience who would like to share their sources with the rest of the group? You could have heard a pin drop. So I upped the ante — "I'll pay anyone $10 for one solid source" — still silence. Business is business.

TIP

When someone is willing to sell you attendance to a webinar or a list of merchandise sources, you can bet the list contains old, fairly public vendors. Also, these folks are in the business of selling lists. If they were so successful, why aren't they filling their coffers with eBay profits?

The bottom line is that all successful sellers seek out their own sources. What works for one may not work for another. Methods for finding goods that I include in this chapter are gleaned from my own research, as well as from interviews with successful online retailers.

Tips for the Modest Investor

If you're interested in making money in your new eBay venture but you're starting with limited cash, follow this list of inventory dos and don'ts:

» **Do** start small. Think about the many collectibles that are sitting around your home. Earn your eBay stripes by selling things where it's safe to make a mistake or two. Consider finding collectibles at garage sales and resale stores as well.

» **Don't** spend more than you can afford to lose. If you shop at boutiques and expensive department stores, buy things that you like to wear yourself (or give as gifts) in case they don't sell.

» **Do** try to find something local that's unavailable nationally. For example, if you live in an out-of-the-way place that has a local specialty, try selling that on eBay.

» **Don't** go overboard and buy something really cheap just because it's cheap. Figure out who would want the item first.

» **Do** consider buying in bulk, especially if you know the item sells well or is inexpensive. Chances are good that if you buy a couple and they sell well on eBay, the item will be sold out by the time you try to buy more. If an item is inexpensive (say $.99), I always buy at least five. If no one bids on the item when you hold your auction, you're only out $5. (Why not check the store's return policy?)

As a citizen of the Internet, no doubt you'll receive unsolicited emails guaranteeing that the sender has the hottest-selling items for you to sell on eBay. Think about this for a second. If you had the hot ticket, wouldn't you be selling it on eBay and making the fortune yourself? These people make money by preying on those who think there's a magic way to make money on eBay. There isn't. It takes old-fashioned elbow grease and research.

Buying for Retail: The Basic Course

If you're not sure what you want to sell for profit — but you're a shop-till-you-drop person by nature — incorporate your advanced shopping techniques into your daily routine. If you find a bargain that interests you, chances are you have a knack for spotting products that other shoppers would love to get their hands on.

FIGURING OUT WHO'S WHO IN THE INDUSTRY

Industrial-strength sourcing is not for the faint-hearted, nor for those who lack the needed licenses and sales permits. (Book 9 fills you in on how to get those; to play with the big boys, you'll have to produce these documents just to get in the door.)

It would be so very simple if you could just buy merchandise from a manufacturer. But that's rarely the case. The wholesale game requires a full team of players to participate, and each player performs a different task, as follows:

- **Manufacturers:** Buying directly from a manufacturer may get you great prices, but that may not be the place for a beginner to start. Manufacturers usually require large minimum orders from retailers. Unless you have a group of other sellers (perhaps a friend who owns a retail store?) to split your order with, you may have to make your purchase from a middleman.

  An exception to the large-quantity requirement may be in the apparel industry. Because apparel has distinct, rapidly changing fashion seasons, a quick turnover in merchandise is a must. Apparel manufacturers may allow you to make small purchases toward the end of the season to outfit your eBay Store. It never hurts to ask.

- **Wholesalers:** Here's your first step to finding your middleman. Wholesalers purchase direct from the manufacturer in large quantities. They sell the merchandise to smaller retailers who can't take advantage of the discounts offered by manufacturers for large orders.

  Find a wholesaler who is familiar with (or better yet, specializes in) the type of merchandise you want to sell. Obviously, someone who specializes in movies on DVD and Blu-Ray probably won't have a clue about the nuances of the fashion market — and vice versa.

  Don't forget to check local wholesalers, as described in the "Finding merchandise locally" section later in this chapter.

(continued)

(continued)

- **Manufacturer's reps:** These are generally the type of people you'll meet at trade shows or marts. They represent one or many noncompeting manufacturers and sell their merchandise to retailers for a commission.

- **Jobbers or brokers:** These independent businesspeople buy merchandise anywhere they can, at distressed prices. They deal mostly in liquidation or salvage merchandise. To find out more about this source, see Chapter 4 in this minibook.

Don't forget to negotiate. Almost everything in the wholesale merchandise world is negotiable. Although merchandise may have a set price, you may be able to get a discount if you offer to pay on delivery or within ten days. Ask whether you can get help with shipping costs and perhaps promotions. Or you may earn a discount if you promote wholesalers' products through banner ads. Ask, ask, ask. The worst you can hear is no.

When you're new at ecommerce, you probably want to get your feet wet first before shelling out large sums for wholesale merchandise. Some great deals are available in the open market for resale!

Joining the hunt for inventory

Check your favorite product category and see what the top selling item is. Better yet, go to your favorite brick and mortar store and make friends with the manager. Store managers will often tell you what's going to be the new hot item next month. After you're armed with the information you need, search out that item for the lowest price you can, and then give it a shot on eBay.

Keep these shopping locales in mind when you go on the product hunt:

» **Upscale department stores, trendy boutiques, outlet stores, or flagship designer stores** are good places to do market research. Check out the newest items — and then head to the clearance area or outlet store and scrutinize the bargain racks for brand-name items.

» **Discount club stores** such as Sam's Club and Costco made their mark by selling items in bulk to large families, clubs, and small businesses. In case you haven't noticed, these stores have upscaled and sell just about anything you could want. And both Sam's Club and Costco have websites: `http://auctions.samsclub.com` and `www.costco.com`.

Just now I visited the Sam's Club auction site, `https://auctions.samsclub.com/auction/endingsoon/today/`. I found a group of items that, when I searched prices on Google, were selling for way below the going price. Locking in items like this could be very profitable. (See Figure 2-1.)

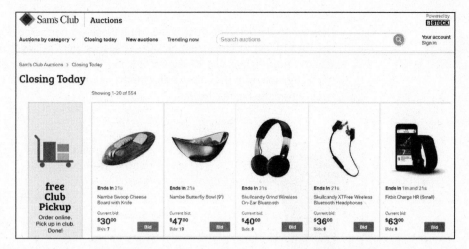

FIGURE 2-1:
Auctions on the Sam's Club website.

I made a quick jump to eBay and searched for the Fitbit HR (black, small) in sold items. Take a look at closing prices shown in Figure 2-2. This example represents a pretty sweet profit potential.

FIGURE 2-2:
The same items sold for a lot more on eBay.

AUTHOR SAYS

In another book, I talked about a special on the Costco website, www.costco.com, for a new *Snow White & the Seven Dwarfs* DVD. For $18.49, you could pre-order the *Snow White* DVD and get a second Disney DVD for *free*. When there's an offer like this, you can sell two items on eBay for the price of one. If I had followed my own advice — bought a case of this deal and held some for future sales — I'd be in the money today. It seems that Disney movies are released for a limited time only.

Now, when checking the Costco site, I find these women's Bodymagic skirts on sale for $14.99 (with free shipping). On eBay they were selling in multiple listings for as high as $34.99. Figures 2-3 and 2-4 show you how profit can be made. By looking at the completed listings, I could even see which colors and sizes netted the highest profit.

FIGURE 2-3: Women's skirts at Costco.

FIGURE 2-4: Profits to be had on eBay.

TIP

Stores like Costco have a 90-day return policy. Keep track of your merchandise cycle and return when you need to.

» **Dollar stores** in your area. Many of the items these places carry are *overruns* (too many of something that didn't sell), *small runs* (too little of something that the big guys weren't interested in stocking), or out-of-date fad items that need a good home on eBay. I've found profitable books, Olympics memorabilia, and pop-culture items at this type of store.

TIP

It's not unusual for dollar-store warehouses to sell direct to a retailer (that's you). Find out where the distribution warehouse is for your local dollar store chain and make contact. The 99¢ Only stores, for example, have a wholesale unit called Bargain Wholesale that runs out of their City of Commerce, California offices. Bargain Wholesale also has a website (see Figure 2-5) which is open to anyone with legitimate resale credentials.

FIGURE 2-5:
Download Bargain Wholesale's catalog on the company site.

>> **Thrift stores** are packed with used — but often good-quality — items. And you can feel good knowing that the money you spend in a nonprofit thrift shop is going to a good cause. Some branches of Goodwill and the Salvation Army receive merchandise from a central warehouse. Ask the manager (whom you've befriended) when the truck regularly comes in.

Goodwill Industries is definitely geared up for the 21st century. You can shop at its online auctions (see Figure 2-6) and get super values on the best of their merchandise. Don't forget to check the going prices on eBay before you buy. Have fun at www.shopgoodwill.com.

>> **Garage, tag, moving, and estate sales** offer some of the biggest bargains you'll ever come across. If you watched the Netflix show, *GirlBoss,* you'll see that the hero started her online business with this advice from my books. The stuff you find at estate sales is often of a higher quality. Keep an eye out for "moving to a smaller house" sales. These are usually people who have raised children,

accumulated a houseful of stuff (collectibles? old toys? designer vintage clothes?), and want to shed it all so that they can move to a condo in Palm Springs.

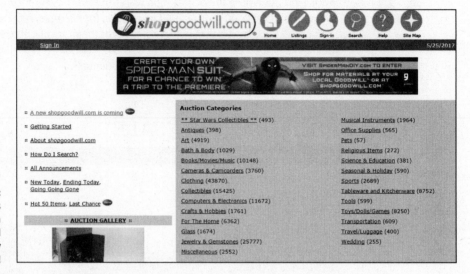

FIGURE 2-6:
Goodwill's auction site even sells scrap gold in the jewelry category!

TIP

When an item is new but has some collectible potential, I suggest you buy in bulk, sell some of the item to repay your investment, and save the balance for later. This strategy has paid off for me a good many times with Disney films, Barbies, and Andy Warhol dinnerware.

>> **Liquidation and estate auctions** are two types of auctions where you can pick up bargains. Before you go to any auction, double-check payment terms and find out whether you must bring cash or can pay by credit card. Also, before you bid on anything, find out the *hammer fee,* or *buyer's premium.* These fees are a percentage that auction houses add to the winner's bid; the buyer has the responsibility for paying these fees.

When a company gets into financial trouble, its debtors (the people to whom the company owes money) obtain a court order to liquidate the company to pay the bills. The liquidated company then sells its stock, fixtures, and even real estate in a liquidation auction. Items sell for just cents on the dollar, and you can easily resell many of these items on eBay. Use Google or Bing and search *auctioneers: liquidators.* You can also contact local offices to get on mailing lists.

Estate auctions are the higher level of estate garage sales. Here you can find fine art, antiques, paper ephemera, rare books, and collectibles of all kinds. These auctions are attended mostly by dealers, who know the local going prices for the items they bid on. But because they're buying to sell in a retail environment, their high bids will generally be the wholesale price for your area. And local dealers are buying what's hot to resell in your city — not what's going to sell across the country. That entire market will probably be yours.

>> **Community newspaper auction listings** are an excellent source of merchandise for resale, particularly the listings of liquidations and estate auctions in the classified section, which often has ads that announce local business liquidations. Do not confuse any of these with garage sales or flea-market sales (run by individuals and a great source for one-of-a kind items). Liquidation and estate sales are professionally run, usually by licensed liquidators or auctioneers, and involve merchandise that may be new but is always sold in *lots* (in a quantity) rather than one item at a time.

TIP

If your local newspaper has a website, use its online search to view the classifieds for major liquidations, estate auctions, or other similar deals. Right there online, you can often find just what you're looking for locally. I typed in a Google search for *Newspaper classified Los Angeles*. The *Los Angeles Times* (and other local papers) showed up. There was a link to garage sales in the *Times* listing. I clicked it and came to a wealth of sources shown in Figure 2-7.

FIGURE 2-7:
A Google search for *newspaper classified los angeles* lists plenty of sales to check out.

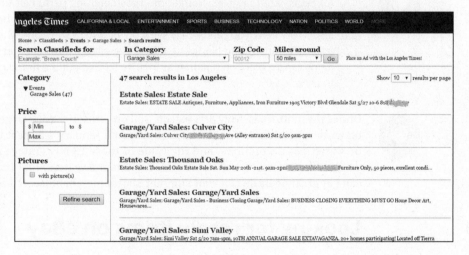

>> **Going-out-of-business sales,** some of which run week by week, with bigger discounts as time goes by. Don't be shy about making an offer on a quantity of items.

WARNING

Going-out-of-business sales can be a bonanza, but be careful and don't be misled. Many states require businesses that are putting on a going-out-of-business sale to purchase a special license that identifies the business as *really* going out of business. Some store ads may read "Going Out for Business" or some similar play on words, so you need to be sure that you're going to the real thing.

» **Flea markets or swap meets** in your area may have some bargains you can take advantage of.

» **Gift shops at museums, monuments, national parks, and theme parks** can provide eBay inventory — but think about where to sell the items. Part of your selling success online is *access*. People who can't get to Graceland may pay handsomely for an Elvis mini-guitar with the official logo on the box.

» **Freebies** are usually samples or promotion pieces that companies give away to introduce a new product, service, or, best of all, a media event. Hang on to these! If you receive handouts (lapel pins, pencils, pamphlets, books, interesting napkins, flashlights, towels, stuffed toys) from a sporting event, premiere, or historic event — or even a collectible freebie from a fast-food restaurant — they could be your ticket to some eBay sales. For example, when *Return of the Jedi* was re-released in 1997, the first 100 people to enter each theater got a Special Edition Luke Skywalker figure. These figures are still highly prized by collectors — and when the next part of the *Star Wars* saga was released, the prices on this figure went up yet again.

TIP

When you go to the cosmetic counter and buy a way-too-expensive item, ask for tester-sized samples. Name-brand cosmetic and perfume samples of high-priced items sell well on eBay. Also, look for *gift with purchase* deals. If it's a specialty item, you can usually sell it on its own to someone who'd like to try a sample, rather than plunge headlong into a large purchase. Less-special items can be grouped together as lots. Be sure to put the brand names in the title.

TIP

One of my mottoes is "Buy off–season, sell on–season." You can get great bargains on winter merchandise in the heat of summer. January's a great time to stock up on Christmas decorations, and the value of those trendy vintage aluminum trees doubles in November and December. Cashmere sweaters, too! In the winter, you can get great deals on closeout summer sports merchandise. It's all in the timing.

Looking for resale items on eBay

Another place to find items to sell is on eBay itself. Look only for good-quality merchandise to resell. Remember that the only way to make a living on eBay is to sell quality items to happy customers so that they'll come back and buy from you again.

Be sure to search eBay auction titles for the following:

» **Keywords:** wholesale, resale, resell, closeout, surplus

» **Key phrases:** case of, wholesale lots, case quantity, "lot of," "pallet of" (see Figure 2-8)

FIGURE 2-8:
A "pallet of" search reveals lots of buys. Narrow down by category to find just what you want.

Also be sure you check out the wholesale categories on eBay. After noticing how many sellers were buying from other sellers, eBay set up wholesale subcategories for almost every type of item. You can find the wholesale items in most categories. Go to the eBay home page and click Shop by Category. Then click See All Categories at the bottom of the pop-up window that appears. Search the page for instances of Wholesale, then select the favorite category in which you sell, and find the Wholesale Lots subcategory. Just click that link to get to the deals. If you're looking for the category featured in Figure 2-9, you can also go to www.ebay.com/b/Clothing-Shoes-Accessories-Wholesale-Lots/41964/bn_1852124.

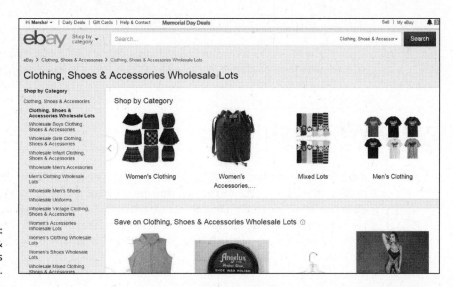

FIGURE 2-9:
Clothing, Shoes & Accessories Wholesale Lots.

CHAPTER 2 **Sourcing Merchandise Like a Pro** 301

TUESDAY MORNING

One of my editors is going to kill me for mentioning one of her favorite eBay merchandise sources, but here it is: Tuesday Morning, which has more than 500 stores scattered over the United States. They sell first-quality designer and brand-name closeout merchandise at deep, deep discounts — 50 to 80 percent below retail. The key here is that the store sells recognizable brand names, the kind of items that eBay shoppers look for. I've seen items at their store from Samsonite, Gucci, Limoges, Wedgwood, Royal Doulton, Madame Alexander, and even Barbie! Find your local store or shop at their website, www.tuesdaymorning.com. The following is a great example of the bargains you can find. On the left, see the item on the Tuesday Morning site at $49.99; on the right, it's close to $117 in an eBay listing. Nice profit margin!

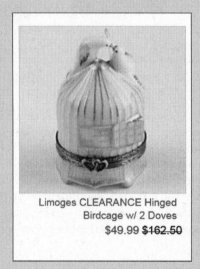

Limoges CLEARANCE Hinged
Birdcage w/ 2 Doves
$49.99 $162.50

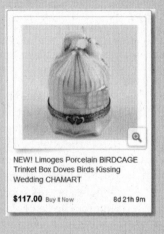

NEW! Limoges Porcelain BIRDCAGE
Trinket Box Doves Birds Kissing
Wedding CHAMART

$117.00 Buy It Now   8d 21h 9m

These prices are from a few years ago. I saw this item selling on eBay today for $159. Which shows if you hold on to limited-edition items, they can go up nicely in value.

Buying Wholesale

After you get the hang of finding items in stores to resell on eBay, it's time to move to the wholesale source. As a side note, I want you to know that although my eBay business is based on wholesale merchandise, I still love going to the sources mentioned in the last section and finding great deals to resell. It's become a fun hobby! Don't we all love to find a piece of merchandise that we *know* we can sell for a profit?

Okay, you want to set up shop on eBay. You kind of know what type of merchandise you want to sell, but you don't know where to turn. Anyone in the brick-and-mortar world who plans to open a new store faces the same quandary: finding merchandise that will sell quickly at a profit.

Merchandise that sits around doesn't give you cash flow, which is the name of the game in *any* business. (*Cash flow* = profit = money to buy better, or more, merchandise.) I spoke to several successful retailers and they all gave me the same answers about where they began their quest. The upcoming sections give you a look at the answers these retailers shared.

Setting up to buy

Purchasing wholesale merchandise may require that you have your state's *resale license,* which identifies you as being in the business. Be sure that you have one before you try to purchase merchandise directly from another business. Also, when you have a resale number and purchase merchandise from another business — known as a *business-to-business* (B2B) transaction — you probably won't be charged sales tax when you purchase your stock because you'll be *paying* sales tax when you sell the items. Go to Book 9, Chapter 1 to find out how to get that magic resale number.

When you have your resale number, you can go anywhere you want to buy merchandise. If you want to buy direct from a manufacturer, you can. Unfortunately, many manufacturers have a minimum order amount, which may be more than you want to spend (and you'd get more of a particular item than you'd ever want at once). To remedy that, see whether you can find independent retailers who buy in quantity — and who will (perhaps) let you in on some quantity buys with manufacturers. I often buy in with a couple of local shops when they purchase their orders.

REMEMBER

To gain access to legitimate wholesale sources, you must be a licensed business in your city or county. You also usually have to have a resale permit and tax ID number from your state. (See Book 9, Chapter 1 for details.)

Finding merchandise locally

Always remember that the cost of shipping the merchandise to you adds a great deal of expense. The higher your expense, the lower your return may be. The more you buy locally to resell, the more profit you can make.

The first place most potential retailers go is to the local wholesale district. These are immediate merchandise sources, within driving distance of your home.

Regional merchandise marts

Your next stop — should you be lucky enough to live in a major metropolitan area — is to find out whether there's a merchandise or fashion mart near you. These are giant complexes that hold as many as several thousand lines of merchandise in one area.

Merchandise marts are hubs for wholesale buyers, distributors, manufacturers, and independent sales representatives. They have showrooms within the property for manufacturers or their representatives to display their current merchandise. Under one roof, you may find both fashion and gift merchandise for your eBay business.

See Table 2-1 for a representative sprinkling of the many marts across the country. This is not a comprehensive list, just one to get your mind moving; I have a much more thorough list in the Tools area of my website www.coolebaytools.com. You can contact the individual marts for tenant lists and more information. If you're a legitimate business, the marts will be more than happy to teach you the ropes and get you started.

TABLE 2-1   **Wholesale Merchandise Marts**

Name	Location	Website Address	Trade Shows
AmericasMart	Atlanta, GA	www.americasmart.com	Apparel, jewelry, shoes, fashion accessories, gifts, home furnishings
California Market Center	Los Angeles, CA	www.californiamarketcenter.com	Apparel, accessories, textiles, toys, gifts, furniture & décor, garden accessories, stationery, personal-care products
theMART	Chicago, IL	themart.com	Apparel, office, home, decorative accessories, textiles, gifts
Columbus MarketPlace	Columbus, OH	www.thecolumbusmarketplace.com	Gifts, garden, home furnishings, décor
Dallas Market Center	Dallas, TX	www.dallasmarketcenter.com	Apparel, gift products, decorative accessories, home furnishings, lighting, garden accessories, floral, and gourmet
The Denver Mart	Denver, CO	www.denvermart.com	Apparel, gifts, souvenirs, gourmet, collectibles, home décor

Name	Location	Website Address	Trade Shows
LA MART	Los Angeles, CA	`www.lamart.com`	Gifts, home décor, furnishings
Miami Merchandise Mart	Miami, FL	`www.miamimerchandisemart.com`	Apparel, gifts, accessories, home décor
MinneapolisMART	Minneapolis, MN	`www.mplsmart.com`	Gifts, home décor, accessories
FortyOne Madison	New York, NY	`www.41madison.com`	Gifts, home décor, accessories
San Francisco Gift Center & Jewelry Mart	San Francisco, CA	`www.sfgcjm.com`	Apparel, jewelry, home furnishings, gifts, stationery
The New Mart	Los Angeles, CA	`www.newmart.net`	Contemporary clothing and accessories

TIP

When you go to each mart's website, you'll find hundreds of links to wholesale sources. Many marts also send you a directory of the manufacturers represented in the mart.

Wholesale trade shows

By checking out the links to the marts listed in Table 2-1, you'll also end up with links to the thousands of wholesale trade shows that go on across the country each year. Trade shows are commonly held in convention centers, hotels, and local merchandise marts.

A super source for finding gift shows is the `greatrep.com` website, shown in Figure 2-10. Here you find a list of all the major gift shows — with clickable links to contact information for the show coordinators. For more on GreatRep.com, see the "Buying Online for Resale" section later in this chapter.

TIP

When visiting a show or a mart, view all merchandise before you place an order. Bring a notebook with you to make copious notes of items you find interesting and where you find them.

These trade shows are gargantuan bourses of hundreds of wholesale vendors all lined up and ready to take your orders. The vendors have samples of the merchandise in the lines they carry and are delighted to answer all your questions about their products, credit applications, and minimum orders. These shows are designed to move products to retailers like you!

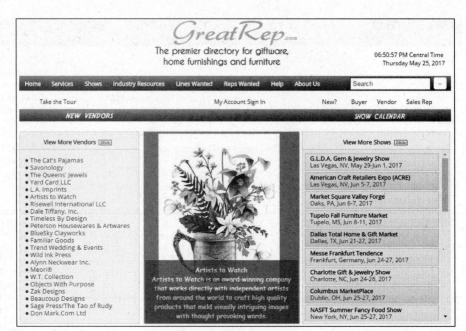

FIGURE 2-10:
Check the
GreatRep.com
website for an
updated trade
show schedule.

NECESSARY ID FOR TRADE SHOWS AND MARTS

Professional trade shows and marts are not open to the general public, and they want to keep it that way. When you attend these venues, they want to be sure that you represent a business. Following is a list of items that you may be asked to provide, as proof that you are a retailer:

- Business cards

- A copy of your current resale-tax certificate or state tax permit

- Current occupational or business tax license

- Proof of a business checking account or a letter of credit from your bank (if you're applying for credit)

- Financial statement

- Cash and checks

Be sure to check with the organization sponsoring the trade show or mart before attending so that you'll have everything you need. Don't let this list scare you — wholesale marts are fun, and the organizers and vendors will do everything they can to help you make your retailing venture a success!

Few trade shows are more exciting than the Consumer Electronics Show (CES), sponsored by the Consumer Electronics Association. If you buy breakthrough technologies to sell online, this show is a must! You'll find the latest in everything high-tech, including digital imaging, electronic gaming, home electronics, car audio, home theater, and satellite systems. You'll see what's new — but more important, you'll see what will be passé in a hurry — great merchandise to sell (in a timely way, of course) on eBay.

CES draws more than 100,000 buyers each year, and the vendors are there to sell their goods to *you*. Visit the CES website at `http://www.ces.tech` to get an idea of the excitement that the show generates.

TIP

See whether the item is selling on eBay before you make your purchase. Bring your tablet or laptop and conduct online research, either on the spot or later in the day for next-day purchases. *Getting* a good deal is one thing — selling it on eBay is another.

Buying Online for Resale

I've come across many legitimate sources of goods on the Internet. But the Internet is loaded with scam artists; it's up to you to check vendors out for yourself before spending your hard-earned money. Even if I mention sellers here, I want you to check them out as if you know nothing about them. I can't guarantee a thing; all I know is that at the time of this writing, they were reliable sources for eBay merchandise.

Craigslist

If you haven't visited Craigslist in a while, you're missing quite a bit. You'll find anything and everything listed in the free local classifieds, and you never know when there will be something worthwhile to resell. This site is always worth at least a once-a-week visit (to find a local version near you, visit `www.craigslist.org`). Much of the stuff on the site is listed by people who are too afraid (or maybe just technophobic) to sell on eBay. Focus on your category of interest and go to town. I did exactly that and found the item shown in Figure 2-11, a Cartier Love bracelet selling for $150. This item sells on eBay for up to $3,000!

TIP

Before buying an item like the one pictured in Figure 2-11, definitely check the authenticity. Buyer beware — it's most likely a fake.

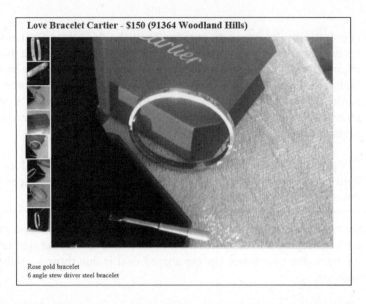

Love Bracelet Cartier - $150 (91364 Woodland Hills)

Rose gold bracelet
6 angle stew driver steel bracelet

FIGURE 2-11:
Craigslist is a super source for purchasing used items from technophobes.

TIPS FOR BUYING WHOLESALE ONLINE

Because the online world can be fraught with problems, keep in mind the following:

- **Protect your email address.** Check every site you sign up with for a privacy policy. Watch out for wording like this in the privacy policy: "Our Privacy Policy does not extend to our affiliated sellers or advertisers. They are free to maintain their own privacy policy independent of us." Again, get an *anonymous* email address to spare yourself spam.

- **Look for an *About Us* page.** Be sure the site has an address and a phone number. Call the number to see whether it is a "real" business, not a fly-by-night. While you're at it, see how you're treated on the phone.

- **Look for safety seals.** Seeing the Better Business Bureau Online, TrustE, or SquareTrade logo on the website can bolster trust in the company.

- **Check out the shipping costs.** Sometimes the shipping can cost more than the item. Before placing your order, make sure you know all the shipping costs and terms.

You must have a Federal tax ID number (that's your identification to do business) to even register on most legitimate wholesale sites. Finding wholesale websites with this restriction is a *good* thing. It's another way to verify that you're dealing with a true wholesale supplier.

B2B wholesale clearinghouses

Legitimate online sites for retailers are rare. Many of the business to business (B2B) merchants and wholesale directories reflect nothing but flea-market goods and highly marked-up drop-shipping items. Don't be disappointed. That doesn't mean you can't find a deal on some great merchandise. The benefit of the Internet is that you have access to many sources. The challenge is to find the good, solid, reliable sources of information, like the following:

» **MadeInUSA.com:** One of the best ways to find an item to sell is to find that item in your everyday life. If you have the manufacturer's name but no contact information, go to the company website at www.madeinusa.com (see Figure 2-12), which has a huge database of manufacturer contact info.

FIGURE 2-12:
Search more than 300,000 manufacturers at this website.

» **GreatRep.com:** At www.greatrep.com, you find a website directory (refer to Figure 2-10) where buyers (that's you) can hook up with manufacturer's representatives that carry lines of merchandise in the wholesale giftware, home furnishings, and furniture industries. It's fantastic! After you register (and provide your state resale license), you have access to listings of thousands of manufacturers. In the listings you may find out how much they require for a minimum order, and you can also request a catalog.

Buying directly from online wholesalers

Following are a few sources that have some unusual merchandise. I've bought from almost all of them:

» **Liquidation.com:** If you like auctions (and I *know* you do), check out www.liquidation.com. This is a massive all-auction website that has incredible deals on all types of merchandise. One of the things that I love about this site is that most individual auctions provide a link to the *manifest* — a list of every piece of merchandise in the lot. If you click the View Manifest link at the top of the auction page, you see a piece-by-piece list of the items included in the lot you're bidding on. Find more on buying liquidation merchandise in Book 4, Chapter 4.

It's best to buy from vendors closer to your geographic area because after you add the shipping fee, you might be paying too much for your lot. Liquidation. com can refine your searches to your location in the country, and it has a shipping calculator to help you know ahead of time how much your shipping may be.

» **Oriental Trading Company:** The Oriental Trading Company has been in business for a long time. I used to buy from their catalog for school and charity affairs. This site offers everything from crafts to costumes to party goods — and all priced perfectly for resale on eBay. Use your practiced eye (and completed search) to ferret out the unique items that will sell. Visit them at www.orientaltrading.com.

» **Big Lots Wholesale:** If you're familiar with the Big Lots stores scattered around the country, you have an idea of what you can buy at www.biglotswholesale.com. A quick click to their website showed me that they were loaded with great deals on everything from health and beauty items to toys to lawn and garden tools. A seller's tax ID number is required to get pricing on this site.

Chapter **3**

Profiting by Selling for Others Online

Consignment sales are a popular way for you to help non-techie types by selling their items on eBay. These people consign their merchandise to you and once it sells, you take a percentage of the profits. Lots of sellers do it, and a few retail locations base their business on it. This chapter gives you a close-up look at consignment selling. In this line of work, you're responsible for taking photos and marketing someone else's items on eBay — for a fee. In addition to the money you earn selling on consignment, you also get excellent experience for future sales of your own merchandise.

Getting Organized to Sell for Others

To set up your business for consignment sales, you should follow a few guidelines:

1. Design a consignment agreement (a binding contract) and send it to the owners of the merchandise before they send you their items. Doing so ensures that all policies are set up in advance — and that no questions need arise after

the transaction has begun. See the end of this chapter for what you should include.

2. Have the owners sign and give the agreement to you (the consignor) along with the item.

3. Research the item based on historic sales so you can give the owners an estimated range of what the item might sell for on eBay.

4. Photograph the item carefully (see Book 5 for some hints) and write a thoughtful, thorough description.

5. Handle all inquiries as though the item were your own; after all, your fee is based on a percentage of the final sale and the feedback you receive is your own. Traditional auction houses handle consignment sales in a similar fashion.

Competing with the Drop-Off Stores

Many stores have opened up across the country with brick-and-mortar locations accepting merchandise from the general public to sell on eBay. By developing your own consignment business, you can compete with the big boys in your own area.

The best part is that if you're running your eBay business out of your home, from a garage, or from a low-rent industrial office, you're a step ahead of the brick-and-mortars who have to pay rent in fancy neighborhoods to get their drop-in business. They also have to hire people who are familiar with running sales on eBay — and aren't you *already* set up for that?

Don't worry about the competition! You may hear about the many eBay consignment stores that are opening up. As a matter of fact, some are selling franchises for this business for up to $21,000, not including training. You already know how to sell on eBay. (Franchise? You don't need a stinkin' franchise!) Use your good sense (and positive feedback) to build your own eBay consignment store.

Retail locations have a much higher cost of business than you do. They need to be open for set hours per day and have several employees on duty at all times. Many of these stores won't accept an item worth less than $75. There's still a lot of profit left for you in the realm of under-$75 items.

Consider all your expenses — remember to take eBay, PayPal, and shipping fees into account. Keep an eye out in your own area should a store open, so you can keep up with the competition.

What do you charge for all your work? I can't give you a stock answer for that one. Many sellers charge a flat fee for photographing, listing, and shipping that ranges from $5 to $10 per item, plus as much as a 40-percent commission on the final total (to absorb fees). Other sellers base their charges solely on the final sale amount and charge on a sliding scale, beginning at 50 percent of the total sale, less eBay and payment service fees. You must decide how much you think you can make on an item.

Table 3-1 gives you some ideas based on the input I've received from some successful eBay consignment sellers. (These percentages may be in addition to the eBay fees.)

TABLE 3-1

Sample Progressive Commission Schedule

Final Value ($)	Your Commission
Under 50	40%
50.01–150.00	35% of the amount over $50
150.01–250.00	30% of the amount over $150
251.00–500.00	25% of the amount over $250
501.00–1000.00	20% of the amount over $500
Over 1000	15%

Remember that you can always choose to charge a flat commission, if that works best in your area. Check out the eBay consignment sellers in your area to see what they charge.

Understanding the "eBay Valet" Program

What is eBay Valet? Simply, the eBay Valet program is an automated system for people who want to sell merchandise on eBay without bothering to learn the ropes. I guess it would be (as you would be as a consignment seller) a way for those who are not familiar with eBay to get their items sold.

You'll find the Valet home page (see Figure 3-1) on the eBay site at

```
www.ebay.com/s/valet
```

You may remember that eBay used to have a Trading Assistant program where they promoted consignment sellers; but that's no more.

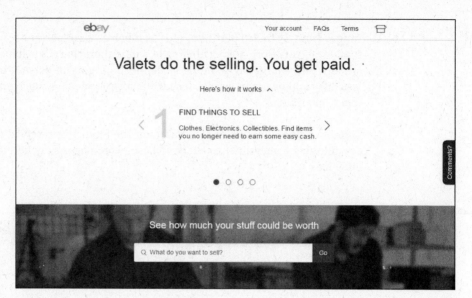

FIGURE 3-1:
The portal for eBay's Valet program.

I have read reviews on the web and found not much to recommend it for sellers. If you want to try it, you can read more about its procedures directly from eBay here:

```
www.ebay.com/s/valet/faq
```

If you're still interested, the requirements to become an "eBay Valet" are listed below. eBay stresses that you must go through a rigorous screening — and the points below are not the only requirements:

1. Ability to list 100,000 listings each month

2. Storage capacity sufficient to hold and manage items received for at least 21 calendar days

3. Ability to list items across all eBay categories

4. Physical presence in all major metropolitan hubs in the U.S.

5. Demonstrated ability to consistently deliver the highest standards of buyer experience to eBay shoppers

If you can fulfill all of those requirements — especially number 3 — well, frankly, you should be making a bundle on your own.

Promoting Your Consignment Business

When I was working in the newspaper advertising business, we had a saying about someone who opened a new store: If all the advertising they do is their Grand Opening ad and nothing after, it won't be long before you'll be seeing the Going Out of Business sale ad. The same is true with your consignment business.

Get creative! Why not design a flyer that you print on your own printer. Put it up at the supermarket, the car wash, the cleaner — anywhere and everywhere flyers are allowed.

Even if you don't see flyers in a retail location, ask the owner of the business if you can put one up — maybe even offer a discount to the business owner for selling his or her items on eBay in exchange.

You might want to make a flyer that includes small tear-off strips where you can place your contact information. When people see your promotion, they can just snip off your phone number (or email address) and contact you when they get home.

Handling Your Business Professionally

How you conduct your business can demonstrate to your customers that you're a responsible person. You need to present a professional appearance when you meet your client, and you should have a professional attitude in your dealings.

Being professional also means anticipating possible problems. In addition to being very clear about financial issues with your clients (especially fees and the realistic selling value of your clients' merchandise), you may want to consider getting additional insurance to cover the merchandise you're holding in your home.

You may also want to consider designing a few forms to reinforce your clients' awareness that this is your business and that you know it well. For example:

>> **Inventory form:** This form lists the entire inventory you receive from the client and should include as detailed a description of the item as your client can supply. Also, include the minimum amount (if any) the client will accept for the item — this will be your reserve price if necessary.

>> **Sales agreement:** Professional consignment sellers who expect to remain in business have their clients sign a sales contract. Read on for some good suggestions about what to put in your contract. It's also a potentially wise investment to have a lawyer look at your contract before you use it.

The below includes quotes from several contracts I've found over the years. They cover many things that you might overlook when you put together your own contract. This, of course, is not a full agreement, but it provides some of the salient points not to forget. Be sure to include an explanation of the consignment process:

>> The Consignor will bring item(s) to the Seller, who, upon both parties signing this contract, will take possession of the items for the duration of the sales.

>> Acceptance of any item consigned will be at the Seller's sole discretion.

>> The Seller will inspect the item(s) for quality and clean if necessary (a fee may apply).

>> The Seller will take quality photographs and write an accurate description of item(s).

>> The Seller will research eBay for similar items to ensure proper pricing.

>> The Seller will start the listing(s) and handle all aspects of the sale including correspondence with bidders.

>> The Seller will collect payment from the winning bidder ("Buyer") at the end of the auction and will ship the item(s) in a timely manner, once funds have cleared.

>> The Seller will follow up the sale by contacting the Buyer to make sure the Buyer is satisfied with the transaction.

>> Once the Seller and Buyer are satisfied with the transaction, payment will be made to the Consignor.

>> The Seller will keep the Consignor aware of the sales progress by telephone or email and by supplying the Consignor the listing number(s) to track the item(s) themselves.

>> The Seller will return unsold item(s) to the Consignor upon payment of outstanding fees.

It's also a good idea to provide the consignor with a statement of items sold, summarizing the total purchase price, all fees, and the amount the consignor receives.

>> **Outline your fees:** "The Consignor will be billed the actual rates and fees as incurred for all services, to include the Seller's *00%* Commission. Any services or upgrades requested by the Consignor will carry the exact fee and will be deducted from payment, or after three (3) failed auction listings, will be due to the Seller payable in cash. If the auction sells, these fees will be subtracted from the winning bid before the Consignor receives payment."

In addition to specifying your nonzero commission, be sure to include a copy of current eBay fees: listing, options, reserves, PayPal, and final value fees.

>> **Outline the terms of your commission:** "The Seller's commission for this service is a percentage based on the final selling price. If an auction does not sell, the Consignor is only responsible to pay the applicable insertion and reserve-price auction fees. An Unsold Reserve fee of *$0.00 [fill in your amount]* will be due to the Seller for a reserve-price auction that does not sell."

>> **Be sure you don't guarantee the item will sell:** "If an item does not sell, the Seller will re-list it two additional times. The Seller may contact the Consignor to discuss combining individual items into lots to attract buyers. The Consignor's verbal consent, or email consent, will be documented in the Consignor's file and will serve as a revision to this contract. After a third unsuccessful listing, the Consignor will be billed for the fees associated with all three listings, plus a $5.00 surcharge. Items will be returned to the Consignor upon payment of those fees. Items not claimed within 14 days from the end of the final listing will become the property of the Seller."

>> **Protect yourself and your eBay reputation:** "The Consignor of said item(s) consents to the sale of said item(s) based on the terms described in this agreement. The Consignor also attests that said item(s) are fully owned by the Consignor and are not stolen, borrowed, misrepresented, counterfeit, etc."

TIP

You might also mention that you will only sell the item if eBay policies allow the item to be sold.

"The Seller will do everything possible to secure the safety of the Consignor's item(s); however, the Seller is not responsible for any damage to the item, including fire, theft, flood, accidental damage or breakage, and acts of God. The Consignor releases the Seller of any such responsibility for any unforeseen or accidental damage."

TIP

I choose to protect myself additionally, because reputation on eBay is paramount. I have a small-business rider on my homeowner's insurance that covers merchandise in my home up to $5,000 in value. It's an inexpensive addition to your policy — *definitely* worth looking into.

>> **Ending a sale prematurely:** "If such an instance arises that the Consignor demands the item(s) to be pulled, the Consignor will pay a cancellation fee of $75. Items will not be surrendered to the Consignor until this fee is paid in cash."

>> **Protect yourself from possible shill bidding:** An important line you should add protects you from possible shill bidding. How about something like this: "The Consignor also agrees not to place a bid on an auction that the Seller has

listed for the Consignor (hereafter 'Shill Bid') on eBay, nor to arrange for a Shill Bid to be made on the behalf of the Consignor by a third party. If the Consignor or an agent of the Consignor submits a Shill Bid on an auction listed by the Seller, the Consignor agrees to pay all fees, commissions, and penalties associated with that auction, plus a $75 fine, and the Seller may refuse to grant consignment services to the Consignor in the future."

Again, I strongly suggest that you get professional advice before, during, and/or after putting together your own contract or agreement. Protect yourself and your business.

Chapter **4**

Sourcing, Liquidation, and Drop-Shipping

You're likely to find various levels of quality when you look for merchandise to resell on eBay. Receiving a box of ripped or stained goods when you expected first-quality merchandise can be disheartening. If you take the time to evaluate the condition of the merchandise you're interested in buying, you save time (and money) in the long run. But to make that evaluation, you need to know what the industry language tells you about the quality of the merchandise.

In addition to qualifying the goods you buy, take the time to qualify the processes and partners you use. For example, *drop-shipping* (shipping goods straight from the manufacturer or distributor to the consumer) has become a popular method for moving merchandise sold on eBay, but it comes with many caveats. For example, eBay has a policy about preselling items you don't have in stock, so be sure to check it out in advance; make sure your drop-shipper has the merchandise ready to go when you place your order. Use this chapter to become a savvy buyer of goods to resell — *and* an effective mover of those same goods.

TIP

Many people use an elaborate practice called *eBay arbitrage*. They put items sold on Amazon up for sale on eBay, and have Amazon ship direct to the customer — or vice versa. This process can go very wrong or very right — sometimes at the same time. If your customer gets a packing slip from another seller, perhaps even indicating a lower price than they paid, you might be in for some very bad feedback. This is a stressful and tricky way to go. I only recommend this if you buy the goods on another site and sell directly from your own purchased stock on eBay.

Know the Lingo of Merchandisers

To help ensure that industry jargon won't trip you up, this section describes the merchandising lingo you need to know — and offers pointers on making the right decisions about your merchandise and methods. Here are some terms you're likely to come across:

>> **Job lots:** A *job lot* simply refers to a bunch of merchandise sold at once. The goods may consist of unusual sizes, odd colors, or even some hideous stuff that wouldn't blow out of your online store if a hurricane blew through. Some of the merchandise (usually no more than 15 percent) may be damaged. Super discounts can be had on job lots — and if the lot contains brand names from major stores, you may be able to make an excellent profit.

TIP

A good way to find a *jobber* (someone who wants to sell you job lots) on the Internet is to run a Google search on *wholesale jobber*.

>> **Off-price lots:** If you can get hold of top-quality, brand-name items in off-price lots, you can do very well on eBay. These items are end-of-season *overruns* (more items were made than could be sold through normal retailers). You can generally find this merchandise toward the end of the buying season.

Many eBay sellers, without having untold thousands of dollars to buy merchandise, make friends with the salespeople at manufacturers' outlet stores (which is where the merchandise may land first). Others haunt places like TJ Maxx, Marshall's, and Burlington Coat Factory for first-rate deals.

TIP

Search the classified ads of genuine trade publications for items to buy in bulk. Publications such as *California Apparel News* have classifieds that are accessible online. Visit their website at www.apparelnews.net and click Classifieds.

>> **Liquidations:** All eBay sellers think of liquidations as the motherlode of deals. And yes, they may *be* the motherlode of deals — if you can afford to buy and store an entire 18-wheeler truckload of merchandise. That takes a great deal of money and a great deal of square footage, plus the staff to go through and test each and every item.

The merchandise can be an assortment of liquidations, store returns, salvage, closeouts, shelf pulls, overstocks, and surplus goods. Some items may be damaged but repairable; others may be perfectly salable. As much as 30 percent or more of a truckload may be useless. Buying liquidation merchandise is a gamble but can have advantages. By buying a full truckload, you have a wide breadth of merchandise, you pay the lowest amount for it, and some of it may be good for spare parts. Just make sure beforehand that you have a place to put it all.

TIP

Save yourself some money. Don't go on eBay and buy some wholesale list for $5. You can get the same names by running a Google search on the term *wholesale*. Every true wholesaler's website has a place where authorized dealers (that could be you) can log in. Try searching for *dealer login* along with a category name, such as *dealer login golf* (as I've done in Figure 4-1).

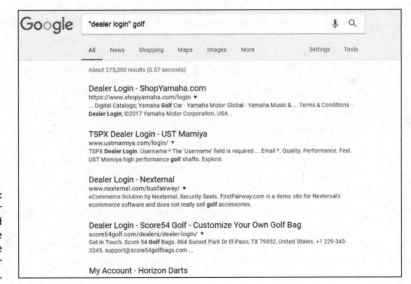

FIGURE 4-1:
I've found over 275 thousand legitimate wholesale resources for golf items.

GETTING THE 411 ON REFURBISHED GOODS

You can find great deals on refurbished electronic merchandise on eBay. Unfortunately, refurbished merchandise gets an unnecessarily bad rap. Very smart people may tell you to be wary of refurbished merchandise. Great advice . . . I guess. I tell people to be wary of *all* merchandise.

The way I figure it, refurbished merchandise has been gone over by the manufacturer twice — new merchandise has been gone over only once. I buy refurbished merchandise all the time. Let me explain what refurbished merchandise is and why it can be such a bargain. Refurbished merchandise can fall into one of these categories:

- **Canceled orders:** This is merchandise in perfectly good shape. Say a customer makes a special order and then changes his or her mind, or the order is somehow mucked up ("I ordered a PC. You sent me a Mac!"). Something has to be done with the merchandise. Enter you, the savvy shopper.

- **Evaluation units:** An evaluation unit is a piece of equipment that is sent to a member of the media or to a corporation for testing or review. Evaluation units must be returned to the manufacturer, and the manufacturer may decide to unload (after thoroughly going over) them.

- **Store returns:** This is probably pretty obvious to you, right? Joe Customer buys something in a store, takes it home, and opens it, only to decide that he doesn't really want it. By law, as soon as the box is opened, a piece of merchandise can never be sold as new again, even if the merchandise was never used.

- **Defective units:** This is a piece of merchandise deemed defective by either the store or by the user and returned to the manufacturer.

- **Overstocks:** When a manufacturer comes out with a new model, the company may take back the older models from retailers in an effort to encourage them to stock more of the newer, faster, cooler model.

Whenever an item is returned to the manufacturer for any reason and the original box has been opened, the item (whether it's a television, a computer, a camera, or some other technical device) must be reconditioned to the manufacturer's original quality standards. Any nonfunctioning parts are replaced with functioning components and the item is repackaged. The manufacturer usually gives refurbished items a 90-day warranty.

When buying refurbished goods, be sure the original manufacturer was the one doing the reconditioning. I'm sure that some tech geeks can fix things just fine in their garages, but you don't have the same level of protection (as in, you don't have a warranty from a reliable source) if you buy a piece of equipment that wasn't fixed by the manufacturer.

Salvage: Liquidation Items, Unclaimed Freight, and Returns

The easiest to buy for resale, *salvage merchandise* is retail merchandise that has been returned, exchanged, or shelf-pulled for some reason. Salvage can also encompass liquidation merchandise and unclaimed freight. Generally, this merchandise is sold as-is and where-is — and may be in new condition. To buy this merchandise directly from the liquidator in large lots, you must have your resale (sales tax number) permit and be prepared to pay the shipping to your location.

Several types of salvage merchandise are available:

>> **Unclaimed freight:** When a trucking company delivers merchandise, a manifest accompanies the freight. If, for some reason, a portion of the shipment arrives incomplete, contains the wrong items, or is damaged, the entire shipment may be refused by the merchant. The trucking company is now stuck with as much as a truckload of freight. The original seller may not want to pay the freight charges to return the merchandise to his or her warehouse (or want to accept blame for an incorrect shipment), so the freight becomes the trucker's problem. The trucking companies arrive at agreements with liquidators to buy this freight in the various areas that the liquidators serve. This way, truckers are never far from a location where they can dump, er, drop off such merchandise.

>> **Returns:** Did you know that when you return something to a store or mail-order house, it can never be sold as new again (in most states anyway)? The merchandise is generally sent to a liquidator who agrees in advance to pay a flat percentage for goods. The liquidator must move the merchandise to someone else. All major retailers liquidate returns, and much of this merchandise ends up on eBay or in closeout stores.

TIP

If you're handy at repairing electronics or computers, you'd probably do very well with a specialized lot. You may easily be able to revitalize damaged merchandise, often using parts from two unsalable items to come up with one that you can sell in like-new working condition.

>> **Liquidations:** Liquidators buy liquidation merchandise by truckloads and sell it in smaller lots. The merchandise comes from financially stressed or bankrupt companies that need to raise cash quickly.

The liquidation business has been thriving as a well-kept secret for years. As long as you have space to store salvage merchandise and a way to sell it, you can acquire it for as low as ten cents on the dollar. When I say you need storage space, I mean *lots* of space. To buy this type of merchandise at bottom-of-the-barrel prices, you must be willing to accept truckloads — full 18-wheelers, loaded with more than 20 pallets (4 feet x 4 feet x 6 or 7 feet) — of merchandise at a time. Often these truckloads have *manifests* (a document detailing the contents of the shipment) listing the retail and wholesale price of each item on the truck. If you have access to the more-than-10,000-square-feet of warehouse that you'll need to unpack and process this amount of merchandise, you're in business.

I'm a fan of Liquidatation.com (www.liquidation.com) and often find myself scrolling their home page to see the current offerings (see Figure 4-2). Buying from them at a good price can mean healthy profits.

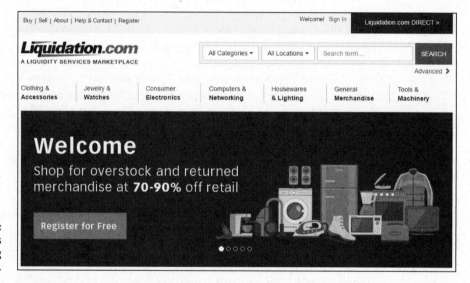

FIGURE 4-2: Liquidation.com's currently closing returns auctions.

>> **Seasonal overstocks:** My motto is "Buy off-season, sell on-season." At the end of the season, a store may find its shelves overloaded with seasonal merchandise (such as swimsuits in August) that it must get rid of to make room for the next season's stock. These brand-new items become salvage merchandise because they're seasonal overstocks.

>> **Shelf-pulls:** Have you ever passed up one item in the store for the one behind it in the display because its box was in better condition? Sometimes the plastic bubble or the package is dented, and you'd rather have a pristine one. That box you just passed up may be destined to become a *shelf-pull*. The item inside may be in perfect condition, but it's cosmetically unsalable in the retail-store environment.

WARNING

Some liquidation items, unclaimed freight, and returns may be unsalable. Although you'll acquire many gems that stand to bring you profit, you'll also be left with a varying percentage of useless items.

Some liquidation sellers sell their merchandise in the same condition that it ships in to their location, so what you get is a crapshoot. You may lose money on some items while making back your money on others. Other sellers who charge a bit more will remove less-desirable merchandise from the pallets. Some may even make up deluxe pallets with better-quality merchandise. These loads cost more, but if they're filled with the type of merchandise that you're interested in selling, you'll probably write better descriptions and subsequently do a better job selling them.

BUYING LIQUIDATION MERCHANDISE ON eBay

Liquidation merchandise can be new, used, or trashed. Searching through a liquidator's eBay listings is like digging through the "Final Sale" bin at a store, where prices are marked down to absurd levels.

Liquidators buy merchandise from companies that are in financial distress and need to raise cash quickly. The kinds of issues companies face can vary — the why isn't important. All you need to know is that you can get access to some astonishing deals because some of it is sold in lots on eBay.

Merchandise arrives by the truckload. From there the merchandise is unloaded, inspected, and sorted — and then the fun begins. Some of the merchandise can be put together in wholesale *lots* (the goods are grouped by the pallet or by the case and sold to wholesalers or retailers), and some of the merchandise may be put aside to be sold to sellers for resale on eBay.

Buying items from liquidators can be a risky enterprise. There's no warranty, and no one you can complain to if something is wrong with the item. All items are always sold *as is* and *where is*. Essentially, what you see is what you get; if it works, it's a bonus.

Here are some tips for buying this type of item:

- **Look for "sealed in the box":** Look at the picture and read the description carefully. If the description states that the item is sealed in the manufacturer's packaging, you have a pretty good chance that the item is in new condition.

- **Don't spend a bundle:** This kind of goes without saying, right? It's supposed to be a bargain.

WARNING

Before you glaze over and get dazzled by a low, low price on a lot, check the shipping cost to you *before* you buy. Many so-called wholesalers will lure you in with bargain-basement prices, only to charge you three times the normal shipping costs. Do your homework before you buy!

Staying Safe When Buying Online

WARNING

Nobody offers a quality or fitness guarantee when you buy liquidation merchandise. You could end up with pallets of unsalable merchandise, and you must steer quickly away from anyone who guarantees that you'll make money. Remember that liquidation merchandise is always sold as-is.

WARNING

Unfortunately, this market can be rife with unscrupulous sellers who are middlemen. They buy the truckloads, go through everything with a fine-tooth comb, and pull out all the saleable merchandise. Then they repack the pallets with what's left, and sell those to unsuspecting newbies who think that they *may* get a good deal.

When buying online, it's hard to know about the company you're dealing with because you've probably just found them after performing a web search. When you find a source from which you want to buy merchandise by the pallet, check out a few things before spending your hard-earned cash:

>> **Get an anonymous free email address from Gmail before signing up for any mailing lists or newsletters.** Some websites that offer these publications make most of their money by selling your email address to spammers. If you give them an anonymous email address, the buckets of spam will never end up in your *real* mailbox. (I learned about that the hard way.)

>> **Raise your shields if the wholesalers also link their websites to miscellaneous make-big-profits-on-eBay websites.** They may be making most of their money from commissions when the ebook of "road-to-riches secret tips" is sold to you.

>> **Be sure the site has a phone number.** Give them a call and see how you're treated. It's no guarantee of how they'll treat you if you're unhappy with a purchase, but you may get a human being on the phone (rare and precious these days).

>> **Look for a physical address.** Do they have a place of business or is the company running out of some guy's pocket cellphone? (Often it's not a good sign if there's no place to *hang* a sign.)

>> **Ask for references.** Seeing the Better Business Bureau Online BuySafe or SquareTrade logo on the website can bolster trust in the company. (They have to qualify for those seals.)

>> **Before you purchase anything, go to eBay and see whether that item will sell — and for how much.** Often you find hundreds of listings for an item with no bids. Check completed listings and be sure that the item is selling for a solid profit over what you expect to pay for it (including shipping).

>> **Never buy anything just because it's cheap.** That was true in Thomas Jefferson's day and is still true today. Be sure you can actually *sell* the merchandise. (I also learned *this* the hard way.)

>> **Look for a guarantee.** Does the source guarantee that you *will* make money or that you *can* make money by buying the right merchandise? Remember that no one can guarantee that you'll make money.

>> **Check for references.** Does the supplier offer on its website references that you can contact to find out some usable information on this seller's items and the percentage of unsalable goods in a box or pallet?

>> **Look for *FOB*.** That means *freight on board*. You will be charged freight from the location of the merchandise to your door. The shorter the distance, the cheaper your freight costs.

WARNING

Before doing business on any website, be sure its owners have a privacy policy that protects your personal information. Also check for an About Us page and make sure the page talks about the business and the people behind it. I hate to be repetitive, but be sure you can reach a human being on a phone or in person (with a street address) if need be.

Dealing with Drop-Shippers

A *drop-shipper* is a business that stocks merchandise, sells the merchandise to you (the reseller), but ships it directly to your customer. By using a drop-shipper, you transfer the risks of buying, storing, and shipping merchandise to another party. You become a *stockless* retailer with no inventory hanging around — often an economical, cost-effective way to do business.

The following steps outline the standard way to work with most drop-shippers on eBay:

1. Sign up on the drop-shipper's website to sell their merchandise on eBay or in your web store. Check out their terms before you sign up; make sure there's no minimum purchase.

2. Select the items from their inventory that you want to sell. The supplier gives you descriptive copy and photographs to help make your sales job easier.

3. Post the item online and wait (fidgeting with anticipation) for someone to buy it.

4. As soon as your buyer pays you for the item, email the drop-shipper (or fill out a special secure form on their website) and pay for the item with your credit card or PayPal.

5. Relax while the drop-shipper ships the item to your customer for you.

6. If all goes well, the item arrives quickly and safely.

You make a profit and get some positive feedback.

TIP

The drop-shipper's website provides you with descriptions and images. Fine. But you and everybody else who sells that item on eBay will have the same photos and descriptive copy. Do yourself a favor and get a sample of your item, take your own pictures, and write your own description. Then at least you have a chance at beating the competitive sameness on eBay.

DROP-SHIPPING TO YOUR CUSTOMERS

Some middlemen, wholesalers, and liquidators specialize in selling to ecommerce sellers through a drop-ship service. Some crafty eBay sellers make lots of money selling lists of drop-shipping sources to eBay sellers — I hope not to you. Dealing with a drop-shipper means that you don't ever have to take possession of (or pay for) the merchandise. You're given a photo and, after you sell the item, you give the vendor the address of the buyer. They charge your credit card for the item plus shipping, and then ship the item to your customer for you.

This way of doing business costs *you* more and lowers your profits. Your goal as a business owner is to make as much money as you can. Because the drop-shipper is in business too, they'll mark up the merchandise (and the shipping cost) so they can make their profit. (When dealing with a manufacturer, you will not have this markup.)

Be careful when using a drop-shipper. Ask for references and search Google for reviews. See whether a zillion sellers are selling the same merchandise on eBay — and not getting any bites. Also, what happens if a drop-shipper runs out of an item that you've just sold? You can't just say "oops" to your buyer without getting some nasty feedback. It's your online reputation at stake. If you find a solid source and believe in the product, order a quantity and have it shipped to your door. Don't pay for someone else's mark-up just for the convenience of having them ship to your customers.

Drop-shipping works especially well for web-based retail operations. Web stores can link directly to the drop-shipper to transmit shipping and payment information. When you're selling on eBay, it's another thing. There's more competition and you can't list hundreds of items at no additional cost.

Listing items on eBay costs time and may build up your expenses before you make a profit. You can't just select an item from a drop-shipper and throw hundreds of listings on eBay without losing money — that is, unless your item is selling like gangbusters at an enormous profit. If that were the case, believe me, there would be another eBay seller buying directly from the manufacturer and undercutting your price.

WARNING

I must interject that I bought (for research) several drop-shipper lists from eBay sellers. I am saddened to report that I couldn't find *any* that fulfilled my security requirements for doing business with an unknown business online. The drop-shippers whose merchandise I could track had a penchant for flooding the eBay market by selling the same item to way too many sellers — thereby driving down the price. I also found little brand-name merchandise available. If any of my readers find a reputable drop-shipper who allows room for profit on eBay, please email me through my website. I think this is a business that *could* work, but only if the right businesses (and business practices) were involved.

WARNING

It's one thing to sign up for a free newsletter — or even to register with a particular site — but it's something else to have to pay to see what the drop-shipper intends to offer you. *You should not pay anything in advance for the opportunity to check out a drop-shipper's merchandise.*

Finding a good drop-shipper

Thousands of web companies are aching to help you set up your online business. Some of them are good solid companies with legitimate backgrounds, but others are just trying to get your money. These guys hope you don't know what you're doing; they're betting you'll be desperate enough to send them some cash to help you get your share of the (har, har) "millions to be made online."

Consider the following when you're choosing drop-shippers to work with:

>> **Skepticism is healthy.** When you come across websites that proclaim that they can drop-ship thousands of different products for you, think twice. *Thousands?* I don't know many stores that *carry* thousands of items — if they do, they have vast square footage for storage and hundreds of thousands of dollars to invest in merchandise. Most drop-shipping services don't. A much

smaller offering of merchandise may indicate that the drop-shipper has the merchandise ready to ship and isn't relying on ordering it from someone for you.

>> **Look out for long lines of distribution.** Drop-shippers are often middlemen who broker merchandise from several sources — for example, from other middlemen who buy from brokers (who in turn buy from manufacturers). The line of distribution can get even longer — which means that a slew of people are making a profit from your item before you even buy it "wholesale." If even one other reseller gets the product directly from the distributor or (heaven forbid) the manufacturer, that competitor can easily beat your target selling price. If you're considering doing business with drop-shippers, verify that they actually stock the merchandise they sell.

Coping with the inevitable out-of-stock

What happens when you sell an item and you go to the distributor's site and find that it's sold out? Before your heart stops, call the drop-shipper. Perhaps those folks still have one or two of your items around their warehouse and took the item off the website because they're running too low to guarantee delivery.

If that isn't the case, you're going to have to contact your buyer and 'fess up that the item is currently out of stock at your supplier. I suggest calling your custom-ers directly in this situation; they may not be *as* angry as they might be if you just emailed them. Offer to refund the money immediately. Somebody else's foul-up may net you bad feedback, but that risk goes along with using drop-shipping as a business practice. Handling foul-ups honorably is good business.

5

Presenting Your Items

Contents at a Glance

Chapter **1**

Your eBay Photo Studio

Welcome to the world of *imaging*, where pictures aren't called pictures but *images.* Pictures taken with a digital camera or a smartphone — or scanned on a scanner — can be cropped, color-corrected, and made near-perfect with simple software. Crisp images draw attention to your listings and grab viewers by the lapels.

Sellers, take heed and read why you should use numerous, well-made digital images in your listing pages:

» If you don't have a crystal-clear picture, potential customers may wonder whether you're deliberately hiding something about the item from view because you know something is wrong with it. Paranoid? Maybe. Practical? You bet.

» Many fickle shoppers don't even bother reading an item description if they can't take a good look the item.

» Aside from using eBay's catalog photos (when available), taking your own pictures shows that you actually have the item in your possession. Lazy sellers take images from a manufacturer's website to illustrate possibly bogus sales on eBay. Why risk being suspect? Snap a quick picture!

» Everyone's doing it. I hate to pressure you, but depending on the category, several images are expected by eBay shoppers. So if you're not using more than one, you're not reaching the widest possible number of people who would consider your item. From that point of view, you're not doing the most you can to serve your potential customers' needs.

So which is better for capturing images — a digital camera, smartphone, or a digital scanner? As with all gadgets, here's the classic answer: It depends. For my money, it's hard to beat the latest smartphones for close up images. Today's smartphones take pictures that rival older digital cameras, but new phones can be expensive. You might be able to justify the cost of a new smartphone if you consider that it will be your eBay camera as well.

But before you go snag one, decide what kind of investment (and how big) you plan to make in your eBay business. If you're already comfortable taking photos with your camera and it does a good job for now, keep on using it. Using an all-in-one printer with a scanner can balance out your photo needs. The scoop on the alternatives is coming right up.

Setting Up Your Studio

Taking pictures for eBay? No problem! You have a digital camera and you know how to use it. Just snap away and upload that picture, right? Sorry, but no. There are good ways and bad ways to take photos for eBay — and believe it or not, the techniques taught by many ecommerce instructors aren't necessarily the best way.

I recommend that you set up a mini photo studio for your eBay pictures. That way, you won't have to clean off your kitchen counter every time you want to take pictures.

TIP

If you must use the kitchen counter, a desktop, or even a chair (as in Figure 1-1), be sure to use an inexpensive infinity photo background, which you can find on — where else? — eBay.

You need several basic things in your photo studio; the extras you need are based on the type of merchandise you're selling. An eBay *generalist*, someone who sells almost anything online — like me! — should have quite a few extras for taking quality photos.

I often use a photo cube combined with small clamp lights (shown in Figure 1-2), true color lamps, or tall floodlights. An inexpensive photo cube works well for larger detailed and collectible objects — as well as any object that will fit in it. By using a translucent fabric cube, you can fully illuminate your item and have no resulting glare, harsh shadows, or detail burnout.

Hands down, the equipment for photographing jewelry and teeny, tiny items is the Cloud Dome (see "Other Studio Equipment" further on). It not only helps with lighting, but also holds your camera or smartphone steady for difficult to light or super-magnified (*macro*) shots.

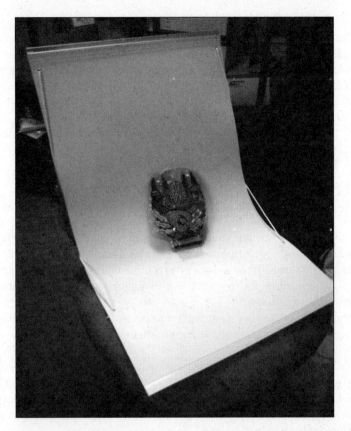

FIGURE 1-1:
Sometimes even
a chair works —
add some light
and voilà!

FIGURE 1-2:
Using a fabric
cube in the
dining room
to photograph
antiques.

What you find in this section might be more than you thought you'd need to produce good pictures. But your photographs will help sell your merchandise, so you need to consider this part of your business seriously. Of course, if you sell only one type of item, you won't need such a varied selection of stuff, but you should have the basic photo setup.

Your #1 Tool: A Digital Camera

Digital cameras, whether smartphone or point-and-shoot, are mysterious things. You may read about *megapixels* (a million pixels) and think that more is supposed to be better, but that doesn't apply to eBay or to web images. Megapixels measure the image resolution that the camera is capable of recording. For eBay use, all you need from a camera is a miniscule 2 megapixels, or 1600 x 1200 in size, which allows for cropping — although my current smartphones take a minimum of 6 megapixels (3264 x 1840). Images uploaded to eBay's picture hosting are optimal when they're at least 500 pixels wide. The eBay servers will perform magic on your pictures and reduce them down sharply.

WARNING

If you're going to self-host because you want to show multiple images of your items within a listing description, beware! With so many online shoppers using mobile devices, your images may not show up clearly on smaller screens. If you use a high-resolution camera, you'll have a pixel-bloated picture that takes a looooong time to load online.

The camera you use for eBay is a personal choice. Would-be big-time sellers starting out in an eBay business (with no experience on the Internet) usually go out and buy the most expensive digital camera they can find. Maybe having lots of megapixels is a macho thing, but a camera with a bunch of megapixels is the last thing you need for eBay images.

You don't need a million pixels, but you do need the following:

>> **Quality lens:** I'm sure anyone who has worn glasses can tell the difference between a good lens and a cheap one. Cheap cameras have flimsy plastic lenses, and the quality of the resulting pictures is accordingly lousy. Your camera will be your workhorse, so be sure to buy one from a company known for making quality products.

>> **Removable media:** Most cameras (and smartphones) can connect to your PC with a USB cable, and many sellers are happy with that type of connection. Whether you choose to transfer images is your choice. Some sellers edit on devices and send pictures direct to eBay. Some find that using cables to

download pictures to the hard drive is annoying. Based on your device, you can also use SD cards of varying sizes.

» **Optical zoom versus digital zoom:** When shopping for your camera, find one with the highest-power optical zoom that you can afford. *Optical zoom* is magnified by the camera's lens (using the camera's internal optics), producing a vivid picture.

Digital zoom is valuable when you have quality software in the camera. When your camera uses digital zoom, it does the same thing as enlarging a picture in photo-editing software: The camera centers the focus over half the focal plane, and uses software interpolation to enlarge the picture. If the algorithm is lacking, your image may be slightly fuzzy.

» **Tripod mount:** It's simple to mount a camera on a stable tripod — although I prefer holding a camera to take shots at varied angles. Tripods can help you avoid blurring your pictures if your hands are a bit shaky. To use a tripod, you need a *tripod mount,* or a clamp to attach your device.

Modern smartphones have OIS (Optical Image Stabilization) built in, thereby making tripod use unnecessary for some.

» **Macro setting capability:** These features will come in handy if you plan to photograph coins, jewelry, or small detailed items. A camera's macro setting enables you to get in really close to items while keeping them in focus. Usually the macro mode can focus as close as 1 inch and as far away as 10 inches.

TIP

The average camera's *focal length* (focus range) is from three feet to infinity. If you have a camera that says the macro focus range is set at 5.1 inches, it means you can't focus it clearly on an object any closer than 5.1 inches. Macro pictures require a steady hand (or you can affix your camera to a Cloud Dome); any vibration can blur your image.

» **Battery life:** When you're choosing your camera (or smartphone), be sure to check into the length of time the camera's battery will hold a charge. The last thing you want to do is run out of juice at the wrong moment. Consider the following:

- Keep a spare battery on hand so you'll be prepared if your camera battery runs low while you're shooting multiple items.

- Invest in a portable charger. These rechargeable batteries last a long time and are worth the investment.

» **White-balance setting:** This is a tricky feature. Most eBay photographers set the camera to Auto (if there is a setting) and hope for the best. If you can adjust the white balance, do so. Manufacturers use different presets. The list of options can include settings for incandescent lights, twilight, fluorescent lights, outdoor, indoor, or shade. All these lighting situations have different color temperatures, as I discuss in the "Lighting" section later in this chapter.

TAKING PICTURES WITH YOUR SMARTPHONE

Whether you use an Android or an iPhone, smartphone cameras are packing in many of the features previously only found in expensive cameras.

My Huawei Mate 10 Pro sports a 20-megapixel Leica camera with optical image stabilization, auto and professional camera control for ISO, WB, metering options, and more. When it's on a clamped tripod, I can say cheese and it will take a picture, so I don't have to fumble to tap the touchscreen.

Fair warning regarding any product pictures you take with any smartphone: Never use the flash. Using the standard lights as I recommend in this chapter will give you a better outcome.

If you're shooting jewelry or other detailed, small items you want to combine in a shot, I don't recommend that you rely on your smartphone alone for taking all such eBay images. I use my phone with a Cloud Dome; the manufacturer of these light-diffusing domes now makes a teeny version of the product for smartphone photography. Named Nimbus, this diffuser has a 4.5-inch focal length.

In most cases, make it easy on yourself — use your smartphone to get good results.

REMEMBER

It's worthwhile to take the time to play with the various white-balance settings of your camera in the different places where you normally photograph eBay merchandise. Make notes on settings that give you the truest colors in your digital images.

>> **Autofocus and zoom:** These options just make life easier when you want to take pictures, and should be standard features.

The bottom line is that you should buy a brand-name camera or smartphone. Occasionally I still use an older Wi-Fi Samsung camera for shooting; lately I prefer my smartphone for its larger visual display. My camera is technically outdated, but it's also loaded with all the bells and whistles I need for eBay photos and for some reason, I can always find it. My smartphone camera comes in handy when I want to get a picture taken quickly because it is always at hand.

I bet you could find a camera or used smartphone that fits your needs right now on eBay. Keep in mind that in our tech-savvy society, many camera and smartphone users chase the latest trends and buy the newest available device. They then sell their older devices on eBay for a pittance. Many tech stores also sell used and refurbished equipment.

Scanning Your Wares

Scanners have come a long way in the past few years. A once-expensive item can now be purchased new for as little as $100 (or as part of an all-in-one printer). If you sell books, autographs, stamps, or documents, a scanner may be all you need to shoot your images for eBay.

When shopping for a scanner, don't pay too much attention to the resolution; the higher the resolution, the bigger the file, and (often) the slower the load. Some scanners can provide resolutions as high as 12,800 dpi, which is more data than you need when you print the image. But to dress up your eBay listings, all you need is (are you ready?) 96 to 150 dpi! That's it. Your images will look great, won't take up much storage space, and won't take forever to load when a buyer looks at them. Basic scanners can scan images up to 1200 dots per inch (dpi), so even they are more powerful than you need for your eBay images. As with smartphones and digital cameras, I recommend you stick with a brand-name flatbed wireless scanner.

Other Studio Equipment

What you find in this section might be more than you thought you'd need for photographing your items. But photographs can help sell your merchandise, so you need to take this seriously. Of course, if you sell only one type of item, you won't need such a varied selection of stuff, but you should have the basic photo setup.

Tabletop tripod

A *tripod* is a three-legged stand that holds your camera or smartphone. The legs should stand on a surface and extend to your desired height or tilt to an angle. The latest ones have a Bluetooth remote so you don't have to touch the camera (or phone) to get the best angle to snap pictures. You can purchase one like this online for as low as $15.

Power charger

If you've ever used digital cameras for any length of time, you know that they can blast through batteries faster than sugar through a 5-year-old. Smartphones, too, can run out of juice at the most inopportune of moments. A portable power charger is a must, especially if you take product photos away from your home base. You can find them online reasonably priced. I use the brand Anker, but it's like I always say: Read the feedback and reviews on the product before purchasing.

Lighting

Trying to take good pictures of your merchandise can be frustrating. If you don't have enough light and use the camera's flash, the image might be washed out. If you take the item outside, the sun might cast a shadow.

Many digital cameras don't work well in low light. I've seen some eBay sellers use a flash and instruct their children to shine a flashlight on the item as they photograph it from different angles — all the while hoping that the color isn't wiped out.

After consulting specialists in the photo business to solve the problem of proper lighting for digital cameras, I put together an inexpensive studio lighting set for online product photography. It's the same one that I successfully use in my home photo studio (refer to Figures 1-1 and 1-2).

Professional studio lights can be expensive, but you might be able to find a set for around $100. (You need at least two lights, one for either side of the item, to eliminate shadows.) Search eBay for used studio lighting; I'm sure you'll find a good deal.

In lieu of a professional set-up, you can successfully use an Ott-Lite or a less expensive, generic true-color version, as shown in Figure 1-3. The lamp's bulb is a full-spectrum, daylight 5000K florescent tube, good enough for jewelry photography. This same light is used for grading diamonds.

FIGURE 1-3:
True-color and folding diamond-grading flip lights.

TIP

The *color temperature* of a light, which ranges from 2500°K to 7800°K, is a number given to a lighting condition. The K after the number signifies the Kelvin color temperature range. Actual daylight color temperature is about 5500°K, and it's best to get your lighting as close to that as you can. Using a bulb with a daylight number is important because it's a *pure neutral*, which means that it throws no blue or yellow cast on your images.

Photo cube

How much do I love my photo cube? I could write a poem! But I'd rather take another picture with it. It allows me to take the most detailed photos of antiques and specialty items at night in my home. It works incredibly well wherever I use it, because my kit includes two true-color lights. The nylon cube diffuses the light so that there are no harsh shadows and I don't burn out minute details with too much light. Take a look at the details in Figure 1-4.

FIGURE 1-4:
The fine details in this antique carving really show up due to the spectacular lighting diffused by the photo cube.

Photo background and stage

Backgrounds come in many shapes and sizes. You can get paper, fabric, or use one of the portable photo stages for smallish items:

>> **Seamless:** In professional photo-talk, *seamless* is a large roll of 3-foot (and wider) paper that comes in various colors and is suspended and draped behind the model and over the floor. (Ever wonder why you never see the floor and wall come together in professional photos?) Photographers also drape the seamless over tabletop shots. Some people use fabrics such as muslin instead of seamless.

>> **Fabrics:** I recommend using neutral fabrics (such as white, light gray, natural, and black) for photographing your merchandise so the color of the fabric doesn't clash with or distract from your items. Some of the photo cubes on eBay come with great low-wrinkle fabric backgrounds as well.

>> **Portable photo background:** A portable photo stage is another valuable tool for taking pictures indoors or out. Textured ABS plastic is manufactured so you can set it in a curve shape (see Figure 1-5); the stage can be set on any surface — and will permit you to take a clean picture without extraneous backgrounds. You can store it flat on a bookshelf till you need it next. Some experts recommend using poster board, which is prone to getting unsightly dirt and dents; it's not worth it. Spend the money and get a cleanable tool you will use forever.

FIGURE 1-5:
Easy kitchen-
counter eBay
photography
(just crop out the
back-ground).

Cloud Dome

If you're going to photograph a lot of jewelry, collectible coins, or other metallic items, you'll probably become frustrated at the quality of your pictures. Metallic objects seem to pick up random color from any kind of light you shine on them for picture-taking. Bad results: Gold jewelry will photograph with a silver tone, and silver will look gold-ish!

After conferring with lots of eBay photo gurus, I was told the secret of getting crisp, clear, close-up pictures: Use a Cloud Dome. It stabilizes your camera (just as if you were using a tripod) and filters all unwanted color tones, resulting in image colors that look like your item.

The Cloud Dome is a specially designed plastic bowl on which you mount your camera. You take your pictures through the dome. The translucent white plastic diffuses the light so your item is lit evenly from all sides, eliminating glare and bad shadows. Check out the manufacturer's website at www.clouddome.com to see some amazing before-and-after pictures.

Cloud Dome makes a smaller version for smartphone photography, called the Nimbus. The Nimbus also manages to get the best images from gems. You can actually capture the light in the facets! Pearls, too, will show their luster. Several eBay members (including yours truly) sell the Cloud Dome; I highly recommend it! In Book 5, Chapter 2, I show you how to use it.

Props

To take good photos, you need some props. Although you may think it strange that a line item in your accounting program will read *props,* they do qualify as a business expense. (Okay, you can put it under "photography expenses" — *props* just sounds so Hollywood!)

How often have you seen some clothing on eBay from a quality manufacturer, but you just couldn't bring yourself to bid more than $10 because it looked like it had been dragged behind a car and then hung on a hanger before it was photographed? Could you see how the fabric would hang on a body? Of course not.

Mannequin

If you're selling clothing, you'd better photograph it on a mannequin. If you don't want to dive right in and buy a mannequin, at least get a body form to wear the outfit. Just search eBay for *mannequin* to find hundreds of hollow forms selling for less than $20. If you sell children's clothing, get a child-size mannequin form as well. The same goes for men's clothes. If worst comes to worst, find a friend to model the clothes. There's just no excuse for hanger-displayed merchandise in your listings.

TIP

I got my mannequin (Midge) at a department store's liquidation sale here in Los Angeles. I paid $25 for her. Her face is a little creepy, so I often crop her head out of the photos. She has a great body and everything she wears sells at a profit. Many stores upgrade their mannequins every few years or so. If you know people who work at a retail store, ask when they plan to sell their old mannequins; you may be able to pick one up at a reasonable price.

Display stands, risers, and more

Jewelry doesn't photograph well on a person's hand and looks a lot better when you display it on a stand or a velvet pad. If you're selling a necklace, display it on a necklace stand, not on a person. You can find these stands on eBay by searching *jewelry display stand*; they can be bought for under $10.

Risers can be almost anything that you use to prop up your item to make it more attractive in a picture. Put any riser pieces that aren't attractive under the cloth that you use as a background. Keep a collection of risers and propping materials in your photo area so they're always close at hand.

You wouldn't believe what the back of some professional photo setups look like. Photographers and photo stylists think resourcefully when it comes to making the merchandise look good — from the front of the picture, anyway! Throughout my years of working with professional photographers, I've seen the most creative things used to prop up items for photography:

>> **Bottles of heavy stuff:** A photographer I once worked with used little bottles of mercury to prop up small boxes and other items in a picture. Mercury is a heavy liquid metal — but also a poison, so I suggest you try the same technique with small bottles (prescription bottles work well) filled with other weighty stuff (how about sand?).

>> **Beeswax and clay:** To set up photos for catalogs, I've seen photographers prop up fine jewelry and collectible porcelain with beeswax (the kind you can get from the orthodontist works great) or clay. Beeswax is a neutral color and doesn't usually show up in the photo. However, you must dispose of beeswax afterward, often because it picks up dirt from your hands and fuzz from fabric.

>> **Museum Gel or Quake Hold:** These two products are invaluable when you want to hold a small object at an unnatural angle for a photograph. (They're like beeswax and clay, but cleaner.) Museums use this puttylike product to keep breakables secured in one place — even during an earthquake! Museum Gel can sometimes be difficult to remove from items (and can leave a residue), so that's why I use Quake Hold putty for my eBay items.

>> **Metal clamps and duct tape:** These multipurpose items are used in many photo shoots in some of the strangest places. For example, if your mannequin is a few sizes too small for the dress you want to photograph, how do you fix that? Don't pad the mannequin; simply fold over the dress in the back and clamp the excess material with a metal clamp, or use a clothespin or a small piece of duct tape to hold the fabric taut.

Chapter **2**

Mastering eBay Photography

Photography has always been a passion for me. The hobby led me (at the age of 10) from developing film in a tiny storage-closet darkroom through my first side-advertising job for a camera store (yes, I was always a moonlighter) to a great professional gig taking photographs of NASCAR auto racing for magazines and newspapers. When designing catalogs, I worked with professional catalog photographers and picked up pro tricks for setting up pictures, buffing up the merchandise, and making everything look picture-perfect. In this chapter, I pass on the tips and shortcuts to you. Use these ideas to take great pictures that flatter your merchandise and help you sell!

Photo Guidelines

The idea behind using images in your auctions is to pull the eyes of potential buyers from other listings to yours. With that goal in mind, you should try to create the best-looking images possible, no matter what kind of technology you're using to capture them.

Point-and-shoot may be okay for a group shot at a historical monument, but illustrating your item for sale is a whole different idea. Whether you're using a traditional digital camera or a smartphone to capture your item, some basic photographic guidelines can give you better results:

>> **Do** take the picture of your item outside, in filtered daylight, whenever possible. That way the camera can catch all possible details and color. If you can't take your images during the day, use a diffuser and a good set of true-color lights, either on clamps or stands indoors.

>> **Do** forget about fancy backgrounds; they distract viewers from your item. Put small items on a neutral-colored, nonreflective background or cloth; put larger items in front of a neutral-colored wall or curtain. You'll want to crop out almost all the background before uploading the image.

>> **Do** avoid getting yourself in the photo by shooting your pictures from an angle. If you see your reflection in the item, move and try again.

AUTHOR SAYS

One of my favorite eBay pictures featured a piece of fine silver taken by the husband of the lady selling the piece on eBay. Silver and reflective items are hard to photograph because they pick up everything in the room in their reflection. In her description, the lady explained that the man reflected in the silver coffeepot was her husband and not part of the final deal. She handled that very well! To solve this reflective problem, take pictures of silvery objects in a photo cube or dome.

>> **Do** use extra lighting. These days, a digital camera's flash will only wash out most colors. Most newer smartphones are expert at bringing out details in low-light situations. Turn off the flash and add extra photo lighting if you need to. The extra lighting acts as *fill light* — it adds more light to the item, filling in some of the shadowed spots.

>> **Do** try to zoom in as close to the item as you can. This will permit you to upload your images immediately — without the need for photo editing.

>> **Do** upload your photos to the eBay Mobile app direct from your smartphone, as shown in Figure 2-1.

>> **Do** take extra close-ups of detailed areas that you want buyers to see (in addition to a wide shot of the entire item), if your item relies on detail.

>> **Do** make sure that the items are clean. Cellophane on boxes can get nasty-looking, clothing can get linty, and all merchandise can get dirt smudges. Not only will your items photograph better if they're clean, they'll sell better, too. Further along in this chapter, I give you some tips on cleaning specific items.

WARNING

If you're selling coins, *don't* clean them! If your coin is of any value at all, cleaning the coin will cause its price to plummet (and your selling reputation to be ruined) once the savvy coin collector discovers your efforts.

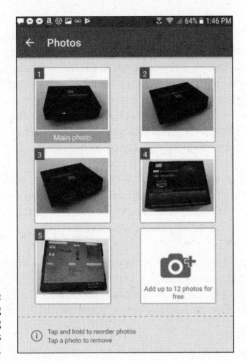

FIGURE 2-1:
Uploading
and cropping
photos in eBay's
mobile app.

WARNING

When you list a used item other than in the categories of books, movies, music, and video games, you cannot use the eBay catalog stock photo in the primary photo position. You *must* upload your own photo, and I recommend that it be a picture of the actual item you're selling.

Photographing the Tough Stuff: Coins and Jewelry

I've been selling on eBay since 1997 and thought I was pretty good at showing off and selling my wares. But then I purchased a small lot of Morgan silver dollars to resell. I figured, no problem — I'd take my standard digital picture and sell away. Oops, my mistake. The digital pictures made my beautiful silver coins look gold!

Then came my next challenge: photographing some silvertone and goldtone costume jewelry. My setup — with its perfect positioning, beautiful lighting, and black velvet jewelry pads — looked stunning. The pictures should have been perfect. But the silvertone looked gold, and the goldtone looked silver. What's the deal?

The deal is lighting — specifically, the need for ambient lighting. *Ambient* light (light that occurs naturally) is the best light for photographing many types of items, especially shiny items. I thought back to when I worked with catalog photographers who took pictures of jewelry — and I remembered the elaborate setup they used to produce the sparkling images you see in the ads. And although I can attempt to re-create the experts' silk tents with photo cubes, the minimalist lighting and multiple light flashes per exposure that are part of the professional photographer's setup can't be duplicated easily at home.

Enter the Cloud Dome, a bowl that you place upside-down over the object you want to photograph. This bowl evenly diffuses ambient room light over the surface area of the object. This way, you can produce quality digital images in average room lighting. The Cloud Dome also helps with the following:

>> **Eliminating camera shake:** When taking close-focus, highly zoomed-in pictures, holding your camera steady is of utmost importance. Using a tripod is difficult with close-up pictures, so using a Cloud Dome is the best option because your camera mounts directly to the Dome and is held as still as if you were using a tripod.

>> **Consistent lighting:** When you use flash or flood lighting alone (without a Cloud Dome) for pictures of metallic objects, your photographs can include shiny hotspots from reflections (off walls and ceilings), washed-out areas from the glare of the lights, shadows, and loss of proper color.

Shooting with the Cloud Dome

The Cloud Dome looks like a giant Tupperware bowl with a camera mount attached. Figure 2-2 shows a Cloud Dome being set up to photograph jewelry (on the right). The image next to it shows the new version for smartphones, the Nimbus.

FIGURE 2-2:
Taking pictures with the Cloud Dome and the Nimbus.

Follow these steps to take a picture with the Cloud Dome:

1. **Attach your camera to the Cloud Dome Nimbus' mount with the lens positioned so that it peers into the hole at the top of the dome.**

2. **Place your item on top of a contrasting background.**

   See the following section, "Further tips for taking pictures," for ideas on choosing a background.

3. **Place the dome — with camera attached — over your item.**

4. **Check the item's position through your camera's viewfinder or LCD screen.**

   If the item is not in the center, center it. If you feel you need additional lighting to bring out a highlight, use a lamp outside the dome.

5. **Focus on your subject and shoot the picture.**

Many items benefit from being photographed through a Cloud Dome, especially the following:

» **Jewelry:** I've found that taking pictures with the Dome keeps the gold color gold and the silver color silver. Also, using the Cloud Dome helps your camera pick up details such as engraving and the metal surrounding cloisonné work. It also gives pearls and gold their unique luster and soft reflection, as shown in Figure 2-3.

FIGURE 2-3:
A quartz stone with gold inclusions and diamonds, photographed with the Cloud Dome.

>> **Gems and stones:** I've seen some beautiful pictures taken of gems and stones with the Cloud Dome You may also want to focus a floodlight or lamp on the outside of the dome for extra sparkle.

>> **Coins and stamps:** The Cloud Dome allows you to hold the camera steady for extreme close-ups. It also allows you to photograph coins without getting any coloration that is not on the coin. For both coins and stamps, you achieve sharp focus and true color.

>> **Holographic or metallic accented items:** If you've ever tried to photograph collector cards, you know that the metal accents glare and holograms are impossible to capture. Also, the glossy coatings confuse the camera's light sensors, causing overexposed highlights.

>> **Reflective objects:** Items such as silverware or even computer chips reflect a lot of light when lit properly for photos. The Cloud Dome diffuses the light so that the pictures become clear.

Further tips for taking pictures

Surprisingly, there's little learning curve to using a Cloud Dome or taking product photos in general. The simple steps in the preceding section attest to this fact. What may take you more time is discovering the tips and tricks that help you achieve professional-looking results. This section should kick-start your discovery process:

>> **Focus, focus:** Due to the focus limitations of many of today's digital cameras, I found it best to use the Cloud Dome with the extension collar (often sold along with the dome), which allows you to have your camera 17 inches away from the item if you're photographing on a flat surface.

>> **Get in close to your item:** When attempting *macro* (extreme close-up) photography, use a tripod or Cloud Dome if possible to steady the shot. If you prefer, after you've centered your item, stand away and take the picture using your camera's self-timer.

>> **Keep background where it belongs:** When selecting a background for your item, choose a contrasting background that reflects the light properly for your item. Make it a solid color; white is always safe, and black can add dramatic highlights.

Prepping and Photographing Clothing

When photographing apparel for eBay, the one rule is: Take the *best picture* you can and move on to the next item so that you can hurry up and list all the items for sale. Period.

And even though I've just said there's only one rule, I also know that taking the *best picture* involves a bit of preparation on your part. Take a moment and perform an eBay search for the keyword *dress*. How many items do you see laid out on the floor or hanging loosely from a hanger? Those items can't compete with items shown on a person, a mannequin, or a dress form. A dress properly staged would probably have sold for twice the amount!

REMEMBER

One of the worst ways to photograph clothing is on a tabletop or folded on the floor. The camera misses essential details in the folded items, and you miss the opportunity to show off the clothing in all its glory — as worn on a body. To get the highest final price, give your clothing an authentic, lifelike appearance.

WARNING

Lifting photographs from the manufacturer's website can be a copyright violation. eBay may end your listing if such a violation is reported.

Apparel photography can be tricky by all measures, especially when you don't have a model. Using a model is a great idea if you have plenty of time to spare. When you work with a model (even if it's a son or daughter or a friend), you'll have to take many shots of the person wearing the same item, because you want the model to look as good as the clothing, and vice versa. Not a timesaver.

What's the best way to shoot fashion for eBay? Assembly-line style. Henry Ford had it right. Have everything assembled in one area and the process can go smoothly and quickly. In this section, I tell you about how to prepare your studio, your props, and your clothing to get the best picture for the least effort. And best of all, the time you spend preparing the clothes to photograph also makes them customer-ready. Now, *there's* a timesaver!

Cleaning and pressing essentials

Before you photograph your clothing, make sure the clothing itself imparts the image you want your buyers to see. For example, remove any loose threads and lint that have accumulated on the fabric.

Have the following items handy to help you with the cleaning and pressing chores:

>> **Garment rack:** When you unpack your merchandise from the carton it was shipped to you in, it can look pretty ragged. And if you've purchased some hanging merchandise and it's in tip-top shape, you'll want to keep it that way. Hanging the merchandise on a garment rack (as shown on the left in Figure 2-4) keeps it fresh-looking so it looks great when you get ready to ship.

FIGURE 2-4: Making clothes look their best for listing on eBay.

TIP

>> **Steamer:** Retail stores, clothing manufacturers, and drycleaners all use steamers. Why? Because steaming the garment with a steam wand is kinder to the fabric and takes wrinkles out in a hurry. Steam penetrates the fabric (not crushing it, as does ironing) and seems to make the fabric look better than before.

Steaming is also five times *faster* than ironing (and not as backbreaking), so that's why it's truly the professional's choice. Steaming garments is a breeze; see for yourself on the right in Figure 2-4.

A handheld travel steamer will work for beginners who sell a few apparel items a month. Although you can steam a garment with a professional-style steamer in a minute or two, you might have to work on a garment with a travel steamer for 15 minutes. If you're thinking about selling a quantity of clothes on eBay, a professional-style, roll-base steamer is what you should look for.

I use a Jiffy Steamer that I've had for quite a while. (I bought it on eBay and got a great deal.) It's the same kind they use in retail stores, only slightly smaller.

>> **Dryel:** A popular, reasonably priced, home dry-cleaning product you use in your dryer, Dryel can be used with almost any type of garment (be sure to double-check the packaging before you use it). After going through a Dryel treatment, clothes come out of the dryer sweet and clean. The starter kit comes with a spray spot remover.

According to eBay rules, all used clothing must be cleaned before it is sold on the site. Even if the vintage garment you have up for sale is clean, it can always benefit by a roll in the dryer with Dryel. New garments, too, benefit; Dryel removes any smells that have clung to the garment during its travels.

>> **Spot cleaners:** I recommend that you use spot cleaners only if you know what you're doing. Some really great ones out there will remove a small spot, but you'd best practice first on items that you're *not* selling.

STEAMING HOT TIPS

Keep these tips in mind when steaming the clothes you sell on eBay:

- Always keep the steam head in an upright position so that the condensation inside the hose drains back into the steamer.
- Run the steam head lightly down the fabric.
- Hang pants by the cuff when steaming.
- Don't let the steam head come directly in contact with velvet or silk; otherwise you may spot the fabric.
- Steam velvet (or any fabric with a pile) from the reverse side.
- Heavy fabrics may do better by steaming from the underside of the fabric.
- When you're through steaming your clothes for eBay, try steaming your mattresses and furniture. Steaming has been proven to kill a majority of dust mites and their accompanying nastiness.

Assembling your fashion photo studio

Photographing fashion right takes a little time, but the right tools make the project easier. Here's a list of some of the items you'll need when photographing clothing:

» **Mannequin body double:** You don't want to deal with supermodels and their requirements for nonfat vanilla lattes, so you have to find someone who will model the garments and not give you any grief. Figure 2-5 pictures my mannequin Midge, who has sold lots of dresses on eBay for me.

FIGURE 2-5:
Midge modeling a vintage fur (photo was cropped before listing).

Full-body mannequins can be purchased on eBay for under $100. (Dress forms go for as little as $25). I bought Midge from a local store that was updating their mannequins. Major department stores often liquidate their display merchandise through online sales, so keep your eyes peeled for sales of store fixtures.

Keep in mind that you needn't spend a mint on a brand-new model. If your mannequin is used and has a few paint chips — so what?

Following are some less expensive alternatives to a mannequin:

● **Molded body form:** Before you decide to jump in with both feet, you might want to try using a hanging *body form* — a molded torso that has a hanger at the top. You can find molded styrene forms on eBay for as little as $20. If you decide to stay in the apparel-vending business, you can always upgrade to a full-size mannequin.

- **Dressmaker's adjustable form:** You can also use a dressmaker's form to model your eBay clothing. The best part about using these is that you can adjust the size of the body to fit your clothing. You can often find new or good-condition used ones on eBay for under $40.

» **Vertical photo lights on stands:** To light your merchandise, you'll do best to invest in some floodlights. You don't have to spend a mint, but as you'll see when you start taking pictures, the little flash on your camera can't accentuate the good parts of your apparel. Stop the flash on your camera from going off when you take pictures of clothes, because too much light coming from the front will wash out the detail in the fabric.

TIP

Place the mannequin in the middle of your studio area. Situate a floodlight on either side, closer to the camera than to the mannequin. Your setup will be a V-shape, with your mannequin at the point, your floodlights at the top of each V-side, and you (or a tripod) holding the camera in the middle at the top of the V. Adjust the distance that you place your lights as needed. Be sure to tilt the light heads to pick up extra detail in the clothing.

» **Clothespins:** To fit your clothing on the mannequin, use clothespins to take up any slack in the garment (be sure to place the clothespins where the camera won't see them). Before you think I'm crazy, I'll have you know that clothespins were used in almost every professional apparel photo shoot that I've participated in. Think about it: The clothing you're selling will come in different sizes and may not always hang right on your mannequin.

eBay Gallery of Horrors

This section shows you a bunch of big-time don'ts. We've seen images like these all over eBay at one time or another.

Mistake #1

Figure 2-6 shows a nice item, but the picture suffers from two major flaws:

» **A glare from the camera's flash shows in the cellophane on the item.** This can be avoided by turning the item slightly at an angle so that the flash doesn't give off such a bright glare, or take the photo in a fabric cube.

FIGURE 2-6:
Glaring errors
here!

>> **The price sticker is smack on the front of the item.** Often you'll buy
things for resale that have stickers. Be a pro — use a commercial product
(see Chapter 1) to remove stickers.

Mistake #2

Don't dress your picture with props to decorate the scene. Your photo should
be a crisp, clean image of the product you're selling, and only that. Figure 2-7
shows a common eBay seller mistake. What a cute teddy — but what are you
selling here?

FIGURE 2-7:
You're selling
what?

Mistake #3

I never knew how much colorful upholstery people had in their homes. I've seen items photographed on plaid, floral, and striped fabrics (see Figure 2-8). It distracts from your item. Don't do it.

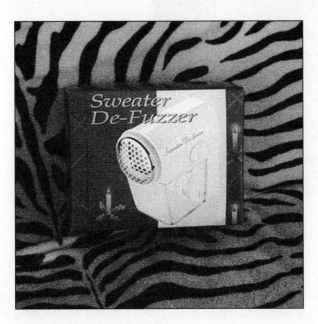

FIGURE 2-8: Nice sofa!

Mistake #4

I'm sure the item in the box shown in Figure 2-9 is desirable, but who can make that judgment without seeing the item? Take the item out of the box. If the box is a crucial part of the deal (as in collectibles), keep it in the box and mention that the item is Mint In Box.

REMEMBER

If you can't open the box without ruining the value of the item, pull in for a macro close-up. When you have a quantity of the item, bite the bullet and open one up. A good picture gets you higher bids, and perhaps that loss of one item will be made up by the higher bids on the sales with good pictures.

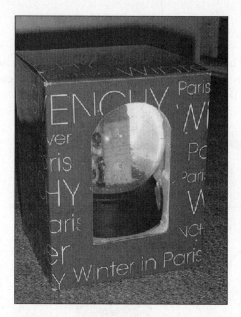

FIGURE 2-9:
Peek-a-boo.

Mistake #5

Can you say *close-up?* Use the zoom on your camera to fill the frame with a full picture of your item. Draw your camera close to the item so the prospective customer can see some detail. Don't take a wide picture of the area around the item, like the shot shown in Figure 2-10. Don't just rely on cropping the picture in an image-editing program; that only makes the image smaller.

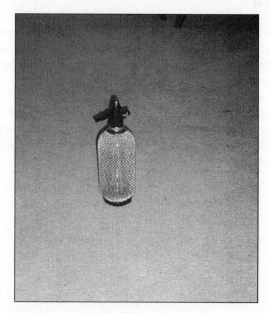

FIGURE 2-10:
Pay no attention
to the object on
the carpet.

Chapter **3**

Writing Listings that Sell, and Using HTML

I must admit, the very thought of coding used to terrify me. HTML sounds terribly geeky. Yet HTML isn't all that scary after you realize that it's just a fancy name for HyperText Markup Language, an easy-to-use language for creating online content. All you need to know is the markup part. You'll find knowing HTML even helps with using WordPress.

HTML uses tags to mark pages to include elements such as text and graphics in a way that web browsers understand. A web browser sees the tags, and knows how to display the document (that is, the web page). HTML also makes possible the whole world of links. When you click a link, you jump to another place: another web page, document, or file, for example.

TIP

HTML can save you money when it comes to your blog or website. A little knowledge of HTML will allow you to build your own online store quite simply and insert PayPal Buy Now (or Add to Cart) buttons. By learning a few HTML tricks, beginners won't have to pay extra for an ecommerce-enabled store from your domain host.

Luckily, you don't have to be a coder to produce enticing web pages or eBay listings. My personal knowledge of HTML gets me only so far, so I often use tools like Mozilla's SeaMonkey to create designs for my emails, blog, website, or eBay listings. I've developed several templates so that all I have to do is replace the text each time I want to repeat a layout. Imparting a specific "look" to all your online business makes your outreach appear far more professional. This chapter shows you how to do that, too.

In addition, the eBay listing-creation form has an area where you can input your own HTML, as well as a designer that you use like a word processor to format text. I show you how to make this convenient tool do magic with your listings.

Writing Descriptions that Sell

Many eBay sellers somehow think that putting colorful graphics and lots of logos in their listings will entice more customers to buy. Unfortunately, that's pretty far from the truth (these listings look especially bad on mobile devices). Customers go to your listings to find information and a great deal on something they want, not to be entertained. They need to see the facts, placed cleanly and neatly on the page.

WARNING

The addition of many unrelated images to your description may cause another problem: A slower-than-normal page-load time for visitors with slower connections. If loading your page takes too long, most people will go to another listing.

So what should you do to attract buyers? I spent most of my career in the marketing business, and the byword of good promotion is, "Keep it simple!" An organized and well-written selling description will outsell dancing bears and random pictures every time.

REMEMBER

When you write the descriptions for your items, be sure that you describe your items clearly and completely. Mention everything about the item; be honest and even mention flaws or damage. When you're honest up front, you'll have a happy buyer.

When your item is a collectible, after you list all the facts, get excited and add a short bit of energetic text in your description. Think infomercial! Think Shopping Channel! They make things sound so good that you feel that you *must* have whatever item they're selling. You can do the same, if you make the effort. In Book 3, Chapter 3, I give you basic pointers on writing the best descriptions possible.

HTML the Easy eBay Way

Luckily, you don't have to know a lot of code to produce attractive eBay descriptions. The listing form has an excellent (but basic) HTML generator that has features similar to a word processor, as shown in Figure 3-1 (click the words *Advanced editing* on the right to access the tool).

FIGURE 3-1:
Getting to eBay's HTML code generator.

Once you click Advanced editing, you'll get to a description text box with all the attributes, such as the one in Figure 3-2.

FIGURE 3-2:
Here you can apply basic HTML without going into coding.

To apply any of these features (such as bold or italic) to your text, you simply highlight the text and click one of the buttons.

TIP

When inputting text, you may notice that eBay's tool inserts a line space after text when you start a new paragraph. If you want the text to wrap and not have a blank space between text lines, hold down the Shift key while you press the Enter (or Return) key. That forces an HTML line break (`<br>`) instead of a paragraph break.

There will be four drop-down lists. Click to the right of each box and the following options appear:

Starting at the left, you see a powerful tool. Do you have text (or an HTML template) that you'd like to have in all your listings for uniformity? Some of your listings? Click the Insert custom template box.

When you click this option, you'll see another option to Create a custom template. Click that and another text box opens. Place your cursor in the text box and paste a predesigned template in the box. Give your template a custom name, and you'll be able to access it for future listings.

After you create your custom template, you can add it to any of your descriptions with a click of your mouse. How convenient! At the end of the chapter, you'll see instructions on how to build your own templates!

Next you'll come to the drop-down lists on the Standard tab shown in Figure 3-2. After you use the leftmost one to specify a template, click to the right of each box going rightward and the following options appear:

>> **Font name:** Apply different fonts to your text. Play around with the different fonts to see which ones you prefer. Stick to web-friendly fonts and don't get *too* creative. Readability is your goal.

>> **Font size:** You can increase or decrease the size of the type. It reads in numbers, or point size. The smallest is 8-point and the largest is 36-point.

>> **Color:** Want to add some color to your text? Just highlight the text and select black, blue, red, green, yellow, or brown from the plethora of colors available.

Just below these drop-down lists, you see a row of buttons. Here's what they do:

>> **Boldface** text

>> *Italicize* text

>> <u>Underline</u> text

>> Align text to the left

» Center text

» Align text to the right

» Create a numbered list

» Create a bulleted list

» "Outdent," or move indented text back to the left

» Indent text to the right

At the upper right, you'll see eBay's *Mobile-friendly checker*. Once you've typed in your simple description or HTML code, click the checker, and eBay will evaluate your code as shown in Figure 3-3.

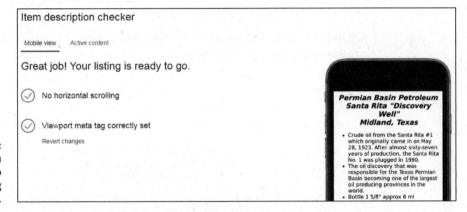

FIGURE 3-3:
eBay will let you know (and help you fix) any coding errors here.

Getting Friendly with HTML

When you want to fancy up any page that appears on the web, knowing a bit of HTML will be a valuable tool in your arsenal.

TIP

You can also use HTML to insert multiple pictures into your descriptions to better promote your item. This won't cost you extra, and you can still use up to 12 free photos from eBay for your top-of-listing images. According to eBay policy, any images with descriptive text on them must appear in your description. For information on how to upload your images to a server for inclusion into your description, see Book 5, Chapter 4.

What HTML can do

Take a look at Figure 3-4. It contains an item description I typed in the listing-description box with HTML.

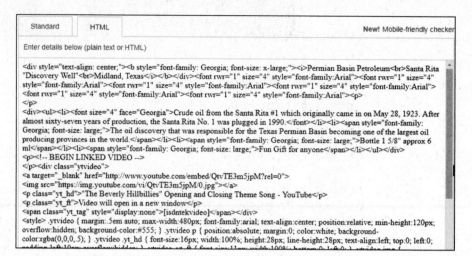

FIGURE 3-4:
Raw HTML
description text.

When I switch to *Standard view,* the description looks a whole lot different, as you can see in Figure 3-5. Pretty cool, eh?

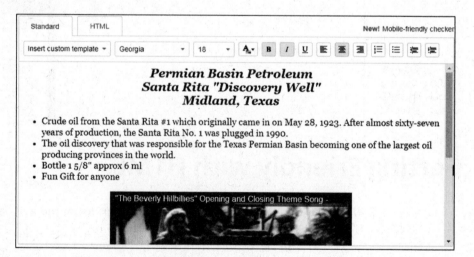

FIGURE 3-5:
Listing
description dolled
up with HTML.

How HTML works

HTML uses a series of codes to give the browser information (commands) about how to display items, such as when text should be bold or italic, or when text is actually a link. And HTML uses angle brackets (< >) to mark those command codes. What's within the brackets is an instruction rather than actual text; only the text of your description will appear on your page.

In the example that follows, the *b* and *i* in brackets indicate that text between them should be formatted bold and italic, respectively. Notice that there are indicators to specify both a start and end to specific formatting (<b> starts bold formatting and </b> ends it). Here's one example:

HTML start and end tags: <b><i></i></b>

Tags with text between them: <b><i>eBay tools</i></b>

The resulting text on your page: ***eBay tools***

TIP

Table 3-1 lists many common HTML tags to get you started. If you want to stay compatible with XHTML (Extensible HyperText Markup Language) and the latest HTML5, start getting in the habit of using lowercase for your tags.

TABLE 3-1   ## Basic HTML Codes

Text Codes	How to Use Them	What They Do
<b></b>	<b>eBay tools</b>	**eBay tools** (bold type)
<i></i>	<i>eBay tools</i>	*eBay tools* (italic type)
<b><i></i></b>	<b><i>eBay tools</b></i>	***eBay tools*** (bold and italic type)
<font color=red></font>	<font color=red>eBay tools </font>	Selected text appears in red. (Because this book is in black and white, you can't see it on the page here.)
<font size=+1></font>	<font size=+3> eBay tools</font>	eBay tools (font size normal +1 through 4, increases size *x* times)
 	eBay tools	eBay tools (inserts line break)
<p>	eBay<p>tools	eBay tools (inserts paragraph space)
<hr>	cool eBay<hr>tools	cool eBay ——— tools (inserts horizontal rule)
<h1><h1>	<h1>eBay tools</h1>	**eBay tools** (converts text to headline size)

(continued)

TABLE 3-1 *(continued)*

List Codes	How to Use Them	What They Do

`<ul><li></ul>`	`<ul><li>I accept`
	`<li>PayPal`
	`<li>Money Orders`
	`<li>Checks</ul>`
		I accept
		• PayPal
		• Money Orders
		• Checks

`<ol><li></ol>`	`<ol><li>I accept`
	`<li>PayPal`
	`<li>Money Orders`
	`<li>Checks</ol>`
		I accept
		1. PayPal
		2. Money Orders
		3. Checks

Linking (Hyperlink) Codes	How to Use Them	What They Do

`<img src>`	`<img src="http://`
	`www.yourwebsite.com`
	`/imagename.jpg">`
		Inserts an image from your server into the description text

`<a href= >`	`<a href= http://`
	`www.yourwebsite.com/`
	`shippinginfo.htm>`
	`Click here for`
	`shipping info</a>`
		When selected text is clicked (in this instance, *Click here for shipping info*), the user's browser goes to the page you indicate in the URL.

`target=_blank`	`<a href= http://`
	`www.yourwebsite.com/`
	`shippinginfo.htm`
	`target=_blank>`
		When inserted at the end of a hyperlink, it opens the page in a separate browser window.

Table Codes	How to Use Them	What They Do
`<table border>`	`<table border=4>`	Puts a border around your table at a width of 4 pixels
`<table></table>`	`<table> sample text` `sample text</table>`	Specifies a table. (The table command must surround *every* table.)

`<tr></tr><td></td>`	`<tr><td>text</td>`
	`<td>text</td></tr>`
	`<tr><td>text</td>`
	`<td>text</td></tr>`
		Table row `<tr>` must be used with `<td>`. Table data to end and open new boxes:
		text text
		text text

A few things to keep in mind about HTML:

>> Don't worry about affecting your design when you press Enter at the end of a line in HTML. You must use a command to go to the next line on the final product, so pressing Enter on your keyboard has no effect on what the page looks like.

>> Most HTML coding has a beginning and an ending. The beginning code is in angle brackets <>. To end the formatting, you repeat the code in brackets, only this time with a slash to end the command </>.

>> It's not necessary to put the paragraph command at the beginning and at the end of the paragraph. This is one command that doesn't need a close. Just put the command <p> where you want the breaking space to occur. This applies also for a horizontal rule, <hr>. Just place the command where you want the line, and it will appear.

REMEMBER

>> People have different fonts set up on their computers, so they may not have the special, unique style of font you want to display. Be sure to use the eBay standard fonts for your text. If you don't, different browsers may substitute other fonts that might look *really* funky on some readers' pages.

Following is a listing description showing the HTML code in bold so it's easier to spot:

```
<center><font face="verdana,helvetica,arial" color="crimson"
    size=5>
<b>Portable Photography Backdrop Stage<br>from Cloud Dome</b>
</font></center>
<center><font face="verdana,arial,helvetica,sans serif"
    color="black" size=4>
eBay Sellers! This is for you! Are you tired of trying to find a
    nice clear spot to take your pictures for eBay sales? Sure,
    you could spend a fortune on backdrops and muslin, but this
    handy, portable stage works (without glare) flawlessly every
    time. This is the most versatile product that I've found for
    tabletop photography. </font>

<br><center><font face="verdana,arial,helvetica,sans serif"
    color="black" size=2>
The Infiniti Board is white-textured, washable, and
    scratchproof. It can be used flat or curved; the height and
    curve are adjustable with the attached locking cords. The
    total size is 19 inches wide by 28 inches long. <p>
<img src="http://www.collierad.com/whiteboard.jpg">
<font face="verdana,arial,helvetica,sans serif" color="black"
    size=2><center>
```

```
I scour the country looking for new reasonably priced tools for
    the eBay seller. Check my feedback to see that customer
    service is the byword of my eBay business. Winning bidder to
    pay calculated Priority Mail (2- to 3-day) shipping based on
    distance. Credit cards accepted through PayPal.<br>
<b>This item is NOT being drop-shipped by another party. We have
    these in stock and will ship immediately - directly to
    you!<br></font>
<font face="verdana,arial,helvetica,sans serif" color= "crimson"
    size=2><i>
GET IT QUICKLY! I ship via 2 - 3 day Priority Mail.</b> </i></
    font><p>
<i><font face="verdana,arial,helvetica,sans serif" color="black"
    size=3><p>
Click below to... <br>
<a href= http://cgi6.ebay.com/ws/eBayISAPI.dll?ViewSellersOtherI
    tems&include=0&userid=marsha_c&sort=3&rows=50&since=-1&rd=1
    target=_blank>
Visit my eBay Store <b><i>for low prices</i></b>on handy seller
    tools and Cloud Dome Products</a></b></font></center>
```

Add Pictures to Your Description

"How do I put pictures in my listing's description area?" Here's the answer to the question I'm asked most when I teach a class on eBay. Many sellers add additional pictures within the auction description area. By putting extra images in the description, they can show more of the item details that may coincide with the verbiage in the description. This isn't magic; you can do it too. Just add a tiny bit of HTML code. Don't freak out on me, now; you can do this. Here is the HTML code to insert one picture in your auction:

```
<img src=http://www.yourserver.com/imagename.jpg>
```

Be sure to use the angle brackets (they're located above the comma and the period on your keyboard) to open and close your code.

When you want to insert two pictures, just insert code for each picture, one after the other. If you want one picture to appear below the other, use the HTML code for line break, <br>. Here's how to write that:

```
<img src=http://www.yourserver.com/imagename1.jpg> <br>
<img src=http://www.yourserver.com/imagename2.jpg>
```

Note that the HTML code shown here is boldfaced to help you spot it, but it's not necessary to bold your HTML code when you *use* it.

Add Videos to Illustrate Your Item

In June 2017, eBay made any active content *verboten* on the site. Basically this means that people had to remove product-demonstration videos from their listings.

Until eBay publishes a new way to post listings, here's a website that can help. Get the URL for a YouTube video and post it on the form at

```
http://www.isdntek.com/tagbot/YouTubeConverter.htm
```

and follow the instructions on the page. Once you've pasted in the YouTube URL, click Make eBay Code and the site will generate eBay-approved code to insert on the HTML view of the description.

Videos help products sell! Anytime you can add a video to your description, it increases sales.

Using HTML Table Codes to Make Templates

Have you ever noticed how some people manage to have a photo on either the right or the left sides of their descriptions? It's not that difficult to do. You add a little HTML code to the listing using a feature called *tables*.

For example, Figure 3-6 shows a picture contained in a table on the left side of the description. (By the way, when the full version of this auction ran on eBay, with the kind cooperation of the people on *The View*, we raised more than $1,000 for UNICEF!)

FIGURE 3-6:
A listing using tables with the picture on the left.

The HTML code for this description goes like this. (The `<tr>` and `<td>` codes create the table format.)

```
<table align=center cellpadding=8 width="80%" border=7
   cellspacing=0 bgcolor="white">
<tr><td>
<center><font face="verdana,helvetica,arial" color="crimson"
   size=5>
<b>"The View"<br>Cast Autographed<br>Coffee Mug</b></font><p>
<img width=250 src="http://images.auctionworks.com/viewmug.jpg">
</td>
<td>
<center><font face="verdana,helvetica,arial" color="crimson"
   size=3>
<b><i>Signed by</i><br><b>Joy Behar<br>Star Jones<br>Barbara
   Walters<br>Meredith Vieira</b>
</font><p>
<font face="verdana,arial,helvetica,sans serif" color="black"
   size=2>
<b>All you fans of <i>The View </i>, this is your chance to own
   a coffee cup autographed by all four stars of the show. The
   proceeds from this auction will be donated to UNICEF. The
   winner will be announced on ABC's <i>The View</i> TV show on
   Monday. We'll be checking this auction live on the show on
   Wednesday, April 23rd, 2003 with Marsha Collier, the author of
   <i>"eBay for Dummies"</i></b>.</font><p>
<font face="verdana,arial,helvetica,sans serif" color="black"
   size=1>
Shipping will be via Priority Mail. Credit cards are accepted
   through PayPal. </font>
</center></td></tr></table>
```

After you get the hang of it, tables aren't scary at all. As a matter of fact, if you want to use my templates for your listings, be my guest!

WARNING

Think twice before loading up your description with buckets of pictures. List the item and take a look at it in the eBay Mobile checker to be sure it looks OK.

Creating Your Own HTML Designs and Templates

When you're ready to take on design in earnest, it really helps to have a few item-description templates all set up and ready to go. This is what the big brands do (granted, some do a better job than others). Although it's fun to play around with using different graphics as you sell on eBay — and I must admit, I've seen some cute ones — having a standardized look establishes you as a branded, professional seller. After all, how often does eBay change its look? The answer is, not too often. The colors and the basics of design remain the same because such is eBay's (very valuable) brand.

What might go into a template? You can insert your logo within your description, or put links to your Profile page or your store, for example. Think of your template becoming your brand. Many auction-management services offer pre-designed templates for descriptions, but their services can often cost big bucks. Save yourself the money, put together your own template, and update it as design trends change.

REMEMBER

Keeping things simple and showing off your product will result in more sales. Getting carried away with graphics that have nothing to do with your item is distracting.

In this section, I show you how to design simple templates using SeaMonkey. It's an all-in-one (like this book), free Internet application suite that grows with you. I use it for the Composer module (a WYSIWYG — What You See Is What You Get — HTML editor). The more HTML you understand, the more you can do with Composer. To make life even easier, in the next section, you use an HTML generator on my website to create a template that you can customize with a little extra knowledge of HTML.

Downloading SeaMonkey

Few things in this life are absolute necessities, but photos and good design definitely are. It's a good idea to start developing templates by building a simple one that includes a space for a photo. Because I like to use much of what the Internet offers for free . . . I use a Mozilla program called SeaMonkey Composer to do just that.

SeaMonkey is a free, fully functional Windows or Mac Internet suite from Mozilla (the same folks who brought to you Firefox). It consists of a web browser, an email and news-client program, and an HTML editor. In other words, you can get all these programs in one. Many people enjoy occasionally switching from Chrome or Firefox to the feature-rich, faster, less-memory-hogging SeaMonkey. I use it because I like the HTML editor Composer.

You can download the free suite at `www.seamonkey-project.org`.

Because SeaMonkey is a *suite* (meaning it has several programs all in one), you decide which program you want to run when you click the SeaMonkey icon. If you just want to use the HTML editor Composer (as I do), take the following steps:

1. **After downloading the software, install it by double-clicking the SeaMonkey icon.**

   You might just want to play with its superfast web browser and maybe get a feel for its other features . . . but right now? I'm using the Composer.

2. **Click the Window link in the toolbar.**

3. **Select Composer from the drop-down menu.**

   A blank new window will open with the Composer ready to go.

Adding text and graphics

After you open SeaMonkey Composer, you'll see that it looks like an eBay or Word page layout, but it has far more features. The most important for you to see are the four tabs at the bottom of the screen. These tabs enable you to view your template in several ways:

>> **Normal.** This is your standard design mode, where you can highlight text — change it or color it — and add pictures or tables, as shown in Figure 3-7.

>> **HTML Tags.** This view shows you your template with the symbols of the tags you have created. Check out Figure 3-8.

>> **HTML Source.** Figure 3-9 shows the raw HTML code that you see when you click the Source tab. From this view, you can save the template to your hard drive and change the text at will through the Normal tab.

>> **Preview.** This tab displays your work in pretty much the same way as the Normal setting, but it's good to double-check that everything is perfect before you save it.

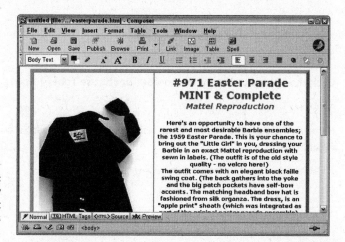

FIGURE 3-7:
It took just a few seconds to put together this simple template.

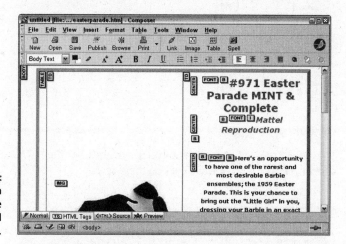

FIGURE 3-8:
How easy to learn HTML when the tags are spelled out for you.

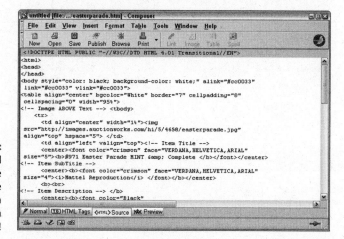

FIGURE 3-9:
Just copy and paste this source code into the eBay description HTML form and voilà!

In the following steps, you create a table that contains a photo on the left and text on the right:

1. **Click the Table button on the toolbar or choose Tools ⇨ Insert Table.**

An Insert Table screen appears.

2. **If you want a photo next to your text, indicate 1 row with 2 columns, as in Figure 3-10.**

This creates a table with two cells side by side.

FIGURE 3-10: Creating a table with two cells.

3. **Click OK.**

The table screen disappears, and you see the table or the HTML coding (as shown in Figure 3-11) for two cells on the screen.

FIGURE 3-11: Coding for a 2 x 1 table in the SeaMonkey screen.

4. **Click the Row 1 Cell 1 on the screen (in Source mode this would be between the HTML opening and closing codes — <td> and </td>), and then click the Image button (it looks like a little picture) on the toolbar.**

The Image Tag dialog box appears.

5. **In the Image Properties box, type the Internet address (URL) where your image is stored.**

You can get the URL from your image hosting service, from your website, or by locating the image on the Internet and copying the URL from the top of your browser screen. If you want to alter the size of your image, you can also type the width or height (or both), in pixels, in the Dimensions boxes.

6. **Click OK.**

The HTML code for the image appears inside the text area.

7. **Click the Row 1 Cell 2 on your screen, and enter the description text you want to appear next to the picture.**

For convenience, you can also open a listing description you've already written in Windows Notepad, and copy and paste it into the space.

Adding HTML formatting

If you've already written your description text, you can paste it into the open window. But if you do that (as Figure 3-12 shows), all the sentences run together in one mammoth paragraph.

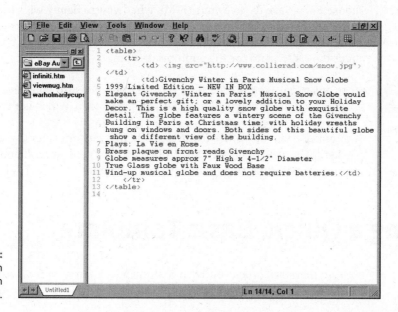

FIGURE 3-12:
Shows the screen filled in with straight text.

To distinguish and emphasize parts of your description — and to simply make it look better — you can add HTML text attributes as follows:

1. **Highlight the text you want to change.**

2. **Click the button on the toolbar for the text formatting style you want to apply.**

   The *B* button is for **bold**, *I* is for *italic,* and *U* is for underline. The formatting is applied automatically.

After some final tweaking, the final description looks like Figure 3-13.

FIGURE 3-13:
A beautiful, quickly created listing!

Choose File ⇨ Save to save your HTML when you're happy with the results. When you're ready to use that auction description, just open the file, copy the code, and paste it into the eBay auction-description area (be sure you're typing in the area under the HTML tab) for the appropriate item.

When inserting HTML code into your listings, be sure you have the HTML tab selected, or your listing will look like a bunch of code (which isn't very attractive).

WARNING

SeaMonkey has many other features, including custom colors, anchors, and spell checker. After you've created a template or two, poke around and see how fancy you can get with this small (but powerful) program.

Getting a Quick, Basic Template

Because there are times you're in too much of a hurry to fool with *anything*, I've put a free ad tool on my website:

When you land on my home page, click the link in the navigation bar labeled Tools. On the resulting page, click the Cool Free Ad Tool link and you jump to the instant template page, shown in Figure 3-14.

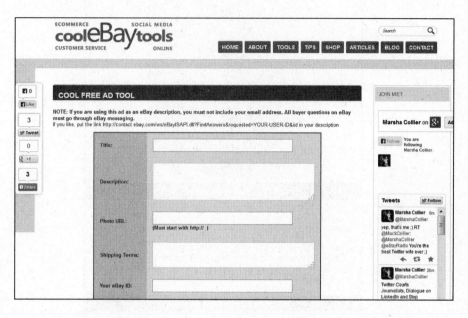

FIGURE 3-14:
The Cool Free Ad Tool page on my site.

To set up a quick eBay template using this tool, follow these steps:

1. **In the Title box, type the headline for your description.**

2. **In the Description box, enter a description.**

   You can copy and paste prewritten text from Notepad or any plain text app, or just write your copy text as you go along.

3. **In the Photo URL box, enter the URL of your image.**

4. **In the Shipping Terms box, type the pertinent information (optional).**

5. **Enter your eBay User ID.**

   The address is used to put code in your description that links to your My eBay messages.

6. **Select the border, background, and navigation font colors from the drop-down lists. Type a size for the navigation font as prompted.**

7. **Click the View Ad button.**

   You see how your new listing description looks. Mine is shown in Figure 3-15.

Scroll down until you see a box containing the description's HTML code, as shown in Figure 3-16.

Givenchy Winter in Paris Musical Snow Globe

Description

Elegant Givenchy "Winter in Paris" Musical Snow Globe would make an perfect gift; or a lovely addition to your Holiday Decor. This is a high quality snow globe with exquisite detail. The globe features a wintery scene of the Givenchy Building in Paris at Christmas time; with holiday wreaths hung on windows and doors. Both sides of this beautiful globe show a different view of the building. Plays: La Vie en Rose. Brass plaque on front reads Givenchy Globe measures approx 7" High x 4-1/2" Diameter True Glass globe with Wooden Base Wind-up musical globe and does not require batteries.

Shipping & Payment Terms

Winning bidder to pay calculated Priority Mail (2 to 3 day) shipping based on distance. Please use the eBay Shipping Calculator below. Type your zip code in the box below to determine your shipping rate. If time is not of the essence, please email and we will quote a lower FedEx Ground shipping rate. Please submit payment within a week of winning the auction. Credit cards graciously accepted through PayPal.

HAVE A QUESTION?

FIGURE 3-15:
Your instant eBay ad.

Copy & Paste the following code into the auction's description box:

```
<CENTER><table border="3" bordercolor="navy"
cellspacing="0" cellpadding="0" width="500"
bgcolor="#ffffff"><tr><td colspan="3"
bgcolor="#ffffff"><center><font face="arial black"
color="navy" size="+2">Givenchy Winter in Paris
Musical Snow Globe </font><br><br><table border="0"
width="500" bordercolor="#000000" cellspacing="0"
cellpadding="5"><tr><td width=500 align="center"><img
src="http://www.collierad.com/snowglobe.jpg"
hspace="0" vspace="0" border="0"></td></tr><tr><td
align=center bgcolor="navy"><font color="white"
size="+1"
face="arial"><b>Description</b></font></td></tr><tr><td
align=center><font face="arial">Elegant
```

FIGURE 3-16:
HTML coding for your listing.

You can copy and paste this code directly into the eBay description area of the Create a listing form (or any eBay listing tool). You can also add HTML codes and even another picture to your item description.

Chapter **4**

Getting the Most from Your Photos

In this chapter, I show you how fast you can get the photos you take — or the scans you make — ready for presentation online. No ecommerce seller should spend hours playing with and perfecting images for listings (although some do). One pass through a simple image-editing software program gets any reasonable picture Internet-ready. In this chapter, I tell you only what you need to know to appropriately resize and touch up.

Size Matters

The prime concern to have about the pictures you put on eBay is size — that's right; in this case, size does matter. If you are using eBay's Picture Hosting services, images must be at least 500 pixels on the longest side because the service converts them to optimal resolution for the page. When you use your own hosted images in the listing description, you need to optimize the files to a reasonable size yourself. Limiting the size of each picture file means you don't bog down the prospective buyer's viewing of your description (especially if you're using multiple images). Why? That's easy. The larger your item's picture files, the longer the browser takes to load the item page. And four out of five eBay users will click back out to avoid a long page load. (I'm guessing that you don't want your listings to elicit that behavior.)

WARNING

Keep in mind that images placed with eBay's picture hosting will expire (disappear) automatically 90 days after the end of the listing. Be sure to save copies of any images you may need in the future on your own computer.

Remember that scanned images are measured in dpi (dots per inch). Do not confuse this with a monitor's pixels per inch (ppi). The average monitor is only 72 to 96 ppi, so why scan your images any higher? Consider that a Facebook cover photo is 851 pixels wide; when displayed full-width at 72 ppi, the image would be over 11 inches wide.

REMEMBER

The higher the resolution, the smaller the text and images will appear on any device. To see your images clearly on a mobile device, the viewer may have to zoom to enlarge. They don't want to squint!

If you use eBay picture hosting for your all eBay items, setting your image size is not an issue. eBay picture hosting applies a compression algorithm that forces your pictures into eBay's prescribed size.

The more compression put into computer images, the less sharp they appear. So you might as well use your camera or image-editing program to set your images to a monitor-friendly size before uploading them.

Here's a checklist of tried-and-true techniques for preparing elegantly slender, fast-loading images to display on eBay:

» **When scanning, set your image resolution at 72 pixels per inch.** Although 72 ppi may seem like a super-low resolution, it only nibbles computer space, shows up fast on a buyer's screen, and looks great on eBay.

» **When using a digital camera, set it (if possible) to no higher than the 2MB, 1600 x 1200 format.** That's about perfect for any monitor. You can always crop the picture if it's too large.

» **For use in your description, make the finished image no larger than 480 pixels wide.** When you size your picture in your image software, it's best to keep it no larger than 300 x 300 pixels or 4 inches square. These dimensions are big enough for people to see the image without squinting, and the details of your item show up nicely.

>> **Crop any unnecessary areas of the photo.** You need to show only your item; everything else is a waste.

>> **If necessary, use your software to darken or change the photo's contrast.** When the image looks good on your computer screen, the image looks good on your eBay page.

>> **Save your image as a JPG file.** When you finish editing your picture, save it as a JPG file. (To do this, follow the instructions that come with your software.) JPG is the best format for eBay; it compresses information into a small file that builds fast and reproduces crisply on the Internet.

Adding the Artist's Touch

Pictures don't always come out of the camera in perfect form. However, you can do a few tweaks to bring them within range of perfection:

>> **Alter the size:** Reduce or increase the size or shape of the image.

>> **Change the orientation:** Rotate the image left or right; flip it horizontally or vertically.

>> **Crop the background:** Sometimes there's a little too much background and not enough product. Don't waste precious bandwidth on extraneous pixels. To *crop* your image means to cut away the unnecessary part of the picture.

>> **Adjust the brightness and contrast:** These two functions usually work together in most photo programs. By giving your picture more brightness, the picture looks brighter (duh). Raising contrast brings out the detail, and lowering it dulls the difference between light and dark.

>> **Sharpen:** If your camera was not perfectly in focus when you took the picture, applying a photo-editing program's sharpening feature can help. If you sharpen too much, however, you can destroy the smoothness of the image.

If your image needs any more help than these alterations, it's probably easier and faster to just retake the picture.

Image-Editing Software

eBay sellers use a wide array of image-editing software. As a matter of fact, some listing software has built-in mini-editing capabilities. Choosing software for your images is like choosing an office chair: What's right for some people is dreadful for others. You might want to ask some of your friends what software they use — and take a look at it.

When you buy a camera, or even when you buy a smartphone, it will no doubt arrive with features that include some type of image-editing software. Give the software a try. If it works well for you, keep it. If not, check out the two options I mention later.

TIP

Every image-editing software program has its own system requirements and capabilities. Study the software that comes with your camera or scanner. If you feel that the program is too complicated (or doesn't give you the editing tools you need), investigate some of the other popular programs.

I used to be happy using Photoshop, but it's a large and expensive program. It's also a bit of overkill for eBay images. Two other new tools have caught my eye: Microsoft Office and PhotoPrep.

Using Microsoft's simple photo editor

Microsoft Office Picture Manager is a software program included with Microsoft Office suite starting with the 2003 version through the 2010 version. (It replaced Microsoft Photo Editor, which had been included with the Microsoft Office suite since Office 97.) Picture Manager offers basic picture-editing features, and it may be a good place to start. If you have Microsoft Office (2003, 2007, or 2010), you find Picture Manager on your Start menu under Microsoft Office Tools. For Office 2013, 2016, or 365, you can download a copy of SharePoint Designer from Microsoft here: `www.microsoft.com/en-us/download/details.aspx?id=16573`.

To edit an image in Microsoft Office directly on your computer, follow these steps:

1. **Right-click the image in one of your folders.**

2. **From the menu that appears, select Open With and then choose Microsoft Office.**

   Although it seems a less-than-intuitive tweak, Microsoft chose to remove the reference to Picture Manager from the menu options. Go figure. Meanwhile, your image opens in the photo editor, as shown in Figure 4-1.

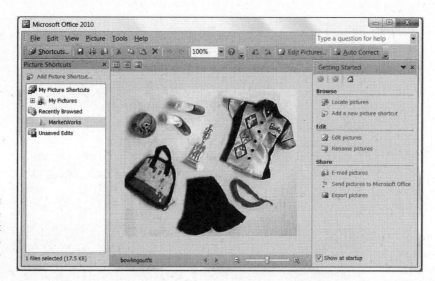

FIGURE 4-1:
A hidden feature
in Microsoft
Office makes
quick photo
edits easy.

3. **If the toolbars and panes don't appear when the photo editor opens, click View⇨Task Pane.**

4. **In the Task pane, click Edit Pictures and all the necessary commands to complete your masterpiece appear.**

Microsoft Office Picture Manager gives you some useful tools: You can auto-correct, fix "red eye," enhance color, adjust brightness and contrast, compress, resize, crop, and rotate. It's about all you need if you take a good photo to begin with. Clicking the Auto Correct button works well to correct the quality of an image. Click Export Pictures, and in the resulting Export task pane, you can choose the exact size for the final image.

Quick touchup and FTP in PhotoPrep

If Photoshop is too expensive and complex (and it really is for eBay purposes), you might be happy giving PhotoPrep by Pixby Software a try. It's a simple, all-in-one photo-editing program designed especially for ecommerce and eBay sellers. The developer of the software knew exactly what processes online sellers need for their images and included just those — and nothing else. There are tools for cropping, JPG compression, sharpening, resizing, enhancing, rotating, and adding watermark text and borders.

The software is a PC application that runs on Windows (versions 7, 8, 10, and XP). For a 30-day free trial, visit the PhotoPrep website at www.pixby.com.

Editing an image for eBay in PhotoPrep is simple (see Figure 4-2).

FIGURE 4-2:
Editing a photo
in PhotoPrep.

After you get your image perfected, it's time to emblazon it on the web for all the world to see. Uploading the images you use for your online networks, website, and blogs is a fairly straightforward process. But when it comes to photos for eBay sales, you have a few choices.

Finding a Home for Your Pictures

Because your image needs an address, you have to find it a good home online. You have several options:

>> **eBay picture hosting:** This is eBay's stock and trade for storing your listing images. To place up to 12 images on a listing at no charge (you can even zoom and enlarge features), this is what you need to use. Images from eBay picture hosting appear at the top left of your listing. Visitors can click the individual photos to show one in the main photo frame. When a potential buyer views your item on eBay's Android mobile app, the pictures scroll horizontally at the top of the screen when the user swipes. iPhone and iPad users must tap a photo to scroll through.

>> **An image-hosting website:** Websites that specialize in hosting pictures are all over the Internet. Some charge a small fee; others are free. The upside here is that they're easy to use.

>> **Your website:** If you have your own website, it's easy to make a separate folder there to store your images for eBay listings. You can name your photos and access them with a URL directing eBay to the picture hosted on your site's server.

Using eBay's Picture Hosting

I highly recommend that your first move be to take advantage of the 12 free pictures per listing from eBay's picture hosting. First, it's available at no charge; second, eBay's picture hosting offers many other benefits, such as ease of uploading — a capability included in eBay's selling tools (see Figure 4-3).

FIGURE 4-3: eBay's selling tools include a photo uploader.

At this point, I'll go back to my basic assumptions about you. I assume you know how to list an item on eBay — or, at the very least, you can make your way through the Create a listing form and get to the photos step.

When you get to this step, you need to upload a picture to eBay, whether or not you have pictures in your description. Why? Because eBay requires at least one image in the listing (remember, you can upload up to 12 pictures for free) and because your uploaded picture becomes part of the ultra-important top area of the item page, as shown in Figure 4-4. Also, shoppers on mobile devices will see this photo at the top of their listing. This picture will also be the default for use as your all-important image in search results.

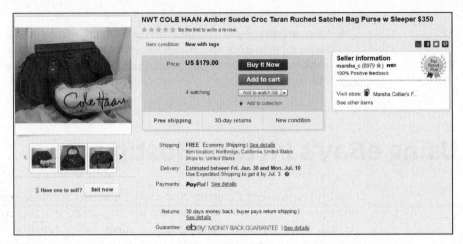

FIGURE 4-4:
The item image
is where the
prospective buyer
looks first.

Always use eBay's picture posting for your primary images. The 12-image limit that eBay offers should suffice for most listings. If you want to include more photos in the description because the item is rare or detailed, host the other images elsewhere.

Uploading your picture to eBay

In this section, I assume that you've already taken a picture, uploaded or scanned it, and saved it somewhere on your computer's hard drive.

TIP

For organization's sake, you might consider making a subfolder called *eBay Photos* in your Pictures folder. That way you can always find your eBay pictures quickly, without searching through photos of your family reunion.

Clicking the Add photos button opens a window on your computer to find the photo in your hard drive's folders you wish to use. Find and select the eBay-ready images you want to upload. After you select the images from your computer, they appear in the Photos area of this window.

To get more options — for example, cropping, rotating, and minor editing functions — click the icons at the bottom of the window to edit the picture, which is shown in Figure 4-5.

FIGURE 4-5:
Note the icons at
the bottom of the
photo that's been
uploaded.

Then, to edit your picture, follow these steps:

1. **To rotate the image, click the circular arrow tool.**

2. **Crop the image as needed:**

   a. *Click the crop box below the larger image.*

   Two squares appear at opposite corners of the image.

   b. *Click the frame on the outside of your image, and move the bar until the unneeded area is cropped out.*

   You can crop from the sides, top, and bottom of the picture.

3. **To brighten or increase contrast:**

   a. *Click the sun icon below the larger image.*

   b. *A pair of sliders will appear; use them to interactively change the look of your image.*

4. **When you're finished, click Save.**

   The main picture will now appear with your edits.

eBay's uploader automatically makes your pictures the perfect size for eBay. But don't forget that you get the best picture quality when you use images with 1600-pixel height or width (minimum is 500 pixels).

When most people first get the urge to dazzle prospective buyers with additional pictures, they often insert more images in the description area. Let's talk about where you can host these images.

TIP

You will find that several third-party sites will also host your eBay images. There's more on those options in Book 8, Chapter 2.

Using Your Free Web Space

REMEMBER

If you have a website, no doubt you have plenty of storage space, but check with your host before you inundate it with images, okay? If you have the space, make a new folder and store your images for your eBay sales there.

In this section, I show you some easy ways to upload your pictures to your website and import them into your eBay listings. Doing so gives you the opportunity to maintain an archive of the items you have (and have had) up for sale.

Internet service providers may supply you with an image-upload area, but they may require you to use File Transfer Protocol (FTP) to upload your images. You may be able to find a free or shareware (requiring a small fee) FTP program on sites such as the following:

TIP

In the eBay picture uploader, you can import pictures from your photo storage area by using their individual URL.

I've been using the Firefox browser, and I really like it. It has a free FTP program, FireFTP, that's reliable and easy to use. FireFTP has never given me a whit of a problem, and I highly recommend it.

You can add FireFTP to your Firefox browser (Mac or PC) by choosing Tools⇨ Add-ons from the Navigation menu. Doing so takes you to a web page where you can search for FireFTP (and lots of other interesting add-ons). You can download the add-on directly by visiting

```
http://fireftp.net/
```

After you install the program, open it and follow these steps to upload a file to your server:

1. **Choose Manage Accounts⇨New.**

The Account Manager appears.

2. **Type in the name of your website in the Account Name box.**

3. **Where prompted, type the FTP address for your account and then click Next.**

4. **Type the user name and password that you use to log in to your website account. Then click OK.**

5. **Click the Browse button (shown in Figure 4-6) to locate the directory on your computer where you store your eBay images.**

FIGURE 4-6:
Selecting your default directory.

6. **Click OK and you're good to go.**

From this point on, every time you click the Connect button, FireFTP logs on to your web space and displays the screen shown in Figure 4-7. Note that the left side of the program is open to the directory you selected as the default for your eBay images. The right side of the screen shows what is currently on your ISP-provided home page.

To upload an image, highlight it and click the transfer arrow in the center. Faster than I could take a screen shot (okay, I took it anyway, and it's Figure 4-8), the image is uploaded to my web space.

FIGURE 4-7:
Signing on to
your FTP space.

FIGURE 4-8:
Instant image
upload!

6 Extending Your Reach

Contents at a Glance

Chapter **1**

Developing Your Own Web Presence

Your eBay Store is important to your business, but it doesn't replace a web-site (preferably an ecommerce site). You should establish your own presence on the web, outside of eBay. And although you might want to link your site to eBay, don't miss out on the rest of the Internet population. You could have some more customers out there.

You *don't* have a website yet? Perhaps you're spending all your spare online time commenting on Facebook? (If that's true, I suspect it's time to get down to business. Call it a gentle hint.) You might consider starting a blog to back up your online selling efforts. Even if you don't sell directly from anywhere other than eBay (although I wish you would), a blog can help build your reputation as an online seller.

You *do* have a website? Have you taken a good look at it lately to see whether it follows new trends? (I recently gave my site a facelift and love the new look.) Does your blog link to your eBay listings or have its own online store? I hope so.

Whether or not you have a website or blog, give this chapter at least a once-over. I provide a lot of detail about websites, from thinking up a name to choosing a host. If you don't have a site, I get you started launching one. If you already have a site, read the pointers about finding the best host. For the serious-minded web-based entrepreneur (that's you), I also include a few important marketing tips.

Know Why Your Web Presence Is Important

Having even a small blog (at the very least) gives you experience in setting up and establishing a web presence. When you're ready to jump in for real, you can always upgrade to a full-on ecommerce site and provide a link to your old site. I've had a blog on Blogger at `mcollier.blogspot.com` since 2004, and when I upgraded my `coolebaytools.com` site, I linked the Blogger site on the naviga-tion bar within it, as shown in Figure 1-1.

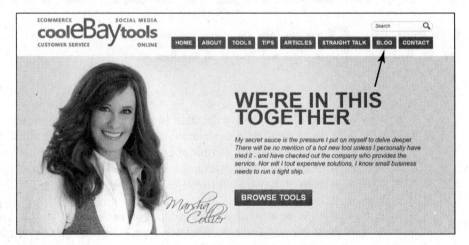

FIGURE 1-1:
My website with a
link to my blog.

My example brings up a classic question: What is the difference between a blog and a website? The term *blog* is shortened from the term *web log*, which originally meant that someone published a journal online on a regular basis. The online journal was a web log of that person's life. In today's world, a blog is not just for emotional meandering; most businesses have one to give a personal touch to cus-tomer experience and share news with their readers.

The main difference between a blog and a website is that a blog is meant to be updated regularly with new content; whereas a website's content is more static and changes as needed. Of course, if you have a blog linked to your website, you can update your content on the blog while keeping the static, evergreen content on the website intact. Take a look at almost any brand's site; you will probably see a link to an accompanying blog in the navigation bar. A blog is now considered a *type* of website.

A blog is a more touchy-feely communication tool; a website is a more concrete representation of your business as a whole. Think of a website as a digital storefront for your business. And keep in mind that a website is of utmost importance if you have a retail location. In my book, *Social Media Commerce For Dummies* (also published by Wiley; you can find it at www.dummies.com), I give you all the up-to-date information on how to make your website shine — and convert visitors to buyers.

REMEMBER

Your customers need to visit your blog and actually read its content to make it a valuable resource for your business. Countless blogs receive just a few hits a day; if your customers are busy, a marketing-oriented blog may be the last place they want to visit. The goal is to engage reader's interest, so don't just write about business; write about topics that you enjoy and that your readers will find interesting — and if you can tie 'em in naturally with the business, so much the better. You might want to direct your blog's focus to a range of broader-interest topics. Bottom line: Have a plan for regular postings and an objective to focus on before you start writing your blog entries.

Free Web Space — A Good Place to Start

Although I love the word *free*, in real life it seems like nothing is *really* free, starting with lunch. Realistically, *free* generally means something won't cost you too much money — but may cost you a bit more in time. When your site is free, you may give up the opportunity to have your own direct URL (Universal Resource Locator) or domain name. That handy feature is available usually for a small extra fee. You may also have to put up with ads appearing on your site, or not; it depends from whom you get the (ahem) free space.

I much prefer a free web space with no ads, but that seems to be asking a lot. Surprisingly, there are a few very good, reliable places. Take a look at Table 1-1, where I compare some popular options for free web space.

TIP

I highly suggest that you do *not* take advantage of "free trials" when it comes to a website. There's a lot of time and effort to put in when you're getting a site ready. By the time you figure out that a particular host isn't best for your site, you may be stuck with a site that's impossible to export to another platform.

TABLE 1-1   **Free Web Space**

Site	Blog or Website	Total Storage	Sharable Images with URL	Design Tools
Weebly.com	Blog/Website	500MB	No	Yes
Webs.com	Website	500MB	No	Yes
Wix.com	Website	500MB	No	Yes
Google Blogger.com*	Blog	15GB*	No	Yes
WordPress.com	Blog	3GB	No	Yes

Storage on all Google Apps is shared from your Google Drive total storage of 15GB.

When it comes time to set up your website, you might want to consider using a quick-and-easy HTML generator such as the one in Mozilla's free SeaMonkey. You can use this tool with the Firefox FireFTP upload extension for a complete web hookup. (See Book 5, Chapter 3 for more information on the SeaMonkey program.)

Your first web pages may be simple, and that's okay. You have to get used to having a website before you can really use it for commerce. Put up a home page that links to a few product-related pages and your eBay listings, and voilà! You're in business. If you're feeling more adventurous about your website, check out the next section, where I describe a handful of website hosts.

Paying for Your Web Space

If you've been on the Internet for any length of time, you've been bombarded by hosting offers through your daily spam. A *web-hosting company* houses your website code and electronically doles out your pages and images to your web page's visitors.

REMEMBER

If you take advantage of PayPal's free Pay Now buttons or shopping cart, you can turn a basic-level hosted site into a full-on ecommerce store without paying additional fees to your hosting company. The PayPal tools are easily inserted into your pages with a snippet of code provided by PayPal. (See Chapter 3 in this minibook for more information.)

Before deciding to spend money on a web-hosting company, check it out thoroughly. Go to that company's site to find a list of features offered. If you still have questions after perusing the website, look for a toll-free number to call. You won't find any feedback ratings on web hosts like you find on eBay, but the following are a few questions to ask (don't hang up until you're satisfied with the answers):

>> **How long has the company been in business?** You don't want a web host that has been in business only a few months and operates out of the founder's basement. Deal with folks who have been around the Internet for a while (hence know what they are doing). Is the company's website professional-looking? Does the company look like it has enough money to stay in business?

>> **Who are some of the company's other clients?** Poke around to see whether you can find links to sites of other clients. Take a look at who else is doing business with the hosting company; visit and analyze their sites. Do the pages and links come up quickly? Do all the images appear in a timely manner? Websites that load quickly are a good sign.

>> **Does the company offer mobile optimization?** With more and more people accessing the Internet on mobile devices (tablets, smartphones) it's more important than ever to have a mobile version of your website. How much do they charge for this? Is it automatic, or do you have to go through a laborious setup?

TIP

Google diminishes the search ranking of websites that are not mobile-friendly. To see whether yours (or any website) fulfills this requirement, you can test it at `https://search.google.com/search-console/mobile-friendly`. Figure 1-2 below shows my website (in Figure 1-1) as it passes the Google mobile-friendly test.

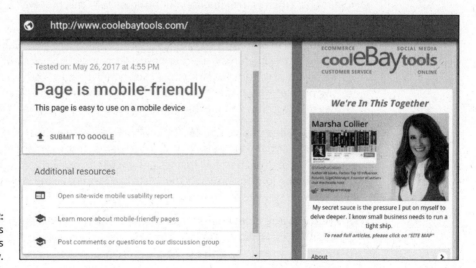

FIGURE 1-2: Google certifies my website as mobile-friendly.

>> **What is the downtime-to-uptime ratio?** Does the web host guarantee *uptime* (the span of time its servers stay operational without going down and denying access to your site)? Expecting a 99-percent-uptime guarantee is not unreasonable; you're open for business — and your web host needs to keep it that way.

>> **How much web space do I get for my money?** For the most basic website on www.web.com (not to be confused with www.webs.com — similar name, different service) you can get 300GB of storage for $5.95 a month; you'd better be getting a *lot* more space if you're paying more for it.

>> **Does the web host offer toll-free technical support?** When something goes wrong with your website, you need it corrected immediately. You must be able to reach tech support quickly, without hanging around on the phone for hours. Does the web host have a technical support area on its website where you can troubleshoot your own problems (in the middle of the night, if needed)?

TIP

Whenever you're deciding on any kind of provider for your business, take a moment to call its tech-support team with a question about their services. Take note of how long you had to hold and how courteous the techs were. Before plunking down your hard-earned money, you should be sure that the provider's customer service claims aren't merely that — just claims.

>> **What's the policy on shopping carts?** In time, you may need to install a shopping cart specific to your site. Does your provider charge extra for that? If so, how much? In the beginning, a convenient and professional-looking way to sell items on your site is to set up a PayPal shopping cart or PayPal Pay Now buttons. When you're running your business full-time, however, a shopping cart and a way to accept credit cards is a must.

>> **What kind of statistics will you get?** Visitors who go to your website leave an electronic bread-crumb trail. Your host collects these statistics, so you'll be able to find out which are your most and least popular pages. You can know how long people linger on each page, where they come from, and what browsers they're using. How your host supplies these stats to you is important.

>> **Is there a desktop design tool?** If you're not a web-design expert, having a WYSIWYG (What You See Is What You Get) design tool will make life a lot easier. If your web host has themes or templates, you're good to go. Using a ready-made (but customizable) template can help make the initial site setup somewhat painless for the non-technically inclined.

>> **Are there any hidden fees?** Does the web host charge exorbitant fees for setup? Charge extra for statistics? Impose high charges if your bandwidth suddenly increases? Are there charges for extras you may need?

>> **How often will the web host back up your site?** No matter how redundant a host's servers are, a disaster may strike, and you need to know that your website won't vaporize. *Redundancy* (having duplicate copies of your data and site functionality) is the safety net for your site.

Table 1-2 provides a comparison of the costs for the most basic offerings. In the rest of this section, I fill you in on the details about the four web-hosting companies listed in the table. Make sure you check out the company websites for the most current information because the features offered change (almost as often as eBay does).

REMEMBER

Keep in mind that **200MB of disk storage space can host as many as 6,000 HTML pages**. My entire website, coolebaytools.com, including WordPress plugins, fills only 55MB!

TABLE 1-2   ## Comparing Entry-Level Hosting Costs*

Feature	GoDaddy	NetworkSolutions.com	Web.com	Yahoo! Small Business (Aabaco)
Monthly plan cost	$7.99	$9.96	$5.95 monthly term	$4.99
Disk space storage	100GB	300GB	300GB	100GB
Data transfer/month	Unlimited	Unlimited	Unlimited	1000GB
DIY web-design tools	Yes	Yes	Yes	Yes
24/7 toll-free tech	Yes	Yes	?	?
Email	?	1000	100	250

Does not take into account any promotional first-year discount offers.

Naming Your Baby

What to name the baby, er, website? It's almost as much of a dilemma as deciding on your eBay user ID or eBay Store name. If you don't have an existing company name that you want to use, why not use the same name as your eBay Store? Register and lock it up now so that you can keep your brand forever.

Name your site with a word that identifies what you do, what you sell, or who you are. And be sure you like it — because once it's yours and you begin operating under it and establishing a reputation, it'll be with you 20 years from now when you're still selling online. (I know, it should only happen!)

If you watched the Netflix series *GirlBoss*, the lead character reads an older edition of my eBay business book and spends an entire episode trying to figure out her website name. This is serious business.

A few websites offer wizards to help you decide your domain name. You can find a particularly intuitive one at the following:

```
http://snapitnow.com/
```

In a small, web-based form, you input your primary business type and keywords that describe your business. The wizard then displays a large number of options and also lets you know whether the options are available. Very convenient.

Before you attempt to register a name, you should check to be sure it isn't anyone else's trademark. To search an updated list of registered United States trademarks, go to the following and use the electronic trademark search system:

```
www.uspto.gov/trademarks-application-process/
search-trademark-database
```

After a search, you may want to trademark your site name. I suggest you consult an attorney to file your trademark. Filing a trademark is a complex proposition.

DOMAIN PARKING

Suppose you've come up with a brilliant name for your site and your business gets really big and famous. Then someone else uses your website's name but registers it as a .net — while yours is a .com. To avoid this situation, make sure you register both domains (.com and .net) and park them with your registrar. That way any permutations of your domain will point to your active website. For example, www.ebay.net and www.ebay.org are registered to (guess who?) ebay.com. You can check the owner of any domain name at any of the web-hosting or registrar sites.

Registering Your Domain Name

Talk about your junk email. I get daily emails advising me to Lose 40 pounds in 40 days, accept credit cards now, and of course REGISTER MY NAME NOW! The last scam seems to be geared to obtaining my email address for other junk mail lists rather than trying to help me register my website. Choosing a *registrar* (the company that handles the registering of your site name) is as important as choosing the right web host. You must remember that the Internet is still a little like the Wild West — and that the cyber-equivalent of the James Gang might be waiting to relieve you of your hard-earned cash. One of the ways to protect yourself is to understand how the registry works (knowledge *is* power), so read on.

Before you decide on a registrar for your domain name, take a minute to see whether the registrar is accredited by ICANN (Internet Corporation for Assigned Names and Numbers — the international governing body for domain names) or is reselling for an official ICANN-accredited registrar. (You'll have to ask who they register with.) The Accredited Registrar Directory is updated constantly at the U.S. Department of Commerce's InterNIC site, so check the following for the most recent list:

    www.internic.com/regist.html

Registering a domain name can cost from between nothing (free with a web hosting package) to around $30 a year. When you're ready, search the top web-hosting companies for deals.

REMEMBER

You'll usually get a substantial discount from the more expensive registrars when you register your domain name for multiple years — a good idea if you plan on staying in business. Also, if you register your name through your hosting service, you might be able to cut the regular prices in half! The only drawback is that your prepaid registration might go out the window if you choose to change hosting companies.

TIP

If you're registering a new domain name but already have a site set up with your ISP, you need a feature called *URL forwarding*, or *web address forwarding*. This feature directs any hits to your new domain name from your existing long URL address. Some registrars offer this service, but watch out for hidden surprises — such as a "free" offer of the service, which means they'll probably smack a big fat banner at the bottom of your home page. Your registrar should also have some available tech support. Trying to troubleshoot DNS issues is a job for those who know what they're doing! Remember, sometimes you *do* get what you pay for.

MAKING YOUR PERSONAL INFORMATION PRIVATE

ICANN requires every registrar to maintain a publicly accessible whois database that displays all contact information for all domain names registered. Interested parties (or, for that matter, fraudsters) can find out the name, street address, email address, and phone number of the owner of the site by running a whois search on the domain name. You can run a whois search by going to https://whois.icann.org/en and typing the domain name in question.

Unfortunately, this information can be useful to spammers who spoof your email address as their fake return address to cloak their identity; identity thieves, stalkers, and just about anyone up to no good may also take an interest. To protect yourself, it's always smarter to register a website in a business name or as a private registration.

Chapter **2**

Marketing Tools for Your Web Presence and Social Media

After you set up your website (whether blog or business site) and eBay Store, it's time to let the world know about it. Having spent many years in the advertising business, I can spot businesses that *want* to fail. They open their doors and expect the world to beat a path to them and make them rich. This doesn't happen — ever.

You must take a proactive approach to letting the world in on the goodies you have for sale. This means spending time promoting your site by buying keywords on Google, getting your URL into a search engine, and taking advantage of social media. There are no shortcuts.

In this chapter, I tell you about ways to exploit the promotional opportunities you find online.

TIP

In my book *Social Media Commerce For Dummies*, I go deeply into using social media to reach new customers. (You can find it at www.dummies.com.)

Advertising with Google AdWords

Wouldn't it be cool if you could run ads all over the Internet at a low price? You can!

Google's cost-per-click (CPC) offering, AdWords, is used by nearly every business on the web. If you are a regular user of Google search, you should be noticing small ads embedded in the search results with a tiny AD icon. I used to think these ads were expensive links from high-dollar operations — until I found out the truth. If you take a look at the ads I found in the results of a Google search in Figure 2-1, you'll see the ads that companies bought to show up on searches for my name.

FIGURE 2-1:
Okay, I googled myself.

According to numerous sources, 1.2 trillion searches were performed on Google in 2016; or about 3.5 billion per day. Google AdWords allow you to create the profitable little ads that accompany each of these searches. You choose keywords to let Google know where to place your ads. Certainly you can come up with some relevant keywords to promote your website or eBay Store.

You pay for such an ad only when someone clicks on it. Want to know more? Go over to `https://adwords.google.com`. Once you're there, you can go over the details and set up your own campaign.

For your campaign, keep the following in mind:

>> **Keywords and keyword phrases:** Come up with a list of keywords that would best describe your merchandise. Google allows you to estimate, based on current search data, how often your selected keyword will come up every day. Google will also estimate your daily cost, based on how many people click

that word. That can be a shocking number. Don't worry — not everyone who sees your ad will click it — but if they did, eeyow!

>> **CPC (cost-per-click):** You determine how much you'll pay for each click on your keywords. You can pay as little as $.05 a click. The dollar amount you place on your clicks makes the basis for how often your ad appears.

>> **CTR (click-through rate):** This statistic reflects how many people click your ad when they see it. If your CTR falls below a certain percentage after 1,000 impressions, AdWords may slow or even discontinue your ad views. When one of your keywords isn't passing muster, it will be indicated on your reports.

>> **Daily budget:** You can set the cap in dollars on how much you'll spend a day. Otherwise, if you had some really hot keywords, you could spend thousands on clicks.

Setting up an AdWords account takes a while and some thinking. So wait until your mind is clear (Saturday morning?) and sit down at the AdWords site with a cup of coffee.

Google gives you excellent step-by-step instructions after you're signed in at `https://adwords.google.com`. This is the general process:

1. Decide whether you want to target your ads geographically.

You can pinpoint your market if you'd like, or you can blast the entire world. Choose from a list of 14 languages, 250 countries, or as far down as 200 United States regions.

2. Create your ad.

This is not as easy as I thought. You can create only three lines of ad text with a total of 95 characters. Be as concise as possible. Don't throw in useless adjectives. Figure out the perfect 95 characters that will sell your site to the world. You must also supply the URL for your website or eBay Store.

3. Select your keywords.

Type your keywords and key phrases in the box provided. You can use Google's Keyword Suggestion tool to help you out. Because this is your initial pass and won't be etched in granite, feel free to take some wild stabs and see what happens.

4. Choose your maximum CPC (cost per click) and then click Calculate Estimates.

Here's where the sticker-shock gets you. The displayed data lets you know which keywords you can afford to keep and which ones must be discarded.

If you want to change your CPC amount, do so and click Recalculate Estimates. The Traffic Estimator calculates how much, on average, you'll end up spending in a day.

5. **Specify your daily budget.**

   There will be a prefilled amount that would ensure that your ad stays on top and gets full exposure every day. (No, Mr. Google, I do not want to spend $50 a day on my keywords.) Set a cap on your budget and Google will never exceed it. You may make it as low as you want; there's no minimum spending amount, but it has to be more than zero.

6. **Enter your email address and agree to the terms.**

7. **Enter your billing information.**

   You're minutes away from your ads going live on the Google index.

TIP

Here's an intriguing fact: Your ads may also appear on other places on the Internet where Google feeds ads.

Getting Your Site Visible on a Search Engine

For people to find your site (and what you're selling), they must be able to locate you. A popular way people do this is by searching with a search engine, so you should submit your site to search engines (they can't find it unless it has a meta tag, which I talk about in a minute). Go to the search engines that interest you and look for a link or a help area that will enable you to submit your site. Be sure to follow any specific instructions on the site; some may limit the amount of keywords and the characters in your description.

To submit your URL to search engines, you need to do a little work (nothing's easy, is it?). Write down 25 to 50 words or phrases that describe your website; these are your *keywords*. Now, using as many of those keywords as you can, write a description of your site. With the remaining words, create a list of keywords, separating each word or short phrase with a comma. You can use these keywords to add meta tags to the header in your document for your home page. *Meta tags* are identifiers used by search-engine *spiders*, robots that search the Internet for new sites to classify on search engines. Specifying a meta tag looks like this:

```
<meta name = "insert your keywords here separated by commas"
   content = "short description of your site">
```

Catch attention on Google

Have you ever googled your eBay Store or website? I did, by searching for the name of my eBay Store, which includes my name. Figure 2-2 shows you the top results.

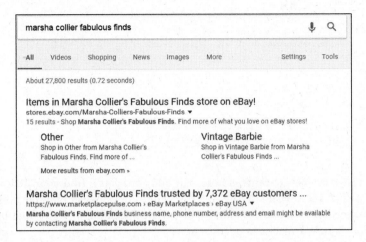

FIGURE 2-2:
Wow! My eBay
Store shows up!

You, too, should Google yourself, your website, and eBay Store to see where and if it's listed. If you find nothing, you're missing out on a huge opportunity for free promotion. Google runs spiders (just picture the way a spider runs — swiftly and all over the place) that scour the Internet on a monthly basis, looking for data to add to the Google index.

Thousands of sites (and you do know that since your eBay Store has a unique URL, it's considered to be a website) are added to the Google index every time its spiders crawl the web.

If your eBay Store or website *isn't* listed, go to

    www.google.com/submityourcontent/#

as pictured in Figure 2-3. When you get to this page, follow the instructions to get your eBay Store URL indexed. To find your store's URL, click the red *store* tag next to your eBay user ID to go to your store, and then copy and paste the URL (in the address line of your browser) into the URL line on the form. When I went to my eBay Store, I got this URL:

    http://stores.ebay.com/Marsha-Colliers-Fabulous-Finds

That's the URL I use in my email and printed propaganda to promote my store.

FIGURE 2-3:
Get your free shot at the big time.

There are no guarantees here, but odds are you'll find your little shop on Google within a few weeks. To get the full benefit of Google's massive power, once you're signed in to Google (or Gmail), be sure to register and verify your business website on Google's Webmaster Tools at

    www.google.com/webmasters/tools

Get listed on Bing and Yahoo!

You will find that dealing with certain webmaster tools entails a fairly strong learning curve. So if you just want to get your site in line to appear in Bing's search, just go to

    www.bing.com/toolbox/submit-site-url

The simplest form on the Internet — shown in Figure 2-4 — appears. Just type in the URL of your homepage, type in the captcha code you see, and you are good to go. Notice, too, that on the right of the form are some handy links to help you with your website.

To be listed on Yahoo! it takes a bit more effort. Bing has taken over the submission chores for Yahoo! I'm afraid things will get a bit complex here. You need to sign up for Bing Webmaster Tools at

    www.bing.com/toolbox/webmaster

By signing up here, you will be able to improve your site's performance in both Bing and Yahoo! searches.

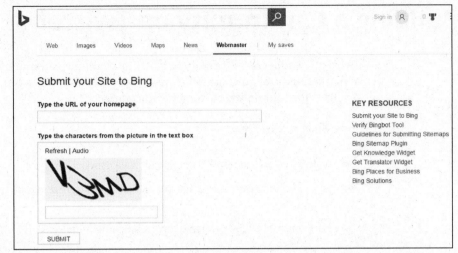

FIGURE 2-4: Submitting your site's URL.

Casting for Customers in Social Media

Social media hosts networking conversations on many sites around the web — for example, on Twitter, Facebook, Pinterest, Google+, and a myriad others. These sites are places where easy engagement can lead to customer enticement.

In this conversational atmosphere, you can expect to

>> **Sell:** Promote online and offline sales by posting promotions, discounts, and offers.

>> **Find new customers:** Find people who are interested in a new vendor. Unhappy customers tend to be verbal on social media; maybe you're the new vendor *they* are looking for.

>> **Build community:** Join with others in your industry to share information. Connect with prospective and current customers to ultimately help drive new business.

>> **Observe the competition:** Follow friendly (or unfriendly) competition to see how they handle social media outreach.

>> **Engage in customer service:** Through connecting online, you can successfully engage with customers who are in need of help.

Your investment in social media networking may take a bit of time to pay off, but pay off it will. (Just stick with it.) I fully cover topics related to conversing through social media in my book *Social Media Commerce For Dummies*.

Building a Community on Twitter

Twitter is a convenient format for building an online community. If the thought of marketing through short-and-sweet messages appeals to you, Twitter may be the place for your online customer connections.

Some quick Twitter stats:

» Twitter has an estimated 310 million active users.

» Estimated total tweets average 500 million per day; that's 6,000 tweets per second.

» Thirty percent of Twitter users have an income of more than $100,000.

» Twitter handles more search queries than Microsoft's Bing and Yahoo! combined.

For Twitter to work for your social commerce, you have to follow people, listen, and take action by engaging in the conversation. Take the time to interact and foster relationships within the Twitter community. (Later on, I show you how to find people to follow who are likely to compliment your brand.)

Participating is not terribly hard because Twitter's tweets are limited to 280 characters. If you send text messages on your phone, you're given room for 160 characters, so moving from text messages to tweeting isn't a big jump. After you get the hang of short messaging, tweeting can become second nature.

When promoting on Twitter

Your plan for Twitter should be to engage a good number of followers, drawing them to your business and brand. Become their virtual friend and give 'em a chance to turn into evangelists for your businesses. Twitter is not a numbers game unless you're a multinational company (and have the staff to run the account).

TIP

When you Tweet, be discreet: Participate, be friendly, and limit promotional tweets to a low number. People usually don't go on Twitter to be sold to; they are there to engage. If your account is constantly sending out marketing-style Tweets, you'll find that relatively few people will follow your account back — or you may be overrun by other promotional bots.

Social media scientist and data-cruncher Dan Zarrella from Hubspot studies social media posts to find out which get the greatest attention. In contrast to Twitter — where information is exchanged among personal tweets — Facebook posts with a higher number of self-referential words (such as *I* and *me*) tend to get more Likes. Note that these posts aren't marketing messages; they're posts that involve you and your involvement with your business and customers.

Choosing who to follow

Twitter can work only when you follow other people and they follow you back. How do you get people to follow you? By commenting on another tweet, re-tweeting, tweeting content, or just jumping into a conversation that interests you.

Your first step is to go to the Twitter home page, at `https://twitter.com`, and click Sign Up for Twitter. On the resulting page, type your full name, your mobile number or email address, and a password, as shown in Figure 2-5.

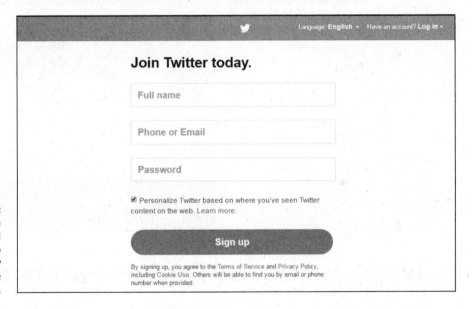

FIGURE 2-5:
Enter a bit of data and you're in! Fill out your bio (add your eBay store URL) on the following page.

After you register on Twitter, things may seem a little lonely for awhile. I signed up in early 2008 and was befuddled by the blank page that stared back at me. Twitter will post suggestions for people you might want to follow.

You can also try searching within Twitter. In Figure 2-6, I searched for the word *eBay*. Notice in the Navigation bar that you can select

>> **Top:** Which would be most popular Tweets with the word *eBay* in them.

>> **Latest:** Tweets mentioning eBay, shown in chronological order with the latest at the top.

>> **People:** Here you will find other popular Twitter users who have the word *eBay* in their user ID or bio.

Using this tool, you're sure to find an interesting group of people to follow. Try inputting the type of merchandise you sell as well. For example, find out who's talking about (say) golf, baseball, jewelry, or fashion.

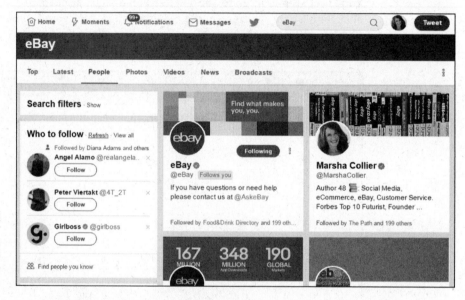

FIGURE 2-6:
Using Twitter search helps you find people interested in your product.

Making Friends and Fans on Facebook

Making friends with strangers can feel creepy, especially on a personal Facebook page. But your prospective customers are all strangers until you interact with them.

I hope you have a personal Facebook page where you connect with friends and family. I do, and since I had a personal page long before Facebook allowed business pages, I have many business contacts there as well. This is the perfect way to get a feel for how Facebook works. When you post personal items, however, be sure to post them to appear only on the news feeds of close friends and family.

But to build your brand on Facebook, you have to start a business page. The hard part is moving business friends away from your personal page to your fan page. As I've said before, in today's social media, business has become personal. So unless you're new to Facebook, you will have some adapting to do.

Facebook business page benefits

A personal page is fun for connecting and sharing, but Facebook business pages have far more flexibility. The trade-off is that your business page will take a bit more finesse to maintain because it blends personal contact and marketing.

>> You can have more than 5,000 friends (fans or Likes on your business page). Do you want that many? The answer is yes if you plan on selling any-thing online.

>> You can use your business name as the page title, making it easier for the page to be indexed by Google. This helps your business's SEO (search engine optimization) and may add strength to the listing position of your business website.

>> Those who Like the page are opting in for your updates. Treat this valuable resource with respect and don't barrage them with promotions.

>> You can customize the page into a mini-site that includes contact forms, sales pages, blog feeds, contests, and even a store.

>> Statistics are available on each individual post on your page.

>> You can open a Shop on Facebook, adding products you carry in stock. Go to the Promote link and add products.

>> Status updates are filtered by Facebook's algorithm, which places what it deems to be the most relevant content in news feeds. Business pages can use a paid ad tool to enhance the number of views a single post garners. (I have seen success with a budget as small as $5 a day.)

>> You can purchase ads that point to your business page or your website. These ads, which appear in Facebook's right-side border, can be targeted using 15 criteria and even more subcriteria. You can narrow the audience to a city and even to a specific Zip code.

As a subtle touch on my business page, I use an application called *Auction Items* (despite the name, the app also posts your fixed-price listings). Applications such as this can only be used on business pages (see Figure 2-7). The application will be listed in the links on the left side of your business page. I find this app gives my items punch, and yet isn't as "in your face" as other marketing programs. You can find it to put on your page at https://www.facebook.com/AuctionItems.

FIGURE 2-7:
The Auction
Items app on
my Facebook
business page
has clickable links
that go directly to
my eBay listings.

Engaging and building your audience

It's time to be your charming self. As the head of your business, your business page should reflect you. In the beginning, you may feel as though you're talking to yourself and a dozen or so family and friends. But don't give up. Slow and steady wins the race.

Only one in five posts on your Facebook business page should be promotional. The other four posts should be about something your audience will appreciate but not directly about your business.

TIP

Find other businesses, perhaps in your field or neighborhood, with which you are friendly and Like their pages from your business page.

Chapter 3

Tapping PayPal to Expand Sales

PayPal was founded with a desire to give its customers plenty of extras for their loyalty — and it offers tons of tools to enhance a seller's online selling experience. The tools on PayPal are still unmatched by any other online payment service.

I've been using PayPal since it started for all my eBay and web sales. I also use it when I shop online, because it doesn't expose my credit card data to new sites that might end up being hacked. PayPal allows you to receive and send payments personally or for your business website. In this chapter, you discover how to build revenue by expanding sales to your own site — and even going mobile — with the help of PayPal.

Enabling PayPal Payments on Your Website

After you get a few items in your garage or business location that you stock in quantity, you've got the makings of your own webstore. Don't let the thought of this spook you. You *can* do it! Aside from selling in your eBay Store, you can sell directly from a website or even from a Facebook store. In time, as your eBay business grows into your own website, you'll find that using PayPal as your payment provider is a great deal. And you pay the same transaction fees — to PayPal only — for processing your credit card sales.

Build business by including your website URL in your email signature, letting the world know you're open for business 24/7.

The first step is to create a website (see Chapter 1 in this minibook). When you have the site up and running, here's what you need to know about using PayPal as a payment tool:

>> **Incorporating payment buttons is easy:** Buy Now or Add to Cart buttons are the most basic way to enable sales through PayPal from your site. These buttons are easy to insert (see the next section) — you don't have to be a computer whiz to create the links because PayPal makes that process almost automatic.

>> **The fees are what you're used to:** There's no fee to use this service beyond the standard processing fee that PayPal charges when someone buys an item on eBay. All you need is a verified PayPal Premier or Business account. (Check out Book 2, Chapter 4 for information on the various types of PayPal accounts.)

>> **The procedure is familiar, too:** When someone buys something from your website, the procedure is the same as when someone pays for an eBay item. You receive an email from PayPal telling you that a web payment (versus an eBay payment) has been received. The email subject includes the item number that you've assigned to the product sold.

PayPal also integrates with shopping-cart and ecommerce software for an additional charge. In this chapter, you examine the free options for new or smaller sellers. If you need help integrating PayPal into shopping-cart software, your website provider will have all the information you need.

Incorporating the Payment Buttons

Enabling your website to accept PayPal payments is as simple as placing the PayPal button on your site. To create a payment button on your site, first sign in to your PayPal account. From there, follow these steps:

1. Click the Tools tab, then All Tools at the top of the page, as shown in Figure 3-1.

You arrive at the Tools.

FIGURE 3-1:
Finding PayPal tools.

2. **Scroll down the page and click the PayPal Buttons box.**

3. **On the resulting page, click Create New Button.**

   You see the page where you create buttons for the items you're selling on your site, as shown in Figure 3-2.

FIGURE 3-2:
Creating a web-payment button.

4. From the drop-down list, select the type of button you want to use to accept payments.

In this example, I chose the Buy Now button, but you can choose any from the following table.

Button	What It Does
Buy Now	With this Buy Now button, customers can click and immediately be brought to PayPal to complete their payment. Use Buy Now for merchandise or if your customer is buying services (for example, a psychic reading, bookkeeping, or consulting).
Small - $25 / Add to Cart	Customers can use the Add to Cart button to select one or more items from your website and place them in a shopping cart when you're selling physical merchandise.
Subscribe	Associate the Subscribe button with your items if you're selling subscriptions to a newsletter or collecting dues for a membership.
Donate	If you have a website where you'd like to get donations — here's the right button. It's an excellent way for nonprofits to get additional funds.
Buy Gift Certificate	Choose the Buy Gift Certificate button if you're selling gift certificates to your store.
Sign up for Installment Plan	The Installment Plan button allows your customers to purchase your item and pay over time with PayPal.

REMEMBER

PayPal enables you to customize the buttons by clicking the Customize Text or Appearance link under Customize Button on the left.

5. Enter your item information, including the item name, ID, price, currency, shipping amount, and tax.

Here's a list of all the items you're asked to enter:

- **Item name:** Type in the name of the product (or service) you will sell with this button.

- **Item ID (optional):** Give your item an ID number or use the standard SKU for the product.

- **Price:** Enter the item price here.

- **Currency:** Decide what currency you're accepting for your purchases. (If you're in the United States, go for the dollars.)

- **Customize Button options:** If your item has options (if, for example, it comes in different sizes or colors), you can create a custom drop-down list for your payment page so the customer can choose.

- **Shipping**: Enter the amount you charge to ship the item.

- **Tax:** Select your state and enter the appropriate sales tax to be applied to your in-state purchases. If you already have a sales-tax provision in your PayPal profile, you see it listed here. PayPal automatically applies the sales tax for sales shipped within your state.

6. **If you don't like the button you chose as it's pictured, click the Customize Text or Appearance link in the Customize Button section to see more options.**

REMEMBER

I like using the buttons that include the different credit card icons so that folks who aren't familiar with PayPal will know that they can use any credit card.

7. **Click the Step 2 tab for the option to track inventory.**

Unless you want to update your button every time you receive new merchandise, I suggest that you leave this option blank.

8. **If you want to add custom features, click the Step 3: Customize Advanced Features (Optional) tab.**

On this tab, you can add extended options for your button. Included (definitely use these!) are the following:

- **Quantity:** If you'd like your customers to be able to purchase more than one of your item at a time, you may indicate that here by giving the buyers a quantity field to fill in.

- **Allow customer to add special instructions:** If you'd like your buyers to be able to write you a note (40-character limit), select the Yes check box.

- **Shipping address:** Select the Yes check box if you'd like the customer's shipping address. (I guess it would be kind of useless *not* to ask for a shipping address when you're expected to ship the item somewhere, huh?)

- **Insert your logo:** To add a logo to your payment page, type the URL where the file is stored. PayPal will place the logo on your payment page.

REMEMBER

The logo you use must be sized at 150 x 50 pixels or PayPal won't accept it.

- **Checkout landing page:** If you want your customers to land on a specific page after they've purchased an item — setting up a thank-you page on your website is a nice idea, for example — enter that URL here.

- **Cancel Transaction page:** If you want to include a page where people are taken if they cancel the transaction before completing it, you can insert that address here. If you don't specify a page, they will land at a PayPal web page that allows cancellation of the transaction.

9. **Click Preview.**

   You see a sample of the page your customer will see after making a web payment to you.

10. **If the page is okay, click the Create Button Now button.**

11. **If you want to go back and edit, click the Edit button.**

That's all there is to creating your first Buy Now button and the payment page that appears when it's clicked. When you get the hang of it for one item, you can reuse many of the settings for other items that you sell.

Repeating the PayPal Button Process

When you have created a payment button, there's no need to go through the entire process for each item. Just familiarize yourself with the various button options and change those entries as needed for each item.

When shoppers click a payment button on my site, they land on my Cool eBay Tools customized PayPal payment page (shown in Figure 3-3, complete with custom logo). The PayPal payment page is a secure page (as indicated by the lock icon) that users access directly from PayPal. The URL for the page begins with https; the s at the end indicates that the site is secure.

FIGURE 3-3:
The customized payment page.

Going Mobile with PayPal Here

In today's mobile-enabled world, you may find an opportunity to sell goods or services through means other than your website accessed on a desktop computer. You can now accept credit cards processed though PayPal on your smartphone with the PayPal Here credit card reader, shown in Figure 3-4.

The card reader is available for free to any PayPal account; just go to www.paypal.com/webapps/mpp/credit-card-reader. It plugs into (and works through) the microphone jack of almost any of the current smartphones. The magic happens when the reader is combined with a free app that's downloadable from the iOS (iPhone) or Android Play Stores; it enables you to swipe a credit card to deposit the funds immediately into your PayPal account.

FIGURE 3-4:
The PayPal Here
card reader.

Although other smartphone credit card readers are available, none have PayPal's support behind them. Other benefits come with PayPal Here:

>> **Low transaction fee.** Although using PayPal Here does incur slightly higher transaction fees than processing a payment online, the current rate (2.7 percent plus $.15 per transaction per U.S. card swipe) beats the competition. Book 2, Chapter 4 gives you more information on how PayPal works.

>> **You can manually enter credit card numbers.** Entering a credit card number manually is handy for phone transactions, but the fee is considerably higher: 3.5 percent plus $0.15.

>> **You can accept checks online.** You can accept and process check payments without going to the bank. The app enables you to accept check payments of $1,000 or less by typing in the check amount. At this time, there is no charge for accepting check payments.

>> **You can send receipts to customers by email or text message.** This feature gives your customer a receipt for the transaction.

WARNING

Always accept payments via PayPal online whenever possible. A customer may want to pay you with a credit card when picking up (or when you deliver) an item, and that's a convenience for them. But realize that your seller protection through PayPal exists *solely on the web*. PayPal Here transactions are not eligible for Seller Protection — so, if possible, have your customers pay you on the web before they get their items.

7

Storing and Shipping

Contents at a Glance

Chapter **1**

Organizing Your Product and Shipping Area

The more SKUs (Stock Keeping Units) you sell, the more confusing the storing and packing of all those items can get. As you build your eBay business, the little side table you use for storing eBay merchandise isn't going to work anymore (and I know you'll want your dining room back). You need to begin to think industrial. Even part-time sellers can benefit by adding professional touches to their business organization.

In this chapter, I emphasize the importance of setting up and organizing your back office. I cover everything from stacking your stock to keeping inventory to getting those indispensable packing materials and saving time by buying postage online. Organization will be your byword. Dive right in. The sooner you read this chapter, the sooner you can organize your eBay back office and get down to business.

The Warehouse: Organizing Your Space

Whether you plan to sell large or small items, you need space for storing them. As you make savvy purchases, maintaining an item's mint condition will be one of your greatest challenges. In this section, I cover the details of what you'll need to safeguard your precious stock.

Shelving your profits

Before you stock the shelves, it helps to have some! You also need a place to put the shelves: your garage, a spare room, or somewhere else. For the home-based business, you have a choice between two basic kinds of shelves:

>> **Plastic:** If you're just starting out, you can always go to the local closet-and-linen-supply store to buy inexpensive plastic shelves. They're light and cheap, but they'll buckle in time.

>> **Steel:** If you want to do it right the first time, buy steel shelving. The most versatile steel shelving is the wire kind (versus solid steel shelves), which is light and allows air to circulate around your items. Steel wire shelving assembles easily; I put mine together without help. You can combine steel-wire shelving units to create a full wall of shelves. Each shelf safely holds as much as 600 pounds of merchandise.

TIP

To save you time, I researched the subject and found some readily available, reasonably priced shelves. Just go to Target or Costco and look for Seville Classics four-shelf commercial shelving, sold in 36- and 48-inch-wide units. Seville Classics also has an eBay store where you can buy from them direct. Look for them at

    http://stores.ebay.com/Seville-Classics

You can easily convert a garage or a spare room to a professional and functional stock room. Figure 1-1 shows a portion of my stock area.

Box 'em or bag 'em?

Packing your items for storage can be a challenge. For smaller items, pick up plastic bags in sandwich, quart, and gallon sizes. When items are stored in plastic, they can't pick up any smells or become musty before you sell them. The plastic also protects the items from rubbing against each other and causing possible damage. If you package them one item to a bag, you can then just grab one off the shelf and put it directly into a shipping box when a listing sells.

FIGURE 1-1:
A portion of my merchandise storage area.

Your bags of items will have to go into boxes for storage on the shelves. Clear plastic storage boxes, the kind you often find at superstores, are great for bulky items. They're usually 26 inches long, so before you buy these big plastic containers, make sure that they'll fit on your shelving comfortably and that you'll have easy access to your items. Smaller see-through plastic boxes with various compartments (such as the type home-improvement stores carry for storing tools) work great for storing very small items.

Using cardboard office-type file storage boxes from an office supply store is another option. These cardboard boxes are 10 x 12 x 16 inches, which is a nice size for storing medium-size products. At around $1 each, they're the most economical choice. The downside is that you can't see through cardboard boxes, so if your label falls off, you have to take the box off the shelf and open it to check its contents. The upside is that they are inexpensive.

TIP

When using these large plastic bins, it's always a good idea to tape a pad of Post-it® notes on the end of the box so you can quickly identify the contents. For more advanced users, how about using a Dymo label maker to re-create the bar code as well as the product name? That way you can scan the code when you remove an item to keep track of inventory.

Speaking of bins, Figure 1-2 shows you the bins in the small-parts area of the warehouse of an eBay seller. His setup isn't exactly what the home seller will need, but it sometimes helps to see how larger sellers do it.

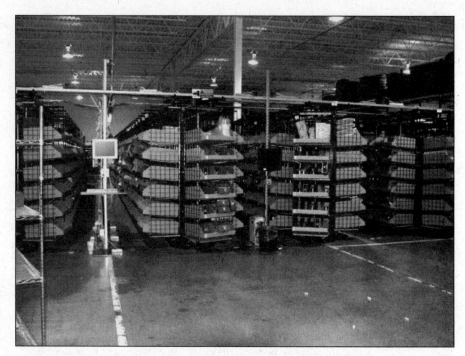

Keeping Track of What You Have

Savvy sellers have different methods of handling inventory. They use everything from spiral-bound notebooks to sophisticated software programs. Although computerized inventory tracking can simplify this task, starting with a plain ol' handwritten ledger is fine, too. Choose whichever works best for you, but keep in mind that as your eBay business grows, a software program that tracks inventory for you may become necessary.

Most of these systems wouldn't work for a company with a warehouse full of stock — but will work nicely in an eBay sales environment. Many sellers tape sheets of paper to their boxes to identify them by number, and use that as a reference to a simple Excel spreadsheet for selling purposes. Excel spreadsheets are perfect for keeping track of your listings as well, but if you're using a management service or software, you don't need both for physical inventory.

You may also want to use Excel spreadsheets for your downloaded PayPal statements, to hold information waiting to transfer to your bookkeeping program. I post my sales each time I make a PayPal withdrawal (a couple of times a week). I keep the PayPal downloads only for archival purposes.

When you're running a full-time business, however, you have to keep Uncle Sam happy with a dollars-and-cents accounting of your inventory, so keep your inventory records in a standardized program such as QuickBooks (discussed in Book 9, Chapter 3). I describe a variety of auction-management software and websites, many of which include physical inventory tracking features.

In my eBay business, I keep my inventory record in QuickBooks. Each time I purchase merchandise for my business, I post it in the program. When I post my sales each week, QuickBooks automatically deducts the sold items from my inventory. I then do a physical inventory as product stock runs low.

AUTHOR SAYS

PLANNING: THE KEY TO GOOD ORGANIZATION

When I had to put my eBay merchandise in order, I was busy with my regular business, so I hired a friend to organize my eBay area. This decision turned out to be one massive mistake. My friend organized everything and put all my items in boxes — but didn't label the boxes to indicate what was stored in each. To this day I still haven't recovered — and don't know where a bunch of my stuff is!

A bit of advice: Think things out and plan where you'll put everything. Organize your items by theme, type, or size. If you organize before planning, you might end up with organized disorganization. The figure shows some merchandise organized, labeled, and stored at an eBay seller's warehouse.

The Shipping Department: Packin' It Up

In this section, I review some of the things you might have for a complete, smooth-running shipping department, such as cleaning supplies and packing materials. The *handling fee* portion of your shipping charges pays for these kinds of items. Don't run low on them — and pay attention to how you store them. They must be kept in a clean environment.

Pre-packaging clean up

Be sure the items you send out are in tip-top shape. Here are a few everyday chemicals that can gild the lily:

>> **WD-40:** This decades-old lubricant works very well at getting price stickers off plastic and glass without damaging the product. And if the plastic on a toy box begins to look nasty — even when stored in a clean environment — a quick wipe with a paper towel and a dash of WD-40 will make it shine like new. It also works well for untangling jewelry chains and shining up metal-lic objects.

>> **Goo Gone:** Goo Gone works miracles in cleaning up gooey sticker residue from nonporous items.

>> **Vamoose:** Is there a smoker in your house? Cigar or cigarette smoke can permeate most items. Vamoose is a chemical miracle that totally removes these stale, smoky smells. Read up about it on the web at www. vamooseproducts.com and find it in their eBay store at

   http://stores.ebay.com/cigaretteandtobaccoelimination

>> **un-du Adhesive Remover:** This amazing liquid easily removes stickers off cardboard, plastic, fabrics, and more without causing damage. It comes packaged with a patented miniscraper top that you can use in any of your sticker-cleaning projects.

Packing materials

The most important area where sellers drop the time-and-money ball is in shipping. I buy hundreds of items from eBay and have seen it all when it comes to packing, padding, and shipping. I've seen money thrown out the window by ecommerce retailers who used incorrect packing materials; too often the wrong stuff is expensive in the first place, and increases the final weight of the package — and shipping cost.

The packing materials that you use for your shipments can either make or break your bottom line in the Shipping Income/Expense column of your business reports.

Prudent packing can be a boon to your business because having lower shipping costs can often make the difference between a profit and none (and offering free shipping affects your position in eBay's search). This is especially true when several people have the same item up for sale, with a minuscule difference in the item's selling price. *Hint:* Free shipping always wins.

Pay attention to packing. It's only expensive if you don't know what you're doing. You can ship your items in quality packing, keep buyers happy, and look forward to positive feedback.

Buying your shipping materials online is very economical. eBay shipping-supply e-tailers make their living selling online. Their overhead is much lower than that of any retail outlet. Even after paying shipping to get the bubble wrap to your door, you save money and time. Most of these sellers ship the same day they get your order.

Using void fill

Nope! Void fill is not a new drug to prevent hunger pangs when dieting. *Void fill* is the industry term for the stuff you use to fill up space in shipping boxes to keep items from rolling in transit. (It's really the modern term for the old-fashioned word *dunnage*.)

REMOVING MUSTY SMELL FROM APPAREL ITEMS

Clothing can often pick up odors that you just don't notice. I recently bought a designer dress on eBay from a seller who had the typical disclaimer in her description: "No stains, holes, repairs, or odors. Comes from a smoke-free, pet-free home."

Unfortunately, the minute I opened the box I could smell the musty odor of an item that had been stored for a very long time.

To prevent that stale storage odor, keep a package of Dryel in-dryer dry cleaning sheets around. This is a safe, do-it-yourself product. Just toss your eBay clothing items in the patented Dryel bag with the special sheet and toss it in the dryer as per the instructions on the box. Your garment will come out smelling clean — and wrinkle free. For more information, visit their website at www.Dryel.com.

There are many forms of void fill, and the best kind depends on the item you're shipping. Here are the most popular types, and a description of their pluses and minuses.

So that you can always be sure that your items will arrive at their destinations in one piece, you'll want to keep the following on hand at all times:

>> **Air packing pillows:** I found out about these nifty little pillows because they seem to come in packages from all the major online stores. I store them as they come in — in my packing area — and recycle them in my outgoing packages.

Buying air packing pillows from sellers on eBay is economical, mainly because the manufacturing and shipping costs are low. What these folks are essentially shipping you is 99 percent air (something the post office hasn't yet figured out how to charge for). You can find air pillows in the Business and Industrial category. Some sellers sell the uninflated pillows with a small hand-size air pump to fill the pillows.

Air packing pillows are perfect for filling in the area around smaller boxed items that you want to double-box. They are also handy if you have break-ables that you've prewrapped in bubble wrap; just use the pillows to fill out the box. They're crushproof and can support about 150 pounds without a blowout.

TIP

I purchase household items from Amazon on a subscription basis. Amazon sends me tons of air packing pillows and I reuse them in my outgoing eBay packages.

>> **Bubble wrap:** Made up of air-filled cushions of polyethylene, bubble wrap is supplied in rolls of different widths and lengths (see Figure 1-3). It shines for those who wrap delicate, breakable items. When wrapping an item with bubble wrap, wrap it one way and then the other, and then affix some packing tape to make your item an impenetrable ball. Depending on your product, you may have to carry more than one size of bubble wrap to properly protect the goods. Bubble wrap is reasonably priced (check out the many vendors on eBay) and adds next to no weight to your packages.

TIP

When you purchase bubble wrap, be sure you buy the perforated, or tear-off, kind. Cutting a giant roll of bubble wrap with a box cutter can be a dangerous proposition.

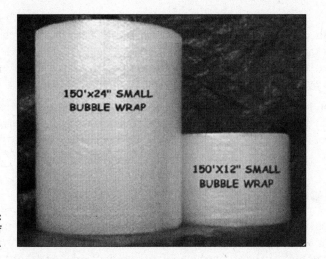

FIGURE 1-3: Different sizes of bubble wrap.

>> **Plain old white newsprint:** In the right shipping situation, plain white newsprint is fantastic. eBay sellers dealing in glass, china, and breakable knickknacks often use white newsprint to wrap each piece before placing it in a box full of packing peanuts.

White newsprint is cheap and easy to store. The bad news? It's heavy when you use too many sheets to wrap the product. If you feel you would like to use newsprint, I suggest you buy it by the roll and use a table-mounted roll cutter to cut the exact size you need. This setup helps you to avoid using too much paper.

>> **Packing peanuts:** Every serious eBay seller has to have a stock of packing peanuts. When properly placed in a box, peanuts fill every nook and cranny and cushion your shipment to make it virtually indestructible. They're handy for padding Tyvek envelopes and filling boxes so that items don't shift around. A bonus: They're cheap and if you recycle them, they don't hurt the environment.

TIP

When packing with peanuts, the key is to not go short in the land of plenty. Use enough peanuts to fill the box completely; leaving any airspace defeats the point of using the peanuts in the first place.

More packing supplies

Your shipping department needs just a few more items. Don't forget to include the following at the outset of your packing career:

>> **Plastic bags:** Buy plastic bags in bulk to save money. Make sure you buy various sizes and use them for both shipping and storing. Even large kitchen or trash bags are good for wrapping up posters and large items; the plastic protects and waterproofs the item from inclement weather.

» **Two- or three-inch-wide shipping tape:** You'll need clear tape for securing packages and to place over address labels to protect them from scrapes and rain. I once received a package with an address label soaked with rain and barely legible. Don't risk a lost package for want of a few inches of tape.

» **Hand-held tape dispenser:** You need a way to get the tape off the roll and onto the box. Using a tape dispenser can be a bit tricky to the uninitiated, but once you get than hang of it, you'll be sealing up boxes in no time flat!

Shipping in mailing envelopes

You'll be shipping your stuff in an envelope or a box. Don't be quick to discount shipping in envelopes. Any item under 13 ounces (15.9 ounces if you print electronic postage) can be shipped via First Class mail — and that can represent quite a savings.

STORING PESKY PACKING PRODUCTS

Storing shipping supplies is the tricky part. I store peanuts in the bags they were shipped in (note the ones in the figure) or in 33-gallon plastic trash bags, and then hang the bags on cup hooks around the garage rafters. To store my bubble wrap from Bubblefast, I hung a broomstick with wire from the rafters. I made the broomstick into a dispenser (of sorts).

MECHANIZING YOUR LABELING

Printing labels on your printer is convenient until you start sending out a dozen packages at a time — then cutting the paper and taping the label gets too time-consuming. Plus, those cut-out labels are not professional. I highly recommend you do yourself a favor and get a thermal label printer. Yes, they can be expensive, but you can find some great deals on eBay. I bought my heavy-duty, professional Zebra 2844 thermal label printer on eBay for one-fourth the retail price. It's saved me countless hours. Another good label printer for beginners is the Dymo LabelWriter 4XL.

Mailing envelopes come in many types of materials. Some are sturdier than others. Here's what many eBay sellers use:

>> **Polyvinyl envelopes:** If you've ever ordered clothing or bedding from any of the television-shopping clubs, this is what they came in. Polyvinyl envelopes are lightweight and puncture- and tear-resistant. They are the most durable envelopes available. Who says you *have* to ship in boxes?

>> **Tyvek envelopes:** You know those really cool, indestructible white envelopes you get from the post office or FedEx? They're made of DuPont Tyvek, a spun-bonded olefin fiber. Tyvek has all the benefits of vinyl envelopes, plus it breathes (allows air to reach your product) and has a higher strength-to-weight ratio than other envelope materials. (That "ratio" business means it's very strong, yet feather-light.)

>> **Bubble-padded mailers:** These envelopes are lined with small bubbles, similar to bubble wrap. They're great for shipping a variety of items and are the most popular with eBay sellers (see Figure 1-4).

Bubble-lined mailers come in different materials:

- Plain-paper bubble mailers are the cheapest way to go, but they can be damaged in the mail if you use them to ship heavy items. The way around that problem is to wrap cheap, clear packing tape once around the envelope in each direction.

- Vinyl bubble mailers aren't expensive and are a super protective way to ship. They're 15 percent lighter than paper bubble mailers and are water-resistant.

If you send items that can fit nicely into bubble-padded envelopes, use them. This type of envelope is perfect for mailing small items or clothing using First Class mail. The envelopes are available in quantity (an economical choice) and don't take up much storage space. Table 1-1 shows you the industry-standard sizes of bubble envelopes and their suggested use.

Box of 25 10-1/2" x 16"
(Industry Size #5)
SELF SEALING BUBBLE MAILERS(Internal Dimensions 9-1/2" x 14-1/2")

bubble*FAST!*'s Bubble Lined mailers are lightweight, yet hold up under the toughest mailing conditions. Air cushioning offers maximum protection. These Mailers are Self-Seal with a 1" Peel and Seal Strip.

And by the way, did you see the price from that national **Office** store? It sure is **MAX!**

FIGURE 1-4:
Bubble-wrap-lined envelopes for sale from eBay seller Bubblefast.

Standard Bubble-Padded or Poly Mailer Sizes

TABLE 1-1

Size	Measurements (in Inches)	Suggested Items
#000	4 x 8	Collector trading cards, jewelry, coins
#00	5 x 10	Postcards, paper ephemera
#0	6 x 10	Doll clothes, DVDs, BluRay, video games
#1	7¼ x 12	Cardboard-sleeve VHS tapes, jewel-cased CDs and DVDs
#2	8½ x 12	Clamshell VHS tapes, books
#3	8½ x 14½	Toys, clothing, stuffed animals
#4	9½ x 14½	Small books, trade paperbacks
#5	10½ x 16	Hardcover books, dolls
#6	12½ x 19	Clothing, soft boxed items
#7	14½ x 20	Much larger packaged items, framed items, plaques

Boxing your items

Depending on the size of the items you sell, you can purchase boxes in bulk at reliable sources. Because you have a resale number, look in your local yellow pages for wholesale boxes (you still have to pay tax, but the resale number identifies you as a business and often can result in lower prices). Try to purchase from a manufacturer that specializes in B2B (business-to-business) sales. Some box companies specialize in selling to the occasional box user.

REMEMBER

You also need to know a little about what it takes to make a sturdy box. The *de facto* standard for quality in general-use shipping boxes is 200-pound double-wall corrugated.

You can save big money if your items fit into boxes that the post office supplies and you plan on using Priority Mail. The U.S. Postal System (USPS) will give you all the boxes and mailing envelopes you need free, and it offers plenty of sizes. See Table 1-2 for available sizes.

TABLE 1-2

Free Priority Mail Packaging

Size (in Inches)	Description
$7\frac{9}{16}$ x $5\frac{7}{16}$ x $\frac{5}{8}$	DVD box
$9\frac{1}{4}$ x $6\frac{1}{4}$ x 2	Large video box (#1096L)
$5\frac{3}{8}$ x $8\frac{5}{8}$ $1\frac{5}{8}$	Small flat-rate
$11\frac{1}{2}$ x $13\frac{1}{8}$ x $2\frac{3}{8}$	Medium (#1097)
$11\frac{7}{8}$ x $3\frac{3}{8}$ x $13\frac{5}{8}$	Flat-rate medium (FBR2)
$12\frac{3}{8}$ x $15\frac{1}{4}$ x 3	Large (#1095)
$12\frac{1}{8}$ x $13\frac{3}{8}$ x $2\frac{3}{4}$	Medium (#1092)
10 x 7 x $4\frac{3}{4}$	Regional Rate A1
$10\frac{15}{16}$ x $2\frac{3}{8}$ x $12\frac{13}{16}$	Regional Rate A2
12 x $10\frac{1}{4}$ x 5	Regional Rate B1
$14\frac{3}{8}$ x $2\frac{7}{8}$ x $15\frac{7}{8}$	Regional Rate B2
6 x 38	Large triangle tube
6 x 25	Small triangle tube
7 x 7 x 6	Small square (BOX4)

(continued)

TABLE 1-2 *(continued)*

Size (in Inches)	Description
12 x 12 x 8	Medium square (BOX7)
11 x 8½ x 5½	Medium flat-rate (FBR1)
23¹¹⁄₁₆ x 11¾ x 3	Large board game flat-rate
12 x 12 x 5½	Large flat-rate box
7½ x 5⅛ x 14⅜	Priority Mail shoebox
11⅝ x 15⅛	Tyvek envelope
9½ x 12½	Padded flat-rate envelope
6 x 10	Cardboard envelope
12½ x 9½	Flat-rate cardboard envelope
5 x 10	Cardboard window envelope

To order your boxes, labels, forms, and just about anything else that you'll need to ship Priority Mail, go to the Postal Store (see Figure 1-5) at

```
https://store.usps.com/store
```

Orders can take up to a month to arrive, so be sure to order before you need more boxes.

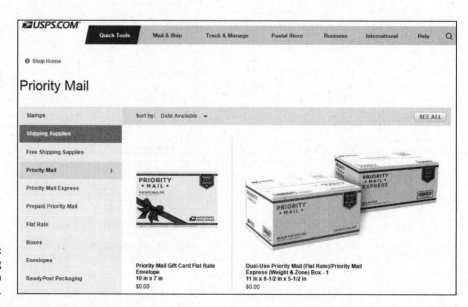

FIGURE 1-5: Order shipping supplies from the USPS.

Buying Postage Online

In 1999, the United States Postal Service announced a new service: *information-based indicia* (IBI) postage that you can print on envelopes and labels right from your PC. In this section, I give you the details on the two main Internet postage vendors:

>> Endicia at

www.endicia.com

>> Stamps.com at

www.stamps.com

You can buy postage and print your labels directly from eBay. If you have plans to sell on other platforms or your website, it may be best to have your own software on your computer.

WARNING

Okay, I'm a savvy-enough consumer and businesswoman that I don't believe in paying for extras — nor do I believe in being a victim of hidden charges. The online postage arena — while providing helpful tools that make running your eBay business easier — is fraught with bargains, deals, and introductory offers. I urge you to read these offers carefully so you know what you're getting yourself into: Evaluate how much it will cost you to start *and to maintain* an ongoing relationship with the company. Although you may initially get some free hardware and pay a low introductory rate, the fine print might tell you that you've *also* agreed to pay unreasonably high monthly prices six months down the line. I always double-check pricing before getting into anything, and I urge you to do the same.

Endicia

At the beginning of PC graphics in the early '90s, I attended a cutting-edge industry trade show. I had a successful graphics-and-advertising business, so I was interested in the latest and greatest innovations to bring my business off the light table and onto my computer. In a smallish booth were a couple of guys peddling new software that enabled artists to design direct-mail pieces from the desktop. What an innovation! Their inexpensive software even let you produce your own bar-coding for the post office. I fell in love with that software and used it throughout my graphics career.

That program (which started life as DAZzle and now wears the Endicia brand), combined with the originators' patented Dial-A-Zip, became the basis for today's software that is distributed to all Endicia customers. There isn't a more robust mailing program on the market.

FREE USPS PACKAGE PICK UP

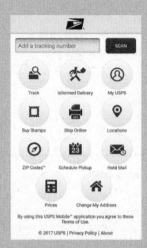

Yes! Some things *are* free! If you print electronic postage for just one Priority Mail or Priority Express package through one of the vendors mentioned in this section, you can request a free pickup for all your packages. Go the post office's website at www.usps.com and type *carrier pickup* in the search box — or go directly to www.usps.com/pickup. The USPS also has a mobile app. I have it on my phone so when I find out I need to ship the next day, I open the app and request a pickup.

You can request a next-day pickup as late as 2:00 a.m. CT.

GETTING THE "COMMERCIAL BASE" DISCOUNT

Printing your postage electronically (online) gives a real benefit: the Commercial Base Price reduction, which is available for First Class packages, Priority Mail, Priority Mail Express, and International services. For Priority Mail packages, Commercial Base price discounts can save up to 39 percent off retail (at the post office) prices, and are based on zone and weight. First Class packages can save up to 18 percent, and Express Mail up to 13 percent off the retail prices.

Endicia has all the features of PayPal shipping and more:

>> **Buy your postage online:** With a click of your mouse, you can purchase your postage instantly using your credit card or by direct debit from your checking account. You can register your preferences when you sign up with Endicia, and you get a Packaging Advisor, as shown in Figure 1-6.

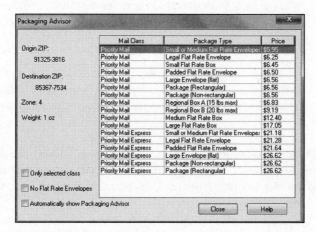

FIGURE 1-6:
Endicia offers a
Packaging Advisor
that checks
for the lowest
shipping rates.

>> **Print postage for all classes of mail, including international:** From Anniston, Alabama, to Bulawayo, Zimbabwe, the DAZzle software not only prints postage but also lists all your shipping options and applicable rates. For international mailing, it also advises you as to any prohibitions (for example, no prison-made goods can be mailed to Botswana), restrictions, necessary customs forms, and areas served within the country.

>> **Print customs forms:** You no longer have to go to the post office with your international packages. Just print the customs form from the Endicia shipping software and give the package to your letter carrier.

>> **Print prepaid return labels:** Should you need to accept a return from a customer, you can send them a prepaid label. Professional accounts can print Pay-on-Use Returns™ labels which are not pre-paid. Postage is only deducted from your postage account if and when the return label is scanned in the mailstream.

>> **Mailpiece design:** Endicia Internet postage is based on the original DAZzle, which was already an award-winning mailpiece design tool that lets you design envelopes, postcards, and labels with color graphics, logos, pictures, text messages, and rubber stamps. You can print your mailing label with postage and delivery confirmation on anything from plain paper (tape it on with clear tape) to fancy 4 x 6 labels in a label printer from an extensive list of label templates.

>> **Integration with insurance:** If you're saving time and money using U-PIC (a private package insurer — see Chapter 3 in this minibook) or Endicia's own insurance, you can send your monthly insurance logs electronically at the end of the month — a service integrated into the Endicia shipping software. There's no need to print a hard copy and mail in this information.

>> **No cut-and-paste necessary:** Endicia software integrates with most common software programs. With Endicia shipping software open on your computer, highlight the buyer's address from an email or the PayPal site and then press Ctrl+C. The address automatically appears in the Endicia postage software. No pasting needed.

Endicia offers two levels of service. All the features just listed come with the Premium plan. Their Professional plan adds enhanced online transaction reports and statistics, Pay-on-Use Returns™ return shipping labels, and stealth indicias.

TIP

The *stealth indicia* (also known as the *postage-paid indicia*) can be an awesome tool for the eBay seller. By using this feature, your customer will not see the exact amount of postage you paid. This permits some of your trade secrets to remain . . . um, secret.

With all these professional features, you'd think that Endicia's service would be expensive, but it's not. The Premium plan is $15.95 a month, and the Professional Plan is $34.95 a month.

eBay and PayPal shipping services

eBay continues to add great features for sellers. Now you can not only buy postage and ship with USPS through eBay but also print labels on your own printer. If you ship lots of items and use a different service for printing your postage, both eBay and PayPal allow you to input tracking information on the site. Just click the Add Tracking Info link for the transaction on PayPal, as shown in Figure 1-7. Input the USPS, UPS, or other shipping company's tracking or delivery-confirmation information (see Figure 1-8), and PayPal sends an email to your buyer with that information.

The information you added appears in both the record of your PayPal transaction and the buyer's record in their account, as shown in Figure 1-9.

FIGURE 1-7:
Choosing to add tracking information on PayPal Activity.

FIGURE 1-8:
Adding the shipper's tracking number on eBay.

FIGURE 1-9:
Tracking becomes part of the sales record on your My eBay page.

eBay shipping services work great when you're just starting out in your business — but after you get rolling, you need a mailing service that includes email and recordkeeping, such as Endicia or Stamps.com. The issue connected with using eBay for shipping is important: When you process your shipping (UPS or USPS), the shipping amount is deducted from your PayPal (sales revenue) balance. I like to keep my expenses separate in my bookkeeping process.

WARNING

If you're starting a business in earnest, you need to keep track of your online expenses separately. Allowing PayPal to deduct your shipping costs from your incoming revenue can create a bookkeeping nightmare. You need to have exact figures for expenses and income — and it helps keep confusion to a minimum when your deposits (withdrawals from your PayPal account to your bank) match your sales receipts. If you want to ship through eBay, be sure you withdraw your sales amount to your checking account *before* you process your shipping. That way your shipping can be charged to your business credit card for easier tracking.

To purchase postage and print your label for a specific purchase, click the Print Shipping Label button next to the payment record in your PayPal account overview. You'll be taken through a step-by-step process for paying for your shipping and printing the appropriate label on your printer.

Stamps.com

Stamps.com purchased 31 Internet postage patents from e-stamp, making its services a combination of the best of both sites. (e-stamp discontinued its online postage service late in 2000; I was a big fan.) Many eBay sellers moved their postage business over to Stamps.com, which purchased Endicia in 2015 for $215 million in cash. Today, the Endicia site continues its own operation and is geared toward more professional shipping solutions.

Stamps.com works with software that you probably use every day, such as Microsoft Word, Outlook, and Office; Corel WordPerfect; and Intuit. Here are some features you might enjoy:

>> **Use your printer to print postage.** If your printer allows it, you can even print your envelopes along with bar-coded addresses, your return address, and postage. This saves quite a bit in label costs.

TIP

The Stamps.com Envelope Wizard permits you to design your own envelopes, including a logo or graphics. You can purchase a box of 500 #10 envelopes for as little as $4.99 at an office supply store.

>> **Have Stamps.com check that your addresses are valid.** Before printing any postage, the Stamps.com software contacts the USPS database of every valid mailing address in the United States. This Address Matching System (AMS) is updated monthly.

>> **Have Stamps.com add the extra four digits to your addressee's ZIP code.** This nifty feature helps ensure swift delivery while freeing you of the hassle of having to look up the information.

Purchasing postage is as easy as going to the Stamps.com website and clicking your mouse. Your credit card information is kept secure on its site. With Stamps.com, you don't *need* any extra fancy equipment, although most introductory deals come with a free 5-pound-maximum postal scale. The scale also functions on its own. Serious users should get a better-quality postage scale from a seller on eBay or through Office Depot.

TIP

Because Office Depot delivers any order more than $50 free the next day, it's a great place to get paper and labels. Better buys on scales, though, can be found on eBay, especially if you search *postage scale*. I use a super-small, 50-pound-maximum scale that I bought on eBay for under $20.

Stamps.com charges a flat rate of $15.99 per month. The site regularly offers sign-up bonuses that include as much as $20.00 free postage or a free 5-pound-maximum digital postage scale. To find the Stamps.com deal of the month, visit its website at www.stamps.com.

Chapter **2**

Shipping without Going Postal

The best part of an eBay business is making the sale and receiving payment. After that comes the somewhat tedious process of fulfilling your orders. You shouldn't feel bad if this is the point that makes you pause and sigh. Order fulfillment is one of the biggest challenges that face any online enterprise.

But as an eBay entrepreneur, you *must* attend to these tasks, however much you'd rather not. In this chapter, you explore your shipping options. I give you the lowdown on the three major carriers — FedEx, United Parcel Service, and the U.S. Postal Service — so you can see who fits your requirements. (For the scoop on insurance coverage, see Chapter 3 in this minibook.)

Shipping: The Heart of Your Business

Shipping can be a make-or-break point for eBay sellers. Being expert at knowing the correct carrier, box size, and packaging will affect your bottom line. Even if the selling portion of your transaction goes flawlessly, the purchased item has to get to the buyer economically and in one piece. If it doesn't, the deal could be ruined — and so could your reputation.

The best way to avoid shipping problems is to do your homework beforehand, determine which method is likely to work best for the type of items you sell, spell out how you intend to ship the item, and charge accordingly. I offer more than one shipping option — including overnight — to satisfy the buyer who may want a specific method of shipment.

AUTHOR SAYS

U.S. POSTAGE AT A BIG DISCOUNT!

I just had to share this with you! The figure shows a picture of an envelope I received for an eBay purchase. I had to email the seller to find out how and why she used so many stamps.

The seller is a collector of U.S. postage. She checks out eBay auctions and buys deals on collections and old sheets of mint state stamps. United States stamps, no matter how old, are always good, so she buys these stamps at discount and uses them on her eBay packages. However, she did mention that when she brings her packages to the post office, all the clerks scatter to take a break!

As a footnote, I checked eBay and found a whole lot of United States postage stamps selling for under face value! Like a *1997 Mars Rover* Pathfinder $3.00 Sheetlet that went for $1.99. The hint to finding these deals is to search for the type of stamp — but don't include the word *stamp* in your keyword search — and then select the Stamps category. Other sellers for this sheetlet grossed as much as $15.00 for the stamp. I guess some sellers will never learn.

Shipping is the heart of an ecommerce business like yours. Don't even think of selling an item without evaluating your shipping options:

1. Before listing the item, figure out how the package will ship.

You don't have to package it up right away, but you should review your options. The two critical factors in shipping are weight and time. The more a package weighs — and the faster it has to be delivered — may or may not reflect higher costs. The time to think about packing and shipping is *before* you put the item up for sale.

2. Know your carrier options.

In the United States, the three main shipping options for most eBay transactions are the U.S. Postal Service, FedEx, and UPS. See the section "Shopping for a Shipping Carrier" for information on how you can get rate options from each service, painlessly and online.

3. Before estimating shipping costs to price your item, make sure that you include all possible fees.

Keep in mind that if your item will sell for over $750, both eBay and PayPal require signature delivery in case the package goes missing and the buyer makes a claim. Paying for this option for United States Postal Service (USPS) packages will currently set you back $2.90. You should also include any insurance costs. (For more on insurance, see Chapter 3 in this minibook.)

TIP

If you offer free shipping, your item will receive preference in eBay's search. Consider this option by building shipping costs in the item price. This works best when an item is light and can be shipped cheaply — while not sacrificing speed. At the very least, offer a flat rate to all your customers.

TIP

If you offer free shipping in your listing and eBay can confirm that the buyer did not pay extra for shipping, you will automatically receive a 5-star rating on your shipping and handling charges as part of your Detailed Seller Ratings.

Posting a flat shipping amount is easy for the customer to figure out. With heavier items, use the eBay online shipping calculator at

`www.ebay.com/shp/Calculator`

to give buyers an idea of how much shipping will cost. This way, buyers can consider the extra cost when comparing different sellers who offer the same item. Figure out what the packed item will weigh and then estimate shipping costs.

Keep in mind, though, that if your idea of "reasonable" shipping costs doesn't jibe with that of your buyer, you may end up with a ding in your DSR feedback rating for shipping fees.

TIP

If the item is particularly heavy and you need to use a specialized shipping service, be sure to say in your listing description that you're just giving an estimate and that the final cost will be determined prior to shipping.

REMEMBER

Shipping calculations can be off target, and you may not know that until after you take the buyer's money. If the mistake is in your favor and it's a biggie, notify the buyer and offer a refund. But if shipping ends up costing you a bit more, take your lumps and pay it. You can always let the buyer know what happened and that you paid the extra cost. Who knows, it may show up on your feedback from the buyer!

4. **Ship the item as soon as you receive payment; eBay bases transit time on your selection of carrier and your proximity to the buyer, as shown in Figure 2-1.**

   Make sure you ship the item to arrive in the time that eBay estimates. Ship that package within your stated shipping time (after payment clears). If you can't, immediately message the buyer on eBay and explain the delay.

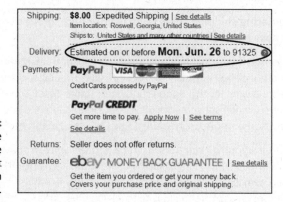

FIGURE 2-1:
The estimate shows the customer up front when the item should arrive.

TIP

When you input the tracking number into the PayPal transaction detail, a follow-up email will automatically be sent to let the buyer know the item's on the way.

TIP

Why not include a thank-you note (a receipt would be a businesslike addition) in each package you send out? I always do. As a customer I also appreciate this courtesy. It always brings a smile to the recipient's face. It never hurts to take every opportunity to promote goodwill (and future business and positive feedback).

Shopping for a Shipping Carrier

When you're considering shipping options, you must first determine what types of packages you'll generally be sending (small packages that weigh less than two pounds or large and bulky packages) and then decide how you'll send your items.

Deciding on your carrier can be the most important decision in your eBay business. You need to figure out which one is more convenient for you (located close to your home base, provides pick up service, gives better customer service) and which is the most economical. Settling on one main shipper to meet most of your needs is important because all your records will be on one statement or in one area. However, you may also need a secondary shipper for other types of packages.

Shipping is an extension of your customer service. Whoever delivers the package to the buyer represents your company. Professional labels, clean boxes, nifty packing peanuts — those are the things you control. Safe and timely delivery falls into the hands of complete strangers, but the buyer will blame you for the tardiness or sloppiness of the shipping. Simple equation: Irate customers = lousy feedback.

So what's a seller to do? Do you use the shipper that other sellers rave about? Perhaps opt for convenience or low price? After you decide on a shipper, how often do you re-evaluate its services?

The rest of the chapter will help you with this decision.

Meeting your front line

Who constitutes the front line of your eBay business? My shipping front line is Scott, the UPS man; Neil, the Post Office carrier; and Ken, who picks up for FedEx Ground. I know the front-line guys because they help my eBay business run smoothly. They don't leave deliveries outside under a bush, and they deliver packages to my neighbor if I'm not home. Neil picks up my eBay packages with a smile and a lighthearted "They're sure buying things, aren't they?" I respond with a smile and a bit of friendly chat.

Wait, are you telling me that you don't get the same service? Have you ever taken a moment to chat with your delivery person? When you personalize a business relationship (such as addressing the person by name), you become more than a street address, you become . . . well . . . a *person*. When you're no longer a number, you become a fellow human being with needs and wants. Believe it or not, people *want* to make other people happy.

I leave a signal when there are packages to be picked up, and every one is picked up. When somebody delivers a big box, it goes to the back door near my studio; that way I don't have to drag it through the front door and across the house.

Try building a relationship with your shipping front line. I've invited them to holiday parties and offered them a cool drink on a hot summer day. The result? My shipping is the easiest part of my business.

Location, location, location

The USPS offers free package pickup at your door (I set my pickups the night before shipping, using the USPS mobile app), but you do have to bring an occasional package in to the post office or use a different carrier. What happens if you have to drop off your packages for shipment? It's important to consider the closest local drop-off point for your carrier. Each of the major carriers has a search feature on its website to find the nearest drop-off location. You input your address or Zip code, and the feature tells you the locations closest to you.

To get the location lowdown quickly, go to the following sites:

>> **FedEx:** www.fedex.com/us/dropoff

>> **USPS:** www.usps.com/locator/welcome.htm

>> **UPS:** www.ups.com/dropoff

TIP

Be sure to read the details about each location online. Different fees may be involved in dropping off packages. Some locations may accept certain types of packages and not others. Read the fine print.

Comparing prices

The powers that be would like you to believe that a particular method of shipping is cheaper for large items and another is cheaper for small packages. There is a good shipping calculator on eBay (www.ebay.com/shp/Calculator) where you can compare parcel shipping prices across the vendors. There's some truth there, but a few more things come into consideration.

>> **Dimensional weight pricing (DIM).** Beginning in 2017, UPS and FedEx instituted dimensional pricing surcharges based on the size of the boxes used. Rather than just using weight and distance, they found that calculating the volume or area that the box will occupy on the carrier is equally important. The USPS has something similar, Cubic Pricing, but it isn't a surcharge; it's a discount that's only available to very large-volume shippers.

>> **USPS Retail rate.** This is the rate you pay when you bring a package to the post office, or print a label online through the USPS Click N Ship website. It is the highest rate that the USPS charges. UPS and FedEx also have retail (or in-store) rates, but discounts are doled out on an individual basis. To calculate (and compare) retail pricing, go to https://postcalc.usps.com.

>> **Discounts and offers.** You will no doubt see online — and on eBay — that you are being "offered" special discounts on shipping. The USPS offers no discounts (except the one mentioned below) for small shippers. UPS and FedEx attempt

to confuse the small seller into thinking they are getting a preferred discount. Don't be fooled: Check the pricing you're offered head-to-head with USPS similar services. You can't compare USPS Priority Mail to UPS Ground. They're not even close. Read carefully before signing up for anything.

>> **Upcharges and extras.** UPS and FedEx have additional charges to consider (for example, the *surge pricing* later in this list). There are fuel surcharges, extra charges for delivering to residences, pickup charges, Saturday charges, and more.

>> **Electronic Commercial Base Pricing.** When you use an online postage vendor like Endicia, Stamps.com, Pitney Bowes SendPro, PayPal, or eBay, you will receive a discounted rate on USPS postage. This is the best deal you can get. Using a third-party postage vendor gives you other advantages as well (as outlined in Chapter 1 of this minibook).

>> **Surge Pricing.** Just as you pay more when you hail an Uber car during a storm, you'll find that both UPS and FedEx have announced ground surcharges as high as 3.4 percent during Black Friday and holiday seasons. A surge in traffic means a surge in price.

>> **USPS First Class Shipping.** First class parcels travel through the mail system nearly as fast as Priority Mail. Now the USPS allows packages up to 15.9 ounces to be shipped First Class. This is when switching from a box to a plastic envelope saves you more than packing costs.

Take a look at Table 2-1 and compare the pricing for a package going cross-country; the prices are based on your business having an account (or printing USPS postage electronically). Retail counter rates are the highest; daily pickup rates will be somewhat less. Trying to translate the rate charts for some major carriers can be a real challenge. I recommend you get pricing estimates directly from their websites or software after you open your account.

TABLE 2-1 **Business to Residence 12 x 10 x 6 Package USPS Priority Mail versus Ground (NY to LA)**

	USPS Priority: 2–3 Days	FedEx Ground	UPS Ground 4 days
Actual Weight (lbs)	2 pounds	2 pounds	2 pounds
DIM Weight	N/A	6 pounds	5 pounds
Base Charge	10.28	13.18	13.10
Fuel Surcharge	N/A	.53	.69
Residential Surcharge	N/A	3.85	3.40
Total cost	**$10.28**	**$17.58**	**$17.19**

Table 2-2 shows you the value of shipping via USPS First Class Package Service.

Know that there are extras for some services, so become familiar with the variations and hidden costs like preferred customer rates and gas fees. Home delivery adds up to $3.85 per package for UPS and FedEx packages. For example, USPS offers regional and flat-rate discounts (more about those further on).

TABLE 2-2　**Business to Residence 8 x 6 x 4 Package USPS First Class Package versus Ground (NY to LA)**

	USPS First Class	FedEx Ground	UPS Ground
Actual Weight	13 ounces	13 ounces	13 ounces
DIM Weight	N/A	2 pounds	2 pounds
Base Charge	3.88	9.32	9.39
Fuel Surcharge	N/A	.37	.49
Residential Surcharge	N/A	3.85	3.40
Total cost	**$3.88**	**$13.53**	**$13.28**

TIP

If you plan on shipping a lot of packages via FedEx or UPS, it would behoove you to contact a representative to find out if they can offer you further discounts.

SHIPPING THE BIG STUFF

When it comes to shipping heavy or big stuff, you have a few options. Because I like using FedEx, I check with FedEx Freight first. A friend once purchased four large heavy-equipment tires on eBay, and there was no way they could go with a regular carrier. We told the seller to place the tires on a pallet and secure them. They were picked up by FedEx Freight. Shipping was reasonable, but the caveat was that the shipment had to be delivered to a place of business, not a residential location.

The www.freightquote.com website negotiates rates with several major freight-forwarders. Before attempting to sell a heavy item, sign on to their website with the weight and dimensions of your shipment, and they'll give you a free quote on the spot.

Shipping with USPS

I'm a big fan of the U.S. Postal Service. Just ask my wonderful letter (er, multiple parcel) carrier Neil. I (as well as the bulk of eBay sellers) use the post office for the bulk of online sales because it's convenient and saves money. In my over 20 years selling items on eBay, they've never lost a package.

The USPS is open to everyone. You don't have to set up an account to use its services. To get a basic idea of what you'll pay to send a package, you can access a retail-rate calculator on the USPS website (https://postcalc.usps.com), shown in Figure 2-2.

FIGURE 2-2: The United States Postal Service retail-rate calculator.

Convenient and fast

The post office has worked hard to keep up with the competition in the parcel business by offering many online features and custom pickup. They also offer many classes of service, with a weight maximum of 70 pounds. Table 2-3 shows the transit times for services that are most popular with eBay sellers. Note that the USPS delivers packages seven days a week; the other major carriers offer only five business days a week.

TABLE 2-3

Most Popular USPS Services

Service	Time to Cross the Country (Days)	What You Can Ship
First Class	3–5	First Class mail can be used to mail anything, as long as it weighs 15.9 ounces or less. You can send a letter, a large envelope, or a small package.
Priority Mail	2–3	Priority Mail is just First Class mail on steroids (for heavier items).
Parcel Select	2–8	Parcel Select is cheaper (and slower) than Priority Mail.
Media Mail	2–8	Media Mail is the least expensive way to mail heavy items. The only caveat is that you can use Media Mail to ship only books and educational items.

Read on for details on the most popular forms of mail used by eBay sellers.

First Class

Good old regular mail — in particular, First Class — is the way we send bills and letters. It works also as an economical alternative for eBay items weighing up to 15.9 ounces.

TIP

Sending items in bubble wrap or plastic envelopes will often get the shipping weight under the ounce maximum for First Class mail.

Too many sellers make the jump to Priority Mail because they don't take the time to think about the weight of their items. It doesn't have to ship in an envelope to go via First Class mail.

Priority Mail

The two-to-three-day Priority Mail service is the most popular form of shipping for eBay packages. There are three price options: Flat Rate, Regional Rate, and Weight/Distance. You can get free cartons from the post office. You can also print postage online through Endicia (www.endicia.com) or Stamps.com at www.stamps.com. See Chapter 1 in this minibook for more about these postage options and for a complete list of what the USPS supplies for your mailing needs.

The Priority Mail rates are perfect for 1-pound packages (starting at $5.95 cross-country when printed online). They also have a flat-rate Priority envelope in which you can jam in as much as possible (regardless of the package's final weight) for $5.95 (retail rate $6.65).

Because USPS rates are based on distance and weight, you can save money by using their new flat-rate Priority Mail boxes. (I've been able to jam quite a bit into them!) The Regional Flat Rate boxes (sizes A and B) can be a deal with the medium-size B box starting at $7.17 ($9.42 retail). Flat-rate boxes ship anywhere in the United States for as little as $12.40 ($13.60 retail) for a medium box.

REMEMBER

The Priority Mail rates (including free shipping materials) are attractive until you get into heavier packages.

Parcel Select Ground

If you want to use the USPS and have a heavy package (up to 70 pounds) that doesn't fit the requirements for Media Mail, use Parcel Select Ground (formerly Parcel Post). Even with the latest rate changes, USPS Parcel Select Ground rates can be highly competitive when you compare them to the UPS or FedEx Ground rates.

When you print your postage electronically, this service is called Parcel Select. Standard Post is for those who buy postage at the Post Office.

Media Mail

To stay new and hip, the post office renamed its old Book Rate to Media Mail, causing many eBay sellers to mistakenly miss out on this valuable mailing tool. The savings are immense. The drawback is that you must mail only books and/or educational media. Transit time on Media Mail is at least 7 to 10 days, but the cost savings on heavy packages may be worth it — as long as your customers realize how long transit time can be.

Understanding the costs

The Postal Service levies additional charges for some often-used services but also gives free services to online postage customers:

>> **Pickup:** If you print your own postage from an online service (see Chapter 1) or print direct from eBay or the PayPal site, the post office offers free pickup, as shown in Figure 2-3. You have to give your packages to your carrier at the time of your regular delivery or schedule a pickup on the USPS Mobile App or on the site at

  `https://tools.usps.com/go/ScheduleAPickupAction!input.action`

FIGURE 2-3:
Put in your
request for
pickup the day
before your
pickup day.

>> **Insurance:** This guarantees that you're covered if your package doesn't arrive safely; USPS will reimburse you up to the value you declare when purchasing the insurance, up to a maximum of $5,000. If your package gets lost or severely mangled in shipping, the Postal Service will, after a thorough investigation (see Chapter 3 in this minibook), pay your claim. Fees start at $1.95 for packages up to $50 in value. Also see Chapter 3 for discounted insurance.

>> **USPS Tracking:** Previously known as Delivery Confirmation, USPS Tracking gives you point-by-point tracking details. It also provides you with proof of delivery or attempted delivery. This number is included free for most postal services when you print your postage electronically. You can check the status of any package by submitting the number online at

`https://tools.usps.com/go/TrackConfirmAction!input.action`

You can also verify a package's delivery by calling a toll-free number, 800-222-1811.

TIP

For a quick way to find out postal zones from your place of business, go to

`http://postcalc.usps.gov/Zonecharts`

You, Too, Can Use FedEx

FedEx is world-famous for its reliable service. It's the number-one choice for all major companies who have to get packages on time. In 1978, FedEx introduced the slogan "When it Absolutely, Positively has to be there overnight" and has built its business on that promise. FedEx acquired Roadway Package Service (RPS) and formed FedEx Ground, which has a separate division called FedEx Home Delivery that delivers to residences. For the services they provide, you'll be happy to know they are still devoted to their on-time promise. Read on.

TIP

If you ever have an issue or a question about a FedEx shipment, you can reach their award-winning customer service staff on Twitter. Just address your Tweet to @FedEx.

FedEx Ground and Home Delivery

When FedEx's Home Delivery began, their slogan was "The neighborhood-friendly service that fits the way we live, work, and shop today." Although I rarely get warm fuzzies from my package delivery, this slogan brought meaning to the philosophy behind their service: to bring professional shipping to your home residence. Now FedEx Home Delivery is part of FedEx Ground, and offers low rates and high-quality service. They're the only shipper that offers a money-back guarantee on home service. They deliver until 8:00 p.m. *and* on Saturdays, but not on Mondays.

To open an account, visit the `FedEx.com` site. To learn more about FedEx, visit the Ground website, shown in Figure 2-4, at

`www.fedex.com/us/fedex/shippingservices/package/ground.html`

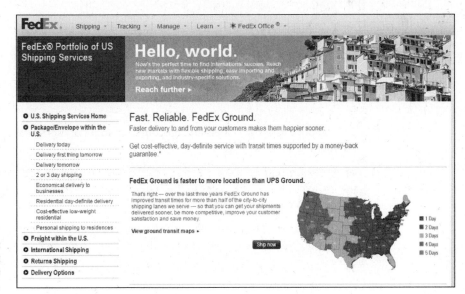

FIGURE 2-4:
The FedEx Ground home page.

Even if you have a current FedEx account, you need to sign on to add the Ground service (which includes Home Delivery). Registering for Ground service is even easier than registering on eBay, so give it a shot.

I opened my FedEx Ground account through a link on the FedEx home page, and got the skinny on how to use the service. FedEx gives you a service schedule to let you know how long it will take your package to arrive at its destination (see Figure 2-5). The online calculator allows you to choose the option of home delivery, so you don't even have to look up alternative rates and charts.

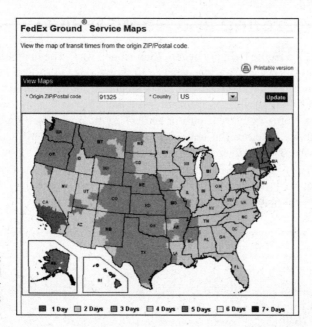

FIGURE 2-5: FedEx Ground service map for delivery from Los Angeles.

Here are a few fast facts about FedEx Ground services:

>> You print your own labels and barcodes for your packages and track them online.

>> FedEx Ground works on a zone system based on your Zip code and how far the package is going. Refer to the FedEx Ground zone chart or get the cost online through the online calculator.

>> Each shipment is covered for $100 in declared value. Additional insurance can be purchased (see Chapter 3 of this minibook).

>> Residential deliveries are limited to 70-pound packages.

>> Daily pick-up service adds an additional charge.

>> Dropping off packages at FedEx counters (this includes all those handy FedEx Kinko's locations) incurs no additional charge.

TIP

To find the closest drop-off location for your FedEx packages, go to www.fedex. com/us/dropoff and type your Zip code. Check that the location accepts Ground, and check the cutoff times.

FedEx online

FedEx has one of the most intuitive online apps for shipping. The FedEx Ship Manager (or Ship Manager Lite for the non-account holder with a credit card) interface will turn your computer into a one-person shipping machine. You can search for rate quotes, track packages, and use the shipping notification option to send tracking information emails to your recipients.

To ship your item from the FedEx website, just sign in and go to the online Ship Manager by clicking the Ship link. You'll be presented with a simple, all-in-one online waybill. Figure 2-6 shows you what it looks like.

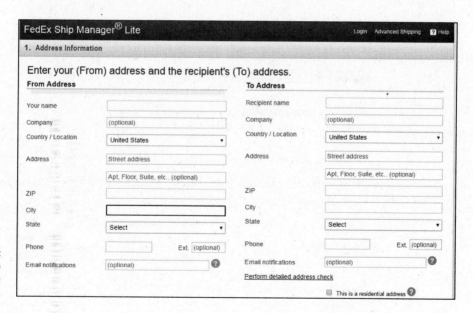

FIGURE 2-6: FedEx Ship Manager Lite online shipping.

TIP

You can copy and paste addresses from your PayPal account into the online form. Just highlight the text you want to copy and press Ctrl+C. To paste the text, place your cursor in the area you want to fill and press Ctrl+V.

When you're filling out the form, note some important entries must be made:

>> **Service type:** If you're shipping to a residence via Ground, select Ground in the service type and be sure to place a check mark in "This is a Residence Address."

>> **Dimensions:** Be sure that you know the proper dimensions for the package you're sending.

TIP

If you sell repeat items in your eBay business, why not measure the boxes ahead of time and keep a list near your computer so you'll know the size? (For example: *Light kit 14 x 12 x 26.*)

>> **FedEx Ship Alert:** Select the email option to send the buyer (and yourself) a notice that the package was shipped and when it is delivered.

After you fill out the form, you can click the Courtesy Rate button at the bottom to get a shipping-cost estimate (not including any special discounts).

REMEMBER

When shipping with FedEx online, if your package is valued over $100 and you use U-PIC for your insurance (see Chapter 3 in this minibook), put $0 in the Declared Value box. Make note of the package on an insurance log and submit it to U-PIC.

SAVING MORE BY PAYING WITH AMERICAN EXPRESS

If you have an American Express Business credit card (which also allows you access to the American Express Open Network), you can save even more on your FedEx shipments!

- **Save 5 percent** of all FedEx Ground shipments with your Open Savings Discount.

- **Save up to 21 percent additionally** on your FedEx Express shipments with the Advantage program. Sign up for this program at

    www.fedex.com/us/open-savings/index.html

To be sure your American Express card is officially linked so you get the discount, call the FedEx/Open Network desk at 1-800-231-8636. As a member of the Open Network, you can also save money on other business needs.

Getting on the UPS Bandwagon

Today's UPS is a $51 billion revenue company focusing on enabling commerce around the world. Every day UPS delivers more than 19.1 million packages and documents worldwide — and I'm sure much of that total represents eBay transactions.

REMEMBER

UPS considers neither Saturday nor Sunday to be delivery days. So when your package is quoted for a 5-day delivery and those five days cross over a weekend, add two days to the delivery schedule. (The USPS and FedEx Ground deliver packages on Saturday.)

Here are some quick facts about UPS:

>> Shipping with UPS requires that you pay a different rate for different zones in the country (zones 1–8). The cost of your package is based on its weight and size, your Zip code (where the package ships from), and the addressee's Zip code (where the package is going). To figure out your cost, use the handy UPS cost calculator shown in Figure 2-7.

Shipping without Going Postal

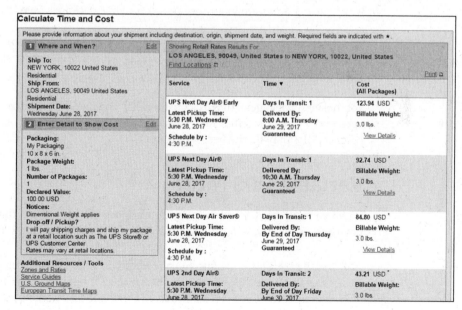

FIGURE 2-7:
The UPS cost (and transit time) calculator.

» UPS offers a chart that defines the shipping time for your ground shipments.

» Each package has a tracking number that you can input online to verify location and time of delivery.

» UPS delivers packages Monday through Friday.

Comparing costs

Although we always complain when the U.S. Postal Service raises their rates, you should know that all other shipping carriers raise their rates every year.

Annual rate increases are one reason that being lulled into complacency can be dangerous. Evaluate your shipping charges and your shipper's fees every year to keep up with the increases and their possible cuts into your bottom line.

While we all *think* that UPS Ground is cheaper than the post office, it's not true in every case.

Every UPS package is automatically insured for up to $100, assuming you declare a value. The post office charges extra for this service, but you can save money either way by using a private insurance policy for your packages (see Chapter 3).

The de-facto standard for eBay shipping is Priority Mail. Compared to UPS 3-Day Select, Priority Mail is the clear cost-saving winner if you must ship packages for swift delivery.

For heavier packages, UPS is considerably cheaper than Parcel Post for packages over 6 pounds. After your packages pass that point, and if time is *not* of the essence, UPS may be the best way to go.

Variable UPS rates

When you ship via UPS and are trying to figure out how to get the best rates, you have quite a conundrum. UPS basically has three rates for small-time shippers:

» **Retail rate:** This is the rate you pay when you go to the UPS Customer Center and they create the label for you. It's the most expensive. With the eBay/ PayPal solution, you can save yourself some bucks by printing your own bar-coded labels and dropping the packages at the Customer Center or giving the packages to a UPS driver.

» **Standard rate:** Use UPS for the rare large box or heavy shipment. An on-demand, or occasional, shipper can call UPS for a next-day pickup. You have to pay an additional $2.75 per package for the driver to pick up from you if you don't feel like bringing the package to the UPS local counter.

» **Daily account:** When you hit the big time, you're able to get the lowest UPS rates and have a driver make daily stops to pick up your packages. Are you worrying that it costs a bundle to have regular UPS package pickup service? (I was, too.) Surprise — it doesn't really if you ship a lot.

Shipping Items through PayPal or eBay

I consider PayPal to be *de rigueur* (a *must have*, to all you non-French speakers) for all online sellers. By using PayPal, a seller can streamline the buyer's shopping experience, making it simple to buy, click, and pay. Along with all the timesaving tools PayPal supplies for the seller, they now offer online shipping services for items through the United States Postal Service or UPS at no extra charge. This is a convenient system for those who don't ship many packages each week because there's no need to use additional software or sign up with an additional service.

Sounds good so far, but (I hate the *buts* — don't you?) the PayPal postage system can make bookkeeping a nightmare for large-scale shippers. That's because PayPal withdraws the postage amounts directly from your PayPal account balance. This is problematic because the result is that your books won't balance: Your final deposits won't match your posted eBay or web sales.

TIP

You can make this arrangement work more efficiently by posting your PayPal sales to your bookkeeping program and *then* withdrawing your money before processing your shipping. Then you simply charge your shipping to a credit card, which will help you balance your books at month's end.

When you're ready to deal with shipping, you simply sign on to your PayPal account and handle it right on the site. To begin the shipping process, follow these steps:

1. **Log in to your PayPal account page.**

2. **Click the Print Shipping Label button next to the item in the row.**

3. **If this is your first time using PayPal labels, set up your printer preferences by clicking in the upper-right corner.**

Default printing preferences are set for any laser or inkjet printer with an 8.5 x 11 standard paper size.

Chapter **3**

Insuring That Your Package Arrives

This chapter reveals the practical link between insurance and timely delivery — and how the wise seller can use both to ensure a better experience for both buyer and seller. The key is an assumption: When someone buys an item from you, the buyer assumes that the item will be shipped in 24 to 48 hours (customers prefer a quick 24-hour turnaround). A little-known rule of the online world is the Federal Trade Commission's *30-day mail-order rule* (16 CFR Part 435) that applies to all online sales, as well as to mail-order businesses.

REMEMBER

Unless you (as the seller) state a specific shipping time, all items must be shipped within 30 days.

Adopted in 1975, this FTC rule proclaims these buyer's rights:

» The buyer must receive the merchandise when the seller says it will arrive, or earlier.

» If delivery is not promised within a certain time period, the seller must ship the merchandise to the buyer no later than 30 days after receiving the order.

» If the buyer doesn't receive the merchandise within that 30-day period, the buyer can cancel the order and get his or her money back.

This rule must be part of the reason why eBay won't allow items on the site for presale (or *drop-shipping*, detailed in Book 4, Chapter 4) unless you can guarantee that the item will be shipped within 30 days. In each of those cases, you must indicate in your description that the item is a presale or drop-ship.

TIP

Note the rule states the merchandise must be delivered in 30 days. The rule doesn't say "unless the item gets lost in the mail." This means that *you*, the seller, are responsible for your packages arriving at their destinations. This makes insurance more important than ever, especially on expensive items.

Insurance Options

When you're shipping a large amount of merchandise on a regular basis, you're going to have to deal with the issue of whether you buy insurance against damage or loss. The lost-in-the-mail excuse doesn't cut the mustard, and having a tracking number doesn't guarantee anything, either.

I ship via USPS for the bulk of my eBay orders, and use Priority Mail often, for one reason. Priority Mail includes up to $50 of insurance with most shipments. That saves me a lot of worry.

WARNING

Buyers who don't receive items that they've paid for can file an "eBay Money Back Guarantee" report against you if the package hasn't arrived within the stated time (based on your shipping mode). Buyers can also have the payment removed from your PayPal account, and you have no defense against this.

Self-insuring your items

Some sellers on eBay self-insure their packages. In other words, they take the risk and use money out of their own pockets if they have to pay a claim. In this sense, *self-insuring* is considered seller's jargon, not an official legal status (only licensed insurance agents can offer insurance).

These sellers are usually careful about packing their items to prevent damage. (Check out Chapter 1 in this minibook to find out about choosing and finding packing materials.) They also always use tracking numbers when using the Postal Service.

TIP

Savvy self-insurers usually do *not* self-insure items of high value. If you sell mostly lower-priced items (under $100) and decide to self-insure, consider making an exception when you do occasionally sell an expensive item. Bite the bullet and pay for the shipping insurance; doing so could save you money and hassle in the long run.

ENSURE PEACE OF MIND BY INSURING YOUR SHIPMENT

Sure, "lost in the mail" is an excuse we've all heard hundreds of times, but despite everyone's best efforts, sometimes things do get damaged or misplaced during shipment. The universe is a dangerous place; that's why we have tracking numbers and insurance. I *always* get insurance on expensive, one-of-a-kind, or very fragile items.

- Be sure your U.S. Postal Service package labels have a tracking number. The tracking shows when an item has been delivered.

- When you sell an item to a customer that has a value over $750, both eBay and PayPal require Signature Confirmation and tracking for delivery.

The major shippers offer insurance that's fairly reasonably priced, so check out their rates at their websites. But don't forget to read the details. For example, many items on eBay are sold MIMB (mint in mint box). True, the condition of the original box often has a bearing on the final value of the item inside, but the U.S. Postal Service insures only what is *in* the box. So, if you sold a Malibu Barbie mint in a mint box, USPS insures only the doll and not the original box. Pack carefully so your buyer gets what's been paid for. Be mindful that shippers won't make good on insurance claims if they suspect that you caused the damage by doing a lousy job of packing.

Alternatively, when you're selling on eBay in earnest, you can purchase your own parcel-protection policy from a private insurer.

Insuring through the major carriers

All the major shippers are in the shipping business (duh), not in the insurance business. Insuring is an annoying — but necessary — sideline to their package-transit businesses.

Most carriers, other than the United States Postal Service, cover all shipments automatically (and at no extra charge) for the first $100 of package value. By the way, the *package value* of an item sold on eBay is the final bid (or Buy It Now) amount. Of course, you can always buy additional package insurance for your shipped items. Should a package get lost or damaged, making a claim opens an entirely new can of worms.

TIP

Note that FedEx and UPS clearly state that they offer "Declared Value Liability" instead of "insurance." Declared value indicates the carrier's liability for a shipment. Both carriers only cover up to $100, and you must pay the fees shown in Table 3-1 for their additional liability coverage.

TABLE 3-1 **Insurance/Liability Domestic Retail Rates for Commercial Carriers**

Shipper	Shipper Rate
FedEx Declared Value	$0.85 per $100 (after first $100 of value) $2.55 minimum
UPS Declared Value	$100.01 to $50,000.00 (after first $100.00 of value) plus $0.65 per each $100.00 (or part of $100.00) up to $50,000.00 $1.95 minimum
USPS	$2.10 for $0.01 – up to $50.00 value
	$2.65 for $50.01 – $100.00 value
	$3.35 for $100.01 – $200.00 value
	$4.40 for $200.01 – $300.00 value
	$5.55 for $300.01 – to $400.00 value
	$6.70 for $400.01 – to $500.00 value
	$9.15 for $500.01 – to $600.00 value
	$9.15 for up to $600.00 value plus $1.25 for each additional $100 of value over $600.00

Getting private, discounted shipping insurance

If you think that printing your own postage is slick, you're gonna love electronic insurance. eBay offers insurance through their ShipCover division at www.shipcover.com. When you purchase postage and print labels through eBay, you can purchase their package insurance. Your insured value may be declared in any amount from the selling price of the item to a maximum of $1,000.

When you purchase ShipCover insurance to cover your USPS parcels through eBay, you are also charged a surplus line tax and stamping fee, as shown in Table 3-2.

TIP

To dissuade "porch pirates" and other nefarious types, consider purchasing private insurance; it's safer. There is no INSURED sticker on the package to draw attention to the value of the item inside the box.

TABLE 3-2 ShipCover Insurance Prices (Domestic and International)

Insured Value	Price in Addition to Postage	Surplus Line Tax	Stamping Fee
$0.01 to $100.00	$1.65	3%	None
$100.01 to $200.00	$3.30	3%	0.20%
$200.01 to $300.00	$4.95	3%	0.20%
$300.01 to $400.00	$6.60	3%	0.20%
$400.01 to $500.00	$8.25	3%	0.20%
$500.01 to $600.00	$9.90	3%	0.20%
$600.01 to $1,000.00	$9.90, plus $1.65 for every additional $100.00 over $600.00	3%	0.20%

A less expensive alternative is used by a large population of professional eBay sellers: Universal Parcel Insurance Coverage (U-PIC) has provided discounted package insurance to sellers since 1989. U-PIC removes the post-office-insurance hassle because you can handle your insurance electronically. You can insure packages that you send through USPS, UPS, FedEx, and other major carriers — even internationally. If you use U-PIC insurance on USPS-shipped packages, you can save up to 85 percent on the carrier's rates.

TIP

U-PIC caters to individual eBay sellers amidst its many big-business clients independently and through its relationship with Endicia. The insurance is also built in to many online postage software platforms.

Here are some great features of the U-PIC service:

>> **No time wasted standing in line at the post office:** The U-PIC service is integrated into online postage solutions or can be purchased on a per-package basis on their website.

>> **Quick payments on claims:** If you have a claim, U-PIC pays it within 7 to 10 business days of receiving all required documents from the carrier.

REMEMBER

As with any insurance policy, assume that if you have many claims against your packages, you can be dropped from the service. (This thought only gives me more impetus to package my items properly — I never want to be banished back to the counter lines!)

>> **Blanket approval:** U-PIC is approved by all major carriers. And turnabout is fair play: All carriers covered must be on the U-PIC approved carrier listing.

>> **Savings:** Again, depending on the quantity and type of items you ship, using U-PIC may save you up to 85 percent on your insurance costs.

FedEx Ground Declared Value and Limits of Liability (Not Insurance Coverage) covers packages up to $100.00. What they charge for items valued over $100 is a bit murky and buried in legalese. UPS coverage for declared value is free for $100 worth of declared value. After $100.01 in value, it's a $2.70 minimum. UPS, too, is not very transparent about exactly what they will charge.

By using U-PIC (see Figure 3-1), you can insure your FedEx and UPS domestic packages for $0.65 to $1.00 per $100.00 value. You can find all their on-demand, online insurance rates at https://u-pic.com/buy-now/item/127Itemid=118.

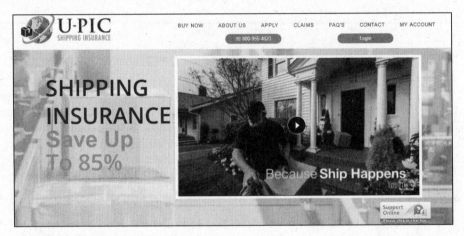

FIGURE 3-1:
The U-PIC
home page.

You can try them out, if you don't want to set up an account yet, by insuring single shipments; do so by clicking the Buy Now tab on their website.

To apply for your own U-PIC policy — with no charge to apply and no minimum premium — click the Apply Now button.

They're a great bunch of people — tell 'em you learned about them in this book!

To place a claim with U-PIC on a shipment, just go to the U-PIC website, click the Claims link, and then choose an option from the File a Claim Online menu. You may need to supply the following:

>> A signed letter, stating the loss or damage from the consignee

>> A completed U-PIC claim form (one claim form per claim)

>> A copy of the original invoice or the end-of-item form

If you're a high-volume shipper, you can negotiate an even lower rate with U-PIC. Call their toll-free number at 800-955-4623. A sales representative will explain to you exactly how to declare value based on your present system.

AUTHOR SAYS

A COUPLE OF CLAIM STORIES

Several years ago, I purchased an original-wardrobe uniform tunic from the *Star Trek* series that was framed and autographed by Leonard Nimoy. When it came, in an appropriate large box surrounded with lots of Styrofoam peanuts and bubble wrap, it also sported a 4-x-4-inch hole in the side of the box, and it looked like someone had taken a sword to the box! Not only that, but there was a sad sound of glass tinkling when I shook the box. Oh, yes — the delivery man had dumped the box, rung the bell, and run.

The carrier couldn't argue about the damage. The claim department tried to give me the line that the item was packed incorrectly. (Does that mean it was sent with a big hole already in the side of the box?) Then they offered me a partial payment. Gee, I really wanted the glass-particle-infested, ripped tunic now. It took a while, but the damages were so obvious that the carrier had to give in and agreed to send a check to the seller. Upon hearing this decision, the seller refunded my payment. (I wonder how long the seller had to wait for *his* payment?)

There was also a dress that I sold and shipped Priority Mail. It never arrived. I had a boiling-hot buyer on the other end, but luckily, I had proof of mailing in the form of a tracking number to show her. I nagged the post office about the package, but as you'll read in the section, "Filing a claim with the post office," you have to wait 30 days for a package to be *officially* declared lost. On the 29th day, the box was returned to me with no explanation or fanfare, and just a return-to-sender stamp on the front.

TIP

If you have the Google toolbar (which I highly recommend in Book 8), or go to www.google.com, you can type any UPS, post office, or FedEx tracking number and find the current tracking information from the carrier's website. Just copy and paste the tracking number into the Google search box and start your search. You'll come to a page that presents a link to package tracking — with your number and carrier showing. Click the link and you end up at the carrier's site with all the current tracking information. Nice!

Making a Claim When Shipping Goes Bad

If you've been selling or buying on eBay for a while, there's a chance that you've made a claim for lost or damaged packages. The process is often grueling — with all the paperwork that's involved — and the decision of the carrier is final. If you don't agree with the carrier, you could try small claims court. But realize that you'll lose a day of work — and when you're in court, you'll face all the legalese you find in the teeny-tiny print on the carrier's terms of service.

I understand the hassles because I've had to make several claims myself. I'd like to help you avoid similar unpleasant experiences, or at least make them less unpleasant. I present information about the U.S. Postal Service first because their claim process is more stringent than that of the other carriers. With any carrier, however, you need to gather the same type of backup information before making a claim.

Filing a claim with the post office

Making a claim with the post office: Oh man, talk about a hassle. But making a claim with any carrier isn't a bowl of cherries on any day. Before making a claim with the USPS, check to make sure your package was covered by postal insurance, purchased at the time of mailing. If you use private insurance instead, you make a claim with your insurance carrier, not the post office.

When a package is lost in transit, you generally must wait a minimum of 21 days after the mailing date before you make the claim; for Priority Mail, you have to make the claim within 15 days. If an item arrives at the buyer's door damaged, you may make a claim with the post office immediately.

There's always a question as to who makes the claim:

>> **Damaged or lost contents:** Either the seller or the buyer can file the claim.

>> **Complete loss:** When a package has not turned up within 30 days, the seller files the claim.

You can file your claim online direct on the USPS site at

    www.usps.com/help/claims.htm

To make a damage claim, you must produce evidence of insurance. This can be either of the following documents:

>> **Original mailing receipt:** The receipt that was stamped at the post-office counter when the item was mailed.

>> **Original box or wrapper:** This must show the addresses of both the sender and the recipient along with whatever tags or stamps the post office put on the package to say it's insured.

You might also be asked to produce evidence showing the value of the item *when it was mailed*. The following list shows some of the documents accepted by the post office for damage claims (however, they may ask for more thorough proof):

» Sales receipt or descriptive invoice

» Copy of your canceled check or money order receipt

» Picture and description of a similar item from a catalog if your receipt isn't available

» A letter from the seller stating the value of the item

» Your own description of the item, including date and time the item was purchased and whether it's new or vintage

For missing packages, you (the seller) should get a dated letter from the buyer stating that the buyer never received the package.

If your buyer is too cranky to cooperate, go to the actual post office where you mailed the package. Ask for a written statement that there is no record of the delivery being made. Postal employees can look up the insurance or delivery confirmation numbers to find whether the delivery took place, but the post office will charge you $6.60 for their efforts. That amount will be reimbursed *if* the post office decides to pay your claim because it doesn't locate your package under a bale of hay in Indiana. If all goes well and your claim is deemed legit, you should get your payment within 30 days. If you don't hear from the post office within 45 days (maybe the payment got lost in the mail?), you have to submit a duplicate claim using the original claim number.

TIP

Note to self (and to you): Always make a copy of any form you give to the government.

AUTHOR SAYS

FINDING OR BUYING LOST PACKAGES

When the post office pays your claim, it will usually ask to keep your item. Your item and thousands of others will end up at one of the Mail Recovery Centers across the country. Here it joins the other lost and salvage mail to be sold, usually at auction.

Items valued over $5 are held for three months, and Registered Mail and insured packages are held for six months. Then they're auctioned. Formerly the "Dead Letter Office," the MRC has had several consolidations that have centralized the operation from four centers into one. The post office Mail Recovery Center is in Atlanta, GA.

The post office sells the stuff via online auctions. If you'd like to check them out, go to www.govdeals.com and search for *USPS*.

Filing a claim with UPS

Whoa! The stories of filing claims with UPS are legendary. Almost any eBay seller can tell you quite a story. I must admit that making a claim with UPS is a good deal easier than making a claim with the post office. After UPS files and accepts your damage claim, you get a check within five days.

For damaged packages, UPS recently streamlined the process, although the buyer must make the claim. You *can* (if you really want to) call 1-800-PICK-UPS (cute, eh?) to file your claim. The better idea is to try the online reporting feature by going to `https://wwwapps.ups.com/webClaims/create?loc=en_US&report_type=1&WT.svl=SubNav` and filling out the form. Be sure you make a damaged item report to UPS immediately.

On the online claim form, you'll be asked to input all information about the package and/or the damage. UPS seems to be familiar with its own handiwork because you get to select your particular type of damage from a menu. After you've filled out and submitted the form, just sit on your haunches and wait for the UPS claims department to contact you.

TIP

I recommend that you print your form after filling it out so you can keep all claim reference information in one place.

REMEMBER

Save the damaged item and all the packaging that it came in. UPS may send an inspector out to look at the package before they approve a claim.

If a UPS shipment appears to be lost, the seller must call UPS to request a package tracer. If UPS is unable to prove delivery, the claim is paid.

Filing a claim with FedEx

Filing a claim with FedEx is similar to the UPS procedure, except FedEx gives you a little more leeway as to time. Instead of the 48-hours-after-delivery deadline, you have 15 business days to make your claim. (This extra time sure helps out when a package is delivered to your house and you're out of town.) FedEx processes all Concealed Loss and Damage claims within five to seven days after receiving all the paperwork and information.

REMEMBER

As with UPS, keep all packaging, along with the item, in case FedEx wants to come and inspect the damage.

You can make your FedEx claim in a couple of ways:

- **By fax:** You can download a PDF claim form with instructions at `http://images.fedex.com/us/customer/claims/Claims_Form_2012.pdf`. Fill out the form and fax it to the number on the form.

- **Online:** Fill out the online claim form by going to `http://www.fedex.com/us/customersupport/managing/claims`.

You must have a FedEx login to begin your claim. (See Chapter 2 in this minibook for instructions on how to get your login.) You still have to mail or fax your supporting documentation. When you file online, you can also choose to receive email updates from FedEx regarding your claim (good idea).

8

Power Selling on eBay

Contents at a Glance

Chapter **1**

Going Pro with Seller Hub

Once the selling bug has bitten you, it's a natural transition to go from listing a few items a month to 20, or 50, or more. And that, dear reader, means you are officially running an eBay business. Congratulations! There's a good and a bad side to this increase. The good is that you're making considerably more money than you did before signing up with eBay. The bad? Well, call it challenging instead: It's time to start using tools to streamline how you do business. This chapter gets you started with some of the best available tools.

Seller Hub is a suite of tools for managing your selling business from your My eBay page.

Getting Seller Hub

As I write this book, eBay is in flux. Currently if you have an active seller account, eBay will opt you in automatically to Seller Hub. If you are a new user who registers as a business, you may already have Seller Hub as your My eBay link.

If you've been on eBay for a while and yearn for the days of using a simpler format, you can still access the old My eBay: All Selling page by scrolling to the Selling Tools box in Seller Hub and clicking *View My eBay Selling.*

Seller Hub Features

Seller Hub allows you to monitor or automate many of the more tedious eBay tasks. The page is divided into several boxes, which I break down here.

You can click the Orders link to view a summary of your sales activities. The Overview page lists at-a-glance statistics so you can see what's going on with your sales quickly, at any time (see Figure 1-1). Links to other pages are enabled by clicking the arrow in the title bar of each box of data.

FIGURE 1-1:
A freshly hatched
Seller Hub
Overview page as
it populates.

Aside from the boxes, there are some powerful links at the top of the Hub after the Overview tab. Each of these headers has a drop-down menu to link you to more data.

» Orders

» Listings

» Marketing

» Performance

Both Orders and Listings have summary boxes on the Overview page, but more detailed information appears when you mouse over the link. I describe the important details of each section further on.

Customize

Looking at the page initially may seem a little disorienting. Scroll up and down the page, and look at the data boxes. If you think you'd prefer not to see some of the options, just click *Customize* in the upper right and you'll be able to remove those areas you don't think you need. You can always click *Customize* again to get them back.

We all like to know how we're doing, and the *Sales (Last 31 days)* area allows you to do just that. A bar chart with percentages shows a sales summary that compares your sales to previous periods and to the market in general.

Seller Level

Once you have received ten Detailed Seller Ratings, the Seller Level Summary box gives you a quick way to check your status on eBay. Clicking on the arrow (or title) on the right of Seller Level will take you to your Seller Dashboard page.

Your Seller Dashboard Summary covers the all-important results of the DSR ratings you get from your buyers. (Find more about Detailed Seller Ratings in Book 1, Chapter 5.) It also keeps you apprised of whether you're following eBay's policies or, instead, have violated any in the recent past.

TIP

If you feel that any of the defects listed on this page are erroneous, go to Help & Support and call eBay to get marks against your reputation expunged. Honest mistakes happen, and you don't want to lose your seller status because of a mistake. Click Help and Support, and click the *Contact us* button at the bottom of the page. After clicking on topics, you'll be presented with the option to call eBay at 866-540-3229 and a passcode with an expiration time. (You can call without the passcode, but it might take longer to get to the right human.)

If you're a Top Rated Seller Plus, you also see your DSR-based Final Value Fee discount (more on that in Book 8, Chapter 3).

On your official Dashboard, like the one in Figure 1-2, you can find out the details of what makes you a good seller in eBay's eyes — and in your customers' eyes, too. Scroll all the way to the bottom to get all the details.

FIGURE 1-2:
My Seller
Dashboard page,
showing details
of my eBay
reputation.

Listings

An important box on Seller Hub Overview page is Listings. You'll get some valuable information there. It references what you did — or didn't — sell, along with even more stats on your sales. This section points out the most important activities you will view once you've got some transactions in progress.

Create Listing

Click the top link on the drop-down menu to put a new item up for sale.

Active Listings

Click the Active Listings link, and you can observe the bidding action just as you can from the My eBay Selling page. The color-coding that indicates auction bidding activity is the same as on the My eBay Selling page. (If the current price is in green and bolded, your item has a bid and the number reflects the high bid. The current price is in red if there are no bids.) Your listings are accessible with a click of your mouse.

You have the option to sort and see only auctions or fixed-price listings on the Active Listings page. You can also search your own listings by keyword or item number.

Unsold Listings

You can access your Unsold ended listings from the links on the left side of the page for easy relisting. You can relist either as an auction or as a fixed price listing.

TIP

You need to know that to be eligible for relisting credit (once you have exceeded your free listings and have to pay insertion fees), the item gets only one shot at reselling. If it's being relisted for a second time, you need to start the listing again by using the Sell Similar link. The Sell Similar link (versus the Relist link) starts the transaction in a new cycle for the sale, thereby making it eligible for the relisting credit if it doesn't sell.

Scheduled Listings

The Scheduled Listings link takes you to any auction or fixed-price listing you've asked eBay to begin at a later time or date. You can also view these pending (scheduled) listings through links that narrow them to listings that start within the next hour — or start today.

When you enter the Scheduled Listings area (by clicking the Scheduled Listings link), you can go directly to any of your listings.

From the Scheduled Listings page, you can confirm all information about the sale, as well as make any changes to the listing or to the scheduling time.

Orders

The Orders link shows you the details of the past 90 days' worth of transactions. You can get to the details by clicking appropriate links in the Orders box (refer to Figure 1-1). You'll find quite a bit of information here, including

>> **Awaiting payment:** This is where items that have been won or bought are shown before a payment is made.

>> **Returns:** Here you'll see the status of your returns. This area can go back as far as the prior 18 months.

>> **Awaiting Shipment:** When a buyer has sent payment through PayPal, the transaction automatically moves to this category.

>> **Paid and Shipped:** After an item is paid for, a reference to it appears here so you can keep abreast of the feedback you need to leave. When you've shipped an item and posted your tracking number, you can also check to see when the item is delivered.

>> **Cases:** This is your Resolution Center where you turn in non-paying buyers and see whether a buyer has opened a complaint on one of your transactions.

WORKING YOUR RESOLUTION CENTER

I hate to see items in the Awaiting Payment area of the Orders page, because it means there's a good chance I might not get paid for an item. I always keep an eye on my Sold, Awaiting Payment items and send out a payment reminder after a day has passed. If you haven't received payment for an item that ended at least two days ago, you can open an Unpaid Item case by clicking the Resolution Center link. Here's a description of some options you see once you've opened a case in the Resolution Center:

- **Open cases:** This is where the items awaiting payment fall when they become eligible for you to file an Unpaid Item case. This happens when seven days have passed without a payment being received.

- **Awaiting other member's response:** After you've filed an Unpaid Item case, the item goes into this area. It links to a dispute page that lists all outstanding disputes. The buyer is expected to answer your dispute here — and you can answer that answer.

- **Final Value Fee credit:** This is the category where buyers go if, after all your attempts to get action, they haven't responded and haven't sent payment. (If they don't cough up within ten days after you file a case, the listing moves to this category automatically.)

- **Items not received or significantly not as described:** Here's where you can see whether a buyer has notified eBay of an item that hasn't shown up when expected or arrived and wasn't what the buyer expected.

In the Resolution Center, you will also be able to handle any cases (cancel transactions when a buyer makes a mistake) that occur during your eBay business.

Selling Tools links

Scroll down the page and you'll see the Selling Tools box on the Overview page. It's a powerful group of links that allow you to download and export your sales history to your computer. Depending on your eBay business, you also have quick links to PayPal, Manage your Store, Sellers you follow, Apps, and to the good old My eBay Selling page — in case you get nostalgic for the old, pre–Seller Hub days.

Getting More from Seller Hub

Within Seller Hub, you'll find lots of handy tools to run your business more efficiently. In this section, I mention some of the most-used features.

Handling order activities

One of my favorite features is that I can follow the progress of my Paid and Shipped sales from this page. When an item has been won or paid for using PayPal, I can click the appropriate link to see the list of items ready for some sale-related action (such as shipping).

Notice the record number next to the buyer's information. To send an eBay message or combined invoice, follow these steps:

1. **Click the record number to the left of the buyer's User ID and name.**

The Transaction Detail record for the sale appears. The Buyer information appears at the top of the page (name, email address, street address, phone number) and any items sold to that buyer are below. (If the buyer has made more than one purchase, you'll see a notation stating as much. You then have the option to click the link to combine purchases in the sales record.)

2. **To send an eBay message to the buyer:**

1. *Click the feedback number next to the buyer's User ID.* This will take you to the buyer's Feedback profile.

2. *On the Feedback profile, click Contact Member.* A window will open, showing the item you have sold to the buyer.

3. *Click the item, then click continue.* An eBay Message contact form appears.

4. *Write your message and click Send the button.*

3. **To send a combined invoice (prior to payment):**

1. *Click one of the record numbers attributed to the buyer's purchase.*

2. *Find the combined purchases button and click it.* Purchases are combined into one transaction, with each item showing its own record number.

3. *Return to the Sold: Awaiting Payment area and click Send Invoice next to the transaction.*

Tracking payments and shipping

Seller Hub makes many selling processes considerably easier. Take a look your Orders⇨All Orders page. From here, you can see how many buyers have paid for their purchases — and how many haven't.

If you've sold items and you're expecting payments, be sure to check this page several times a day. When a buyer makes his or her payment using PayPal, eBay will update your records. (PayPal also sends you a payment-received email.)

After you ship the item, you can indicate any pertinent information on the Sales Records screen. The transaction information is available when you click the record number next to the item that's been shipped. After you ship the item, select the check box next to Shipped On and the date will appear automatically. Now, type in the tracking number (I do this from PayPal as I double-check for buyers' notes before I print a label), and click Save; the record moves from the Sold: Awaiting Shipment page to the Paid and Shipped page. This change is also reflected on the Summary page.

Relisting and Selling Similar Items

Wouldn't it be better if you could select a whole bunch of items and relist them all together? Step up to Seller Hub for a one-click option. You can access items that have not sold, logically enough, from the Unsold Items area. Relisting is accomplished with a click of the mouse.

To relist an item through Seller Hub, follow these steps:

1. **Click Unsold Listings.**

   To do so, click the appropriate tab at the top of the page in Seller Hub (or just link through the Overview page box).

2. **Mark the items to relist (or Sell Similar from the drop-down menu) by selecting the check box next to each item's Title.**

   You may select any or all of the items listed on the page.

3. **Click the Relist button (or the Sell Similar link).**

   The Relist Multiple Items page appears.

4. **Review all the items listed (along with the fees).**

5. **Submit the items by clicking the Submit All button.**

Accessing Seller Hub Reports

I like the Hub because it gives you the opportunity to keep all your selling information in one place. It also provides a downloadable report — in spreadsheet format — that you can archive for your records. Here's the information you can expect to find in the reports:

» **Sales record number:** The number assigned to the transaction by Selling Manager for identification purposes.

» **User ID:** The eBay User ID of the person who purchased the item from you.

» **Buyer zip:** The buyer's Zip code.

» **State:** The state the buyer resides in.

» **Buyer country:** The country your buyer lives in.

» **Item number:** The eBay number assigned to the item when you listed it for sale on the site.

» **Item title:** The title of the listing as it appeared on eBay.

» **Quantity:** The number of items purchased in the transaction.

» **Sale price:** The final selling price of the item.

» **Shipping amount:** The amount you charged for shipping the item.

» **Shipping insurance:** If the buyer paid insurance, it's listed next to his or her sales record.

» **State sales tax:** If you've set up Selling Manager to calculate sales tax for your in-state sales, and sales tax was applied to the item when it was sold, that amount is listed here.

» **Total price:** The GSA (gross sales amount) for the transaction.

» **Payment method:** The method of payment used by the buyer. This is inserted automatically if the item is paid through PayPal, or manually inserted by you into the sales record if paid by another method.

» **Sale date:** The date the transaction occurred on eBay.

» **Checkout:** The date of checkout. This is usually the same as the transaction date.

» **Paid on date:** The date the buyer paid for the item.

» **Shipped on date:** The ship date you entered in Selling Manager.

» **Feedback left:** Whether you left feedback for the buyer is indicated by a Yes or No in this column.

» **Feedback received:** The feedback rating left for you by the buyer (positive, negative, or neutral).

» **Notes to yourself:** If you input any personal notes regarding the transaction in the sales record, they appear here.

Keep in mind that Seller Hub reports are available on the site for only four months, so be sure to download your information regularly.

Notice that there is no column reflecting the eBay fees you paid for listing and selling the item. If you have plenty of time on your hands, you can create another column and input the fees from your eBay invoice for each item. Save time by posting the monthly total once a month in your bookkeeping program.

To get the file from eBay to your computer, follow these steps:

1. **Go to Seller Hub Overview.**

2. **Under Seller Tools, click the File Management Center link.**

   This takes you to the File Management Center.

3. **Click the Create a Download Request link.**

   A Create a Download Request page appears.

4. **Select the records you want from the links provided.**

5. **Select the time period you want to include in your report.**

   It's best to generate monthly or quarterly reports, so that your reports coincide with specific tax periods. You can always combine more than one report in your spreadsheet program to show different periods of time.

6. **Click the Save button.**

   You then see a confirmation page and a confirmation number for your request. eBay will send you an email when your report is ready.

7. **You will receive an email (almost immediately).**

   Click the link in the email, and you're taken to the View Completed Downloads page.

8. **Click the link to download the file.**

   The Save As dialog box appears so you can save the file on your hard drive.

9. **Rename the file to reflect the sales month and year, and then click Save.**

   After the file is downloaded, you'll see a confirmation with your new filename.

It's a good idea to create a directory on your computer with a name such as eBay Sales. In this directory, you can store all the reports you download from eBay, PayPal, or any other online service. Be sure to include this directory when you perform regular data backups.

Now you can open the new file in Microsoft Excel.

With simple spreadsheet commands, you can customize the look of your report. For example, if the column for Buyer Country is unnecessary for your records (for example, if you ship only within the United States, that information is not useful), you can delete the column in two quick steps:

1. **Highlight the column by clicking the column letter.**

2. **Choose File⇨Cells⇨Delete.**

    Voilà! The offending column is no more.

TIP

All spreadsheet tasks mentioned here can be performed in similar fashion in Google Docs.

The spreadsheet generated by Seller Hub is much more useful if you total the columns. That way, you can see your total sales at a glance. To total a spreadsheet column:

1. **Click in the blank cell at the bottom of the column you want to total.**

2. **Click and drag over the cells you want to sum.**

3. **Click the AutoSum (Σ) button (also found under Formulas tab).**

4. **The total appears.**

If you want to total the columns next to the one you just totaled, you don't have to re-input the formula. Just highlight the results cell from your last formula, and highlight cells in the same row that you want to contain totals of the columns. Then under Editing, click below the Σ symbol to fill cells to the right. This copies the formula to the connecting cells and all the columns are totaled.

Chapter **2**

Managing Sales with eBay Apps and Third-Party Tools

When you get to the point of running up to 20 listings at a time, I highly recommend that you begin to use a management tool. At that point, eBay will most likely port your account from My eBay to Seller Hub. But when your eBay business begins to push 100 listings a week, I recommend that you consider getting additional help in the form of an app or software.

Whether you use an online service (SaaS) or software residing on your own computer is a personal decision. You may find it easier to use an online system because you can log on to your selling information at any time from any computer. But if you want to archive your work locally (as I do), you may prefer an app that does the work on your computer and uploads the final products to eBay.

Most desktop-based software packages have features that enable you to do your work on your computer and then upload (or download) your data when you go online.

In either case, if your business has reached the level where you need a listing or management tool, congratulations! In this chapter, I want to save you some time finding the service or software that's right for you. I outline some of the tasks that a management product would preferably provide, and compare prices of several services.

Finding Function-Specific Apps

A visit to the eBay Apps Center will dazzle you with hundreds of third-party applications that have all been verified by eBay. Such verification means that these apps should always be up to date and ready for any of eBay's changes.

You'll find apps designed for many functions that fall into categories such as checkout, customer support, finance and accounting, inventory listing, marketing and merchandising, research and reporting, shipping and payments, and sourcing. They integrate directly with the eBay.com interface for sellers in the United States.

The apps in the center are the brain-children of developers who have been vetted to join the eBay Developers program, and they're offered in the eBay Apps Center only after rigorous testing. When you visit the Apps Center, you find reviews and ratings from other eBay sellers. Take the time to read these comments to see whether an app is right for you.

Find the eBay Apps Center (shown in Figure 2-1) from your My eBay page by clicking Applications and then the Apps Center link. You can also find it by going directly to

```
https://applications.ebay.com/
```

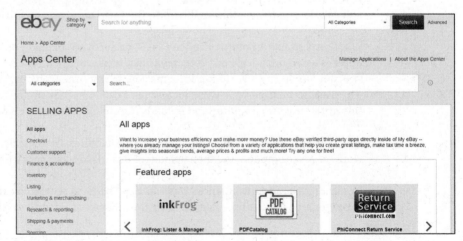

FIGURE 2-1:
Many handy apps
are available at
the Apps Center.

Although the Apps Center has many choices, you may find that some of them just don't fit your business style. The remaining sections in this chapter give you tips and ideas on saving time and money by using such software.

Choosing Your Management Tools

If you searched the Internet for eBay management services and software, you'd come up with a bunch. After speaking to many sellers, I've found online services that offer two important features:

>> **Uptime reliability:** Uptime is vital here; you don't want the server that holds your photos going down or mislaunching your sales.

>> **Regular updates:** Ask if their software is continually updated to match eBay changes.

Using a site or software to run your sales takes practice, so I suggest you try any that appeal to you and that offer free preview trials. As I describe a few different applications, I include a link so you can check them out further.

REMEMBER

Some software and services work on a monthly fee; others work on a one-time purchase fee. For a one-time-purchase software application to truly benefit you, it must have the reputation for updating its software each time eBay makes a change to its procedures and policies. The programs I discuss in this chapter have been upgraded continually to date.

WARNING

Most services have a free trial period. Be sure that you don't spend a bunch of your precious time inputting your entire inventory, only to discover you don't like the way the service works. Instead, input a few items to give the service a whirl.

There's a huge difference between auction-*listing* software and sites and auction-*management* products. When your business activity level increases and you turn to an auction-management solution for your eBay business, you should look for certain standard features (described next). Also consider what information-management features you currently have through your bookkeeping program (see Book 9). You have the data there, regardless of whether you use it in a management solution.

Looking for Essential Features

Here are some important features to look for when you evaluate the offerings of auction-management services and products:

>> **Image hosting:** Some hosts dazzle you with gigabytes of image storage. Keep one thing in mind: eBay requires images now to be at least 500 pixels on one side; this means your images will hover around 1MB in size. This means you could store approximately 1,000 pictures in a 1GB storage space. Since most people upload their pictures to eBay, you will probably not have a need to use an image host. If you have a website, you might just host your own images in a folder there. (Read more about this option in Book 5.)

TIP

All your eBay images should ideally be archived on your computer (or removable drive) — how about in a folder called *eBay Images*?

>> **Listing design tools:** The basis of most of these products is a good listing function. With the advent of mobile, people are not looking as much for great design. They want a listing with the facts — and good images. Be sure to use a spell checker. There's nothing worse than sloppy spelling in a listing.

>> **Listing uploading tools:** Most products have a feature that launches a group of listings to eBay all at once. They may also allow you to schedule auctions to get underway at a prescribed time.

>> **Bulk listing:** You can also expect to be able to put together your listings at your leisure offline and upload them to your service. Most products archive your past listings so that you can relist at any time. Many services also offer bulk relisting.

>> **Email management:** You may be provided with editable email letters (templates) that you can customize with your own look and feel.

>> **Feedback automation:** Post feedback in bulk to a number of your buyers, or leave pre-designed feedback for each, one by one. Some products support automatic positive feedback that kicks in when a buyer leaves you positive feedback.

Exploring Advanced Features

Depending on the type of business you run, you may need some of the more advanced features offered by management products:

>> **Inventory tools:** Management products may allow you to create inventory records for your different products, such that you can click a bunch of them to list them automatically. When an item is sold, the tool deducts the item from your inventory automatically.

>> **Sales-tax tracking and invoicing:** With full management, you can expect your sales tax to be calculated into your invoices and complete line-item invoices to be sent automatically. Multiple items, when purchased by the same buyer, will be combined.

>> **Consignment tracking:** If you sell on eBay for others, be sure to look for a product that enables you to separately track the products you sell for your clients. You should also be able to produce reports of consignment sales by customer.

>> **Shipping:** Most of the services will give you the option of printing your packing lists and shipping labels directly from the product.

Finding More to Automate

Now that eBay has become a world marketplace, a single-page auction or item listing is becoming an increasingly valuable piece of real estate. Millions may view your sale, and the more auctions and fixed-price items that you can list, the better your chance to make a good living. Time is money: You need to post quickly and accurately.

Posting auctions, keeping records, cataloging inventory, managing photos, and gathering statistics are all tasks that you can automate. The more your business grows, the more confusing details may become. Automated tools can help you keep it all straight.

REMEMBER

However, the more paid tools you use, the more expense you may be adding to your business. Always keep your bottom line in mind when evaluating whether to use fee-based software and services — eBay's beginner Seller Hub is free.

You'll have to perform back office tasks, no matter how few (or how many) listings you're running. Depending on your personal business style, you may want to automate any or all of the following tasks. You may choose to use a single program, a manual method, or use some features from one program and some from others. For those who aren't ready for the automated plunge, I offer alternatives here. Where appropriate, I insert references that guide you to places in this book (or on the web) where you can find more information about the automated services I discuss.

Setting up a link to your eBay listings

Until you get an eBay Store, set up a link to your listings from your website or blog as a great alternative. That way, visitors to your site can browse your listings directly on eBay. You can produce your own listing gallery without any fancy programs or auction-management software, and at no additional cost.

To make a link to your eBay listings without installing fancy scripts, you need to do two things:

1. **Test the following URL in your browser, substituting your own User ID in place of the bold italics:**

   ```
   www.ebay.com/sch/merchant/yourUserID
   ```

   Figure 2-2 shows a sample of what you'll see.

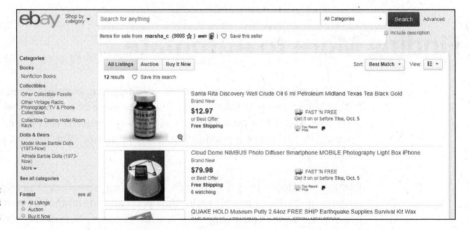

FIGURE 2-2: My eBay listings from the link.

2. **After checking your link, insert the following HTML into your site to include a link to your eBay sales:**

   ```
   <a href="http:// www.ebay.com/sch/
     merchant/yourUserID"><b>Click <I>here</I> to view
     YourUserID Gallery</b></a>
   ```

   You can also use this in your emails to customers to show them just what's for sale at any given moment.

Automating end-of-auction email

If you want to set up emails to be sent automatically after an auction ends, you must use a software application. The software should download your final auction results, generate the email, and let you preview the email before sending it out. Many of the online sites discussed later in this chapter send out winner confirmation emails automatically when an auction is over.

Keeping inventory

Many eBay sellers depend on the notebook method — crossing off items as they're sold. If that works for you, great. Others prefer to use an Excel spreadsheet to keep track of inventory.

Most of the management packages handle inventory for you. They automatically deduct an item from inventory when you launch an auction or when the item ships. You have your choice of handling inventory directly on your computer or keeping your inventory online with a service that's accessible from any computer, wherever you are.

I handle my inventory on my desktop through QuickBooks. When I buy merchandise to sell, and I post the bill to QuickBooks, it automatically puts the merchandise into inventory. When I post my sale, it deducts the items sold from standing inventory. I can view a status report whenever I want to see how much I have left — or have to order.

Composing HTML for listings

Fancy descriptions are nice, but fancy doesn't make the item sell any better. Competitive pricing and low (free?) shipping rates work in your favor — especially with Best Match search. Also, a clean listing with as many photos as necessary goes a long way toward selling your product. Some software and services offer a large selection of templates you can use to gussy up your descriptions.

The use of simple HTML doesn't slow the loading of your page, but the addition of miscellaneous images (decorative backgrounds and animations) can make viewing your item a distasteful chore.

Don't fret; you can make do by repeatedly incorporating two or three simple HTML templates, cutting and pasting new text as necessary. Most listing programs offer you several template choices. I recommend that you stick with a few that are similar, giving a standardized look to your listings — which is just the way major companies give a standardized look to *their* advertising and identity.

Your customers will get used to the look of your auctions and feel comfortable each time they see one.

I use SeaMonkey Composer (a free program from the people who brought us the Firefox Internet browser) to generate much of my code for auction descriptions. Visit Book 5, Chapter 3 for more information on this handy program.

TIP

An important line of code that everyone seems to forget is the one that inserts a picture into your auction description. You need (due to eBay policy) to embed any images that have text you inserted within your description. These types of images are no longer allowed as your main eBay pictures. On the Sell an Item page, click the tab to view in HTML mode, and insert the following line below where you'd like your image to appear in your description:

```
<img src="http://www.yourwebsiteserver.com/imagename.jpg">
```

Be sure to substitute your own server and image name. If you want to put one picture above another, type `<p>` and then repeat the HTML line with a different image name.

Scheduling listings for bulk upload

If you're a store owner and want to schedule a future automated launch of your listings without incurring eBay's $.10 fee, you must use an online management service (check out the "Opting for Third-Party Management" section).

Checking out

When someone wins or buys an item, eBay's checkout integrates directly with PayPal. If you're closing less than 100 sales a day, that's all you need. eBay and PayPal will also send an email to you and the buyer so that you can arrange for payment.

A personalized winner's notification email can easily contain a link to pay, making a checkout service unnecessary.

Printing shipping labels

Printing shipping labels without printing postage can be the beginning of a laborious two-step process. I recommend alternatives: Endicia (for Mac and Windows), Stamps (Windows), and eBay for all operating systems — all of which can print your labels and postage in one step. Check out Book 7, Chapter 1 for information on how this works.

Generating customized reports

Sales reports, ledgers, and tax information are all important reports that you should have in your business. Online services and software supply different flavors of these reports.

PayPal allows you to download your sales data into a format compatible with QuickBooks. You can also choose to download your data in Excel spreadsheet format. PayPal reports are full of intensely detailed information about your sales and deposits. Putting this information in a standard accounting software program on a regular basis can make your year-end calculations easier to bear.

Opting for Third-Party Management

You may want to run your business from any computer, anywhere in the world. If that's the case, you might do best with an online service. Auction-management websites handle almost everything, from inventory management to label printing. Some sellers prefer online (or hosted) management sites because you can access your information from any computer. You might use every feature a site offers, or you might choose a bit from column A and a bit from column B and perform the more personalized tasks manually. Read on to determine what service might best suit your needs.

Although quite a few excellent online services for automating sales are available, I have room here to show you only a few. Many services are similar in format, so in the following sections I point out some of the highlights of a few representative systems.

SixBit Software

The developers at SixBit are no newcomers to eBay business. I first used their original Auction Assistant software in 1997, and they have been upgrading their game with new versions ever since. The founder, John Slocum, has changed with the times and offers a full-featured desktop ecommerce tool for multiple selling platforms, as shown in Figure 2-3. You'll be able to expand your business (if you want to) to venues such as Etsy and Amazon as well as eBay.

FIGURE 2-3:
SixBit Software
has every level
of ecommerce
businesses
covered.

At SixBit you'll find pricing for different levels of sellers. The software can grow with your business by unlocking newer features on each level as your revenues progress. You'll find a trove of instructional videos on the site to help you learn the software.

You'll find all the previously listed important features in their packages, including some of the most rare: consignment selling (with full reporting), product pricing research, and drop-shipping management.

To learn more and get a free trial, visit

```
www.sixbitsoftware.com
```

Vendio

I have fond memories of the early days on AuctionWeb (the forerunner of eBay). Some are especially about the other folks I met when we were all starting out with the online selling experience. The site (originally AuctionWatch) was founded in summer of 1998 as a message board for online sellers. Hard work pays off, because today that site is Vendio (www.vendio.com) — and it has served more than a million sellers over the years to improve their bottom line.

One of the things that makes Vendio unique is its range of offerings. In addition to auction management, Vendio has a full complement of research tools and other offerings. Each tool, should you choose to use it, is offered *a la carte*.

TIP

Vendio offers a customizable store you can place on your own web space — at no additional charge. When you set up your store, all your listed items are seamlessly integrated. To get current information and sign up for a free trial, go to `www.vendio.com`.

Auction Wizard 2000

Way back in 1999, Standing Wave Software developed a product that would handle large inventories and meet the needs of the growing eBay population. Enter Auction Wizard. In 2000, the company introduced a more robust version, Auction Wizard 2000, to meet the challenges presented by changes on eBay.

This software is an auction-management workhorse, whose pieces are integrated into one program. Some of its special features enable you to

>> **Handle consignment sales.** Keep track of consignment sales by consignees, including all fees.

>> **Edit your images before uploading.** The software allows you to import your images, and crop, rotate, or resize images for your auctions.

>> **Upload your pictures with built-in FTP software.** You can do this while you're working on your auctions, eliminating the need for another piece of auction-business software.

The program interface is straightforward. I always plunge into new programs without reading the instructions, and I was able to use this program right off the bat. I'm still not a whiz at it, but that's probably because Auction Wizard 2000 has so many features that I haven't had the time to study them all.

Visit the Auction Wizard 2000 website for a trial:

`www.auctionwizard2000.com`

Chapter **3**

Attaining PowerSeller and Top Rated Seller Status

When you browse through items on eBay, you're bound to notice a Top Rated Plus icon next to a member's User ID. To the uninitiated, this may look like an award given to a seller for selling thousands of items on eBay — but it's not. The eBay Top Rated Plus status is given only to those sellers who uphold the highest levels of professionalism and customer service on the site. Take a look at mine in Figure 3-1.

FIGURE 3-1:
My Top Rated Seller Plus badge as proudly displayed on an item page.

Seller information
marsha_c (8982 ⭐) **me**
100% Positive feedback

There are three levels of upgraded status for eBay sellers:

>> **PowerSellers:** These members have to maintain certain levels of gross merchandise sales (total dollar amount of eBay sales — GMS in eBay-speak), and they must get there by providing excellent customer service.

>> **Top Rated Sellers:** eBay sellers at this level don't have to have as large a volume of sales as an eBay PowerSeller, but they face stricter customer service requirements.

>> **Top Rated Seller Plus:** Only the sellers who fully commit to their businesses get this status. In searches, only Top Rated Plus sellers have badges next to their listings.

You may notice that many sellers on the site with feedback ratings in the tens of thousands do not have the Top Rated Plus badge on their listings. That isn't a comment on whether they're good people; it's just that some of their transactions may have gone not-so-good. In this case, be sure to check the seller's feedback and thoughtfully evaluate it. Many times buyers do not read the seller's policies before they buy — and then give negative feedback (as in the case of buyers not reading the seller's warnings when buying liquidation merchandise). See Book 4, Chapter 4 for more on that type of product.

In this chapter, I tell you what it takes to join these exclusive eBay sellers — and the benefits that the status offers. To check for new updates on these seller requirements, visit eBay at

```
http://pages.ebay.com/br/en-us/services/buyandsell/powerseller/
criteria.html
```

eBay COMMUNITY VALUES

The eBay community values aren't taken lightly by the eBay community and eBay employees. The values were set out early on by the company's founder, Pierre Omidyar.

- We believe people are basically good.

- We believe everyone has something to contribute.

- We believe that an honest, open environment can bring out the best in people.

- We recognize and respect everyone as a unique individual.

- We encourage you to treat others the way that you want to be treated.

All eBay sellers are expected to uphold these tenets in all their dealings on the site. Okay, no snickering from the peanut gallery; we all know that quite a few sellers don't follow these precepts. But then, they're not PowerSellers or Top Rated Sellers, are they?

Becoming an eBay Elite Seller

Aside from the benefits mentioned throughout this chapter, consider this very important reason to be recognized on eBay: eBay's Best Match search algorithm weighs every item and every seller. Attaining recognition as a seller who is in business seriously makes a difference in how prominently your listings are displayed on eBay.

Joining PowerSeller ranks

The ranks of PowerSellers have five levels of membership, depending on your monthly sales, as shown in Table 3-1. Each PowerSeller tier gives the seller more privileges from eBay. One of the most valuable benefits is that when an issue needs to be addressed with eBay, PowerSellers can access priority customer-service support.

TABLE 3-1

PowerSeller Tier Sales Volume Requirements

Tier	Annual GMS ($)	Transactions
Bronze	$1,000	or 100
Silver	$3,000	or 300
Gold	$10,000	or 1,000
Platinum	$25,000	or 2,500 items
Titanium	$150,000	or 15,000 items

To become a PowerSeller on eBay, you must fulfill the following requirements:

>> **Be an active eBay member for at least 90 days.**

>> **Sell a minimum of $1000 in sales and 100 transactions, over the past 12 months.**

>> **Buyer Protection cases must have no more than 0.30 percent of transactions result in the eBay Money Back Guarantee and PayPal Purchase Protection cases closed without seller resolution.**

>> **Maintain at least a 98 feedback percentage in the past 12 months.**

>> **Keep your eBay account current.**

>> **Comply with all eBay policies.** To obtain or keep PowerSeller status, you must not exceed the following:

- *Bronze level:* 4 violations in a 90-day period
- *Silver/Gold levels:* 5 violations in a 90-day period
- *Platinum level:* 6 violations in a 90-day period
- *Titanium level:* 7 violations in a 90-day period

>> **Maintain a minimum rating of 4.5 or higher for the past 12 months in all four Detailed Seller Ratings (DSRs).** Occurrences of 1s and 2s on DSRs with U.S. buyers may not exceed the following rates and counts:

- *Items as described:* 3 percent and a count of 3
- *Communication:* 4 percent and a count of 4
- *Shipping time:* 4 percent and a count of 4
- *Shipping & handling charges:* 4 percent and a count of 4

>> **Run your business by upholding eBay's community values (see the earlier sidebar).**

PowerSeller eligibility is reviewed every three months. You can track your progress on your Seller Dashboard. (I tell you more about Seller Dashboard in Book 2, Chapter 5.)

Becoming a Top Rated Seller

Becoming a PowerSeller is good, but Top Rated Seller status gives you better ranking in searches and more benefits (read on). Top Rated status is reviewed monthly. As a Top Rated Seller, your Feedback profile page will show your ranking (Figure 3-2 shows an example).

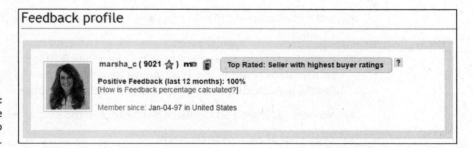

FIGURE 3-2:
Feedback profile page of a Top Rated Seller.

To become a Top Rated Seller on eBay, fulfill the following requirements:

» Be an active eBay member for at least 90 days.

» Complete 100 or more transactions with U.S. buyers within the past year.

» Sell a minimum of $3,000 in annual sales to U.S. buyers.

» Buyer Protection cases must be less than .5 percent of your total number of transactions with U.S. buyers.

» Maintain at least a 98 feedback percentage.

» Keep your eBay account current and comply with all eBay policies.

» You must have less than 3 percent of your transactions show late shipping.

» Your *defect rate* is the percentage of your transactions that close with some violation of the eBay Money Back Guarantee or the PayPal Purchase Protection. No more than .5 percent of your transactions may have one or more defects.

» Tracking numbers must be uploaded to eBay/PayPal for at least 95 percent of your transactions within your promised Handling Time.

» 1 Business Day Handling Time. Handling time is measured in business days (Monday through Friday). You must upload tracking information no later than 11:59:59 p.m. Pacific Time the next day. If purchases are made on weekends, tracking must be uploaded Monday before 11:59:29 p.m. Pacific Time.

TIP

All the above shipping requirements are based on whether your carrier (USPS, FedEx, or UPS) has scanned the package into its system. Sometimes the USPS is lax in this regard. Be sure to ask the person receiving your package to scan it. I often stand there and watch them. No, really. It matters. eBay receives this electronic information from the post office and bases your ratings on the scan times and dates.

Top Rated Seller eligibility is reviewed every three months. You can track your progress on your Seller Dashboard (more on the Dashboard in Chapter 1 in this minibook).

Getting highlighted on eBay: Top Rated Plus

To align with evolving consumer expectations, eBay updated the Top Rated Seller status to "Plus." These are the only sellers that receive a badge; the Top Rated Plus seal (see Figure 3-3) appears on all these seller's listings.

FIGURE 3-3:
The eBay Top
Rated Seller Plus
badge appears
in item search
results.

Also, on the Feedback profile page of all Top Rated Sellers, this recognition is displayed: "Top Rated: Seller with highest buyer ratings."

It isn't a very big jump to attain "Plus" status after you're a Top Rated Seller. After you meet the Top Rated Seller requirements, you have to meet only these two additional requirements:

>> **One-day handling:** Include one-day handling in your listings (meaning you ship within one day of purchase) and post the tracking.

>> **Money-back return policy:** Offer a money back, 30-day (or longer) return policy.

Many sellers find these last two requirements too onerous and don't even attempt Top Rated Plus status. That's a bit short sighted. Read on to find out about a benefit that affects your bottom line.

The Benefits of Membership

As an eBay recognized seller, you get a few perks that can help you build your business. The efforts you put into servicing your customers and selling on eBay are rewarded through the PowerSeller and Top Rated Seller programs.

PowerSeller perks

As a PowerSeller member, you have privileges. There are several invitation-only PowerSeller groups and you benefit from things that boost your bottom line like unpaid item protection.

AUTOMATIC FIVE-STAR DETAILED SELLER RATINGS (DSRs)

eBay has come to value that the highest-quality sellers give people the best buying experience on the site. So they've devised a plan (tied into those gnarly Detailed Seller Ratings) to reward those who play by the rules.

A distinct benefit of following good customer-service policies is that you boost your positive feedback if you follow the rules given here. (Note that some of the stars in the rating will be grayed out when your buyer goes to leave you feedback.)

- **Communication:** If there is no contact between you and your buyer (you provide complete, relevant descriptions — to the point that the buyer gets all the information right from your listing) and you specify one-day handling time, when the buyer leaves you feedback, you will automatically receive a Five-Star rating.

- **Shipping Time:** Buyers will not be able to leave a score of less than five stars if you specified one-day handling and upload the tracking numbers by the end of the next business day (11:59 p.m. Pacific Time) after the buyer's payment clears. Also, delivery must be confirmed (via the tracking numbers) within four business days from when the payment clears, or within your shipping mode's estimated delivery time if less than four days.

- **Shipping Cost:** If you offer free shipping and the buyer takes advantage of that option, the buyer cannot lower your rating in this category.

In addition to participating in their own discussion board, eBay PowerSellers get other benefits:

» **Unpaid Item Protection:** PowerSellers not only get credit for the Final Value Fee and listing fee when faced with a non-paying buyer, they also get a credit for any Listing Upgrade Fees (for example, Buy It Now, Bold, or Subtitle) — you know, all that extra fluff. It adds up.

» **Shipping rate discounts:** You can save on UPS, USPS, and FedEx shipping when printing through eBay Labels. Please note that the Commercial base pricing may be cheaper when printing your own labels.

Top Rated Seller benefits

Top Rated Sellers have entered a high level of eBay benefits. They get the Unpaid Item Protection as PowerSellers do, as well as access to the discussion board and the shipping discounts. There are added benefits:

>> **Increased visibility in Best Match search:** Now eBay gives the advantage to the listings of the upper half of sellers in terms of buyer satisfaction. Sellers with highest detailed seller ratings within the last 30 days receive more exposure than the average seller.

>> **USPS Commercial Plus pricing:** Top Rated (or sellers who ship 300 or more transactions per month) get this rate when you print labels on eBay.

Top Rated Seller Plus benefits

When you have met all requirements and attain the Top Rated Seller Plus status, you get these additional perks:

>> **Badge:** eBay will display the Top Rated Seller Plus badge on your listings.

>> **Higher search ranking:** You get maximum exposure in searches.

>> **10-percent discount on Final Value Fees:** eBay discounts the Final Value Fees on the monthly bill to those who maintain high standards and meet the Top Rated Seller Plus requirements.

Chapter 4

Deciding When You Need an eBay Store

I f you're doing well selling your items on eBay, are you itching to open an eBay Store? Have you used the eBay Buy It Now feature in one of your listings? Have you sold via Fixed Price listings? Did either work for you? If you're a highly active seller, having an eBay Store may help your business (plus you get more free listings a month and other benefits).

Opening an eBay Store can expand a successful business. An eBay Store provides you with your own little corner of eBay where you can leverage your good relationships with your customers and sell directly to them. But the eBay Stores platform is not a total solution, and having an eBay Store is no one-way ticket to Easy Street. (There's no such ticket anyway. But you knew that.)

I get emails all the time from people who open their own eBay Stores and are still not successful in moving merchandise. Why? Because running an eBay Store is not an instant key to success. And because you can sell on eBay without having a designated eBay Store. No matter how many money-back guarantees you receive from online gurus promising magical success on eBay, the only magic is putting your shoulder, nose, and whatever else to the grindstone — and exerting the effort necessary to bring customers to your store.

If you're running many listings and your business is doing well, the discounts on fees, upgrades, and more may be reason enough to open a store. The decision should be financial. This chapter should give you all the information you need to make a thoughtful decision.

TIP

If you're just beginning on eBay, the best advice I can give you is to hold off on opening an eBay Store until your feedback rating is over 100. Participating in transactions on eBay is a natural teacher; you'll see mistakes that sellers make when they sell to you. Some sellers are plain unfriendly, and by buying and selling on eBay you'll have a true understanding of how quality customer service will help you build your business. You'll also learn from your own mistakes and be able to provide better service to your customers.

Locating Your Special Place Online

When you're opening an eBay Store, you have just three main rules to remember and apply: location, location, location. If you were going to open a brick-and-mortar store, you could open it (for example) in the corner strip mall, at a shopping center, or even in a suburb. You'd have to decide in what location your store would do best; that goes for an online store as well. You'll find tons of locations where you can open an online store, including sites such as Amazon.com, Etsy, and (of course) eBay.

You have to pay rent for your online store, of course, but opening and running an online store isn't nearly as expensive as doing the same for a tangible store in the real world (where you also have to pay electrical bills, maintenance bills, and more). Plus, the ratio of rent to (hopefully successful) sales makes an online store a much easier financial decision, and your store's exposure to the buying public can be huge.

Checking Out Online Stores Galore

According to comScore, in June 2017, these ecommerce sites garnered an astounding number of *unique* visitors (counting *all* of one person's visits to the sites just *once* a month) from home, work, and university locations:

>> **Walmart:** 89,322,000

Think about this when you consider whether people are still shopping the web looking for bargains.

>> **eBay:** 90,145,000

>> **Craigslist:** 61,580,000 (October 2016)

>> **Apple, Inc.:** 140,939,000

>> **Amazon.com:** 180,032,000 (This total includes all Amazon sites.)

Back in the day, eBay must have felt competition from the Yahoo! Small Business feature and from Amazon.com — and so decided to open its doors (in July 2001) to sellers who wanted their own online stores. Originally, those stores represented fixed-price sales and were a normal progression so eBay could continue as the world's marketplace.

eBay itself is a kind of online store that specializes in selling *your* stuff, not *theirs.* You're not competing with your landlord. In addition to its staggering number of visitors, eBay offers different levels of store rent and benefits; some are shown in Table 4-1.

TABLE 4-1   **Costs for an eBay Store**

	Basic	Premium	Anchor
Basic rent	$19.95 (or $24.95 on a month-to-month basis)	$59.95 (or $74.95 on a month-to-month basis)	$299.95 (or $349.95 for month-to-month)
Unlimited insertion fee for auctions that end in a sale	✔	✔	✔
Discounted auction insertion fee (unsuccessful)	25¢	15¢	10¢
Number of free fixed price insertion fee listings	250	500	1,000
Additional fixed price listing insertion fee	20¢	10¢	5¢
Final value fees	3.5% - 9.15%	3.5% - 9.15%	3.5% - 9.15%
Vacation hold to put listings and Store "on hold" while you're away	✔	✔	✔

eBay Stores can feature both auctions and fixed-price listings — happily, the Buy It Now items you list are as easy to handle as auctions. To review the prices and rules before you open your eBay Store, go to

`http://pages.ebay.com/seller-center/stores/subscriptions.html`

When you're ready to get down to virtual brass tacks, the details of setting up your eBay Store are available on this web page:

http://pages.ebay.com/seller-center/stores/branding.html

Choosing Between Store Types

All eBay Stores are on a level playing field. All your items are equally searchable on eBay, so you can be right up there with the big guys and compete. The first cost differential is the type of store you want to open.

Even the basic eBay Store ($19.95 per month when paid yearly) gives you a lot of options; higher-level stores build on these. Here are my favorite highlights:

>> **Listings:** All your eBay listings, whether auction or fixed-price, will appear in your eBay Store.

>> **Custom URL (web address):** Your eBay Store will have its own Internet address that you can use in links in promotional material — even to promote your store on the Internet. (My eBay Store address is http://stores.ebay.com/Marsha-Colliers-Fabulous-Finds.)

>> **Store search:** When customers visit your eBay Store, they will be able to search within your listings for their desired item — with your own personal search engine.

>> **Three hundred store categories:** You can sell (say) sporting goods in one category, women's fashion in another, fine art in one more . . . you have up to 300 custom categories for your varied merchandise.

>> **Custom store header:** Get your own brand by designing a graphic store header.

>> **Markdown Manager:** Hold a sale in your store! Select items to discount for a period of time and offer discounted pricing.

>> **Vacation hold:** Ever wish you could make your listings temporarily unavailable, or let your customers know you'll be out of town? This great feature allows you to do just that.

>> **Create Promotional Flyers:** Online tool to help you design a flyer to promote other items and include in your shipments.

>> **Search engine keyword management:** You may customize search engine keywords in Manage My Store to improve your store's page rankings in the search engines to which eBay feeds.

REMEMBER

When people visit your eBay Store, they have no way of knowing whether you have a Basic, Premium (or Featured), or Anchor Store. The design of your store is up to you — you can make it as fancy as you want.

Knowing the Fee Structure

When you have an eBay Store, other fees are involved (are you surprised?). In addition to the monthly fee, you'll have to take note of options fees and Final Value Fees. These fees are different for eBay Store sellers than for those selling on eBay without a store.

Items sold by eBay Store owners carry a fee structure similar to that of items listed on the eBay site, but the actual numbers and percentages are different. The difference in cost helps you decide which items to put in your store, your auctions, or on your website. Knowing the prices in Tables 4-2, 4-3, and 4-4 upfront helps you to decide what you need to get for each item in the different sales formats.

TABLE 4-2   **Store Inventory Listing Upgrades**

Upgrade	Starting or Buy It Now price: under $150		Starting or Buy It Now price: over $150	
Upgrade	1-, 3-, 5-, 7-, and 10-day duration	30-day and Good 'Til Cancelled	1-, 3-, 5-, 7-, and 10-day duration	30-day and Good 'Til Cancelled
Gallery Plus	0.35	1.00	0.70	2.00
Item subtitle	0.50	1.50	1.00	3.00
Listing Designer	0.10	0.30	0.20	0.60
Bold	2.00	4.00	3.00	6.00
Value Pack (Gallery Plus, Listing Designer, and Subtitle)	0.65	2.00	1.30	4.00

TABLE 4-3

Store Final Value Fees

Categories	Final Value Fee (Maximum $250)
Computers/Tablets & Networking Video Game Consoles	4%
Consumer Electronics Cameras & Photos Coins & Paper Money Stamps	6.15%
Musical Instruments & Gear	7.15%
Motors Parts & Accessories	8.15%
Clothing, Shoes, & Accessories	9.15%
Collectibles	9.15%
Home & Garden	9.15%
Camera & Photo Accessories	9.15%
Cell Phone Accessories	9.15%
All Other Categories	9.15%

TABLE 4-4

Advanced Upgrade Fees

Option	Price	FEE
Buy It Now	$0.99-$9.99	$0.05
	$10-$24.99	$.10
	$25 - $49.99	$.20
	$50 or more	$.25
Reserve Price	$0.01-$74.99	$3.00
	$75.00 or more	4% of reserve price (Maximum $100)

Selecting Your eBay Store Name

If you saw the show *GirlBoss* on Netflix, you'll know that the main character, after reading this section in one of my early books, spent an entire episode deciding on her eBay Store's name. Yes, it's that important.

So once you've decided to take the plunge and open an eBay Store, you need to think of a good name. The name doesn't have to match your eBay User ID, but both names are more recognizable if they relate clearly to each other. You can use your company name, your business name, or a name that describes the soul of your business. I recommend that you use the same name for your eBay Store that you plan to use in all your online businesses. By doing so, you begin to create an identity (or, as the pros call it, a *brand*) that customers will come to recognize and trust.

REMEMBER

Your online eBay Store should not replace your ecommerce-enabled website (see Book 6), but instead, should be an extension of it. When people shop your eBay Store, take the opportunity to make them customers of your website through your package inserts. Good deal!

Setting Up Shop

It's time to get down to business. You get to the eBay Stores hub page as follows: At the bottom of the home page, you'll find a link menu. Click the Stores link from the Buy area of this menu, and on the right side of the resulting page, click the Open a Store link on the right. This takes you to the Seller's Hub of eBay Stores. If you click all the links you see here, you get the eBay company line about how good an eBay Store can be for your business. Okay, you already *know* how good an eBay Store can be for your business, so skip the propaganda and get right down to business (but don't forget to check for any policy changes that may affect your store's operations).

WARNING

Before you click that link to open your eBay Store, ask yourself two questions:

>> **Can I make a serious commitment to eBay?** Any store — especially this one — is a commitment; it won't make money for you unless you work for it. You have to have the merchandise to fill it and the discipline to continue listing your fixed-price *and* auction items. Your store is a daily, monthly, and yearly obligation.

When you go on vacation, you can use the eBay Store's Vacation Feature and eBay will either close your item listings or put up a notification letting your customers know that you're on vacation until a specified date.

You can close your eBay Store temporarily, but eBay will reserve your store name for only 30 days. After that, you have to come up with a new name (and your competition may have taken over your old store name, especially if it's famous).

>> **Will I work on my eBay business even when I don't feel like it?** You have to be prepared for the times when you're sick or just don't feel like shipping but orders are waiting to be shipped. You have to do the work anyway; it's all part of the commitment.

eBay gives you the venue, but it's in your own hands to make your mercantile efforts a success. If you can handle these responsibilities, read on!

Subscribing to eBay Stores

If you're serious and ready to move on, go to the very bottom of the home page, and look for the link to Stores, under Buy. You can also go to the page at

    http://stores.ebay.com/

and click the Open a store link in the upper-right corner of the page. On the resulting page, click Subscribe Now. You're taken to subscription page.

eBay wants to ease you into this eBay Store thing. Make you feel comfortable, so you'll get the easy stuff first. Figure 4-1 shows you the initial sign-up screen, where you get to select the level of store you want. It's an easy choice: Start small with the $19.95 (when paid yearly) version. Come to think of it, many sellers have been running the Basic version for years and have been very happy with it.

FIGURE 4-1:
Taking the big step — go ahead and just do it.

You don't have to do anything but click.

The resulting page is where eBay starts to get serious. It shows your monthly charges and the User Agreement. Here eBay changes the friendly *Continue* button to the businesslike *Subscribe*. That's to let you know that this is serious. When you click Subscribe, the clock starts to tick on your monthly fees.

Don't subscribe to an eBay Store unless you're ready to get started immediately. Fees start the day you sign up, so why not read this chapter first and get centered on what you want to do? While you're thinking, the next section offers some pointers.

Making the required decisions

You need to make a few decisions to create a good store. So before building your eBay Store, read the following sections. Depending on the whims and changes that move through eBay, the order in which you have to implement these decisions can vary, but these are choices that you must make:

1. Type your new eBay Store's name.

You've decided on a store name, right? Your eBay Store's name can't exceed 35 characters. Before you type it, double-check that you aren't infringing on anyone's copyrights or trademarks. You also can't use any permutation of eBay trademarks in your store's name.

2. Type a short description of your store.

When I say short, I mean *short*. You have only 300 characters to give a keyword-filled description of your store and merchandise. You can't use HTML coding to doll up the description, and you can't use links. Just the facts please, and a *little* bit of dazzle.

The importance of this description is huge. When people use search engines such as Google and Bing, this is the area where those programs look to find the keywords they use to classify and list your store.

Consider writing your copy ahead of time in Word. Then, still in Word, highlight the text and choose Tools ⇨ Word Count. Word gives you the word count of the highlighted text. Check the character count with spaces, to be sure your text fits.

3. Select a graphic to jazz up the look of your store.

Create a custom 1200-x-270-pixel banner of your own. (See the text after this set of steps for info on designing your own graphics — or hiring someone to do it.)

If you're wondering in which category your store will be listed on the eBay Stores home page, it's up to you to make that choice. eBay checks the items as you list them in the standard eBay category format. For example, if you have

Deciding When You
Need an eBay Store

six books listed in the Books: Fiction and Nonfiction category and five items in the Cameras & Photo category, you'll be in the listings for both categories. Your custom Store categories (read on) are used to classify items only in your store.

eBay has a web page for eBay Store FAQ (frequently asked questions) that may have answers that you need. You can find it at

http://pages.ebay.com/seller-center/faq/stores.html

Designing an eBay Store logo

If you use one of eBay's prefab graphics and just leave it there, people shopping your eBay Store will know that you aren't serious enough about your business to design a simple and basic logo. I've had many years of experience in advertising and marketing, and I must tell you that a custom look will beat clip art any day. Your store is special — put forth the effort to make it shine.

If you have a graphics program, design a graphic with your store's name. Start with something simple; you can always change it later when you have more time. Save the image as a GIF or JPG file, and upload it as you would any other image.

A bunch of talented graphic artists make their living selling custom web graphics on eBay. If you aren't comfortable designing, search eBay for *ebay store banner* or *ebay store template*. Billboard banners on eBay sell for about $10 to $150 — certainly worth the price in the time you'll save. eBay even certified some designers to work on stores. You can find them listed at

http://pages.ebay.com/cr/en-us/storefronts/designdirectory.html

Running Your Store

You can customize your store at any time by clicking Manage My Store, which is a link on your Seller Hub page, or just go to your store through the link on your Feedback Profile page.

The page shown in Figure 4-2 appears, with headings describing important tasks for your store.

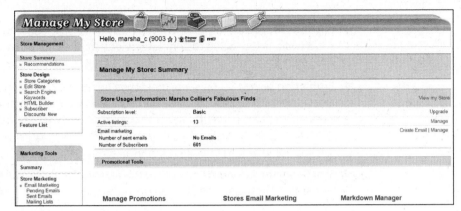

Store design

In the Store Design area, you can perform tasks required for your store design.

Here are a just few of the tasks you should consider revisiting:

>> **Store design:** You can always go back to the design area and change the name of your store or the theme of your pages. You can also change the way your store items are displayed: Gallery View (as shown in Figure 4-3) or List View. Neither view is inherently better, but I like the Gallery View because it shows the thumbnail gallery pictures of my items.

You should also select the order in which your items will sort. Highest Priced First, Lowest Priced First, Items Ending First, or Newly Listed First. I like Items Ending First as my sort, so buyers can get the chance to swoop in on items closing soon.

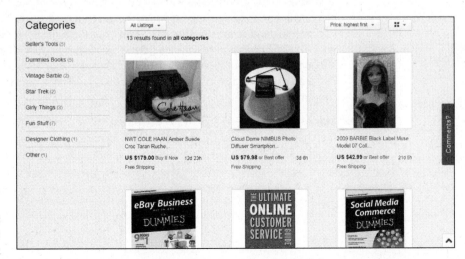

FIGURE 4-3:
My eBay Store in Gallery View.

Deciding When You Need an eBay Store

>> **Custom categories:** Here's where you really make your eBay Store your own. You may name up to 300 custom categories that relate to the varied items you sell in your store.

>> **Promotion boxes:** Set up some promotion boxes and change them every month or so to keep your store's look fresh. Select items for promotion that work well with the particular selling season. You have the option of inserting a filmstrip of your items, as I do on my store's home page. When your prospective buyer mouses over one of the photos, it expands.

>> **Search engine keywords:** Check out this area to see the keywords that eBay forwards to the major web shopping and search feeds. If you think there are better keywords, be sure to add them.

Marketing tools

Under the Marketing tools heading, you can perform many tasks that help bring customers to your store. You have the option of clicking a Summary page, which gives you a quick look at how your store's marketing features are currently set. You have a lot of options in this area. Here are a few of the many offered:

>> **Email marketing:** When you want to design an email campaign to your buyers, you have all the tools here. Create an email newsletter, create one for sending later, and manage your subscriber lists — all from one convenient area.

>> **Listing frame:** Select this option after you set up an eBay Store. Don't ask questions, just do it. The custom listing-header display is one of the best tools you can use to bring people into your eBay Store. Since I don't believe in cluttering up my listing pages with a lot of graphics, I use the option to have a store invitation message appear above the description in my item listings. Click the link and select the option to Show Your Custom Listing Header on all your eBay auctions and fixed-price sales. This custom header encourages shoppers to visit your eBay Store when they browse your eBay listings. When customizing, you may include your store logo, as well as a search box specific to your eBay Store.

>> **Markdown Manager:** So you say you have to raise some cash to buy new merchandise? Why not run a sale? By clicking here, you can select items to put on sale. After they've been marked down, they'll appear as "On Sale."

Office and Legal

Contents at a Glance

Chapter 1

Getting Legal with the State and the Feds

I f you've bought and sold on eBay, had some fun, and made a few dollars, good for you — enjoy yourself! When you start making serious money, however, the government no longer considers your business to be a hobby. It's time to consider some issues such as business structure, tax planning, and licenses; this chapter offers as painless an entrée as possible.

When you're concentrating on fulfilling multiple orders and keeping your customers happy, the last thing you need is a G-man breathing down your neck. Worst-case scenario: How about getting audited in December when you haven't been keeping up-to-date records all year? I know this sounds like stripping the fun out of doing business on eBay, but taking a bit of time and effort now can save you a ton of trouble later on (and will save you money in penalties).

Giving Your Business an Official Name

In most states in the United States, you used to be able to find liner ads in the classified section of the local newspaper. They're called *fictitious name statements*.

No, the statements aren't fictitious, but in effect, the names are — and as such, they need to be registered with your state before you can open a bank account in a business's name. This is also referred to as your DBA (or Doing Business As) name. They let the state know who owns and operates a business.

In California, you must file a fictitious name statement within 40 days of the commencement of your business. (Other state laws vary, so check the websites listed later in this chapter for more information on your state's requirements.) Your statement must also include a physical address where the business is operated — not a post office box address.

WARNING

Before you assume that registering a name isn't required in your state, check with your state's business code. (Links to all 50 states are presented later in the chapter.) Some states, such as Indiana, require that you register the assumed name of your business with the Secretary of State.

DON'T WASTE MONEY ONLINE!

All kinds of expensive services on the Internet are more than willing to handle the work for you for a fat fee. Don't spend too much of your money if you don't have to. If newspaper publication is required, look for a small community newspaper or business journal (if they still exist in your part of the world) and call them to see whether they handle this type of legal ad. Most small publications are 90 percent supported by the money they make on filing legal ads. They're the experts on this type of filing. Plus, you get to help out another small business in your community. Every five years, it's a good thing to file your company's DBA (Doing Business As) with the nice lady at the local newspaper office.

When my DBA came up for renewal, I noticed that my state had a $26 renewal fee — which was about one-fifth of what an online legal site wanted to charge me. I couldn't believe they were charging so much; I figured I must be missing something, so I called my State office. The lady who answered was actually grateful that I called; she said it was a shame that so many businesses mark up the cost of this service so much. So, when it comes to renewals, consider going to your state's website (you can find it in the state links listed in Table 1-1) and you may be able to renew for a small fee online or through the mail.

In the states requiring publication, your fictitious name statement must be published in an adjudicated (officially approved) newspaper for a certain amount of time. Ostensibly, this is to let the community know that a business is starting and who owns it. The newspaper supplies you with a proof of publication, which you keep in your files as a record of your filing. You generally have to renew the statement after a prescribed number of years.

After you have your officially stamped proof of publication, you can bring that to the bank and open an account in your business name, which is an important step in separating your personal living expenses from the business.

Taking Care of Regulatory Details

Let me give you some important advice to make your life easier in the long run: Don't ignore city, county, state, and federal regulatory details. Doing so may *seem* to make life easier at the get-go, but if your business is successful, one day your casual attitude will catch up with you. The usual attitude of government is that "Ignorance of the law is no excuse." You must comply with all the rules and regulations that are set up for your protection and benefit.

Business license or city tax certificate

Business licenses are the official-looking pieces of paper you see behind the register at brick-and-mortar businesses. Every business must have one, and depending on your local laws, you may have to have a *city license* or a *city tax registration certificate*. Yes, even if you're running a business out of your home and have no one coming to do business at your home, you may still need this. If you don't have one, the authorities may charge you a bunch of penalties if they ever find out. Avoiding this step isn't worth that risk.

TIP

To save you hanging on the phone, listening to elevator music, and being transferred and disconnected ad nauseam, I supply you with the direct links for business portals for each state to apply for your licenses and permits in Table 1-1. These URLs are accurate at the time of this writing, but as everybody knows, URLs change frequently. Check the following for updates:

    www.sba.gov/content/what-state-licenses-and-permits-does-
    your-business-need

TABLE 1-1   ## Websites for Business License Information

State	Link
Alabama	http://revenue.alabama.gov/licenses/munbuslic.cfm
Alaska	www.commerce.alaska.gov/web/cbpl/businesslicensing.aspx
Arizona	www.azdor.gov/Business/LicensingGuide.aspx
Arkansas	http://asbtdc.org
California	www.calgold.ca.gov
Colorado	www.sos.state.co.us/pubs/business/main.htm
Connecticut	www.ct-clic.com/Content/Smart_Start_for_Business.asp
Delaware	https://onestop.delaware.gov/osbrlpublic/Home.jsp
District of Columbia	https://dcra.dc.gov/service/about-business-licensing
Florida	www.myflorida.com/taxonomy/business/business%20licenses,%20permits%20and%20regulation/
Georgia	https://georgia.gov/popular-topic/applying-business-license
Hawaii	http://hawaii.gov/dcca/areas/breg
Idaho	www.idaho.gov/services/?subject=business
Illinois	www.illinois.gov/business/Pages/default.aspx
Indiana	https://inbiz.in.gov/BOS/Home/Index
Iowa	https://tax.iowa.gov/starting-business
Kansas	www.kansas.gov/business/
Kentucky	http://onestop.ky.gov/start/Pages/occupational.aspx
Louisiana	http://geauxBiz.com/
Maine	www.maine.gov/portal/business/licensing.html
Maryland	http://commerce.maryland.gov/start/the-process
Massachusetts	www.mass.gov/dor/businesses
Michigan	www.cityapplications.com/business-licenses/MI-Michigan/biz-Michigan.html
Minnesota	https://mn.gov/deed/business/
Mississippi	www.mssbdc.org/resources/faqs
Missouri	www.sos.mo.gov/business

State	Link
Montana	https://revenue.mt.gov/home/businesses/starting_business
Nebraska	www.nebraska.gov/osbr/index.cgi
Nevada	https://nvsilverflume.gov/home
New Hampshire	www.nh.gov/business/index.html
New Jersey	www.nj.gov/njbusiness/starting/
New Mexico	www.newmexico.gov/business/
New York	www.businessexpress.ny.gov/
North Carolina	https://edpnc.com/start-or-grow-a-business/start-a-business/
North Dakota	www.nd.gov/businessreg/license/index.html
Ohio	http://business.ohio.gov/licensing/
Oklahoma	http://okcommerce.gov/business/startup/
Oregon	http://sos.oregon.gov/business/Pages/starting-business.aspx
Pennsylvania	www.pabizonline.com/Register/Pages/default.aspx
Rhode Island	www.ri.gov/taxation/BAR/
South Carolina	http://sc.gov/Business/Pages/licensePermitsAndRegistration.aspx
South Dakota	https://sosenterprise.sd.gov/businessservices/
Tennessee	www.tn.gov/ecd/topic/how-to-start-a-business
Texas	https://texaswideopenforbusiness.com/start-business
Utah	www.utah.gov/business/starting.html
Vermont	www.vermont.gov/portal/business/
Virginia	https://bosapp.cyberdatainc.com/bos/
Washington	www.dol.wa.gov/business/
West Virginia	www.wvcommerce.org/(S(egl0nun5bc2elv55hryzc2rr))/business/businessassistance/smallbusiness/gettingstarted/business_license/default.aspx
Wisconsin	www.revenue.wi.gov/Pages/Businesses/New-Business-home.aspx
Wyoming	http://soswy.state.wy.us/Business/Business.aspx

State sales tax and resale number

If your state has a sales tax, a *sales tax number* (the identifying number you use when you file your sales tax statement with your state) is required before you officially sell anything. If sales tax applies, you may have to collect the appropriate sales tax for every sale that ships within the state that your business is in.

Some people also call this a *resale certificate* because when you want to purchase goods from a wholesaler within your state, you must produce this number (thereby certifying your legitimacy as a seller) so the dealer can sell you the merchandise without charging you sales tax.

To find the regulations for your state, if you can't find the information on the web pages listed in Table 1-1, try the following site that supplies links to every state's tax board, which should have the answers to your questions (look for a link to sales and excise taxes):

www.taxadmin.org/state-tax-agencies

Accessing online regulatory shortcuts

If you're going to be paying anyone a salary (or even hire a contractor), you'll need an *employer identification number* (EIN), also known as a *federal tax identification number*. Every business has one. It's like a Social Security Number for a business, identifying your business on all government forms: a nine-digit number assigned to all businesses for tax filing and reporting. You may also need one for your state.

If you have employees, you need to file *withholding forms* to report that you collected the necessary withholding taxes. You must send these reports to the state and the IRS on behalf of your employees. You're also expected to deposit those tax dollars with the IRS and your state on the date required, which may vary from business to business. Many enterprises go down because the owners just can't seem to keep their fingers out of withheld taxes — which means the money isn't available to turn in when the taxes are due. (This is another reason you should have a separate bank account for your business.)

No need to dawdle, and don't waste your money with a third party who charges for their service. Why not get the number direct from the source, while you have the time:

1. There's no charge to get your employer ID number (EIN).

An employer ID number can be assigned by filing IRS form SS-4. Go to the IRS website to apply online:

www.irs.gov/businesses/small/article/0,,id=102767,00.html

Or if you'd rather mail in the form, the details and downloadable form are available as a PDF file.

2. State employer ID numbers for taxes may depend on your state's requirements. Visit the following for an overview of the requirements for every state in the country:

`www.taxadmin.org/state-tax-forms`

3. Register for the Federal Government Electronic Federal Tax Payment System® (EFTPS) service where you pay any tax due to the Federal Government online without paying an extra fee to a third party. Once you have your FEIN, head over and register at

`https://www.eftps.gov/eftps/`

Selecting a business format

After you've fulfilled all the regulatory details, you need to formally decide how you want to run your company. You need to set up a legal format and to make a merchandise plan. (For more on merchandise planning, visit Book 4, Chapter 2.)

When you have a business, any type of business, it has to have a legal format for licensing and tax purposes. Businesses come in several forms, from a sole proprietorship all the way to a corporation. A "corporation" designation isn't as scary as it sounds. Yes, Microsoft, IBM, and eBay are corporations, but so too are many businesses run by individuals.

Each form of business has its pluses and minuses — and costs. I go over some of the fees involved in incorporating later in this chapter. For now, I detail the most common types of businesses, which I encourage you to weigh carefully.

WARNING

I'm not a lawyer (I don't even play one on TV), so be sure to consult with a professional in the legal and financial fields to get the latest legal and tax ramifications of the various business formats.

Sole proprietorship

If you're running your business by yourself part-time or full-time, your business is a *sole proprietorship*. Yep, doesn't that sound official? A sole proprietorship is the simplest form of business; you don't need a lawyer to set it up. Nothing is easier or cheaper. Most people use this form of business when they're starting out. Many people often graduate to a more formal type of business as things get bigger.

TIP

If a husband and wife file a joint tax return, they *can* run a business as a sole proprietorship (but only one of you can be the proprietor). However, if both you and your spouse work equally in the business, then running it as a partnership — with a written partnership agreement — is a much better idea. (See the next section, "Partnership," for more information.) A partnership protects you in case of your partner's death. In a sole proprietorship, the business ends with the death of the proprietor. If the business has been a sole proprietorship in your late spouse's name, you may be left out in the cold.

Being in business adds a few expenses, but many things that you spend money on now (relating to your business) can be deducted from your state and federal taxes. The profits of your business are taxed directly as part of your own income tax, and the profits and expenses are reported on Schedule C of your 1040 tax package. As a sole proprietor, you're at risk for the business liabilities. All outstanding debts are yours, and you could lose personal assets if you default. Also, as your business becomes profitable, this business format forces you to pay an additional self-employment tax.

Also, you must consider the liability of the products you sell on eBay. If you sell foodstuffs, vitamins, or nutraceuticals (new-age food supplements) that make someone ill, you may be personally liable for any court-awarded damages. If someone is hurt by something you sell, you may also be personally liable as the seller of the product.

TIP

In a sole proprietorship, as with any form of home-based business, you may be able to get an insurance rider to your homeowner's insurance policy to cover you against some liabilities. Check with your insurance agent.

Partnership

When two or more people are involved in a business, it can be a *partnership.* A general partnership can be formed by an oral agreement. Each person in the partnership contributes capital or services and both share in the partnership's profits and losses. The income of a partnership is taxed to both partners, based on the percentage of the business that they own or upon the terms of a written agreement. Any losses are also split. The partnership must file its own tax return (Form 1065) reporting the business financials to the IRS.

You'd better be sure that you can have a good working relationship with your partner: This type of business relationship has broken up many a friendship. Writing up a formal agreement when forming your business partnership is an excellent idea. This agreement is useful in solving any disputes that may occur over time.

TIP

In your agreement, be sure to outline things such as

>> How to divide the profits and losses

>> Compensation to each partner

>> Duties and responsibilities of each partner

>> Restrictions of authority and spending

>> How disputes should be settled

>> What happens if the partnership dissolves

>> What happens to the partnership in case of death or disability

One more important thing to remember: As a partner, you're jointly and severally responsible for the business liabilities and actions of the other person or people in your partnership — as well as for your own. Again, this is a personal liability arrangement. You are both personally open to any lawsuits that come your way through the business.

GETTING LEGAL DOCUMENTS PREPARED

Many of the required business documents do not require a lawyer, but some do, depending on the complexity (and size) or your business situation. I have set up a folder with some free sample documents that you can print or download from my collection of Small Business Forms at www.scribd.com/lists/4150612/Small-Business-Forms.

If you're thinking of setting up one of the business formats described in this chapter, you can get the proper documents filed without hiring an attorney. Because of variations from state to state, online document services have proved to be tricky. I recommend that you go to Google and search for a local Legal Document Service near you. These companies handle legal document preparation for business incorporation, partnerships, and more for reasonable prices. You meet with a real person, usually a paralegal or a Certified Legal Document Assistant. They interview you and fill out the appropriate documents for your state.

When it comes to setting up an official company format, you may just want to (at the very least) consult with an attorney. Perhaps you can find one who is also a member of your local Chamber of Commerce.

Getting Legal with the State and the Feds

REMEMBER

The partnership has to file an informational return with the IRS and the state, but the profits of the partnership are taxed to the partners on their personal individual returns.

LLC (limited liability company)

A *limited liability company,* or LLC, is similar to a sole proprietor or partnership but also has many of the characteristics of a corporation. An LLC differs mainly in that the liabilities of the company are not passed on to the members (owners). Unless you sign a personal guarantee for debt incurred, the members are responsible only to the extent of the total amount they have invested in the company. But all members *do* have liability for the company's taxes.

TIP

A limited liability company doesn't require as much of the legal red tape and obsessive-compulsive bureaucracy as a regular corporation requires. For example, while a corporation will require a board of directors, board meetings, an annual stockholders' meeting, and meeting minutes of all these events, a limited liability company won't.

You'll need to put together an operating agreement, similar to the partnership agreement. Doing so also helps establish which members own what percentage of the company for tax purposes. Most states will require you to file Articles of Organization forms to start this type of business.

An LLC is taxed like a sole proprietorship, with the profits and losses passed on to the members' personal tax returns. An LLC may opt to pay taxes like a corporation and keep some of the profits in the company, thereby reducing the tax burden to individual members. Although members pay the LLC's taxes, the LLC must still file Form 1065 (just like a partnership) with the IRS at the end of the year. This gives the IRS extra data to be sure that the individual members properly report their income.

WARNING

Some states levy additional special or minimum taxes on an LLC. Be sure to check with your state's business department.

Corporation

A corporation has a life of its own: its own name, its own bank account, and its own tax return. A *corporation* is a legal entity created for the sole purpose of doing business. If you're a sole proprietor and you're incorporating, one of the main problems you face is realizing that you can't just help yourself to the assets of the business. Yes, a corporation can have only one owner — but that owner is the shareholder(s). If you can't accept that you can't write yourself a check from your corporation — unless it's for a specified salary or for the reimbursement of legitimate expenses — then you may not be cut out to face the responsibility of running your own corporation.

There are two types of corporations; it's best that you consult your accountant or lawyer to decide which is best for you.

>> **C corporations** are what we normally consider as corporations. This is the business format of the big guys, although depending on your sources of income, it might work for you. It is taxed as a separate entity and is subject to corporate income tax.

>> **S corporations** are corporations that have filed a special election with the IRS. They are not subject to corporate income tax, but are treated similarly (not identically) to partnerships for tax purposes.

The state in which you run your business sets up the rules for the corporations operating within its borders. You must apply to the Secretary of State of the state in which you want to incorporate. Federal taxes for corporations presently range from 15 to 35 percent, and they're generally based on your net profits.

TIP

Employee owners of C corporations can use the company to shelter income from being taxed by dividing the income between their personal and corporate tax returns. This is frequently called *income splitting*; it involves setting salaries and bonuses so that any profits left in the company at the end of its tax year will be taxed at only the 15 percent rate.

Be sure to check the current corporate taxes and compare what you pay and how much you'd pay in taxes if you left profits in a small corporation — important to know if you're going that route.

TIP

Considering that the individual Federal tax-rate percentages for incomes up to $75,000 annually can go as high as 28 percent, the trouble of keeping a corporation for your business may be a huge money-saver.

The Tax Foundation (http://taxfoundation.org/) offers its annual State Business Tax Climate Index that lists the ten highest- and ten lowest-ranked states:

>> **Ten best states** in this year's Index are Wyoming, South Dakota, Alaska, Florida, Nevada, Montana, New Hampshire, Utah, Indiana, and Oregon. Many of these states do not have one or more of the major taxes, and thus do not have the associated complexity and distortions.

>> **Ten lowest-ranked, or worst, states** from highest taxes to lowest are New Jersey, New York, California, Vermont, Minnesota, Ohio, Rhode Island, Connecticut, Maryland, and Louisiana.

The full index report and state-by-state ranking can be found at

https://taxfoundation.org/2017-state-business-tax-climate-index

Most states also have their own taxes for corporations. In Table 1-2, you see the basic tax for C Corporations (assuming your corporation makes money after payroll and other expenses). Please check with your tax professional; many states have franchise taxes, inventory taxes — and goodness knows what else — as well.

TABLE 1-2

2017 State Corporate Income Tax Rates

State	Tax Rates and Brackets	Note This . . .
Alabama	6.5%	Federally deductible
Alaska	2.0% > $25K	
	3.0% > $49K	
	4.0% > $74K	
	5.0% > $99K	
	6.0% > $124K	
	7.0% > $148K	
	8.0% > $173K	
	9.0% > $198K	
	9.4% > $222K	
Arizona	4.90%	Minimum tax $50
Arkansas	1.0%	> $0
	2.0% > $3K	
	3.0% >$6K	
	5.0% > $11K	
	6.0% > $25K	
	6.5% > $100K	
California	8.84%	Minimum tax $800
Colorado	4.63%	
Connecticut	7.5% or higher	Additional 20% surtax applies businesses with at least $100 million annual gross income

State	Tax Rates and Brackets	Note This . . .
Delaware	8.7% on the first $20 million	
District Of Columbia	9.0%	Minimum tax $100
Florida	5.5%	
Georgia	6%	
Hawaii	4.4% > $0	
	5.4% > $25K	
	6.4% > $100K	
Idaho	7.4%	Minimum tax $20
Illinois	7.75%	Sum of corporate income tax rate of 5.25% plus a replacement tax of 2.5%
Indiana	6.25%	
Iowa	6.0% > $0	50% of federal income tax is deductible
	8.0 > $25K	
	10.0 > $100K	
	12.0 > $250K	
Kansas	4% > $0	In addition to the flat 4% corporate income tax, Kansas levies a 3.0% surtax on taxable income over $50,000
	7.0% > $50,000	
Kentucky	4.0% > $0	
	5.0 > 50K	
	6.0 > 100K	
Louisiana	4.0% > $0	Federally deductible
	5.0 > 25K	
	6.0 > 50K	
	7.0 > 100K	
	8.0 > 200K	

(continued)

Getting Legal with the State and the Feds

TABLE 1-2 *(continued)*

State	Tax Rates and Brackets	Note This . . .
Maine	3.5% > $0	
	7.93 > 25K	
	8.33 > 75K	
	8.93 > 250K	
Maryland	8.25%	
Massachusetts	8%	Minimum tax of $456
Michigan	6%	
Minnesota	9.8%	
Mississippi	3.0% > $0	
	4.0 > $5K	
	5.0 > $10K	
Missouri	6.25%	50% is deductible
Montana	6.75%	Minimum tax is $50
Nebraska	5.58% > $0	
	7.81 > $50K	
Nevada	None	
New Hampshire	8.2% > $0	
New Jersey	6.5% > $50K	
	7.5 > $50K	
	9.0 > $100K	
New Mexico	4.8% > $0	
	6.2 > $500K	
	7.6 > $1,000,000	
New York	6.5%	Small business taxpayers in New York pay rates of 6.5%, 7.1%, and 4.35% on three brackets of entire net income up to $390,000
North Carolina	3.0%	

State	Tax Rates and Brackets	Note This . . .
North Dakota	1.41% > $0	Federally deductible
	3.55% > $25K	
	4.31% > $50K	
Ohio		Ohio no longer levies a tax based on income, but instead imposes a Commercial Activity Tax (CAT) equal to $150 for gross receipts sitused to Ohio of between $150,000 and $1 million, plus 0.26% of gross receipts over $1 million (the *situs* is the place to which, for purposes of legal jurisdiction or taxation, a property belongs)
Oklahoma	6.0%	
Oregon	6.6% > $0	Minimum tax $150 for sales up to $500,000
	7.6% > $100K	
Pennsylvania	9.99%	
Rhode Island	7.0%	
South Carolina	5.0%	
South Dakota	None	
Tennessee	6.5%	
Texas	1.0%	
Utah	5.0%	Minimum tax $100
Vermont	6.0% > $0	Minimum tax $250
	7.0 > $10K	
	8.5 > $25K	
Virginia	6.0%	
Washington	Varies	
West Virginia	6.5%	
Wisconsin	7.9%	
Wyoming	None	

TIP

Often, in small corporations, most of the profits are paid out in tax-deductible salaries and benefits. The most important benefit for a business is that *any liabilities belong to the corporation.* Your personal assets remain your own, because they have no part in the corporation.

Chapter **2**

The Necessity of Taxes and Value of Business Reports

You'll get no argument from me that bookkeeping can be the most boring and time-consuming part of your job. You may feel that you just need to add your product costs, add your gross sales, and bada-bing, you know where your business is. Sorry, I wish that's how it worked, but it's not that easy.

Did you add that roll of tape you picked up at the supermarket today? Although it cost only $1.29, it's a business expense. How about the mileage driving back and forth from suppliers, garage sales, and resale shops? Those are expenses, too. I suspect that you're not counting quite a few other seemingly "inconsequential" items like these in your expense column.

I must confess that I enjoy posting my expenses and sales once I actually get into the task. It gives me the opportunity to know exactly where my business is in its course at any given moment. Understand, I'm not using a pencil-entered ledger system to do that; my tool of choice is a software program that's fairly easy to use. But the concepts behind the tools matter too. In this chapter, I give you the lowdown on the basics of bookkeeping — and emphasize the importance of keeping records in case Uncle Sam comes calling. Keep reading: This chapter is *required*.

Dealing with a Professional

Have you ever wondered why businesses have CFOs (chief financial officers), vice presidents of finance, CPAs (certified public accountants), and bookkeepers? It's because keeping the books is the backbone of any company's business. Once you have a business, trusting your taxes to an online service can be problematic, because your relationship with your tax preparer is a personal one.

Do you have a professional going over your books at least once a year? You should. A paid professional experienced in your type of business knows what to do when it comes to your taxes. Due to the complexity of the tax code, not just any paid preparer will suffice when it comes to preparing your business taxes. Here's a list of possible people who can prepare your tax returns.

WARNING

>> **Tax preparer (or consultant):** This is the person you visit at the local we-file-for-you tax office. Did you know that a tax preparer could be anybody? There is no licensing involved. H&R Block hires as many as 70,000 seasonal workers as tax preparers each year. I'm sure that some may be familiar with the tax code, but the sheer number of tax preparers and the lack of regulation can make using a we-file-for-you tax office a risky proposition for business-people who want to minimize their tax liability.

   The United States General Accounting Office report once estimated that 2.2 Americans overpaid their taxes by an average of $610 per year because they claimed the standard deduction when it would have been more beneficial to itemize. Half of those taxpayers used paid preparers who clearly were not cognizant of the full tax law as it applied to these individuals. Scary, huh?

>> **Volunteer IRS-certified preparers:** AARP (American Association of Retired Persons) does an outstanding job of assembling nearly 35,000 tax preparers to serve the needs of low-to-middle-income taxpayers (special attention going to those over 60). Their goal is to maximize legal deductions and credits, resulting in "tangible economic benefits" for their clients. These volunteers have to study, take a test, and become *certified by the IRS* before they can lend their services to the cause.

In recent years, AARP volunteers served a total of 2.6 million seniors in the United States. My mother was a retired corporate comptroller, and she volunteered in this program for many years. (She was disappointed when she made her lowest score on the IRS test — a 94 percent!) They staff nearly 5,000 sites nationwide. To find the one near you, call 1-888-227-7669 and select Tax-Aide Information or go to the AARP Foundation Tax-Aide locator at

`www.aarp.org/applications/VMISLocator/searchTaxAideLocations.action`

>> **Public accountant:** A public accountant, or PA, must fulfill educational, testing, and experience requirements and obtain a state license. PAs must take an annual course to maintain their status.

>> **Enrolled agent:** Often called one of the best-kept secrets in accounting, an enrolled agent is federally licensed by the IRS. (CPAs and attorneys are licensed by the state.) EAs must pass an extensive annual test on tax law and tax-return preparation every year to maintain their status. (They also have to pass annual background checks.) Enrolled agents are authorized to appear in place of a taxpayer before the IRS.

Many EAs are former IRS employees. To find an enrolled agent near you, go to `www.naea.org` and click the *Find a Tax Expert* button at the top of the page.

>> **Certified public accountant:** Certified public accountants (CPAs) must complete rigorous testing and fulfill experience requirements as prescribed by the state in which they practice. Most states require every CPA to obtain a state license.

CPAs are accountants. They specialize in recordkeeping and reporting financial matters. Their important position is as an advisor regarding financial decisions for both individuals and businesses. CPAs must take an annual course to maintain their status.

Keeping the Books: Basics to Get You Started

Although posting bookkeeping entries can be boring, clicking a button to generate your tax information is a lot easier than manually going over pages of sales information on a pad of paper. That's why I like to use software, particularly QuickBooks (more about that program later).

I suppose that you *could* use plain ol' paper and a pencil to keep your books; if that works for you, great. But even though that might work for you now, it definitely won't in the future. Entering all your information into a software program now — while your books may still be fairly simple to handle — can save you a lot of time and frustration in the future, when your eBay business has grown beyond your wildest dreams and no amount of paper can keep it all straight and organized. I discuss alternative methods of bookkeeping in Chapter 3 in this minibook. For now, I focus on the basics of bookkeeping.

Tracking everything in and out

To effectively manage your business, you must keep track of *all* your expenses — down to the last roll of tape. You need to keep track of your inventory, how much you paid for the items, how much you paid in shipping, and how much you profited from your sales. If you use a van or the family car to pick up or deliver merchandise to the post office, you should keep track of this mileage as well. When you're running a business, you should account for every penny that goes in and out.

Bookkeeping has irrefutable standards called GAAP (Generally Accepted Accounting Principles) that are set by the Financial Accounting Standards Advisory Board. (It sounds scary to me, too.) *Assets, liabilities, owner's equity, income,* and *expenses* are standard terms used in all forms of accounting to define profit, loss, and the fiscal health of your business.

Understanding double-entry accounting

Every time you process a transaction, two things happen: One account is credited while another receives a debit (think yin and yang). To get more familiar with these terms (and those in the following list), see the definitions in the chart of accounts in Chapter 3 in this minibook. Depending on the type of account, the account's balance either increases or decreases. One account that increases while another decreases is called *double-entry accounting:*

» When you post an expense, the debit *increases* your expenses and *decreases* your bank account.

» When you purchase furniture or other assets, it *increases* your asset account and *decreases* your bank account.

» When you make a sale and make the deposit, it *increases* your bank account and *decreases* your accounts receivable.

>> When you purchase inventory, it *increases* your inventory and *decreases* your bank account.

>> When a portion of a sale includes sales tax, it *decreases* your sales and *increases* your sales tax account.

Manually performing double-entry accounting can be a bit taxing (no pun intended). A software program, however, will automatically adjust the accounts when you input a transaction.

Separating business and personal records

As a business owner, even if you're a sole proprietor (see Chapter 1 in this mini-book for information on business types), you should keep your business books separate from your personal expenses. By isolating your business records from your personal records, you can get a snapshot of which areas of your sales are doing well and which ones aren't carrying their weight. But that isn't the only reason keeping accurate records is smart; there's the IRS to think about, too. In the next section, I explain Uncle Sam's interest in your books.

REMEMBER

Okay, posting bookkeeping can be boring. But at the end of the fiscal year, when you have a professional do your taxes, you'll be a lot happier — and your tax preparation will cost you less — if you've posted your information cleanly and in the proper order.

Records Uncle Sam May Want to See

One of the reasons we can have a great business environment in the United States is because we all have a partner, Uncle Sam. Our government regulates business and sets the rules for us to transact our operations. To help you get started with your business, the IRS maintains a small-business website (shown in Figure 2-1) at the following address:

www.irs.gov/businesses/small-businesses-self-employed

In this section, I highlight what information you need to keep and how long you should keep it (just in case you're chosen for an audit).

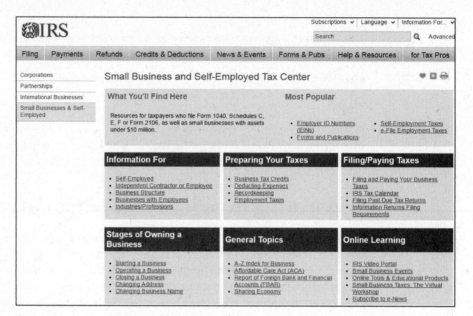

FIGURE 2-1:
IRS page for small businesses, complete with handy links.

Supporting information

Aside from needing to know how your business is going (which is really important), the main reason to keep clear and concise records is because Uncle Sam may come knocking one day. You never know when the IRS will choose *your* number and want to examine your records. In the following list, I highlight some of the important pieces of supporting information (things that support your expenses on your end-of-year tax return):

» **Receipts:** Please heed this advice: *Save every receipt you get.* If you're out of town on a buying trip and have coffee at the airport, save that receipt — it's a deduction from your profits. Everything related to your business may be deductible, so you must save airport parking receipts, taxi receipts, receipts for a pen that you picked up on your way to a meeting, *everything.* If you don't have a receipt, you can't prove the write-off.

» **Merchandise invoices:** Saving all merchandise invoices is as important as saving all your receipts. If you want to prove that you paid $400 and not the $299 retail price for that PlayStation 2 that you sold online for $500, you'd *better* have an invoice of some kind. The same idea applies to most collectibles, in which case a retail price can't be fixed. Save all invoices!

>> **Outside contractor invoices:** If you use outside contractors — even if you pay the college kid next door to go to the post office and the bank for you — you should get an invoice from them to document exactly what service you paid for and how much you paid. This is supporting information that will save your bacon, should it ever need saving.

>> **Business cards:** It may sound like I'm stretching things a bit, but if you use your car to look at some merchandise, pick up a business card from the vendor. If you're out of town and have a meeting with someone, take a card. Having these business cards can help substantiate your deductible comings and goings.

>> **A daily calendar:** This is where your smartphone or tablet comes in. Every time you leave your house or office on a business-related task, make note of it on your calendar. Google Calendar syncs easily with your mobile devices. Keep as detailed a hoard of minutiae as you can stand. At the end of the year, I print out my Google calendar by month for tax backup. Staple the pages together and include the hard copies in your files with your substantiating information.

>> **Credit card statements:** You're already collecting credit card receipts, right? Why not just download your credit card statements from the web at the end of every month — and back them up. If you have the statements, you have a monthly proof of expenses. When you get your statement each month, post it into your bookkeeping program and itemize each and every charge, detailing where you spent the money and what for. (QuickBooks has a split feature that accommodates all your categories.) File these statements with your tax return at the end of the year in your year-end envelope.

To check for new information and the lowdown on what you can and can't do, ask an accountant or a CPA. Also visit the IRS Tax Information for Businesses site (they even have videos), shown in Figure 2-2, at

```
www.irs.gov/businesses
```

How long should you keep your records?

How long do you have to keep all this supporting information? I hate to tell you, but I think I've saved it all. I must have at least ten years of receipts and statements. But you know, I'm not too extreme; the period in which you can amend a return or in which the IRS can assess more tax is never less than three years from the date of filing — and can be even longer.

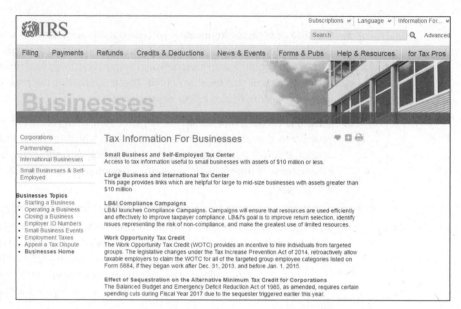

The IRS wants you to save anything related to your tax return for three years. But if you take a look at Table 2-1, the IRS may want backup documentation for up to six years. So for safety's sake, keep things for six years, if only to prove you're innocent. (As an aside, because I'm paranoid, I still keep everything for the maximum mentioned by the IRS — seven years.)

TABLE 2-1   **Keep Records for This Length of Time**

Circumstance	Keep Records This Long
You owe additional tax (if the following three points don't apply)	3 years
You don't report all your income and what you don't report is more than 25% of the gross income shown on your return	6 years
You file a fraudulent tax return	Forever
You don't bother to file a return	Forever
You file a claim of refund or credit after you've filed	3 years or 2 years after the tax was paid (whichever is longer)
Your claim is due to a bad debt deduction or worthless securities	7 years
Employment Tax records	At least 4 years after the date that the tax becomes due or is paid, whichever is later
You have information on assets	Life of the asset

Even though I got the information in Table 2-1 directly from the IRS website and literature (Publication 583, "Starting a Business and Keeping Records"), it may change in the future. You can download a PDF copy of the booklet by going to the following address:

> www.irs.gov/pub/irs-pdf/p583.pdf

It doesn't hurt to store your information for as long as you can stand it and stay on top of any changes the IRS may implement.

Getting the Most from Your Reports

After you're up and running with your business, you can look forward to having lots of reports to evaluate. Of course, you get a bunch of reports from PayPal, eBay, and so on, but the most important reports are those you generate from your bookkeeping program, whether it's software such as Excel or QuickBooks, or an online service such as GoDaddy Online Bookkeeping (formerly Outright).

Because my business consists of more than eBay sales, I use QuickBooks to manage my business records, and it keeps several common reports (Balance Sheet, Accounts Payable, P&L, and so on) in an easily accessible area. If you check out the Reports tab in your bookkeeping program, I'll bet you find similar items. Before your eyes glaze over, though, check out this section for straightforward descriptions of these reports and the information they provide.

Similar sales and financial reports are common to all businesses, and reviewing them on a monthly basis can help you stay on top of yours.

To get your business reports when you need them, you must post your sales receipts regularly — and thereby update the "money in" and "inventory out" figures. Post your payments as often as you can (especially on your company credit card — post those transactions the minute you get the statement) — and reconcile your bank account the moment your bank statement arrives.

What does posting and reconciling tasks get you? The opportunity to press a button and get a complete picture of your business. From the reports you generate, you find out whether your business is profitable, what products are selling, and if you're spending too much money in a particular area. Keeping your books up to date allows you to find problems before they become unmanageable.

If you run your sales and financial reports only quarterly rather than monthly, a problem — such as not pricing your items high enough — could be mushrooming out of control before you can detect and correct it.

Understanding the balance sheet

Your balance sheet provides the best information on your business. It pulls data from all the other reports and gives you a complete look at the financial condition of your business.

Your balance sheet shows all your assets:

» **Cash in bank:** The money in your business bank account.

» **Accounts receivable:** If you've invoiced anyone and not received payment as yet, that amount is reflected here.

» **Inventory assets:** This is the value of the merchandise you've purchased for resale but have not sold yet.

» **Other assets:** Things owned by your business (not by you), such as furniture and vehicles. These are long-term assets that build accumulated depreciation. They're not considered in the current asset figure.

» **Accumulated depreciation:** This is depreciation, over time, of your long-term assets. This is either calculated by your accounting program or given to you by your accountant.

Your balance sheet also shows your liabilities:

» **Accounts payable:** Money you owe vendors and money due on unpaid credit cards show up here.

» **Sales tax:** The money you've collected on sales tax (that is due to your state) is a liability.

» **Payroll liabilities:** If you haven't made a bank deposit (it's faster to make payment on the Federal online payment system at www.eftps.gov/eftps) covering the money you've withdrawn from employees (withholding taxes, Social Security, Medicare, and so on), it shows up here.

Your equity shows up in the (literal and figurative) bottom line. It will include the initial investment in your business and the net income total from your profit-and-loss statement.

TIP

An important business ratio — the *net working capital ratio* — is drawn from your balance sheet. Subtracting your current liabilities from your current assets gets you the *net* dollar amount of your *working capital* (that is, how much capital you have left to work with). But to get the net working capital *ratio*, divide your current assets by your current liabilities. Any value over 1.1 means you have a positive net working capital. If you need a loan from a bank, this is the first figure a loan officer will look for.

Tracking your accounts payable

When bills come in, post them in your accounting program. This will generate the *accounts payable* report. Accounts payable is the area that shows how much you owe and when it's due. This is crucial information for meeting your obligations on time.

When you pay an outstanding bill, the bookkeeping program deducts the money from your checking account and marks the bill as paid. That bill will no longer appear on this report.

Knowing your sales-tax liability

One of the vendors you'll owe money to is your state. (In California, the State Board of Equalization collects such debts.) Every time you post an invoice or sales receipt that charges sales tax, that amount shows up in the *sales-tax liability report*. You run this report on a timeframe determined by the state; you may be required to report monthly, quarterly, or yearly. Also, how often you report may depend on your total in-state sales. Just make sure you match your reporting with your state's requirements.

REMEMBER

COGS — the cost of goods (merchandise) sold — is a separate consideration from sales tax. For a closer look at COGS, see *Intermediate Accounting For Dummies* by Marie Loughran (Wiley), available at www.dummies.com.

Analyzing your profit and loss statement

If your accountant asks for your income statement, he or she is asking for your *profit-and-loss statement*, or *P&L*. This report lays out clearly every penny you've spent and brought in. You can set these reports to generate by any period of time; usually eBay sellers produce them by calendar month.

A summary P&L itemizes all your income and expense accounts individually and totals them by category. This way, you'll be able to isolate individual areas where you may notice a problem, such as spending too much in shipping supplies.

Please use the following list of income and expense accounts as a guide, and not as gospel. I am not a tax professional, and I suggest that when you set up your own income and (especially) expense accounts, you go over them with a licensed tax expert. Here's a glimpse at the kinds of accounts and categories you see on a P&L statement:

- » **Income:** Every dollar you bring in is itemized as income. For many sellers, this can break down into several individual accounts. These figures are automatically generated by your bookkeeping program from the sales receipts you input. The total of all these income areas is subtotaled at the bottom of this area as total income.

  - **Sales:** This totals eBay sales and shipping income in separate totals. These figures subtotal as total sales.

  - **Website advertising:** If you're a member of any affiliate programs (Google Ads on your site count here too) or have a newsletter that takes advertising, this income posts here.

  - **Consulting:** Income from providing consulting services or teaching others.

- » **Cost of goods sold (COGS):** This area itemizes by category all the costs involved in your eBay (and website) sales only. None of your business operating expenses, such as your telephone bill, show up here; they're farther down on the report. To get the current information from the IRS as to what constitutes COGS, visit their website here:

  www.irs.gov/publications/p334

  Your cost of goods sold is subtotaled under the heading total COGS.

- » **Gross profit:** Your bookkeeping program magically does all the calculations — and you'll be able to see in a snapshot whether your eBay business is in good, profitable health. This particular figure is the gross profit *before* you figure in your company expenses (often called G&A, for *general and administrative costs*).

Now come your expenses. Listed in individual accounts, you have subtotals for your various business operating expenses, as follows:

- » **Payroll expenses:** The total amounts you pay your employees.

- » **Taxes:** Broken out by state and federal, the taxes you've paid to the regulating agencies for running your business.

- » **Supplies:** Computer and office supplies. How much paper goes through your printer? Not to mention those inkjet cartridges, pens, computers, telephones, copiers, and network equipment. All those expenses appear here.

- » **Seminars and education:** Did you buy this book to educate yourself on your eBay business? It counts. Have you attended a seminar to educate yourself on eBay? Going to a business conference? Those count too.

» **Contract labor:** This is the money you pay to anyone who is not an employee of your company, such as an off-site bookkeeper or a company that comes in to clean your office. The federal government has stringent rules as to who classifies as an independent contractor. Check this website for the official rules:

```
www.irs.gov/businesses/small-businesses-self-employed/
independent-contractor-self-employed-or-employee
```

» **Automobile expenses:** This is where you post expenses, such as parking, gas, and repairs for an automobile used for your eBay business. If you have only one vehicle that you also use for personal transportation, your tax person may have you post a percentage of its use in this area.

» **Telephone:** Do you have a separate phone line for your business?

» **Advertising:** Expenses you incur when running advertising campaigns, such as in Google AdWords or in your eBay banner program.

Your expenses will come to a whopping total at the bottom. Then, at the very bottom of the page, will be your net income. This is your *bottom-line profit.* I wish you all a very positive bottom line!

Keeping Your Records and Data Safe

If the hazard of not backing up your computer isn't a tired subject, I don't know what is. Whenever you hear someone talking about their latest computer crash, all the person can do is stare blankly into the distance and say, "I lost everything!" I admit it's happened to me — and I'm sure that you've heard this cry from others (if you've not uttered it yourself): "If only I'd backed up my files!"

What about a natural disaster? It can happen, you know. When I went to sleep on January 16, 1994, I didn't know that the next day, when I attempted to enter my office, everything would be in shambles. My monitors had flown across the room, filing cabinets turned over, and oh, did I mention the ceiling had collapsed? The Northridge earthquake taught me some solid lessons about keeping duplicate records and backed-up data copies *in an offsite location.*

TIP

Reasonably priced, secure backup can be accomplished in the cloud these days through Microsoft OneDrive, Google, Amazon, or any one of a group of providers for a reasonable cost. Consider these — along with a backup drive on premises — for your own peace of mind.

If a computer crash or natural disaster has happened to you, you have my deepest and most sincere sympathy. It's a horrible thing to go through.

WARNING

What's another horrible thing? A tax audit: It can make you feel like jumping off a cliff if you've been filing your hard documentation with the shoebox method. (You know, one box for 2011, one for 2012, and so on.) Filing or scanning your receipts and PDF backup documentation in an organized, easy-to-find format can pay off in future savings of time (and nerves). (Again: Back up these PDFs to the cloud.)

I want to tell you up front that I don't always practice what I preach. I don't always back up my stuff on time. I do make an attempt to back up to OneDrive every time I remember. Following best practices for backing up your computer data and safeguarding the hardcopy documents that you inevitably will have just makes life easier.

Backing Up Your Data

I'm not specifically suggesting that you go out and buy backup software (though I think it's a good idea). I *am* suggesting that you back up the eBay transaction records and other data on your computer *somehow*. Consider the following points when choosing how to back up the data you can't afford to lose:

» Regularly back up at least your data folder onto an external hard drive.

» Backup software can make your backup chores less *chorelike.* Most packages enable you to run backups unattended and automatically, so you don't have to remember anything. (External hard drives come with their own sync software to handle this for you.)

» Backup software doesn't have to be expensive; System Image is included in Windows and will back up your entire hard drive. If you really need software, search Google with the term *backup Windows.* This query returned more results than I could ever need!

» Consider making monthly backups of the info from your PayPal account. You can download the data directly from the site and can archive several years' worth on the drive.

Saving Your Backup Paperwork

Some business records are still paper, and until such time as the entire world is electronic, you'll have some paperwork to store unless you scan in every document. You can buy manila file folders almost anywhere. If you don't have filing cabinets, office supply stores sell cardboard boxes that are the perfect size to hold file folders. An external hard drive is a must for backup documentation as well.

And just what do you need to scan and file in your new organized office? Here are a few important suggestions:

>> **Equipment receipts and warranties:** You never know when some important piece of your office hardware will go on the fritz, and you'll need the receipt and warranty information so you can get it fixed. Also, the receipts are backup documentation for your bookkeeping program's data.

>> **Automobile expenses:** Gasoline receipts, parking receipts, repairs — anything and everything to do with your car. You use your car in your eBay business (for example, to deliver packages to the post office for shipping), don't you?

>> **Postal receipts:** Little slips of paper that you get from the post office. If you use an online postage service, print a postage report once a month and file it in your filing cabinets or boxes as well.

>> **Merchandise receipts:** Merchandise purchased for resale on eBay. Documentation of all the money you spend.

>> **Licenses and legal stuff:** Important! Keep an active file of anything legal; you will no doubt have to lay hands on this information at the oddest moment. It's reassuring to know where it is.

>> **Insurance information:** Policies and insurance proposals should all be kept close by.

I'm sure you can think of some more things that can benefit from a little bit of organization. When you need the information quickly, and you can find it without breaking a sweat, you'll be glad you kept things organized.

Chapter **3**

Taking Care of Your Finances

When you meet with one of the professionals described in Chapter 2 in this minibook, you'll need to bring a complete and accurate set of books. To prepare accurate books, you can hire a bookkeeper (who will use accounting software) or you can learn how to use accounting software yourself. Don't shy away; you *can* do this.

Lots of folks who are successfully using bookkeeping software today knew nothing about bookkeeping before they set up their own accounts. I'm one of them. I keep my books and file quarterly taxes myself and send the year end reports to my accountant. This chapter paves the way into professional and relatively painless bookkeeping.

Keeping an accurate accounting of your business gives you one major benefit: You can, at any time, look at your bookkeeping and have an idea of how well (or not) your business is doing.

REMEMBER

When your business gets so busy that you have no time to post your bookkeeping, hire a part-time bookkeeper to do your posting for you. A site like UpWork (www.upwork.com) is invaluable in finding the right person. With the advent of cloud computing and the rise of software as a service (SaaS), numerous online tax-preparation and payroll apps have popped up. Many of them are good and will do a good job for a small startup.

I researched to find which software was the best selling and easiest to use. I had many discussions with CPAs, enrolled agents, and bookkeepers. The software that these professionals most recommend for business — generally considered the best, which is why I devote so much of this chapter to it — is Intuit's QuickBooks.

According to the National Small Business Association's 2017 Small Business Taxation Survey, one in three small businesses report spending more than 80 hours — two full work weeks — each year on federal taxes. Plus, they spend a bunch of money. My goal, in my 20 years in business, is to spend the least time and money on these tasks. The advice in this chapter is based on my experience and current research.

QuickBooks is also available in an online version. I personally use the desktop version and their Payroll for my business. Whether you use the (subscription) SaaS service or desktop (fixed cost) is a personal decision. I can say that the desktop version has more features for ecommerce businesses. If QuickBooks Online is what you'd like to start with, give it a try. Especially if you've never used an accounting program before. If you find you need more features in the future, you can easily move to the desktop.

What? Double-Entry Accounting?

You already understand double-entry accounting if you keep your checkbook up to date. Professional-level business bookkeeping is quite similar, done through a similar double-entry system.

Double-entry accounting requires each transaction to be recorded in two accounts. From one account there is a debit (minus) and the other gets a credit (plus), as shown in Table 3-1. When the books are reconciled, this method minimizes errors as the sum of the accounts with debit balances should equal the sum of credit balance accounts.

TABLE 3-1   **Double-Entry Bookkeeping Transactions**

Account	Debit	Credit
Assets	Increase	Decrease
Expenses	Increase	Decrease
Liabilities	Decrease	Increase
Owner's Equity	Decrease	Increase
Revenues	Decrease	Increase

Stephen L. Nelson (MBA, CPA MS in Taxation), the author of *QuickBooks 2017 All-in-One For Dummies* (Wiley), describes it this way: "The formula [behind double-entry accounting] says that a business owns stuff and that the money or the funds for that stuff come either from creditors (such as the bank or some vendor) or the owners (either in the form of original contributed capital or perhaps in reinvested profits)."

To be honest, this whole double-entry bookkeeping makes my head spin and makes me a little sick to my stomach. That's why I use QuickBooks software to do the work of debiting and crediting for me automatically. If you really want to understand in depth how this all works, I recommend you read Stephen's book.

QuickBooks: Professional Bookkeeping

QuickBooks offers several versions, from basic to enterprise (company-size) solutions tailored to different types of businesses. The various versions have a few significant differences. QuickBooks Pro adds job costing and expensing — and the capability to design your own forms. QuickBooks online does a darn good job, too, so check out the comparison at

```
https://quickbooks.intuit.com/products/
```

and see which version is best for you. I use QuickBooks Pro (the least expensive desktop edition), so that's the version I describe in the rest of this section. If you're just purchasing QuickBooks Pro, you may have an updated version that works a bit differently. But the accounting basics that the software provides for your business don't change.

I update my QuickBooks software every few years, and the product improvements continue to save me time in performing my bookkeeping tasks. If you find that you don't have time to input your bookkeeping data, you may have to hire a part-time bookkeeper. The bonus is that professional bookkeepers probably already know QuickBooks. Also, at the end of each year, the QuickBooks program will supply you with all the official reports your enrolled agent (EA) or certified public accountant (CPA) will need to do your taxes. (Yes, you really *do* need an EA or a CPA.) You can even send your preparer a backup on a flash drive or a CD. See how simple bookkeeping can be?

QuickBooks Pro

When you first fire up QuickBooks Pro, you must answer a few questions to set up your account. Among the few things you need to have ready — before you even begin to mess with the software — are the following starting figures:

>> **Cash balance:** This may be the amount in your checking account (no personal money, please!) or the amount of money deposited from your eBay profits. Put these profits into a separate checking account to use for your business.

>> **Accounts receivable balance:** Does anyone owe you money for some auctions? Outstanding payments make up this total.

>> **Account liability balance:** Do you owe some money? Are you being invoiced for some merchandise that you haven't paid for? Total it and enter it when QuickBooks prompts you.

If you're starting your business in the middle of the year, gather any previous profits and expenses that you want to include because you'll have to input this information for a complete annual set of diligently recorded books. I can guarantee that this is going to take a while. But you'll be thanking me for insisting that you get organized. It just makes everything work smoother in the long run.

QuickBooks EasyStep Interview

After you've organized your finances, you can proceed with the QuickBooks EasyStep Interview, shown in Figure 3-1. The EasyStep Interview is designed to provide a comfort level for those with accounting-phobia and those using a bookkeeping program for the first time. If you mess things up, you can always use the Back arrow and change what you've input. If you need help, simply click the Help button and the program will answer many of your questions. Hey, if worst comes to worst, you can always delete the company file (including your erroneous inputs) and start over.

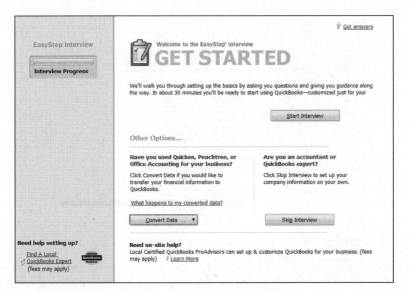

FIGURE 3-1:
A QuickBooks Pro
EasyStep Interview
start page.

For the whirlwind tour through the QuickBooks EasyStep Interview, just follow these steps (which are only a general guideline):

1. **Start QuickBooks, and choose the Create a New Company option.**

   You're now at the EasyStep Interview.

2. **On the first page of the interactive portion of the interview, type your company name (this becomes the filename in your computer) and the legal name of your company.**

   If you've filed a fictitious name statement (see Chapter 1 in this minibook), the fictitious name is the legal name of your company.

3. **Continue to follow the steps, answering other questions about your business, such as the address and the type of tax form you use.**

4. **When QuickBooks asks what type of business you want to use, choose Retail Shop or Online Commerce (as I did in Figure 3-2).**

TIP

   If you have a business other than your eBay sales — perhaps consulting or teaching others — you may want to just leave the Company box blank in QuickBooks, specify no business option, and build your own chart of accounts from the one they give you — that's what I did.

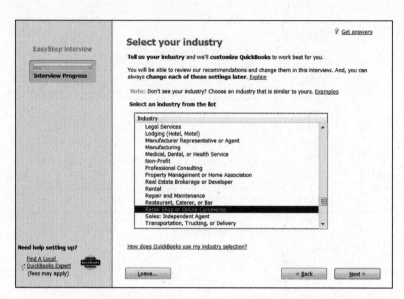

FIGURE 3-2:
Selecting your
company type.

5. **When QuickBooks asks whether you want to use its chosen chart of accounts, choose Yes.**

You can always change the accounts later. If you want to spend the time, you can input your entire custom chart of accounts — more about that in the next section — manually (but I *really* don't recommend it, since the generated chart is easily edited).

6. **Answer some more general questions, which I'm sure you can handle with the aid of the intuitive QuickBooks help feature.**

7. **When the preferences pages appear, I recommend that you select the option that says, "Enter the bills first and then enter the payments later."**

TIP

This is a handy option; if you input your bills as they come in, you can get an exact idea of how much money you owe at any time by just starting the program.

8. **Click the box to indicate that you collect sales tax.**

9. **On the Sales Tax preferences page, indicate the agencies for which you collect sales tax, and then set up the tax-collecting information.**

10. **Decide whether you want to use QuickBooks to process your payroll.**

Even if you're the only employee, using QuickBooks payroll information makes things much easier when it comes to required deductions and filling out your payroll deposits. I subscribe additionally to QuickBooks Enhanced Payroll — which files reports and sends my business' Federal and State payments for me, electronically and automatically. This saves hours of labor and pays for itself over a year's time.

11. **Answer a few more questions, including whether you want to use the cash basis or accrual basis of accounting.**

The *accrual* basis posts sales the minute you write an invoice or post a sales receipt, and posts your expenses as soon as you post the bills into the computer. Accrual-basis accounting gives you a clearer picture of where your company is financially than does cash-basis accounting. The *cash basis* is when you record bills by writing checks — expenses are posted only when you write the checks. This way of doing business may be simpler, but the only way you'll know how much money you owe is by looking at the pile of bills on your desk.

12. **If you're comfortable doing so, just click Leave and then input the balance of your required information directly into the program without using the Interview feature.**

Setting Up a Chart of Accounts

After you've finished the EasyStep Interview and have successfully set up your business in QuickBooks, the program presents a *chart of accounts* — essentially an organization system, rather like file folders, that keeps all related data in the proper area. When you write a check to pay a bill, it deducts the amount from your checking account, reduces your accounts payable, and increases your asset or expense account if that's appropriate.

You have a choice of giving each account a number. These numbers, a kind of bookkeeping shorthand, are standardized throughout bookkeeping. Believe it or not, everybody in the industry seems to know what number goes with what item. To keep things less confusing, I like to use titles as well as numbers.

To customize your chart of accounts, follow these steps:

1. **Choose Edit⇨Preferences.**

2. **Click the Accounting icon (on the left).**

3. **Click the Company preferences tab and indicate that you'd like to use account numbers.**

An editable chart of accounts appears. Because QuickBooks doesn't assign account numbers by default, you'll need to edit the chart to create them.

4. **Go through your QuickBooks chart of accounts and add any missing categories.**

You may not need all these categories — and you can always add more later. In Table 3-2, I show you a chart of accounts that a CPA wrote for an eBay business. To get an idea of how you can customize the chart of accounts, also look at Figure 3-3, which shows you the chart of accounts from my own business.

TABLE 3-2   **eBay Business Chart of Accounts**

Account Number	Account Name	What It Represents
1001	Checking	All revenue deposited here and all checks drawn upon this account.
1002	Money market account	Company savings account.
1100	Accounts receivable	For customers to whom you extend credit.
1201	Merchandise inventory	Charge to cost of sales as used, or take periodic inventories and adjust at that time.
1202	Shipping supplies	Boxes, tape, labels, and so forth; charge these to cost as used, or take an inventory at the end of the period and adjust to cost of sales.
1401	Office furniture and equipment	Desk, computer, telephone.
1402	Shipping equipment	Scales, tape dispensers.
1403	Vehicles	Your vehicle if it's owned by the company.
1501	Accumulated depreciation	For your accountant's use.
1601	Deposits	Security deposits on leases.
2001	Accounts payable	Amounts owed for the stuff you sell, or charged expenses.
2100	Payroll liabilities	Taxes deducted from employees' checks and taxes paid by company on employee earnings.
2200	Sales tax payable	Sales tax collected at time of sale and owed to the state.
2501	Equipment loans	Money borrowed to buy a computer or other equipment.
2502	Auto loans	This is for when you get that hot new van for visiting your consignment clients.
3000	Owner's capital	Your opening balance.
3902	Owner's draw	Your withdrawals for the current year.
4001	Merchandise sales	Revenue from sales of your products.

Account Number	Account Name	What It Represents
4002	Shipping and handling	Paid by the customer.
4009	Returns	Total dollar amount of returned merchandise.
4101	Interest income	From your investments.
4201	Other income	Income not otherwise classified.
5001	Merchandise purchases	All the merchandise you buy for eBay; you'll probably use subaccounts for individual items.
5002	Freight in	Freight and shipping charges you pay for your inventory, not for shipments to customers.
5003	Shipping	Shipping to your customers: USPS, FedEx, UPS, and so on.
5004	Shipping supplies	Boxes, labels, tape, bubble wrap, and so on.
6110	Automobile expense	When you use your car for work.
6111	Gas and oil	Filling up the tank.
6112	Automobile repairs	When your business owns the car.
6120	Bank service charges	Monthly service charges, NSF charges, and so on.
6140	Contributions	Charity.
6142	Data services	Does an outside firm process your payroll?
6143	Internet service provider	What you pay to your Internet provider.
6144	Website hosting fees	Fees paid to your hosting company.
6150	Depreciation expense	For your accountant's use.
6151	eBay fees	What you pay eBay every month to stay in business, based on your sales.
6152	Discounts	Fees you're charged for using eBay and accepting credit card payments; deducted from your revenue and reported to you on your eBay statement.
6153	Other auction site fees	You may want to set up subcategories for each site where you do business, such as Yahoo! or Amazon.
6156	PayPal fees	Processing fees paid to PayPal.
6158	Credit card or merchant-account fees	If you have a separate merchant account, post those fees here.
6160	Dues	Membership fees you pay if you join an organization (relating to your business) that charges them.

(continued)

Taking Care of Your Finances

TABLE 3-2 *(continued)*

Account Number	Account Name	What It Represents
6161	Magazines and periodicals	Books and magazines that help you run and expand your business.
6170	Equipment rental	Postage meter, occasional van.
6180	Insurance	Policies that cover your merchandise or your office.
6185	Liability insurance	Insurance that covers you if (for example) someone slips and falls at your place of business (can also be put under Insurance).
6190	Disability insurance	Insurance that will pay you if you become temporarily or permanently disabled and can't perform your work.
6191	Health insurance	If you provide it for yourself, you may be required to provide it to employees.
6200	Interest expense	Credit interest and interest on loans.
6220	Loan interest	When you borrow from the bank.
6230	Licenses	State and city licenses.
6240	Miscellaneous	Whatever doesn't go anyplace else in these categories.
6250	Postage and delivery	Stamps used in your regular business.
6251	Endicia.com fees	Fees for your eBay business postage service.
6260	Printing	Your business cards, correspondence stationery, and so on.
6265	Filing fees	Fees paid to file legal documents.
6270	Professional fees	Fees paid to consultants.
6280	Legal fees	If you have to pay a lawyer.
6650	Accounting and bookkeeping	Bookkeeper, CPA, or EA.
6290	Rent	Office, warehouse, and so on.
6300	Repairs	Can be the main category for the following subcategories.
6310	Building repairs	Repair to the building you operate your business in.
6320	Computer repairs	What you pay the person to set up your wireless network.
6330	Equipment repairs	When (say) the copier or the phone needs fixing.
6340	Telephone	Regular telephone, fax lines.
6350	Travel expenses	Business-related travel, business meals.

Account Number	Account Name	What It Represents
6360	Entertainment	When you take eBay's CEO out to dinner to benefit your eBay business (don't forget to invite me too).
6370	Meals	Meals while traveling for your business.
6390	Utilities	Major heading for subcategories that follow.
6391	Electricity and gas	Electricity and gas.
6392	Water	Water.
6560	Payroll expenses	Wages paid to others.
6770	Supplies	Office supplies.
6772	Computer	Computer, tablets, software, and supplies.
6780	Marketing	Advertising or items you purchase to give out that promote your business.
6790	Office	Miscellaneous office expense, such as bottled water delivery.
6820	Taxes	Major category for the following subcategories below.
6830	Federal	Federal taxes.
6840	Local	Local (city, county) taxes.
6850	Property	Property taxes.
6860	State	State taxes.

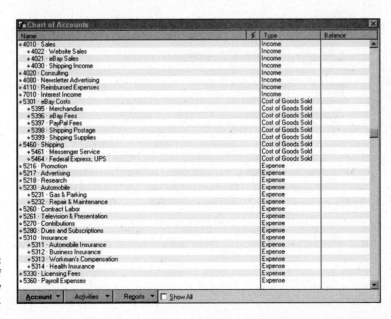

FIGURE 3-3:
The chart of accounts from my eBay business.

Having QuickBooks Report on Your eBay Business

QuickBooks can give you up-to-the-minute reports about the status of your eBay business and keep track of everything — including payroll and sales-tax liability — in the background. Here are a few things that I like about using QuickBooks to streamline an online business:

» **Inventory reports:** As you purchase inventory, aside from deducting the money from your checking account and expensing your merchandise account, QuickBooks adds the purchased merchandise to your inventory. Every time you sell an item, QuickBooks deducts the item from your inventory.

Figure 3-4 shows you a part of an inventory report that I pulled out of the program. You can see how valuable the data is. With a click of my mouse, I can see how much I have left in stock and the average number of items I've sold per week.

5:48 PM
03/01/13

The Collier Company, Inc.
Inventory Stock Status by Item
April 2012 through March 2013

	Item Description	Pref Vendor	Reorder Pt	On Hand	Order
Inventory					
Cloud Dome Angle	Cloud Dome Angled collar	Cloud Dome, Inc		1	
Cloud Dome 7 collar	Cloud Dome 7 collar	Cloud Dome, Inc		7	
Cloud Dome	Cloud Dome NO COLLAR	Cloud Dome, Inc		7	
Brush Set	Pur Minerals Brush Set	Santa fe Produc...		7	
Ossential	Obagi Ossential	Santa fe Produc...		9	
Obagi	Obagi Kit			1	
Black SY lamp	True color sy			3	
Singelringen	Singelringen			0	
QVC xmas	QVC Christmas Jewlery			6	
5550 Bulb	Full SPectrum Bulb			14	
PBS					
Online Business	Your Online Business Plan			11	
MYFOL	▸ Making Your Fortune Online			24	
PBS - Other				0	
Total PBS				13	
Calendar	Fraggle Rock			-9	
20" Tent	20" Photo Tent			1	
28" Tent	28" Photo Tent			9	
Angled Collar	Cloud Dome Angled Collar	Cloud Dome, Inc		34	
Black Infiniti	Black Infiniti Board	Cloud Dome, Inc		9	

FIGURE 3-4:
A portion of an inventory-tracking report.

» **Sales-tax tracking:** Depending on how the program is set up (based on your own state sales tax laws), you can request a report that has all your taxable and nontaxable sales. The report calculates the amount of sales tax you owe. You can print this report for backup information of your sales-tax payments to the state.

>> **Payroll:** Whether you use the Enhanced Payroll Service to prepare your payroll or input the deductions yourself, QuickBooks posts the appropriate withholdings to their own accounts. When it comes time to pay your employees' withholding taxes, QuickBooks can generate the federal reporting form (all filled in) for submitting with your payment.

>> **Sales reports:** QuickBooks gives you a plethora of reports with which you can analyze your sales professionally. One of my favorite reports is the Sales by Item Summary. This report gives you the following information for every inventoried item you sell, in whatever time period you choose:

- Quantity sold

- Total dollar amount sold

- Percentage of sales represented by each item

- The average price the item sold for

- COGS (cost of goods sold) by item

- Average cost of goods sold by total sales per item

- Gross profit margin in dollar amounts

- Gross profit margin expressed as percentage

TIP

Depending on how you post your transactions, you can analyze your eBay sales, website sales, and brick-and-mortar sales (individually or together). You can also select *any* date range for your reports.

Posting Sales from PayPal My Way

Some sellers import PayPal data into QuickBooks; I don't. The problem with that import process is that a new customer file is set up for each of your sales.

Saving each sale as a new customer will make your database huge in no time. Last time I checked, the maximum number of names (employees, customers, vendors) for QuickBooks Pro is 14,500. QuickBooks is a large program to begin with, and if you're going to use it (and update it) for several years, the database might explode.

If you've ever worked with large files, you know that the larger the data file, the more chance there is for the data to become corrupt. That's the last thing you want. Besides, a successful online business can max out QuickBooks with over 14,000 customers in just a few years.

TIP

To keep track of your customers, you download a PayPal monthly report and import it into an Excel spreadsheet to build your customer database.

Posting sales to match deposits

In this section, I show you a procedure I developed to process my PayPal sales. I've run it past several accountants and QuickBooks experts, and it's garnered rave reviews. I'm sharing it with you because I want you to be able to run your business smoothly. Lots of sellers use this method. It shortens your inputting time.

Rather than post an invoice for every customer, I input my sales into a customer sales receipt as shown in Figure 3-5. Whenever I make a PayPal deposit into my business checking account — which is every few days, depending on how busy sales are — I post my sales into QuickBooks. This way, the total of my sales receipt equals the amount of my PayPal deposit. (If you've ever tried to reconcile your PayPal deposits with your sales *and* your checking account, you know how frustrating it can be.)

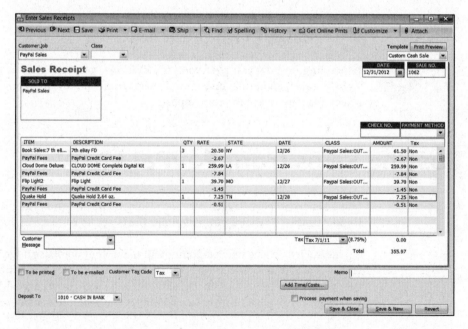

FIGURE 3-5:
My customer sales receipt.

In my QuickBooks, I designate PayPal as the customer. It makes no difference who bought what; the only thing that matters is which item sold (to deduct from inventory) and for how much (to post to my financial data).

Customizing the sales data

The program gives you the flexibility to customize forms, and Figure 3-5 shows my customized sales receipt for PayPal sales. PayPal is a taxable customer when sales are made in the State of California, and the appropriate sales tax is applied automatically. I added the following when I customized the form:

TIP

>> **PayPal fees:** I set up PayPal fees as a credit against sales. (In Figure 3-5, you can see they are applied as a negative.) This helps me match the total amount of the sales receipt to my PayPal deposit. It also gives me a discount line in my sales reports that tracks my total paid in PayPal fees. The PayPal fees line also appears in the "cost of goods sold" area of my financial statements.

In case you're wondering about eBay fees, they have their own line in my chart of accounts. I charge eBay fees to my company credit card. When the credit card expenses are posted, eBay fees post as an expense to the eBay fees account.

>> **State:** I type the two-letter state abbreviation of the shipping location with each item. This serves as backup information for my State Board of Equalization (the California sales tax board) and also allows me to run reports on what has sold in which states.

>> **Date:** The date at the top of the sales receipt is the posting date. The date in the product posting indicates the date the PayPal payment was posted.

>> **Class:** Every item posted in QuickBooks can be part of a defined class to make it easier for you to isolate certain types of transactions. I set up two classes of PayPal sales: California sales and out-of-state sales. California sales are classified as taxable; out-of-state sales are classified as nontaxable. QuickBooks calculates the tax liability automatically.

Although PayPal does send a Form 1099 at the end of the year, it does not break out sales tax.

REMEMBER

>> **Tax classification:** When I type the first two letters into the class area (OU for out-of-state sales and CA for in-state sales), the tax line changes automatically to Tax or Non-Tax. QuickBooks would do this whether I show this field in the sales receipt or not, but by having it appear, I can use it as a secondary reminder to post the taxable class properly.

By inputting my eBay sales data in this way, I streamline the process in several ways. I post data to only one program, only once. From this sales receipt, I get updated inventory reports, accurate sales tax data, and accurate expense and income tracking. It also eases the process of reconciling my checking account.

Chapter 4

Keeping You and Your Business Secure Online

Online security is something everybody worries about, but few people do anything about it. When people's accounts are hacked, they whine and moan about online security, but they don't give a moment's thought as to why using a user ID as a password (tell me you didn't do that) *wasn't* the best choice.

Even if you avoid such classic blunders, you have to keep your wits about you online. Sad to say, some people out there *are* trying to dupe you; it's time to take charge of our own security and fight back in the best ways we can. Some phishing scams pretend to be from eBay, PayPal, Citibank, and others — and try to bilk you out of your personal information. I show you a fairly foolproof way to recognize those. I also show you how spammers get your email address. Even if you never give it out, they have ways of getting it from you. In this chapter, I hope to teach you how to be a little more savvy about which emails you open — and how to fight back.

Staying Away from Spam

I used to spend at least an hour every day cleaning spam out of my daily emails; but no longer. Read on to see how I've cut my spam-scanning time!

Spam is sneaky, and antispam software can cause you to lose email that you need because it seems that the word *eBay* is a favorite of spammers. I want *news* on eBay, but I don't want to get those make-a-fortune-on-eBay emails.

I also would rather not hear from Mr. Felix Kamala, son of the late Mr. A.Y. Kamala. It seems his family lost millions in Zimbabwe to a scammer in the government, and he wants me to help him get his secret stash of "Fifteen million five hundred thousand united state dollars." He was going to give me 20 percent just for helping him — how thoughtful! (In case you didn't know, this email is part of what the FBI calls the *Nigerian email scam* — also called the 419 scam — named after the African penal code violated with this crime.)

TIP

Know that most email providers, your ISP, and the free providers install spam filters so we are not quite as exposed as much as we were in the past. I have found that the free providers actually do a better job than one might expect.

Figure 4-1 is an example of such a message found in my Gmail spam filter.

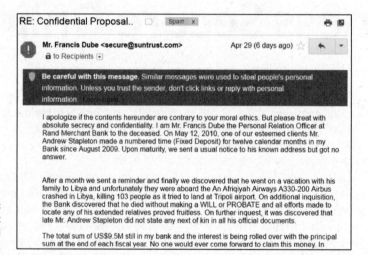

FIGURE 4-1:
The classic 419 scam is still circulating.

Keeping your email address quiet

Have you ever signed up for anything on the Internet? Before you signed up, did you check to see whether the site had a posted privacy-policy page? Did you notice a tiny check box surreptitiously placed at the bottom of the page that says you agree to receive emails from the site? You probably didn't.

After you type your name in a box on the Internet agreeing to accept email, expect to receive a *lot* of mail. Check any site for a Privacy Policy and read how they treat email addresses. Many sites openly admit that they share your address. You are now an opt-in customer. *Opt in* means that you *asked* to be on a list, and a site with a loose Privacy Policy can even sell your address to spammers.

Take a look at Figure 4-2. It's a description from an eBay listing for a CD containing 14,000,000 email addresses. Yes, you can buy access to all those potential suckers for only $7.00.

FIGURE 4-2:
A tempting offer to violate people's privacy.

Just opening your email and loading images can give you away as well. Spammers will often make up return email addresses to mask their true locations (as you can tell by some of the "From" addresses). If you open and view their email, the email sends a notice to the spammers' server, and then they know that the email address is valid. This practice can also be masked in the HTML to occur when the email consists of merely a picture — when it goes back to grab the picture for your email, it reports that your email address is good.

Recognizing Scams and Phishing

Much of the spam you get can be recognized by the subject line. I used to check my email after I downloaded it to my computer. That's a dangerous procedure, though, considering that some emails do their real job by delivering malware that's set up to self-install if the attachment — or even the email itself — is opened.

I now use Gmail with its very effective spam filters. Since not everyone uses Gmail (I recommend you do), you can also forward email from another email account to a Gmail address to take advantage of their advanced security. Let me take you through some steps to maintain your security.

It may seem you've received an email from PayPal. They say your account needs to be renewed? Oh my! You certainly don't want to lose access to your PayPal account — which, by the way, does not expire.

Or how about an email, supposedly from PayPal, that says:

> *We recently reviewed your account and suspect that your PayPal account may have been accessed by an unauthorized third party. Protecting the security of your account and of the PayPal network is our primary concern. Therefore, as a preventative measure, we have temporarily limited access to sensitive PayPal account features.*
>
> *Click below in order to regain access to your account:*

Uh-huh. Right. As in, STOP RIGHT THERE!

Take a good look at the email you have received. Who is it addressed to? When PayPal sends you an email, the opening line says "Dear (*your registered name*)." In my case, a real email from PayPal read, "Dear Collier Company." Spam emails are usually more generic, addressed to "Dear Valued User" or "Dear *youremailaddress.com*." PayPal will *never* address an email to your email address.

Take a look at this email, purportedly from eBay, in Figure 4-3. Notice the eBay return address; I don't think that's quite right.

FIGURE 4-3:
This email is addressed to my email address, not my customer account ID.

Responding to these emails is tantamount to giving away your information to a stranger. Don't do it. I did some very careful investigating so I could show you how the scam works. Please read about what I found, but please read this first:

If you suspect a message is spam, just delete it.

In Gmail, you can click the arrow at the top right of the email return address. In a drop-down menu, as shown in Figure 4-4, you will see several options.

FIGURE 4-4:
Gmail options for dealing with emails.

To confirm whether the email is real, click *Show Original*. At the top of the original, you get a short synopsis of the email. Note that in Figure 4-5 the return email address for eBay is *not* eBay.com.

Original Message	
Message ID	<34915d02d02d893d8pmj91377280d8@i327.angjrmob.us>
Created at:	Sat, May 6, 2017 at 7:09 PM (Delivered after 18 seconds)
From:	
To:	
Subject:	marsha.collier, your recent purchase got a reward
SPF:	PASS with IP 93.76.157.132 Learn more
DKIM:	PASS with domain i327.angjrmob.us Learn more

FIGURE 4-5:
This email is not from eBay.

Below the synopsis will be the code for the email, which can also be used to confirm your suspicions. I scrolled to the bottom, finding the line that said *Sign in now* (followed by a URL, as shown in Figure 4-6).

FIGURE 4-6:
If you click Sign In Now you will be redirected to the scammer's website.

```
<a href=3D"http://i327.angjrmob.us/b/b1cef52c7ec85611cd6b775beb884baa.h=
tml?c=3D59001">
```

Take a good long look at the link, and at the URL embedded in the email. Look just before it in the source code and you can see that the link *really* redirects whoever clicks it to `http://i327.angjrmob.us/b/b1cef52c7ec85611cd6b775beb884baa.` `h=tml?c=3D59001` — *not* to the eBay secure URL! Liar, liar, pants afire.

WARNING

When it comes to the authentic PayPal website URL, it begins with `https`, not `http`. The `s` in `https` stands for *secure*.

If you want to find out for sure whether your PayPal or eBay (or bank account) account has a problem, or whether you actually should view a recent charge, play it safe: Close the email, go directly to the real site, and log in at the *real* URL. If your account does have a problem, you'll know right away.

Fighting Back!

There's quite a bit that you can do to help stop spam. According to Federal law, every email should have an Unsubscribe link that does not require you to enter your email address to stop getting the sender's emails. Sound good? Well, there's a nasty catch. Read on.

Often the link that says, "Click here to have your name removed from the list" goes directly to a site where the spammers actually collect emails from people and then exploit them. Have you ever clicked one of those? I have. I found out that those links are the gold standard for collecting valid email addresses! If you respond to the spam in any way, shape, or form, they know they've reached a valid address — and watch the spam (or worse) to your mailbox increase. In the case of Gmail, you can just click to report Spam or Phishing. That's all you need to do.

TIP

When signing up for some sort of newsletter with an organization you're new to or unsure of, use an anonymous Yahoo!, Gmail, Hotmail, or Live address. It's easy enough to sign up for one, and if spammers get hold of that address, they will not be privy to your private address.

Also, no matter how curious you are about enlarging certain parts of your anatomy, don't even open the emails you receive on those topics. And certainly don't respond.

Last, report spammers. Several legitimate sites take reports and forward them to the appropriate authorities. Don't bother trying to forward the spam to the sender's ISP. These days they're mostly forged with aliases, and all you'll do is succeed in clogging up the email system. Here are a couple of places you can go to report spammers:

>> **Federal Trade Commission:** Yes, your tax dollars are at work. The FTC would like you to forward unwanted or deceptive messages to spam@uce.gov; and you can find details at

`www.consumer.ftc.gov/articles/0038-spam`

There the message becomes available to law enforcement (especially vital if the email is trying to get your personal information).

>> **SpamCop.net:** This outfit's been around since 1998 and reports spam emails to ISPs and mailers. A Report Spam tab appears on the home page (`www.spamcop.net`) and these folks work hard to get spammers out of the loop.

Keeping Your Password (and Accounts) Secure

When was the last time you changed your passwords? I mean the whole enchilada: eBay, PayPal, your online bank account? Hey, I'm not the keeper of the *shoulds*, but you *should* change your critical passwords every 30 days — rain or shine. That's not just me saying that. It's all the security experts who know this kind of stuff. The world is full of bad-deed-doers just waiting to get their hands on your personal information. Password theft can lead to your bank account being emptied, your credit cards being pushed to the max, and worst of all, someone unsavory out there posing as you.

You've probably seen commercials on TV poking fun at the very real problem of identity theft. If you ask around your circle of friends, no doubt you'll find someone who knows someone who's been in this pickle. It can take years to undo the damage caused by identity theft, so a better plan is to stay vigilant and protect yourself from becoming a victim. It can also take a lot of money — a post on Bankrate.com says "a recent study from Javelin Strategy & Research, fraudsters stole $16 billion from 12.7 million U.S. consumers in 2014, with a new identity fraud victim popping up about every two seconds."

In this section, I give you some tips for selecting good passwords and other personal security information. I also show you the type of passwords to stay away from and what to do if (heaven forbid!) your personal information is compromised.

Reporting hijacked accounts

If someone gets hold of your personal information, the most important thing to do is report it immediately. If you see any items that aren't yours on the

Bids/Offers or the Selling area of your My eBay page, it's time to make a report — and *fast!*

Okay, you know that something hinky is going on with your eBay account because *you* never placed a bid on the Britney Spears stage-worn T-shirt. (Did you? Let's say you didn't.) And you can't imagine that your spouse did, either (but double-check just to be sure). Here's what to do immediately:

>> **Change your personal email account password with your ISP or email provider.** Go to their home page and look for an area called Member Center, settings, or something similar. In this area, access your personal account information — probably through a link called something like My Account. You should be able to change your password there.

>> **Change the email account password on your home computer.** Don't forget to change the password on your computer's email software as well (Outlook, Firefox, and the like), so you can continue to download your email from the server.

Perhaps you discover that your private information has been compromised when you suddenly can't log in to your eBay or PayPal account. If this happens on eBay, follow these steps to request a new password:

1. **Go to the eBay Sign In page.**

   Don't type your password. You just tried that and it doesn't work.

2. **If you have your mobile number registered to your eBay account, click the *Text a temporary password* link, as shown in Figure 4-7.**

FIGURE 4-7:
The Text a temporary password link on the Sign In page.

If you have a land or office line registered to your eBay account, click the *Forgot your password* link. Doing this takes you to a page where you're prompted to type in your user ID or registered email address. Those silly security questions that you answered when you registered for eBay become very important now.

3. **Alternatively, you can use your PayPal login credentials to change your eBay password.**

Choosing a good secret question

If you read the harrowing procedure in this chapter's "Act quickly but don't freak out" sidebar, you know that having someone sabotage your eBay account is something you never want to go through. But if your secret question is easy to figure out, someone with bad intentions can wreak havoc on your account even more easily.

TIP

Your password is only as secure as the secret question, so *don't relate your password and secret question to each other in any way.* For example, do not make your secret question a clue to your password — and *especially* don't make your password answer the secret question. Better yet, think of your secret question as a separate, auxiliary security device for your account.

Here are some tips for setting a secure secret question:

» **Never use your mother's maiden name.** That is most likely the *secret* that your bank uses as your challenge question. (They usually ask when you open the account.) So that is definitely out — you don't want to give *anybody* that word.

» **Select a question and provide a *creative* answer:**

- **What is your pet's name?** Give an answer such as Ralph the Rhino or Graak the Pterodactyl or something a bit more wildly creative. Don't give your actual pet's name (or species). Anyone who knows you is likely to know your pet's name.

- **What street did you grow up on?** Name an unusual landmark from your hometown. Don't use a street name.

- **What is the name of your first school?** Make up a good one — perhaps Elementary Penguin Academy? School of Hard Knox?

- **What is your father's middle name?** Make up a goodie or skip it.

- **What is your school's mascot?** There's a lot of creativity that can go on here. How about red-and-white-striped zebra? Pink elephant?

REMEMBER

ACT QUICKLY BUT DON'T FREAK OUT

If you can't seem to get a new password for your eBay account, and you're unsuccessful at contacting eBay, there's still hope. Remain calm, follow these steps, and take notes as you go:

1. Scroll all the way to the bottom, and on the left side of the page you will see a light-colored tab labeled *Legal & more*. Click there and links to all eBay interior pages appear (see the figure).

    Alternatively, you can go to any eBay item page (or any page on the site) and find a link at the very bottom to the Security Center. Whichever set of links you go to, click the link to the Security Center.

2. **When you get to the Security Center, find the Report a Concern category.**

3. **Under the Report a Concern headline, click *Report an Account Theft*.**

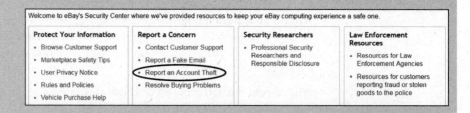

4. **On the following page, find the boldface headline that reads *If you can't sign in, contact us immediately*. Click the link to contact eBay immediately.**

    The page that appears has a link you can use to call eBay.

5. **Click the *Call us* link (they are on duty 24/7).**

    You will be presented with a number to call and a customer service representative will help you sort things out.

Your bylaws for selecting answers to a secret question are two: Be creative, *and* be sure you remember the darned thing! (And here's one more: Don't use any of the examples I just used. Make up your own.)

Avoiding easily hacked passwords

Poorly chosen passwords are the number-one loophole for hackers. If you think that hackers are just a small group of hypercaffeinated teenagers, think again. It's now also the domain of small- and big-time crooks who hack into an account, spend a few thousand dollars that belong to someone else, and move on.

I searched Google for hacking software and came up with over 2 million matches. Many of these websites offer an arsenal of free hacking tools. They also provide step-by-step instructions for beginners on how to crack passwords. The Internet can be its own worst enemy.

Here are some industrial-strength tips for setting a secure password:

>> **Number of characters:** Compose your password of more than eight characters.

>> **Case sensitivity:** Because passwords are case-sensitive, take advantage of the feature. Mix lowercase and uppercase in your passwords.

>> **Letters, numbers, and symbols:** Combine these to make your passwords harder to crack.

>> **Proper words:** Don't use proper words that appear in the dictionary. Think of the title of your favorite book. Make your password the first two letters of each word with numbers in the middle (*not* sequential).

TIP

It should go without saying, but what the heck: Don't use any of the sample passwords shown here. It's safe to say that lots of people will be reading this book, and anything seen by lots of people isn't secret. (I know you know that, but still.)

STAY SMART: DON'T BE A MAKE-IT-EASY!

Any beginning hacker (or tech-smart teenager) can figure out your password if it falls into the following categories. Don't use 'em! They are pathetically easy!

- **The obvious:** The word *Password*. D'oh!

- **Birthdays:** Don't use your birthday, your friend's birthday, or John F. Kennedy's birthday. Not only are these dates common knowledge, but so is this truism: A series of numbers is easy to crack.

- **Names:** Don't use your first name, last name, your dog's name, or anyone's name. Again, it's common knowledge and easy to find out. (Most people know my husband's name; it's been in many of my books!)

- **Contact numbers:** Nix on *any* Social Security Number (if they get hold of *that* one — watch out!), phone numbers, your email address, or street address. For classic phone-book information, try sites like Spokeo (http://www.spokeo.com/), pipl (https://pipl.com/), or PeekYou (http://www.peekyou.com/).

- **Any of the lousy (easily cracked and most frequently used) passwords in the table:** The words in this table have been gleaned from password dictionaries available from hackers. Note that this is *not* a complete list by any means; there are thousands of common (lousy) passwords, and "unprintable" ones are a lot more common than you may think. If you really care to scare yourself, Google the phrase *common passwords*.

!@#$%	!@#$%^&	!@#$%^&*(	0	0000	00000000	0007
007	01234	123456	02468	24680	1	1101
111	11111	111111	1234	12345	1234qwer	123abc
123go	12	131313	212	310	2003	2004
54321	654321	888888	a	aaa	abc	abc123
action	absolut	access	admin	admin123	access	administrator
alpha	asdf	animal	biteme	computer	eBay	enable
foobar	home	Internet	login	love	mypass	mypc
owner	pass	password	passwrd	papa	peace	penny
pepsi	qwerty	secret	superman	temp	temp123	test
test123	whatever	whatnot	winter	windows	xp	xxx
yoda	mypc123	powerseller	sexy			

Chapter **5**

Networking Your Home or Office

The first time I spoke to my editors about putting information in my books about networking a home business, they scoffed. People who worked at home back in the day didn't need computer networks (as if networks were solely for big companies with lots of cubicles). Since we're now well along in the 21st century, home and small office networks are required to do business.

I started writing about eBay in 1998, and now it's close to twenty years later. A lot of technology has washed under the bridge, and many advances have been made. Setting up a network in 1999 meant spending hours (maybe days) changing settings, testing, checking computers, and cursing. That was if you were lucky enough to finally get it right. Otherwise — as was the case for most home users, including me — you'd give up, take the whole thing as a loss, and go on with your life.

Luckily for the rest of us, networks are considerably more user-friendly than in the old days. Also, more pleasant modes of networking (other than having miles of Ethernet cables snaking around the walls of your house) came to the fore of technology.

By networking your home (or office) you'll save time by having the flexibility to work from different rooms or locations. You can run your business out by the pool (or in your backyard) in summer!

This chapter is a quick-and-easy discussion of home networks installed on Windows-based PCs. Happily, since I have a Mac user in my home, I've found that networking is pretty universal. In this chapter, I give you a lesson on what I know works for most people.

REMEMBER

At this point, I want to remind you that I'm not a super nerd, even though I do host a `Computer and Technology Radio` show (just like I'm not a lawyer or an accountant). Ping me on Twitter (@marshacollier) if you're having trouble — I'll try to help.

The What and Why of Networks

What is a network? These days it doesn't mean a TV channel nor a group of colleagues: A *network* is a way to connect devices and computers so that they can communicate with each other — as if they were one giant computer with different terminals. The best part is that a network enables all those devices to share a single high-speed Internet connection, as well as the sharing of printers and other peripherals. When you set up a network, you can give Internet access to multiple appropriately equipped devices — computers, tablets, smartphones, or TVs. From each networked device, it's possible to access other networked devices.

You can connect as many devices as you like and run your business from anywhere in your home — you can even hook up your laptop, tablet, or smartphone from the bedroom if you don't feel like getting out of bed.

Now for the *whys* of a home network. A network is a convenient way to run a business. All businesses use them, and so should you. You can extend your DSL line, fiber-optic, or Internet cable connection so that you can access it anywhere in your home — as well as in your office. Besides, you can stream YouTube videos direct to your television.

In networked computers, you can set directories in each computer to be *shared.* That way, other computers on the network can access those directories. You can also password-protect specific files and directories to prevent others (your children or your employees) from accessing them.

Variations of a Home Network

You have a choice of three types of home networks: Ethernet, powerline, and wireless. See Table 5-1 for a quick rundown of some pros and cons of each.

TABLE 5-1   **Network Pros and Cons**

Network Type	Pros	Cons
Traditional Ethernet*	Very fast, cheap, and easy to set up	Computers and printers must be hardwired; cables run everywhere
Powerline	Fast; your home is prewired with outlets	Electrical interference may degrade the signal
Wireless Mesh	Modular nodes placed throughout the home extend the signal wirelessly	Expensive
Wireless network**	Pretty fast; wireless (no ugly cords to deal with)	Might need extenders to carry the signal throughout your home

*Connects computers over a maximum of 328 feet of cabling

**Several flavors of wireless are available. See "Hooking up with wireless," later in this chapter.

Many people still use an Ethernet connection to hardwire the network's main (desktop) computer to connect to a wireless router. If you have an office, it's nice to know that Ethernet cabling will work over 300-foot distances. You can then connect laptops (and desktops) throughout the house via wireless and powerline.

The wireless network is the hot ticket — the new standard, and, er, assimilating more households all the time. However, in a home office setting, the wireless signal may experience interference because many networks run with the same 2.4 GHz (or conflict with 5 GHz) technology as some appliances. I have a wireless network and it works great. My primary network hookup is via Ethernet. But it's actually a hybrid, combining Ethernet and wireless (with an extender).

With broadband over powerline, you get high-speed Internet directly into your home electrical system. Just plug in your powerline boxes (more on that later) and you're up and running.

All networks need the following two devices:

>> **Router:** A router allows you to share a single Internet IP address among multiple devices. A router does exactly what its name implies; it routes signals and data to and from the different devices on your network. If you have only one computer, the router can act as a firewall or even a network device leading to a wireless print or media server.

>> **Modem:** You need a modem for an Internet connection. You get one from your cable or phone company and plug it into an outlet with cable (just like your TV) or into a phone jack if you have DSL. The modem connects to your router with an Ethernet cable.

TIP

If you have broadband, you don't need to have a main computer powered on to access the connection anywhere in the house. If you keep a wireless-enabled printer turned on, you can also connect to that and print from your laptop, tablet, or smartphone in another room — right through the wireless network.

Extending wireless with powerline

An ingenious invention, a *powerline wireless extender* uses your existing home powerlines to carry your network and your high-speed Internet connection. You access the network by plugging a powerline adapter wired to your router into an electrical outlet on the wall. Then another little box can be placed farther away in your home to broadcast an additional wireless signal. Standard powerline networks have been around for a while; this is the second round of technological advances for them.

I have used a powerline wireless extender so I could bring my network out to the garage and to far points in my home.

Hooking up a powerline network or extender is so easy that it's a bit disappointing — you'll wonder why it isn't more complicated. Most installations work immediately right out of the box. Figure 5-1 shows you the base setup. Other rooms need only a powerline wireless adapter.

Home Office

65 Mbps Powerline
Network Adapter

Router

Broadband
modem

85 Mbps Powerline
Network Adapter
(XET1001)

Set-top box

Gaming
console

or

85 Mbps Powerline
Network Adapter

Laptop

Living Room

FIGURE 5-1:
The main
computer setup
for a powerline
network.

Powerline graphic courtesy of Linksys

Hooking up the wireless/powerline network goes like this:

1. **The high-speed connection comes in through your DSL or cable line.**

2. **Plug the cable line (or phoneline for DSL) into your modem.**

3. **Connect one "in" Ethernet cable from your modem to a router.**

4. **Connect the "out" Ethernet cable to the wireless powerline extender.**

5. **Plug the wireless powerline extender into a convenient wall outlet.**

6. **Plug the wireless powerline receiver box into a convenient wall outlet wherever you want to extend the signal.**

That's it!

The benefits of using powerline as a Wi-Fi network *or* as a network extender are as follows:

>> **It's fairly inexpensive.** The requisite powerline magic box costs around $50, but you'll need one for each computer you connect.

>> **It's fast — as fast as (or faster than) other network connections.** You could stream movies from one room to another.

>> **The networking connection is made through your existing electrical wiring.** It doesn't consume extra electricity.

>> **Installation is easy.** Just plug a cable into your computer, and connect the cable to the powerline box. Plug in the powerline box.

If you have a high-speed Internet connection, no doubt you received a modem when you signed up. Because it's not common to connect the modem directly to your computer (a router does the network routing for you), you may already have a router.

The network integration works like this:

>> The high-speed connection comes in through your DSL or cable line.

>> The cable (or DSL) line plugs into your modem.

>> An Ethernet cable goes from your modem into a router.

>> One "out" Ethernet cable connection from the router goes to a local computer.

>> Another "out" Ethernet cable goes to the powerline adapter.

>> The powerline box plugs into a convenient wall outlet.

When you want to connect the computers in other rooms to the network, just plug in a magic powerline box.

Hooking up with wireless

Wireless networking — Wi-Fi (or, to the more technically inclined, IEEE 802.11) — is the go-to standard for all kinds of wireless networks. It's an impressive system when it works, with no cables or connectors to bog you down.

If you're worried about your next-door neighbor hacking into your computer through your wireless connection, stop worrying. Wireless networks are protected by their own brand of security, called WPA2 (Wi-Fi Protected Access 2). Although super-hackers have cracked this system, it's the best currently available for the home office user.

WPA2 utilizes a *pre-shared key* (PSK) mode, where every user on the network is given the same passphrase. In the PSK mode, security depends on the strength and secrecy of the passphrase. So, to link your laptop or desktop to a wireless network with WPA2 encryption, you need the pre-determined passphrase. Just enter it during setup — on every computer that uses the network — and you should be good to go.

TIP

Most free Wi-Fi hotspots you come across may have no encryption, so never send personal information in such an environment without using a VPN (Virtual Private Network) app.

The different flavors of wireless

If you've ever used a wireless telephone at home, you've used a technology similar to a wireless network. Most home wireless phones transmit on the radio frequency band of 2.4 GHz and have the option to choose from several channels automatically to give you the best connection.

You may get confused when you see the different types of wireless available. Here's the lowdown on the variations:

>> **802.11a:** This is a wireless format that works really well — fast with good connectivity. It's used when you have to serve up a wireless connection to a large group of people, as in a convention center or a dormitory. It delivers data at speeds as high as 54 Mbps (megabits per second). It also runs at the 5 GHz band, so it doesn't compete with wireless phones or microwave ovens for bandwidth.

>> **802.11b:** My laptop has a built-in 802.11b card, so I can connect to the ever-popular hotspots in Starbucks and airports. It's a fairly common wireless type and is used on most platforms. It travels over the 2.4 GHz band. The 802.11b version is slower than the 802.11a version, transferring data at only 11 Mbps.

TIP

The lower frequency of 2.4 GHz drains less power from laptops and other portable devices. Also, 2.4 GHz signals travel farther, and can penetrate walls and floors more effectively than 5 GHz signals.

>> **802.11g:** This flavor is based on the 2.4 GHz band. It speeds data up to a possible 54 Mbps, and it's backward-compatible with 802.11b service.

» **802.11n:** The newest mode builds on the previous standards by adding multiple-input multiple-output (MIMO). MIMO is a technology that uses multiple antennas (usually built into the router) to carry more information than previously with a single antenna. It uses the 5 GHz band (versus the 2.4 it used previously). It can increase speed through your TCP/IP connection to 450 Mbps.

» **802.11ac:** The very latest iteration comes in two speeds: 867 Mbps and 1300 Mbps. It also works only on the 5 GHz band, and dual-band routers can only operate on 2.4 GHz band at speeds of 802.11n. Theoretically, 802.11ac can go up to speeds of 6.93 Gbps and beyond, but since it's so new, we'll have to wait and see. For a peek at what's coming, go to

`http://blogs.cisco.com/wireless/cisco-will-ride-the-802-11ac-wave2`

TIP

For maximum speed at this time, your entire network needs to be an 802.11n 5 GHz network. Some of my legacy devices only work at 2.4 GHz, so I run a dual system and let the device make its own choice of connection speed. Also consider getting a wireless USB antenna adapter for older laptops to upgrade their wireless connection to match the speed of your router.

Setting up your wireless network

Installing your wireless network isn't a gut-wrenching experience either (although it can be if the signal doesn't reach to where you want it). You hook up your computer (a laptop works best) to the wireless access point (the gizmo with the antenna that broadcasts your signal throughout your home or office) to perform some setup tasks such as choosing your channel and setting up the WPA2 code. (The wireless access point often comes with a preset WPA2 code.)

After you complete the setup and turn on your wireless access point, you have a Wi-Fi hotspot in your home or office. Typically, a hotspot provides coverage for about 100 feet in all directions, although walls and floors cut down on the range.

Here are some simplified steps on configuring your network:

1. **Run a cable from your DSL or cable line to your modem.**
2. **Connect an Ethernet cable from your modem to your router.**
3. **Connect another Ethernet cable to your wireless access point.**
4. **Type in the passphrase to all computers on the network.**

Take a look at the network diagram in Figure 5-2.

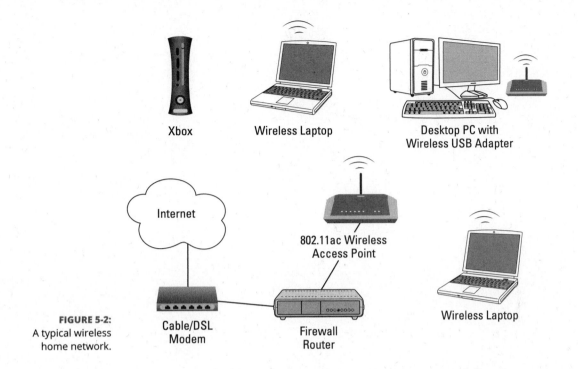

FIGURE 5-2:
A typical wireless home network.

Xbox Wireless Laptop Desktop PC with Wireless USB Adapter

Internet

802.11ac Wireless Access Point

Cable/DSL Modem Firewall Router Wireless Laptop

Internet Security and Your Home Network

Broadband Internet connections are always on — which means your computer is exposed to possible invaders. You should shield your computer with a strong firewall and an antivirus program.

When you're connected to the Internet, you're exposed not only to hackers but also to threats such as *Trojan horses,* programs that can get into your computer when you innocently view an infected website. Once inside your computer, the Trojan horse, like ET, phones home. From there, an evil-deed-doer, who now has a direct line to your computer, may be able to wreak havoc with your precious data.

Visit the website for Gibson Research Corporation at www.grc.com. Gibson Research is the brainchild of an early PC pioneer, Steve Gibson, who's renowned in the world of codes and programming. Steve is *the* expert when it comes to exposing the vulnerabilities of systems over the Internet. A few free diagnostic programs on this site will check your computer's vulnerability to Internet threats.

Shields UP! (at www.grc.com/x/ne.dll?bh0bkyd2) and LeakTest (www.grc.com/lt/leaktest.htm) test your computer for vulnerabilities — and terrify you with results that expose your Internet connection as a sitting duck. Which is an excellent reason to use them — and then get to fixing the holes.

Index

C

C corporations, 538

cable Internet connections, 13

California Apparel News, 320

California Market Center, 304

cash-basis accounting, 567

central processing units (CPUs; chips), 8

CertaPay, 253

certified public accountants (CPAs), 547, 563

CES (Consumer Electronics Show), 307

CGC (Comics Guaranty, LLC), 156

charity auctions, 61

check-out process
  credit cards, 101
  general discussion, 101–102
  integration with PayPal, 502

checks
  eChecks, 108, 167
  personal, 253

chips (central processing units [CPUs]), 8

cigarette and tobacco odors, 432

Cisco, 596

city tax certificates, 531

Classified Ads feature
  fees, 203
  general discussion, 135
  Real Estate category, 224
  selecting for your listing, 237

Cloud Dome, 335, 338, 343, 350–352

COGS (cost of goods sold), 555–556

Coin World, 151–152

coins
  authentication and grading, 151–153, 155–156
  photographing, 337, 348–351

collectibles
  asking questions before buying, 149–151
  authentication services, 155–156
  considerations before buying, 148–149
  general discussion, 141–142
  grading terminology, 145–146
  online resources, 152–154

pricing
    via barcode scanning, 142–144
    via eBay, 144, 146–148
  reading about, 151–152

Collectors.com, 153

Columbus MarketPlace, 304

Comcast, 12

Comics Guaranty, LLC (CGC), 156

communication
  Auto Answers feature, 159–161
  contact information
    false or missing, 39
    finding, 110, 129, 138
    publishing, 39
  contacting buyer, 270–271
  contacting seller
    asking questions, 49, 110, 149–151
    via phone, 109
  friendly, helpful, and productive, 163
  general discussion, 157
  on-site vs. email, 164
  personalizing, 163–164
  preferences management, 189
  responding to questions, 161
  signing up for mailing lists/newsletters, 326
  spelling and grammar, 158
  thank-you notes, 164, 452
  viewing messages, 22
  writing descriptions to pre-answer initial inquiries, 158

computers
  browsers
    defined, 13
    keyboard shortcuts, 14–15
    most-used, 13–14
  buying
    refurbished, 9–10
    used, 9
  essential components of
    CPU, 8
    external backup drive, 8
    hard drive, 8
    keyboard, 8–9

About the Author

Marsha Collier, one of the world's foremost experts and educators in the fields of eBay and ecommerce, is also a top-selling eBay author with over 1 million copies of her books in print (including special editions for the UK, Germany, France, Canada, Australia, China, and an edition in Spanish). Her name frequently crops up in the same breath as ecommerce and customer service. She's the author of the *For Dummies* series on eBay (*eBay For Dummies, Starting an eBay Business For Dummies, eBay Business All-in-One For Dummies*) plus many other related, best-selling titles.

Marsha is especially proud of two books: *eBay For Dummies,* the bestselling book for eBay beginners now in its 9th edition, and *eBay Business All-in-One For Dummies,* the bestselling title on operating an online business. She intermixes her writing about eBay with her role as experienced spokesperson. While traveling across the United States and around the world, she makes regular appearances on television, radio, and in print to discuss online commerce and customer service.

In her spare time, Marsha writes about technology and co-hosts *Computer and Technology Radio.* You can live tweet during the #techradio show on `www.computerandtechnologyradio.com`.

Marsha earned her eBay stripes as a longtime seller on the site. She began her eBay selling career in 1996 to earn extra money for her daughter's education (and eventually paid for university with her eBay earnings). She continued her business as a part-time venture and was one of the first eBay PowerSellers. Nowadays, you can find everything from autographed copies of her books to Barbie items in her eBay Store ("Marsha Collier's Fabulous Finds") at `http://stores.ebay.com/Marsha-Colliers-Fabulous-Finds` and on her website, `http://www.coolebaytools.com`.

In 2004, Marsha began publishing a blog, Marsha Collier's Musings (`http://mcollier.blogspot.com`) to talk about timely topics she thinks her readers will enjoy. An early innovator in social media, Marsha penned several books; two of her favorites are *The Ultimate Online Customer Service Guide* and *Social Media Commerce For Dummies.* Her online brand has grown as she shares her thoughts on how businesses can make the most of the Internet. She has recently been awarded several honors:

Onalytica 2017: Consumer Electronics Show Top Influencers

IBM 2017: #NewWayToWork Futurist

Brand Quarterly Magazine 2016: 50 Marketing Thought Leaders Over 50

Forbes 2016: The Top 20 Influencers of Chief Marketing Officers

Inc. Magazine 2015: 8 Great Role Models for Wowing a Crowd

2013 Forbes: *Top 20 Women Social Media Influencers*

2013 Forbes: *Top 50 Social Media Power Influencers*

Marsha currently resides in Los Angeles, CA. You can contact Marsha via her website, `www.coolebaytools.com`.

Publisher's Acknowledgments

Executive Editor: Steve Hayes

Development Editor: Barry Childs-Helton

Technical Editor: Patti Louise Ruby

Production Editor: Tamilmani Varadharaj

Project Manager: Scott and Maureen Tullis

Cover Image: © TZIDO SUN/Shutterstock

Acknowledgments

Writing a book is a monumental task. Lots of people have helped, but the lion's share of assistance comes from the encouragement that I receive from social media friends and the eBay community.

I've had unending support from my husband, Curt Buthman. We've had to put our lives on hold while I've been writing this book, and he's been really swell (yes, I said swell) putting up with my crazy writing schedule. I am ever grateful for his love and understanding.

If it weren't for Patti "Louise" Ruby's friendship and support as the tech editor for this book, I think I might have lost my mind. She helped me keep on top of the many changes on the eBay site and never said no to my seemingly endless requests.

Once again, I worked with Maureen Tullis and Barry Childs-Helton who were my editors on this book. Maureen put up with my obsession for getting this book right and understanding my crazy. And Barry cleans up after us both. You'd almost think there's no one on earth with such vast experience with the English language. I'm honored to have them as my editors; they help create the very best in the *For Dummies* series. Thank you, Maureen and Barry.

Then, of course, I thank the management at John Wiley & Sons, Inc., and my publisher, Steven Hayes, for having faith that we can continue to fill the world with instructional and entertaining books.